Protecting Soldiers and Mothers

Protecting Soldiers and Mothers

The Political Origins of Social Policy in the United States

Theda Skocpol

THE BELKNAP PRESS OF
HARVARD UNIVERSITY PRESS
Cambridge, Massachusetts
London, England

Library of Congress Cataloging-in-Publication Data

Skocpol, Theda.
    Protecting soldiers and mothers : the political origins of social policy
in the United States / Theda Skocpol.
        p.   cm.
    Includes bibliographical references and index.
    ISBN 0-674-71765-1
    1. Public welfare—United States—History—19th century.
2. Public welfare—United States—History—20th century.   3. United
States—Social policy.   I. Title.
HV91.S56   1992
361.973—dc20   92-8062
                        CIP

Dedicated to the memory
of my mother, Jennie Mae Becker Barron,
and my father, Allan Ernest Barron

This book grew out of the most exciting things that can happen to a scholar: the discovery of startling new facts and the reworking of preconceived notions to accommodate new possibilities. Let me introduce *Protecting Soldiers and Mothers* by recounting the unexpected turns of thought and investigation that led to its creation.

More than a decade ago, I plunged into the study of public social policies in the United States, planning in due course to produce a book about the roots and subsequent evolution of the Social Security Act and other economic and welfare programs of the New Deal. I intended to trace U.S. policies from the 1930s and 1940s, through the War on Poverty and the Great Society, to the present, and to situate U.S. policies by comparing them with those of the major "welfare states" of Europe. As "background" for this study, I decided to spend a bit of time—one summer—coming to terms with the failure of the United States to adopt European-style social insurance policies between 1900 and 1930. That would be a prelude to my discussion of the "real action" in U.S. social politics, from the 1930s to the present.

In the midst of the summer of 1982, happily in residence at the Institute for Advanced Study in Princeton, I encountered Isaac Max Rubinow's *Social Insurance, With Special Reference to American Conditions*. Much of Rubinow's book was, as I had expected, an attempt to hold out European examples for the United States to emulate. But then I arrived at the chapters on old-age pensions and found Rubinow claiming in 1913 that many elderly Americans were *already* receiving public benefits under the rubric of pensions for Union veterans of the Civil War. Fascinated by his description of the breadth and expense of these old-age benefits, I asked myself how historians of U.S. social welfare could have overlooked them—assuming that Rubinow was even close to correct in his empirical description, a matter which I soon set out to investigate. I was even more intrigued with Rubinow's belief in 1913 that Civil War pensions would serve as an "entering wedge for a national system of old-age pensions." Why hadn't that turned out to be true?

Before long, I found contemporaries of Rubinow's, fellow reformers such as Henry Rogers Seager and Charles Richmond Henderson, who argued that Civil War pensions were actually an obstacle rather than an entering wedge for broader systems of old-age pensions and workingmen's insurance. These progressives acknowledged that many elite and middle-class Americans of their day were repelled by the "political corruption" associated with the expansion of Civil War pensions from the 1870s to the 1910s. I realized that Civil War pensions were fascinating, not only because they were America's first national system of public old-age and disability benefits, but also because the politics associated with them might have helped to prevent Americans during the early twentieth century from adopting European-style old-age pensions and social insurance.

Over the next few years, my studies of the expansion of Civil War benefits and the politics that grew up in reaction to them led me toward many of the arguments now embodied in Parts I and II of this book. Drawing insights from empirical investigations, as well as from the "state-centered" theoretical frame of reference for which I had already become known, I was able to link the original expansion of Civil War pensions to the dynamics of nineteenth-century U.S. patronage democracy. And I was able to understand the reaction *against* this precedent by many reform-minded groups during the Progressive Era. Their reaction was part of a fundamental reorganization of U.S. government and politics.

But established mind-sets resist change. For several more years, as I made a difficult transition from the University of Chicago to teaching at Harvard University, I still thought I was working on a modified version of my original book plan. A first major part of my book in progress would, I imagined, deal with the expansion of Civil War pensions and the subsequent failure of proposals for social insurance and general old-age pensions during the Progressive Era; later parts would move on to the roots and consequences of the New Deal and of the War on Poverty. There was still no hint that gender would play a central role in my understanding of U.S. political history. I was writing about the changing U.S. formal polity, and about (mostly) male officials, politicians, and intellectuals. Weren't these, after all, the stuff of "state-building," my primary focus?

As I drafted chapters for this modified book, I set off on what I expected would be another very brief detour. Realizing that the 1910s was not only a period when proposals for general old-age pensions and workingmen's social insurance were defeated in the United States but also a period in which various social policies for women and children were actually enacted, I felt I should devote a part of one of my chapters to the positive legislative outcomes. I was particularly intrigued by "mothers' pensions"—laws authorizing social expenditures for widowed mothers that were rapidly enacted across forty U.S. states during the 1910s. How was it, I wondered, that this exception to the general progressive bias against public social spending had occurred? At first I thought the protagonists of mothers' pensions would turn out to be judges of the juvenile courts, new agencies of government established by reformers in many states prior to the 1910s. But I soon confronted the extensive involvement of women's voluntary groups, not only as advocates for mothers' pensions, but also as supporters of protective labor laws for women workers and of the federal Children's Bureau and the Sheppard-Towner programs of maternal health education. How could women have had so much influence over social legislation even before most of them had the right to vote in American democracy?

Believing—still!—that all I was doing was preparing to write one section of a single chapter, I delved into the rich, recently created literature on U.S. women's history, hoping to make sense of what American women's organizations had been doing politically in the early twentieth century. My excitement grew as I came to understand that the distinctive institutional arrangements and historical formation of the U.S. polity could help to explain why voluntary groups of (mostly nonvoting) women were able to play a stronger role in U.S. social politics around the turn of the century than movements of industrial workers. Impressed with the extensive organization achieved by nationwide federations of local women's clubs in the early 1900s, I began to hypothesize that these far-flung federations might have enjoyed an unusual degree of leverage in agitating for social legislation in a period when the U.S. polity was undergoing a transition away from party-dominated patronage democracy. To see if some of my hunches were correct, I explored patterns of legislative enactments and searched for records from the National Congress of Mothers and the General Federation of Women's Clubs. Just for the fun of it, I started tallying what I could learn about the legislative activities of the major women's federations in each U.S. state. Before long, it became something of an obsession for me to track down more and more reports of national women's conventions and, where possible, state-level records of women's club activities.

When it came time to start writing about my conceptual and empirical discoveries, I thought I perhaps had enough for a separate chapter (rather than just a section of the original chapter on the Progressive Era). But when the draft of this "chapter" was done, it was already over a hundred pages; and I still had more ideas—and leads on data—about the involvement of women's groups in achieving social legislation during the Progressive Era. What was I to do? The original plan for one book stretching from the 1870s to the present was becoming more and more unwieldly. The more I did fresh research—and the more I discovered—the further I seemed to be from moving on toward the present.

During 1989, I finally experienced the gestalt switch that allowed me to pull together *Protecting Soldiers and Mothers*. At last, I understood that I had not just discovered more "background information" about why the United States had not launched a European-style welfare state for workers prior to the New Deal. I had positive stories to tell—and analyses to offer—about the first major phases of modern U.S. social provision, the creation of policies intended to protect, and honor, soldiers and mothers. Gender relations and identities were not just a footnote to my overall story; they were centrally intertwined with the structural and cultural patterns of American politics from the nineteenth into the early twentieth century. My state-centered theoretical frame of reference had evolved into a fully "polity-centered approach" as I had grappled with a central issue in the study of any nation's political development: the transformations over time in the issues, social identities, and styles of politics that succeed (or fail) at influencing agendas of political debate and public policymaking. From the time I realized these things, completing the research and writing for *Protecting Soldiers and Mothers* was like doing the last parts of a huge, complex jigsaw puzzle: the pieces were finally fitting together, and the emerging picture was (to me, at least) lovely.

I have written so far as if I were solely responsible for producing this book—as, indeed, I alone *am* to be held accountable for all of its shortcomings. But, of course, no scholarly project is ever completed apart from social support, or without intellectual inspiration from colleagues. And I have been blessed with much of both.

Over many years I have had the privilege of collaborating with excellent younger scholars, both before and after they completed Ph.D.'s in sociology or political science at Harvard University, the University of Chicago, Princeton University, and the Massachusetts Institute of Technology. Most of these collaborations have culminated in joint presentations and publications, and they have also nourished the research and ideas for this book. Let me therefore offer thanks first and foremost to those who have worked closely with me on research about U.S. social politics: Marjorie Abend-Wein, Edwin Amenta, Bruce Carruthers, Elisabeth Clemens, Kenneth Finegold, Christopher Howard, John Ikenberry, Susan Lehmann, Ann Shola Orloff, Sunita Parikh, Gretchen Ritter, Libby Schweber, and Margaret Weir. In addition, I am grateful for specific research assistance from various students, including Bridget Asay, Daniel Ernst, James Johnsen, Debra Minkoff, Sina Mandalinci, and Mark Templeton.

As a native Midwesterner, I have always felt that most of U.S. politics is rooted outside the major urban centers of the East. Working on this book reinforced that conviction, especially as I gathered facts about Civil War veterans and women's groups across forty-eight states. But it has been very difficult to gather such data, because national records invariably leave out a lot, and the rest of what may be available is scattered in libraries and historical societies all over the United States. Therefore I owe a special debt to those who have gone out of their way to help me dig up difficult-to-find information at places where I could not go in person. Eleanor Gehres and Phil Panum at the Denver Public Library sent me information on the Grand Army of the Republic in Colorado and Wyoming. Ken Finegold and his assistant Thomas Regan, Jr., dug up facts about the politics of mothers' pensions in New Jersey; Elisabeth Clemens and her assistant Douglas Adams looked for information about social policies in Arizona; and both Lis Clemens and Ann Orloff sent me similar information for Wisconsin. Kathy Wyatt of Omaha did extensive research for me on women's groups and social legislation in the state of Nebraska. My sister, Jane Barron Hughes, sent information about women's club activities in West Virginia. Ronald Schaffer, a historian I have never met except through his writings, responded to a phone call by sending old research notes about women's politics in Montana. Michael Wallace sent me from Ohio State University at Columbus a copy of a dissertation about the Grand Army of the Republic in Ohio. Libby Schweber helped me obtain materials from the Princeton University Library. And at the last minute, just before this book went into production, the Registrar of the Vermont Historical Society, Mary Labate Rogstad, working with Nancy Coone, found handwritten records of endorsements of mothers' pensions and hour laws by the Vermont Federation of Women's Clubs.

Other scholars have sent me important information, often from their own as-yet-unpublished works-in-progress. John Sutton generously shared quantitative data sets on the U.S. states, and he has collaborated with me and others in a study of the expansion of Civil War pensions across the states between 1870 and 1920. Joanne Goodwin sent information from her dissertation on women's politics in Illinois. Mary Ellen (Waller) Zuckerman shared data and insights from her book about early-twentieth-century women's magazines. And Earl Mulderink kindly drew on his dissertation research about Civil War veterans in New Bedford, Massachusetts, to enlighten me about the fate of African-Americans in the pension system. Additional facts or references came from Robert Asher, Gary Cross, Louisa Bertch Green, Patrick J. Kelly, Roland Marchand, and Suzanne Marilley. As the notes to the book indicate, I have also benefited greatly from having access to many unpublished Ph.D. dissertations through the reproduction service of University Microfilms.

While I was writing and rewriting, many fellow scholars were kind enough to read all or part of the manuscript and give me—often extremely detailed—comments and suggestions. Although I was not always able to take every bit of their advice, I did take a great deal of it. Many errors have been avoided and many arguments honed because of the sharp eyes and engaged minds of these generous colleagues. I am thankful to James Alt, Edwin Amenta, Edward Berkowitz, Elisabeth Clemens, Nancy Cott, Matthew Crenson, Desley Deacon, Morris Fiorina, Ellen Fitzpatrick, Linda Gordon, Peter Hall, William Hixson, Jennifer Hochschild, Carole Joffe, Richard John, Mary Katzenstein, Ira Katznelson, Morton Keller, Barbara Laslett, Seymour Martin Lipset, Steven Mintz, Eileen McDonagh, Sonya Michel, Carol Mueller, Earl Mulderink, Ann Shola Orloff, James Patterson, Susan Pedersen, Paul E. Peterson, Paul Pierson, Jill Quadagno, Wendy Sarvasy, Ann Schofield, Martin Shefter, Kathryn Kish Sklar, Charles Tilly, Ellen Kay Trimberger, and Viviana Zelizer.

Over the many years that I worked on this book, I benefited greatly from fellowships and grants that gave me precious time to write and paid for some of my research costs. I was fortunate to be a Member during 1980–81 of the School of Social Science of the Institute for Advanced Study in Princeton, New Jersey; and I returned to the School as a Visitor for the next three summers. The Russell Sage Foundation awarded me grants during 1983–84 and again during 1990–92; some of the research funded by these grants has contributed to this book. My research on the legal aspects of U.S. social policymaking was aided by a grant from the Mark DeWolfe Howe Fund of the Harvard University Law School. During 1986 and 1987, I benefited from a major grant from the Ford Foundation's Project on Social Welfare and the American Future. And from January through June of 1990 I was able to devote full time to completing the draft of this book, thanks to a John Simon Guggenheim Fellowship. I am extremely grateful for the help—and encouragement—received from all of these sources.

Still others have helped to turn my manuscript into a publication. At Harvard University Press, Michael Aronson arranged the contract and supervised the scholarly review process, and I am especially grateful to Camille Smith for doing a careful job of copyediting and coordinating the production process. My friend Walter Lippincott, Jr., gave me much good advice about contracts and the publishing process. A number of individuals and institutions assisted me in assembling camera-ready copies of the historical illustrations that appear throughout the book. Thanks go to Bonnie Hardwick and Peter Hanff at the Bancroft Library of the University of California at Berkeley; to Katherine Dibble and John Dorsey at the Boston Public Library; and to Patricia King and Marie Helene Gold at the Schlesinger Library of Radcliffe College. I am also grateful to Philip Heymann and his assistant Tom Potter. My secretary, Juliet Sanger, did a great deal of careful typing and double-checking to prepare tables for the book. And my husband, Bill Skocpol, mastered new software in order to create the state-by-state maps.

Finally, let me acknowledge how embedded this book has been in my family relationships. Bill Skocpol has always been extraordinarily supportive of all my scholarly and professional endeavors. His marvellous engagement as the father of our four-year-old son, Michael Allan, meant that the arrival of our beloved child only spurred this book to completion. My "second mother," Marie Halstead Barron, has been a constant source of love and encouragement—as was my late father, Allan Barron, who I wish could have lived a few more years to see this book completed. He knew it was going to be dedicated to him. Throughout his life, my father was a Civil War buff, and his enthusiasm surely helped to pique my interest in American history. My late mother, Jennie Becker Barron, was a champion of women's special homemaking skills, and she often spoke with reverence of the female professors who had taught her home economics in college. In *Protecting Soldiers and Mothers*, I hope that I have at last found a way to express, in my own distinctive scholarly way, some of what my mother and father each gave to me.

CONTENTS

ILLUSTRATIONS

The legislation of Congress should . . . be so enlarged and extended as to provide against the possibility that any man who honorably wore the Federal uniform shall become the inmate of an almshouse, or dependent upon private charity.

Republican Party Platform, 1888

I hold it to be a hideous wrong inflicted upon the republic that the pension system instituted for the benefit of the soldiers and sailors of the United States has been prostituted and degraded . . . As things are, Gentlemen, one cannot tell whether a pensioner of the United States received an honorable wound in battle or contracted a chronic catarrh twenty years after the war. One cannot tell whether a pensioner of the United States is a disabled soldier or sailor or a perjured pauper who has foisted himself upon the public treasury. I say that to put the pension system of the United States into this condition is a crime . . . against Republican Institutions.

President Charles Eliot of Harvard, 1889

Many of the old men and women who, in Europe, would be in almshouses are found in the United States living upon pensions with their children or in homes to which paupers are not sent, and they feel themselves to be honored guests of the nation for which they gave the last full measure of devotion . . .

This [military pension] system is instructive in relation to workingmen's insurance both as a precedent and as a warning . . . The pension idea itself, in spite of faults of law and administration, has already prepared the way for insurance of old age for wage earners . . . [But the] extravagance and abuses of this military pension system have probably awakened prejudices against working-men's pensions.

Professor Charles Richmond Henderson, 1909

In this country, owing to partisan politics, the authorities are prone to spend so much time wrangling over the spoils of office that they have little left for civic improvement.

The initiative has to come from the citizens; and since men are more or less closely absorbed in business, it has come to pass that the initiative in civic matters has devolved largely upon women.

Mrs. Imogen B. Oakley, 1912
Chairman, Civil Service Reform Committee,
General Federal of Women's Clubs

We cannot afford to let a mother, one who has divided her body by creating other lives for the good of the state, one who has contributed to citizenship, be classed as a pauper, a dependent. She must be given value received by her nation, and stand as one honored . . . If our public mind is maternal, loving and generous, wanting to save and develop all, our Government will express this sentiment.

Mrs. G. Harris Robertson, 1911
President, Tennessee Congress of Mothers

Understanding the Origins of Modern Social Provision in the United States

In October of 1889, President Charles Eliot of Harvard University—a prominent Mugwump located in the very heartland of that status-conscious movement for good government reform—delivered a speech to the Bay State Club of Boston.[1] The speech explained why he, formerly a loyal Republican, was switching his allegiance to the Democratic Party. Eliot's preference for the Democratic stand on tariffs and his great respect for the efforts of Democratic President Grover Cleveland on behalf of civil service reform were cited as two reasons for the shift. The third reason was Eliot's sense that patronage-oriented Republican politicians were leading the way in "prostituting and degrading" the Civil War pension system into what was becoming, in effect, America's first large-scale nationally funded old-age and disability system.

Eliot knew whereof he spoke. By the time the elected politicians—especially Republicans—had finished liberalizing eligibility for Civil War pensions, over a third of all the elderly men living in the North, along with quite a few elderly men in other parts of the country and many widows and dependents across the nation, were receiving quarterly payments from the United States Pension Bureau.[2] In terms of the large share of the federal budget spent, the hefty proportion of citizens covered, and the relative generosity of the disability and old-age benefits offered, the United States had become a precocious social spending state. Its post–Civil War system of social provision in many respects exceeded what early programs of "workingmen's

1

insurance" were giving needy old people or superannuated industrial wage earners in fledgling Western welfare states around the
turn of the century.

Early in the twentieth century, a number of U.S. trade union
officials and reformers hoped to transform Civil War pensions into
more universal publicly funded benefits for all workingmen and
their families. Charles Richmond Henderson, a professor at the
University of Chicago and a prominent member of the American
Association for Labor Legislation, argued for this program in his
1909 book, *Industrial Insurance in the United States*.[3] But it was not to
be. From Mugwumps to progressive reformers, many elite and middle-class Americans viewed Civil War pensions as a prime example
of governmental profligacy and electorally rooted political corruption. During the Progressive Era, public opinion was preoccupied
with curbing the fiscal excesses of patronage-oriented political parties. In this political climate, various social reforms were enacted into
law, but not those calling for new public spending on old-age pensions or other kinds of workingmen's social insurance. America's
first system of public social provision for men and their dependents
died with the Civil War generation, and was not to be replaced by
other measures until the Great Depression and the New Deal of the
1930s.

The United States thus did not follow other Western nations on
the road toward a paternalist welfare state, in which male bureaucrats would administer regulations and social insurance "for the
good" of breadwinning industrial workers. Instead, America came
close to forging a maternalist welfare state, with female-dominated
public agencies implementing regulations and benefits for the good
of women and their children. From 1900 through the early 1920s,
a broad array of protective labor regulations and social benefits were
enacted by state legislatures and the national Congress to help adult
American women as mothers or as potential mothers.

Most American women did not gain the right to vote until 1920
or a few years before, so they were outside the party politics that
had fueled the expansion of Civil War benefits. Even so, nation-
spanning federations of local women's clubs were the chief proponents of such maternalist policies as mothers' pensions, minimum
wage regulations, and the creation of the federal Children's Bureau.
In European nations, well-established bureaucracies and program-

matic political parties devised and administered programs for civic betterment, as Mrs. Oakley of the huge General Federation of Women's Clubs explained in her 1912 article.[4] But in the United States, most men were preoccupied with partisan politics or business and "the initiative in civic matters . . . devolved largely upon women" organized into voluntary associations. As they took the lead in U.S. social-welfare politics during the first decades of the twentieth century, moreover, American clubwomen acted from a broadly shared, gender-based vision that Mrs. Roberts of the National Congress of Mothers nicely articulated when she spoke in 1911 about a maternal public mind, "loving and generous, wanting to save and develop all" American families.[5] Women aimed to extend the domestic morality of the nineteenth century's "separate sphere" for women into the nation's public life. For a while, this vision was a remarkable source of moral energy and political leverage for the female instigators of the first U.S. programs of public social provision destined to endure (despite unintended transformations) through the New Deal and down to the present day.

American Social Provision in Historical and Comparative Perspective

Parts of the historical sketch I have just offered will come as a surprise to many readers. Properly schooled citizens of the United States, scholars of American history, and social scientists who analyze the growth of Western "welfare states"—all take for granted certain received truths about the American past. America in the nineteenth and early twentieth centuries was supposedly a land of rugged individualists, profoundly distrustful of government and engaged in free-wheeling market competition to gain the fruits of an expanding capitalist economy. Individual dependency was little recognized—and socially stigmatized—in this land of plenty. Such public provision as there was for the needy, disabled, or elderly was virtually always local, provided through poor houses, or private charity, or niggardly public assistance outside of institutions. State governments did little beyond setting up a few custodial institutions and, especially in the industrializing areas of the country, regulating "charities and corrections" toward the end of the nineteenth century. Above all, we have been taught that the U.S. federal government did virtually nothing about public social provision until the Great Depression and the New Deal of the 1930s. Then at last, in a "big bang" of social reforms that accompanied many extensions of federal power into the country's economic and social life, the United States enacted nationwide social insurance and public assistance policies.[6] At that point, most scholars presume that the United States joined the evolutionary mainstream of Western social progress—as a "laggard" on the universal road to "the modern welfare state."

What eventually came to be called "the welfare state" grew up in successive phases in parts of the industrializing Western world.[7] In an initial phase between the 1880s and World War I, many European nations, along with Australia, New Zealand, and Brazil, launched the social spending policies that have come to be considered at the core of modern welfare states; and many countries also passed laws regulating hours and wages and (in New Zealand and Australia) the arbitration of industrial labor disputes. Early social spending measures included noncontributory public pensions for the elderly such as those established in Denmark in 1891, New Zealand in 1898, Australia from 1900 to 1908, and Britain in 1908. They also included partly contributory and partly publicly funded social insurance measures such as those established in Germany during the 1880s, Britain in 1911, Brazil in 1923, and quite a few other countries during the same period. In the years accompanying and following such programmatic beginnings, certain benefits were mandated for middle-class citizens. But at first most social expenditures were devoted to "workers' insurance," or they were meant to keep "respectable" old people, usually former workers and their spouses, out of demeaning local poor houses.

From the 1920s onward, many of the early welfare states for workers (as we might call them) evolved into comprehensive welfare states for all citizens, or for many categories of them. Nations with early commitments to pensions and social insurance soon began to expand and reorganize their efforts, continually improving benefits and extending elibility to new social groups. Under the impact of Depression and World War, certain liberal democracies also proclaimed bold new ideals of national social provision and took steps to implement them. In beleaguered wartime Britain, planning for social life after the conflict combined with intense feelings of democratic solidarity to spur a self-conscious sense of national pride in "the welfare state" as opposed to the Nazi "warfare state."[8] The sentiments born of war received legislative expression in its aftermath, when British social provision attempted to blend public assistance, social services, and social insurance into a seamless national system of basic protections, creating a uniform floor of protection for all citizens.[9] In Sweden and the other Scandinavian democracies, meanwhile, somewhat different ideals and policies took firm hold before and after World War II, as "full employment welfare states" coordinated generous social benefits designed to further social equality with Keynesian macroeconomic management and targeted labor-market policies.[10]

Despite the desire of many scholars to view its social policy history in universal evolutionary terms, the United States has never come close to having a "modern welfare state" in the British, the Swedish, or any other positive Western sense of the phrase.[11] It did not institute social benefits for workingmen or the elderly during the early twentieth century. The Social Security Act of 1935, still the framework for nationwide public social provision in the United States, included only one national program, contributory retirement insurance. Unemployment insurance was a federally mandated program with the states left in charge of taxes, coverage, and benefits. Public assistance programs were offered federal subsidies with the states left responsible for devising and administering policies. National health insurance was not included in the Social Security Act, and it was not enacted in the late 1940s or afterward, either. No comprehensive American welfare state emerged from the New Deal and World War II. Nor was any such welfare state "completed" during the next "big bang" of U.S. social policy innovations, the War on Poverty and the Great Society of the 1960s and early 1970s.

Down to the present day, the word "welfare" has a pejorative connotation in the United States. It refers to unearned public assistance benefits, possibly undeserved and certainly demeaning, to be avoided if at all possible by all "independent," self-respecting citizens. Americans recurrently debate "welfare reforms," along with new kinds of policy departures such as "family leaves" and federal subsidies for day care. But whatever new social policies the future may bring, it seems highly unlikely that the United States will ever converge with the Western welfare states fashioned between the 1880s and the 1960s.

That the United States has never really approximated an ideal-typical Western welfare state has not prevented scholars from discussing the history of its social policymaking almost single-mindedly in relation to that model—something encouraged by the assumption that national and state governments in the United States were little involved in public social provision prior to the 1930s. Social scientists debating alternative theories of welfare state development have primarily examined U.S. social provision from 1935 onward.[12] They have offered a variety of hypotheses about why the United States was a "welfare laggard," that is, why it started its welfare state so late by international standards. Comparativists have also offered hypotheses about why the United States still has fewer programs, less comprehensive social coverage, and lower expenditures on social insurance than most other highly industrialized nations. To explain these things, comparative models of welfare state development draw our attention to the factors *absent* in American history compared to other national histories, or else to factors only weakly apparent.

To bring into sharper focus things distinctively *present* in the history of American social policy, we should presumably turn to historians who have looked closely at happenings before as well as after the 1930s. But here too the model of evolutionary progress toward a modern welfare state holds sway, directing our attention to some realities and away from others. Historians of American welfare politics from the nineteenth century to the 1930s paint a picture of heroic reformers endeavoring to pull the country away from local poor law practices and toward national social insurance. The title of Roy Lubove's classic book *The Struggle for Social Security, 1900–1935* captures this perfectly.[13] Such historical accounts are teleologies keyed to the eventual triumph of what Daniel Levine calls America's "own version of the capitalist welfare state" in the Social Security Act of 1935[14]—although sometimes the stories proceed from what James Patterson calls America's "early welfare state" fashioned during the New Deal to discussion of the further innovations of the antipoverty war launched in the 1960s.[15] Historical accounts treat the period before the 1930s as one in which "obstacles"—such as liberal values or business power—frustrated early reformers' attempts to create an American welfare state. Interestingly, even a recent book written from a different perspective than many earlier social policy histories, Michael Katz's *In the Shadow of the Poorhouse*, retains some of the traditional narrative structure.[16]

My purpose is hardly to make light of scholars who note absent conditions in American history or obstacles to social insurance before the New Deal. Part II of this book focuses on such matters. Still less do I mean to dismiss the many insights that appear in excellent histories of U.S. social policy and in cross-national studies of welfare states that include the American case. The end notes for this book attest to the many things I have learned even from authors with whose central theses I disagree. What I do wish to suggest is that received wisdom about the past of U.S. social provision—framed as a struggle to move the country along an evolutionary path from nineteenth-century local poor relief to the modern welfare state as embodied in the Social Security Act—blinds us to important patterns that need to be explained.

Inspired by fresh descriptions of what did and didn't happen in the development of social policies from the 1870s through the 1920s, we can pose new questions about U.S. social provision in comparative perspective.

Why did the United States provide such expensive and generous benefits for many disabled and elderly men and their dependents under the rubric of Civil War benefits? And how did the resulting U.S. system of social benefits compare to early modern social policies in other Western nations?

Civil War benefits were offered by the federal government and by state and local governments. They cannot be set aside as mere unavoidable concomitants of the human damage inflicted by the original military conflict, for the extension of Civil War benefits came after claims directly due to wartime casualties had peaked and were in decline.[17] From the 1880s through the 1910s, federal veterans' pensions became the keystone of an entire edifice of honorable income supplements and institutional provision for many northern Americans who were longstanding citizens. In many ways, the extent and terms of these disability and old-age benefits compared favorably to the coverage and terms of early social insurance and pension policies in other Western nations. Yet there were also crucial differences of form, coverage, and justification between U.S. policies and the programs of fledgling welfare states.

If the United States by 1900 had costly old-age and disability benefits outside the poor law, why did the nation subsequently refuse to build

*on, or replace, this early system of public social provision, transforming
it into workingmen's insurance or more general pensions for the elderly?*

Inspired by European precedents, proposals for need-based old-
age pensions, for health and unemployment insurance covering
wage earners, and for labor regulations to protect all adult male
workers received considerable intellectual justification and political
support in the early-twentieth-century United States. Yet even
though reform ferment peaked during the Progressive Era, and even
though Civil War pensioners were visibly dying off, such proposals
were defeated or deflected by the legislatures and the courts. From
the overall agenda of workingmen's social provision, only laws mandating compensation for industrial accidents succeeded. They were
enacted by forty-two U.S. states between 1911 and 1920, and by two
more during the 1920s. We need to learn why workmen's compensation laws were successful. But the larger mystery remains. Once
we realize that the U.S. federal government (along with many states)
was centrally involved in offering social benefits to respectable citizens long before the New Deal, then we need to wonder anew about
the failure of most proposals for social benefits and labor regulations
for workingmen and the elderly during the early 1900s. The failure
of these proposals is obviously not simply attributable to inherent
obstacles to overcoming local poor relief in industrializing America.
There must be more to it than that.

> *If proposed social policies for workingmen were not successful during
> a period when all U.S. adult white males had the suffrage, then why—
> mostly at times and places where women could not vote—did U.S.
> legislatures enact, and the courts sustain, social spending for mothers
> and certain protective labor regulations for adult female wage earners?
> And why did the federal government establish the Children's Bureau
> and expand its mission until the middle of the 1920s?*

In U.S. politics during the early decades of the twentieth century,
the story is not only one of social policies that failed to be enacted.
Beginnings were made in creating public social provision not tied to
generational entitlements, even if these beginnings were later to be
reworked and superseded. As Table 1 illustrates, social policies for
women alone loomed much larger in early modern U.S. social provision than they did in the pioneering Western welfare states for

Table 1   Early modern social policies, 1880–1929

Nation	Workmen's compensation	Old-age pensions or insurance	Sickness insurance	Unemployment insurance	Labor regulations for men*	Labor regulations for women	Mothers' pensions
Germany	1884	1889	1883	1927	No	1908	No
Australia	1900–1914 Laws in all 6 Australian states	1908	No	No	Hour laws by late 19th century Arbitration of industrial disputes Minimum wage from 1919	1908	No
New Zealand	1900	1898	No	No	Hour laws by late 19th century Arbitration of industrial disputes Minimum wage from 1918		1912
Britain	1906	1908 1925	1911	1911 1920	Trade Boards 1909–1918 for minimum wages	Hour laws from 19th century; Trade Boards for minimum wages	No
United States	1911–1920 42 states 1920s 2 more states	No (except 6 states in 1920s)	No	No	No	Hour laws in 41 states by 1929 Minimum wage laws, 1912–23, in 15 states	1911– 1920 40 states 1920s 4 more states

* Laws applying only to special dangerous occupations are not included here.
Sources: Peter Flora and Arnold J. Heidenheimer, eds., *The Development of Welfare States in Europe and America* (New Brunswick, NJ: Transaction Books, 1981), table 2.4, p. 59; Francis G. Castles, *The Working Class and Welfare: Reflections on the Political Development of the Welfare State in Australia and New Zealand, 1890–1980* (London: Allen and Unwin, Port Nicholson Press, 1985), ch. 2; George Steinmetz, "Workers and the Welfare State in Imperial Germany," *International Labor and Working-Class History*, Special Issue on "Workers and the Welfare State," no. 40 (Fall 1991): 18–46; T. H. Kewley, *Social Security in Australia, 1900–72*, 2d ed. (Sydney: Sydney University Press, 1973), ch. 4; and Elizabeth Brandeis, *Labor Legislation*, in Vol. 3 of *History of Labor in the United States, 1896–1932*, by John R. Commons and Associates (New York: Macmillan, 1935), chs. 3–5.

workers. The pioneering paternalist welfare states might emphasize social insurance, as did Germany; or regulations to establish a "living wage," as did Australia and New Zealand; or a combination of both, as did Britain. But all of them focused on helping the breadwinning male wage earner. While they sometimes had laws for mothers or for women workers comparable to those enacted in the United States, they invariably had many laws covering male workers that the United States did not enact during this period.

America's first publicly funded social benefits other than military pensions and poor relief were mothers' pensions. These were laws passed in forty states between 1911 and 1920 to enable localities to provide payments for needy widowed mothers (and occasionally others) in order to let them care for children at home. Four more states passed mothers' pensions during the 1920s (along with two in the early 1930s). Protective labor regulations for women wage-workers understood as potential mothers also proliferated during this period. New or improved limits on women's hours of work passed in thirteen states between 1900 and 1909; in thirty-nine states between 1909 and 1917; and in two more states before 1933. Minimum wage laws for women workers were enacted by fifteen states between 1912 and 1923. In addition to state-level laws for women, in 1912 the U.S. federal government established a Children's Bureau, headed and staffed not by the usual male officials but by reformist professional women who aimed to look after the needs of all American mothers and children. Across the nation, women's groups campaigned for the creation of the Children's Bureau, just as they pressed for the enactment of mothers' pensions and protective labor regulations. In the 1910s, a national government bureau "run solely by women" was "without parallel elsewhere in the world."[18] And by 1921 the Children's Bureau had successfully spearheaded a campaign for the first explicit federal social welfare program, one that offered grants-in-aid to the states. The Sheppard-Towner Infancy and Maternity Protection Act encouraged the creation of federally subsidized pre- and postnatal clinics to disseminate health-care advice to mothers, in the hope of reducing the high infant mortality rates that the Children's Bureau had documented for the United States compared to other industrial nations.

Finally, we will need to ask about the larger implications of developments and nondevelopments in U.S. public social provision from the 1870s to the 1920s. In this book I do *not* treat U.S. social provision in the late nineteenth and early twentieth centuries in the usual fashion, as an evolutionary backdrop to the eventual triumph of Social Security in the 1930s. But the past did matter for the future of American social policymaking. The goals and political capacities of later proponents of social insurance were influenced by memories of Civil War pensions, and by the very restricted achievements of campaigns during the Progressive Era for workingmen's insurance. At the federal and state levels, institutionalized social programs from the maternalist era survived to become parts of America's new nationwide system of public social provision launched in the 1930s, although this happened in unintended ways. All in all, the roots and consequences of the earliest phases of modern American social politics hold lessons applicable to the politics of social provision in the United States right down to the present day.

Clearly this book has its work cut out for it. Before plunging into the description and explanation of U.S. social politics between the 1870s and the 1920s, however, it behooves us to sharpen our analytical tools. What can we learn from existing works by historians and social scientists who have sought to explain the origins and early patterns of American social provision in temporal depth and cross-national perspective? Where received arguments and theories seem inadequate, how do I propose to do any better? With the aid of what frame of reference, what concepts and hypotheses, will I interrogate the American past and offer fresh arguments about why early U.S. social provision developed as it did? The remainder of the chapter addresses these matters, suggesting ways in which the analysis of U.S. social policymaking from the 1870s to the 1920s can prompt reworkings of received scholarly approaches to explaining the origins and growth of national systems of social provision.

The Limitations of Existing Perspectives

Working from various points of view, thoughtful scholars have endeavored for many years to make sense of the origins and development of modern social policies in the United States. Until the middle 1970s, debates oscillated between two perspectives that avowedly were polar opposites theoretically and methodologically—but that were also complementary in certain ways. The first stressed that modern social policies develop in response to the *logic of industrialism*. This approach held sway among social scientists who did research on large numbers of nations, using statistical techniques and highly aggregated data for restricted slices of time. The second approach countered with an emphasis on *national values,* and understandably it found special favor among scholars who preferred to use historical methods.

Just as the books elaborating the findings of the logic of industrialism school made their appearance, scholars (often younger ones) found fault with its deemphasis of political conflicts. Nor were the critics satisfied with the national values approach as an alternative, for it was perceived as offering little systematic analysis of the political struggles that have underpinned the emergence and growth of social policies. A sea change therefore occurred during the middle 1970s. Attention to the effects on social policymaking of trade unions and labor-based political parties became the vogue in cross-national studies of welfare states, with comparisons limited to six to eighteen advanced-industrial countries. This happened at the same time that many historically oriented scholars were turning to an emphasis on business hegemony to explain U.S. social provision in particular. Thus various political-economy arguments about class struggle or class domination have taken center stage in recent debates about the politics of social policymaking in the United States.

In the last few years, feminist scholars have started to invoke ideas about patriarchal domination and women's politics to interpret aspects of the development of modern social policies in the United States and elsewhere. This literature is in its infancy, but after other theoretical perspectives have been discussed, I will highlight the issues raised by feminists and indicate which lines of reasoning seem more promising than others for explaining U.S. developments.

Are Modern Social Policies a By-product of Industrialization?

"Economic growth is the ultimate cause of welfare state development."[19] This has been the guiding assumption for those who understand modern social policies as rooted in a universal logic of industrialism. As countries develop economically, the reasoning goes, industries emerge, labor forces shift out of agriculture, and cities grow. Regardless of ideologies or political regimes, the populations of economically developing nations face broadly similar problems and dislocations. Once families are off the land and dependent on wages and salaries, they cannot rely only on their own resources or local community help to cope with injuries at work, with episodes of illness and unemployment, or with the upkeep of elderly relatives no longer able to be economically productive. Social demands for pensions and social insurance thus inevitably grow with industrialization and urbanization. At the same time, improved economic productivity makes it possible for governmental authorities to respond to the new needs with appropriate programs. According to this view, therefore, all economically developing countries should institute similar sequences of social policies.[20] And they should expand social expenditures and the coverage of policies in tandem with further economic growth.[21]

Plausible arguments along these lines understandably inspired a lot of cross-national research, although this is not the place to review the results in any detail. Suffice it to say that the hypotheses fared well only with data for the 1940s, 1950s, or 1960s, especially when large numbers of countries at all levels of development were studied at once and the object was to account for variance in highly aggregated dependent variables.[22] Once scholars began to inquire about the origins and changes of specific kinds of social policies, once they studied global patterns over long stretches of time, and once they focused on the long-term experiences of twelve to eighteen leading industrial-capitalist nations, then the logic of industrialism approach was soon undermined as a sufficient guide to causal processes.[23]

U.S. patterns do not accord well with the expectations of the logic of industrialism perspective, a situation which has usually led scholars of this persuasion to supplement their arguments with ideas from the national values school, to be discussed shortly. Prior to the 1930s the United States is an awkward extreme "outlier" on the graphs; it was one of the world's industrial leaders yet lagged far behind other nations—even much less urban and industrial ones—when it came to instituting nationwide pensions or social insurance.[24] Perhaps we could fix things up by counting Civil War pensions as modern social benefits, for they certainly expanded simultaneously with American industries and cities during the decades following the end of the

Great Rebellion. Civil War pensions, however, did not chiefly benefit the denizens of the greatest U.S. industrial centers; they were more likely to help farmers and townsmen in turn-of-the-century America.[25]

Even if we leave aside Civil War pensions, how can such a profoundly determinist and evolutionist theory handle the early 1900s? Social provision for old soldiers faded, yet the U.S. federal government did not continue old-age pensions, and state governments did not enact pensions, health insurance, or unemployment benefits. It is especially misleading to juxtapose the U.S. national government to foreign national governments in this period, because until the mid-1930s the various states were the arenas where social legislation was enacted, and certainly where debates over social insurance were centered. Within the United States, the state of Massachusetts closely resembled Britain in tempos and levels of industrialization and urbanization up to the 1920s. Thus the failure of Massachusetts to enact proposals for British-style pensions and social insurance cannot be attributed to the variables that the logic of industrialism school prefers to invoke.[26] Bringing additional U.S. states into the picture only raises further questions for this perspective, because less industrialized and less urbanized states were often pioneers in social legislation.[27]

In the final analysis, socioeconomic modernization not only is a poor predictor of the timing of enactment of social policies across nations and across states within the United States; it also says little about the content of specific national or state-level policy profiles, ignoring the particularities of program constituencies and the public rhetoric used to legitimate them. We can hardly learn from this perspective why many other Western nations launched paternalist welfare states between the 1880s and the 1920s, while the United States primarily enacted maternalist regulations and social benefits. Of course it was important that industrialization and urbanization were transforming America around the turn of the twentieth century. These processes threw up new issues and social groupings that entered into political conflicts. But they did not determine patterns of political contention or policy outcomes. What is needed is an approach much more sensitive to the political causes and the substantive contents of social policies.

Can National Values Explain Social Policymaking?

Rather than assimilate the U.S. case to a worldwide logic of industrialism, there have always been those who highlight "American exceptionalism," tracing it to the country's extraordinarily strong liberal values. In a classic formulation, Louis Hartz argued that the United States, a nation born in rebellion against British rule and a country supposedly without class divisions or a feudal heritage, developed an all-encompassing liberal culture in which individual rights are sacred, private property is honored, and state authority is distrusted.[28] As one of the world's "new societies," America in Hartz's view was a pure "bourgeois-capitalist" fragment, broken off from Europe and lacking the ideological dynamism occasioned by the clash of feudalism, liberalism, and socialism back on the Mother Continent.[29] Since Hartz, others have used the hegemony of liberal values to account more specifically for American social politics in contrast to the development of European welfare states.

Scholars point to different aspects of "liberalism" as the chief obstacle to governmental social provision in the United States. The comparative economic historian Gaston Rimlinger treated individualist values as central.[30] In a slightly different formulation, the cultural historian Daniel Levine characterizes the nineteenth- and early-twentieth-century United States as a "land of abundance," a market-oriented society whose citizens saw "no reason for people to be poor and therefore no reason for any but the most minimal, mostly private, charity."[31] The social welfare historian Roy Lubove attributes the failure of most social insurance proposals in the Progressive Era to the strength of voluntarism, the aspect of the American liberal tradition that he chooses to emphasize. He argues that in "the broadest sense voluntary association provided an alternative to politics and governmental action. It enabled groups of all kinds to exert an influence and seek their distinctive goals without resort to the coercive powers of government."[32] The fundamental theme of distrust of government is also highlighted by the political scientist Anthony King, who argues straightforwardly that "the State plays a more limited role in America than elsewhere because Americans, more than other people, want it to play a limited role." King explains that "Americans' beliefs and assumptions about government . . . can be summarized in a series of catch phrases: free enterprise is more efficient than government; governments should concentrate on encouraging private initiative and free competition; government is wasteful; governments should not provide people with things they can provide for themselves; too much government endangers liberty; and so on."[33]

For scholars of the national values persuasion, the underlying dynamics posited by the logic of industrialism approach are considered to be necessary but not sufficient to explain national variations. These socieconomic processes do indeed push all nations toward modern social policies. At the same time the cultural and ideological conditions inherited from each country's preindustrial past either facilitate or delay governmental actions to promote social security. Many scholars who talk about national values are vague about the processes through which they influence policymaking. From scattered explicit and implicit remarks, however, we can surmise that inherited values are thought to influence the actions that political leaders choose to take, as well as the ease with which reformers outside government can build popular support for proposed new policies. Cultural and ideological factors are also said to affect the programmatic design and the official rationales of the modern social policies that, sooner or later, must emerge in all nations undergoing economic development.

Scholars of the national values school point convincingly to overall correlations between major cultural traditions and the forms and rationales of social policies. The arguments are especially plausible when countries at the opposite poles of "authoritarianism" versus "liberalism" are contrasted, as they often are by these scholars. Germany versus the United States is a favorite comparison.[34] Nevertheless, proponents of this approach have so far failed to pinpoint exactly how cultural values, intellectual traditions, and ideological outlooks have concretely influenced processes of political conflict and policy debate. Nor have these scholars addressed the most difficult puzzles about political culture and the development of social policies in America.

Along with others, scholars who regard the dominance of U.S. liberalism as an impenetrable obstacle to public social provision prior to the 1930s have failed to consider Civil War pensions. When liberal values of individualism, self-sufficiency, voluntarism, distrust of government, and market competition were supposedly at their height in the late nineteenth century, how was it that Americans countenanced such widespread and relatively generous benefits, delivered directly by the federal government, and often to people not suffering from war wounds or economic privation of any kind? Almost all proponents of the liberalism argument seem to regard nineteeth-century America as a "self-adjusting" market economy with a minimalist government not capable of much involvement in either economic or social life.[35] But U.S. public policies in the nineteenth century were actually quite interventionist—for distributive purposes. There simply never was a "night watchman state" in U.S. capitalism or in American society.

There are also problems with less economistic arguments that treat U.S. voluntary associations as inherently morally opposed to government action. Why was it that the Grand Army of the Republic, in many ways a voluntary fraternal association like others that proliferated in the nineteenth century, became within a few years of its founding deeply involved in lobbying for participation in the implementation of governmental social benefits for veterans? And why did women's voluntary associations end up deemphasizing private charitable solutions to social problems in favor of campaigns for new public social legislation in the early twentieth century? Clearly, distrust of the state was not an absolute even for those Americans who placed great value on voluntary association. Voluntarism and governmental action have never been simple opposites in the United States. Voluntarism often leads toward involvement with government, and gives rise to new demands for public social provision.

Arguments about national values are too holistic and essentialist to give us the explanatory leverage we need to account for variations in the fate of different social policies, or for changes over time in the fate of similar proposals. Why did public education spread early and extensively in the United States, but not social insurance?[36] Anthony King answers, simply, that public education is more congruent with American values about equality of opportunity and supporting individual initiative.[37] Perhaps. But, then, why have public policies to support full employment opportunities and employment training not been much more readily instituted in the United States than straightforward public benefits for the elderly and the poor? Throughout U.S. history, American citizens have preferred public help to get jobs over other kinds of public assistance. Proposed employment policies have been accompanied by compelling rhetoric about the need to help citizens help themselves, but only sometimes have such policies been enacted.[38] Obviously, the mere value-content of arguments made on behalf of policy proposals is not enough to explain their fate.

Nor is the value-content of arguments made *against* proposed policies sufficient to explain legislative outcomes. Perhaps the clearest example of ideologically imbued opposition to a U.S. social policy innovation was the strong resistance of most charity organizations during the 1910s to the enactment of pensions for poor mothers and children. Eloquent appeals were made to fundamental liberal values of voluntarism and individual responsibility, as charity spokespersons argued that private help was best for the poor, who should not become "dependent" on governmental handouts.[39] Despite such appeals, mothers' pensions were enacted.

Obviously, other forces can override whatever obstacles to public social provision are inherent in American liberalism—assuming that such a value complex really has held sway in the nation's social and political life. This, however, may be an assumption in need of critical reexamination. A swelling strand of historical scholarship has questioned the Hartzian notion of an all-encompassing individualist-liberal culture in the American past. Coming together in the 1960s, what Robert Shalhope called "the republican synthesis" in American historiography fundamentally revised understandings of political thought in the late colonial, revolutionary, and early national periods, arguing that Lockean liberalism was not the primary current. Rather, early

> Americans believed that what either made republics great or ultimately destroyed them was not the force of arms, but the character and spirit of the people. Public virtue became preeminent . . . Easily acquired wealth had to be gained at the expense of others; it was the whole body politic that was crucial, for the public welfare was the exclusive end of good government and required constant sacrifice of individual interests to the greater needs of the whole.[40]

A thoughtful recent commentary by James T. Kloppenberg argues that this "republican virtue tradition" was not the only ideological influence at work in the early national period. It coexisted and mingled with Protestant Christian religious ideals and with "a tradition of liberalism based on responsibility rather than cupidity."[41] All of these traditions could be used to justify public policies expressing civic ideals.

"The ethical thrust" of early American political culture, Kloppenberg suggests, diminished into the "flattened discourse of nineteenth-century individualism and democracy" with its accompanying celebration of the unfettered pursuit of market advantages.[42] Sean Wilentz describes this as a process that at first unfolded among elites:

> Between the Revolution and 1850 changing class and social relations led to recurring reinterpretations of republicanism and battles over what the republican legacy meant. During that period, some groups of Americans—preeminently, so far as we know, the nation's leading politicians and jurists but certainly many more— came increasingly to interpret the republican framework as one or another form of liberal capitalist polity and economy. They did not reject republicanism in favor of liberalism; they associated one with the other.[43]

Yet echoes of republican civic virtue certainly reverberated through the century. Starting during the Jackson period, such values inspired movements to create the public "common schools" that proliferated across communities and states in nineteenth-century America. The purpose of widespread basic education, the early school reformers declared, was not to help individuals get ahead but to educate a virtuous American citizenry to serve as the democratic backbone of the Republic.[44] Ideals of civic virtue were also unmistakably present in antislavery crusades, in the Republican call to arms for the Civil War, and in the Mugwumps' efforts to reform party politics in the later nineteenth century. Interestingly enough, both supporters and critics of Civil War pensions invoked civic values in support of their positions. As the Grand Army of the Republic argued for the sacred obiligation of the Nation to protect the Union veterans who had saved it, reformers such as Charles Eliot argued that the profligacy of the ever expanding pension system would have pernicious effects on the public morals of officeholders and citizens alike.[45]

What is more, as a number of U.S. labor historians have recently argued, "labor republicanism" flourished in movements of American artisans, wage-workers, and small property holders from the Jackson era through the nationwide mobilization of the Knights of Labor in the 1880s.[46] Describing what he calls "a nation-wide expression of . . . nineteenth-century American class consciousness" in the Knights, Wilentz explains that it

> was not, in any way, a sharply defined proletarianism . . . It was a consciousness of class in which the demise of the American republic and growing concentration of wealth and power were attributed to the inequalities and unnatural dependencies of the wages system. Fundamental to this consciousness was the belief that these inequalities should be removed not by returning to some (apocryphal) traditional "golden age," but by democratizing the political and economic relations of industrializing America.[47]

Significantly, the Knights of Labor called for many governmental policies to promote social welfare in a "cooperative commonwealth" of producers.[48] Even after the Knights were superseded by the American Federation of Labor with its dominant ideology of "pure and simple" trade unionism, some state-level labor movements, such as the Washington State Federation of Labor, remained so imbued with the ideals of working-class republicanism that they were at the forefront of struggles for labor regulations and state-funded accident insurance in the early twentieth century.[49]

Reworked republican ideals, surviving at least through most of the nineteenth century, were not the only source of legitimation for public social provision in industrializing America. The normative political thought of middle-class women's associations remains to be analyzed by scholars far more qualified in this field than I. Yet it is obvious that women, who were deliberately left out of the original independent, patriarchal, property-holding conception of republican citizenship, developed in creative tension with republican and liberal ideals their own values to sustain civic participation and action for community welfare.[50] Originally assigned the strictly domestic yet thoroughly moral role of "republican motherhood," many American women—especially white, middle-class, Protestant women—extended their domestic sphere outward to fill much of the civic space left behind by elite men, who were turning to the individualist-liberal pursuit of market wealth and partisan party power.[51] The nation itself, women's ideologists sometimes argued, could be saved only through the full extension of selfless and nonmaterialistic domestic values into public life. As Rheta Childe Dorr put it in 1910: "Woman's place is in the Home . . . Her task is homemaking. Her talents, as a rule, are mainly for homemaking. But Home is not contained within the four walls of an individual home. Home is the community. The city full of people is the Family. The public school is the real Nursery. And badly do the Home and the Family and the Nursery need their mother."[52] Such women's ideologies of "social housekeeping," particularly when expressed by charitable and temperance movements or in widespread federations of local women's clubs and mothers' clubs, eventually served to justify calls for governmental policies designed to help, first underprivileged women, then all mothers and children, and finally all of America's families.[53] As we shall see in Part III, arguments based on notions of women's special morality accepted by most Americans of both genders did much to shape public opinion and legislative agendas in the early twentieth century.

Recent intellectual and cultural historiography, in sum, undermines any essentialist, timeless, and holistic notion of "American liberal values," and points to coexisting ideals of religious and republican virtue, as well as feminine ideals of "social housekeeping," as alternative sources of legitimation for public social provision. What is more, recent historiography underlines how unfruitful it is to think of liberalism itself as merely a set of laissez-faire, individualist tenets starkly opposed to possibilities for social provision.

Early welfare state measures could in fact be intellectually justified and morally valued through internal reworkings of liberalism itself. Liberal values were in many respects just as hegemonic in nineteenth-century Britain as they were in the nineteenth-century United States. Yet before World War I, Britain enacted a full range of social protective measures, including workers' compensation (1906), old-age pensions (1908), and unemployment and health insurance (1911). These innovations came under the auspices of the British Liberal Party, and they were intellectually and politically justified by appeals to "new liberal" values of the sort that were also making progress among educated Americans around the turn of the century.[54] Under modern urban-industrial conditions, the "new liberals" argued, positive governmental means must be used to support individual security; and this can be accomplished without undermining individuals' liberty or making them dependent on the state. If British

Liberals could use such ideas to justify both state-funded pensions and contributory social insurance in the second decade of the twentieth century, why couldn't American progressives do the same? In both Britain and the United States by the turn of the twentieth century, sufficient cultural transformation within liberalism had occurred to legitimate fledgling welfare states without resort to either conservative-paternalist or socialist justifications.[55] Eventually, indeed, U.S. New Dealers used just such new-liberal arguments to justify the nationwide social security policies that they successfully launched during the 1930s.

As this book proceeds, we can retain the salutary emphasis on historical process that scholars of the national values school have introduced in response to logic of industrialism arguments. Yet general deductions from national values—however defined—simply cannot give us the answers to many crucial questions about public policymaking. To explain varying policy outcomes, and to compare U.S. developments to those in other countries—especially liberal Britain—we must find more precise analytical tools than those offered by this approach. *Whose* ideas and and values? And ideas and values *about what* more precisely? We must identify the groups active in politics, analyze the resources that they can bring to bear in allying or conflicting with one another. These are matters we will need to take seriously—along with the comingling of cultural traditions and the possibility of variable interpretations of each tradition's central ideas.

We must also investigate how the changing institutional configurations of national polities advantage some strategies and ideological outlooks and hamper others. Too often, national values explanations one-sidedly derive political outcomes from values, without revealing that experiences with governmental institutions and political processes profoundly affect the way people understand and evaluate alternative policy possibilities within a given cultural frame. Thus a central theme in this book will be the impact of nineteenth-century party politics on elite and popular understandings of what was possible and desirable in U.S. social politics during the early twentieth century. Within the broad bounds of "liberal" politics, the outlooks and policy proposals of reformist professionals, trade unionists, and women's groups were all profoundly influenced by their diverse socially situated experiences with U.S. political institutions. Moreover, the British counterparts to these American groups developed different outlooks and policy goals because of their interactions with a contrasting set of political institutions.

Working-Class Weakness?
The United States and the Social Democratic Model

Recently, debates among scholars doing cross-national studies of six to eighteen Western industrial nations have converged on what Michael Shalev calls the "social democratic model" of welfare state development.[56] According to the boldest form of this model put forward by such theorists as Walter Korpi and John Stephens, "the welfare state is a product of the growing strength of labour in civil society."[57] For these authors, a fully developed welfare state coordinates social benefits (such as social insurance, welfare transfers, and public housing, education, and health services) with industrial regulations (enforcing minimum wages, workplace safety, and unionization) and with Keynesian and labor-market policies aimed at ensuring economic growth with full employment.[58] Such a full-employment welfare state is the historical construction of

> a highly centralized trade union movement with a class-wide membership base, operating in close coordination with a unified reformist-socialist party which, primarily on the basis of massive working class support, is able to achieve hegemonic status in the party system. To the extent that these criteria are met, it is hypothesized that the welfare state will emerge earlier, grow faster, and be structured in ways which systematically favor the interests of labor over those of capital.[59]

For the adherents of this social democratic approach, Sweden since World War II is the epitome of a fully developed welfare state—while the United States repeatedly appears in their studies at the opposite pole, as the exemplar of a minimally developed welfare state. A straightforward explanation is offered: American public social provision commenced later and has not become as generous as European public social provision, because of the relative weakness of U.S. industrial unions and the complete absence of any labor-based political party in American democracy. Given these weaknesses of working-class organization, U.S. capitalists have been unusually able to prevent governments at all levels from undertaking social-

welfare efforts that would reshape labor markets or interfere with
the prerogatives or profits of private business. In short, if the welfare
state is the product of the strength of labor in civil society, then a
weak or nonexistent welfare state must be the product of the weakness of organized labor and the relatively unchallenged hegemony
of capitalists.

Plausible as the social democratic model may seem, if our intention
is not merely to contrast the United States with Sweden from the
1940s onward but also to explain the overall trajectory and specific
patterns of U.S. social provision since the nineteenth century, then
this model is misleading or insufficient in several ways.

In the first place, the social democratic model does not adequately
illuminate historical events and sequences prior to the 1940s for
either the United States or Europe. In the late-nineteenth-century
United States, the expansion of Civil War pensions owed little to
trade unions or working-class-based politicians; and the benefits that
fully enfranchised American workers gained from nineteenth-century politics are not captured by the social democratic model. Meanwhile, between the 1880s and 1920s in Germany, Sweden, Britain,
and other nations that launched pioneering paternalist welfare
states, social insurance programs were devised by conservative or
liberal politicians and bureaucrats, not by trade unions and social
democratic political parties.[60] During this period, trade unions everywhere were preoccupied with other kinds of public policies, such as
the legal rules affecting union organization. And unions realistically
worried that social insurance programs might undercut their autonomy and empower bureaucrats. Only after early European social
insurance programs were launched did trade unions and labor-
oriented political parties become strong advocates of their expansion—especially if benefits could be increased without commensurate
"contributions" taken directly from the paychecks of workers.

Indeed, the social democratic model cannot explain the stances
taken by U.S. trade unions on proposals for British-style social policies during the Progressive Era. It is true that craft unions dominated the American Federation of Labor (AFL) during this period,
and the national AFL leadership opposed contributory social insurance. Nevertheless the AFL did call for noncontributory old-age pensions, just as the British unions did in the early 1900s. Moreover,
Federations of Labor in many U.S. states, including relatively strong

ones in the leading industrial states with many unionized workers, supported calls for both old-age pensions and social insurance. As Chapter 4 will show, differential labor strength as a single, unmediated factor cannot account for the divergent policy patterns of the United States and Britain between the 1890s and the 1920s. The British and U.S. trade union movements began with similar orientations toward social legislation, and then diverged because of their experiences in very different national polities. In general, institutional influences on working-class political outlooks need to be considered along with measures of working-class strength in cross-national explanations of social policy development.

Additional problems with the social democratic model flow from its overemphasis on political conflicts between capitalists and industrial workers. This deflects our attention from other social classes and from cross-class coalitions that have played major roles in the development of modern social provision. Cross-class coalitions between professionals and popular groups have been crucial to the enactment of all modern social policies in every nation. What is more, for Sweden and the other Scandinavian democracies—on the home turf of the social democratic model, so to speak—Francis Castles, Gösta Esping-Andersen, and others have recently stressed the role of agrarian parties and agrarian-urban alliances in launching and expanding social provision, noting that alternative urban-rural coalitions blocked or retarded comparable policies elsewhere in Europe.[61] Similarly, for the United States from Civil War pensions through Social Security, regionally differentiated agrarian interests have always been crucial arbiters of the extension and limitation of public social provision.[62]

Social identities and conflicts based on ethnicity, race, and gender also tend to be overlooked in the social democratic perspective, with its primary focus on working-class organization. Along with other theorists of modern welfare states to date, proponents of the social democratic model have tended to assume that all significant social policies are targeted on wage-workers or employees (or perhaps "citizens" in general, with a tacit assumption that they are employees or economic dependents of employees). But this conception of the policies to be explained is misleading. As this book emphasizes, certain major phases and sectors of U.S. social provision, such as Civil War pensions and workingmen's benefits, have been constructed around male roles—including the noneconomic role of the soldier-veteran, as well as the role of wage-earning family breadwinner—while others have been focused on the female roles of mother and working woman understood as a potential mother.

When accounting for policy developments in Europe and the United States, social democratic theorists prefer to treat racial, ethnic, or gender factors simply as potential "divisions" that may undercut the unified class organization of wage- and salary-workers. Of course, these social differences do often function to subdivide workers. But such a view is not sufficient for the analysis of any country's policy history, and especially not for understanding the United States, where political forces grounded in ethnic and gender identities positively shaped early patterns of public social provision.[63] Competing political parties rooted in regional and ethnic differences, and in white male fraternalism, fueled the expansion of Civil War benefits. Federated white women's clubs expressing a certain kind of gender ideology agitated for maternalist social policies during the early 1900s. To make sense of all of this, we must have a theoretical frame of reference that sensitizes us to the full range of identities and relationships, including class but not restricted to it, that may figure in a nation's social politics.

Business Hegemony?
Welfare Capitalism and U.S. Public Social Provision

If an organized working class was not the primary actor in the dramas of U.S. social provision, what about that perennial deus ex machina of American history, big business? While some business interests opposed social policies as the social democratic model presumes, perhaps others actually *propelled* the limited and often market-oriented social policies that have developed in the United States. This sort of class argument has able proponents. As comparative social scientists have debated the social democratic model, which necessarily regards the United States as a "negative" case where the working class is weak, scholars who have analyzed U.S. social provision outside of any explicit cross-national context have elaborated the "welfare capitalism" approach.

Proponents of the welfare capitalism approach take for granted that corporate capitalists have dominated U.S. political processes since the late nineteenth century, and they look for economically grounded splits between conservative and progressive capitalists, or between regional economic blocs, as the way to explain social policy developments.[64] Jill Quadagno analyzes the expansion of Civil War pensions in the context of the regional dominance of the North over the South, and grounds Republican support for rising pension expenditures in the desire of many northern manufacturers to retain high protective tariffs.[65] To explain twentieth-century social policy developments, she and other welfare capitalist theorists argue that certain U.S. corporations preceded the public sector in evolving principles of modern organizational management, including policies for stabilizing and planning employment and for protecting the social welfare of loyal employees. When public social insurance measures were finally legislated in key states and at the federal level, these policies supposedly responded to the suggestions of the welfare capitalists, and were designed to meet the needs of progressively managed business corporations.

Advocates of this perspective have produced many studies showing that particular capitalists advocated this or that social policy—usually a program to be voluntarily implemented by their own or other people's corporations, yet occasionally a provision of a law actually enacted by government. Welfare capitalist theorists have been even more successful at demonstrating influences by corporations over the implementation of laws, once passed by governments.[66] Nevertheless, these theorists have failed to demonstrate that significant *groups or categories* of U.S. capitalists—as opposed to maverick individuals not representative of any class or industrial sector—ever supported mandatory public old-age pensions or social insurance in the United States. Nor have they acknowledged the many times when business actors, even the most "progressive" ones, failed to have their preferences realized in the political process. Indeed, theorists of this school have remarkably little to say about actual political processes and legislative battles. They often present amazingly naive pictures of "policymaking" that amount to little more than documenting a personal contact between a capitalist and a legislator or an executive official.

As the social democratic model posits, American business groups have almost always opposed old-age pensions and social insurance legislation, along with most other federal and state-level social and regulatory measures favorable to workers or consumers.[67] The one clear-cut exception to this statement—the workmen's compensation laws of the 1910s—can be explained only by taking into account preexisting governmental structures and public policies. As we shall see in Chapter 5, U.S. business groups along with others sought a change from governmental regulation through the courts to another form of public regulation. Yet business groups that supported workmen's compensation did not always get the kinds of laws they preferred. More to the point, they did not ask for government to intervene *de novo* in an area where it was not previously involved. No matter how adaptable American capitalists have proven to be after the fact, the historical evidence is overwhelming that they have regularly opposed the initial establishment of new public policies that (in their perception) would either interfere with managerial prerogatives or in any way raise the cost of doing business. As a consequence, forces other than U.S. capitalists have propelled the development of American social policies that embodied significant extensions of governmental regulation, taxing, and spending.

To be sure, some advocates of the welfare capitalism perspective acknowledge that policy intellectuals (including social scientists or lawyers or social-work leaders) have defined agendas of public debate and decided upon the details of proposed social policy innovations. Nevertheless, in welfare capitalism accounts, such policy intellectuals are treated as agents acting for enlightened business interests, and evidence is offered of the financial and organizational ties between big business and particular intellectuals or groups of policy experts. For example, the leading group of reformist intellectuals active in research and the advocacy of new social policies during the Progressive Era was the American Association for Labor Legislation. Scholars of the welfare capitalism school have labeled it business-dominated, citing financial gifts from capitalists and the presence of some business people in the organization in support of this conclusion.[68]

The welfare capitalism perspective on policy-oriented intellectuals downplays the distinctive orientations that these intellectuals, along with other educated middle-class people, often bring to the politics of social policymaking. A major shortcoming of most political economy approaches, not just this one, is the tendency to posit zero-sum relations of domination or struggle between only two classes, capitalists and industrial workers. Not only does this overlook agrarian groups along with social groups based on race and gender; it also forces "professionals" and all sorts of educated workers into the two-class mold. Such groups must be seen as aligned with, or agents of, either capital or labor. In the American case, for obvious reasons, professionals and policy intellectuals have tended to be seen as allies of capital—particularly big business, whose financial hand can always be found in the universities, research institutes, and foundations from which new policy ideas frequently emanate. Certainly there have been instances where organizations of policy intellectuals were on very short financial leashes from vigilant business interests and, as a result, avoided certain findings or recommendations.[69] Often, however, the financial leashes are not so short, and the business overseers not so vigilant. In those instances, self-sustaining groups of American policy intellectuals have developed relatively autonmous conceptions of "the public interest" and pursued policies accordingly.[70] For such groups of intellectuals and professionals, we need to probe directly the outlooks, the organizational settings, and the career patterns that have underpinned their pursuit of lines of policy distinct from those favored by either business or labor.

As we avoid simply assuming that intellectuals and professionals are thinking for someone else, we must also avoid the proclivity of welfare capitalism theorists to treat political parties and politicians as mere agents of business. It is certainly true that American political parties have always had intimate financial connections with businesses and wealthy individuals. It is also true that close connections can often be documented between legislators or executive agencies and businessmen. But these facts do not mean that voters and elections, or nonbusiness groups, can be ignored in analyses of policy debates or legislative processes. Still less do they mean that politicians or governmental officials respond only to the demands or needs of business. Elected politicians and appointed officials in the United States look for ways to aggregate or compromise the interests of diverse groups who have various nonoverlapping resources—votes, money, public statements of approval—that the politicians and officials need. Moreover, politicians and officials seek to forge these compromises of social interests in ways congruent with the operating needs of the political institutions within which they pursue their careers.

Indeed, we should finally keep in mind that "business interests" themselves cannot be defined, and certainly not realized, outside of the context of historically existing political institutions or apart from prior public policies. Like industrial workers and other social groups, capitalists always define their interests, form political alliances, and achieve (or fail to achieve) policy goals through given political arrangements at particular times and places. Welfare capitalist theorists ground capitalist interests in market and corporate dynamics, paying too little attention to the impact on business goals and capacities of governmental arrangements, party systems, and preexisting public policies.

How Should Gender Enter the Analysis?

We have seen that existing theoretical perspectives on modern social policies ignore gendered dimensions of politics, as well as the roles that women's organizations may have played in bringing about particular sorts of measures. In the welfare state literature, as in standard U.S. welfare historiography, "public" life is typically presumed to be an exclusively male sphere, with women regarded as "private" actors confined to homes and charitable associations. Debates have centered on the relative contributions of male-dominated unions, political parties, and bureaucracies to the shaping of labor regulations and social benefits designed to help male breadwinners and their dependents. Established approaches often overlook social policies targeted on mothers and women workers. And they fail to notice the contributions of female-dominated modes of politics, some of which are not dependent on action through parties, elections, trade unions, or official bureaucracies. The unconsciously gendered premises of cross-national research on the origins of welfare states have blinded scholars to patterns of politics and policy that were especially important in the United States between the 1870s and the 1920s. In this book I try to improve our perception by keeping gendered social policies, especially Civil War pensions and maternalist policies, very much at the center of explanatory attention.

Are there *theories* that make gender relations or identities central to the explanation of social policies in the United States and across nations? Serious scholarship on gender and welfare states is so new that much of it is either historically descriptive or devoted to sensitizing readers to matters previously overlooked. Interpretive essays abound in a very recent, lively literature about women and welfare, but it is difficult to find straightforward causal propositions about gender and social policies. Nevertheless, a few things can be said about theoretical frames of reference and tentative arguments already in the literature.[71]

Much as the early neo-Marxist debates about "the capitalist state" found myriad ways to repeat the insight that all kinds of governmental actions could express capitalist class interests or reproduce capitalist class relationships, so many of today's fledgling feminist theories of the welfare state argue that modern social policies express dominant male interests and reproduce "patriarchal" relations between the genders in ever changing ways. The focus may be on gendered relations of domination in families or in paid workforces, or (most often) on shifts in the linkages between the two spheres of patriarchal domination. Regardless, governmental actions, including social policies, are portrayed as functioning to reinforce or rework male domination of women. Thus, Eileen Boris and Peter Bardaglio argue in "The Transformation of State Patriarchy" that the

> nineteenth and early twentieth centuries . . . saw not the decline
> of patriarchy but its transformation from a familial to a state form
> . . . [T]he emergence of the welfare state did not erode the family
> as such, but it did begin to undermine the patriarchal structure of
> relations between men and women within many families . . . Laws
> and public policies—as well as governmental institutions and
> professional supervision by doctors, educators, social workers, and
> other so-called family experts—developed as part of a larger sup-
> port system that reproduced patriarchal social relations. Conse-
> quently, male-dominated—even male-headed—families became
> less important to the maintenance of male domination in the social
> arena outside the family . . . [I]ncreasingly egalitarian legal rela-
> tions in families were counterbalanced by the continued economic
> exploitation of women at home and in the workplace.[72]

In a slightly different patriarchal formulation, one combined with elements of Marxist analysis, Mimi Abramovitz argues in *Regulating the Lives of Women: Social Welfare Policy from Colonial Times to the Present* that American social policies have functioned to enforce a "family ethic" about women's proper roles. In response to the economy's changing needs for women's extrafamilial labor, governmental policies have varied in the degree to which they pushed marginal women into the paid labor force. Such "programs have tended to reward women whose lives included marriage, motherhood, and homemaking but to penalize women who did not or could not choose such pursuits."[73]

Patriarchal domination perspectives have been used to interpret various kinds of U.S. social legislation in the early twentieth century. Protective labor laws for women workers have been presented as devices to keep women from competing equally on labor markets with male wage earners.[74] And mothers' pensions have been presented as devices to keep women at home and away from well-paid wage-labor.[75] Above all, scholars working from patriarchal presumptions have focused on the local implementation of mothers' pensions from the 1910s onward. In most localities where mothers' pensions were funded at all, decisions were made about which mothers were morally "fit" to receive benefits, and about how to define the "suitable homes" that mothers had to maintain to continue to qualify for benefits. Widows rather than unmarried mothers were the ones who qualified, and there may have been cultural discrimination against widows from subordinate racial and ethnic groups (although many foreign-born and some black widows did receive benefits). Widowed mothers had to avoid or give up full-time paid jobs outside the home to stay at home with their children. At the same time, their pensions were so small that they often had to do low-paid part-time wage-work or else tasks (such as laundry) that could be carried on at home. Obviously, this overall situation accords well with patriarchal domination perspectives, which stress that welfare policies such as mothers' pensions should favor formerly married women, enforce domestic norms, and restrict women who work for wages to marginal, low-paid jobs.

Nevertheless, in their interpretations of mothers' pensions and protective labor regulations, patriarchal theorists have little to say about variations in the timing or contents of legislation or about differences in patterns of implementation. The "reproduction of patriarchy" and the "enforcement of the family ethic" are too vague to explain such variations. More important, patriarchal theories are positively misleading about the origins of maternalist social policies during the Progressive Era. Thus, Mimi Abramovitz's chapter "Poor Women and Progressivism" portrays reformers and public social service workers as the sole moving force behind mothers' pensions and protective labor regulations for women workers.[76] While the benign intentions of some of these advocates are acknowledged, Abramowitz has practically nothing to say about the political processes that led to the enactment of such laws by many state legislatures. She primarily emphasizes the ways in which the Progressive Era laws allegedly channeled women out of the paid labor force and into domestic duties. Like other patriarchal theorists who write from the perspective of American equal-rights feminists of the 1960s, Abramowitz leaves the strong impression that these laws created a more repressive situation for poor widows and wage-workers.

We do not learn from this and other patriarchal domination accounts that prior to the enactment of mothers' pensions, poor widows usually faced worse options, including more repressive forms of low-wage toil and governmental intervention to take away their children.[77] Nor do we learn (as we shall see in Part III of this book) that many women's groups, including women's trade unions as well as elite and middle-class women's clubs, mobilized politically to press for the enactment of protective labor laws and mothers' pensions— even if the practical implementation of these laws eventually belied the hopes of many of their original supporters. When patriarchal theorists do mention the role of elite and middle-class women in pressing for new social policies, they present this situation as the imposition of middle-class norms on poor women. We do not learn of the celebration of the universal civic value of mothering—by mothers of all classes and races—that was so central to women's movements for mothers' pensions and protective labor legislation in the early 1900s. Or if such ideas are described, they are treated cynically as a disguise for more fundamental system-functions of patriarchal, class, and racial domination.[78]

Theories highlighting patriarchal domination have also tended to obscure crucial variations among early modern social policies relevant to women. Many scholars have insightfully argued that most (although not all) early social policies in Europe, Australasia, and the Americas idealized the "family wage," that is, the notion that male wage earners should earn enough to sustain their families. Empirically speaking, adequate family wages were rarely actually earned by working-class males during industrialization; and for military and demographic reasons certain nations such as France created social policies that helped women to combine wage-earning and motherhood. But professional reformers as well as male trade unionists in many nations—including the United States and Britain—did tend to believe in the family wage earned by a male breadwinner as an ideal. Along with many other forces, this ideal devalued women's wage-work and played up the value of their unpaid roles as housewives and mothers. When applied to early modern labor regulations and social spending policies, the family wage ideal encouraged measures that would, on the one hand, increase male wages and, on the other hand, sustain women and children who lacked "male breadwinners." Feminist scholarship about social policies enacted from the late nineteenth through the mid-twentieth centuries constantly emphasizes that labor regulations, social insurance, and relief policies usually presumed the family wage as an ideal norm. This situation has been labeled "patriarchal."

But we should not allow an insight about the similar breadwinner-led family norms on which most modern social policies were originally based to obscure crucial differences between what I call "paternalist" and "maternalist" versions of such policies. Besides being devised by male politicians, bureaucrats, and trade unionists, paternalist measures—such as those that dominated British social policy during the early 1900s—attempted to shore up the working condition of all workers in ways that reinforced male trade unions, and attempted to channel public benefits to women and children through male wage-earning capacities. Thus British wives gained rights to maternity benefits under the 1911 National Insurance law if they were married to wage earners who "contributed" to the system; and the same was true for survivors of British male breadwinners under the 1925 Widows, Orphans, and Old Age Contributory Pensions Act. In contrast, early U.S. labor regulations were not only devised and implemented primarily by female professionals and women's groups, they also applied directly to women. U.S. labor regulations covered women workers. U.S. mothers' pensions went directly to widowed mothers (and occasionally to nonwidowed mothers) regardless of the previous wage-earning status of their dead or departed husbands. And the educational services of Sheppard-Towner clinics went directly to all mothers, including many who were not tied to wage earners. All of these are properly understood as "maternalist" versions of policies that presumed breadwinner ideals.

Broader categories of women were reached by these measures than would have been reached if they had been oriented more exclusively toward the dependents of wage-earning men. There are, in short, policy variations within "patriarchy" that need to be fully understood and analyzed, along with variations in the timing and geographical spread of legislative enactments.

Interpretations highlighting patriarchal domination are, however, not the only way in which feminist scholars are seeking to understand the social policies of the United States and other nations. Much as abstract, functionalist, neo-Marxist theories of the capitalist state came to be challenged by comparative-historical studies that stressed the agency of working-class organizations, so are feminist debates about social policies beginning to be informed by historical and comparative studies that focus on the institutionally and culturally conditioned activities of women's groups in shaping early modern social policies.

Historians of middle-class women's activities and outlooks in the industrializing United States have produced a rich literature on which I shall draw in Chapter 6. This literature highlights not patriarchal oppression but American women's political agency and what historian Paula Baker calls the "domestication" of American politics.[79] It probes the ways in which many elite and middle-class Protestant women (mostly white, yet including some black women) created organizations infused with aspirations to extend women's domestic values into civic and national life. One scholar who operates within this women's agency framework, Kathryn Kish Sklar, goes so far as to argue that "women reformers . . . used gender-specific approaches to social problems as surrogates for class-specific strategies" in the course of launching an early American welfare state.[80] Sklar has developed her ideas while working on a massive biography of the social-democratic reformer Florence Kelley, who did indeed use women's mobilization and gender-specific laws as ways to work toward working-class welfare. But however appropriate Sklar's instrumentalist formulation—stressing gender as a straightforward surrogate for class—may be for Florence Kelley in particular, it does not capture the full complexity of the ideals that American women brought to social politics around the turn of the twentieth century. Nor can a focus on intellectual reformers alone alert us to the remarkable leverage that coalitions of many different forces, including diverse women's movements, achieved in U.S. social policymaking during this period. We must compare various women's organizations to one another, and to organizations of unionized male workers and male professionals. And we need to analyze the interplay between U.S. political institutions and variously structured social movements and political coalitions. Sklar's provocative scholarship makes an important start in these directions, challenging us to explain why the U.S. polity in the early twentieth century was more receptive to women's movements for social policies targeted on mothers than it was to bureaucratic, professional, or trade union efforts on behalf of social policies targeted on all wage-workers.

Methodologically, Sklar's work can be called a cross-nationally informed case study, because she brilliantly uses comparisons between Britain and the United States to analyze the sociocultural and political contexts within which Florence Kelley became so influential in early modern social policymaking. Unfortunately, most historiography of women and early-twentieth-century U.S. policymaking remains very insular, relying on archival sources about particular individuals or organizations—usually intellectuals based in New York, Massachusetts, Illinois, and Washington, DC—and not making use of systematic comparisons. But very recently some fully comparative studies have appeared, analyzing the place of gender relationships and women's agency in the social politics of various U.S. states, and in the launching of different national systems of social provision within the Western world.[81]

An example of this valuable new comparative scholarship is Seth Koven and Sonya Michel's "'Womanly Duties': Maternalist Politics and the Origins of Welfare States in France, Germany, Great Britain, and the United States, 1880–1920," a synthetic article that draws upon a range of historical studies by its authors as well as others.[82] Koven and Michel stress that women's voluntary groups developed models and proposals for early welfare state policies across all of these Western nations. Women's groups were often "maternalist" in orientation—that is, devoted to extending domestic ideals into public life—and they demanded benefits and services especially targeted on mothers and children. In Koven and Michel's view, maternalist women's politics was strongest in the nations that had the "weakest," least bureaucratic states. Thus they group Britain and the United States together in contrast to France and Germany, where "strong" bureaucratic states tended to crowd out women's politics. Yet Koven and Michel also point to a supreme irony in early welfare state formation. They argue that the countries that had stronger women's movements ended up with less generous social benefits for mothers and children as their national systems of public social provision matured.

I do not fully agree with Koven and Michel's analysis. Their contrast between "weak" and "strong" states is too crude to get at the differences among national political systems that affect how likely women are to become politically active and (a separate issue) in what ways women can have an impact on policy decisions. In particular, Koven and Michel fail to analyze crucial differences between the ways class and gender identities figured in the social politics of Britain and the United States between the 1870s and the 1920s. Although both of these nations had "weak states" in Koven and Michel's terms, they actually had very different governmental institutions, administrative systems, and electoral and political party systems. The different patterns of British and U.S. political organizations encouraged class-oriented social policymaking for workingmen in the former nation, and gender-oriented social policymaking, from Civil War pensions to maternalist regulations and social benefits, in the United States.[83]

Still, along with recent U.S. women's history, the comparative-historical approach used by Koven and Michel suggests analytical possibilities that students of gender and social policies need to keep in mind. For one thing, gender is not just a relation of social domination or social inequality, as the patriarchal theorists emphasize. Female gender identities—which are not all the same, and which change over time—can also be sources of social solidarity, organization, and moral purpose. The nineteenth-century social identity of the domestically oriented wife and mother functioned in this way for the maternalist women's groups that figured so prominently in turn-of-the-century social politics in the United States and elsewhere. Male gender identities also sustain solidarities and outlooks, as they did in nineteenth-century U.S. political parties and election rituals and in the politics of Civil War pensions; and as they did for many trade unionists who advocated early workingmen's social benefits as a way to buttress the wage-earning role of the male family breadwinner.

Like other social identities, gender identities are not only historically changing and cross-nationally variable; they are always defined
and expressed in relationship to various social structures, economies,
and political institutions. As Desley Deacon has argued, "the struggle
between the sexes over the construction of the gender order" may
be "universal and ongoing," yet we must direct our "attention to
what might be called intermediate structures, that is to institutions
specific to certain times and places through which the particular
gender order of that time and place is shaped."[84] Systematic comparisons across nations and states, moreover, can help us to find
regularities in the ways in which institutional arrangements influence
and respond to gendered forces that aim to shape public policy
outcomes.

Finally, historical and comparative-historical studies sensitive to
gender concerns suggest that the results of policies cannot be read
back historically into their causes. Women's groups, for example,
may achieve legislative victories, but then be unable to control the
implementation of social policies, so that they end up doing harm
rather than good to many women. Or social policies may be supported by bureaucrats, or parties, or unions, or upper social classes,
with the intention of "controlling" women, but then end up having
beneficial primary or secondary effects on the situations of mothers
or female workers. Indeed, policies pursued for very different purposes, such as increasing national population or integrating workers
into the polity, may end up having beneficial effects for women
within the bounds of given gender relationships.[85]

In sum, explorations of gender and social policies must be historically grounded and institutionally contextualized, and must allow
for the possibility of unintended outcomes and changing configurations of causally relevant processes over time. Gender identities
and relationships, no matter how theorized, are unlikely to explain
everything about the origins and development of U.S. social policies
in comparative perspective. But any approach to explaining the
history of U.S. social provision will certainly have to bring gender—
as identity, agency, and relationships—fully into the analysis.

The Shared Limits of Existing Theories

Scholars inspired by the perspectives we have just examined see
themselves as arguing about basic causal issues; and so they are. At

the same time, all of these perspectives share problematic assumptions about the evolutionary nature of "the welfare state" and the socioeconomic roots of political processes.

"The modern welfare state" has been seen by scholars in all camps as unified and inherently progressive, growing in recognizable stages in all industrializing and urbanizing nations. According to certain schools, national values or balances of social strength may affect the pace and comprehensiveness of welfare state development. Nevertheless, most scholars presume that some approximation to the welfare state necessarily, progressively, and irreversibly develops in every country that undergoes industrialization or capitalist development. Ideal-typical conceptions of the welfare state have been abstracted from certain understandings of a few national histories, and then turned into general explanatory variables. Applied to the American case, such conceptions have been especially harmful. They have ruled Civil War pensions and maternalist policies out of the analysis altogether, and they have distracted attention from the disjunctures between major phases and configurations of national social provision.

An incomplete conception of long-run social change underpins progressivist visions of the welfare state. Social policies have been seen as "responses" to long-term change conceived in socioeconomic terms. The motors that transform societies are thought to be industrialization and urbanization—or if one has Marxist proclivities, capitalist development, which also involves changing class (and perhaps gendered) relations of production. Right after World War II, some British writers speculated on the possible relationships between stages of modern war and the expansion of social provision.[86] But recent students of social policies have less and less to say about geopolitics and warfare.[87] What is more, hardly anyone acknowledges that long-run processes of state formation—processes which include sequences of wars and revolutions, along with constitution-making, electoral democratization, and various forms of administrative bureaucratization—might have had as much or more impact as socioeconomic transformations on the contexts within which social policies have been fashioned.[88] Yet only by taking processes of state formation and patterns of political organization seriously, and noticing that these intersect in varied ways with economic and social transformations, can we can break with the progressivist notion of social policies as aspects of societal evolution.[89]

Scholars from the schools we have reviewed not only ignore long-run processes of state formation; they also presume that governmental activities express social conditions and straightforwardly respond to social demands. Although class analysts are the only ones who explicitly discuss the political processes that tie social change to policy outcomes, we may safely infer from less systematic remarks that those who emphasize industrialism or national values or patriarchy also view politics in socially determinist ways. The following diagram captures the shared vision of social change and the political process:

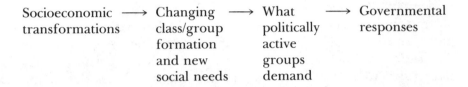

Socioeconomic ⟶ Changing ⟶ What ⟶ Governmental
transformations   class/group   politically   responses
                     formation   active
                     and new   groups
                     social needs   demand

According to this socially determinist frame of reference, politically active groups, including parties, are considered vehicles for the expression of demands that arise from underlying socioeconomic conditions. After groups and parties weigh in at the political arena—some perhaps more effectively than others because of class, racial, or gender advantages—then governments generate policy outputs to meet the social demands. In this view of the political process, if modern social policies do not emerge or mature, it must be because economic development has not yet created sufficient needs or resources, or because for cultural reasons the citizenry has not yet demanded new social policies, or because the industrial working class is not sufficiently organized to have its preferences met in the face of capitalist resistance. We have already noted the many puzzles about American social provision left unresolved by arguments such as these.

Without discarding the valid insights of the various perspectives reviewed in this section, we need to correct our angle of vision. State formation, political institutions, and political processes (understood in non–economically determinist ways) must move from the penumbra or margins of analysis and toward the center. The following section offers my strategy for accomplishing this shift in our analytical angle of vision.

A Polity-Centered Analysis of
American Social Provision

As research on social policies has become more historical in recent years, a few scholars have begun to forge what I shall call a "structured polity" approach to explaining the origins and transformations of national systems of social provision. This approach views the polity as the primary locus of action, yet understands political activities, whether carried on by politicians or by social groups, as conditioned by the institutional configurations of governments and political party systems.[90] Political scientists such as Peter Hall, Hugh Heclo, and Martin Shefter; historians such as Paula Baker, Richard McCormick, and Richard Oestreicher; and historical sociologists such as Seymour Martin Lipset and Charles Tilly, all have contributed fundamental ideas to this emergent appoach. Drawing upon their insights as I present my own formulations, I can sketch an analytical frame of reference that suggests hypotheses about the patterns and tempos of U.S. social provision. This framework draws our attention to four kinds of processes: (1) the establishment and transformation of state and party organizations through which politicians pursue policy initiatives; (2) the effects of political institutions and procedures on the identities, goals, and capacities of social groups that become involved in the politics of social policymaking; (3) the "fit"—or lack thereof—between the goals and capacities of various politically active groups, and the historically changing points of access and leverage allowed by a nation's political institutions; and (4) the ways in which previously established social policies affect subsequent politics. Let me explore these in turn, moving from the theoretical rationale for taking each process seriously to illustrations of how it illuminates important aspects of the history of U.S. social provision during the time period of interest in this book.

State Formation and the Initiatives of Politicians

A structured polity perspective holds that politicians and administrators must be taken seriously. Not merely agents of other social interests, they are actors in their own right, enabled and constrained by the political organizations within which they operate. Political officials can therefore make independent contributions to the development of a nation's social policies.

Because states are authoritative and resourceful organizations—collectors of revenue, centers of cultural authority, and hoarders of means of coercion—they are sites of autonomous action, not reducible to the demands or preferences of any social group. Both appointed and elected officials have ideas and organizational and career interests of their own, and they devise and work for policies that will further those ideas and interests, or at least not harm them. Of course, elected or appointed officials are sensitive in many ways to social preferences, and they normally want to promote the health of the economy. Yet politicians and officials are also engaged in international and domestic (including intrastate) struggles among themselves, and they must pursue those struggles by using the capacities of the organizations within which they are situated. If a given state possesses no existing (or readily adaptable) capacities for implementing given lines of policies, political leaders are not likely to pursue them. But such leaders are quite likely to take new policy initiatives—conceivably well ahead of social demands—if the capacities of state organizations can be readily adapted or reworked to do things that they expect will bring advantages to them in their struggles with political competitors, at home or on the international scene.

If the foregoing arguments make sense, we need to understand the historical formation of various states as a prelude to explaining contributions to social policymaking by their politicians and officials. Yet here we run up against an interpretive barrier. The notion that the United States has "a state" that could independently affect patterns of policy strikes many people as absurd, or at least rhetorically strained. Through many centuries Continental Europeans built up a sense of "the state." Europeans experienced the activities of centralized, standing bureaucracies, and heard the confidently proclaimed self-justifications of the enduring corps of officials that staffed those bureaucracies.[91] The United States, however, is a relatively young country born of a revolution against British and Continental European patterns of concentrated political sovereignty. Except for judges sitting on state and federal high courts, groups of public officials in America have been less unified, enduring, and self-confident than those in European states. Thus both the American people and their social analysts lack a sense of the state. Americans typically write and speak of their country as if it were, and ever had

been, just a collection of self-reliant individuals and local or occupational communities, tied together by a competitive market and an
impersonal Constitution.

This self-perception is an important part of American political
culture that cannot be ignored. It would be a big mistake, however,
to restrict our own analytical tools to those implied by America's
inherited sense of "statelessness," as all too many students of U.S.
social provision have previously done.

A state is any set of relatively differentiated organizations that
claims sovereignty and coercive control over a territory and its population, defending and perhaps extending that claim in competition
with other states.[92] The core organizations that make up a state
include the administrative, judicial, and policing organizations that
collect and dispense revenues, enforce the constitutive rules of the
state and society, and maintain some modicum of domestic order,
especially to protect the state's own claims and activities. According
to this definition, not all societies have had states, and states have
coexisted with—and persisted across—different "modes of production." Properly speaking, there is no such thing as a generically
"feudal state" or "capitalist state." Rather there are variously organized states coexisting with various patterns of economic production
and exchange. By this definition, plenty of room is left for variation
across time and space, within as well as between types of socioeconomic systems, in the ways states are organized and the mix of activities they undertake. Only some states, for example, have institutions of representative decisionmaking linked to their core organizations. When they do, it is important to understand how their
constitutional, legislative, and electoral arrangements intersect
with the coercive, administrative, judicial, and policing organizations.

If the state is so defined, then certainly the United States has
always had one. We can identify the distinctive and changing organizational features of the U.S. state, the resources its officials have
commanded, and the ways the resources and organizational features
have influenced official proclivities and abilities to shape U.S. social
policies. The following relationships need to be explored:

State   ⟶ Political organizations ⟶ Policy
formation   with given capacities   contributions
           and operating needs   of officials

The processes that have formed the U.S. state include the revolution and constitutional settlement that founded the nation, the wars in which it has engaged, and its adaptation to special geopolitical environments. By modern times, many Continental European nations possessed centralized bureaucracies and standing armies, because their states had been build by absolute monarchs who warred constantly with one another and had to wrest the men and most of the fiscal resources for warmaking from locally entrenched landlords and peasantries.[93] In contrast, through a loosely coordinated revolution against British colonial rule, the American colonies forged a federalist constitutional republic.[94] After some years of continued sparring with Britain, the fledgling nation found itself facing westward toward a huge continent available for conquest from always worrisome yet militarily unequal opponents. Wars have never had the same centralizing effects for the U.S. state as they have had for many European states, in part because America's greatest conflict was the Civil War about itself.[95] In addition, mobilization for both the World Wars of the twentieth century relied heavily on the organizational capacities of large business corporations and trade associations.[96] Only after World War II, when the United States took on global functions, did a federal "military-industrial complex" emerge, nourished by the persistence into peacetime of substantial direct federal taxation.[97]

The U.S. state was also formed by, in comparative terms, early mass electoral democratization and late, fragmentary administrative bureaucratization within a three-tiered federal system of nonhierarchically arrayed national, state, and local governments. As we shall soon see in greater detail, nineteenth-century America developed a federal "state of courts and parties."[98] In this polity, the patronage-oriented politicians who coordinated the workings of parties, administrative agencies, and legislatures elaborated social and economic policies as cross-class distributions rather than as class-oriented categorical measures.[99] Not until the late nineteenth and early twentieth centuries—decades after the establishment of electoral democratization for men, and well after capitalist industrialization had created private corporate giants operating on a national scale—did federal, state, and local governments in the United States make much headway in the bureaucratization and professionalization of their administrative functions.

With the greatest changes coming first in certain cities and states, bureaucratic transformations happened in piecemeal ways through reform movements spearheaded by executive officials and professionalizing elements of the American middle classes.[100] As the various levels of U.S. government were partially bureaucratically and professionally reorganized, the fragmentation of political sovereignty built into U.S. federalism, and into the divisions of decisionmaking authority among executives, legislatures, and courts, was reproduced in new ways during the twentieth century.[101] Rather than becoming lifelong governmental civil servants, U.S. professionals, and particularly policy-oriented intellectuals among them, tended to spend but short periods in governmental agencies, while pursuing careers predominantly anchored outside of governments, in corporations or private associations or universities. While competing with professionals and bureaucrats for control over new realms of public policymaking, twentieth-century U.S. political parties became perhaps even more decentralized in their basic operations; and in many localities and states the major parties uneasily combined patronage-oriented and interest-group-oriented modes of operation.[102]

Indeed, contrary to the image offered by some scholars that the United States became bureaucratically centralized in response to industrialism, one could argue that U.S. social politics became less centrally coordinated around the turn of the twentieth century. The federal government's Civil War pensions were no longer the major arena of social policy; and the New Deal would not arrive until the 1930s. Political parties became less nationally competitive and patronage-oriented. And the U.S. Constitution was judicially interpreted as leaving jurisdiction over industrial and social policies largely to the forty-eight state legislatures. Meanwhile, within the federal government, Congress, with its strong roots in state and local political establishments, has remained pivotal in national domestic policymaking throughout the twentieth century.[103] What is more because of its limited fiscal and bureaucratic capacities, the U.S. national government has often relied for policy implementation on subsidies or activities channeled through business enterprises, state or local governments, or "private" voluntary associations.

Because the U.S. federal state was slow to develop modern administrative capacities, reformers opposing "political corruption" and advocating civil service reform had to reorganize or bypass the en-

trenched arrangements of nineteenth-century patronage democracy.[104] At the same time, they had to wrest substantive jurdisdiction
from the courts. When new agencies empowered to administer social
legislation were finally established, they were typically isolated islands
of expertise within local, state, and federal governments, limited by
ongoing jurisdictional disputes among legislatures, executives, and
courts. Initially, these agencies were limited to information-gathering
and regulation. Even so, if they developed continuities of personnel
and a sense of collective purpose, some of these agencies became
capable of promoting social programs.

Understanding the historical formation of the U.S. state, and its
disjoint reorganization at the turn of the twentieth century, helps us
to see the ways in which different kinds of political officials have
promoted social policies of particular sorts, and with varying degrees
of success. In nascent Western welfare states, labor regulations and
social benefits for workingmen were pursued by central officials of
governmental bureaucracies and by politicans in charge of governments with national administrative capacities. In the United States,
by contrast, democratically elected legislators and patronage party
politicians were the propellers and shapers of widespread distributive social policies—including Civil War benefits—during the nineteenth and early twentieth centuries. Thus the Republican Party, the
U.S. Pensions Bureau, and Congress and state legislatures (pressured
by the Grand Army of the Republic) were all central to the propelling
and shaping of generous social benefits for veterans of the Civil War
and their dependents.

From the turn of the century onward, collectively oriented social
insurance programs and labor regulations were promoted across the
states by reformist professionals with aspirations to build new administrative agencies, as well as by established governmental agencies
(such as bureaus of labor statistics) serving as relatively stable centers
of professional-bureaucratic expertise. In addition, some female
professional reformers eventually managed to achieve a bureaucratic
beachhead within the Childen's Bureau of the federal government,
from which they pursued a program that would administer maternal
health education services in partnership with state and local governments and voluntary groups.

Nevertheless, as we shall see in Parts II and III of this book, the
efforts of turn-of-the-century U.S. reformist professionals to pro-

mote new social policies succeeded only when they were allied with popular constituencies associated across many localities and legislative districts. While the major political parties were less important than they had been in the nineteenth century, Congress and state legislatures remained pivotal arbiters of social legislation. In contrast to European reformers who could work through national bureaucracies and parliamentary political parties, U.S. reformist professionals—including actual or would-be government officials—could make headway toward new social policies only if they could gain decentralized political leverage on legislatures. When this happened at all—as, for example, in the instances of the U.S. Department of Agriculture and the U.S. Children's Bureau—it happened because ongoing political alliances were formed between professionals and officials, on the one hand, and widespread local voluntary groups, on the other.

Political Institutions and Social Identities in Politics

Socially determinist theories overlook the ways in which the identities, goals, and capacities of all politically active groups are influenced by political structures and processes. Patterns of bureaucratic development influence the orientations of educated middle-class groups as well as the possibilities for all social groups to "do things" through public authority. In addition, the scope of the electorate, along with changes in rules about electoral access and voting routines, affect the popular social identities that figure in political debates at different periods. The institutional arrangements of the state and political parties affect the capabilities of various groups to achieve self-consciousness, organize, and make alliances. Thus socioeconomic theories about group consciousness and class conflicts have to be reworked to take into account the effects of changing governmental and party organizations.

The following diagram suggests the dual lines of determination that should enter into any analysis of the social identities and relations involved in political processes. Notice that socioeconomic relations and cultural patterns are important parts of the analysis. I am not trying to substitute "political determinism" for "social determinism." I propose to explore how social and political factors *combine* to affect the social identities and group capacities involved in the politics of social policymaking.

State and party structures
and scope of electorate

Socioeconomic relations
and cultural patterns

Politicized social identities and
group political orientations and
capacities

With the aid of this frame of reference, we can make sense of a fundamentally important aspect of U.S. social politics in the early twentieth century: the relative weakness of "working-class" political consciousness, and the simultaneous prominence of middle-class women's gender consciousness and female determination to project domestic and maternal values into national politics.

Among the major theoretical perspectives reviewed earlier, the social democratic model has the most to say about working-class-based politics. Yet, tellingly, this theory has been elaborated with certain political arrangements implicitly in mind, namely centralized and bureaucratized states with parliamentary parties dedicated to contending over public programs in the name of broad, nation-spanning collectivities. The European nations for which the social democratic model works best have had such centralized bureaucracies and parties, in addition to the class relationships and union structures emphasized by the theory. Historically, moreover, voting rights in Europe were extended step by step to class-based social groups. The United States, however, does not have similar patterns of state and party organization; nor did it historically experience comparable phases of electoral democratization on a class-by-class basis.

As the comparative-historical scholarship of Martin Shefter has demonstrated, the kinds of appeals political parties have made, and the sorts of group identities they have helped to politicize, have depended on sequences and forms of state bureaucratization and electoral democratization.[105] In certain European countries, state bureaucratization preceded the emergence of parliamentary parties, or the democratization of the male electorate, or both. When political parties emerged in such circumstances, they could not get access to the "spoils of office" and instead had to make programmatic appeals to collectively organized constituents, including organized workers. But circumstances were sharply different in the nineteenth-century United States, where no premodern centralized bureaucracy held sway, and where full democratization of the electorate for white males was virtually completed nationwide by the 1840s. The intensely competitive political parties that mobilized this mass American electorate colonized all levels of public administration, and used the spoils of office to motivate party cadres. The parties also relied heavily on distributions of public jobs and publicly funded divisible benefits to appeal to locally situated constituents. What is more, since no class-defined group of American males was excluded from the democratic electorate, there was little space—much less than in Continental European countries or even nineteenth-century Britain— for old or new parties to appeal on ideologically or programmatically collectivist lines to newly mobilizable, socioeconomically defined groups of men.

Ironically, as American workers were transformed from artisans into wage-workers or migrated from rural into industrial and urban settings, they were discouraged from becoming politically class conscious, because of their full incorporation into democratic electoral and party routines rooted in local communities that were often ethnically defined.[106] Because they were already voting, American workers did not *need* to mobilize along class lines to overcome exclusion from the suffrage. At the same time, workers' organizations *could not* call on autonomous bureaucrats for help in their struggles with capitalists. And trade unions soon learned to distrust the U.S. state, because of the increasingly vigorous efforts of one of its arms, the judiciary, to block union activities.[107] Given all of these circumstances, the American trade unions that eventually became most successful on "bread and butter" workplace issues did not forge stable ties to labor-based political parties during the period around the turn of the century when European social democratic movements, linking unions and parties, were formed. As the historian Richard Oestreicher has summed up the situation in a brilliant analysis of the disjunction between "class sentiment" and "political consciousness":

From the 1870s until the 1930s, class sentiments were widespread among American workers, but before the 1930s the structure of political power in American society . . . made it harder to mobilize class sentiments in the political arena than in the workplace . . . In an entrenched party system, with winner-take-all elections and an electorate highly mobilized on a different [that is, nonclass] basis, political mobilization around class sentiments demanded far greater resources and involved greater risks than the labor movement was able or willing to muster while workplace mobilization around work-related issues needed far fewer resources. Without a tradition of successful political mobilization, class sentiment could not be translated into an articulated political consciousness.[108]

In short, longstanding political structures—including early democratization for white males, along with a federal state that divides authority and gives legislatures and courts pivotal policymaking roles—have not encouraged U.S. industrial workers to operate as class-conscious political forces. The operations of political parties have also persistently discouraged class consciousness, even though parties have become less patronage-oriented during the twentieth century. Local and state-based party politicians work out individually varied, ad hoc relationships with specialized "interest groups." As both Robert Salisbury and Graham K. Wilson have concluded from their reflections on "Why No Corporatism in America?" U.S. state and party structures function in a mutually reinforcing fashion to encourage a proliferation of competing, narrowly specialized, and weakly disciplined interests—rather than the disciplined, centralized national associations representing entire functional-economic categories that have figured in European corporatist politics, whether social democratic or not.[109]

While political forces claiming to represent the industrial working class had (in cross-national perspective) relatively little presence in U.S. social politics around the turn of the twentieth century, national and local groups claiming to speak for the collective interests of women were able to mount ideologically inspired efforts on behalf of maternalist social policies. Patterns of exclusion from—and tempos of incorporation into—electoral politics shaped the possibilities for women's political consciousness—just as they influenced possibilities for working-class consciousness. But the results for women were quite different. Middle-class American women fashioned an ambitious and influential maternalist consciousness at the turn of the century, during a period when mainstream U.S. workers' organizations were eschewing class-oriented ideologies and programs.

In major European countries during the nineteenth and early twentieth centuries, either no one except monarchs, bureaucrats, and aristocrats had the right to participate in national politics, or else property ownership, education, and other class-based criteria were used to limit electoral participation by categories of men. Thus European women were not the only ones excluded from the suffrage and, at least at first, economically privileged women did not have to watch lower-class men exercise electoral rights denied to them. Class-defined political cleavages tended to proliferate and persist in Europe, and even politically active women's organizations oriented themselves to class issues. In the United States, by contrast, for almost a century the rights and routines of electoral democracy were open to all men (even to the black ex-slaves for some decades after the Civil War), while they were denied to all women.[110]

By virtually universal cultural consensus, woman's "separate sphere" in the nineteenth century was the home, the place where she sustained the highest moral values in her roles as wife and (especially) mother. Yet this did not mean that American women stayed out of public life. Through reformist and public-regarding voluntary associations, American upper and middle-class women, joined by some wives of skilled workers, claimed a mission that they felt those of their gender could uniquely perform: extending the moral values and social caring of the home into the larger community. In the process, reformist women took a special interest in social policy issues that they felt touched the well-being of other women. By the Progressive Era, moreover, women's associations concluded that women must have the suffrage in order to reform all of politics, acting as "housekeepers for the nation."

Although "maternalist" ideas about social welfare spread across the industrializing world in the late nineteenth and early twentieth centuries, they loomed politically largest in the United States, for three major reasons. First, women's community organizations started out tied to churches and synagogues in the United States as in other Judeo-Christian nations. Yet institutional religion was less of a restraint on the eventual emergence of transdenominational and autonomously female-led voluntary associations in the United States than elsewhere, because America was an overwhelmingly Protestant nation with no established church.[111] No Catholic bureaucracy as in France, and no established Protestant church as in England, was present to channel and limit female social activism.

Second, it was crucial that American women gained more and better higher education sooner than any other women in the world. This prepared a crucial minority of them for voluntary or irregularly recompensed public leadership, especially since regular elite career opportunities were limited. Widespread education also set the stage for strong alliances between higher-educated professional women and married housewives scattered across the nation, many of whom were relatively well educated, and some of whom in every locality had been to college and worked as schoolteachers before marriage.

Finally, as I have already stressed, American women reacted more intensely, both ideologically and organizationally, against their relatively sharper exclusion from a fully democratized male polity. Throughout the nineteenth century, no major industrializing country differentiated worlds of politics—understood in the broadest sense as patterns of participation in public affairs—so sharply *on strictly gender lines* as did the United States. Given the absence in the United States of bureaucratic and organized working-class initiatives to build a pioneering paternalist welfare state for industrial workers and their families, there was more space left for maternalism in the shaping of fledgling modern social policies. Thus the policies and new public agencies especially for women and children sponsored by American women's associations loomed especially large on the overall agenda of issues that Progressive Era politicians took seriously.

As self-conscious protagonists in the shaping of social policies, organized American women made their strongest showing around the turn of the century, just as one would expect from a model that focuses on the mobilization of excluded groups to gain access to core political routines. Exclusion from the suffrage for most American women (prior to the late 1910s and early 1920s) stimulated collective consciousness and counter-organization outside of the parties and regular electoral politics. The mobilization leading into the granting of new access, as well as the immediate aftermath of the extension of rights, should be the moments when ideological and programmatic self-consciousness are greatest for any excluded social category in a polity. After formal inclusion, on the other hand, most members of the category may move toward accommodation with standard political routines. How soon this happens depends on the degree to which the group retains its own self-consciousness and organization after being granted access to the electorate. For the most part, American women failed do to this after they began to participate fully in elections and regular party and bureaucratic politics in the 1920s.

Using the same perspective we have just applied to understand the possibilities for working-class and women's political consciousness, we can also gain insights about the political outlooks of U.S. capitalists. To a greater degree than business people in many other capitalist nations, U.S. capitalists (in the apt phrase of David Vogel) "distrust their state."[112] This is, of course, somewhat ironic, given that American capitalists have not had to contend with a highly mobilized, nationally politically conscious working class, and they often get their way in governmental affairs. Yet U.S. business owners have had to operate in a long-democratized polity prone to throw up periodic moralistic "reform" movements, including farmers' movements and women's movements inclined to challenge business prerogatives. What is more, the distrust that U.S. capitalists feel toward government reflects the frustrations that they have recurrently experienced in their dealings with a decentralized and fragmented federal state—a state that gives full play to divisions within business along industrial and geographical lines.[113]

Conflicts within the ranks of U.S. business were (and still are) readily politicized, since losers can always "go to court"—or back to the legislatures, or to another level in the federal system, or to a new bureaucratic agency—for another round of battle in the interminable struggles that never seem to settle most public policy questions. For American capitalists, the state has seemed neither coherent nor reliable. Indeed, the uneven and inconstant effects of U.S. political structures help to explain why—contrary to the expectations of the "welfare capitalism" school—"progressive" corporate leaders have always found it difficult to inspire broad business support for national social policy initiatives, even those that might benefit the economy as a whole on terms favorable to the dominant sectors of business. With a few individual exceptions American capitalists have never seen government as a positive means to achieve class-wide purposes. For the most part, various industries and smaller as well as larger businesses have concentrated on fighting one another through politics. Different sectors of business have come together only episodically, and then usually in efforts to block reformers or popularly appealing social movements that want to extend government regulation or taxation and spending for social welfare purposes.

The "Fit" between Political Institutions and Group Capacities

Historically developing governmental institutions, political party systems, and electoral rules of the game not only affect the political consciousness and orientations of various social groups. At the same time, the overall structure of political institutions provides access and leverage to some groups and alliances, thus encouraging and rewarding their efforts to shape government policies, while simultaneously denying access and leverage to other groups and alliances operating in the same national polity. This means that the degree of success that any politically active group or movement achieves is influenced not just by the self-consciousness and "resource mobilization" of that social force itself.[114] As the following diagram suggests, degrees of success in achieving political goals—including the enactment of social legislation—depend on the relative opportunities that existing political institutions offer to the group or movement in question (and simultaneously deny to its opponents and competitors).

Politicized social identities and group political orientations and capacities ⟩———⟨ Governmental institutions; political party system; rules of the game

"Fit?"
How much access?
How much leverage?

This kind of perspective has been used to explain why U.S. business interests, past and present, often successfully oppose new public social policies. Multiple points of access to legislatures, committees within legislatures, executives and agencies, and—if necessary—state or federal courts, give well-organized and resourceful groups such as business many opportunities to delay or block undesired legislation. If one point of access does not work, another often does. What is more, as David Robertson has recently emphasized, especially during the early twentieth century business interests gained considerable negative leverage from the fact that forty-eight states, rather than one national government, were the loci for legislative struggles.[115] Business groups could argue that each state's business climate and economic competitiveness would be harmed if it enacted regulations or taxes not matched by other states.

Nevertheless, we cannot treat the prominence of the states within the federal system as an absolute bar to strong legislation in individual states, still less as simply an impediment to nationwide social policy innovations. In 1911, for example, the state of Massachusetts enacted a workmen's compensation law with very broad workforce coverage, overriding vociferous arguments by businessmen and other conservatives that the local business climate and the ability of Massachusetts enterprises to compete with out-of-state firms would thereby be grievously harmed.[116] In other states, too, versions of workmen's compensation that business groups vigorously opposed were sometimes enacted during the Progressive Era. Moreover, both women's hour laws and mothers' pensions were very rapidly enacted across forty-some U.S. states during the 1910s. In these instances, most of the U.S. states engaged in what might be called competitive emulation, a process in which interstate rivalry promoted rather than retarded nationwide social policy enactments within the nonparliamentary and decentralized U.S. federal system.

In general, U.S. political structures allow unusual leverage to social groups that can, with a degree of discipline and consistency of purpose, associate across many local political districts. From the nineteenth century onward, what I call "widespread federated interests" have weighed heavily on particular issues in U.S. social politics, sometimes without regard to partisan alignments on those issues. U.S. trade unions during the early twentieth century were *not* effectively organized in this way; they were concentrated in certain urban centers rather than spread out across thousands of localities, and they were functionally organized rather than nested in local-state-national organizational hierarchies.[117] In isolation, big corporations or associations of big businesses did not function as widespread federated interests either. Yet big and small U.S. businesses have often been allied through federated associations such as the National Association of Manufacturers. And by the 1920s, private medical doctors in the United States had created a powerful three-tier federation, the American Medical Association, that could easily rival the legislative leverage of business in opposing new public social policies such as health insurance or the 1926–27 renewal of the federal Sheppard-Towner program.

Significantly, widespread federated interests have also included cross-class movements advocating the enactment or extension of major U.S. social policies. The Grand Army of the Republic was such a federated association that fought very successfully for generous Civil War benefits. Huge women's federations that successfully promoted social legislation in the late nineteenth and early twentieth centuries included the Women's Christian Temperance Union, the General Federation of Womens' Clubs, and the National Congress of Mothers. Such women's federations were influential in the rapid diffusion of maternalist social legislation across many states during the 1910s. And a cross-class federation of men's clubs, the Fraternal Order of Eagles, conducted many state-level campaigns for need-based old-age pensions during the 1920s. Tying together clubs based in local legislative districts into statewide and nationwide networks of social communication, all of these widespread associations were well situated to promote specific kinds of social policies, especially as proposals had to make their way through many different state legislatures, or through the House of Representatives in the national Congress.

A fundamental question addressed in this book is why maternalist forces promoting social policies for mothers and women workers were considerably more effective in U.S. politics during the early 1900s than were paternalist forces that simultaneously worked for the enactment of policies targeted on male wage-earners. As the book unfolds, this question will be answered in significant part through explorations of the "fit" between the organizational capacities of maternalist and paternalist forces, and the opportunities afforded by U.S. political institutions.

As we shall see in Part II, support for for certain paternalist social policy proposals came from reform-minded public administrators and social scientists, and support for certain other paternalist proposals came from national or state-level trade unions. But male reformers and trade unionists often operated at ideological and organizational cross-purposes during the early twentieth century; they did not form effective political alliances on behalf of new social policies, except in a few individual states. What is more, neither reformist professionals nor trade unions were organized as widespread federated associations reaching into localities across the nation. Supporters of paternalist social policy proposals in the early-twentieth-century United States usually found it difficult to conduct simultaneous legislative drives across many states.

By contrast, as we shall learn in Part III, women's groups were able to form broad alliances between reformist professionals and locally rooted women's groups. These alliances could press legislatures to enact new social policies for women workers and for mothers and children. As U.S. unions and reformist male intellectuals could not, female intellectuals and popular groups *could* work together in early-twentieth-century U.S. social politics, in ways analogous to intellectual-worker alliances in the social democratic movements of other nations.[118] In addition, American maternalist alliances achieved considerable leverage in the national polity. Because the largest women's associations of the day, especially the General Federation of Women's Clubs and the National Congress of Mothers, had been built up out of voluntary associations created by elite and middle-class women excluded from the nineteenth-century routines of U.S. electoral politics, they developed as autonomous federations *paralleling* the three-tier local-state-national structure of U.S. federalism. In turn, this happened at a historical juncture when male-only U.S. political parties were weakened, when state legislators were more sensitive to moralistic waves of public opinion than to partisan party controls, and when U.S. courts were willing to accept labor regulations for women but not for men.

Thus U.S. women's political mobilization through nationwide federations of voluntary groups faced a receptive governmental context during the 1910s and early 1920s. For a time, the structures of U.S. politics rewarded broad maternalist alliances with many (although not invariable) legislative successes. And this happened even as the same political arrangements were quite unreceptive to the importunings of the social scientists and trade unionists who worked for paternalist social policies.

Policies Transform Politics

Beyond examining official initiatives and the effects of political institutions on social politics, we need, finally, to keep in mind a fourth process—policy feedbacks—highlighted by a structured polity approach. Too often social scientists who study national systems of social provision forget that policies, once enacted, restructure subsequent political processes. Analysts typically look only for synchronic determinants of policies—for example, in current social interests or in existing political alliances. In addition, however, we must examine patterns unfolding over time (and not only long-term macroscopic processes of social change and polity reorganization). We must make social policies the starting points as well as the end points of analysis: As politics creates policies, policies also remake politics.

Once instituted, policies have feedback effects in two main ways. In the first place, because of the official efforts made to implement new policies using new or existing administrative arrangments, policies transform or expand the capacities of the state. They therefore change the administrative possibilities for official initiatives in the future, and affect later prospects for policy implementation. In the second place, new policies affect the social identities, goals, and capabilities of groups that subsequently struggle or ally in politics. Thus, as summed up in the following diagram, social policies feed back into the processes we have already posited within the polity-centered frame of reference:

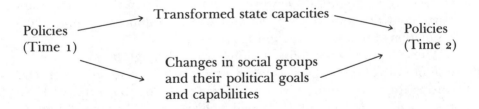

We can take our analysis of policy feedbacks a bit further by asking whether any given policy has effects on state capacities and politics that serve either to promote or to frustrate the further extension of that line of policymaking. This is a way of getting at the "success" of policies in terms of ongoing political processes. It contrasts with other ways of discussing the success or failure of policies, for example by assessing their "efficiency" according to some external economic criterion, or by assessing their moral worth according to a given normative standard. According to this political-process approach, a policy is "successful" if it enhances the kinds of state capacities that can promote its future development, and especially if it stimulates groups and political alliances to defend the policy's continuation and expansion.[119] Indeed, public social or economic measures may have the effect of stimulating brand new social identities and political capacities, sometimes groups that have a stake in the policy's expansion, sometimes groups that seek to repeal or reorient the policy in question. What is more, positive or negative policy feedbacks can also "spill over" from one policy to influence the fate of another policy proposal that seems analogous in the eyes of relevant officials and groups. Tracing these feedback processes is crucial for explaining the further development of social provision after initial measures are instituted.

The importance of policy feedbacks is one of the best reasons why any valid explanation of the development of a nation's social policies must be genuinely historical, sensitive to processes unfolding over time.[120] Certainly, policy feedbacks figure in many of the arguments of this book, above all those dealing with positive and negative feedbacks from Civil War pensions.

The expansion of Civil War pensions included powerful positive feedbacks. After initial legislative liberalizations, veterans became self-consciously organized and mobilized to demand ever improved benefits; and the Bureau of Pensions became one of the largest and most active agencies of the federal government. By the early twentieth century, moreover, many American workers and citizens appear to have wanted to extend this policy precedent into more widely available old-age pensions. Yet at the same time, Civil War pensions set in motion reactions against future public social provision along similar lines. Because the very successes of Civil War pensions were so closely tied to the workings of patronage democracy, these successes set the stage for negative feedbacks that profoundly affected the future direction of U.S. social provision. During the Progressive Era, the precedent of Civil War pensions was constantly invoked by many American elites as a reason for opposing or delaying any move toward more general old-age pensions, even though such pensions could have allowed elite reformers to build alliances with trade unions similar to those achieved by contemporary British reformers. Moreover, the party-based "corruption" that many U.S. reformers associated with the implementation of Civil War pensions prompted them to argue that the United States could not administer any new social spending programs efficiently or honestly.

Stepping back to gain an overview of U.S. social policymaking in the late nineteenth and early twentieth centuries, we can trace feedback processes that added up to relative political success or failure for particular types of efforts. Some of the policies enacted back then proved politically viable in American democracy, at least for a time. Civil War benefits and the programs of the Children's Bureau are examples of such relatively politically viable measures (even if Civil War pensions did have negative spillover effects for other policy proposals debated during the Progressive period). In their own right, Civil War benefits and Children's Bureau programs inspired geographically widespread popular constituencies that crossed class lines, and their expansion was promoted by politicians and by dynamic administrative agencies. But other early U.S. social policies fizzled administratively and politically—even some like mothers' pensions that had originally been enacted at the behest of the same groups that fought for more successful maternalist social policies. The less successful policies were targeted on impoverished people, and failed to encourage broad political coalitions dedicated to expanding their funding and scope. Mothers' pensions deteriorated into inadequate and often demeaning "welfare" benefits, destined to constitute the underside of U.S. public social provision down to the present day.

Looking Ahead

Arguments from a polity-centered frame of reference have been introduced in this chapter in dialogue with other major theoretical approaches used to explain social provision in the United States. From now on, however, the presentation will be chronological. How did changing U.S. state capacities and the proclivities of politicians contribute to the patterns of social policymaking outlined in the first part of this chapter? How did U.S. political institutions and their transformations, along with feedbacks from previous policies, influence agendas of debate and social conflicts over policies between the 1870s and the 1920s? Only a genuinely historical analysis can tackle these issues, probing the interaction of social and political transformations, and exploring the sometimes ironic unfolding of political processes over time.

Methodologically, this book offers a "comparatively informed historical case study" of the development of U.S. social provision. Only one national case, that of the United States, is analyzed in depth; but comparisons of relatively independent historical trajectories also figure at many points in the discussion. Where useful and valid, both quantitative and qualitative comparisons are made across states within the United States. These help us to account for variations in legislative timing, contents, and implementation. In addition, I make some comparisons between the United States and other nations. Britain figures most consistently in these comparisons, but a number of other countries are also discussed at one point or another. Still, no other national history besides that of the United States is fully explored or explained, for the purpose of the cross-national comparisons is not to validate a general argument. These comparisons are used to clarify patterns distinctive to the United States, and to help sort out causes of American patterns that are either unique or shared with other countries.

Evidence of several types has been pulled together in this book. For some issues I have been able to prepare fresh cross-state quantitative data good enough for the statistical testing of hypotheses. Mostly, however, I have synthesized carefully analyzed primary evidence with "secondary" evidence from published historical studies. Where books and articles published by historians have been plentiful and, upon some probing into their sources, convincing, I have happily relied on them. But for issues where the existing secondary works have been sparse or not fully convincing to me, I have worked with various associates to find and analyze telling primary sources, in order to gain a more adequate picture of what happened as well as why. I have made much use of government records. Perhaps most uniquely, the organizational records of women's groups and of the American Federation of Labor have been thoroughly probed for insights about these groups' political capacities and their stances on policy issues. Where possible, I have tracked down the activities of key women's groups in scattered state records as well as in national compendia. I have also spent many enjoyable hours gaining a "feel" for the perspectives of policy actors, and digging up the occasional piece of support for (or evidence against) a working hunch.

Except for the Conclusion, the chapters to follow are grouped into three parts. Part I analyzes the nineteenth-century U.S. "state of courts and parties," highlighting its proclivity to create and expand distributive social policies, including Civil War benefits. Part II asks and answers why the United States did not enact proposals for old-age pensions, general labor regulations, and workingmen's social insurance during the Progressive Era. And Part III explores the roots of U.S. women's political mobilization around the turn of the century, focusing closely on the various maternalist social policies enacted in the 1910s and early 1920s. Each part begins with an overview of the central issues it addresses. The book concludes ten chapters from now with a reflection on the successes, failures, and legacies of the earliest phases of U.S. social provision.

PART I

A Precocious
Social Spending Regime

In America the great moving forces are the parties. The government counts for less than in Europe, the parties count for more . . . Their ingenuity, stimulated by incessant rivalry, has turned many provisions of the Constitution to unforeseen uses, and given to the legal institutions of the country no small part of their present colour.

James Bryce, 1895

Let Grover talk against the tariff tariff tariff
  And pensions too.
We'll give the workingman his due
  And pension the boys who wore the blue.

Republican campaign ditty, 1888 presidential election

What tells in holdin' your grip on your district is to go right down among the poor families and help them in the different ways they need help . . . If there's a family in my district in want I know it before the charitable societies do, and me and my men are the first on the ground. I have a special corps to look up such cases . . .

Another thing, I can always get a job for a deservin' man. I make it a point to keep on the track of jobs, and it seldom happens that I don't have a few up my sleeve ready for use . . .

It's philanthropy, but it's politics, too—mighty good politics . . . The poor are the most grateful people in the world, and, let me tell you, they have more friends in their neighborhoods than the rich have in theirs.

George Washington Plunkitt, 1905

Most of us hold to a nostalgic image of a smaller-scale and less complicated American past, believing that federal and state governments in the United States did not become significant providers of social welfare until the middle of the twentieth century. This received portrait of yesteryear contains much truth, yet it hardly prepares us for some startling facts. Between 1880 and 1910, the U.S. federal government devoted over a quarter of its expenditures to pensions distributed among the populace; aside from interest payments on the national debt in the early 1880s, such expenditures exceeded or nearly equaled other major categories of federal spending.[1] By 1910, about 28 percent of all American men aged 65 or more, more than half a million of them, received federal benefits averaging $189 a year.[2] Over three hundred thousand widows, orphans, and other dependents were also receiving payments from the federal treasury.[3] During the same period, thousands of elderly men and a few hundred women were also residents of special homes maintained by the federal government or their respective states.

Officially these benefits were granted under federal and state laws dealing with veterans of the Civil War. After 1890, what amounted to disability and old-age pensions were paid quarterly from the federal Treasury to all applicants who could claim to be Union veterans, as well as to others claiming to be dependents of soldiers who had died during or after the war. In addition, the federal government ran homes for disabled and elderly soldiers; both northern and southern states provided individual benefits and domiciliary care for especially needy veterans of the Civil War armies; and the northern states received federal subsidies for their veterans' homes.[4]

The dimensions to which this complex system of Civil War benefits ultimately grew, along with the timing of that growth, show that it was no mere military program and no simple mopping-up operation in the direct aftermath of the 1860s conflict. The human after-effects of the Civil War interacted with intense political party competition between the 1870s and the 1890s to fuel public generosity toward a fortunate generation of aging men and their family dependents. As a result, the United States during the late nineteenth century became for many of its citizens a kind of precocious social spending state: precocious in terms of the usual presumption of an absence of federal involvement in social welfare before the New Deal, and precocious in terms of how the United States around 1900 compared to other Western nations.

The fascinating story of the elaboration of Civil War benefits into an early U.S. regime of public social provision will be told in Chapter 2. This story cannot be understood, however, except in the context of the distinctive governmental institutions and political organizations that patterned public policymaking and political participation in the nineteenth-century United States. In Chapter 1, therefore, I analyze the characteristics of early America's federal and democratic "state of courts and parties," contrasting it to the more bureaucratic and centralized monarchical and aristocratic polities that held sway in much of contemporary Europe. I also discuss the kinds of "distributive" public policies that were favored by U.S. legislatures and by competitive, patronage-oriented political parties rooted in a highly mobilized democratic male electorate.

Even setting aside Civil War benefits for a time, we shall soon learn that several kinds of public social provision flourished in nineteenth-century America. Common schooling for white citizens of all social classes spread across the land, putting the United States into the international forefront of countries offering public education. Some charitable and welfare institutions received subsidies from federal and state legislatures, payments arranged by party politicians to reward favored local constituencies. Opportunities for economic advancement were faciliated for fortunate Americans of all social classes through public distributions of land and other resources, regulatory adjustments, and job opportunities arranged by the dominant political parties. And certain American workers were buffered in adversity or saved from destitution by the discretionary welfare efforts of urban political machines in the great cities.

All of these sorts of benefits and opportunities—along with Civil War benefits to old soldiers and their dependents from the 1870s onward—flowed to Americans through the nineteenth-century U.S. polity. Clearly, it behooves us to understand the distinctive institutional arrangements and political routines of this polity. That is the task to which we now turn.

CHAPTER 1

Patronage Democracy and Distributive Public Policies in the Nineteenth Century

At first glance, it might seem sufficient to characterize the polity of the youthful United States as "stateless." The American Revolution was a revolt not only against the British Empire but also against any European-style notion of concentrated political sovereignty— whether focused in a supreme parliament, as in Britain after the English Revolution, or in an official bureaucracy built up under absolute monarchy, as in much of Continental Europe. After years of political skirmishes between colonists and royal governors, a confederation of thirteen colonies separated America from Britain. Then the Founding Fathers sought to cement a precarious national unity by designing a new federal government. Under the Constitution adopted in 1788, the powers of the states and the central government were carefully divided and balanced against one another in a "compound" arrangement that left many ambiguities for the future, while the new rules for the federal government spread cross-cutting responsibilities among Congress, the President, and a system of courts.[1] In Samuel Huntington's words, "America perpetuated a fusion of functions and a division of power, while Europe developed a differentiation of functions and a centralization of power."[2]

Skeptical of the desirablity of any one center of authority acting in the name of the national good, the sponsors of the Constitution aimed for a governmental system that would protect against executive arbitrariness and check majorities in legislatures, yet at the same time give renewed informal hegemony to gentlemen embodying civic ideals of disinterested republican virtue.[3] Antifederalists were even more distrustful of centralized authority and almost defeated the proposed Constitution. Within a decade after ratification, however, early American political factions converged on a shared language of "constitutionalism" to articulate sharply conflicting ideals about the scope of governmental authority; each contending faction argued that it was correctly implementing the Constitution's provisions.[4]

Henceforth, Americans looked to "the Constitution" and "the rule of law," as the loci of fundamental sovereignty.[5] Especially in pre–Civil War America, these functioned as a "roof without walls" in the apt words of John Murrin, as "a substitute for any deeper kind of national identity," because "people knew that without the Constitution there would be no America."[6] While never-ending rounds of legislation in Congress and the states expressed shifting sets of special interests, the sovereign ideals of constitutionalism and the rule of law could reign impersonally above an economically expansionist and socially diverse country. Only during the Civil War did a Republican-run crusade to save a northern-dominated nation temporarily transfer the locus of sovereignty to an activist federal government. But even the Civil War did not generate a permanent autonomous federal bureaucracy; localism, divisions of powers, and a distrust of governmental activism never disappeared even in the North. The U.S. "Tudor polity" reemerged in full force after the southern states rejoined the union in the 1870s.[7]

An American State of Courts and Parties

It will not do, however, to leave the matter here, stipulating that Europeans had concentrated sovereignties and a sense of "stateness" while nineteenth-century Americans had neither. If "the state" is understood only as a European construct, then "Americans may be defined," in the insightful words of Albert Frederick Pollard, "as that part of the English-speaking world which instinctively revolted against the doctrine of the sovereignty of the State and has . . . striven to maintain that attitude from the time of the Pilgrim Fathers to the present day."[8] In a more analytic vein, however, Stephen Skowronek has placed the totality of early American political arrangements in a framework that helps to highlight their distinctive features.

Skowronek points out that the United States certainly did have a state, both in the sense of "an organization of coercive power" and in the sense of "stable, valued, and recurring modes of behavior within and among institutions":[9] "The early American state maintained an integrated legal order on a continental scale; it fought wars, expropriated Indians, secured new territories, carried on relations with other states, and aided economic development. Despite the absence of a sense of the state, the state was essential to social order and social development in nineteenth-century America."[10] To be sure, this early American state was not a set of locality-penetrating bureaucracies headed by a monarch or a parliament. Rather, in Skowronek's telling phrase, it was a "state of courts and parties." Operating across the formal state and federal levels with elected executives and legislatures, courts and parties were the key organizations—and judges and party politicians were the crucial "officials in action"—that constituted the American state in the nineteenth century.[11] "Party procedures lent operational coherence to the disjointed institutions of the governmental apparatus, [and] court proceedings determined the meaning and the effect of the law itself."[12]

Courts were not very prominent in the original debates over Constitutional design, yet as the nineteenth century progressed they carved out a more authoritative role than the Founders had envisaged or than British courts enjoyed. "There is hardly a political question in the United States," observed Alexis de Tocqueville, "which does not sooner or later turn into a judicial one."[13] To be sure, early American judges and lawyers needed to adjust English common law precedents to U.S. circumstances, and they had to fend off various movements to codify the laws and reduce judicial discretion.[14] Yet these elites and the courts through which they operated also enjoyed important advantages. They could take advantage of their countrymen's regard for the Constitution and legal procedures as common points of reference in a polity racked with jurisdictional disputes, where fundamental issues regularly required adjudication. And there was no national civil bureaucracy that could compete with the courts by promoting "the national interest" in a more substantive fashion.

In the 1803 landmark case of *Marbury v. Madison* the Supreme Court successfully claimed prerogatives to review executive decrees and declare legislation "unconstitutional." These prerogatives were used infrequently before 1864, but much more frequently afterward.[15] Over the course of the nineteenth century, moreover, both the exercise of powers of judicial review and the common law case interpretations of federal and state judges and lawyers added up to substantive lawmaking. Private property rights and norms of market behavior were instrumentally adjusted to the needs of an entrepreneurial and rapidly growing capitalist economy.[16] To limit the activities of labor unions, the courts used conspiracy doctrines, and then contract and equal-protection doctrines and interpretations of antitrust laws. In spheres from the economy to the family, U.S. courts sought to maintain the boundaries of public versus private authority in American democracy. By the late nineteenth century, the jurisdiction of federal courts had expanded in relation to state courts and legislatures; and judicial activism was reinforced by the assertion of quasi-administrative powers through writs and injunctions.[17]

Arnold Paul has summed up late-nineteenth-century legal developments as "a massive judicial entry into the socioeconomic scene" effecting "a conservative-oriented revolution" in the name of concentrated private property. "From the 1890's through the mid-1930's," Paul writes, the courts engaged in "judicial superintendence and frequent intervention against the legislative discretion in matters of economic regulation and social reform."[18] Indeed, for the turn-of-the-century period, it may be accurate to call the U.S. state "court-dominated," as certain scholars have recently begun to do.[19] Such domination came about, however, not simply because judges and lawyers self-consciously defended the emerging corporations, acting as agents of the capitalist class. As Morton Keller has correctly pointed out, "the rise of judicial activism . . . had as much to do with the structural relationship of the courts to the other sectors of the polity as with the social and economic predilections of the judges."[20] In the nineteenth-century polity, courts and party-dominated legislatures enjoyed complementary as well as competitive relationships, since party politicians (for reasons we shall soon see) preferred to avoid zero-sum decisions about property and regulation.[21]

In addition, the "structural" relationship of courts and legislatures developed over time. Crucially, judges and lawyers could carry on more continuous and intellectually self-conscious conversations with one another than did legislative representatives, who tended to serve only for very brief terms, creating very high rates of turnover in Congress and the state legislatures.[22] Arguably, therefore, the judicial sector of the American polity became the first to achieve the institutional memory that must underpin any sort of continuous policymaking through what Hugh Heclo has called "political learning" or "collective puzzlement on society's behalf."[23] In the European nations Heclo studied, national civil administrators were historically central to processes of political learning; but in the United States judicial officials achieved continuous purview over a broad scope of policy issues well before groups of civil administrators did, for the latter gained independent footholds in local, state, and national governments only from the Progressive Era onward.

The advantages U.S. lawyers and judges enjoyed as bearers of political learning probably became most telling, however, only late in the nineteenth century. This was when elite legal education finally became nationally oriented and somewhat professionally standardized, and when the other great contenders for control in the nineteenth-century American polity, the patronage-oriented political parties, came under sustained attacks from reformers who wanted to pursue "the public interest" in nonpartisan ways.[24] To understand the period before that, from the 1830s until the turn of the century, I agree with Richard L. McCormick that we should center our attention on what may properly be called "the party period" in U.S. public policymaking.[25]

The Triumph of Patronage Democracy

Political parties and vocationally specialized partisan politicians became the pivots of the nineteenth-century American polity. Ironically, this happened even though the Constitution made no mention of them, given that the Founders disapproved "the baneful effects of the spirit of party."[26] Foreign observers of the actual workings of American government noticed the increasing centrality and distinctiveness of U.S. parties. Alexis de Tocqueville had only a little to say on the subject; he toured the country in the early 1830s when democratized parties were just emerging. As an adherent of the republican virtue tradition that had inspired the Founders, Tocqueville strongly disliked the new party men and motives he saw stirring in the Jackson period. Even so, he noted that in "the United States . . . the majority rules in the name of the people . . . [who are]

surrounded by the constant agitation of parties seeking to draw them in and to enlist their support."[27]

At the height of the party period five decades later, James Bryce observed that in "America the great moving forces are the parties. The government counts for less than in Europe, the parties count for more."[28] "A description of them is therefore a necessary complement to an account of the Constitution and government" since "their ingenuity, stimulated by incessant rivalry, has turned many provisions of the Constitution to unforeseen uses."[29] "The party organizations in fact form a second body of political machinery existing side by side with that of the legally constituted government," such that "the whole machinery, both of national and of state governments, is worked by the political parties."[30] American parties, Bryce noted, "have been organized far more elaborately than anywhere else in the world, and have passed more completely under the control of a professional class."[31]

What I shall call patronage democracy was patterned by the predominance of competing party organizations and the professional politicians who ran them. This system did not appear right at the birth of the nation; the critical watershed came from the 1820s to the 1840s. During its earliest decades, American government was a "regime of notables" characterized by "deferential-participant politics."[32] In that phase there were two political factions, proto–political parties, the Federalists and the Jeffersonian Republicans; but these were not specialized political organizations and they did not compete directly in many areas of the country. Each proto-party was a coalition of locally prominent notables—landowners, patrician merchants, and so forth—who relied upon social prestige and economic standing to garner personal followings. Public offices were held by gentlemen, whose tenure was often respected even when the party other than their own was in ascendance. Moreover, rule by notables in the early American republic went hand in hand with restricted electoral democracy and, often, very low rates of voter turnout.[33]

By the 1840s, however, the United States had become the world's first large-scale popular democracy.[34] The franchise was extended to virtually all adult white males and politics became permeated by electoral contests. As America expanded westward, new states were added that lacked property qualifications in their franchise; and there were also movements to remove voting restrictions in many of the older states. Simultaneously, the states emulated one another in according direct elections a greater role. Governors and presidential electors, along with many new offices at lower levels of government, were subjected to direct election, and single-member congressional districts were established.

Presidential electioneering moved to center stage in this period, and encouraged the "two-partyism" that has been such an enduring feature of normal American politics.[35] After the attenuation of the Virginia dynasty in the 1820s left no nationally prestigious successor to James Monroe, political forces in the various regions began to contest the presidency. Innovators like Martin Van Buren and the Bucktails of New York, along with like-minded counterparts in other states, knit together a new, ultimately nation-spanning Democratic Party. This was an interstate organizational coalition through which to capture the presidency for a popular politician, Andrew Jackson, who had been passed over by the notables. By the 1840s, a similarly nationwide counterpoint party, the Whigs, was pulled together to contest for the highest offices on behalf of "Tippecanoe and Tyler too." Pairs of competing specialized party organizations emerged in all major regions of the country; the process started in the Middle Atlantic states and New England, spread to the "West," and finally proceeded, albeit incompletely, into the South.[36]

This unprecedentedly full establishment of electoral democracy in a large country occurred just as America's agrarian-commercial economy entered the early stages of capitalist industrialization, its growth spurred by major improvements in transportation and communication.[37] Full electoral democratization; a growing economy in a society of farmers, smaller merchants, artisans, and some wage-workers; and a polity without an entrenched bureaucratic machinery—these conditions together offered fertile ground for opposition to the political hegemony of notables. Movements against privilege flourished during "the Jacksonian Era," which brought the curtailment of such mercantilist practices as restricted bank charters, regulations on entry to professions, and special grants to particular corporations. Opportunities to get ahead were thenceforth thrown open to many contenders.[38] As part of the overall "opening of American society," younger politicians accomplished fundamental and complementary reorganizations in party politics and public administration, changing the basic character of early American government from a regime of notables to party-run patronage democracy.

Martin Shefter has deftly summed up this transformation as the rise of a new kind of political elite. According to Shefter, the deep-ening of the electoral franchise and the proliferation of elected offices

> turned party management into, if not a full time profession, then at least a vocation that demanded far more time and attention for its successful performance than had been devoted to it by the gentlemen dilettantes of the earlier regime. At the same time, the expulsion of the notables from institutions of policy-making and administration, and the subjection of these institutions to party influence gave middle class lawyers, editors, and businessmen an incentive to devote themselves to the tasks of party management, because these developments made it possible for such men-on-the-make to live off politics by serving as agents for private interests in their dealing with government (the Jacksonian period saw the rise of the lobby), by moving into and out of public office, and by making personal contacts and obtaining private contracts that were useful in their private careers. The Jacksonian reforms, then, placed at the very center of the political system a group of middle class professional or semiprofessional politicians.[39]

A new ethical understanding of political parties and their purposes also came to the fore along with the new men.[40] The political notables of the Founders' generation had tried to practice consensus politics in the national interest (while actually splitting into factions around personalities and ideological principles). In contrast, the regular pol-iticians of the party period celebrated the virtues of organizational loyalty and all-out competition between parties. Disciplined parties were, in their view, agents of democracy and the public good. Yet the new parties were not to be firmly wedded to ideological principles or fixed programs. They would serve primarily the "constituent" functions of filling public offices and sticking together on procedural issues "that in some fashion affected the fortune of the organization itself . . . The practices that tended to preserve the party became the real 'principles' of the party."[41] Of course, this could include making gestures toward particular ideological or issue positions; and regardless of their personal views or previous positions, loyal "party men" were supposed to go along with the party whenever it made such maneuvers in its organizational interest.

The regular American parties of the nineteenth century managed the complex, never-ending processes of nominations and elections for local, state, and national offices.[42] Party conventions became the typical means for nominating candidates, and the nineteenth century's frequent elections required that party supporters be kept in a high state of enthusiasm and readiness through canvasses and rallies. Money also had to be raised from party loyalists and allied businessmen. Party leaders kept in touch with one another across the states, and formed ties to local grassroots leaders who could personally reach voters, often in cities through such neighborhood-based entities as saloons, fire brigades, or ethnic charitable associations. During the formative Jackson period, the basic cadres of the major political parties were ward leaders, perhaps allied with saloon keepers or drill leaders or heads of benefit associations.[43] Later in the nineteenth century, party machines were often able to internalize local cadres and centralize organizational discipline over local ward leaders.[44]

Crucially, from the Jackson era through the end of the century, parties also controlled much of the staffing and functioning of public administration in the United States. Previously public offices were allocated, often informally and for indeterminant periods, to members of the socioeconomic "establishment." Reacting against the arrangements of the republic of notables, however, the Jacksonians introduced limited terms of appointment, the norm of "rotation in office," and partisan party control of the "spoils of office."[45] Such practices, along with formal procedural rules and the supervision of lower by higher officials, made it possible for "new men," not necessarily highly educated or socially well connected, to serve in public offices. On the less salutary side, rotation in office tended to block internal promotions, thus undermining the autonomous *esprit de corps* of the public service.[46]

Administrative staffing through patronage was complementary to the intensified electoral activities of the new political parties.[47] The opportunity to control the allocation of public offices inspired party cadres and allowed national and state party brokers to offer local loyalists influence over appointments allocated from their levels of government. In turn, public officeholders were highly motivated to contribute portions of their salaries and their time to foster the popularity of their party. For only if their party won the next election would their jobs be safe. Otherwise, the opposite party and its appointees would claim the "spoils of office."

Once in place, the parties and their managers proved remarkably resilient, dominating U.S. politics and knitting together the branches and levels of the "Tudor polity" throughout the nineteenth century.

The local roots of the parties sunk deep into particular neighborhoods: "Every precinct and village had its Republican and Democratic clubs" at the height of the party period during the Gilded Age.[48] Yet party efforts simultaneously spanned localities within states and, to a remarkable degree, reached across the nation as a whole. Certainly the party organizations were not top-down hierarchies; rather they were ramified networks fueled by complex and shifting exchanges of favors for organizational loyalty. As such, however, they successfully linked local to state politicians and kept state politicians in touch with one another and with whatever national officeholders their party might have.

The Social Roots of Electoral Politics

Although the parties were essentially leadership networks rather than mass membership organizations, their preeminence in the nineteenth century coincided with unprecedented levels of popular electoral participation. During those periods when two well-established parties were most closely competitive—as the Democrats and Whigs were from 1840 to 1852 at the height of the "second party system," and as the Republicans and Democrats were from 1876 to 1892 at the height of the "third party system"—turnouts, respectively, of almost 70 and 80 percent of the eligible adult male electorate were common in presidential contests. The rates were higher in the North alone, and they fell off remarkably little even in off-year congressional elections.[49] In the words of Walter Dean Burnham, the "19-century American political system, for its day, was incomparably the most thoroughly democratized of any in the world."[50] It was also the most democratically mobilized in American history, since turnout rates in U.S. national elections from the 1840s to the turn of the century consistently remained much higher than either previously or afterward.

In contrast to most nineteenth-century European parties—which either excluded workers and farmers or else mobilized them *as classes* to demand the suffrage[51]—the major political parties of U.S. patronage democracy incorporated popular supporters without encouraging the crystallization of class conflicts or collective class demands. Recently, many social historians have argued that the major nineteenth-century parties expressed different orientations toward "the market revolution"—with Whigs (and later Republicans) favoring governmental efforts to promote orderly commercialization and Democrats fearing that entrenched, wealthy "non-producers" (such as financiers, commercial landowners, and rentier capitalists) would use governmental interventions to the disadvantage of "producers" (such as tradesmen, artisans, wage-workers, and yeomen farmers).[52] Yet the loosely pro- and antimarket orientations of the major parties were a far cry from "class consciousness" in any meaningful sense. Of course, Whigs, Democrats, and Republicans did not have the field entirely to themselves; there were periodic third-party "crusades" on behalf of the socioeconomic interests of "producers" and such causes as nativism or antislavery. But only one third-party crusade—the northern cross-class movement for "free soil, free labor, and free men"—developed into a major party; and these Republicans devolved in due course into a perfectly regular collection of patronage-oriented machines.[53] Leaving apart the early Republicans, moreover, the majority of American wage-workers (that is, initially artisans and then in growing numbers factory workers) probably never flirted with producers' parties or farmer-labor or socialist parties. Instead, because American white male workers were full citizens from the start, their political consciousness was profoundly influenced by the regular parties and, indeed, by the overall routines of patronage democracy as a system of political participation.[54]

For the leading few in the working classes—especially those who aspired to move into the middle class—politics was a matter of "getting ahead." This was possible through the jobs, legal perquisites, connections to businessmen, and opportunities for earning (or skimming) income that were handed out by the major parties as they sought to co-opt and control those local leaders who could best link them reliably into the mass electorate. In fact, the ability of the regular parties to offer such opportunities to aspiring leaders from the working classes was one of the advantages they had in competition with more radical populist or worker parties. Discussing the situation in the last third of the nineteenth century, the historian Richard Oestreicher points out that the

> kinds of talented and ambitious working-class personalities who were struggling to establish the [European] Social Democratic parties of the Second International were by then successful machine politicians in the United States . . . By providing potential access to power, political machines undercut some of the reasons for alternative forms of working-class political mobilization at the same

time that they dramatically raised the costs of effective alternative mobilization. Any effort to mobilize workers politically independent of, or against, existing party organizations faced not only the bourgeois resistance one would expect to any challenge to capitalist power in a capitalist system, but also the implacable opposition of armies of working-class and lower middle-class political professionals who correctly viewed attempts to restructure the basis of party politics as threats to their livelihood.[55]

For most working-class citizens, along with other American citizens, politics involved "getting out the vote" for the regular parties within their local residence communities. Such electoral participation by workers might help attract government services or benefits to their urban neighborhoods.[56] Especially in towns and smaller cities, it also served as a check on any direct repression by local authorities—for example, discouraging them from calling out state militias against strikers.[57] As Oestreicher explains, urban "machine politicians responded flexibly to a range of working-class grievances, both day-to-day problems of individuals at a neighborhood level and, confronted by strong unions, policy demands in the administrative and legislative realms."[58] What is more, especially when class conflicts became intense, the regular parties showed great tactical flexibility. They were willing to make concessions to selected policies advocated by radical movements—until such time as those movements, or the occasional third parties they spawned, faded from the scene or were absorbed into the regular party coalitions.[59]

Yet even when benefits did not flow, or when the connections between voting and public policies were obscure, nineteenth-century politics was highly sociable and lots of fun—for ordinary voters as well as party activists. In an age without television or movies, there were many elections, and voting was a public act accompanied, preceded, and followed by fraternal drills and torchlight parades, mammoth rallies and picnics, and rousing speeches to the party faithful. Nineteenth-century elections were not about isolated individuals "making up their minds." Electoral campaigns helped already partisan communities to express their loyalties and prepare for "battle" with one another. As the historian Michael McGerr recounts: "By the end of the Civil War, Northerners had turned campaigns into spectacular displays of exuberant partisanship . . . Both cause and result of political participation, spectacular campaigns helped to push voter turnout upward toward the record highs of the late nineteenth century."[60] Although "elements of spectacle" first appeared in Northern elections before the Civil War, they peaked during the Third Party system of the 1870s to 1890s:

> Spectacular electioneering in the third party system depended on the activities of clubs and marching companies usually formed for the duration of a campaign. [These groups were set up soon] after the major parties' presidential nominations, often as early as June and July . . . By September and October, clubs and companies marched and counter-marched across the North. In small towns each party typically had a campaign club, a marching company or two, and perhaps companies of veterans, boys, and blacks. There were so many marchers in cities that the parties grouped the companies together in battalions, legions, regiments, brigades, and armies, whose colonels and generals issued "battle orders" to the troops on the eve of parades. The companies and clubs absorbed the energies of millions of Northerners . . . [and] created a partisan spectacle that engulfed Northern communities for three months before election day.[61]

Class relations and differences were often expressed in the process of electoral campaigning during the nineteenth century.[62] But the major parties themselves were far-flung associations of males from different classes. And the parties proudly trumpeted their credentials as representatives of the entire American people. Inevitably, the effect for workers was to dissociate struggles over wages and autonomy that they experienced at workplaces from their activities and outlooks as citizens. Workers shared "politics" not with fellows from faraway workplaces, but with neighbors and with followers of "their party" from other classes and localities. American white men, moreover, shared rituals and symbols of political participation with one another in a way that helped to express their "manhood" in contrast to the feminine domesticity of women, all of whom were formally excluded from voting and core party activities.

Not only did ordinary American men vote with remarkable enthusiasm and consistency in the nineteenth century, they also remained loyal to one major party, in many cases over lifetimes and across generations. Localized communities based on ethnicity or shared religion were the basic building blocks of electoral loyalties in nineteenth-century American democracy.[63] Elections expressed complex mosaics of struggles dividing immigrants from native-born Americans, specific immigrant groups from others, Catholics from Protestants, and, among Protestants, "liturgical" (or "ritualist") believers such as Lutherans from "evangelical" (or "pietistic") believers such as Baptists or Presbyterians. The particular oppositions that aligned ethnocultural groups with the Democrats, or else with the Whigs or Republicans, ultimately depended on local conditions. Imperatives of group defense or competition could lead similar groups to take different sides in different localities.[64] Nevertheless, there were strong and enduring correlations across localities in the partisan orientations of two basic complexes of ethnocultural groups: The Democratic Party was the home of Catholics, including Irish and other urban-immigrant groups, of liturgical Protestants, and of white Southerners after the Civil War. Meanwhile, native-born evangelical Protestants were especially attracted to the Whigs and then to the Republicans.

If the major parties had robust and enduring differences in ethnocultural electoral support they correlatively projected contrasting stances toward the proper role of government in society and the economy.[65] Evangelicals or pietists felt that it was proper for government to regulate social morality by legal means, to purge the world of sin (whether slavery or drunkenness). Correlatively, Whigs and especially Republicans projected activist stances for government, including the federal government. Liturgical ethnocultural groups saw no intrinsic need for such an activist state role. In resonance, the Democrats championed state and local freedoms from federal intrusions, attacked interventions that apparently furthered economic privilege, and championed the defense of immigrant life-styles against nativist efforts at moral regulation.

Shall we conclude, then, that the major parties directly translated into public policies the sociocultural proclivities of their respective supporters? This may often have happened in localities, where such cultural issues were tackled as whether to set up compulsory public common schools and what values to teach in them, and whether liquor sales and saloons should be prohibited. Local branches of Democrats, Whigs, or Republicans could take up the causes most in tune with the values of particular ethnic or religious communities. Yet when the major parties tried to take stands on zero-sum cultural issues at higher levels, as they were periodically brought to do by

factions in their ranks, they faced the prospect of offending some
of the ethnoreligious forces in their complex coalitions, while pleas-
ing others. For example, in the 1890 Wisconsin election the Republicans lost German Protestant support because native-born Republicans had pushed laws enforcing temperance and exclusively
English-language instruction in the schools. Faced with such threats
of cultural imperialism, the German Protestants preferred to vote
with German and Irish Catholic Democrats, with whom they were
normally at odds.[66] On the whole, therefore, extralocal party leaders
tried to avoid taking hard stands on specific, zero-sum cultural issues.
Normally they let implicit allusions and symbolism in their campaigns
evoke the diffuse attitudes toward government activism that resonated with evangelical versus liturgical outlooks, but remained vague
and flexible on specifics, allowing grassroots cadres in different localities to interpret the party's stance in different ways.

The Primacy of Distributive Public Policies

For ordinary American men in the nineteenth century, politics happened through voting and the display of communally shared values
in parades, rallies, and speeches. But for elites oriented above the
local level, politics happened in the halls of legislatures and the
smoke-filled rooms of party gatherings, where fine-grained decisions
were hammered out dealing with the distribution of economically
relevant benefits. Throughout the century, policymaking in Congress and the state legislatures was focused on economic matters.
This happened even though economic questions were usually not
fought through as politically explicit class struggles. On the electoral
stump, Whigs versus Democrats, and then Republicans versus Democrats, contended rhetorically over general orientations toward government promotion of economic development: Was more or less of
it better for the nation or "the people"? Meanwhile, as party cadres
and as elected representatives within legislatures, these same politicians haggled continuously and in minute detail over distributions
of government-controlled resources and privileges to individuals,
communities, or enterprise groups.

Such decisions were the primary stuff of public policymaking in
the nineteenth-century United States, and in the words of Richard
L. McCormick:

The riches that governments bestowed were various indeed. Land was one such resource, and for almost the whole of the century federal and state officials allocated and sold it. Charters and franchises for banking, transportation, and manufacturing likewise were given away, especially by the states. Special privileges and immunities also came from government: For example, tax exemptions, the right of eminent domain, the privilege of charging tolls on roads and bridges, and the right to dam or channel streams and rivers. Public bounties occasionally encouraged privileged private enterprises, just as government investments sometimes funded mixed corporations. The federal government's tariff also represented a kind of public gift to the individuals and corporations whose products received protection. Public authorities at every level distributed aid by constructing or subsidizing highways, canals, railways, bridges, and harbors.[67]

"Except for the abolition of slavery," McCormick concludes, "the distribution of economic benefits probably represents the outstanding achievement of nineteenth-century American government. Certainly it formed the most characteristic achievement."[68]

Theodore Lowi has made a helpful analytic distinction among major types of public policies—including regulatory, redistributive, and distributive types—and we can say some basic things about their political characteristics.[69] Both "regulatory" and "redistributive" policies are aimed at satisfying the needs of collectivities; and they are likely to be zero-sum in their consequences, imposing losses on the disfavored groups whose actions are regulated or whose advantages are redistributed. "Distributive" policies, on the other hand, are often directed at particular individuals or groups; and they are likely to have elements of discretion built into the political decisions about who is eligible and who, among the eligible, actually receives benefits. As the historian Gerald Grob amplifies, "distributive policies are characterized by the ease with which they can be disaggregated" and they tend to be positive-sum in that "the indulged and the deprived, the loser and the recipient need never come into direct confrontation."[70] To be sure, disbursements can fuel resentments among those left out. Yet new recipients can always be added at a later time, just as previous recipients can come back for more. What is more, distributive policies can be positive-sum in a still more fundamental way, as when one policy (such as tariffs or public land sales) generates fiscal dividends that can be used to fund additional distributive policies.

The nineteenth-century U.S. polity was ideally adapted to generating distributive rather than regulatory or redistributive policies. There are several reasons why, which can be discussed in turn. These include the role of official spoils in the political system, the centrality of legislatures in the policy process, and the coalition-building needs of the major parties.

Patronage, a quintessentially distributive phenomenon, was the meat and potatoes of nineteenth-century politics. As soon as politicians gained control of any level or branch of government, the most basic task they performed was the (re)distribution of appointive public offices to fellow party loyalists. We have seen that the original architects of the U.S. polity avoided the construction of any centralized professional bureaucracy, such as would have greatly facilitated the formulation and implementation of regulatory or redistributive policies. Then the Jacksonians consolidated and celebrated partisan party control over the "spoils of office," which meant in effect that the party organizations colonized nineteenth-century U.S. public administration.

From the 1830s onward, the parties staffed federal, state, and local offices in accord with their patronage needs. "Local government officials and state administrators appointed men to fill a number of jobs and also got to dictate the choice of appointees to some federal jobs in return for support of the national party."[71] State governors—and (especially after the Civil War) the senatorial bosses who worked hand in glove with them to tend state party machines—influenced appointments at all levels where their party held sway.[72] Presidents worked with Senators to fill executive branch offices, including those in the customs houses of New York, Boston, Philadelphia, and New Orleans.[73] They also consulted with Congressmen and state and local party leaders about the postmasterships that were "the backbone of political machines." Postmasterships, explains the historian George Mayer,

> provided the party that controlled the Presidency with two-thirds of its [federal] patronage . . . [and] in most communities the postmaster was the sole link between the citizen and the national government. He performed such important functions for the party

as testing local sentiment, smoothing over factional quarrels, distributing campaign material, and raising money. His negative power to withhold information was almost as important as his power to issue it, and pamphlets mailed by the opposition party often wound up in wastebaskets instead of postal boxes.[74]

Nineteenth-century American government had a proclivity for distributive politics not only because its administrative arrangements came to be constituted through patronage. It was equally important that elected legislative bodies—the Congress and the state legislatures—were the centers of public policymaking.[75] Except when their procedures are highly institutionalized and when programmatic parties control their agendas, legislatures most readily decide matters by logrolling, a mode of decisionmaking to which distributive policies especially lend themselves. At the federal level, Skowronek has pointed out, "operations tended to center in Congress, where a logrolling process could best service the states and localities."[76] Furthermore, "at every governmental level, the dominant legislative branch threw open its doors to special, local interests demanding assistance and decrying restraints."[77] Issues frequently came onto legislative agendas when particular citizens, corporations, or communities petitioned a state legislature or Congress for some benefit or regulatory advantage.[78] Elected representatives found it politically wise to respond to many such particular requests, and much legislation took the form of "special" or "private" bills.[79] Over time, accusations of favoritism toward particular interests naturally arose, but they could be fended off by the establishment of broad distributive policy rubrics under which many potential beneficiaries could apply.[80] Ideally from the politicians' point of view, these were designed to leave room for legislators and administrators to exercise some continuing discretion in offering politically visible help to applicants from the approved category.

Finally, distributive policies predominated in nineteenth-century U.S. politics because they served many functions for the major political parties, the keystones of the entire governmental edifice. Aside from the direct distribution of public offices, party leaders used divisible economic resources or regulatory privileges to attract and retain the loyalty of business supporters, leaders of popular associations, locally rooted political brokers, and even "swing" voters in tightly contested areas. Precisely because most legislated benefits and privileges were so divisible and the allocations not inherently zero-sum, complex coalitions could be built up within and across the states. It was possible for each major party to contain interests that might, in general terms, find the governmental philosophy of the opposing party more congenial. Certainly, broad distribution of divisible benefits was one way in which the major parties managed to include local supporters from apparently clashing cultural or economic camps within the same trans-state networks.

Some scholars have treated major distributive policies such as the tariff as evidence of business domination rather than party primacy in nineteenth-century U.S. politics.[81] But this fails to notice important things about the appeal of tariff measures, as well as the precise shape they took. On the first matter, nineteenth-century Whigs and Republicans portrayed tariffs not only as benefits to manufacturers and raw-materials producers, but also as tools for promoting the American national interest by keeping employment steady and wages high.[82] Social historians of the working classes have found that workers in many protected industries and skilled occupations believed such appeals.[83]

Furthermore, industrialists could not always persuade politicians to form tariffs exactly as they wanted, even when party leaders and highly organized capitalists were closely allied with one another. For example, in the early 1880s, the powerful Industrial League of Philadelphia, led by the manufacturer and Republican grandee Joseph Wharton, proposed "a tariff commission plan, which . . . would take the tariff out of politics and place reform in the hands of an impartial body of experts." Republicans, who then controlled both the presidency and the Senate, appointed the commission as "a means of delaying tariff revision," although, predictably, they "were not enthralled by the idea of taking the tariff out of politics." When the Tariff Commission's report appeared, it called for "an ill-disguised revision of the tariff system in favor of the manufacturers and at the expense of the [raw-materials] producers." The industrialists were ecstastic, because "they had been agitating for years to obtain cheaper raw materials by lowering tariff duties on raw materials." But the report "was political dynamite for the Republicans," who "had built up a finely balanced political coalition based on protection for manufacturers and producers."[84]

In the ensuing clash between industrial and party concerns, the party concerns prevailed. Ironically, the agent was William D. "Pig Iron" Kelley of Pennsylvania, Speaker of the House, normally a close ally of his state's industrialists, "especially on tariff matters." Kelley led the House of Representatives in derailing the commission's recommendations (which were embodied in a Senate bill supported by the Iron and Steel Association and the National Association of Wool Manufacturers). As the historian of this incident concludes, "the Pennsylvania Republican protectionists were first of all party men, and secondly protectionists."[85] Kelley's forces substituted the tariff act of 1883, which was "no revision at all." Tariffs would continue to be brokered in Congress, not "taken out of politics" by an expert commission. And the Republican party would continue to balance interests for its own political well-being. It would not just register the demands of its dominant industrial supporters, or of any other economic interest.

As this example suggests, distributive policies in nineteenth-century patronage democracy were above all shaped by the needs and proclivities of parties that were "not merely a 'mirror' of opinion nor a 'medium' through which pressures were transmitted."[86] The major political parties in nineteenth-century America's patronage democracy flourished not as business conspiracies, nor as programmatic representatives of collective interests, but because they were so adept at using governmental resources for widely and eclectically distributing divisible benefits.

An exception must be registered to this characterization of nineteenth-century U.S. political parties, however. During the Civil War crisis from the late 1850s to the early 1870s, one of the major parties—or perhaps I should say a reformist crusade that grew into a major party—*did* operate in a startlingly programmatic fashion, implementing fundamental coercive and redistributive measures. The Republican Party won the most sectionally polarized election in U.S. history in 1860, fashioned a federal war machine eventually capable of defeating the South, and mobilized broad popular support in the Northeast and Midwest for the limitation and then total abolition of slavery. During Reconstruction, the Radical Republicans promoted regulatory and redistributive policies that, had they been fully implented, would have added up to a virtual "revolution from above" in the defeated South.[87]

But to note this exception is also to help delineate by contrast the

"normal" conditions under which the primacy of distributive policymaking held. The Republican party-state was at its most programmatic and redistributive as an emergency war machine and in relation to southern interests at times when they were in rebellion or
under federal military occupation. Arguably, even after the Civil
War and Reconstruction were over, Republican policies retained a
redistributive edge where the South was concerned, for the party
ended up with little support in that region.[88] Yet otherwise, even
during the war itself, much of the North's electoral and party politics
proceeded roughly as usual. This required free-flowing distributive
benefits, including contracts for manufacturers of war materials and
bounties for army volunteers; and the Civil War Republicans were
quite adept at managing these flows. More to the point, once the
southern states rejoined the Union and shook off most Reconstruction controls, the Democratic Party again became closely competitive
for national offices. Then the Republican Party outlived its heroic
phase and settled into the normal distributive routines of patronage
democracy. This system, which had emerged in the Jackson era, not
only revived after the Civil War but reached its climactic height
between the mid-1870s and the mid-1890s.

Social Policies in Nineteenth-Century America

Social security for those hurt or bypassed by the growing market
economy was not the main emphasis of nineteenth-century American
government, for it was geared to helping citizens and enterprises
get ahead economically. Even so, social policies of various sorts were
developed, including schools, institutions to handle the poor and the
impaired, and what I shall label "distributive social benefits" potentially available to many "independent" citizens. Such social policies
were shaped not just by the value-laden responses of Americans to
the massive changes of urbanization and capitalist industrialization
but also by the dynamics of U.S. federalism, the absence of bureaucracies, the preeminence of legislatures, and the activities of patronage-oriented democratic parties.

Coping with unfortunates who were impaired or who had to ask
for poor relief, and teaching children basic skills and values—these
were the "social functions" *explicitly* performed by nineteenth-century
American governments. In a profoundly decentralized society and

political order, both sets of activities were the responsibilities of local governments in the villages, towns, counties, and cities, with only modest involvement by the higher levels of government in the federal system. Yet the contrasting trajectories of poor relief and public education over the course of the century demonstrate a lot about the overall impact of patronage democracy on "the dependent" versus the "independent" majority of a democratic citizenry. American public education grew early and steadily through waves of initiatives by reformist professionals and local communities, and it was encouraged by enabling laws and subsidies from state and federal legislatures. Meanwhile, as the tasks of succoring the dependent burgeoned and proved increasingly complex, reformers' efforts to involve state and national governments succeeded only within strict limits, hampered by legislative fickleness and the absence of bureaucratic capacities. Ultimately, too, American reformers themselves became so ambivalent about government's role in a democratic, patronage-oriented polity that they attacked public spending for the needy with increasing thoroughness and counter-organization.

The Spread of Common Schools

Schooling for All is the apt title of a book by Ira Katznelson and Margaret Weir that describes how public education for white children of all social statuses emerged early and expanded rapidly in the United States.[89] Indeed, this is a realm of social policy in which America was the leader among modernizing nations.[90] During the first half of the 1800s only Prussia rivaled the United States in the expansion of public school enrollments. Yet the Prussian (and later Imperial German) system was highly stratified, separating out a small number of privileged youth for secondary and university educations, typically as routes into bureaucratized civil service positions. European systems in general were institutionalized in some variant of this stratified format. In contrast, the United States proliferated, first, common primary schools, and then relatively unstratified secondary schools. A profusion of colleges and universities also grew up starting in the nineteenth century, to attract unusually large proportions of the relevant age categories into higher education. America early became, and long remained, the world's most schooled society, in terms of sheer proportions of every age cohort attending educational institutions and receiving broadly similar instruction within them.[91]

The early and rapid expansion of U.S. primary schooling ran well ahead of industrialization, and high enrollments occurred first in rural communities, not the great cities.[92] Neither the capitalist class nor the emerging industrial working class took the lead, although many unions and other groups of workers did support the growth of common schooling in their localities.[93] Across the country outside the South, many communities, including the villages and small towns of rural America, built free public schools and sent children to them for at least part of the year. To spread schools across the land, networks of ministers, lawyers, teachers, and other educational promoters worked with whatever local allies they could find in each place, endeavoring (not always successfully) to standardize patterns of schooling across localities. What tied disparate groups of reformers, farmers, small businessmen, and artisans together in the broad social movement for democratic schooling was, in the words of the sociologist John Meyer and his collaborators, a "Protestant-Republican millennial view of the polity, coupled by a particular view of the nature of capitalism." The promoters of common public schooling believed that American competitive-market capitalism and democracy would flourish "in the hearts and minds of individuals, in the purified citizen members of a redeemer nation." "The concern of these nation-builders," as Meyer and his associates label them, "was not so much to control labor as to include everyone in their definition of the polity."[94]

The institutional arrangements of the nineteenth-century U.S. polity can help us understand why common public schooling spread so quickly and extensively; they can also help us make sense of the simultaneous growth of parochial schools, along with the proliferation of both public and private colleges. The early democratization of the white male electorate ensured that masses of ordinary Americans could support public schooling as a right of democratic citizenship, rather than warily opposing educational institutions imposed from above by officials and upper classes, as as happened in Europe.[95] In the United States, moreover, no national bureaucracy existed to regulate, finance, or serve as a central magnet for educational development; and no single dominant church served as a prop or a counter-weight to the state. Thus local and voluntary

forces, including Catholic parishes and a multiplicity of Protestant
and Jewish sects, took more initiatives than they did in other nations.
In a democratic political context, "participatory localism" encouraged many such groups to support free public schools, while others
defended coexisting private schools. Decentralized federalism allowed local, state-level, and private initiatives to compete with one
another—and often to imitate one another as well, in waves of analogous institution-building.[96] As the political scientist Paul E. Peterson
has aptly put it, "competition among ethnic and racial groups sharp-
ened the demand for schooling and contributed to its dispersal at a
rate far surpassing anything occurring in Europe . . . The exceptions
to the pattern confirm this general relationship. When blacks and
Orientals were deprived of their political rights, access to schooling
was also denied them."[97]

Educational promoters in the United States often got bipartisan
support from legislatures and democratically elected politicians.[98] To
be sure, the original champions of common public schools, epitomized by Horace Mann, were worried about the rise of political
parties and hoped that a schooled citizenry would perpetuate the
values of civic republicanism in contrast to party partisanship.[99] Yet
the dominant parties took account of locally rooted ethnoreligious
value differences and also engineered legislation to encourage the
endeavors of their grassroots supporters.[100] Thus, first Whig and
then Republican majorities passed many state-level measures making
primary schooling compulsory, channeling funds to public educational institutions, establishing state regulatory boards, and ensuring
that common school teachers could require readings from Protestant
Bibles. Meanwhile, Democratic politicians resisted centralizing and
"pan-Protestant" initiatives, and state legislators connected to urban
Democratic machines sometimes found ways to channel state funding to parochial schools.

The federal Congress promoted education through distributions
to the states. Even before the full democratization of male electoral
politics, the Northwest Ordinance of 1787 granted each new state
public lands to sell for the support of public education.[101] And in
1862 the Republican Congress passed the Morrill Act, making "land
grants" to states willing to set up at least one college "where the
leading object shall be . . . to teach such branches of learning as are
related to agriculture and the mechanic arts."[102] As for the courts,

they never gainsaid that under the Constitution, local and state governments could tax, spend, and regulate for public schools, and they also accepted the federal government's encouragement of state initiatives in the Morrill Act. In due course, the courts teamed up with Republican-dominated state legislatures to cut off any public subsidies for parochial schools, leaving subsequent encouragement of them up to the wiliest subterfuges of urban party bosses.[103]

Although the early extension of the democratic suffrage and the competition of parties for cross-class electoral support facilitated the founding and rapid geographical spread of common schools in the United States as contrasted to Europe, it is important to note that under some circumstances patronage-oriented parties limited the improvement and reorganization of public school systems. By the later nineteenth century, educational reformers were trying to make enrollments compulsory, improve teacher-student ratios, expand secondary schools, and bureaucratize and professionalize entire systems of schools in states and cities. Reform politicians might be friendly to these goals, even in the face of business opposition.[104] But machine politicians, particularly those associated with mature, centralized urban machines led by Irish Catholics, did not want school systems taken out of local politics, nor did they favor regulatory measures or collective policies to benefit middle-class professionals. During the 1880s and early 1990s, mature city machines faced tight contraints on their abilities to raise taxes or borrow for public spending.[105] The bosses in any event preferred to spend scarce resources on jobs for blue-collar voting males, not white-collar, nonvoting female teachers; and they were often allied with Catholic Church leaders worried about the expansion of Protestant-dominant public schools. All the same, even those leaders of mature, fiscally constrained urban machines who in practice limited the improvement and professionalization of school systems still felt the need to pay rhetorical lip service to democratic schooling. They often continued to build schools, given that public construction was an important source of patronage construction jobs. And they helped all ethnic sectors of their voting constituencies to gain access to teaching positions and to neighborhood schools with culturally congenial curricula.[106]

Let us return to the big picture. Although aspects of nineteenth-century patronage democracy may have limited the improvement and reorganization of U.S. school systems—particularly in cities with centralized machines facing tight fiscal constraints—the structure of the U.S. polity as a whole encouraged the extensive growth of education, from the emergence of common schools prior to the Civil War through the subsequent expansion of primary enrollments and the spread of secondary schools. Not only did the absence of bureaucracy in the United States allow space for democratized schooling. Democratic voting rights and the sense of belonging to the national polity encouraged all citizens to demand more and more access to schooling for their children. And the elected officials who dominated the polity usually supported the creation of all varieties of educational institutions and the broadening of access to them, because schools were widely popular in American democracy.

Welfare Provision for Dependent People

If the structures and dynamics of the U.S. polity facilitated the growth of common public schooling, they often, although not always, impeded governmental provision for dependent people during the nineteenth century. This happened partly because social policies for dependents were not broadly popular. It also happened because American elites and reformers increasingly reacted against the ways in which political parties distributed particularistic subsidies to welfare institutions and "outdoor" relief to the poor.

Americans brought the ideals and practices of the "Old Poor Law" with them from England; these called for local authorities to provide supervision and relief to each community's dependents, those who could not rely on immediate family members for survival.[107] But of course there were always many "little poor laws" in the colonies and, subsequently, in the United States; for there were no direct links between national authority and highly varied local practices. When the English "reformed" their Old Poor Law into the New Poor Law of 1834, which called for the abolition of "outdoor relief" and the establishment of workhouses to deter people from becoming paupers, the United States did not uniformly follow suit, especially when it came to cutting off all outdoor relief.[108] Almshouses were set up in many cities, towns, and counties; yet long-established practices of outdoor relief and "contracting out" the poor also continued.[109] In contrast to what happened with public education, local communities did not so readily compete to emulate and outdo one another in their provisions for the poor and dependent. Help for the poor often depended on local economic and labor-market conditions. Insofar as elements of standardization crept in, they were the work of private crusaders and voluntary groups, often with religious inspiration and backing, who pursued a series of reforms that promised to "cure the ills" of dependent people as individuals, remaking them into worthy independent citizens.

Many reformers placed their hopes in new custodial institutions—almshouses with mandatory work for the able-bodied poor; homes for the wayward; and asylums for the mentally ill—and fought to get them set up and properly operated according to the wisdom of the day.[110] Local or private resources, however reluctantly given, were usually all the institution-builders could muster. Yet when legislative coalitions were propitiously balanced for a particular institution's sponsors, public subsidies might flow directly under governmental auspices or—more likely—indirectly through private charitable intermediaries.

The federal government did a bit of institutional subsidizing. In 1819 Congress passed "An Act in Behalf of the Connecticut Asylum for Teaching the Deaf and Dumb," bestowing an endowment of 23,000 acres of public land to sustain an institution that had been founded with private and church resources and had earlier benefited by a one-time appropriation from the Connecticut legislature.[111] Responding to calls for interregional equity, Congress similarly aided a public institution in Kentucky in 1826.[112]

More often, subsidies were distributed at the discretion of state legislatures and, after the advent of patronage democracy, seem to have responded to shifts in party strength. By the 1860s, the New York legislature's annual charity bill "had become a logrolling instrument to accommodate the political needs of individual legislators . . . granting funds to private orphanages, hospitals, dispensaries, and charity schools."[113] What is more, after Boss William M Tweed arrived in Albany in 1869, he got himself onto the Senate Committee on Charitable and Religious Societies, so that he could increase legislative appropriations and channel them through his New York City Democratic machine to Catholic institutions, which had not previously gained much state largesse.[114] Analogously—although no doubt to the greater benefit of Protestant-sponsored institutions—

Pennsylvania's Republican Party Boss Matthew Quay arranged during the 1880s not only for subsidies to particular corporate capitalist interests but also for

> appropriations to hospitals, school districts, penal institutions, charitable societies, and asylums . . . By controlling the appropriations committees of the state house and senate, Quay influenced the flow of funds . . . and would withhold part, or all, of an institution's share if the legislators and others primarily interested in it did not play the logrolling game according to his rules. Lawmakers working in behalf of a particular institution or program quickly discovered that legislative enactment did not depend upon either the quality of the program or the availability of funds. Quay . . . exacted a price—the commitment of interested legislators to other issues important to him [as party leader] before clearing their measure for passage.[115]

Clearly, public funding for the institutions favored by nineteenth-century welfare reformers remained very vulnerable to legislative and party whims, and thus was highly uneven across places and time. Welfare institutions probably fared best under patronage democracy when they had persistent social networks of crusaders tied to broad ethnoreligious constituencies, as well as mandates to serve more rather than less appealing categories of dependents. A telling case that helps to illustrate this point is the fate of Dorothea Dix's remarkable drive to obtain federal subsidies for the institutional care of indigent insane people. She came close, when Congress in 1854 passed the "Ten-Million-Acre Bill," granting public lands to the states for this purpose.[116] President Pierce vetoed the bill, however, arguing that the federal government's purpose was "not to dispense charities to the indigent . . . If we have the power to grant charities to one class of the community who may be suffering, why not to another? If to the lunatic, why not to the blind . . . the deaf and dumb, and to the whole range of paupers whose provision is now confined to the communities to which they belong?"[117]

Largely on party lines, Congress sustained Pierce's veto that year. But as a historian of this episode rightly points out, this need not have been end of the effort, if only Dorothea Dix had not been such a lonely crusader.[118] Other federal welfare subsidies, such as the law to aid the Kentucky institution for the deaf and the Morrill Act to aid agricultural colleges, needed to come up more than once to gain acceptance from both Congress and a President.[119] In this case, however, Dix did not involve a broader social network, and in all likehood the cause of the indigent insane was not at all politically appealing in a democracy. "No person or organization came forward to carry on the campaign . . . Thus, eight years later, when the political climate had changed to such a degree as to make possible the provision of federal land grants for assistance to other worthy causes, the mentally ill and other pressing welfare problems had no organized voice in the land or champion in Congress."[120]

By the last third of the nineteenth century, elite reformers had become disgusted by the vagaries and "corruption" of patronage democracy and alarmed by the rising costs and complexity of care for dependents in a rapidly industrializing and urbanizing society. Increasingly, therefore, reformers championed measures designed to take public welfare provision out of "politics"—or, more precisely, to take it out of the grip of the patronage-oriented political parties that controlled much of the polity in the post–Civil War decades.

Some reformers called for and achieved state legislation establishing regulatory boards, including Bureaus of Charities and Corrections to oversee and reform local poor relief practices.[121] Such boards were often staffed in an ad hoc fashion by the very persons who had lobbied for them. Unlike their counterparts in contemporary Britain and Continental Europe, these boards were not outgrowths of a bureaucratic state, and they lacked fiscal resources or coercive authority. Insofar as they could maintain continuity of purpose at all— and often they could not—their usual achievement was to gather rough statistics and promote publicity about the specific "social problems" and political malfeasances under their nominal jurisdiction. The boards charged with enforcing regulatory laws, such as those restricting child labor, made very little headway in the nineteenth century.[122]

Another elite strategy for taking welfare out of politics was exemplified by the Charity Organization Societies organized voluntarily by elites in many American cities and towns from 1877.[123] These societies were fiercely devoted to the abolition of public "outdoor relief" for the poor. Practitioners of "scientific philanthropy," the Charity Organization Societies emphasized coordination and investigation. If help for individuals was needed, they preferred to arrange for private "friendly visitors," typically upper-class or middle-class ladies, to counsel poor families on hard work and sobriety. The visitors also sorted out "unworthy" poor people, such as able-bodied male shirkers, from those "worthy" poor, such as widows, who were deserving of tiny bits of private charity leavened with plenty of moral advice.

Charity Organization reformers, along with many other American elites in the late nineteenth century, were especially appalled by the ways in which public relief for able-bodied unemployed men could become enmeshed with grassroots party politics. In their eyes, this situation undermined the integrity of the "public interest" and simultaneously harmed the moral character of the individuals who received the governmental handouts. In the characteristic words of E. L. Godkin, editor of the *Nation,* the woes of America's great cities could be traced to "foreigners . . . ignorant, credulous, newly emancipated, brutalized by oppression . . . [who] learn to look on the suffrage simply as a means of getting jobs out of the public, and taxation as another name for the forced contributions of the rich to a fund for the poor man's relief."[124]

Urban Party Machines as Distributors of Welfare and Jobs

The men and women of the Charity Organization Societies were not imagining things. Patronage democracy in nineteenth-century America did indeed sponsor a sort of distributive, discretionary welfare regime, delivering some benefits directly to individuals (in addition to the subsidies to favored schools and welfare institutions that we have already noted). As noticed both by contemporary reformer critics and by scholars ever since, late-nineteenth-century urban party machines were prime practitioners of what we may call "distributive social welfarism," especially in the Eastern and Midwestern cities where the parties were competitive and solidly rooted in mass electorates, and not just tied to particular business interests as parties were in some Western states.[125] The urban machines were the parts of the party system most directly in touch with the new industrial working class and its many problems of low and uncertain income, bouts of illness and unemployment, and accompanying episodes of family disorganization. Democratic party machines were typically closer to workers, partly because Republican machines, as "urban off-shoots of state-level GOP machines," were organized "in the air" from the "top down," while the Democratic machines were organized from the "bottom up" as well as, wherever possible, with the aid of resources channeled down from the state and federal governments.[126] The Democrats were the party of most of the immigrant, unskilled workers—including those preeminent machine-builders, the Irish.

What sorts of welfare benefits did urban party machines channel to American workers? With the benefit of anachronistic social scientific rhetoric, we can see that the machines offered particularized "regulatory adjustments" and "in-kind income supplements." More important, the party machines also served as primitive "employment agencies," and often provided temporary public employment to cushion their favored constituents against severe episodes of unemployment.

At the grassroots of urban politics, regulatory adjustments and gifts of money, goods, or services helped to warm the relationships between local ward leaders and the families in their neighborhoods, the votes of whose menfolk they reliably had to "get out" for the party on frequent election days. The characteristic kinds of benefits were episodic, particularistic, and at the discretion of the politician: baskets of food to poor families on holidays; money for a casket to a bereaved widow; a cousin sprung from jail; a food shipment to an orphanage; a gift for a working-class wedding; intervention to help immigrants become quickly naturalized.[127] As George Washington Plunkitt of Tammany Hall told the journalist William Riordan from personal experience:

> What tells in holdin' your grip on your district is to go right down among the poor families and help them in the different ways they need help. I've got a regular system for this. If there's a fire in Ninth, Tenth, or Eleventh Avenue, for example, any hour of the day or night, I'm usually there with some of my election district captains as soon as the fire engines. If a family is burned out I don't ask whether they are Republicans or Democrats, and I don't refer them to the Charity Organization Society, which would investigate their case in a month or two and decide they were worthy of help about the time they are dead from starvation. I just get quarters for them, buy clothes for them if their clothes were burned up, and fix them up until they get things runnin' again. It's philanthropy, but it's politics, too—mighty good politics.[128]

The ward leader did not simply trade benefits for votes on a one-to-one basis; that would be too individualistic an interpretation.[129] Thinking about the matter more sociologically, we can see that the ward leader *displayed* his friendly generosity and caring for all the neighbors to see, thus getting a much more robust political payoff than the sum of the piddling favors he handed out to a few of them. "Who can tell how many votes one of these fires bring me?" mused Plunkitt. "The poor are the most grateful people in the world, and, let me tell you, they have more friends in their neighborhoods than the rich have in theirs . . . [T]he poor look up to George W. Plunkitt as a father, come to him in trouble—and don't forget him on election day."[130] An astute settlement house worker, Mary Kingsbury Simkhovitch, observed in 1902 that the machine politician "combines to an unusual degree the qualities of insider and outsider, man of weight and common neighbor."[131] While the elite reformers of the day, Simkhovitch felt, were "outsiders" "working on the people, not with them," the Tammany politician remained a sympathetic friend, talking and living in the same style as his neighbors, even as he used his political connections to arrange help for them.[132]

Jobs, Simkhovitch further argued, were the most important kind of aid that machine politicians provided members of the urban working class. "I can always get a job for a deservin' man," said George Washington Plunkitt; "I make it a point to keep on the track of jobs, and it seldom happens that I don't have a few up my sleeve ready for use."[133] Patronage was the very lifeblood of the regular political parties of the nineteenth century, so it should hardly surprise us that they served as primitive employment agencies for favored working-class supporters, and especially for the Irish who were usually the ethnic fellows of the urban politicians.[134] The kinds of opportunities available to individuals with the right party connections were various: jobs for the lucky few in the political machine itself; jobs in public agencies allocated through patronage; jobs with private enterprises beholden to the machine for contracts or immunity from police action; and jobs on public works projects.[135] Some of these jobs represented fabulous opportunities for upward mobility; loyal, career machine politicians could end up as wealthy as millionaire George Plunkitt. To be sure, most machine-provided jobs, as Steven Erie has vigorously argued, left their holders doing unskilled labor or, especially after the turn of the twentieth century,

lower-level blue- or white-collar jobs in expanded city governments.[136] Yet in turn-of-the century Massachusetts, according to Alex
Keyssar, "positions with the city were desirable not just because they
were jobs but also because they were unusually steady and secure
jobs. The best position that an unskilled Irish laborer could hope to
obtain was a job as a city laborer. Even skilled workers sometimes
abandoned their seasonal trades in favor of the security of the police
or fire departments."[137]

In addition to opening permanent job opportunities, the patronage parties might respond to the cyclical depressions of the capitalist
economy by putting supporters temporarily to work in this way,
although their willingness to launch public works may have been
greater in the early "formative" phases of the machines than later,
when consolidated machines became sensitive to middle-class worries
about taxes during the 1880s.[138] At times, the machines sponsored
public works as unemployment relief in response to the demands by
unions or reformist labor parties, or in response to demonstrations
by the unemployed themselves. American workers, immigrants and
natives alike, strongly preferred work relief to public or private
charity.[139] And if urban party machines could stave off middle-class
pressures against higher taxes or public borrowing, they might respond with emergency employment measures that were in line with
their normal proclivity to dispense public jobs.

While other kinds of favors from the ward bosses might be appreciated, employment opportunities were particularly coveted, for
they were "the necessary centre around which life turns" for tenement dwellers, "and especially for those who live on the margin."[140]
Consequently, the machine politicians as the "job dispensers of the
great city are evidently the greatest friends the poor man has."[141]
Certain modern scholars have stressed that, in the aggregate, the
urban machines provided relatively few jobs, distributed them in
ethnically biased ways, and certainly did not solve the massive problems of unemployment, underemployment, and low-wage drudgery
that many workers faced.[142] All of this is true enough. But I think
it fails to capture the way in which the party machines both appealed
to and helped to shape American workers' preferences for publicly
facilitated employment rather than any other sort of social provision.

If only a few people "got ahead" through machine-provided jobs,
and if only a few others benefited from work-relief during hard

times, nevertheless many of their friends and neighbors could see that the urban party machines were doing something to help people help themselves. Prior to the New Deal, urban machine politicians were just about the only authorities in the United States who responded sympathetically and concretely to problems of unemployment.[143] Whatever the upper-class reformers might think, the alternatives for unemployed workers could be family breakup, crime, or dependence on demeaning private charity. Those workers who were helped to get ahead through patronage, or to get by with jobs on public works, could feel that they had received honorable kinds of help, congruent with their basic values. What is more, jobs arranged through the political machine could be the equivalent of the opportunities for mobility the parties opened through postmasterships for people in rural communities.[144] In terms of relative significance to individual workers and their families and friends, jobs offered by urban machines were analogous to the opportunities the parties created for people at higher levels of the class structure, through business contracts and posts for ever clamoring state and federal officeseekers.[145]

Conclusion

The only Americans who were really forced to be "hardy individualists" in the nineteenth century were the very poor, especially able-bodied men who were not fortunate enough to enjoy ties to party politicians. Such individuals were shunned in principle, and increasingly in practice, if they sought public help in any dignified form. Meanwhile, few if any of the citizens who received special opportunities for jobs, careers, or income through politics felt that they were obtaining illegitimate aid. Certainly, they did not think they were getting anything so demeaning as public "relief." Nor did they think of themselves as objects of charity. Such, of course, was the beauty of patronage democracy. This federal polity structured by competitive parties rooted in a cross-class white male electorate helped many Americans to get ahead economically, without making them feel like clients of a "welfare state."

As we next turn to examine the elaboration of Civil War benefits, we shall see that patronage democracy not only distributed welfare assistance to urban workers and opened economic opportunities to citizens across walks of life; the U.S. polity of the late nineteenth century also extended pensions and other benefits to disabled and elderly men of all social classes, and helped many of their dependents as well. Through Civil War benefits, the federal government—long before the New Deal—became the source of generous and honorable social provision for a major portion of the American citizenry.

CHAPTER 2

Public Aid for the Worthy Many:
The Expansion of Benefits
for Veterans of the Civil War

Histories of U.S. social provision have failed to notice that the national government was a major welfare provider at the turn of the century—no doubt because the relevant expenditures were officially categorized as military costs. Yet as Isaac Max Rubinow declared in 1913, five years after the British launched national old-age pensions,

> when our [American] pension roll numbers several thousand more names than that of Great Britain . . . [and] when the cost of our pensions is over $160,000,000, or more than three times as great as that of the British pension system . . . it is childish to consider the system of war pensions as a sentimental problem only, and to speak of the millions spent for war pensions as the cost of the "Civil War." We are clearly dealing here with an economic measure which aims to solve the problem of dependent old age and widowhood.[1]

Rubinow was right. Over several decades, Civil War pensions evolved from a restricted program to compensate disabled veterans and the dependents of those killed or injured in military service into an open-ended system of disability, old-age, and survivors' benefits for anyone who could claim minimal service time on the northern side of the Civil War.

More than just the demographic givens of a major war brought about this outcome. The political forces of late-nineteenth-century American patronage democracy fueled the expansion of Civil War social benefits. Ultimately, the system became a kind of precocious social security system for those U.S. citizens of a certain generation and region who were deemed morally worthy of enjoying generous and honorable public aid. As we shall see, however, this early American regime of social provision differed in fundamental respects from the old-age pensions and social insurance programs that emerged during the same decades in other Western nations.

The Politics of Civil War Pensions, 1860s–1910s

The basic precondition for the later widespread disbursement of military pensions to military veterans and the survivors of deceased soldiers was the duration, intensity, and mass-mobilizing quality of the Civil War itself. "With the national economies on both sides fully integrated into their respective war efforts, the American Civil War was truly . . . the first 'total' war in the modern sense."[2] The conflict not only joined industrial with human mobilization; the pattern of warfare, especially once Union forces drove deeply into the South, was relatively unlimited in that it was directed against civilians and economic targets as well as military formations. What is more, the American Civil War, like the earlier French revolutionary wars and the later World Wars of the twentieth century, was "democratic," because the entire adult male citizenry was subject to calls to military service. At first, the calls in the North were voluntary; but in March 1863 conscription was instituted for men 20 to 45 years old who could not pay commutation or arrange for substitutes.[3]

The Civil War was also, by far, the most devastating war the United States has ever experienced. Some statistical facts about the North's experience of the Civil War can help to convey how traumatic it was. (White southerners suffered an even greater human impact, as we shall learn below.) About 2,213,000 men served in the Union army and navy.[4] This included about 37 percent of the northern men between the ages of 15 and 44 in 1860[5]—fully comparable to the massive one-third of British men who served in World War I, a quintessential "total modern" war.[6] Overall, the Union side in the Civil War suffered 364,511 mortal casualties (including 140,414 battle deaths and 224,097 other deaths, mostly from disease).[7] These numbers translate into a ratio of about 18 (17.95) northerners killed per thousand in the population, whereas only 1.31 Americans per thousand were to die in World War I, and 3.14 per thousand in

World War II.[8] As for the Union military's wounded who survived, they numbered some 281,881, or about 14 (13.88) per thousand in the northern population.[9]

Throughout this discussion, therefore, we need to remember that the sheer dimensions of the Civil War as a martial event made *possible* the subsequent expansion of a generous pension system. This war created a large number of survivors of dead soldiers, along with many wounded and other veterans who might later claim rewards for latent disabilities or for their service alone. Nevertheless, no examination of the demographics of the war outside of the context of the nineteenth-century U.S. polity can account for the development of the pension system, as a contrast with the other major nation that experienced democratic military mobilization in early modern times can help to dramatize.

From 1792 through 1815, Revolutionary and Napoleonic France experienced mass-mobilizing wars. "Over two and a half million recruits passed through France's armies," most of whom died in combat or (especially) from disease, but some 150,000 of whom survived to be pensioned (along with an unknown number, in the thousands, who survived without pensions).[10] Benefits for French soldiers commenced in generous terms at the democratic height of the Revolution, much as still more generous U.S. veterans' benefits were later to commence in the democratic North in the midst of the Civil War. Laws passed in France in 1793 reflected a historically unprecedented concern to pension not just officers but also disabled and needy common soldiers and the widows of soldiers who died in service.[11] The subsequent historical trajectory of French veterans' benefits was, however, conditioned by fiscal constraints and, even more, by the revival of bureaucratic controls and elite patronage under Napoleon.

In France after 1803, a large backlog of pension applications was efficiently processed by the bureaucracy, but the rates of pensions were sharply lowered, and the eligibility of common soldiers and their widows to receive help was restricted, even as French officers received proportionately more under the 1803 laws and through special grants to favorites from Napoleon himself.[12] Despite the benefit cutbacks, as backlogs of earlier-wounded veterans moved through the system, overall French pension costs attributable to the Revolutionary and Napoleonic Wars continued to rise modestly through the 1810s.[13] France continued during subsequent decades to do more for veteran common soldiers than did other European nations.[14] But its veterans' benefits did not for many years become as generous (in levels or coverage) as they had been at the height of the Revolution. And they would never become anywhere near as legally liberalized, socially far-reaching, or costly as those of the late-nineteenth-century United States. The contrast, I maintain, was between a mass-mobilizing French Revolution that gave way to centralized bureaucracy and only episodically redemocratized postrevolutionary regimes, and a U.S. Civil War that entailed democratic mass mobilization without centralized bureaucratic controls and subsequently gave way to a restoration of full-fledged federal patronage democracy.

A glance backward in U.S. history also suggests the importance of democratic politics for the long-term expansion of veterans' benefits.[15] Back at the time of the American Revolution, the only pensions seriously debated by the Continental Congress were disability pensions for wounded soldiers and lifetime service pensions (at half-pay) for officers. In 1818, pensions were extended more generally to veterans of the U.S. War of Independence—but only to those who could prove the most dire poverty. Significantly, open-ended service pensions for all surviving Revolutionary warriors and widows—as opposed to the stricter disability and need-based pensions—did not emerge until after the advent of patronage democracy, with its universal suffrage rights for all American white males. In 1832, service pensions were legislated for all veterans, benefiting some 33,425 men whose average age by then was 74.5 years. And in 1836, the widows of rank-and-file soldiers who had served during the War of Independence also starting receiving pensions. In contrast to postrevolutionary France, therefore, the postrevolutionary United States can be said to have further liberalized the terms of its military pensions, particularly after the advent of universal white manhood suffrage in its nonbureaucratic polity. But, of course, the expansions of U.S. military pensions prior to the 1860s were minimal compared to what was to come with the mass-mobilizing Civil War and its political aftermath.

Raising Massive Armies in a Democracy

Generous responses by the Union side to the needs of the soldiers and sailors fighting for its cause commenced within the first year of the Civil War, well before anyone imagined that the conflict would drag on so long and become so costly. The United States was a full democracy for white males, and the Republican party had risen to power in the name of "free land, free labor, and free men."[16] Generous treatment for soldiers was in accord with the outpouring of nationalist sentiment in the democratic North. It was also a practical necessity for a nonbureaucratic state, especially once the first rush of patriotic volunteering was over and prior to the institution of conscription in 1863. As John William Oliver, an early historian of Civil War pensions, put it, "our democratic nation was put to a test, the like of which few nations have had to meet. Without a creditable standing army, and lacking the power to compel men to enter upon military service, our Government had to resort to the policy of persuasion" to raise over a million volunteers in 1861 and 1862.[17]

During 1861, preexisting regular army benefits were granted to the first volunteers for the Civil War, yet this was understood to be only a stopgap approach. In February 1862, a new law specifically addressing the needs of Union soldiers and their dependents was enthusiastically enacted by the Republican-dominated Congress.[18] Secretary of the Interior J. P. Ushur proudly declared it "the wisest and most munificent enactment of the kind ever adopted by any nation."[19] Subsequently, the 1862 law was rendered more generous and systematic by a steady stream of legislative tinkering; but it was destined to remain the baseline of the Civil War pension system until 1890. Under the 1862 law, the award of pension benefits was directly linked to disabilities "incurred as a direct consequence of . . . military duty" or, after the close of combat, "from causes which can be directly traced to injuries received or disease contracted while in military service."[20]

Despite "a feeling, shared by several members of Congress, that in an army made up of citizen soldiers rather than mercenaries, it would be unjust discrimination to pension an officer at a higher rate than a private,"[21] disability pensions under the 1862 law were graded according to rank. A lieutenant colonel or above totally disabled for manual labor originally received $30 per month, while at the other end of the gradation of ranks, a private similarly disabled got $8; and "proportionate pensions were to be given in each rank for partial disability."[22] Soon things became much more complicated, however. From 1864 on, new laws mandated special benefits (higher than those for "total disability") for particular kinds of severe mishaps, or for disabled veterans who required special attendants. In 1864, for example, the loss of both hands or eyes entitled a soldier to a pension of $25 a month, and within a decade this was raised to $50. The system soon became rather baroque; for example, by 1872 there were two grades of disability for manual labor; the loss of one arm at the shoulder joint was worth $18.00, while the loss of an arm above the elbow joint was worth $15.00 a month; and "the loss of sight in one eye, the sight of the other having been lost before enlistment" was compensated at $31.25 a month![23] Much room for initiative and interpretation was introduced into the system, for veterans and doctors had to make the case for conditions such as "disability equivalent to the loss of a hand or a foot," and the Pension Bureau had to decide which claims, or combinations of claims, to allow. In later years, such extremely difficult to interpret conditions as "chronic diarrhea" and "nervous prostration" came to be covered by special pension rates.[24]

Under the 1862 law, widows, orphans, and other dependents of those who died for causes traceable to their Union military service also received pensions at the rates their relatives would have gotten for total disabilities.[25] The rates for dependents were very generous by preexisting historical standards in the United States and beyond; and the range of potential beneficiaries also became remarkably broad. According to the 1862 law, for example, dependent mothers and sisters of dead or injured soldiers could, under certain circumstances, receive pensions, and in due course dependent brothers and fathers were also made eligible. Normally, only one dependent relative was eligible at a time (for example, a mother if there was no widow, and so forth). In 1873, however, extra amounts were added to widows' benefits for each dependent child.

Patterns of Pension Growth after the Civil War

Given the generosity of the basic Civil War pension law, as well as the magnitude of the needs immediately generated by the war, it is hardly suprising that each year thousands of former soldiers, and survivors of soldiers who had died, applied for these military-disability pensions. Before pensioners from the Civil War started to be added to the rolls in 1862, the United States was paying benefits to

10,700 veterans and widows at a total cost of about $1 million per year; and beneficiaries and expenditures were declining each year.[26] By 1866, however, the Civil War enrollments had suddenly swelled the pension list to 126,722, with total disbursements mounting to about $15.5 million.[27] From 1866 through 1873 and 1874, the numbers of pensioners and the cost grew steadily, as the human costs to the northern side of America's massive internal bloodletting registered in the public fisc.

The pension costs of the Civil War seemed to peak in the years after 1870—just as one might expect for a benefit system tied directly to disabilities incurred in wartime service. "We have reached the apex of the mountain," declared Commissioner of Pensions James H. Baker in 1872.[28] The numbers of new applications declined after 1870; the total number of pensioners stopped growing in 1873; and the total expenditures reached an apparent upper limit in 1874.[29] Although there were complaints about fraudulent pension claims even in this early period, the political impact of this concern was undercut when the system seemed to stop expanding.

Part of the reason for the mid-1870s pause in the expansion of the Civil War pension system must have been that the subjectively most pressing needs of the (then-youthful) veterans and survivors had already been addressed. True, the Pension Bureau refused to accept about 28 percent of the applications it received between 1862 and 1875.[30] Yet it is important to realize that large numbers of potential pensioners did not apply at all. Although the requirement to demonstrate service-connected disabilities obviously limited applications from veterans, many potentially eligible veterans and survivors failed to apply for pensions during the decade after the war's end. A desire to forget the war and get on with life, an absence of financial need, unfamiliarity with the possibilities or the application procedures, and a reluctance on the part of some to take handouts from the government—all of these factors may have been involved in the initially low "take-up rate" for Civil War disability pensions. And that rate truly was rather low. Among the survivors of the Union soldiers who were killed during the war, plus the survivors of the veterans who died by 1870, only about 25 percent were receiving dependents' pensions in 1875.[31] Also, we know that about 15 percent of the surviving ex-soldiers in 1865 had been wounded during the war.[32] Presumably most of them, if motivated, would

Table 2. Take-up rates for Civil War pensions

	Union veterans in civil life*	Disabled military pensioners**	Percentage of veterans enrolled as pensioners
1865	1,830,000	35,880	1.96%
1870	1,744,000	87,521	5.02%
1875	1,654,000	107,114	6.48%
1880	1,557,000	135,272	8.69%
1885	1,449,000	244,201	16.85%
1890	1,322,000	—	—
1891	—	520,158	39.34%
1895	1,170,000	735,338	62.85%
1900	1,000,000	741,259	74.13%
1905	821,000	684,608	83.39%
1910	624,000	562,615	90.16%
1915	424,000	396,370	93.48%

*Source: U.S. Bureau of the Census, *Historical Statistics of the United States, Colonial Times to 1970*, Bicentennial (Washington: Government Printing Office, 1975), pt. 2, series 957–970, p. 1145.

**Source: William H. Glasson, *Federal Military Pensions in the United States* (New York: Oxford University Press, 1918), pp. 144, 271, 272. The figures for 1865–1885 include a small number of invalids from wars prior to the Civil War. The Pension Bureau's report for 1890 was incomplete, so the 1891 number for disabled pensioners was divided by the 1890 estimate of veterans in civil life.

have been in a very good position to claim some sort of disability benefits (and this does not include many others who could make the case for later disabilities that had remained latent during the war). Yet Table 2 reveals that only 6.5 percent of all veterans, or about 43 percent of the formerly wounded men who might have been especially eligible, had signed up for (disability) pensions by 1875.

Despite the initial reluctance of many veterans and surviving relatives to claim pension benefits, the "apex of the mountain" for Civil War pensions came not in the mid-1870s, as Commissioner Baker declared, but two decades later. Along with Table 2, Figure 1 helps to show what happened to the Civil War pension system as it evolved from a generous, partially utilized program for compensation of

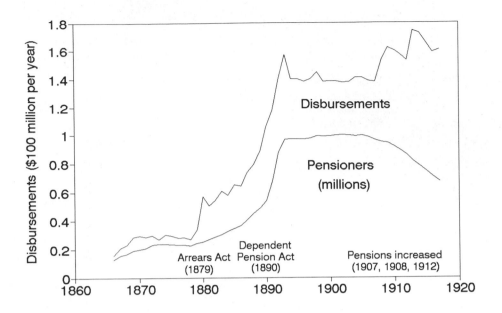

Figure 1   The expansion of Civil War pensions, 1866–1917
Source: William H. Glasson, *Federal Military Pensions in the United States* (New York: Oxford University Press, 1918), p. 273.

combat injuries and deaths into an even more generous system of disability and old-age benefits, which were ultimately "taken up" by over 90 percent of the Union veterans surviving in 1910. In contrast to what happened in France after the Revolution, the terms of eligibility for U.S. veterans' pensions became steadily more liberal in the decades after the Civil War. Accordingly, after the mid-1870s, the numbers of pensioners and the costs resumed upward trajectories and continued to grow until the facts of generational mortality overtook the ingenuity of politicians at channeling ever higher benefits to ever more people.

There were several notable legal watersheds along the way. The 1879 Arrears Act allowed soldiers who newly discovered Civil War–related disabilities to sign up and receive in one lump sum all of the pension payments they would have been eligible to receive since the 1860s. A decade later, the 1890 Dependent Pension Act severed the link between pensions and service-related injuries. Any veteran who had honorably served ninety days in the Union military, whether or not he had seen combat or been in any way hurt during the war, could apply for a pension if at some time he became disabled for manual labor. In practice, old age alone soon became a sufficient disability, and in 1906 the law was amended to state this explicitly.[33] After the turn of the century, moreover, Congress several times significantly raised the general benefit levels for both veterans and surviving dependents.

What happened after the mid-1870s to the Civil War pensions system? Clearly, pensions became caught up in politics, but how, exactly? Certain political mechanisms that might have fueled expansion have been suggested by the small number of social scientists who have examined the matter. Let me comment briefly on their ideas before I develop my own arguments.

One argument about the liberalization of Civil War pensions is a pressure group thesis.[34] After the Civil War, hundreds of thousands of former Union soldiers organized themselves into veterans' associations, which in turn repeatedly lobbied Congress to improve benefits. Indeed, this "social demand" argument gains plausibility from the highly visible role that the most important Northern veterans' organization, the Grand Army of the Republic, played in lobbying for legal liberalization in the years prior to the Dependent Pension Act of 1890, and the glee with which the organization greeted this law when it passed.[35] Other facts militate against simple reliance on the GAR pressure group thesis, however. During the 1870s, when the Arrears Act was urged through Congress, the Grand Army of the Republic was at best limping along, with many of its state-level "departments" in severe disarray and others avoiding political entanglements by concentrating on local fellowship and charity.[36] The national Grand Army of the Republic did not officially endorse or lobby for the Arrears Act, which actually seems to have affected the GAR more than vice-versa.[37] The new law stimulated thousands of applications for membership in veterans' associations (of which the GAR was the strongest), and also intensified the interest of Grand Army leaders in pension legislation and administration. In 1881–82, the GAR set up a Washington-based Pensions Committee to lobby Congress and the Pensions Bureau. The most rapid expansion of the GAR came during the 1880s—"immediately after the society . . .

began its aggressive campaign for government aid to veterans"—
and the organization reached the peak of its membership in 1890,
when it enrolled 39 percent of all surviving Union veterans.[38] After
1890, as during the decade before, the GAR continued to pressure
Congress on behalf of ever more liberalized pension laws. Yet the
GAR never did get all that it asked Congress to give; and even the
Dependent Pension Act of 1890 fell a little short of the straight
"service pension" (that is, for all veterans aged 62 and above, with
no disability clause) that many within the GAR were demanding.[39]

Another argument stresses the link between protective tariffs and
the expansion of pension expenditures. Generous Civil War pensions
become in this view a way to siphon off the embarrassing fiscal
"surpluses" that high tariffs incidentally produced. Those supposedly pulling the political strings were protection-minded businesses
in the northeastern "core" region of the country. The Republican
Party is pictured as controlled by such protectionist business interests, while the Democratic Party opposed both high tariffs and generous pensions because both worked to the fiscal disadvantage of
the South and other places (including New York City) with a stake
in free commerce.[40] Midwestern agricultural areas that might otherwise have had an interest in free trade are considered to have been
"bought off" by the disproportionate flow of pensions, funded by
tariff revenues, to veterans and survivors in those areas. In current
scholarship, this argument is most clearly put forward by the political
scientist Richard Bensel.[41]

The historical sociologist Jill Quadagno adopts basically the same
perspective, but also stresses that the 1890 pension liberalization was
not as complete as it might have been, because provisions for a
straight service/old-age pension were not incorporated into the legislation the Congress finally adopted.[42] She attributes what she calls
the "defeat of a national old-age pension proposal" in 1890 to the
growing strength of free-trade proponents within the ranks of northern big business. In my view, the evidence Quadagno offers for such
free-trade business input to the 1890 legislative process is very
skimpy. But it may not matter, because Quadagno makes too much
of the slight concessions to fiscal responsibility built into the 1890
Dependent Pension Act. This law can hardly be called a "defeat" for
old-age coverage, because it soon became, through administrative
rulings and later legislative tinkering, in effect a pension for all
elderly Union veterans who had served ninety days or more.

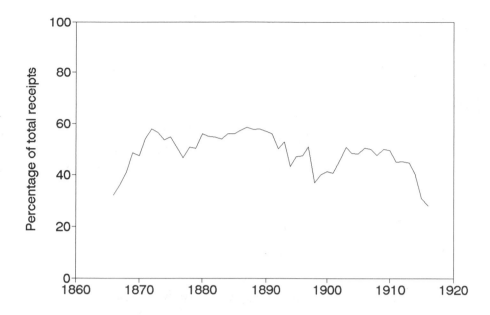

Figure 2   Customs receipts as percentage of total federal receipts, 1866–1916
Source: *Historical Statistics of the United States: Colonial Times to 1970*, Bicentennial ed., pt. 2 (Washington: Bureau of the Census, 1975), p. 1106, series Y 352, Y 353.

What was the relationship between pensions and tariff revenues? Figure 2 shows that customs receipts constituted between 30 percent and 58 percent of federal revenues during the entire period between the Civil War and World War I. Figure 3 shows that there was, indeed, a federal budget "surplus"—that is, an excess of total receipts over current expenditures—from 1866 to 1893. Clearly, the Dependent Pension Act of 1890, designed to make many more veterans eligible for pensions than under previous laws, passed after a decade of spectacular federal surpluses. Curiously, however, the Arrears Act of 1879 passed at a time when there was practically no surplus, that is, when the customs receipts of the day were actually being spent on other items (especially on retiring the debt). Supported by both Republicans and northern Democrats, this critical piece of pension legislation passed without a close connection to spending of surplus revenues, and indeed there were many worries about how to cover

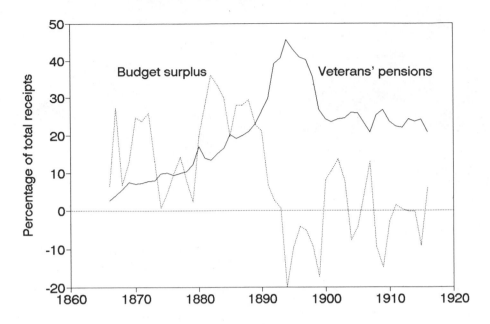

Figure 3   Federal surplus (deficit) and veterans' pensions as per-
centage of total federal receipts, 1866–1916
Source: Historical Statistics of the United States: Colonial Times to 1970, Bicentennial ed., pt. 2
(Washington: Bureau of the Census, 1975), p. 1106, series Y 352; p. 1104, series
Y 337; and William H. Glasson, *Federal Military Pensions in the United States* (New York:
Oxford University Press, 1918), p. 273.

its anticipated cost.[43] One suggestion at that time for paying the
pension bill, a suggestion that surely did *not* appeal to eastern business interests, was to expand the money supply by printing Green-
backs. This notion came from George Lemon, a prominent Washington pension attorney (who would later become a vocal advocate
of linking tariffs and pensions).[44] Apparently Lemon always put
pensions first, which makes sense given that pension attorneys
reaped a fee from every pension application they could drum up,
and Lemon handled tens of thousands of cases.

Arguments pointing to organized veterans or tariff advocacy by
protectionist northeastern industrialists are not so much wrong as
incomplete and underspecified. Such groups were part of the Re-

publican-orchestrated coalition behind the 1890 Dependent Pension Act. But there were other instruments in the band; and the party leaders who set the tune had their own organizational interests above and beyond those of the GAR and business groups. The expansion of Civil War pensions must be understood in relation to the structure of the nineteenth-century U.S. state, and situated in terms of the dynamics of political party competition after the Civil War. Not only did the expansion of Civil War pensions fit the proclivity of the nineteenth-century U.S. polity for distributive policies; the important legal watersheds also reflected the changing competitive strategies of the major political parties; and the forms of new legislation maximized possibilities for using pensions to recruit voters.

After the end of Reconstruction, the Republicans became locked in tight national-level competition with a revived Democratic Party for control of the presidency and the Congress. This was a competition which lasted until after the realignment of 1896, when the Republicans again became nationally dominant. The initial major liberalization of Civil War pensions through the Arrears Act was spurred by the revival of tight party competition. Yet the ensuing expansion of pensioners and pension costs soon worked differentially to the advantage of the Republican Party, which learned the uses of the Pension Bureau in managing the application backlog spurred by the Arrears Act. After the mid-1880s, the national Democrats emphasized tariff reductions and backed off from pension liberalization, while the Republicans became the champions of a politically as well as fiscally complementary set of generous distributive policies, including pensions along with tariffs. The Dependent Pension Act of 1890 was very much a Republican-sponsored measure, an intraparty compromise; and later slight changes in this law also came under Republican auspices.

The Arrears Act and the Competitive Politicization of the Pension Question

The Arrears of Pension Act passed the House on June 19, 1878, went through the Senate on January 16, 1879, and was signed into law by President Rutherford B. Hayes on January 25. Acording to this law (as later amended in the appropriations process), whenever applicants for pensions had been awarded benefits starting some years after the war, their cases should be reopened and payments made back to the date of their discharge from the military or the death of the family breadwinner. What is more, anyone who applied for a new pension (up until July 1880) would, assuming it was eventually granted, automatically receive as part of the first payment all of the "arrears," or previous pension payments, to which he or she would have been entitled from the time of discharge or death. "The average first payment in 1881 to army invalids was $953.62; [and] to army widows, minor children, and dependent relatives, $1,021.51."[45] At a time in U.S. history when the average annual money earnings of nonfarm employees totaled about $400, these were considerable windfalls that could be put to excellent use.[46] As Hayes would later write in defense of signing this legislation: "Look at the good done. In every county of the North are small but comfortable homes built by the soldier out of his arrearage pay."[47]

The Arrears Act originated partly from a genuine desire to rationalize and reform preexisting laws, and partly from a politically well-timed lobbying campaign organized by a few prosperous pension attorneys. For one thing, many Congressmen and officials were perturbed by inequities among veterans traceable simply to the date at which they applied for pensions, and in the current session House members had introduced more than eighteen hundred private bills attempting to address such problems for individuals.[48] New laws often originate in this way, as officials and politicians themselves become dissatisfied with the operation of earlier policies and create revised measures, typically more expensive or interventionist, to correct the situation.

In addition, the leveling off of new applications in the 1870s was a problem for pension attorneys, and some major attorneys saw arrears legislation as an excellent way to stimulate renewed business. Because pension attorneys collected fees limited by statute to $10 apiece for each application they helped assemble and shepherd through the Pension Bureau, they had a strong interest in generating as many applications as possible. "By means of subagents and a very thorough system of advertising they were 'drumming' the country from one end to the other in search of pension claims . . . Claims agents and attorneys were building up an emormous practice. Those most skilled in the system were gradually drifting to the nation's Capital. There they divided their energy between handling claims and lobbying for more favorable pension legislation."[49] In October

1877, George E. Lemon launched the *National Tribune,* a periodical news sheet distributed to Union veterans across the country, in order to agitate for arrears legislation and advertise his own firm's services. Another pension attorney, N. W. Fitzgerald, used the competing news sheet *Citizen Soldier* to the same end. And one Captain R. A. Dimmick set up a lobbying group, the Soldiers' Association, to generate petitions advocating arrears legislation to be sent to Congress and state legislatures.[50]

Pension attorneys did not always get their way, however.[51] Therefore, it was very important that northern elected politicians from both parties were highly susceptible at this juncture to arguments on behalf of the Union soldiers and survivors. From the mid-1870s, with Reconstruction at an end and the Democratic South back in the national electorate, the two major parties became closely competitive both in national elections and in state elections throughout much of the East and Midwest. The Democrats regained control of the House in 1875, and were clearly savoring their renewed prospects for national power. For a time, the Democrats saw the pensioners' cause as a way to prove their nationalist credentials in the North, neutralizing the Republicans' "bloody shirt" tactics.[52] Neither party wanted to appear ungenerous to the widows and disabled soldiers.

The Democratic-controlled House was the first to pass the Arrears bill, with only four nonsouthern Democrats dissenting and no Republicans opposed.[53] While the bill was pending before the Senate, twenty-five senators faced reelection in their state legislatures (which chose senators in those days). Pressure orchestrated by the pension agents was directed to the state legislatures, in order to influence their choices or to encourage incumbent senators to support the Arrears bill. In the end, the Arrears Act passed the Republican-controlled Senate with virtually unanimous support from northern Democrats as well as Republicans. After the passage of the Arrears Act and related appropriations legislation, moreover, Democratic spokesmen competed with Republicans to claim credit. In the words of Illinois Democratic Representative Townsend, "This side of the House deserves commendation for the liberality and zeal with which it has supported legislation in the interest of soldiers engaged in all wars waged in behalf of our government, thereby refuting every accusation against the [D]emocratic party of want of regard for the interest of the soldier."[54]

With the passage of the Arrears legislation, veterans and survivors had new motives to apply for both monthly pensions and the hefty initial lump-sum payments. As a contemporary critic wrote, the "effect of this law was to stir up a multitude of people to apply for pensions who had never thought of the matter before. In one year 141,466 men who had not realized that they were disabled until the Government offered a premium of a thousand dollars or more for the discovery of aches and disabilities, made application."[55] "Before 1879, new claims had been filed at the rate of 1,600 a month; after the new act took effect, new claims rose to over 10,000 a month."[56]

Defeat for an Attempt to Centralize the Application Process

The avalanche of new applications stimulated by the Arrears Act was to be processed by a U.S. Pension Bureau that had few means at its disposal to detect fraudulent claims by pension applicants. Although the Bureau was consistently staffed by "old soldiers" who were favorably disposed toward applicants, few contemporary observers doubted that the details of the application process were relatively honestly managed inside the agency itself. When pension claims arrived by mail in Washington, they were carefully filed and scrutinized for proper execution; then the Adjutant General's Office and the Surgeon General's Office of the War Department were asked to report from their records (which were "beyond change or alteration") all available data on a soldier's military service and wartime medical treatments.[57] Yet the processing of applications was also dependent upon thousands of doctors scattered in communities across the North, along with local witnesses, notaries, and lawyers.[58] From the time of the war, pension applicants were allowed to testify for themselves or find their own witnesses in support of their applications; for example, neighbors might testify to a woman's marriage to a dead soldier, and to her persistent widowed status and proper sexual conduct after his death. To certify the war-related disabilities on which pension awards to veterans depended before 1890, applicants also submitted affidavits obtained from local physicians. These doctors were situated far outside of Washington, perhaps enmeshed in the same social networks as the pension applicants they examined; they were not subject to any effective bureaucratic supervision by the Bureau. As time passed after 1865, it became increasingly difficult for either the physicians or the central Pension Bureau officials to tell whether a wound or disease actually had originated in the war. Besides, without being able to cross-examine witnesses, Pension Bureau officials had to depend upon the honesty of supportive affidavits in the application. There were Special Examiners from the Bureau detailed to look into certain applications, but these were only a minority of instances in which there were either special problems of documentation or glaring reasons to suspect irregularities.[59] The 1879 Arrears Act itself repealed a previous rule that had limited the use of parole evidence (for example, the supportive testimony of kinspeople, neighbors, and former comrades in arms) rather than the records of the War and Navy Department to settle long-pending claims. This "change opened the way for the renewal of many long-standing claims of doubtful character."[60]

More important, during the period when the Arrears Act was passed, Congress refused to enact a major proposal for reforming the administrative system by which pension applications were processed. This was the "Sixty Surgeon Pension Bill," embodying a plan that had been pressed for several years by J. A. Bentley, the Commissioner of Pensions from 1876 to June 1881. In place of the existing system that "permitted claims to be established upon affidavits prepared in secret by the claimants and their friends, and upon the certificate of the neighborhood physician,"[61] Commissioner Bentley proposed the following arrangement:

> The whole country was to be divided into pension districts of such a size . . . that one surgeon devoting his entire time to the duties assigned him could make all required medical examinations in that district. A highly qualified [and generously paid] surgeon was to be appointed for each district, and was to be placed under the direction of the Commissioner of Pensions. Also a competent clerk was to be sent to each pension district, to act in conjunction with the surgeon. The duty of the clerk was to take testimony in each case, review the evidence, and cross-examine the witnesses [in public hearings]. These two officials were to constitute a Commission on the part of the Government, before whom all pension applicants were to appear and submit whatever proof they desired in support of their claim. After obtaining all information relating to each claim, the case and its testimony was to be forwarded to the Pension Office for final settlement.[62]

Commissioner Bentley's remarkable proposal was, in effect, an effort to build up a stronger civil service organization able to conduct judicial-type proceedings, in order to control costs and promote regular standards in the granting of Civil War pensions. The example of France in the nineteenth century suggests that such an organization might have restricted the expansion of pensions. But Congress simply ignored Commissioner Bentley's plan, preferring instead to institute minor modifications in the existing system. During 1881 and 1882, it was stipulated that special pension examiners should hold hearings for those applications dependent upon parole evidence alone; and local boards of examining surgeons were substituted for affidavits from family physicians.[63] During the 1880s, the Pension Bureau in Washington was rehoused in a magnificent new building as it grew into what Commissioner of Pensions Green B. Raum called in 1891 "the largest executive bureau in the world"—with an office force of 2,009 persons, "besides eighteen pension agents, with a clerical force of 419, and 3,795 examining surgeons stationed in various parts of the country."[64] Yet the application process remained rooted in local communities and regions. Applicants for pensions could apply credibly for more benefits than they might strictly deserve, or even for pensions they had not earned at all—as long as they could obtain the collusion of friends and neighbors, who might themselves have an interest in a successful application, and as long as they could secure the help of local doctors and lawyers, whose "natural disposition would be to favor the applicant . . . There is little reason why they should feel called upon to protect the Government treasury."[65] The pension application system remained a classic example of a recurrent pattern in U.S. politics: a central agency linked with constituents and voluntary groups in thousands of local communities across America.

Pensions Become Fuel for Congressional and Party Patronage

The passage of the Arrears Act in 1879, accompanied by the failure in early 1881 of what was known as "Bentley's Sixty Surgeon Pension Bill," transformed Civil War pensions from relatively straightforward compensation for wartime disabilities into fuel for patronage politics. Pension patronage flourished both through Congress and through party controls over the leadership and nonroutine practices of the Pension Bureau. An ideal "distributive" policy, as we have seen, is one in which benefits are given to many particular recipients and politicians have some discretionary control over the timing and targeting of those benefits. Civil War pensions may not seem to fit this profile very well, if one assumes that conditions of eligibility were set by statutory law and potential recipients exercised all the discretion: that once they applied, they would automatically get the benefits if their qualifications fell within the statute. In fact, however, the statutes quickly became so bewilderingly complex that there was much room for interpretation of cases. Interior Department officials and Commissioners of Pensions might apply more or less stringent interpretations of existing statutes; they might even invite whole classes of old cases to be reopened to allow more generous pension awards.[66] In addition, individual cases (or groups of cases) might be speeded up or slowed down in their passage through the Bureau of Pensions. As a result of the many reapplications and new applications stimulated by the Arrears Act, a backlog of several hundred thousand claims piled up for processing, and such massive backlogs continued to hang over over the system into the 1890s. This situation allowed considerable space for the manipulation of the timing of case processing.[67]

If a given applicant did not feel that his or her case had been correctly processed by the Pension Bureau, or if he or she thought that things were moving too slowly or that existing statutes did not quite cover the special merits of the case, a petition to a congressional representative might result. In 1882, Representative Roswell G. Horr of Michigan observed: "I think it is safe to say that each member of this House receives fifty letters each week; many receive more . . . One-quarter of them, perhaps, will be from soldiers asking aid in their pension cases, and each soldier is clear in his own mind that the member can help his case out if he will only make it a special case and give it special attention."[68] Robert M. La Follette estimated in his autobiography that he spent from a quarter to a third of his time in Congress from 1885 to 1891 "examining testimony and untangling . . . records" for the "many old soldiers" in his district. Such help to a veteran from a Congressman could be just as important to the recipient's welfare as help to an unemployed worker from an urban political boss, as La Follette explained: "I recall one interesting case. An old man, by the name of Joseph Wood, living in Madison, very poor, had a claim pending for an injury received at Pittsburgh Landing. His case had been repeatedly rejected because the records of the War Department showed that his regiment had not arrived at Pittsburgh Landing until forty-eight hours after the claimant swore he had been injured." La Follette found that his captain and twenty-five other soldiers agreed with the claimant, and so did the memoirs of General Sherman. But the War Department would not question its records.

> I seemed up against it, when it flashed across my mind that the [War Department] document looked too new to be the original record. Upon inquiry, I found this was true. The old worn records had been stored away years before. Some one was detailed to examine them, and sure enough, there had been a mistake in copying. General Sherman and my old soldier friend were right. Thirty-six hundred dollars back pension brought comfort to that old man and his wife.[69]

With a proliferation of cases such as these, the "volume of correspondence between the Pension Bureau and members of Congress was immense. In 1880 it was reported as amounting to nearly 40,000 written and personal inquiries; in 1888 it had more than doubled (94,000 items); and in 1891 it reached a peak of 154,817 congressional calls for information on the condition of cases, an average of over 500 for each working day."[70]

Usually the Pension Bureau was asked to reconsider or nudged to process cases more expeditiously. Yet when the Bureau and the Secretary of the Interior ultimately ruled against applicants, Congressmen could sponsor "private pension bills" that added individuals to the pension rolls or—more often—increased benefits for existing pensioners. In the aggregate, private pension bills do not seem to have accounted in particular years for more than 0.5 percent to 2 percent of new pensioners or additional pension expenditures.[71] Nevertheless, Congress spent considerable time on them, and their numbers rose dramatically during the 1880s and again after 1900.[72] "In the 49th Congress [1885–1887], 40 percent of the legislation in the House and 55 percent in the Senate consisted of special pension acts. It was customary for Friday evening to be 'pension night' during congressional sessions."[73] "Passage of private pension bills was by general consent. Usually no quorum was present."[74] Eventually, congressional handling of private pension bills became fully routinized: pension committees in each house simply allocated congressmen regular quotas of bills that they could put through without any real scrutiny.[75] When special pension bills were enacted at the highest rates in the early twentieth century, most raised the rates for individuals that congressional representatives found especially meritorious, even though these applicants' situations fell outside of existing statutes. Some special acts, however, actually changed the military records of former soldiers classified as "deserters," in order to make them eligible for pensions.

Pension patronage went beyond congressional interventions in individual cases. During the nineteenth century, when competitive patronage democracy was at its height, party-appointed leaders of the Pension Bureau exercised a certain amount of partisan discretion in the handing of categories of cases. In the words of the historian John Oliver,

> there is evidence that as early as 1880 the influence of the pension system was felt in the political affairs of the nation. According to the testimony of one of the special agents of the Bureau, Mr. Thomas P. Kane, it was quite a common practice for the Pension Office to concentrate its forces on those claims coming from doubtful states, just before the general elections . . . [And a] table submitted by the chief of the Records and Accounts Division shows that during the three months of July, August, and September, 1880, the average number of pensions issued was 1,661; but in October, the month preceding the national election, there were 4,423 original claims allowed.[76]

Appointed in 1881 by Republican President James A. Garfield, Commissioner of Pensions Colonel W. W. Dudley proved to be a key innovator in the political use of the Pension Bureau. Not only did Dudley champion the rapid expansion of the Pension Bureau to facilitate the processing of claims; he also worked with the Grand Army of the Republic to draw up lists of potentially eligible veterans in each state, and he made lists of veterans' addresses available to new applicants so that they could locate witnesses. Commissioner Dudley determined that, as of 1882, over a million living Union veterans and almost 87,000 pensionable relatives had not yet applied for benefits; and he realized that two-fifths of existing pensioners, along with over half of the 300,000 claims then pending at the Bureau, came from the electorally crucial states of Illinois, Indiana, New York, Ohio, and Pennsylvania.[77] Moving from investigation of the political potential of the pension system to practical applications,

Commissioner Dudley directed Pension Bureau officials not to refuse claims until after the 1884 presidential election, and told them speed up the processing of applications from Ohio and Indiana, where the election was sure to be very close. In September 1884, moreover, Dudley went on a paid "leave of absence" from Washington, taking large numbers of pension examiners first into Ohio and then into Indiana. Prospective pensioners were sought out, urged to apply, and told to vote for the Republican ticket to ensure the rapid processing of their claims. Several Democrats later told congressional investigators that they voted Republican in the election out of fear for their pension applications![78]

Commissioner Dudley's efforts may have helped the Republicans to carry Ohio by 15,000 votes, but they failed by about 6,500 votes in Indiana.[79] The Democratic presidential candidate Grover Cleveland was elected, and Dudley had to resign his post. Nevertheless, Colonel Dudley's "performance was not lost on the Republican Party. [Thereafter] the party used its incumbency of the White House as a vehicle for boosting the outputs and generosity of the Pension Bureau . . . If the Republicans were able to create an enduring alliance with the ex-soldiers and build a national political machine, it was largely because they were willing and able to employ the pension bureaucracy in a partisan fashion."[80] There were also reports of Democrats using the Pension Bureau to help old soldiers when they were in office and facing elections.[81] Nevertheless, Heywood Sanders presents rough evidence that the expansion of Pension Bureau budgets and personnel, and higher rates of approval for new pension claims, corresponded to years of Republican control of the executive branch between 1878 and 1899. "For the individual veteran," he concludes, "the choice was obvious . . . Electoral support for Republican candidates promised a better pension, delivered more quickly."[82]

Party Differentiation and Republican Sponsorship of the Dependent Pension Act

Indeed, the Democrats and the Republicans increasingly parted company on the issue of pension generosity after the early 1880s. To be sure, many northern Democrats in Congress continued to vote in favor of private bills and general pension legislation. But from the time of Grover Cleveland's presidency onward, the national Democratic Party and Democratic presidents stressed controls on pension expenditures and the need to attack fraud in the system. Meanwhile, the Republicans waxed ever more eloquent in their advocacy of generosity to the Union veterans. As the 1888 Republican platform put it, "The legislation of Congress should conform to the pledges made by a loyal people and be so enlarged and extended as to provide against the possibility that any man who honorably wore the Federal uniform shall be the inmate of an almshouse, or dependent upon private charity. In the presence of an overflowing treasury, it would be a public scandal to do less for those whose valorous service preserved the government."[83]

"In the presence of an overflowing treasury . . ." This phrase signals an important reason for major party differentiation on the question of further pension liberalization. After the 1870s, the rapid growth of the industrializing U.S. economy brought plentiful revenues into the federal Treasury. As we saw in Figures 2 and 3, tariff revenues accounted for between 30 percent and 58 percent of all federal revenues between the Civil War and World War I, and the decade of the 1880s was a time of huge "surpluses" in the federal budget. Even with efforts made to "retire the outstanding national debt as quickly as possible," nevertheless, in the words of Morton Keller, "the most pressing fiscal problem of the 1880s was the large revenue surplus generated by rising tariff receipts."[84] This rising surplus easily covered the unanticipated costs of the Arrears Act and left high-tariff advocates, mostly Republicans, looking for new ways to spend money, while advocates of lower taxes and tariffs could argue that the revenues were no longer needed.

The Democrats under the leadership of Grover Cleveland championed the cause of reducing "excess taxation" and backed off from competing with the Republicans on generous pensions in order to save money. Protective tariffs, the Democrats argued, constituted hidden taxes on consumers and on most southern and western producers. According to the Democrats, protection should be reduced and, in general, only such moderate customs duties retained as might be necessary to raise revenue for a frugal federal government.[85] To the consternation of many Democratic "regulars," President Cleveland also took up the cause of civil service reform as a way to reduce costly patronage "corruption" and make federal administration more "efficient." For the Republicans of this era, the federal government functioned as a prime source of patronage resources. Of course, the Democrats also had patronage needs, but their most important party machines were centered in states and in major urban centers. In any event, Cleveland was a reformer by personal conviction, and he received support from many formerly Republican Mugwumps (such as President Eliot of Harvard).[86]

Meanwhile, the Republicans understood themselves to be the party of those who had saved the nation and could best represent its postwar interest in a strong, growing economy.[87] The party benefited by the 1880s from an ideally complementary set of distributive policies, using some measures, such as protective tariffs and the expansion of federal services, to generate the money and jobs that could be distributed through other policies, including the pension system. By finding popular new uses for the surpluses piling up in the 1880s, the Republicans hoped to maintain the tariffs that helped them build coalitions across industries and localities. If a way could be found to spread Civil War pensions to still more people, that would be ideal. After the Arrears Act, many veterans and survivors had applied for pensions but could not prove that disabilities or deaths were directly connected to Civil War military service.[88] Additional pensions would flow overwhelmingly to the northeastern and midwestern states where the Republicans were strong (and wanted to stay strong), including states where they found themselves in close competition with the Democrats.[89] Furthermore, pensions apparently would go disproportionately to townspeople and farmers, the sectors of the Republican coalition that did not benefit as directly from tariffs as many workers and businessmen did (or believed they did).[90]

Urged on by the Grand Army of the Republic and facing an electorate in which more than 10 percent of the potential voters were Union veterans, the Republicans moved toward reinforcing protective tariffs and fundamentally liberalizing the original Civil War pension law.[91] George Lemon's *National Tribune* and other Grand Army propagandists warned veterans across the North to beware of efforts at tariff reduction until all their needs were met. Initially elements within the Grand Army, and then in 1888 the national GAR itself, endorsed calls for a new universal "service pension" that would simply make every Union veteran and all survivors eligible for monthly payments, regardless of disabilities or capacity for manual employment. Meanwhile, Democratic President Cleveland helped to galvanize the "old soldier vote" for the Republicans, because he became known as a determined enemy of pension liberality. Not only did Cleveland veto 228 bills (while allowing 1,871 to become law), he also rejected the "Dependent Pension Bill of 1887," a forerunner of the measure that would pass in 1890.[92] Cleveland had earlier appeared to encourage such legislation, but he backed off when he saw what the costs might be and also because he claimed that the 1887 bill was vaguely worded.

For the 1888 election, the Republicans mobilized the Grand Army of the Republic, whose membership stood at 372,960 in 1888.[93] They made strong promises about liberalized pensions and protective tariffs.[94] And they nominated a "soldier president," General Benjamin Harrison, who ran a campaign that linked tariffs to appeals to the veterans, as illustrated by a political song of the day:[95]

> Let Grover talk against the tariff tariff tariff
> And pensions too
> We'll give the workingman his due
> And pension the boys who wore the blue.

This combination worked for the Republican party in 1888. In an across-the-board victory widely attributed to the "old soldiers'" vote, the Republicans took both houses of Congress; and they won the presidency by detaching Indiana and New York from the states that had gone for Cleveland in 1884. In Indiana, the Republican victory was by the extremely narrow margin of 2,300 votes, and Harrison was surely helped by the presence of many thousands of present and potential pensioners along with a successful Republican gubernatorial candidate who was the leader of a major pension lobbying group. In New York, the Republicans won by some 13,000 votes in a state where "there were 45,000 federal pensioners in 1888 and the movement of service-pensions for all the Civil War soldiers was particularly strong."[96] Without controlled statistical studies, we cannot really tell whether pension politics made the differences in these states in 1890, but we do have the necessary kind of evidence for Republican fortunes across 88 Ohio counties in elections from 1892 to 1895. Heywood Sanders found that, even when the veteran population was controlled for, the prior distribution of pensions up to 1890 significantly affected both turnouts and election results in favor of the Republicans.[97]

After the 1890 national election, Republican President Harrison put "Corporal" James Tanner, a legless Union veteran and a member of the GAR Pension Committee, in charge of the Pension Bureau,[98] and he resubmitted liberalized pension legislation to the Congress. During the election, Tanner had, by his own account, "plastered Indiana with promises" of more generous pensions under the Republicans. "God help the surplus revenue!" the new commissioner declared, as he set about handing out new and readjusted pensions with gusto. Indeed, Tanner was so heedless of regular procedures that he soon had to be replaced by a slightly more cautious close friend of the soldiers, Green B. Raum, himself a GAR official and Republican politician from Illinois.[99] Meanwhile, as the Pension Bureau forged ahead with granting pensions under loose interpretations of existing laws, the Republicans' "Billion Dollar Congress" enacted monetary reforms that helped knit together western and eastern Republicans, along with the the Dependent Pension Act, and the McKinley Tariff of 1890, which embodied the highest rates up to that point in U.S. history.

The Dependent Pension Act was a "service-disability" measure, which relaxed the previous requirement that veterans must show disabilities originating in injuries actually incurred during the Civil War. Henceforth, monthly pensions could, in the words of the Act, be obtained by "all persons who served ninety days or more in the military or naval service of the United States during the late war of the Rebellion and who have been honorably discharged therefrom, and who are now or who may hereafter be suffering from a mental or physical disability of a permanent character, not the result of their own vicious habits, which incapacitates them from the performance of manual labor."[100] With this watershed legislation, the door was opened for many new successful applicants—exactly what the Republican party wanted. Even the Grand Army's Pension Committee was pleased, declaring: "While not just what we asked, [the Dependent Pension Act] . . . is the most liberal pension measure ever passed by any legislative body in the world, and will place upon the rolls all of the survivors of the war whose conditions of health are not practically perfect."[101] This was prophetic.

Both the numbers of pensioners and overall expenditures on Civil War pensions leapt upward again after 1890 (see Figure 1). By 1893, there were 966,012 pensioners and the federal government was spending an astounding 41.5 percent of its income on benefits for them. This was the peak of expenditures and, of course, natural attrition was pruning the ranks of actual and potential beneficiaries. But new veteran pensioners also continued to apply throughout the 1890s. As Table 2 documents, the percentage of Civil War veterans receiving benefits grew from 39 percent in 1891 to 74 percent in 1900. By 1915, 93 percent of Civil War veterans who were still living were signed up for federal benefits.

From the 1890s into the 1910s, the old-line Republicans continued to reap political rewards from the complementary interlock of high tariffs and generous pension expenditures. Yet the sudden expansion of pensions right after 1890, accompanied as it was by all-too-evident excesses and corruption, helped Grover Cleveland to be reelected president in 1892. The revenue situation also became tighter in the 1890s. Thereafter, especially once the national Democratic Party went into decline, pension issues became less salient in national party competition.[102]

Over time, Civil War pensions became more and more obviously old-age and survivors' benefits for the veterans. Administrative rulings making age alone a "disability for manual labor" commenced soon after the Dependent Pension Act, and were later confirmed by a 1906 law that declared simply "the age of sixty-two years and over shall be considered a permanent specific disability within the meaning of the pension laws."[103] Further innovations in general pension legislation—the most important of which occurred in 1907, 1908, and 1912—conferred general benefit increases on age-and-length-of-service categories of veteran pensioners, and addressed the needs of widows and other dependent survivors. Even when the Republicans were completely in control, however, a degree of moderation prevailed; not every new idea for more generous pensions was put into effect. In a situation in which huge revenue "surpluses" were no longer present (see Figure 3), we may surmise that the Republicans felt the intense criticism directed against pension profligacy, not only by Democrats but also by Mugwumps and progressive reformers. Besides, since pension eligiblity had already been extended to virtually all Union veterans, further legal changes could not reach out to new categories of voters.

Looking back over the entire expansion of the Civil War pension system, it seems apparent that the dynamics of party-run patronage democracy spurred that expansion. We saw that close competition between the Republicans and the Democrats in the late 1870s helped to bring about the passage of the Arrears Act, whose effects, in turn, fueled the emergence of the Republican "old soldiers'" machine. The major parties continued to be very closely competitive until the mid-1990s, and in this context it was especially advantageous for the Republicans to combine tariff protection with the increased distribution of pension benefits under the Dependent Pension Act.

To be sure, in any polity—and certainly in any democracy—there would have been pressures to to provide for elderly and impoverished veterans toward the end of their lives. Such pressures in the 1830s and 1840s, for example, had led to modest and very belated benefits (more than fifty years after the war!) for nonofficer Revolutionary War veterans and their survivors. For Civil War veterans, however, this expectable movement toward universal-service coverage was speeded up and made much more generous. A military-disability system originally tailored to mobilize unprecedented masses of soldiers eventually became enmeshed in the intense competition of the distributively inclined parties that dominated both legislation and administration in the United States from the mid-1870s to the mid-1890s. Thus Civil War pensions became one of a handful of major distributive policies that helped to fuel and sustain late-nineteenth-century U.S. patronage democracy—and, especially, to further Republican fortunes within it.

A Precocious American Welfare State?
Civil War Benefits in Comparative Perspective

From the 1880s through the early twentieth century, while the United States was elaborating its Civil War pension system, many European nations (as well as Australia and New Zealand) were launching pension and social insurance programs that would later be called the foundation stones of "the modern welfare state." How did the benefits and the coverage of U.S. Civil War pensions compare to those offered by early European social programs? Did the United States really have, however temporarily, its own sort of social welfare state, and, if so, were the same or different groups of Americans benefiting compared to those who would have been reached by early European-style efforts? Evidence on these matters is spotty, but some tentative conclusions can be drawn.

European Beneficiaries and U.S. Pensioners

In this early period, European social insurance was really "working-men's insurance"—a means by which the state enforced and supplemented contributions by entire categories of employees and employers in order to partially protect wage-workers (and later some lower-level salaried people) against the losses of income associated with illness, disability, and old age.[104] The German health, disability, and old-age insurance measures of the 1880s fit this model, as did the 1911 British programs for health and unemployment insurance.[105] Initially, as in Britain, the least skilled or most economically vulnerable workers might not be targeted in the contributory insurance schemes, but the coverage of social insurance did soon tend to spread downward as well as upward in the hierarchies of employed workers. Right from the start in 1889, contribution toward German old-age and disability insurance was "complusory for all wage earners and employees whose annual income did not exceed 2000 M[arks]."[106] Yet benefits were only gradually extended. By 1910, two decades after the start of the old-age and disability system, actual pensions or prospective elibility for them reached 52 percent of the economically active German population and 22 percent of the total population.[107] Most of the 1,122,000 German pensions in force at that point were for disability rather than old age; about 25 percent of Germans over age 60 were pensioned in 1910.[108]

A somewhat different pattern characterized the noncontributory old-age pensions instituted by Denmark in 1891 and by Britain in 1908.[109] These pensions targeted the "respectable" elderly poor, regardless of employment status, and were regarded as ways to contain rising costs of local poor relief and keep former working people of good character from having to enter the dreaded poorhouses in their old age. Instead, needy elderly people would receive modest pensions directly from the national state, as in Britain, or administered by local authorities and reimbursed by the national state, as in Denmark.[110] By the early 1910s, about 25 percent of Danes over 60 and about 35 percent of those over 70 were receiving old-age benefits.[111] About half of Britons over the age of 70 were receiving pensions by 1910, and about two-thirds were getting them by 1914.[112]

In the early years, therefore, European contributory old-age insurance and noncontributory pensions were explicitly meant for

lower-income elderly people or for certain categories of retired employed workers. Against this European background, various features
of U.S. Civil War pensions can be discussed.[113] By the turn of the
twentieth century, Civil War pensions served for many Americans
as an analogue to noncontributory old-age pensions, or to disability
and old-age insurance without the contributions. In 1910 the vast
majority of Civil War veterans were aged 65 or over, and some 90
percent were signed up as pensioners.[114] I estimate that about 18
percent of all U.S. residents aged 65 and over were pensioners in
1910, including 28.5 percent of all elderly men, along with approximately 8 percent of all women 65 and over who were included on
the survivors' pension roll (a roll that also included orphans and
other dependents, as well as younger widows).[115] As Appendix 1 and
Figure 4 indicate, in many states of the North the proportions of
pensioners in 1910 could climb as high as about one-fifth of all
elderly people (and of course higher proportions of the elderly men).
These rates of population coverage for U.S. Civil War pensions fall
well short of the coverage of British old-age pensions, but (particularly the figures for the U.S. North) are in the same range as the
coverage of the German and Danish old-age programs.

For those Americans included in the Civil War system, the terms
of coverage were quite generous compared to European social programs. This was especially true when it came to eligibility for benefits.
Civil War pensioners could automatically claim disability for manual
labor due to old age by age 62, and in practice many started receiving
pensions in their fifties or earlier. Meanwhile, except for the Danes,
who became eligible for old-age benefits at age 60, Europeans had
to wait until age 70 for pensions, although German workers who
could prove disabilities were eligible for pensions at earlier ages, and
large numbers applied for disability payments in their sixties or even
earlier.[116] Only in 1916 did the German state begin to promise eventual old-age benefits to all contributors who reached the age of 65.[117]
Given that skilled and unskilled manual laborers in the nineteenth
century often wore themselves out well before age 65 or 70, the
American veterans had a distinct advantage—above all in relation to
Britons—in being able to draw benefits earlier, especially since the
benefits for those Americans who gained eligiblity before age 62
were not necessarily any lower. Finally, German old-age and disability
insurance failed to cover surviving dependents until 1912, when

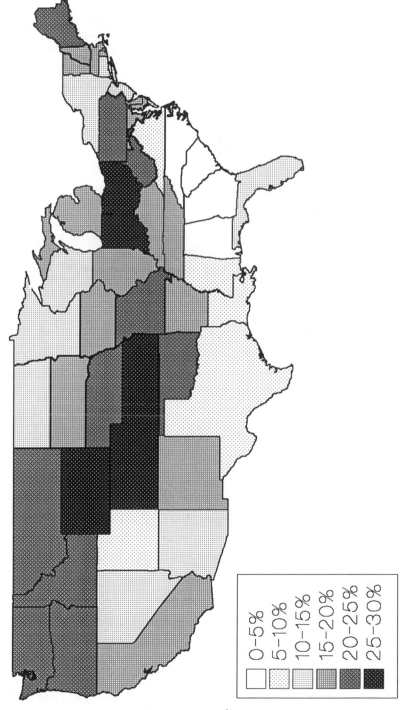

Figure 4   Civil War pensioners as percentage of population aged 65 and older, 1910

0-5%
5-10%
10-15%
15-20%
20-25%
25-30%

Table 3.   Average pensions in U.S. dollars and as a proportion of average annual earnings in the United States (1910), Germany (1912), and Great Britain (1910)

Country and year	Amount of average pension	Average pension as % of average annual earnings
United States, 1910		
all pensioners	$172	30%
widows—1908 law	$144	25%
Germany, 1910		
old-age pension	$39	17%
invalidity pension	$42	18%
Germany, 1912		
widows' pension	$18	7%
Britain, 1910*		
overall	$65	22%

* Pension figure for Great Britain is the maximum rather than the average pension. Use of this figure is warranted by the fact that fully 94.6% of all pensioners during this period received the maximum amount (Ritter, *Social Welfare in Germany and Britain*, p. 155).

Sources:

Germany: Gerhard Ritter, *Social Welfare in Germany and Britain: Origins and Development.* (New York: Berg, 1986), p. 191; Wisconsin Industrial Commission, *Report on Old Age Relief* (Madison: Industrial Commission of Wisconsin, 1915), pp. 56–59; *Sozialgeschichtliches Arbeitsbuch*, II (Munich: Verlag C. H. Beck, 1978), p. 107; H. Phelps Brown and Sheila Hopkins, *A Perspective on Wages and Prices* (New York: Methuen, 1981), pp. 194–195.

Great Britain: Ritter, *Social Welfare in Germany and Britain*, p. 155; Brown and Hopkins, *A Perspective on Wages and Prices*, pp. 194–195.

United States: U.S. Bureau of the Census, *Historical Statistics of the United States* (Washington: Government Printing Office, 1960), pp. 91–92; Brown and Hopkins, *A Perspective on Wages and Prices*, pp. 194–195; U.S. Bureau of Pensions, *Report, 1910.* (Washington: Government Printing Office), p. 147.

widows became eligible for 47 percent of the average disablement pension.[118] In sharp contrast, dependents of U.S. Civil War casualties (or of veterans who died later) could receive payments that became increasingly generous over time, averaging a remarkable 80 percent of the amounts given to invalid pensioners in 1910.[119]

As for the levels of benefits, Table 3 gives some benchmarks for the United States, Britain, and Germany. British old-age pensions averaged about 22 percent of a typical employee's annual income in

1910, and German old-age benefits were only about 18 percent of an average employed person's annual salary. Meanwhile, the average U.S. invalid pension in 1910 was $172 a year, or about 30 percent of the average annual income for all employed Americans. What is more, we should remember that many individual American pensioners had achieved eligibility for much higher benefits—ranging up to some $1,200 a year for a few privileged men in 1910.[120] Unusually high benefits often went to officers and their dependents, and to former soldiers with severe disabilities or elaborate combinations of specific disabilities that added up to high overall rates. In addition, many lucky applicants in the American system got large windfall payments through "arrears" legislation. And quite a number of unusually generous ongoing pensions were arranged through "special" pension acts tailored to individual cases.[121]

If, therefore, Civil War pensions were in certain respects—and for some Americans—as good as or better than European-style social programs, nevertheless they were not a true analogue to "workingmen's insurance." Nor were they full substitutes for need-based old-age coverage. Neither employment status nor income levels were criteria of inclusion and exclusion in the U.S. veterans' pension system, and many workers and poor people were left out altogether. As Isaac Rubinow put it in 1913, "a very large majority of the wage-working class get very little of the war pension, the bulk of which must reach the middle-class American."[122] Instead of working-class status or low income, factors such as territorial residence, timing of arrival in the country, ethnicity, and political connections—along with the official criterion of honorable Union military service for at least ninety days between 1861 and 1865—differentiated those Americans who benefited from those who got nothing out of the system of aid to Civil War veterans.

Who Benefited in the United States?

The most obvious correlate of inclusion in the Civil War pension system was long-time residence in the northern parts of the United States. In 1910, approximately 35 percent of northern men aged 65 and over were on the pension rolls, whereas less than 10 percent of men residing in the South were federal pensioners (some of these were ex-slave veterans, and many others were white Union veterans who had migrated from the North).[123] Obviously, native-born American men from the North, along with those who had arrived in the North as immigrants before the Civil War, were the most likely to have served in the Union armies. Heywood Sanders has done some empirical work on the aggregate characteristics of pensioners in Ohio in 1890.[124] He concludes that they were disproportionately native-born, living in Republican-oriented areas of relative population stability, non-Catholic, and residents of farms rather than big cities. Pensioners also tended to live in counties with relatively less personal wealth per capita. Of course, such statistical findings do not mean that all individual pensioners had these characteristics. Immigrants from Germany, Ireland, and the Austro-Hungarian dominions, including many Catholics, were certainly to be found among Union soldiers and thus also among subsequent pensioners.[125] Moreover, some of these, as well as many native-born veterans, surely lived and worked in smaller and larger cities after the Civil War; and many pensioners must have earned relatively high incomes compared to post–Civil War immigrants.

Figure 5, borrowed from Richard Bensel, uses 1887 county breakdowns of pensioners (which were only made for the years 1886 to 1890) to show the gross disparities in pension densities among areas of the country. Figure 4 gave state-level proportions of pensioners in 1910. In different ways, Figures 4 and 5 reveal how privileged the northern states were, especially the northeastern and lower midwestern states, along with those western states to which northerners migrated after the Civil War. With its added detail, Figure 5 also reveals the lesser concentration of pensioners in major urban-industrial centers like New York, Cleveland, Detroit, and Chicago. Such areas were important destinations of postwar waves of south-central European immigration, and thus many of their industrial workers were not eligible for Civil War pensions. In addition, some cities such as New York had been centers of draft resistance by some of the Irish during the Civil War.[126]

Post–Civil War immigrants who ended up in urban and industrial centers were disproportionately likely to be unskilled and poorer workers around the turn of the century, while the native-born or earlier-immigrant workers (who were more often eligible for Civil War pensions) were more likely to be skilled workers or middle-class white-collar or professional people.[127] Among the middle strata, per-

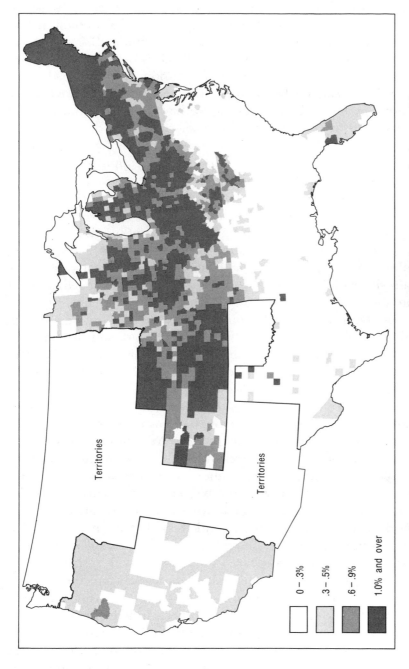

Figure 5 Persons receiving military pensions as percentage of county populations, 1887

Source: Richard Bensel, *Sectionalism and American Political Development* (Madison: University of Wisconsin Press, 1984), p. 68.

0 – .3%

.3 – .5%

.6 – .9%

1.0% and over

Territories

Territories

haps the most privileged occupational group with respect to pensions was government workers. "Veterans' preference" prevailed in federal and many state and local civil services, and public employees could also draw pensions. Other middle-class occupational groups could do the same, since to draw a pension one only had to be "disabled" for *manual* labor, and a pensioner could continue to work at a "nonmanual" job. In any event, we have a strong empirical hint that many old or retired federal workers may have done especially well in the Civil War system: In Appendix 1, notice that among those 65 and older in Washington, DC, in 1910, a whopping 37.6 percent were collecting Civil War pensions!

Beyond the privileged core group of native-born and earlier-immigrant northerners, some 186,017 blacks served in the Union armies, including 7,122 who served as lower-level officers in colored units. Blacks made up about 9 to 10 percent of the Union forces, and almost three-quarters of the blacks who served came from the former slaveholding states, whose freedmen became eligible for Union service late in the war.[128] Although there is no systematic evidence about how black Union veterans fared in the pension application process compared to whites, hints from the historical record suggest that free blacks with stable residential histories in the North probably did as well as their white socioeconomic counterparts, while black veterans and survivors from the ranks of freed slaves may often have lacked the documents they needed to establish claims for pensions.[129] Remarkably unlike most U.S. institutions of its day, the Pension Bureau was not formally racist.[130] Yet both its universalistic procedures and its informal presumptions could create difficulties for former slaves, illiterates, and others with disadvantaged personal histories.[131] Because they had been barred from serving as superior officers, blacks were also ineligible for the more lucrative pensions received by white former officers and their dependents. Despite all of these considerations, we should keep in mind that black Union veterans and their survivors fared much better with respect to pensions than white former-Confederate southerners and the vast majority of black southerners who were not military veterans. These white and black southerners were entirely excluded from the federal pension system, even though they tended to be poorer than than socially comparable northerners—and even though residents of the South helped to pay for the Union pensions through customs duties and higher prices for industrial goods.[132]

State-Level Provision for Confederate and Union Veterans

It would be inaccurate to imply that Confederate army veterans were left entirely without public provision. During the Civil War and during and after Reconstruction, the defeated southern states had no veterans' pensions, although asylums for disabled Confederate veterans and for widows and dependent daughters were established in all the southern states from the end of the war through the 1880s.[133] As the Arrears and Dependent Pension Acts made Union pensions very generous for northerners, the Democratic-controlled southern states felt it necessary to do more for Confederate veterans. During the late 1880s and 1890s, all eleven former Confederate states instituted state-level pensions.[134] These states were poor and had to double-tax their citizens to help the Confederate veterans, so pensions were given only for service-connected disabilities and to truly indigent veterans or widows—much as Revolutionary War pensions had been given in the pre–Civil War United States. There was never any true southern analogue to the Dependent Pension Act of 1890.

Given restrictions on eligibility for Confederate pensions, it is not surprising that less than 20 percent of the former Confederate soldiers still alive in 1905 were receiving benefits, at a time when over 80 percent of the still-living Union veterans were pensioned.[135] Still, a remarkable 58 percent of southern white men between the ages of 15 and 44 in 1860 (as compared to about a third of northerners then in the same age group) did military service during the Civil War.[136] By 1910, therefore, the percentages of people aged 65 and older who were Confederate pensioners (including widows as well as invalids) were sufficiently large, when added to the percentages receiving Union pensions in each southern state, to bring those states into the same range of pension coverage as many northern states.[137] However belated, the response of the southern states to the precedent of Union Civil War pensions arguably brought their region into some degree of parity with the nation as a whole.

This conclusion is too cheery, however. Not only were Confederate pensions restricted to disabled and needy former soldiers and needy dependents; they were also much less generous financially than federal pensions. Georgia was the southern state with by far the most generous pension system, and in a 1907 article William Glasson used 1906 data to dramatize the difference between Georgia's pension rates and those of the federal system.[138] Overall, Georgia gave $60.00 a year to "indigent Confederate soldiers who served at least six months during the Civil War." Meanwhile, Union veterans who had served only ninety days were getting at least $114.33 in 1906.[139] And the different annual rates for ex-soldiers with specific severe disabilities were still more striking:

	Georgia	Federal
For total loss of sight	$150	$1,200
For loss of sight of one eye	30	144
For total loss of hearing	30	480
For loss of a hand	100	360
For loss of both hands or feet	150	1,200
For total disability in one arm	50	432
For incapacity to perform manual labor	50	360
For loss of a thumb	5	96
For loss of a little finger or toe	5	24
For the loss of four fingers	20	192

Even with lower standards of living in the South taken into account, the Confederate pensions were truly penurious. Considering that the Confederate pensions went primarily to southern white men who were in general almost certainly needier than the northern men who received pensions, it is especially significant that the former Confederate states provided much lower benefits than federal pensions.

Nor were federal pensions the only kind of public help that disabled, needy, and—eventually—elderly Union veterans might expect. Federal and state-level soldiers' homes were also available to those who found themselves in the most difficult circumstances and might otherwise have ended up in local poorhouses. Right after the Civil War, the federal government established the National Home for Disabled Volunteer Soldiers in Washington, DC. Four regional branch homes were added by 1871, and in due course there were a total of nine branches in the system of national homes.[140] Originally, only disabled veterans were eligible for care in these homes, and some disabled men also received "outdoor" relief payments channeled through these institutions. For some years after the war, the homes functioned primarily as places for severely disabled, young,

unmarried, and disproportionately foreign-born veterans to stay until their premature deaths, or until they learned to earn their livings
from their own labor plus their pensions, and thus left the homes.[141]
Later, the national homes evolved into old-age asylums, and in 1884
a new law specified that the branches of the National Home could
take in elderly veterans without requiring them to have disabilities
linked to wartime injuries.[142] As they became old-age homes, the
national homes served a higher proportion of native-born veterans,
who became about 60 percent of all clients by the turn of the century.[143] These were men in their late fifties or early sixties in 1900,
who were without living spouses or other relatives on whom to
depend in daily life, and who were typically skilled workers. There
were smaller proportions of former unskilled workers and farmers,
but very few from middle-class occupations.

During the 1880s and 1890s, movements spearheaded by the
Grand Army of the Republic also resulted in the establishment of
de facto old-age homes for soldiers in some 28 states.[144] Congress
decided in 1888 that the federal government should pay these state
homes subsidies (starting at $100 a year) for each Union veteran
they housed.[145] By 1910, some 31,830 Union veterans, or about 5
percent of those still living, were being cared for in these national
and state homes.[146] And these men normally continued to draw their
regular Civil War pensions at the same time.[147] Confederate state
homes, meanwhile, housed about 2,000 men, less than one percent
of their veterans.[148]

While some especially needy Union veterans enjoyed the possibility
of combining institutional succor with their federal pensions, other
veterans and dependents in the North benefited from adding state
or local financial aid to their federal pensions. By 1910 all but six
states provided for relief of needy Civil War veterans.[149] We know
fairly precise facts about state and local aid for the state of Massachusetts, owing to an excellent statistical study on sources of support
for "Aged and Dependent Persons" in 1915 completed by the Massachusetts Bureau of Statistics. As Table 4 shows, impoverished elderly Massachusetts veterans and soldiers' dependents had state or
local aid available to them in addition to federal pensions, and they
fared much better than the Massachusetts elderly on poor relief. On
the average, the elderly Civil War veteran or his widow got about
$125.00 a year from the state or locality—not counting the average

Table 4.   Public provision for Massachusetts elderly in 1915

Type of aid	Recipients (65 and over)	Expenditures
Poor relief (almshouses and "outdoor" relief)	7,856	$722,000
State pauper institutions	995	$79,000
Total relieved under poor laws	8,851	$801,000
State military aid	9,677	$620,000
Local soldiers' relief	4,502	$346,000
Total aided outside poor laws by Massachusetts	14,179	$1,767,000
U.S. military pensions in Massachusetts	29,150	$6,452,000
Total aid to veterans and dependents	29,150+	$8,219,000

Note: Aid to veterans in Massachusetts (state military aid and local soldiers' relief) was given to many individuals who were also receiving federal pensions, but the degree of overlap between state and federal recipients was not calculated in the Bureau's report. I have conservatively assumed that no additional persons were aided by the state. Even on this assumption, the total number receiving all forms of veterans' aid far exceeded those helped under the poor laws. Because I do not know exactly how many people were receiving all forms of veterans' aid, I have not tried to estimate average per capita benefits. Yet it is clear that each form of veterans' aid was more generous to recipients than poor relief. In the United States as a whole in 1915, 92 percent of military pensioners were Civil War veterans or survivors.

Sources: Commonwealth of Massachusetts, Bureau of Statistics, *Report of a Special Inquiry Relative to Aged and Dependent Persons in Massachusetts, 1915* (Boston: R. F. Forster, 1916), pp. 16–34; and *Report of the Commissioners of Pensions to the Secretary of the Interior for the Fiscal Year Ended June 30, 1915* (Washington: Government Printing Office, 1915), p. 16.

of about $190 that many were also getting from federal pensions— while the Massachusetts pauper got an average of $90 a year from the state or locality.

Socially, there were predictable differences between these two categories within the approximately 24 percent of all Massachusetts old people who received public help of any kind (poor relief, veterans' aid, and/or federal pensions) in 1915.[150] Like Union veterans in general—and like the aged men who predominated by the turn of the century in the state and national veterans' homes—the Massachusetts old soldiers and military dependents who received state or local aid must have come disproportionately from the 60.6 percent of the total Massachusetts elderly population in 1915 that was native-born.[151] In contrast, the state's elderly paupers were over 60 percent foreign born, even though the foreign born constituted only 39.4 percent of all the Massachusetts elderly in 1915.[152] Mostly these were elderly men and women without families to help them. They did not qualify for either federal or state aid to veterans, and thus had no choice but to fall back on the poorhouse or outdoor relief.

Individual Initiative, Social Networks, and Political Location

So far I have written as if only legitimate claimants ended up on the federal pension rolls; but there certainly were some fraudulent Union "veterans" and "survivors" receiving payments. By the nature of the case, it is hard to estimate their numbers and social characteristics. Over the years, supporters as well as critics recurrently declared that a quarter or more of already *approved* pension claims were, in fact, fraudulent.[153] Many of these may have been polemically motivated overestimates; in any event they included overly generous pensions as well as those that should not have been paid at all. Investigators from the Pension Bureau occasionally reexamined already-approved cases, seeking to trim overgenerous awards and weed fraudulent claimants from the rolls. According to John Oliver, for example, in "1874, the special agents of the Bureau made an investigation of 1,263 claims, and they discovered that in those cases in which pensions had already been granted, nearly 40 percent—411 cases—proved to be without merit . . . Between 1876 and 1879, there were 5,131 claims investigated, and of this number 1,425 [28 percent] were dropped as being fraudulent."[154] This was a decade when Commissioners of Pensions seem to have been relatively vigilant about weeding out fraud, but there is no way to tell how representative were the cases chosen for reexamination. In any event, the 1,836 cases dropped for fraud in 1874 and between 1876 and 1879 constituted just a little over one-half of one percent of the

314,991 pension claims that had been approved by the Pension Bureau between 1861 and 1876.[155]

Another fraud investigation was conducted in 1893, when a Commissioner appointed by pension system critic President Grover Cleveland proudly reported that

> [w]holesale frauds . . . at Norfolk, Va., in New Mexico, and Iowa . . . were brought to light by intelligent special examiners . . . [H]undreds of fraudulent pension claims had been allowed by the Board on testimony manufactured and forged by the claim agents [that is, attorneys]; and other hundreds of like claims, from the same claim agents, were pending in the Bureau . . . In the Iowa case the claim agent had secured control of several local medical boards . . . by having the claimant, a brief time before [official] examination, come to a member of the board for prescription and treatment, paying his fee therefor. After repeating this so often that the surgeon could not fail to understand that he was really getting extra pay from the claimants, the claim agent was able to procure from him copies of the surgeon's reports to this Bureau and notably high ratings for his clients . . . The result . . . was the allowance of pensions, at notably high rates, to nearly all his clients in the vicinity, bringing into that community a steady influx of money in considerable amount, going into all channels of business. So corrupting was this influence that a strong disposition was manifested to mob the special examiner when . . . [local people learned that his investigation might] unsettle many pensions obtained by fraud and improper practices.[156]

Fascinating as this account is for what it reveals about the possibilities for locally rooted corruption in the pension system, it cannot be used to tell what proportion of all the 966,012 pensions in existence in 1893 were fraudulent. We have no way of knowing whether conditions in Norfolk, New Mexico, and Iowa were in any way typical. It seems doubtful that they were. In most communities, lawyers and surgeons were probably honorable, if only because normal social relationships among ex-soldiers made it difficult for individuals to make false claims about their military service. And even if we suppose (which is highly unlikely) that the "hundreds" of fraudulent cases revealed by the 1893 investigations led to as many as 900 dropped cases, that would still be fewer than one-tenth of one percent of all the pensions on the rolls in that year.[157]

Obviously, the results of intermittent fraud investigations by the Bureau of Pensions depended on the sets of cases chosen for reexamination, the resources and zealousness of the examiners, and the political motivations of the Pension Bureau officials in power at particular historical junctures. After poring over *Annual Reports* of Commissioners of Pensions to find any possible systematic statistics, I have reluctantly concluded that nothing exact can be said about the proportions of illegitimate pensioners or expenditures. We can only speculate that some (undetermined) thousands, or conceivably tens of thousands, of the nearly one million pensioners in 1910 were bogus. Perhaps aided by dishonest pension attorneys, these men and women had exploited the loose and locally rooted application system to obtain fraudulent pensions or—in most cases, I suspect—overly generous benefits.

Whatever their precise numbers, were such men and women socially different from fully legitimate claimants? Critics of "corruption" in the pension system often singled out "cowardly" veterans, blacks, and widows for special ridicule as cheaters.[158] Indeed, applications for widows' pensions seem to have generated the greatest concern among Pension Bureau special examiners and reformist critics alike, especially as the terms of elibility were broadened and the average age of widow beneficiaries went down. As one critic colorfully explained in 1893:

> Until lately widows were mainly those who before the war had been the wives of the soldiers in whose name they made claim, and had resided ever since in the communities whence came the proof of their widowhood. But of late the aggregate of cases has increased year by year, where designing girls have yoked themselves to decrepitude to secure public support for the rest of their lives, or where irregular life is afterward preferred to marriage in order to retain the thus bedraggled pension.[159]

Despite such anecdotal assertions, in the absence of any systematic evidence I tend to doubt that those who cheated in the pension game were socially much different from those who were legitimate claimants. Possibly, socially less connected individuals, or else those from localities with many people who had moved around since the Civil War, were a bit more prone to making false or exaggerated applications. But, in general, the same sorts of experiences and hopes must have inspired applications of all degrees of honesty, thus predisposing the fraudulent, the exaggerated, and the fully legitimate claimants to resemble one another, especially in broad social characteristics such as income, race, ethnicity, and religion.

In the final analysis, indeed, we must guard against overcategorizing the discussion of who benefited from the pension system versus who did not. For of course Civil War pensioners were not *determined* by categorical social characteristics of any kind. This point has several aspects to it.

In the first place, not only whether a person got a (legitimate or fraudulent) pension, but *how soon* he or she starting receiving the benefits, and *how generous* the benefits were, all depended in part on the individual's initiative and social-network connections. One had to find out how to apply and actually do it with some finesse. The payoff of the application could be decisively influenced by the skillful handling of witnesses and doctors, by the hiring of a clever pension attorney, and by communication with one's Congressman (or, best of all, knowing him personally!). Payoffs could also be influenced by creative storytelling about injuries, about the original conditions of military service, or about one's marital and sexual relationships. No doubt, broad social characteristics like income or education correlated with the individual capacities and network connections necessary to get the most out of the pension system. But after all such categorical characteristics are factored into the equation, individual gumption and imaginativeness, as well as the locations of socioeconomically similar applicants in community networks and military peer groups, must also have explained many varying outcomes.

"Exposés" of fraudlent cases, such as the story of "the 'William Newby' Case" discussed in the December 1910 number of *World's Work,* only serve to dramatize possibilities that must have been exploited more successfully—and more subtly—by countless others who were not caught attempting to defraud the system. According to the journalist William Bayard Hale:

> A man named William Newby, of White County, Illinois, was killed at Shiloh, April 6, 1862, and was buried on the battle-field by his comrades . . . His widow moved from Illinois to Texas, and his family had grown up and scattered by the year 1891, when a stranger walked into the streets of the Texan town and announced himself as William Newby. His story was that a wound on the head

had made him insane, that he had wandered, and had only lately regained memory of his identity. The widow Newby was sent for, and after a little talk declared that this was her missing husband. Now Mrs. Newby had for thirty years been pensioned as a veteran's widow. The restored "Newby" immediately applied for a pension. His stake was a large one, his claim [with arrears] being $15,000.[160]

Hale went on to recount how the Pension Bureau investigated, and found that "the new 'Newby's' eyes were of the wrong color, and that he was twenty years younger than he should have been. Further investigation proved the imposter to be a character known as 'Rickety Dan' Benton, who had lived in White County, Illinois as a boy, but had never been in the army, although he had been in poor-houses and jails." Nevertheless, the case was not resolved until after a trial prosecuted by the Pension Bureau in which "140 witnesses, including the widow and one son, testified in behalf of the pretended Newby," while the "Government produced sixty witnesses, including 'Newby's' daughter and brother, who repudiated him and told of marks not shown on the defendant's body." This man was convicted, and kept off the pension rolls. *World's Work* opined, however, that the false Newby's claim "would probably have been allowed without thought of investigation by previous administrations of the Pension Office." Whether or not this is true, the sorts of social support he was able to muster for his rather blatant attempt at fraud must have been much more readily available to countless others who just cheated the system a little bit around the edges.

In addition to individual initiative to fashion a legitimate or illegitimate application, political location mattered as much as social characteristics in determining whether and when pensioners were signed up and how well they did. From the point of view of the polity as a whole, we have already seen how crucial it was to have been a denizen of the North rather than the South: this is obvious for a pension system that exploited the Civil War's losers to care for its winners. Yet within the North and among Union veterans living there, political location also mattered in two other ways. According to Sanders's study of Ohio, it helped to live in counties with long-term propensities to vote Republican, because the party and the Grand Army of the Republic worked together to sign up pensioners in those areas, consolidating the party's electoral base and motivating high turnouts.[161] Moreover, a study I did with several collaborators reveals that political factors helped to explain the differential expansion of numbers of pensioners across the states from 1870 through 1920, even with such obvious explanatory variables as numbers of veterans and Grand Army posts included in the equations.[162] It helped to live in a northern state where the Republicans were relatively strong. It also helped to live in a northern state where the Republicans and the Democrats were closely competitive for votes. Indiana is the perfect case. This state had over 28 percent of its elderly on Civil War pensions in 1910 (see Appendix 1). I would speculate that this was partly because the Republicans were fairly strong, yet also because Republicans and Democrats were closely matched in Indiana, and tried to outdo each other from the 1880s onward in generosity to the "old soldiers."

In short, individual gumption, social connections, and a good deal of outreach by party politicians shaped the specific destinations, timing, and generosity of Civil War pensions. These realities must be taken into account along with analysis of the social characteristics of the eligible pool of Union veterans in our thinking about who benefited from the system. Although individual and partisan-political factors must also have been involved in the early extension of pensions and social insurance in Europe, I would hazard the guess that there the social patterns of eligibility and of actual receipt of comparable benefits were much more *categorical* by occupation or income level. In the United States, by contrast, some individuals among a group of co-workers or neighbors were eligible for Civil War pensions and others were not, simply according to the vagaries of who could and did enter the Union military between 1861 and 1865. What is more, among those who were eligible to apply for pensions, some did and some didn't, some did sooner and others later, and—above all—some got much more than others, regardless of economic need or even of actual physical disabilities. The "system" must have seemed very unsystematic indeed, say for older workers in America around the turn of the century. In Europe, their life chances with respect to pensions or social insurance would have been more objectively similar.

Civil War Pensioners as the Morally Worthy

Perhaps even more important, the European social programs were culturally and politically understood—by authorities and recipients alike—in categorical-economic terms: European benefits were "workingmen's insurance" or pensions for the "respectable elderly of diminished means." Meanwhile, U.S. Civil War pensions (and other forms of public help for veterans and dependents) were not conceptualized in socioeconomic terms at all. Instead they were understood in political and moral terms. Legitimate Civil War pensions were idealized as that which was justly due to the righteous core of a generation of men (and survivors of dead men)—a group that ought to be generously and constantly repaid by the nation for their sacrifices. Politicians constantly spoke of a "contract" between the national government and the Union's defenders in the Civil War, arguing that in return for their valiant service the former soldiers and those tied to them deserved all the public provision necessary to live honorable and decent lives free from want.

By contrast, it was not the national government's role to provide for southerners who had rebelled against it (indeed, during the Civil War, Confederates who had served honorably in previous U.S. wars were removed from the pension lists as traitors). Nor should the federal government concern itself with citizens—however needy or respectable—who had chosen not to serve in 1861–1865, or who had been black slaves not freed before the end of the war, or who had arrived in America too late to have the choice to fight for the endangered Union. Interestingly, this resulted in a moral ordering of claims on the federal government's largesse that crosscut class and racial categories, even if some ethnic and regional divisions were reinforced. Not only were many middle-class and better-off individuals dealt into the system very generously while many needier workers were left out, so were some American blacks (free northerners and freed southerners) included, while certain white-immigrant ethnic groups plus virtually all white southerners were excluded.

Institutional and cultural oppositions between the morally "deserving" and the less deserving run like fault lines through the entire history of American social provision. The late-nineteenth-century system of Civil War pensions sorted people into those opposed categories in a very different way from what would be true in later eras of U.S. public provision. Still, the Civil War pension system, like subsequent provision for "deserving" Americans, was also defined in opposition to charity or public programs for paupers at state and local levels.

The justifications offered for pensions, soldiers' relief, and veterans' homes invoked the need, as the 1888 Republican platform put it, "to provide against the possibility that any man who honorably wore the Federal uniform shall become the inmate of an almshouse, or dependent upon private charity."[163] As Green B. Raum, Republican Commissioner of Pensions in 1891, explained, "an old soldier can receive a pension as a recognition of honorable service with a feeling of pride, while he would turn his back with shame upon an offer of charity."[164] Leaders of the Grand Army of the Republic emphasized similar themes. In their efforts on behalf of veterans' homes in the 1880s, state-level GAR "departments" canvassed poorhouses to find out how many veterans were in them, and then pleaded with legislators and the public, in the words of an Ohio GAR Commander, "to take such steps as might speedily secure for our unfortunate Companions-in-Arms the measure of justice no patriot can question, and to remove the stigma inseparable from a cot in an Alms House."[165] Similarly, the Massachusetts statutes about aid to veterans and their dependents stated quite openly that their purpose was to help persons "who would otherwise be receiving relief under the pauper laws."[166] In short, honorable and generous public provision for Civil War veterans was openly defined in opposition to demeaning provision for paupers. The point was to keep these deserving men and those connected to them from the degrading fates of private charity or the public poorhouse.

Nor was it just a question of keeping worthy individuals away from charity and poorhouses. Proponents of the pension system could also see a justification for its redistribution of public tax revenues toward certain parts of the country and certain local communities. As a Civil War veteran explained in a 1891 letter to the *Century Magazine:*

> The lapse of years, the infirmities incident to age, and casualties of various kinds, had rendered large numbers of our old comrades incapable of self-support. The county poorhouses and other refuges were becoming crowded with such inmates . . . In this manner the citizens of such counties as had been most patriotic and had furnished the largest quotas of their able-bodied sons for the defense of the nation were now being rewarded (?) by the assessment of extra-heavy taxes for the support of their county poor. It was the intent and design of the [Dependent Pension] act of June 27, 1890, to lift that burden . . . and place it on the shoulders of

all taxpayers, to the end that those who had made no sacrifice of life, blood, or treasure might contribute at least equally with those who had given their best and bravest for the maintenance of national life.[167]

Here, finally, is the heart of the contrast between Europe's fledgling welfare-state programs and the United States of America's often equally extensive—and sometimes more financially generous—Civil War pensions. Europe's early social insurance and pension programs reached out symbolically and materially to do modest amounts for whole categories of workers and the less economically privileged. State help was being more or less uniformly offered to those who economically needed it, if not the most, then certainly a lot. In the United States, however, the nation's help was lavished on a selected subset of the working- and middle-class people, citizens of both races, who by their own choices and efforts as young men had *earned aid*—for themselves and their dependents, and even for their communities. If the Republican Party was the special vehicle for delivering this hard-earned help—and if it, in turn, reaped organizational rewards and asked special loyalty from the pension recipients—well that was (in the eyes of the Republican loyalists) only the party's due for having led the forces that saved the Union. The Civil War pension system righteously privileged both the political party and those among the citizenry who had participated victoriously in a morally fundamental moment of national preservation. The Civil War pension system was, in other words, not really a "welfare state" in any objective or subjective sense. It was, rather, an unabashed system of national public care, not for all Americans in similar work or life circumstances, but for the deserving core of a special generation. No matter how materially needy, the morally undeserving or less deserving were not the nation's responsibility.

PART II

The Failure of a Paternalist
Welfare State

Social insurance . . . has been decried as rank paternalism, and this indictment must be readily admitted. For social insurance, when properly developed, is nothing if not a well-defined effort of the organized state to come to the assistance of the wage-earner and furnish him something he individually is quite unable to obtain for himself.

Dr. Isaac Max Rubinow, 1913

Compulsory social insurance is in its essence undemocratic. The first step in establishing social insurance is to divide people into two groups—those eligible for benefits and those considered capable to care for themselves. The division is based on wage-earning capacity. This governmental regulation tends to fix the citizens of the country into classes, and a long established insurance system would tend to make these classes rigid . . . [I]f those who really have the interests of the wage-earners at heart will turn their activities and their influence toward securing for wage-earners the opportunity to organize, there will be no problems, no suffering, and no need that will necessitate the consideration of benevolent assistance of a compulsory character.

Samuel F. Gompers, 1917

The characteristic common to most of the [social insurance] policies that I have advocated is that they call for vigorous governmental action. It is right here that we find the principal source of opposition to them in the United States . . . The truth is that our distrust of them is not due to the form of our government, or even to the size of our country, but to our distrust of government itself—a distrust which is partly inherited and partly the result of painful experience. We do not wish our cities, our states, nor our nation to undertake new and difficult functions, because we know that they functions they now undertake are too often ill performed.

Professor Henry Rogers Seager, 1910

Extensive and generous as they were, Civil War benefits in the turn-of-the-century United States differed in basic ways from pensions and social insurance launched by other Western nations after 1880. Still, these peculiar U.S. benefits might have opened the way for the early enactment of more permanent public benefits for all working and elderly Americans. To invoke this possibility is not to deal in a purely counterfactual logic. During the Progressive Era, a period of political ferment stretching from roughly 1906 through World War I, a number of social reformers in the United States expected just such a smooth transition from Civil War benefits to "workingmen's insurance."

Terms like "industrial insurance," "state insurance," and "social insurance" were used interchangeably with "workingmen's insurance" in the discourse of the 1880s to the 1920s. All of these labels referred to one or more of an array of monetary benefits—industrial accident compensation, old-age pensions, and public insurance against illness, unemployment, and disability—designed to protect workingmen and their families against the hazards of sudden income loss in an industrializing market economy. Often, workingmen's insurance was discussed by reformers in close conjunction with protective labor regulations, through which governments use legal and administrative powers to enforce workplace safety and standard employment practices. As Charles Richmond Henderson put it:

> Protective legislation is an essential part of that social policy in which industrial insurance has a large place. The tendency of protective devices is to lower the cost of insurance, while the tendency of insurance is to offer a constant and ever-present motive to avoid injuries and diseases as well as to provide indemnity when injury is inevitable. The principle underlying both movements is the social interest and duty to care for the welfare of citizens exposed through general conditions to suffering, loss, and death.[1]

Ideally, from the point of view of reformers in the Progressive period, bureaucratically administered protective labor regulations might be extended to include regular payment of wages in money, maximum hours of daily work, minimum wages for unorganized workers, and possibly even arbitration of labor disputes to prevent strikes.[2]

In the United States of the early 1900s, new benefit programs classifiable under the rubric of workingmen's insurance would have been the closest thing to a continuation and extension of Civil War benefits. Indeed, some U.S. reformers justified the hope for workingmen's insurance through moral analogies to military pensions. When Representative William B. Wilson, a leader in the United Mine Workers and the American Federation of Labor, introduced the first national pension plan into Congress in 1909, he made an imaginative symbolic connection to the Civil War system. Wilson proposed to create an "Old Age Home Guard of the United States Army," in which all long-standing American citizens aged 65 and over were invited to enroll as privates, provided that their property was less than $1,500 in value and their income was under $240 a year. In return for "pay" of up to $120 per year, the duty of each elderly "private" would be "to report annually, in writing, to the Secretary of War, on blanks furnished by him for the purpose, the conditions of military and patriotic sentiment in the community where such private lives."[3] As far as protection for the aged was concerned, Wilson's proposal bore out the hopes of the University of Chicago sociologist and reform activist Charles Richmond Henderson, who in his 1909 book *Industrial Insurance in the United States* argued that "the logic of national conduct" on military pensions would lead "straight toward a universal system for disability due to sickness, accident, invalidism, old age, and death."[4] "The nation and the states," Henderson reasoned, "have already declared it to be our duty to shelter the aged and the wounded soldier, why should the victims of the 'army of labor' be neglected? They have also served their country in occupations even more dangerous and destructive than war, and quite as useful."[5]

Henderson's sentiment was echoed by Lee Welling Squier in his 1912 book *Old Age Dependency in the United States*. "The community, as a whole," opined Squier, "owes the disabled soldiers of the nation's industrial army as tender consideration and ample rewards for service as are recognized to be due the veterans of the nation's military service."[6] The moral analogy could stretch even further, Squier felt. Just as the wealthy who invested in government debt rightly earned interest on their loans, "so, also, the soldier in the industrial army has loaned the nation his strength, time, and service; and a pension paid to him by the nation may justly be regarded as interest on his loan."[7]

Isaac Max Rubinow was less moralistic than many of his contemporaries, so he cited demographic and fiscal reasons why "the system of war pensions represents a very important entering wedge for a national system of old-age pensions."[8] Commenting in one of the chapters of his massive and meticulous 1913 treatise *Social Insurance, With Special Reference to American Conditions,* Rubinow examined the matter from a cross-national perspective. "No matter how lenient and extravagant future war-pension legislation may be," he observed, "it is hard to imagine how the rapid decline in the number of surviving invalids of the war can be prevented . . . A large appropriation will, therefore, automatically become available, which will permit of the establishment of a national old-age pension scheme without even any material fiscal disturbance—something which no important European country has been able to accomplish." "Already the first beginnings in the movement for a national old-age pension system have been made," he concluded; "England's precedent on the one hand, and the familiarity with the war pension on the other, have given the straight pension idea a material advantage." Rubinow, moreover, saw old-age pensions as but one part of a comprehensive system of social insurance and labor regulations that he advocated for the United States.

As we now know, Wilson, Henderson, Squier, and Rubinow were mistaken to expect a smooth transition from Civil War pensions to more general benefits for elderly Americans. More than that, along with other advocates of social provision in the Progressive Era, Henderson and Rubinow were frustrated in their hopes for health and unemployment insurance and labor regulations to protect the "army of labor" from the hazards of service in the trenches of the marketplace. Unlike other industrializing capitalist nations, the United States was not to become a fledgling welfare state for workers and the elderly around the turn of the twentieth century. If we juxtapose U.S. social legislation as it existed by 1929 to the legislative profiles of nascent paternalist welfare states of Europe and Australasia, the United States stands out for its lack of nationwide public protection for male workers and elderly people. Neither national nor state-level old-age pensions were successfully enacted before the 1920s; and "as late as 1928 only six states had pension laws [for the very needy elderly], and of these only two, Montana and Wisconsin, were actually paying pensions, even in a few counties."[9] Still more striking, the United States offered little public help to adult male workers before the 1930s—except state-level publicly regulated workers' compensation for industrial accidents. The United States in the 1910s and 1920s offered no sickness or unemployment insurance to workers; and there were no minimum-wage laws that included male workers. Finally, legislative limitations on hours of work were virtually everywhere restricted to women workers and to narrow categories of males in occupations designated as particularly hazardous.[10]

How could Henderson and Rubinow—along with other able social analysts and eloquent advocates of social reform—have been so incorrect in their assessments of what might happen in the early-twentieth-century United States? Why did the United States allow an extraordinary system of publicly funded old-age and disability benefits for many working- and middle-class citizens to pass out of existence with the Civil War generation, without immediately launching workingmen's benefits and associated protective labor laws in its place? Why did new public measures to help "the army of labor" mostly fail to be enacted in the United States between the 1890s and the 1920s, even as they were being instituted in other industrializing capitalist nations across the Old and New Worlds?

That the United States did not move smoothly from Civil War benefits for many elderly people toward general social provision for workingmen and their dependents cannot be attributed to an absence of fully detailed and publicly advocated proposals. Inspired by European and Australasian examples, well-argued proposals were made for old-age pensions, health and unemployment insurance, and protective labor laws covering all American workers. But all such proposals in the early twentieth century failed to be enacted. Laws mandating business to offer compensation to workers injured in industrial accidents were the only part of the agenda of "workingmen's insurance" to achieve legislative success in the early twentieth century.

In this part we shall examine the characteristics, programs, and tactics of the pioneering U.S. social analysts and reformist professionals who advocated new regulations and benefits for workingmen. We shall also explore the complex attitudes of American trade unions toward social legislation, and explain why organized labor and reformist professionals often found themselves at cross-purposes. Most important, with the aid of occasional comparisons to Britain, we shall analyze how the changing institutions and political universe of the early-twentieth-century United States frustrated most of the efforts of those who advocated labor regulations and social spending for workingmen and their dependents. Although much debated, paternalist social policies went against the grain of political and governmental transformations during the Progressive Era. Thus the "army of labor" was not to be included in the honorable tradition of generous public social provision previously established by American democracy for the veterans of the Army of the Republic.

CHAPTER 3

Reformist Professionals as Advocates of Workingmen's Insurance

After Bismarck's Germany took the electrifying step of establishing a series of compulsory insurance programs for workers in the 1880s, policy discussions reverberated across Europe, the Americas, and Australasia. Should new state-run or state-subsidized benefits be enacted to help workers and their families when market incomes were interrupted by old age, ill health, or unemployment? Should new or extended administrative regulations limit hours of wage labor or shore up minimum wages for the most vulnerable and least organized sectors of the working class? The United States participated fully in this transnational discussion. "Collective puzzlement on society's behalf," to use Hugh Heclo's phrase, got under way in the turn-of-the-century United States very much in tandem with similar puzzlement about public social benefits and labor regulations elsewhere.[1]

Popular groups sometimes entered into these policy debates, but the initiative tended to rest with certain governmental officials and politicians, and especially with higher-educated, upper- or middle-class professionals of a reformist bent. At this point in history in industrializing countries, such people were often attracted to social benefits and labor regulations as possible tools for ameliorating class conflict, promoting economic efficiency, and in general furthering the national interest as they understood it. Accounts of the origins of modern social policies in Germany, Sweden, Britain, Australasia, Brazil, and elsewhere trace innovative ideas and proposals to civil servants, social reformers, and social analysts, highly educated persons from the upper and middle classes, who were concerned to address the problems of the emerging urban, industrial working classes.[2] Such policy innovators were self-conscious participants in transnational associations and networks, ever cognizant of foreign precedents that might be reworked to fit conditions in their own countries.

Pioneering American advocates of workingmen's insurance and labor regulations fit this profile. They were reformist professionals who sought to adapt foreign policy precedents to U.S. social needs and governmental conditions.[3] We can see this by looking, first, at those who wrote the earliest U.S. books about social insurance and, secondly, at the investigative and lobbying association, the American Association for Labor Legislation, through which they and other reform-minded social analysts pushed for social benefits and labor regulations in early-twentieth-century U.S. politics.

Early Investigators of Social Insurance

Table 5 provides information about the seven earliest book-length investigations of workingmen's social insurance completed by American authors. For each, I have included data on the author's life as well as information on the auspices and contents of the investigation itself.[4] From the information in this table, and from the ideas and discourse in the books themselves, we can gain preliminary insights into the social and cultural conditions that facilitated initial proposals for public social insurance in the United States.

The authors of America's groundbreaking investigations of social insurance—John Graham Brooks, Miles Dawson, Lee K. Frankel, Charles Richmond Henderson, Frank W. Lewis, Isaac Max Rubinow, Henry Rogers Seager, and William Franklin Willoughby—had a lot in common.[5] All were men.[6] Their fathers were invariably merchants or lawyers. All had gained college and postundergraduate educations at a time when only a minute proportion of all Americans achieved this much formal education. Moreover, most of the investigators (all except Frank Lewis and the co-authors, Lee Frankel and Miles Dawson) eventually developed careers as "social scientists," broadly construed. Indeed, among authors in Table 6 from non-Jewish backgrounds, one can trace the changing nature of careers in U.S. social science during a formative period.[7] For the older men, note John

Table 5. Early investigations of social insurance by Americans

Author and book	Auspices of investigation	Author's life span	Social background	Education	Career	Memberships
BROOKS, John Graham *Compulsory Insurance in Germany* 1893	Fourth Special Report for the U.S. Dept. of Labor, commissioned by Commissioner Carroll D. Wright	b. 1846 d. 1938	Son of a New Hampshire merchant	1867 University of Michigan Law School 1869–71 Oberlin College 1871–75 Harvard Divinity School 1882–85 Berlin, Jena, Freiburg Universities, plus travels in England	Tried to enroll as drummer in Civil War, but failed 1875–91 Unitarian Minister, leader of discussion groups on labor and reform issues 1891–1920 Cambridge, MA, based freelance labor analyst and public lecturer for popular and university audiences	American Social Science Association (President 1904) National Consumers' League (first President, 1899) NYC: Century and 19th Century Clubs Boston: Colonial and St. Botolph Clubs
WILLOUGHBY, William Franklin *Workingmen's Insurance* 1898	Book published in the "Library of Economics and Politics" edited by Richard Ely. Author employed at time by U.S. Department of Labor	b. 1867 d. 1934	Son of a major in the Union Army who later became a lawyer and judge in Virginia	1888 A.B. Johns Hopkins University in History and Political Science	1900–01 Expert investigator for U.S. Dept. of Labor 1901 Lecturer at Johns Hopkins and Harvard	American Association for Labor Legislation (President, 1913) American Political Science Association (Vice President, 1921)

				Positions	Associations
				1901–07 Treasurer of Puerto Rico	American Statistical Association
				1909 Assistant Director, U.S. Bureau of Census	
				1911 Taft Commission on Economy and Efficiency	
				1912–14 Chair of Jurisprudence and Politics, Princeton University	
				1914–16 Constitutional Adviser to the President of China	
				1916–30 Director of Institute for Governmental Research	
HENDERSON, Charles Richmond *Industrial Insurance in the United States* 1909	Revised version of a book originally published in Germany (his Ph.D. dissertation) Similar text published in *American Journal of Sociology*, 1907–1909	b. 1848 d. 1915	Born in Covington, Indiana 1870 A.B., University of Chicago 1895–1896 Ph.D. in Germany	1873–82 Pastor of First Baptist Church in Terre Haute, Indiana 1882–92 Pastor of Woodward Avenue Baptist Church, Detroit 1892–1915 Professor of Sociology, University of Chicago; University Chaplain	National Conference of Charities and Correction (President, 1898) American Association for Labor Legislation American Sociological Society American Economics Association

(*continued*)

Table 5 *(continued)*

Author and book	Auspices of investigation	Author's life span	Social background	Education	Career	Memberships
HENDERSON *(continued)*						American Academy of Political and Social Science
						Trustee of various welfare institutions
LEWIS, Frank W.	Independently published. Thanks Dr. George Zacher of the Imperial Insurance Office, Berlin, for statistical information				Boston lawyer	
State Insurance: A Social and Industrial Need						
1909						
FRANKEL, Lee K. (and Miles M. Dawson)	Commissioned by the Russell Sage Foundation in 1908.	b. 1867 d. 1931	Father came from Germany to Georgia in 1850	1887 B.S. University of Pennsylvania 1893 Ph.D. University of Pennylvania	1887–93 Instruction in Chemistry at University of Pennsylvania 1893–99 Consulting Chemist in Philadelphia	American Public Health Association (President, 1919)
Workingmen's Insurance in Europe						Other national health associations
1910						New York State Conference on Charities and Corrections

1896–99
Chemist of the Retail
Grocers' Association of
Philadelphia

1899–1908
Manager of United
Hebrew Charities in New
York City

1908
Special investigator for
Russell Sage Foundation

1909–31
Organizer of new
welfare section of the
industrial department of
Metropolitan Insurance
Co.

1918–31
Commissioner of New
York State Board of
Charities

Became second Vice-
President of Metropolitan
Life

(continued)

Table 5 *(continued)*

Author and book	Auspices of investigation	Author's life span	Social background	Education	Career	Memberships
SEAGER, Henry Rogers *Social Insurance: A Program of Reform* 1910	Kennedy lectures for 1910, delivered at the School of Philanthropy of the Charity Organization Society of New York City, while Seager was Professor of Political Economy at Columbia University. Book was an extension—and revision—of a reform plan outlined for AALL in 1907.	b. 1870 (Lansing, MI) d. 1930	Great-grandfather: farmer in northern New York State Grandfather: prominent Methodist minister in Rochester and Buffalo Father: lawyer in Michigan	1890 B.A. University of Michigan 1890 Work with H. Adams and Richard Ely at Johns Hopkins University 1891–93 Halle, Berlin, Vienna Universities 1894 Post-graduate studies with S. Patten at University of Pennsylvania; received Ph.D.	1896 Assistant Professor at University of Pennsylvania 1902 Adjunct Professor at Columbia University 1905– Professor of Political Economy at Columbia 1930 Executive Officer of his Department	1906 Founder of American Association for Labor Legislation; President 1911–1912 and 1914–1915 1909 Vice-Chair of Wainwright Committee to Study Employers' Liability 1922 President of American Economics Association

RUBINOW, Isaac Max *Social Insurance; with Special Reference to American Conditions* 1913	b. 1875 d. 1936	Born in Russia, son of a wealthy Jewish textile merchant; came to USA from Moscow in 1893	1885–92 Moscow Gymnasium 1893 Study for B.A. at Columbia University 1898 M.D. New York University Medical College 1900 Part-time graduate student in School of Political Science at Columbia	1899–1903 Doctor in New York City ghettos 1903– Federal bureaucracy: U.S. Civil Service Commission examiner 1904–07 Expert in economics and statistics at Bureau of Statistics, USDA (monographs on Russian wheat) 1908– Bureau of Statistics, U.S. Department of Commerce and Labor; directed research on European workmen's insurance 1911–16 Chief Statistician, Ocean Accident and Guarantee Corporation	American Association for Labor Legislation Socialist (during 1910s)

Independently published. Drew on lectures presented at the New York School of Philanthropy, Spring 1912, and on research for the *24th Annual Report of the Commissioner of Labor*, U.S. Bureau of Labor

(continued)

Table 5 (continued)

Author and book	Auspices of investigation	Author's life span	Social background	Education	Career	Memberships
RUBINOW (continued)					1916– Executive Secretary, Committee on Social Insurance of the American Medical Association 1919–22 Director of medical unit in Palestine for Zionist Organization of America 1923–28 Head of Jewish Welfare Society in Philadelphia 1928–29 Executive Director of Zionist Organization of America 1929–36 Secretary of Independent Order of B'nai B'rith, Cincinnati	

Graham Brooks's "amateur" career as, first, a minister and then a freelance lecturer and social investigator, along with Charles Richmond Henderson's midlife switch from the ministry to a university professorship and chaplaincy. Then note the more purely secular "professional" career of the considerably younger Henry Rogers Seager, who became a lifelong academic economist at Columbia University and, eventually, president of the American Economic Association.

None of the early American investigators of social insurance could be properly described as merely a social scientist, let alone as a narrow specialist, however. Throughout their working lives, all of these men combined social investigation with advocacy of social reforms and public policy innovations. As exemplified by Henry Rogers Seager, who became a founder and four-term president of the American Association for Labor Legislation, these social analysts were centrally involved in reformist political associations even when they also gained the highest professional credentials. Civic men all, they moved readily across institutional settings and audiences in the nominally "public" and "private" sectors.

This becomes still more clear when one probes the roots and auspices of the investigations they completed. The very first U.S. study of social insurance, John Graham Brooks's *Compulsory Insurance in Germany,* was prepared by a private citizen, a "gentleman thoroughly equipped for such a study . . . [who] was about to take up a residence of some years in Germany."[8] Yet as the title page in Figure 6 illustrates, it was commissioned by U.S. Labor Commissioner Carroll D. Wright as a special report for an early federal statistical agency, the U.S. Department of Labor.[9] Just a few years later, a young expert employee of that same federal agency, William Franklin Willoughby, published a second study, *Workingmen's Insurance,* in the commercially published Library of Economics and Politics, a series organized by Professor Richard T. Ely of the University of Wisconsin.[10] The five subsequent books listed in Table 5 were all published under nongovernmental auspices, one by the Russell Sage Foundation and the others by commercial presses.[11] All of these works aimed for broad civic-minded audiences, and both Seager's and Rubinow's books originated as lecture series held at the New York School of Philanthropy, run by the Charity Organization Society of New York City. Rubinow's *Social Insurance,* moreover, drew

FOURTH SPECIAL REPORT

OF THE

COMMISSIONER OF LABOR.

COMPULSORY INSURANCE

IN

GERMANY

INCLUDING

AN APPENDIX RELATING TO COMPULSORY INSURANCE IN OTHER COUNTRIES IN EUROPE.

PREPARED UNDER THE DIRECTION OF

CARROLL D. WRIGHT,

COMMISSIONER OF LABOR,

BY

JOHN GRAHAM BROOKS.

WASHINGTON:

GOVERNMENT PRINTING OFFICE.

1893.

Figure 6 Title page of *Compulsory Insurance in Germany,* by John Graham Brooks, 1893

heavily upon a massive two-volume study of European workmen's insurance that he had completed in 1908–09 while employed at the Bureau of Statistics, U.S. Department of Commerce and Labor, the agency descended from the one that had sponsored Brooks's *Compulsory Insurance in Germany* in the 1890s.[12]

Written in self-conscious dialogue with one another, the early U.S. investigations of social insurance framed the issues in remarkably parallel ways. Every one of these books surveyed recent European (and sometimes Australasian) approaches to workmen's compensation, sickness insurance, and old-age benefits; and several also examined measures to help the unemployed. The authors discussed the situation of the U.S. industrial working class to determine whether similar or alternative policies might be needed in this country. Even though they used terminologies ranging from "compulsory insurance" (Brooks; Lewis) to "workingmen's insurance" (Willoughby; Frankel and Dawson) to "industrial insurance" (Henderson) to "social insurance" (Seager; Rubinow), all of the authors of these early studies agreed that new policies were needed to address the difficulties that wage-workers (and perhaps low-salaried employees) faced owing to the dislocations that inevitably accompanied the advance of urbanization and industrial capitalism. Even skilled, hardworking, and prudent-minded workers, these authors suggested, could not earn enough from private wages to save for unforeseen accidents or illnesses or economic crises, difficulties not of their own making that could plunge their families into poverty. Society owed workingmen and their dependents some systematic help in the face of such contingencies. Help should not take the form merely of charity or of public poor relief, because the object should be to prevent "respectable" workmen from becoming poor and dependent. Rather, "insurance" of some sort should be given partly for ethical reasons and partly to enhance the "efficiency" of the capitalist industrial order, which all the authors assumed was here to stay.

Much as they agreed about the nature of the social dilemmas to be addressed, when it came to making precise policy recommendations for the United States, and when it came to saying which foreign precedents should be adapted to American conditions, the seven pioneering investigators of social insurance arrived at somewhat different conclusions. This happened partly because of their various political sensibilities, but mostly according to how the international and domestic possibilities looked at the time each man wrote his book.

During the 1890s, Brooks examined the German programs of "compulsory insurance" and parallel stirrings in other European countries, while Willoughby self-consciously went beyond Brooks to explore voluntary and publicly subsidized–voluntary approaches to social provision in England, France, Belgium, and Italy. Brooks maintained that the United States should wait at least ten years and watch for the "material" results of the German policies.[13] Yet he also believed that Germany's ethical example would eventually echo in every civilized industrial nation.

> The change of opinion . . . in at least five European countries within ten years has been revolutionary . . . [T]hese nations, wholly irrespective of politics, forms of government, race antipathies, or economic traditions, have rapidly fallen under German influence on this question of insurance . . . The truth is the effect was a moral one. The idea of such insurance being so obviously ethical and falling into touch with the new feeling of social obligation [that arises in industrial society], the example became for this reason contagious.[14]

Germany, Brooks concluded, "is trying this experiment not for herself alone but for the world."[15] Having been higher-educated in Germany like many other American intellectuals of his day, Brooks expected experts in the United States to be influenced by Germany's ethical example, and then to educate public opinion accordingly. Writing a few years after Brooks, Willoughby wanted America to learn from England and France as well, modifying and building upon legal and voluntary approaches to work injuries and sickness insurance. Old-age compensation, Willoughby felt, should be left until later, by which time workers and employers could be educated to the advantages of state action on behalf of social provision.[16] The need for public education about the advantages of policies pioneered abroad was something wholeheartedly agreed upon by all of the early American investigators of social insurance.

By 1909, Henderson and Lewis unabashedly advocated that Americans imitate German contributory and compulsory social insurance for work injuries, ill health, and old age. Henderson proposed innovations for the entire country, while Lewis aimed his recommendations at the state of Massachusetts in particular. Both writers expressed optimism that legal and adminstrative obstacles could be overcome.[17] In 1910, Frankel and Dawson's almost exclusively descriptive *Workingmen's Insurance in Europe* subtly shifted the emphasis away from Germany by fully covering the whole range of European policies, including voluntary measures, and always discussing Britain first. Yet these authors, too, explicitly praised German "comprehensiveness."[18]

Also writing in 1910, Seager shared the admiration of the other writers for certain German precedents, especially in the area of health insurance. But his book was the most U.S.-centered of all the early social insurance studies. As we shall see in greater detail in Chapter 5, Seager was acutely aware of the many administrative and political obstacles to introducing German-style measures in America.[19] He always placed the emphasis in devising policy recommendations on finding methods suited to special U.S. cultural and governmental conditions. Seager was also slightly (but only slightly) less inclined to take "progress" for granted than were others writing at about the same time.

Certainty that the United States would take part in worldwide progress toward social insurance buoyed these early investigators. Frankel and Dawson saw in the industrial world of 1910 a universal "tendency toward a complete and connected system of insurance . . . under which workingmen will be insured against all contingencies where support from wages is lost or interrupted by any cause other than voluntary cessation of labor."[20] Apparently it was to be just a matter of time before the United States would join this tendency, devising its own legally inclusive measures with as much "liberty" in "methods of adminstration" as possible.[21] In his 1913 treatise, *Social Insurance,* Rubinow also posited a transnational movement toward social insurance encompassing all civilized industrial countries, citing not only German and Austrian but also British, French, and Australasian policies as worthy precedents for the United States in particular policy areas. In a tone born of a kind of evolutionist confidence, Rubinow called upon the United States to avoid "childish" replays of arguments and policies that had proved unworkable elsewhere, while joining the international march toward comprehensive social insurance. "The movement for social insurance is one of the most important world movements of our time," he argued.[22]

Along with a faith in worldwide progress, most of the early American students of social insurance shared a conception of the state as a positive agency for implementing social change in the public good. A sense of the state as a paternalist and ethical agency suffused the groundbreaking U.S. studies of social insurance. Brooks spoke of the "duty of the state toward the working classes," and spent most of the first chapter of his book discussing the ideas of German philosophers and economists. He wrote about Fichte, who held that the "state . . . is not to be negative nor to have mere police function, but to be filled with Christian concern, especially for the weaker members," and about Schaeffle, who wanted to replace charity with "nationalized general self provision for the whole life," and about Wagner, who wanted the "state, inspired by strong moral purpose" to act boldly in helping "the laborer into a position where the struggle for existence can be made as fair as the nature of the problem permits."[23] In Brooks's view, any "faithful account . . . of the origin of the boldest experiment in social reform that any state ever tried can not omit the fact of an influence so vast as that of these philosophers . . . upon the general view of the state function in Germany and upon certain men [that is, public officials] who did so much to give the state a paternal character."[24]

Echoing Brooks's admiration for German ideals—while trying to quiet possible American fears about authoritarianism—Frankel and Dawson argued that the "compulsion" in German-style social insurance should not be seen as "coercion," but rather as "the recognition of a responsibility which rests on all citizens alike; namely, the responsibility of providing against the ordinary risks of life . . . [T]here are risks in life, common to all workingmen, against which it is impossible for the individual alone to make provision." This is "not a code of mandatory laws but the highest development of an ethical principle" known to all "enlightened countries," republics as well as despotic monarchies.[25] Similarly, Henderson invoked "the modern conception that the state owes certain duties toward those who are in an economic position of dependence."[26]

Offering perhaps the frankest defense of ethical state paternalism, Rubinow wrote that social insurance "may be and has been decried as rank paternalism, and this indictment must be readily admitted. For social insurance, when properly developed, is nothing if not a well-defined effort of the organized state to come to the assistance of the wage-earner and furnish him something he individually is quite unable to attain for himself."[27] Above all, Rubinow wanted to realize the fullest expression of ethical statism in a democratic context, where social insurance would be "a powerful object lesson of the reality of the new concept of the state as an instrument of organized collective action, rather than of class oppression, the concept of the future state in the making, rather than of the state in the past."[28] Public social insurance had different effects on class conflicts in democratic versus authoritarian states, he explained: "As social insurance is the creature of the state—the 'benevolent' autocratic state in some cases, but more frequently the modern democratic state—it has had the effect of establishing much more peaceable relations between the state and the working class, in so far, that is, as the state is truly democratic. If it does not have that effect in Germany or in Russia it is because there is no democratic state."[29]

Even the author of the most U.S.-centered investigation of social insurance urged a new, positive role for state action. Seager introduced his 1910 lectures and book by arguing that for the

> sections of the country . . . in which manufacturing and trade have become dominant interests of the people, in which towns and cities have grown up, and in which the wage earner is the typical American citizen—the simple creed of individualism is no longer adequate. For these sections we need not freedom from governmental interference, but clear appreciation of the conditions that make for the common welfare, as contrasted with individual success, and an aggressive program of governmental control and regulation to maintain these conditions.[30]

Seager was very worried that traditional American individualist attitudes still stood in the way of many desirable social reforms, but there was no doubt that he wanted his country to move toward a view of the state as a positive moral agency. To become "a truly civilized society," he believed, the United States must develop a "deepening sense of social solidarity and quickening of appreciation of our common interests." And Americans must "begin to think of government as . . . organized machinery for advancing our common interests."[31]

In their positive views of the role of the state, the early U.S. investigators of social insurance resembled many other early American social scientists, for several reasons. For one thing, graduate study in German universities was undertaken by many budding U.S. social analysts in the late nineteenth century (and this general tendency was reflected in the educational experiences of Brooks, Henderson, and Seager).[32] Exposed to the "historical school" of economics then dominant in Germany, young American graduate students often returned to the United States with a view of "the state as an educational and ethical agency whose positive aid is an indispensable condition of human progress," to use the opening words of the 1885 founding platform of the American Economic Association.[33] There were also indigenous American roots for such thinking. Many northerners who had served the Union cause during the Civil War, or whose fathers had served that cause, saw the federal government as potentially an agent of virtuous reform. Moreover, the socially responsible versions of Christianity to which many turn-of-the-century social analysts were exposed in their upbringing could lead to similar hopes for improvement through governmental action.[34] Notice that the backgrounds of many of the writers in Table 5 show evidence of such influences from the Civil War or from religious socialization. These influences, along with the German educational experiences of most of them, explain why pioneering U.S. advocates of social insurance believed so fervently that workingmen and their families should be helped by new compulsory public policies. Social insurance for these writers was not just an expedient, or even just a paternalistic way to help wage earners. It was a way to use state power to promote the social solidarity and moral well-being of the nation as a whole.

The American Association for Labor Legislation

If early American proponents of social insurance saw the need to convince public opinion of the appropriateness of such programs as a response to the insecurities that advancing industrialism was creating for the working population, their efforts were not restricted to the writing of books. Experts on social insurance were also willing to work with one another and with other reform leaders to sponsor a continuous flow of research on industrial problems and to influence the policy choices made by legislators and the public. Prior to the 1920s, the chief organizational vehicle for those favoring social insurance and a variety of other legislative reforms affecting male wage earners was the American Association for Labor Legislation (AALL).[35] This group was officially launched on February 15, 1906, as the American Section of the International Association for Labor Legislation.[36] For some years, U.S. governmental experts and social scientists had been delegates to this international body, and the establishment of the AALL was a concrete way to embody the transnational push toward labor legislation on U.S. soil.

The AALL was founded and propelled by reform-minded social scientists. It grew out of an organizing session held at the December 1905 meeting of the American Economics Asssociation and chaired by Dr. Adna F. Weber of the New York State Department of Labor. This gathering included Professors Richard Ely of the University of Wisconsin, Henry Rogers Seager of Columbia University, and Henry Farnam of Yale University.[37] Throughout the Progressive period, university-based social scientists from Columbia, Princeton, Wisconsin, and Yale served as presidents of the AALL, giving way to businessmen presidents only during the 1920s when the AALL had diminished innovative momentum.[38] By 1908, moreover, the job of secretary had become the lynchpin of the AALL's organizational structure, and this full-time post was to be held from 1909 until 1943 by John B. Andrews, a student and lifelong close associate of the University of Wisconsin labor economist Professor John R. Commons.[39] Andrews worked in conjunction with an assistant secretary, Irene Osgood (who became Irene Osgood Andrews), at the AALL's national office in New York City, where it moved in 1908 from its original headquarters in Madison, Wisconsin.

Never a mass-membership body, the AALL started with 21 members in 1906—including well-known leaders from the worlds of charity, social work, labor, and business, as well as academia. Membership climbed to 903 in 1909, and growth continued to be rapid until a peak of 3,348 was reached in 1913. Subsequently, membership declined a bit and fluctuated around 3,000 until the early 1930s, when the association went into further decline.[40] The halcyon days of the AALL corresponded to the height of the Progressive Era from around 1910 into World War I. Not only was this the period of peak membership and activities, it was also the time when the AALL tapped the enthusiastic energy of prominent social scientists and defined virtually all of the broad programmatic goals that it pursued for the rest of its organizational lifetime.

At first, the leaders of the fledgling AALL hesitated to commit it openly to legislative advocacy in addition to policy-relevant research. But by 1910 the group amended its original statement of purpose—which promised "to encourage the study of labor conditions in the United States"—by adding the phrase "with a view to promoting desirable labor legislation."[41] This transition was also marked—and justified—in the 1910 presidential address to the AALL of Professor Henry Farnam of Yale University.

Speaking about "Practical Methods in Labor Legislation," Farnam celebrated the recent organizational gains of the AALL and the fact that "[we] have issued many valuable publications. Our information bureau is used continually by State Commissioners [of labor], chambers of commerce, librarians, legislators and by the State and national governments," while "many thousands get the benefits of our work indirectly through trade unions, manufacturers' associations, and other organizations which contribute toward the support of the association."[42] Indeed, Farnam was correct to suggest that the AALL was well established as a commissioner and disseminator of policy-relevant research. In the year 1910 alone, the AALL claimed to have distributed some 164,000 copies of circulars, pamphlets, and articles.[43] And in 1911 the Association began the quarterly publication of the *American Labor Legislation Review,* a compendium of facts about social issues in industry and alternative policy proposals to address them. This journal—which every year summarized legislative developments across all of the forty-eight states, the District of Columbia, and the federal government—was a crucial source of regular information as well as labor legislation advocacy for many individuals and organizations during the Progressive Era and afterward.

Building upon its achievements in policy research, President Farnam wanted the AALL to study and apply the arts of careful legislative drafting and lobbying. As to the former, he reasoned that U.S. "legislation which is prodigious in its mass, amounting easily in a single year to 16,000 enactments, is mainly the product of unskilled labor. Hence when it is submitted to the trained minds of our courts, it is not surprising that a great deal of it is condemned."[44] If Farnam felt that the "skilled labor" of the AALL could help proponents of social legislation avoid the "bugaboo of unconstitutionality," he also urged AALL members to study the "art of legislative midwifery"—"the methods by which, when a bill is prepared, the favorable votes of legislators may be obtained." This, he argued, is precisely that part of the art of legislation which has enjoyed a really professional development in our country. Legislators come and legislators go, but the lobby seems to be the one stable element in our legislative halls. Such an assocation as ours does not expect, nor does it desire, to add to the world's knowledge of this subject, though its members may need to be reminded, and reminded emphatically, that since this art has been developed in the service of private interests, those who aim at the public interest are under a peculiar obligation to study and apply its legitimate features.[45]

The Political Methods of the AALL

Although the AALL did add legislative drafting and lobbying to its mission, it never gave up its original view of the policymaking process as a set of rational discussions among experts, officials, and organizational leaders. The first-line audiences for the AALL were other reform advocacy groups, such as the National Consumers' League, as well as the national professional associations of social workers, public-sector officials, and social scientists. The AALL advertised its policy priorities in the *Survey,* the journal of liberal settlement people and social workers.[46] And recurrently it held annual meetings in conjunction with the American Economic Association, the American Political Science Association, the American Sociological Society, and the American Statistical Society. This was done so that AALL presidential addresses would get wide expert audiences, and so that joint sessions could be planned on such topics as the minimum wage or health insurance.[47] What is more, when the AALL undertook major programmatic initiatives, it always started by convening special conferences that featured debates among nationally established reformers and academics.[48]

The philosophy behind the AALL's proclivity for converting fellow professionals first was articulated by Rubinow in 1917, when he optimistically reported in the *Survey* about the results of polls conducted by the California Social Insurance Commission. In these polls, 87 percent of respondents from the American Economic Association and the National Conference of Charities and Correction favored social insurance, while only 4 percent were opposed and 9 percent undecided. "It is true," conceded Rubinow, "that American professors and social workers do not often write our laws; nevertheless any viewpoint gaining such strong support among them must eventually permeate the thought and conscience of the whole American people and lead to some constructive action, for even a superficial review of the history of any progressive tendency in American political, economic, or social life will corroborate the use of this generalization."[49]

More broadly, the AALL sought to influence legislators and public opinion. For this, it relied not only on direct lobbying by experts, and not only on the dissemination of AALL investigations and model bills—although these were crucial tactics for a group that had unbounded faith in the persuasive powers of rational investigations of empirical facts. Characteristically, a quote from Sir Edward Coke, "Reason is the Life of the Law," appeared on the cover of the June 1913 number of the *American Labor Legislation Review* devoted to reporting on the AALL's first American Conference on Social Insurance. In addition, though, the AALL tried to build interorganizational coalitions, chiefly by encouraging leaders of other associations to set up committees to look into matters of social insurance, perhaps with someone from the AALL serving on them. As Rubinow explained this process early in the AALL's national campaign for health insurance: "Charity organizations in New York and other cities, . . . chambers of commerce or boards of trade, actuarial societies and other similar national and local bodies have been appointing committees on social insurance, until one begins to have the uncomfortable feeling of holding membership in a half dozen of them."[50] Hoping that the other associations would end up endorsing something approximating its position on the policy matters at issue, the AALL expended much interpersonal effort to persuade individual leaders from business associations, medical and public health associations, and trade unions to endorse its legislative proposals. During its drive for health insurance, the AALL proudly published endorsements and quotations from any such leaders it could find. These endorsements were highlighted in AALL pamphlets on health insurance, and sections of the *American Labor Legislation Review* were devoted to statements by the following categories of people, organizational leaders and individual public figures: Employers and Financiers; Labor Representatives; Physicians and Nurses; Social Workers; Public Officials; Economists and Statisticians; Jurists and Attorneys; and Newspaper Editors.[51]

Sometimes this technique gave an impression of stronger support

from interest groups than actually existed. Early in the course of
devising and promoting health insurance bills, for example, the
AALL successfully persuaded people within the leadership of the
American Medical Association. The AALL did not foresee that,
within a few years, fuller consideration of health insurance by local
and state medical societies, many of which became very hostile to
the idea, would force reconsiderations of the national AMA's stance
on this issue.[52] What is more, early in the health insurance campaign,
AALL leaders bandied about a quote from the Industrial Betterment
Committee the National Association of Manufacturers (NAM) that
apparently endorsed an element of compulsion in health insurance.
But it soon became apparent that other NAM leaders were speaking
out against the AALL's health insurance proposals and promoting
voluntary industrial plans instead.[53]

Another favorite AALL tactic for promoting model bills was to
encourage governors and legislatures to set up public investigatory
commissions. In order to influence eventual recommendations for
new legislation, the AALL sought to have its own experts engaged
to staff such commissions. As Rubinow explained, the "normal evolution of any movement in social legislation may be roughly outlined
as follows: literary propaganda, lectures and meetings, voluntary
committees, public commissions, drafting of bills, legislative proposals and finally legislative enactment."[54] This approach could be very
successful—up to a point. For example, during the New York State
campaign for workmen's compensation legislation, Governor
Charles Evans Hughes appointed a commission in 1909 that included
President Henry Seager and Secretary Crystal Eastman of the New
York branch of the AALL; and following the commission's recommendations, New York passed a law in 1910. But that law was soon
found unconstitutional; and when another law was passed in 1913,
it conformed not to the proposals of the AALL but to the preferences of New York State's powerful casualty insurance companies.[55]
More telling, the AALL appeared initially to be very successful in
shaping the health insurance campaign in California, when that
state's Social Insurance Commission (SIC) engaged Rubinow as an
expert consultant, and in due course recommended in favor of
compulsory health insurance with a few modifications of the AALL's
specific proposals. But this was far from enough to ensure final
victory, because the SIC's proposed enabling constitutional amend-

ment was overwhelmingly defeated in a popular referendum in 1918.[56] Events in both New York and California, therefore, demonstrated that investigatory commissions could not ensure legislative victories. This basic story was repeated in many states during the AALL's national campaign for health insurance. In addition to California, nine other states appointed investigatory commissions: Connecticut, Illinois, Indiana, New Hampshire, New Jersey, New York, Ohio, Pennsylvania, and Wisconsin. A majority of these official bodies recommended in favor of legislation, but to no avail.[57]

Despite the limitations of its political approach, the AALL rarely ventured beyond rational arguments meant to persuade other elites and voluntary organizations. It did not devise emotional appeals that might have made its legislative campaigns attractive to mass-circulation magazines.[58] It did not engage in systematic grassroots political mobilization. Nor, despite its declared purpose of securing uniform legislation across the states, did the AALL attempt to use its own organizational resources, or those of allied federated associations, to reach directly into the civic life of local communities—and legislative districts—across the United States. For a while after 1907, the AALL officially chartered state branches, which were founded in Illinois in 1908, in New York and Minnesota in 1909, and in Massachusetts in 1912.[59] These were all states where groups of AALL members, mostly university professors and prominent reform leaders, actively pursued legislative agendas. But by 1912, the New York branch voted to dissolve and move its work back into the national AALL office. Soon "the other state branches discontinued functioning as sub-units of the national organization," which thereafter "assumed all duties, delegating specific tasks to permanent or *ad hoc* committee."[60] Certainly the AALL never developed a fully ramified, federated structure of local, state, and national associations, nor even as extensive a network of formally affiliated local groups as the National Consumers' League.[61] Interestingly, in 1910, the outgoing AALL President John R. Commons (the mentor of John Andrews, who took over as full-time AALL secretary in that year) argued that it had been a mistake to place emphasis on creating state branches, because coordinating them would take too much of the secretary's time. Commons urged that the AALL "resolve itself into a scientific bureau to aid other associations in promoting labor legislation."[62]

In practice, the AALL took more initiatives than this formulation implies; yet it operated in the general spirit of Commons's advice as a national center for commissioning policy-relevant research and disseminating model legislative proposals to other experts, interest-group leaders, journalists, and political officials. Unlike the higher-educated women reformers we will meet in Part III of this book, the reformist social scientists of the AALL did not have the political will to take their policy ideas directly to grassroots groups of Americans. Lacking the will, they did not search out the organizational means to do this—as they might have done, for example, by working regularly with the nationwide, locally rooted General Federation of Women's Clubs.[63] Rather, the predominantly male experts of the AALL leadership remained entranced by their view of politics as a rational conversation among elites.

What Social Forces Did the AALL Represent?

Some analysts of U.S. social politics have treated the AALL as an agent of capitalist interests, an interpretation apparently buttressed by certain facts.[64] Some wealthy capitalists were members of the Association, and reformist businessmen normally served as treasurers of the AALL because of their ties to potential donors.[65] During the 1920s, such businessmen were also the presidents of the AALL, but this is not the period with which I am concerned here. The AALL's budget was always modest, ranging from about $16,000 to $32,000 a year, nourished mainly by dues and donations from individuals and by occasional large contributions from "such philanthropic organizations as the Russell Sage Foundation, Carnegie Foundation and the Milbank Fund."[66] The organization did depend upon wealthy benefactors for a significant proportion of its funding. In 1912, for example, the AALL received $27,385 in dues and gifts from 2,260 members; yet 65 percent of the total funding came from twenty-one contributors who gave amounts of $100 or more, including such benefactors as "John D. Rockefeller; Elbert Gary of the United States Steel Corporation; Felix Warburg, a leading banker and philanthropist; Mrs. Madeline Astor; V. Everett Macy . . . ; and Miss Anne Morgan, the daughter of the financier."[67]

Donations to the AALL came from many different sources, however, including diverse wealthy individuals whose families or companies or industries did not agree with one another on issues having to do with industrial labor or the proper role of government in social legislation.[68] Diversification of dependence is a well-known way for a donee to create plenty of room for maneuver in relation to donors. Nor is there evidence that any of the wealthy donors ever successfully pressed his or her views on an otherwise reluctant AALL. Unless one can demonstrate precisely that the AALL consistently subordinated its policies to the goals of particular capitalist contributors, or to the goals of a group of them with common interests, one cannot maintain that merely taking money from assorted wealthy people, including handfuls of them formally affiliated with the organization during the 1910s, was enough to turn the social scientists and middle-class reformers who predominated in the leadership, staff, and membership of the AALL into agents of capitalists.

The AALL often clashed with business groups within the political process. It differed with insurance and other business interests over the scope and form of workmen's compensation bills.[69] Its campaigns for health insurance brought it into bitter conflict with the insurance industry and with such business peak associations as the National Association of Manufacturers, the National Civic Federation, and the Associated Merchants and Manufacturers of New York State.[70] Along with other progressive reformers the AALL persistently differed with very conservative business groups such as the Illinois Manufacturers' Association (IMA). The IMA opposed all new governmental expenditures and regulations to help labor, and it believed that the AALL pursued "semi or boldly socialistic" measures.[71] The AALL also clashed with reformist, "corporate-liberal" business forces, including "progressive" employers in Massachusetts who preferred voluntary to compulsory unemployment insurance, and the National Civic Federation, which orchestrated representatives from business and the national Federation of Labor into vocal criticism of AALL proposals for public health insurance.[72] Certainly there is no evidence at all that the AALL simply tailored its positions to those of even the most "liberal" business groups of the day.

Were the social processes at work more subtle, however? Perhaps those who shaped the AALL's outlook and programs were self-selected and co-opted into the intellectually sincere promotion of fundamentally "capitalist" reforms, because they were pursuing careers "within the system." It is certainly true that the AALL never directly challenged the continued existence of U.S. capitalism, but instead sought to make it more socially just and more efficient at the same time. "The fundamental purpose of labor legislation is the conservation of the human resources of the nation"—this was the motto that appeared on the cover of each issue of the *American Labor Legislation Review.*

Yet to regard acceptance of capitalism as proof of the AALL's co-optation would be to obscure the highly varied ways in which reformers then, as now, could work for changes "within" capitalism. For example, prominent in the AALL's campaigns for health insurance was Isaac Max Rubinow, a Socialist Party member and lifelong social democrat, a man who constantly switched employers throughout his life in order to continue to pursue his reformist ideals.[73] Are we to consider him in the same way we consider Frederick Hoffman, a former president of the American Statistical Association and a third vice president and statistician at the Prudential Insurance Company of America? Hoffman quit the AALL's Committee on Social Insurance in 1916, once it became clear that it would recommend compulsory, government-run health insurance rather than the voluntary, private plans favored by the life insurance industry. While continuing to advocate public health measures and business-sponsored social provision, Hoffman became a persistent, bitter, vocal, and extremely effective foe of the AALL's health insurance proposals. He used Prudential's resources to produce and distribute pamphlets, and generally cited business-sponsored research, all in the service of efforts to counter AALL ideas rationally, and to smear them emotionally as subversive German imports.[74] If we can agree that there was a major difference between Rubinow and Hoffman as two experts who sought reforms "within capitalism," then we can safely locate the early AALL closer to Rubinow, given that he worked closely with the entire AALL leadership throughout the Progressive period and led the decisive health insurance campaign.

The prestigious academics who during the 1910s shared the leadership of the AALL with Rubinow had careers securely anchored in major universities and nationwide professional associations. AALL leaders such as Professors Seager, Farnam, Commons, and Willoughby pursued careers outside of corporations, and they enjoyed general scholarly prestige that also freed them from overdependence on any one university employer. This situation may well have meant, following the argument of the historian Mary O. Furner, that they could not go very far in the direction of advocacy for labor, let alone for socialism.[75] But it also freed them from day-to-day pressures or inducements to promote business interests or take the same points of view as spokesmen for particular industries such as Frederick Hoffman.

Broad governmental and cultural processes underpinned the AALL's existence as a force partially independent of businessmen and the existing institutions of the capitalist economy. Drawing on his "own observations and experience as an officer of the New York Department of Labor," one of the AALL's founders, Dr. Adna Weber, explained in 1907 how the growth of governmental bureaus of labor statistics, along with changes of outlook within U.S. higher education, had laid the historical basis for the formation of the Association. "The promotion of labor legislation," Weber observed, was originally "left mainly to the laboring classes without the assistance and guidance that they should have had from the professional classes."[76] By the early twentieth century, however,

> the ground ha[d] been prepared for its [the AALL's] activity by the work of government labor bureaus and university seminars in the collection and publication of . . . histories and labor legislation in the important commonwealths of New York, Pennsylvania, Massachusetts, and Connecticut. At the same time the study of labor problems . . . reacted upon the minds of university students and teachers, and . . . produced a marked change in their attitudes toward labor legislation.[77]

As a result of these changes, Weber observed, the

> subject of labor legislation is interesting a growing body of citizens, which is being rapidly recruited from the ranks of young college graduates . . . [Such] men are coming to realize the impropriety of calling labor laws class legislation . . . On the contrary, they are realizing that it is vastly in the public interest to enact laws that will not only safeguard the health and morals of the people massed in large factories or employed in small sweatshops, but also protect them from extortion and coercion, and secure to them some leisure in which to prepare themselves for the discharge of the duties of citizenship.[78]

There were socialists and trade union leaders, as well as capitalists, among the AALL's members, but everyone understood that the

Association was not dedicated to any of these forces.[79] Not beholden to any organized class interest, the AALL conceived itself to be a proponent of a higher social good to be realized in practice through socioeconomically interventionist public policies. The requisites of that higher social good, AALL people believed, were not best perceived by businessmen, many of whom were given to fierce competition and exploitation of labor, or by organized socialists, who were too obsessed with class conflict. Nor did AALL people believe that trade union leaders would pursue the general social good, given the unionists' preoccupation with the survival and expansion of their own narrowly based organizations. As AALL Secretary John Andrews expressed this perception in a 1915 letter describing trade unionists in New York:

> We often find the majority of the highly organized workers hand in hand with Tammany [that is, the Democratic Party machine] for their own selfish interests, and in workmen's compensation matters at Albany they fought vigorously against the inclusion within the benefits of the law of more than a comparatively few groups of workers—and those highly organized. This selfish tendency is also noticeable in the attitude of certain prominent leaders of organized labor toward minimum wage legislation for the protection of unorganized poorly-paid women.[80]

Properly reform-minded experts were the ones most likely to understand the general social good—exactly those, in fact, whose activities gave the AALL such élan during the Progressive Era. And the proper audience for reformist experts was "the public," which was outside of class conflict and had a stake in ameliorating it, as John Commons explained: "At the outside guess, not more than 6,000,000 wage-earners, and 1,500,000 employers and investors are in the field where classes are forming. Two-thirds of the voting population are spectators. We call them the public. They may be forced to take sides, but they want fair play. The outcome depends on the way they are brought in."[81]

The AALL's self-conception was part of the cultural rationale being developed in those days for the emerging role of the professional expert: scientific, objective, and able to discern and help bring about policies in the interest of the whole society. Arguably, the AALL took over in a new, transitional era the normative policy advocacy role played in the post–Civil War period by the gentlemanly American Social Science Association (ASSA).[82] The AALL picked up this cause from the faltering ASSA at a time when more specialized national professional associations were emerging in economics, political science, sociology, and statistics, and when some of America's major universities were downplaying traditional religious teaching and promoting empirical social research along German lines. Yet professionalizing American social analysts exposed to German conditions in the late nineteenth century not only admired the German research universities; they also envied the close connections of German professors to public policymaking. Holding together for a time social analysts whose professional successors would later, from the 1920s onward, drift apart into more and more specialized academic worlds, the AALL thus did more than continue reform traditions earlier embodied in the ASSA. It also expressed an aspiration for policy influence by the earliest cohorts of U.S. professional social scientists, experts who remained morally concerned about the problems of industrial society in its entirety. Regardless of their individual disciplinary or research specialties, AALL members believed that the labor regulations and social insurance measures they proposed would improve the living and working conditions of *all* members of the working class. At the same time, their proposals would further the broad "public interest" in social justice and economic efficiency for an orderly, regulated capitalist society. The AALL's members understood themselves to be encouraging and publicizing rigorous scientific investigations to lay the basis for sound labor legislation in the national interest.[83]

Another way to situate the AALL in the social landscape of its time comes from noting that it cared about more than passing new legislation. The AALL was also committed to a certain kind of administrative statebuilding to ensure that labor legislation would be properly enforced by well-trained experts free from partisan economic interests and political corruption. Enforcement of reform laws, once passed, was a problem keenly felt by the AALL, as it had been felt by many of the reformers who gained legislative victories during the nineteenth century. All too often, new U.S. laws made no special provisions for enforcement, leaving it to oversight by legislatures and chief executives and to sanctioning by the courts. This usually meant that laws were not effectively enforced once the publicity that had led to their passage died away. Fearing this, and wanting continuous attention to effective enforcement, reformers of the Progressive Era, including the AALL, advocated the setting up of special public commissions.

Following the enactment of workmen's compensation laws, the AALL, under the inspiration of John Commons, called for the spread across the states of "omnibus industrial commissions" that would unify the enforcement of these and all other industrial regulations, combining functions that had previously been scattered among many agencies. Taken from a 1916 book by Commons and Andrews, Figure 7 contrasts New York's unified industrial commission, which approximated the AALL's ideal, with the extremely fragmented administrative situation in Illinois, which the AALL abhorred.[84] As Commons explained in a key 1913 article, an omnibus industrial commission could engage in continuous studies of practical industrial conditions, "not the academic research of the laboratory and the study, nor the journalistic investigation of the agitator, but the constructive investigation of the administrator" in consultation with appropriate experts and interested parties.[85] Because omnibus commissions would have ongoing capacities to do policy-relevant research, they would in a sense publicly institutionalize the functions voluntarily performed by the AALL itself. Such "constructive investigation," Commons felt, would make administrative findings of fact convincing to the courts, and would lay the basis for recommendations of new legislation by the commissioners. Omnibus industrial commissions would constitute a "fourth branch of government" taking over functions from the courts and from partisan legislatures and executives. These commissions should be led and staffed by professional experts, while also incorporating members or advisory boards "representing" labor and management. In the words of the historians Edward Berkowitz and Kim McQuaid, although AALL "advocates rationalized this new branch of the public sector as a joint labor-managment exercise . . . the industrial commission testified to their belief in the management of industrial processes by a well-educated elite."[86] Reformers wanted to charter agencies from which professional experts like themselves could gain an overview of industrial problems in the public interest.

Hopes for administrative statebuilding also figured in the AALL's campaign for health insurance. As Figure 8 illustrates, the Associa-

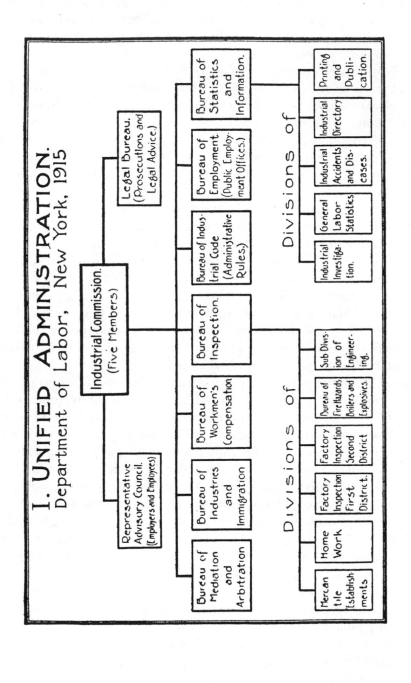

I. UNIFIED ADMINISTRATION.
Department of Labor, New York, 1915

Industrial Commission.
(Five Members)

Representative Advisory Council.
(Employers and Employees)

Legal Bureau.
(Prosecutions and Legal Advice.)

Bureau of Mediation and Arbitration

Bureau of Industries and Immigration

Bureau of Workmen's Compensation

Bureau of Inspection.

Bureau of Industrial Code (Administrative Rules.)

Bureau of Employment (Public Employment Offices.)

Bureau of Statistics and Information.

Divisions of

Mercantile Establishments

Home Work

Factory Inspection First District.

Factory Inspection Second District

Bureau of Fire Hazards, Boilers and Explosives.

Sub Division of Engineering.

Divisions of

Industrial Investigation.

General Labor Statistics

Industrial Accidents and Diseases.

Industrial Directory

Printing and Publication.

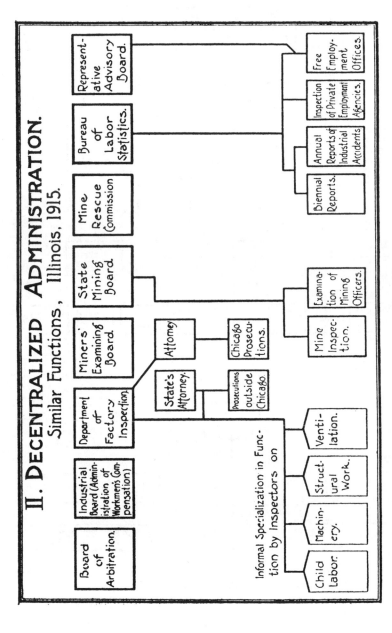

II. DECENTRALIZED ADMINISTRATION.
Similar Functions, Illinois, 1915.

Figure 7 Organizational charts about state labor law administration
Source: John R. Commons and John B. Andrews, *Principles of Labor Legislation*
(New York: Harper and Brothers, 1916), pp. 434–35.

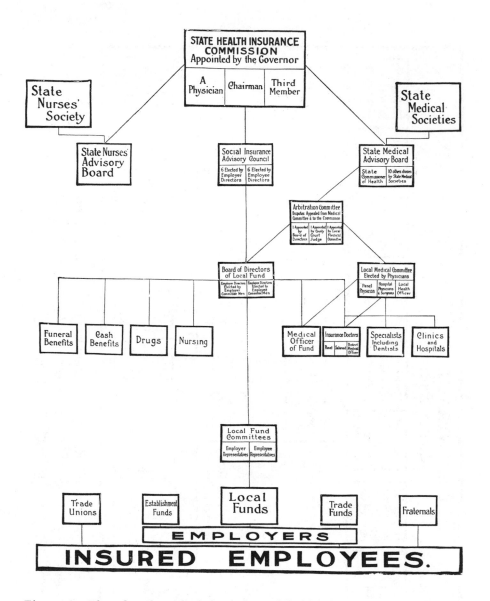

Figure 8   Plan for the administration of health insurance
Source: American Labor Legislation Review 7(1) (March 1917), facing title page.

tion's model health insurance bill included provision for a central commission to collect and disburse contributions from employers and employees and to supervise the actual delivery of illness benefits and medical services by local "approved societies." A council of employer and employee representatives would advise the commission, whose "duties . . . will be principally judicial and supervisory. Its purely administrative functions will be few." There would be three commissioners appointed for six-year terms by the governor, one a physician, and "Each commissioner shall devote his entire time to the duties of his office, and shall not hold any position of trust or profit, or engage in any occupation or business interfering or inconsistent with his duties as such commissioner, or serve on or under any committee of a political party."[87] The images in Figures 7 and 8 portray the aspiration of the AALL to have professional experts in authoritative positions "above" partisan politics and clashing economic interests.

The new administrative agencies favored by progressive reformers including the AALL were in conformance with the sociocultural tendencies toward professionalization that reshaped life for the educated middle classes of the turn-of-the-century United States. These regulatory and investigative bodies would provide occupational opportunities for higher-educated "experts," but without forcing them to commit themselves to the dubious prospect of prolonged careers within government in a country that lacked a national civil service.[88] Experts could move into and out of authoritative commissions, spending some time in them in the midst of careers that took them through universities, civic associations, and perhaps business corporations. This situation would be ideal for the professionalizing elements of the American "new middle class." It would keep those emerging organizational realms of government that reformers of the Progressive Era understood to be best suited for realizing "the public interest" fully accessible to the outlooks and career needs of the social stratum that most fully supported the full range of the period's reforms. It is therefore hardly surprising that the AALL always combined its advocacy of new social benefits and labor regulations with proposals for this type of public adminstration, for it would allow social-scientific experts of its own ilk to gain greater influence in U.S. governmental and social life.

Reformers' advocacy of such new administrative agencies often brought them into disputes with other political and social forces. There were conflicts with party politicians, who preferred to retain partisan control of any agencies created to implement legislation. There were tensions between reformers and the courts, a period of working out to what degree administrative agencies would be able to take over areas of dispute resolution previously handled by on a case-by-case basis under the common law. There were disputes with trade union leaders, who often preferred labor agencies controlled by political appointees particularly tied to them.[89] And there were clashes with business groups, who usually wanted the enforcement of social standards left to market contracts or to the discretion of "voluntary" corporate efforts. Such tensions indicate that the administrative statebuilding efforts of the AALL really were partially independent of established class and political interests in the early twentieth century.

The Social Policies Promoted by the AALL

What sorts of social legislation did the AALL advocate, and when? The AALL's overall programmatic vision was perhaps best articulated by Henry Rogers Seager, who served as president in 1911 and 1912 and again in 1914 and 1915. Just before this period, Seager prepared his comprehensive lectures and book *Social Insurance: A Program of Social Reform.*[90] Even earlier, at the AALL's first annual meeting in December 1907, Seager presented an "Outline of a Program of Social Legislation with Special Reference to Wage-Earners," in which he called for old-age pensions; social insurance benefits to compensate workers and their dependents for industrial accidents, illness, death, and unemployment; improved workplace safety regulations, protective labor regulations for women, children, and unorganized male workers; regulated savings opportunities for workers; and labor exchanges and industrial training programs to prevent unemployment.[91] The AALL's overall program as detailed in the 1922 pamphlet *Labor Problems and Labor Legislation* was not much different from the outline first offered by Seager back in 1907.[92] Figure 9 indicates the scope of this mature program.

Beyond offering a comprehensive vision of desirable labor policies for the United States, the AALL set particular legislative priorities at each stage of its operations. At the start of each phase, investigations might be sponsored and sessions or conferences convened to highlight a particular social problem and to debate the merits of alternative policies for coping with it. Sometimes the AALL left matters at this—as, for example, in the discussions it sponsored about mothers' pensions and minimum wages.[93] But at other times the AALL launched full-blown legislative campaigns with varying degrees of persistence and success. The Association began its quest for legislation by campaigning from 1909 to 1913 for new laws dealing with industrial safety and with compensation for workmen injured in industrial accidents.[94] Buoyed by immediate results as state legislatures enacted many safety and compensation laws, the Association continued for many years to work for new and improved measures in these areas. (Its contributions to the nationwide movement to enact and improve workmen's compensation laws will be analyzed in Chapter 5.) Yet soon after these early efforts were under way, the AALL moved on to advocacy of fully state-enforced and partially publicly funded social insurance, hoping to buffer workingmen against hazards of unemployment and sickness.

The AALL was drawn into advocacy of measures to deal with unemployment after it sent a delegation to the International Conference on Unemployment in Paris in 1910. In 1911 AALL President Seager launched an American Section of the International Association on Unemployment. Chaired by Charles Henderson of the University of Chicago, this auxiliary of the AALL had 84 members by 1914. During that year—amid the national economic recession of 1913–1915—the auxiliary extended its operations by founding the Oregon Committee on Unemployment and the Massachusetts State Section on Unemployment, and by sponsoring the First National Conference on Unemployment in New York City, February 27–28.[95] Research efforts and field investigations followed, and soon led to the the AALL's first major program in this area, "A Practical Program for the Prevention of Unemployment in America," which called for a permanent public employment service, countercyclical public works projects, "regularization" of private employment by businesses, and public unemployment insurance.

When the "Practical Program" was published in the *American Labor Legislation Review* in June 1915, an "Introductory Note" by John Andrews indicated that a "bill establishing public employment insurance . . . is being drafted . . . for early introduction in state

Labor Problems
and
Labor Legislation

JOHN B. ANDREWS, Ph.D.

SECRETARY, AMERICAN ASSOCIATION FOR LABOR LEGISLATION
JOINT AUTHOR, HISTORY OF LABOR IN THE UNITED STATES
MEMBER, PRESIDENT'S CONFERENCE ON UNEMPLOYMENT
EDITOR, AMERICAN LABOR LEGISLATION REVIEW

(Second Edition Completely Revised)

American Association for Labor Legislation
131 East 23d Street, New York City
1922

Figure 9   Title and contents pages of *Labor Problems and Labor Legislation,* by John B. Andrews, 1922

Contents

legislatures."[96] Although this overstated what the national AALL was prepared to do, there were local AALL affiliates already at work, including the Massachusetts Committee on Unemployment. On January 4, 1916, this group introduced into the Massachusetts legislature the nation's first unemployment insurance bill, modeled on the British legislation of 1911.[97] This was part of a series of proposed measures to combat unemployment, which had become acute in Massachusetts during the recession of 1913–1915, arousing the concern of reformers, organized labor, politicians, and reformist businessmen in that state.[98] Massachusetts Governor Samuel W. McCall appointed a Special Commission on Social Insurance to look into the need for unemployment insurance along with old-age pensions and health insurance. In early 1917, this commission rendered a complexly divided report, which included a call for the state to create a permanent board of employment.[99] While suggesting voluntary efforts by businessmen to combat unemployment in the present, the Special Commission also cautiously endorsed the principle of public unemployment insurance for the future. But the Massachusetts recession was over by the time the Special Commission's report was delivered, and no new measures were enacted. After the effort for unemployment insurance faltered in Massachusetts, there was not much more AALL activity on this issue until the Association came out in support of the more regulatory and business-centered "industrial reserves" approach to out-of-work benefits that was recurrently debated in Wisconsin during the 1920s.[100] The 1916 Massachusetts episode was the high-water mark for AALL advocacy of European-style, partially publicly funded unemployment insurance for the United States.

During the Progressive period, the AALL's strongest and most sustained effort in social insurance came after the establishment at its December 1912 Annual Meeting of a Committee on Social Insurance charged "to study conditions impartially, to investigate the operation of existing systems of insurance, to prepare for needed legislation, and to stimulate intelligent discussion."[101] Appointed by AALL President Franklin Willoughby, the new Committee included the pioneering social insurance investigators Miles M. Dawson, Charles Richmond Henderson, Henry Rogers Seager, and Isaac Max Rubinow, along with the chairman, Edward T. Devine of the New York School of Philanthropy; Frederick L. Hoffman, a statistician at

Prudential Insurance; Henry J. Harris of the Division of Documents, Library of Congress; Carroll Doten of the Massachusetts Institute of Technology (replacing the briefly serving John Koren) representing the American Statistical Society; and AALL Secretary John Andrews.[102] Undertaking to guide the AALL's efforts on social insurance legislation, the Committee initially sponsored the first American Conference on Social Insurance in June 1913 in Chicago. "The time is ripe for the careful study of social insurance in America," declared Secretary Andrews, and this event included speeches and debates about social insurance in general, sickness insurance, insurance against unemployment, pensions for mothers, old-age insurance, and the "insurance aspects of workmen's compensation."[103]

Conducted over several years, the deliberations of the Committee on Social Insurance propelled the AALL away from a possible early interest in old-age pensions, and toward an all-out campaign from 1916 through 1919 in support of state-level health insurance bills. Henry Rogers Seager played a major role in focusing the AALL's agenda concerning social benefits. In 1907 and 1908 he wrote favorably about publicly funded noncontributory old-age pensions along the lines of those instituted in Denmark, New Zealand, and Great Britain, and seemed to be suggesting that the United States should soon move along similar lines.[104] By 1910, however, Seager had backed off from advocating public old-age pensions for the United States.[105] Ironically (as we shall see in Chapter 4), this happened just as the American Federation of Labor was indicating that it could accept noncontributory old-age pensions much more wholeheartedly than it could accept contributory social insurance of any sort. In Chapter 5, we shall explore why the AALL and other U.S. advocates of workingmen's social insurance refused to join with trade unions during the 1910s in a push for British-style old-age pensions.

Seager joined others on the AALL's Committee on Social Insurance in concluding during 1914 that sickness coverage was "the most urgent of the remaining social insurance problems."[106] The Committee drew up for discussion a series of "Standards" that should be met by any new legislation. These included the principle that "Sickness insurance should be compulsory [for wage earners below a certain income threshold] and be financed by joint contributions from employers, employees and the public" and the principle that "Benefits should include medical service, supplies, necessary nursing

and hospital care and cash benefits during the period of disability."[107]
By late 1915, the Committee had prepared a model health insurance
bill inspired primarily by German patterns, but named "health insurance" after the British 1911 program (rather than "sickness insurance" as the German program was called). Launched by the
AALL in 1916 with fanfare and an elaborate "Brief for Health
Insurance," the model bill called for compulsory insurance for all
manual employees earning less than twelve hundred dollars a year,
to be be financed two-fifths from employers' contributions, two-fifths
from workers' contributions, and one-fifth from public revenues.
Benefits were to include hospital treatment, medical and surgical
supplies, cash payments in lieu of lost wages, maternity coverage for
both female workers and the wives of male workers, and funeral
expenses for all covered workers.[108]

There were several reasons why the AALL arrived at the conclusion that priority should be placed on this sort of health insurance.
Perhaps the most important was that various investigations—one of
which is graphically summarized in Figure 10—convinced AALL
members and other reformers of the day that much preventable
poverty among wage earners and their families was due to sickness.
Coverage for costly medical services, along with cash benefits paid
while wage earners were recovering, would, the AALL believed, do
a great deal to ameliorate such "dependency" among wage earners
in the United States.

In addition, the AALL Committee on Social Insurance reasoned
that health insurance could function, as workers' compensation regulations supposedly did, to induce employers to maintain safe and
healthy workplaces, in order to reduce their liablity for tax contributions. Employees, too, would be motivated to work for healthier
workplaces and communities. Indeed, for the AALL, contributory
health insurance was intended to lead to "a comprehensive campaign
for health conservation" on the part of workers, employers, and the
public alike.[109] As Irving Fisher of Yale University summed up the
argument in his December 1916 presidential address to the AALL:

> We conclude that health insurance is needed in the United States
> in order to tide the workers over the grave emergencies incident
> to illness as well as in order to reduce illness itself, lengthen life,
> abate poverty, improve working power, raise the wage level, and
> diminish the causes of industrial discontent. It is not a panacea. It
> will not bring the millennium. But there is no other measure now

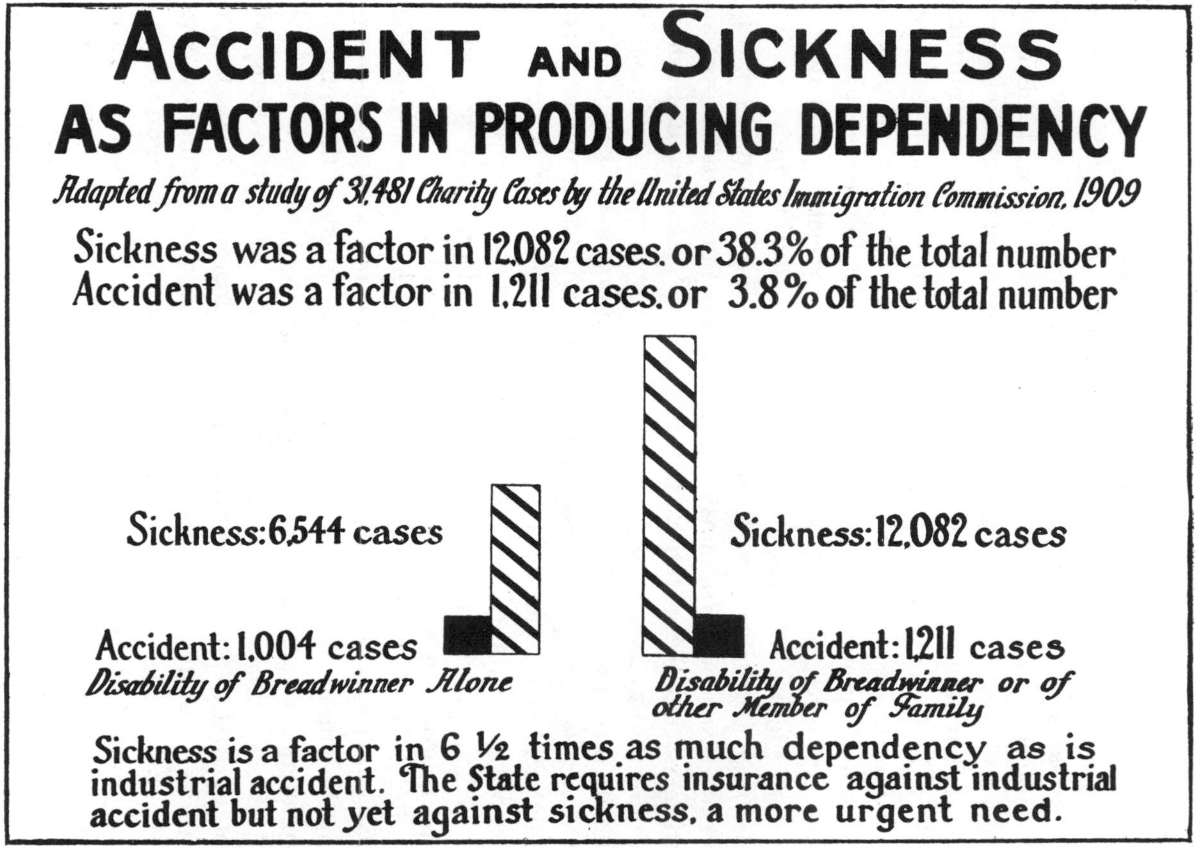

ACCIDENT AND SICKNESS AS FACTORS IN PRODUCING DEPENDENCY

Adapted from a study of 31,481 Charity Cases by the United States Immigration Commission. 1909

Sickness was a factor in 12,082 cases, or 38.3% of the total number
Accident was a factor in 1,211 cases, or 3.8% of the total number

Sickness: 12,082 cases

Sickness: 6,544 cases

Accident: 1,211 cases
Disability of Breadwinner or of other Member of Family

Accident: 1,004 cases
Disability of Breadwinner Alone

Sickness is a factor in 6 ½ times as much dependency as is industrial accident. The State requires insurance against industrial accident but not yet against sickness, a more urgent need.

Figure 10
Source: *American Labor Legislation Review* 6(2) (June 1916), p. 179.

before the public which equals the power of health insurance toward social regeneration.[110]

The AALL was supremely confident that its health insurance campaign would proceed just as smoothly and rapidly toward legislative successes as had the cross-state drive for workers' compensation. Writing in 1917, Isaac Rubinow wonderfully expressed this confidence. "Whether this legislative year will see actual health insurance legislation or not is after all not a matter of very great importance . . . I think even the most bitter opponents of the health insurance movement are willing to admit that the best they can achieve is a certain postponement."[111] An evolutionist faith in the inevitability of social progress through successive and interrelated governmental reforms buoyed the spirits of AALL leaders during the 1910s. The *American Labor Legislation Review* repeatedly published maps showing health insurance programs sweeping across European nations; and the Association concluded that the United States would inevitably follow the transnational pattern.[112] After workmen's compensation, health insurance was "the next great step in social legislation." These ringing words appeared as a slogan on the AALL's stationery during the health insurance drive.[113] Accepting the advice of its Committee on Social Insurance, the AALL of the Progressive period staked its prestige and resources on this particular effort to achieve public social provision for workingmen and their families.

By the early 1920s, however, it was clear that governmentally regulated and funded social insurance was not soon to be enacted in the United States. And the AALL lost much of the spirit and momentum that had propelled it during the 1910s. To be sure, the *American Labor Legislation Review* continued to appear along with other AALL publications; and John Andrews and Irene Osgood Andrews continued to run the national office and communicate with experts, legislators, and associations around the nation on behalf of new and improved labor laws. But the Association ceased to grow, and rarely launched its own new legislative initiatives during the 1920s. It continued to pursue established agendas and sometimes endorsed movements led by others, such as the effort of the Wisconsin Industrial Commission to attain unemployment reserves and the state-level campaigns for old-age pensions waged by organized labor and the Fraternal Order of Eagles.

The AALL of the 1920s no longer engaged—or so exclusively expressed—the civic energies of a range of prominent social scientists. No doubt the failure of the health insurance drive of 1916–1919 was deeply discouraging to many who had given so much time to the effort, especially since the nation entered a period of reaction against many social reforms and statebuilding efforts after World War I. During the 1920s, too, American universities and academic professions were increasingly led by more specialized professionals, who had diverse opportunities to offer technical advice to public agencies or large corporations.[114] The giants of the turn of the century, the men who had founded the fledgling modern social science professions of the United States, and who had maintained a broad, reformist perspective on industrial society in the process, were dying or retiring. The AALL lost momentum as this inevitable generational change proceeded, becoming less of an innovative social movement for reform, and more of a "clearing house" for publication and lobbying revolving around the person of Secretary John Andrews. Often preoccupied with defending previous gains such as workmen's compensation laws, the AALL of the 1920s did little innovative thinking of its own. And even where social insurance was concerned, it became but one advocacy group among many on the national scene.

Conclusion

Reform-minded American intellectuals, especially from the ranks of early social scientists and staff professionals employed by state and federal bureaus of labor statistics, participated avidly in transnational discussions about labor regulations and "workingmen's insurance" around the turn of the twentieth century. Carefully researched books explored German, British, and other foreign precedents. Early American investigators of workingmen's insurance were especially attracted to the possible "ethical" uses of governmental power to buffer workingmen and their families from the disruptive effects of capitalist industrialization. Banding together with other reformers, they formed the American Association for Labor Legislation to investigate social conditions in industry, devise model legislative proposals, and lobby legislatures and civic voluntary associations in favor of their enactment. Throughout the 1910s, the AALL, under the enthusiastic collective leadership of a network of reformist academics, was at the forefront of advocacy for general labor regulations and social insurance in the United States.

From 1916 through 1919, the AALL engaged above all in spearheading the nation-spanning movement for state-level health insurance, using the political tactics that I have analyzed. Had this legislative campaign succeeded, even in one or a few states, the United States would indeed have taken "the next great step" toward a European-style welfare state, in which benefits for employed workers and their dependents were at the heart of partially tax-supported social provision. But as we know, health insurance bills were defeated in the early-twentieth-century United States, just as British-style unemployment insurance failed to make headway either in Massachusetts or elsewhere. Of the AALL-supported legislative campaigns during the 1910s, only those about industrial safety and compensation for workers' injuries were successful.

In Chapter 5, we shall explore *why* virtually all of the AALL's early proposals for general protective labor laws and social insurance failed to become law in the early twentieth century; and we shall learn why the AALL declined to push for noncontributory old-age pensions during the 1910s. Before turning to that discussion, however, let us examine the policy orientations of U.S. trade unions in this watershed period. The AALL expected unions to follow its lead toward new public policies designed "for the good" of industrial workingmen and their dependents. But union leaders had their own ideas about what measures were best for wage earners.

CHAPTER 4

Help for the "Army of Labor"?
Trade Unions and Social Legislation

Because the reform-minded social scientists of the American Association for Labor Legislation (AALL) believed that rational arguments would persuade fellow elites and the general middle-class public about the need for new labor laws, they were not prepared to engage in popular political mobilization. AALL members did, however, expect to provide enlightened and unchallenged leadership for one popular group, namely organized labor. AALL founder Adna F. Weber lamented that throughout the nineteenth century "the trade-union men, through whose initiative most . . . labor laws were placed on the statute books, did not always have the benefit of . . . [professional] advice, and a great deal of that legislation has been crude and ineffective, and has broken down when tested in the courts."[1] Weber cited the fifty-year-old campaign of American organized labor for eight-hour statutes as the best example of this sad situation. "Professional men" were not sympathetic to this legislative objective of workers, and so "the shorter day has been treated as a plaything of politics upheld solely as a bid for the 'labor vote' without any real comprehension of its significance."[2] By the early twentieth century, however, the reformist professionals of the AALL were ready to provide "guidance and advice" to the trade unions. Writing in 1907, Weber seemed to take it for granted that "trade union men" would follow the lead of "professional men" into a better future through governmental policies in the public interest.

American reformers looked approvingly at contemporary political alliances between reformers and trade union men in Britain. In that country, certain trade unionists joined elite and middle-class reformers in 1899 to form the National Committee of Organized Labour on Old Age Pensions, which called for pensions for all needy British citizens over age 65. The same year the mainstream British labor federation, the Trades Union Congress (TUC), endorsed need-based old-age pensions to begin at age 60, and soon the fledgling Labour Representation Commmittee took up the cause as well. Many of the demands of this cross-class campaign for social legislation were met in the British old-age pension law enacted by the Liberals in 1908.[3] In addition, trade unions and Labour representatives in Parliament acquiesced in a series of labor-market regulations and social insurance laws initiated by the Board of Trade and enacted by the governing Liberals between 1906 and 1914.[4] By the end of World War I, the newly ascendant Labour Party had become—along with the mainstream labor federation, the Trades Union Congress (TUC)— the chief supporter of expanded public social provision in Britain.[5] During the first two decades of the century, in short, British reformers and the Liberals had successfully drawn many TUC leaders and Labour politicians into advocacy for a British welfare state for workers and their dependents. Reformist professionals in the United States wanted to be able to do something similar during this watershed period.

U.S. Reformers and Trade Union Leaders at Cross-Purposes

But relations with the U.S. trade unions did not develop as American advocates of workingmen's insurance hoped—especially not at the national level, the level at which the AALL leadership preferred to form alliances with other associational leaderships. To its chagrin, the AALL had to face increasingly vociferous and visible opposition from AFL President Samuel F. Gompers and other national union leaders who pushed the American Federation of Labor into official stances against precisely those contributory social insurance measures and labor regulations on which the AALL placed priority. To be sure (as we shall see below), state-level AFL federations often took more favorable positions on social legislation than the national trade union leaders. And the national AFL itself called for federal noncontributory old-age pensions. Nevertheless, the opposition of the dominant forces within the national AFL to major types of social policy cut off key possibilities during the 1910s for united drives by reformers and organized labor toward a paternalist American welfare state.

The National AFL Opposes Social Insurance

In 1916, AFL President Samuel F. Gompers testified emotionally against social insurance. The occasion was a congressional hearing about a bill to establish an official commission to look into the need for national unemployment insurance. Dismissing the other witnesses at the hearing as those "professors, insurance actuaries, research workers and [labor bureau] commissioners . . . [who] each in turn gave his or her judgement of the bugs [that is, workers] that they had studied microscopically," Gompers insisted that trade unions and their wage demands alone would be enough to protect the entire American working class. He denounced proposals for social insurance and other labor legislation as attempts "to rivet the masses of labor to the juggernaut of government."[6] The AFL's official organ, the *American Federationist,* immediately reprinted Gompers's lengthy congressional testimony under the title "Voluntary Social Insurance vs. Compulsory: Shall the Toilers Surrender Their Freedom for a Few Crumbs?"[7] The journal offered a stream of negative commentary in response to "a persistent, concerted attempt on the part of certain associations and individuals to urge the adoption of compulsory social insurance, both by the federal government and by state governments."[8] Similarly, national AFL conventions throughout the 1910s refused to endorse, and often severely criticized, plans for contributory, government-administered social insurance that were being publicly discussed by reformers, commissions, and legislatures.

The national AFL leadership did not accept public unemployment insurance as a remedy for joblessness, calling instead for actions by trade unions in conjunction with other sorts of governmental policies.[9] The Federation endorsed the provision of out-of-work benefits by its constituent unions, characteristically claiming in 1916, "We are not unmindful of the needs of the workers and of the ills from which they suffer; our unions have, to a large extent, provided for social insurance in cases of sickness, unemployment, superannuation and death."[10] Studies by labor statisticians and reformers during the Progressive Era showed that such voluntary union social benefits were far from adequate even for trade union members, let alone for the vast numbers of unorganized and predominantly unskilled workers of the day.[11] AFL leaders may have resented these studies. Yet the fate of the unemployed did concern them, because "there must be an appreciation of the real menace which a body of unemployed workers constitutes to the standards of wages, working conditions, and living of those who are employed."[12] Trade union demands for eight-hour days would, the AFL leaders felt, spread work more widely among people who might otherwise be unemployed. In addition, the expansion of public works projects during recessions would allow "the general public . . . [to] mitigate the evils of unemployment without devising any elaborate program or social justice or economic reform."[13] At the height of an economic emergency, the national AFL was even willing to countenance straightforward public relief: the 1915 AFL Convention resolved "That the Executive Committee be instructed to prepare measures to be introduced into Congress, state legislatures and municipalities which shall provide for the erection of buildings in which unemployed may find lodging during the winter months and in which they shall be supplied with nourishing meals while unemployed."[14] But unemployment insurance still was not acceptable to the national AFL leadership.

During the nationwide, AALL-led campaign for health insurance from 1916 to 1920, the AFL under Gompers still refused to relent in its opposition to social insurance. At the AFL's November 1916 Convention, the Executive Council denounced the health insurance bills being introduced by reformers in various states, arguing that these "measures themselves and the people who present them represent that class of society that is very desirous of doing things for the workers and establishing institutions for them that will prevent their doing things for themselves and maintaining their own institutions" of voluntary social benefits.[15] Similarly, at a December 1916 Conference on Social Insurance held in Washington, DC, under the auspices of the Federal Bureau of Labor Statistics of the Department of Labor, Gompers spoke against "compulsory social insurance" and Grant Hamilton of the AFL's Legislative Committee delivered a detailed brief against health insurance, maintaining that "it would build up a bureaucracy that would have some degree of control or authority over all of the workers of the State."[16]

By the time of the 1918 AFL Convention, there was recognition that many state labor federations were endorsing health insurance proposals. Nevertheless, although the Convention advocated the extension of workmen's compensation to cover industrial diseases, it defeated a motion from the International Ladies' Garment Workers in support of a "comprehensive national system of Social Insurance." Instead, the 1918 Convention set up an investigatory committee to look into the advantages and disadvantages of health insurance, and also charged it to investigate "the financial resources of the persons and organizations promoting this scheme and what relation they may have with those interests who are opposed to the best interests of the Labor movement."[17] Faced with continuing disagreements about health insurance within the labor movement, AFL Conventions for the following years delayed and equivocated, until the nationwide movement for such legislation died down.[18]

The best summary of Samuel Gompers's passionate reasoning against all forms of workingmen's insurance appeared in a January 1917 article in the *American Federationist* called "Not Even Compulsory Benevolence Will Do."[19] This article commented upon differences between insurance advocates and AFL unionists at the 1916 Conference on Social Insurance mentioned above. According to Gompers, the reformers "wanted to do something *for wage-earners* to relieve their suffering and need. The other group [that is, the AFL] wanted to do something *for itself*, to solve its own problems and to establish itself in a position to take care of the emergencies of life." Gompers, of course, took the trade union perspective, maintaining that "social insurance can not remove or prevent poverty. It does not get at the causes of social injustice. The only agency that does is the organized labor movement" with its emphasis on higher wages and voluntary social benefits.

Gompers emphasized two ways in which social insurance would fundamentally harm American workers. First, it would subordinate them to a state they might not control: "Whoever has control of this new agency acquires some degree of control over the workers. There is nothing to guarantee control over that agency to the employed. It may also be controlled by employers." Secondly (in an interesting argument that has been too little noted by historians), Gompers criticized workingmen's insurance for its departure from universal principles of citizenship. "Compulsory social insurance," he wrote, "is in its essence undemocratic. The first step in establishing social insurance is to divide people into two groups—those eligible for benefits and those considered capable to care for themselves. The division is based upon wage-earning capacity. This governmental regulation tends to fix the citizens of the country into classes, and a long established insurance system would tend to make these classes rigid." Although acknowledging their good motives, Gompers called upon the reformers of the AALL and beyond to change their fundamental policy objectives. If "those who really have the welfare of wage-earners at heart will turn their activities and their influence toward securing for wage-earners the opportunity to organize, there will be no problems, no suffering and no need that will necessitate the consideration of benevolent assistance of a compulsory character," setting workers apart from other citizens.

Labor Regulations for Men are Ruled Out, Too

If they could take scant comfort from AFL pronouncements about social insurance, AALL reformers were equally disappointed in the evolution of the national Federation's stance toward protective labor legislation.[20] From its earliest years, the AFL endorsed American labor's long-standing aspiration for a universal eight-hour day. And it was not until the middle of the second decade of the twentieth century that the AFL formally ruled out legislative means as a way to reach this goal for all workers.

The history of AFL positions was complex. Over the years, the AFL never ceased to campaign for federal and state legislation limiting the hours of workers employed by governments and government contractors and subcontractors. Maximum-hour laws were also endorsed for particularly vulnerable categories of workers, especially women and children; and at the height of the Progressive Era in 1913, the Federation seemed to be cautiously favorable toward minimum-wage laws covering unorganized women workers.[21] Meanwhile, the Federation consistently opposed minimum-wage statutes for adult males, declaring that if "it were proposed in this country to vest authority in any tribunal to fix by law wages for men, Labor would protest by any means in its power. Through organization the wages of men can and will be maintained at a higher minimum than they would be if fixed by legal enactment."[22] From the 1890s onward, too, the AFL preferred to work toward the ideal of an eight-hour day for all workers not through legislative actions or general strikes but through but union campaigns in one industry after another. Even so, the national AFL for many years did not officially rule out eight-hour statutes covering all workers—and, indeed, in the late 1890s the Federation defended eight-hour laws that were enacted and then challenged in the states of Utah and Colorado.[23] There were always many groups within the AFL that continued in the tradition of the Knights of Labor to fight for general eight-hour statutes.

By the 1910s, labor federations in several western states wanted to extend eight-hour laws covering women into general statutory limits for all workers. At the 1913 Convention of the AFL in Seattle, such western unionists appeared to gain the national Federation's endorsement when a resolution was passed declaring that where "women's eight-hour laws already exist an agitation should immediately begin for the enactment of general eight-hour laws."[24] But during the following year, AFL President Gompers spoke out against general eight-hour laws, infuriating unionists in California, Oregon, and Washington, who had to watch business interests put quotes from Gompers on billboards and on pamphlets distributed during successful efforts to defeat eight-hour laws by popular referenda in those states.

At the 1914 AFL Convention, the issue was fully joined in a lengthy, acrimonious debate.[25] Resolutions reaffirming what was thought to be the 1913 position—in favor of following upon the attainment of state-level eight-hour statutes for women with additional campaigns for general eight-hour laws—were presented and passionately argued by delegates from the California and Washington State Federations of Labor, the International Assocation of Machinists, and the International Union of Timber Workers. But the AFL's Committee on Resolutions offered a substitute, saying that "the question of the regulation of wages and the hours of labor should be undertaken through trade union activity, and not made subjects of laws through legislative enactments, excepting in so far as such regulations affect and govern the employment of women and minors, health and morals; and employment by Federal, state, and municipal government."[26] In a convention which, as always, was dominated by representatives of large international craft unions loyal to Gompers, the position of the Resolutions Committee carried by 11,237 votes in favor to 8,107 votes against, with 607 abstaining.[27] At the 1915 AFL Convention, the matter was argued again in response to motions favoring legislative action on the eight-hour day submitted by representatives of the International Machinists and the Illinois State Federation of Labor. Again, however, the Committee on Resolutions prevailed with a restatement of the official AFL endorsement of trade union action as the means for attaining the eight-hour day.[28]

In his presidential address to the American Association for Labor Legislation in 1915, Henry Rogers Seager spoke with dismay about this "reactionary" AFL reversal of American organized labor's historic position on hour laws.[29] Seager urged the AFL to reconsider, arguing that the method of leaving wages and hours to union-won trade agreements alone "takes no account of the great majority of adult male wage-earners who are still unorganized and will probably long remain unorganized . . . There is no sharp dividing line between women wage-earners and men wage-earners as regards their helplessness in the face of adverse industrial conditions."[30] But the national AFL did not reconsider its position, and continued to oppose legislative routes to shorter hours for adult men. Two decades later, looking back on developments from 1935, the labor historian Elizabeth Brandeis would write that this "reversal of position by the A.F. of L. . . . effectively put an end to the movement for general enforceable hour legislation for men and even reduced the amount of legislation sought for special groups."[31]

A Break in the Pattern: The AFL Endorses Old-Age Pensions

Analysts of the national AFL's stands during the early twentieth century typically overgeneralize its hostility toward early welfare-state legislation.[32] They fail to notice that there was one part of "workingmen's insurance" that the U.S. labor federation was prepared to endorse—namely national, noncontributory pensions for needy elderly American citizens. Reformist elites in the United States could not get the national AFL's support for contributory social insurance of any kind, including contributory old-age insurance of the German variety. But had the AALL not backed away from advocating noncontributory old-age pensions during the 1910s, American elite reformers could have joined forces with the AFL in a national Progressive Era campaign for British-style old-age pensions. Despite what many scholars have claimed, the failure of this cross-class alliance to come together in the pre–World War I United States, as it did in Britain, cannot be laid at the feet of the American trade unions.

To be sure, the American Federation of Labor did not immediately accept old-age pensions when they were proposed in its internal debates, probably because its leadership at first identified this idea with the Socialist minority in the federation. At the 1902 AFL Convention, two resolutions favoring national, noncontributory, needs-based old-age pensions were presented, one by Delegate Victor L. Berger, a Socialist from the Milwaukee Federated Trades Council, and the other by Delegate William J. Kelly of the Pittsburgh Central Labor Council. Berger's resolution was phrased in Marxist, class-conflict language, and called very precisely for "a bill which will secure to every wage-worker in the United States who has earned no more than $1,000 average wages per year, a pension of no less than $12 per month at the age of 60, and thereafter for the rest of his or her natural life."[33] Except for the means test, these terms were very close to those of basic Civil War pensions at the time.[34] Delegate Kelly's resolution was more general and evocative of American moral traditions:

> *Whereas,* It is a well-known and as equally humiliating fact that in this age of so-called civilization, when a man gets old and worn out—it may be by many years of useful but so often illy requited toil—he finds it hard and often impossible to get work, which failure tends sometimes to reduce him to pauperism, to an object of charity and to the poorhouse; therefore be it

> *Resolved,* That the American Federation of Labor, in convention assembled, shall fully use its best offices to have Congress enact an old-age pension law that will do for the aged who have given so much to the industrial struggle what the soldier's pension is designed to do for the old soldier.[35]

Following the usual AFL routine, both of these proposals were referred to the Committee on Resolutions, which later reported unfavorably on them.[36]

The resolutions thus died; but not until a bit of debate had occurred, sprinkled with references to precedents in Civil War pensions. According to the Convention record, "Delegate Wheeler expressed surprise that the committee should oppose a proposition of this kind" and "Delegate Sherman . . . said that every man and woman was entitled to recognition for what they have done for the Government. All work as one army to make the country what it is. The old age system is now the mark for trusts and corporations, to relegate old men to the scrap pile. What are we going to do with old age if we do not co-operate?" But in reply "Delegate Lennon said: It will be the working people who will have to pay for the old age pensions, as they are already paying for pensions to war veterans. Why saddle ourselves with a new tax? He compared this country to the countries of Europe. Working people do not want charity from the government—they want justice. He wanted less government by the people and more government by the unions."[37] A few more brief comments followed. But knowing that the decision of the Committee on Resolutions could not be overturned, no one called for a vote; and soon President Gompers moved on to the next order of business.

Victor Berger was embroiled in the AFL's ongoing squabbles between Socialists and pure-and-simple trade unionists, and he was not a man to give up. Later representing the International Typographical Union (or, in 1907, the Wisconsin State Federation of Labor), Berger resubmitted his old-age pension resolution to the AFL Conventions in 1904, 1905, 1906, and 1907.[38] Each year, however, the Committee on Resolutions reported against the Berger resolution, and each year the Committee's position was upheld—until 1907, when a new twist occurred. This time, Delegate William B. Wilson of Pennsylvania from the United Mine Workers intervened to offer an amendment to the usual report of the Committee on Resolutions against the Berger proposal, saying: "We [the AFL] favor the principle of an old-age pension, and advise that the Executive Council be instructed to make an investigation of methods by which that end can be attained under our laws, and report the same to the next convention."[39] After another delegate tried unsuccessfully to have the AFL simply endorse state-level efforts on behalf of old-age pension legislation, the Wilson amendment was accepted by the Convention.

At the 1908 AFL Convention, President Gompers—having been

commissioned by the Executive Council to look into old-age pensions—presented a lengthy report, which principally described old-age pension laws or debates as they then existed in Austria, Belgium, Denmark, Iceland, France, Germany, Italy, New Zealand, New South Wales and Victoria in Australia, and England. When he came to the issue of "the advisability of recommending legislation for old age pensions in the United States," Gompers was cautious. Significantly, he did not denounce the idea of old-age pensions, as he was wont to do with most proposals for social legislation. But he warned that it "would require many years of constant effort to even get this subject seriously considered in the many states of our country, when we take into consideration the stupendous difficulties that have been and are necessary to overcome in order to obtain legislation for the workers of a much more moderate character."[40] Gompers discussed the likely constitutional objections that might be raised to prevent, or judicially overturn, old-age pension laws at either the state or the federal level of government. The Committee on Resolutions then considered the matter of public old-age pensions, and later in the 1908 Convention endorsed the idea in principle and asked that the Executive Council be authorized to draft a bill to be introduced either in the federal Congress or in the states, or both, depending on where it was decided old-age pensions could be "most readily secured."[41] Tactics, not principles, were to govern further AFL consideration of old-age pension legislation.

By 1909, the leadership of the national AFL had decided that the federal government was the place to fight for old-age pensions. At that Convention, the Committee on Resolutions sponsored "an exceedingly adroit draft" of a bill to create an "Old Age Home Guard of the United States Army."[42] This bill had been prepared for the Executive Council by William B. Wilson of the United Mine Workers, who was also a Democratic Congressman from Pennsylvania. Obviously, Wilson's proposal for federal old-age pensions contained many allusions to Civil War pensions. Yet as Wilson explained to his fellow delegates in his lengthy, legalistic "Brief," the bill was also carefully designed to get around a myriad of possible constitutional obstacles in the U.S. federal system. Granted that old-age pensions might be justified as part of the constitutional powers of the states, Wilson nevertheless argued that there "is at least an element of doubt in it" and argued that the "difficulty of securing favorable legislation in 46 separate states is so apparent that it only has to be mentioned to be understood." Instead, Wilson felt that it would be easier to justify old-age pensions through the federal Congress's undoubted constitutional authority "to raise and support armies." "From every point of view," he concluded, "the method herewith proposed seems to be the most feasible. It places the pensioner in the direct employment of the government; . . . it enumerates the duties to be performed . . . and stipulates the compensation to be received for the service required."[43]

According to Wilson's bill, all needy American citizens over age 65 would become "privates" in the Old Age Home Guard and receive, depending on their degree of need, up to "one hundred and twenty dollars per annum, to be paid in quarterly installments, as pensions are now by law paid."[44] These elderly privates were called upon to report yearly to the Secretary of War about "patriotic sentiment" in their communities, but Wilson's bill carefully spelled out that no punishments would follow if they did not so report.[45] Significantly, too, his bill stipulated that "persons related as husband and wife shall not both be eligible for enlistment" at the same time. Following the precedent of Civil War pensions, Wilson proposed an old-age pension for elderly male breadwinners and then, after their deaths, a survivors' benefit for their widows.

The 1909 AFL Convention warmly endorsed Congressman Wilson's proposal for the "Old Age Home Guard," and he introduced the bill in the House of Representatives on December 14, 1909, and again on April 11, 1911.[46] Congress did not pass any old-age pension bill, however, and (for reasons we shall explore in the next chapter) the idea of such pensions did not catch fire in the U.S. public debates during the Progressive Era. Nevertheless, it is worth underlining that the national AFL continued to support the principle of noncontributory and need-based old-age pensions. Further explicit endorsements of old-age pensions for all workers came at the AFL Conventions in 1910, 1911, 1912, 1913, and 1914.[47] Thereafter, probably because there was no warm welcome for the old-age pension idea in Congress or in public debates, the AFL's interest in a national old-age pension law declined. At the 1916 Convention, delegates from the West Virginia State Federation, the Ohio Valley Trades Assembly, and the Amalgamated Association of Iron, Tin, and Steel Workers tried to get the national AFL Executive Council to reintroduce an old-age pension bill in Congress. More significantly, these delegates also asked the Council "to urge upon state branches that they take similar action with regard to their State Legislatures, and assist them in so doing." This resolution was deflected into further study by the Executive Council, and it was not until the 1920s that the AFL endorsed the principle of state-level old-age pensions.[48] Yet there was never any repudiation of support for old-age pension legislation by the national AFL, analogous to its repudiation of hours laws for men.

As we shall see later, the locus of organized labor's activity on old-age pensions in the later teens and the 1920s simply shifted downward to the state labor federations.[49] We can therefore conclude that American organized labor expressed steady official support from 1909 onward for the principle of pensions "for the poor and needy who, during their active years as wage-earners, have contributed to the nation's wealth and prosperity, and are no longer able to do so."[50] Efforts by the national AFL leadership to act on this principle were, however, concentrated in the years between 1909 and 1914, and enthusiasm waned when the Federation's support for national old-age pensions failed to obtain a favorable response from other actors in the U.S. polity at the height of the Progressive Era.

Explaining the Policy Preferences of the National Federation

Why did the nationally federated trade unions in the United States refuse to support reformers' efforts to achieve contributory insurance and general labor regulations? A comparison of the American Federation of Labor to the British Trade Unions Congress (TUC) suggests that the reasons lay to some degree in the characteristics of American unions, but mostly in the experiences those unions had within the U.S. polity around the turn of the century. The political experiences of the U.S. trade unions and their members can also help us understand why the AFL endorsed noncontributory old-age pensions at the national level between 1909 and 1914.

Two Union Movements: Differences and Similarities

The American Federation Labor was founded in 1886 through a revolt by craft unions against the Knights of Labor, a highly politicized association and would-be "universal brotherhood of labor" that did not accept the autonomy of particular trade unions.[51] Unlike its predecessor, the AFL always respected the autonomy of its constituent labor bodies, which initially were mostly locally rooted craft unions and later included many bureaucratized national (or "international") unions that blended craft and industrial principles of organization.[52] As the labor historian Andrew Thomson explains an important difference between the AFL and the British TUC:

> In Britain,. . . the main centers of unionism were in the staple industries of the Industrial Revolution, serving not only national but international markets . . . In the United States, the reverse was true. There were important national product market industries, notably in coal, clothing, glass, and the foundry trades, where unionism was well represented, but for the most part unionism's greatest strenth was in the local product market industries of building, newspaper printing, street railways, baking, and local haulage.[53]

Although certain truly industrial unions, notably the Mine Workers and the Brewery Workers, came over to the AFL from the Knights, by 1910 only about 16 percent of AFL members were organized into industrial unions, which tended to be oriented toward expansion into the unskilled labor force.[54] In comparison, at this time over 60 percent of British workers organized under the Trades Union Congress (TUC) were members of industrial unions.

Certain analysts of social policies have argued that craft unions found it easier to protect the interests of their skilled-worker members through workplace and market actions; thus such unions would not see as much need as industrial unions to work for legislative solutions.[55] This argument does help to make sense of the greater propensity of the British TUC to support public social provision. It also helps explain why the AFL's strongest industrial affiliate, the United Mine Workers (UMW), was the center within the American trade union movement of early agitation for public social provision. As we have seen, delegates from the Mine Workers to AFL Conventions were among the pioneering advocates of AFL endorsements of old-age pensions. Moreover, the Mine Workers conducted official campaigns for pensions in many states during the 1910s and 1920s.[56] The Secretary-Treasurer of the Mine Workers, AFL Vice-President

William Green, was a vocal advocate of contributory social insurance, breaking with President Gompers to offer support to the AALL's drive for public health insurance for workers.[57] Still, one cannot argue that *only* industrial unionists supported public social provision in the early-twentieth-century United States. We have learned that delegates from craft unions, not just leaders of Mine Workers, were among those who supported old-age pension legislation within national AFL debates from 1902 onward.[58]

Was it, perhaps, also the case that British unionists were simply a lot stronger than U.S. trade unionists in this period, thus making the British unions more inclined to work through politics? "Union density"—the proportion of the total labor force organized—was consistently lower in the United States, because fewer workers were available for organization in a country that still had a much higher proportion of its workforce in agriculture.[59] Nevertheless, during the respective period of greatest social-policy innovation in the two nations—1906 to 1911 in Britain and 1910 to 1920 in the United States—the union densities were reasonably similar, ranging from 9 to 16 percent in both countries. And union densities were very similar between Britain and such highly industrialized and urbanized U.S. states as Massachusetts.

As for the proportions of total national electorates that the two union movements could potentially mobilize politically, we must of course consider that only about half of British union members could vote under the male householder franchise that prevailed until 1918. In contrast, virtually all American male unionists were eligible to vote. Taking this and other factors into account, one scholar has estimated that the TUC included about 10 percent of the British electorate in 1906, while the AFL included about 5 percent of the total American electorate (voters plus others eligible to vote). U.S. trade unionists appear, moreover, to have accounted for about 8 percent of those who actually voted in the 1908 election.[60] Although this was a period of electoral demobilization in the United States, organized workers, disproportionately skilled, still turned out for elections more often than the unorganized.[61] What is more, union voters were much more weighty in the industrialized states and localities. Sheer numerical voter potential does not seem to have put the U.S. trade union movement at much of a disadvantage compared to the British movement before World War I.

Neither the American AFL nor the British TUC had anything close to majority power at the time early modern social policies were debated in the two national polities. Both movements had to enter into alliances with non-working-class forces to make headway in extralocal politics. Important questions thus remain to be answered. As minority forces, how much political clout could British and American labor muster—to contribute to the achievement of their own political objectives and to carry their weight in alliances? What were the objectives that these trade union movements pursued in politics? And how and why did those objectives change over time?

Divergent Experiences in Politics

During the 1880s, the British TUC and the American AFL, and their constituent unions, used a mixture of workplace and political strategies to improve the lot of wage-earners under capitalism.[62] Both trade union movements sought legislation such as restrictions on child and sweated labor, arbitration boards to promote union recognition and avert strikes, and legalization of the eight-hour day. Another shared legislative objective was the modification of common-law "conspiracy" doctrines that had for decades been used against unions by the British and the U.S. courts; and after this objective was at least partially achieved, both the British and U.S. unions continued to worry about reversing adverse judicial decisions. Despite similarities in their initial political orientations and continuing worries about the courts, however, the British and U.S. trade union movements reaped contrasting rewards from politics, spurring the British movement to plunge in more deeply, while the American movement, at the level of the national Federation, retreated toward market unionism and collective bargaining. Experiences in two different national political systems explain much about the divergence of British and U.S. trade unionists after the 1880s.

In Britain, mobilizing politically to win victories through Parliament was, of course, difficult for the unions, yet ultimately proved rewarding. Like the American AFL, the British TUC confederation was loose and decentralized; its leadership was originally cautious about potentially divisive political involvements; and many British union members could not vote even after the 1867 enfranchisement

of working-class male householders. Still, English workers traditionally had a certain political class consciousness because they were
originally excluded from the franchise and had to fight for political
rights as a class.[63] Furthermore, the British unions were spurred into
politics by the threats they felt in common from laws and judicial
rulings to which they were all simultaneously subject in the unitary,
nonfederal polity. In response to the convening in 1867 of an official
commission on union matters, the British unions created the TUC,
called upon the working classes to organize for political objectives,
began systematically questioning parliamentary candidates, and set
up a national committee to lobby and monitor Parliament.[64] Soon
after the broadening of the franchise in 1867, Parliament passed
laws between 1871 and 1876 to reverse adverse judicial rulings and
ensure the unions basic institutional security.[65]

After the 1870s, the British unions for a time rested content with
their existing arrangements for political involvement, and they gradually gained more direct representation through working-class MPs
and other sympathizers in the Liberal Party. Then the rise of "new
unions" and moderate socialists, employer offensives against unions,
and a worsening judicial climate all helped bring about the establishment in 1899–1900 of the Labour Representation Committee, pre-
cursor to the Labour Party. But it was still not clear that the British
labor movement as a whole would go much further into politics—
until the Taff Vale decision of 1901 aroused the unions, all of whom
were threatened by this nationally binding ruling by the judicially
supreme Law Lords, a decision that rendered union assets liable to
seizure in damage suits filed by employers who were hurt economically by normal union strike tactics.[66] After Taff Vale, individual
unions and the LRC raised new levies for national political activities,
and renewed emphasis was placed on electing Labour or "Lib-Lab"
MPs, as well as on "pledging" other MPs, especially Liberals, to
support legislation overturning Taff Vale.

Labour Party forces themselves were helped to gain a substantial
early foothold by the structure of the British polity. A useful contrast
can be drawn to the fate of Socialists in the U.S. polity. As Richard
Oestreicher explains, because of winner-take-all elections, large
congressional districts, and one-party dominance in most areas of
the country after 1896, a

minority showing in an American election produce[d] no seats, no officeholders. The 6 percent Socialist vote in 1912 gave the American Socialist party no seats, no officeholders. In December 1910 the British Labour party received 6.4 percent of the national vote and elected forty-two members of Parliament . . . In a parliamentary system, especially if the major parties were relatively balanced as in Britain, local majorities [or pluralities] could give minor parties policymaking leverage in Parliament.[67]

More important than the direct leverage gained by the early Labour Party, the British unions and the LRC entered into explicit political alliances with the Liberal Party prior to the 1906 and 1910 elections, both of which prominently featured programmatic issues of vital interest to labor. The Liberals swept the 1906 election and won more narrowly in 1910; and in both elections Labour forces and Labour-supported Liberals also did well. The Liberal-Labour alliances triumphed electorally across class lines especially in the industrial centers of Britain, which were dispersed across many parliamentary districts, and not as concentrated in large cities as in the United States.[68]

British labor's fuller entry into national parliamentary politics after 1900 was therefore fruitful. The unions were able to work together in ways that led to quick electoral payoffs. The explicit political alliance with the Liberals led at once to the reversal of Taff Vale's consequences in the 1906 Trade Disputes Act, and to the enactment of certain pieces of social legislation, including old-age pensions, for which unions had previously agitated. All of this reconfirmed British labor's historically rooted sense that good things could be done through parliamentary action. This sense, along with short-term needs to continue working with the Liberals, allowed most of the unions and most of the Labour MPs to go along with the enactment of welfare-state measures about which they were not very enthusiastic—especially contributory social insurance—and to participate in implementing these measures once enacted. The British unions could cooperate with a strong administrative elite committed to "rationalizing" labor markets and overcoming the worst exploitative excesses of capitalism. The upshot of the policy orientations mutually worked out during the Liberal-Labour alliance of 1906–1914 was that, later—after World War I switched the relations between Liberals and Labour, making the latter dominant—British labor would become the chief proponent of comprehensive welfare-state expansion, especially in ways that would protect the autonomy of unions and insure the flow of benefits through the male breadwinners who were the most powerful constituents of the unions and the Labour Party.[69] This would likely not have happened if the British TUC, from the 1870s to the 1910s, had not found it both internally feasible and externally rewarding to work through parliamentary politics to attain its most immediate political objectives, particularly the defense against legal threats to union existence.

While British unionists found legislative and party politics, and cooperation with public administrators, increasingly rewarding between the 1870s and the 1910s, their U.S. counterparts faced repeated frustrations in using such political means. During the 1880s and early 1890s, both the Knights of Labor (a labor movement which included more than just wage-earners) and the AFL and other trade unions (which more specifically expressed the outlooks of wage-earners) worked for and achieved many legislative victories. These came in such areas as legal hours limits, measures prohibiting sweated labor in tenement dwellings, laws prohibiting company stores or payment in scrip rather than cash, and laws protecting unions against employer discrimination.[70] At this time in U.S. political history, voter turnout rates were high, and electoral competition between the Republicans and Democrats was very tight throughout much of the North. Mainstream party organizations often courted labor votes and wanted to satisfy fast-growing labor organizations. In addition, independent labor or populist parties flourished for periods in many parts of the country, often bequeathing parts of their programs to established parties.[71]

But U.S. labor's early legislative gains were minimal and not sustained. A major problem was that nineteenth-century labor laws could not be effectively implemented through preexisting administrative arrangements. In proportion to the numbers of industrial workplaces, the United States had far fewer factory inspectors and other labor-law administrators than Britain, and such officials as the U.S. states did have often worked only part time and lacked authority to compel employers to do anything.[72] Successful enforcement of most early U.S. laws required the bringing of civil suits through the courts. Or else it required that initial legislative victories be followed up with futher campaigns to create and empower regulatory bureaucracies—a process which rarely wended its way to the full implementation of protective statutes.

Failures of enforcement and follow-though happened with many early labor laws, but early arbitration laws offer an especially telling example. Between 1878 and 1890, ten states as well as the federal government passed statutes calling for the public arbitration of labor disputes. Labor movements backed such laws as a way to gain official sanction for organized labor—and, indeed, the arbitration boards often did call for the acceptance of unions and some of their demands. The "most significant laws, passed in Massachusetts and New York, established permanent state boards of mediation with . . . investigative powers and the right to offer mediation in response to requests from parties in dispute."[73] It soon became clear, however, that, without the authority and administrative means to compel employers to recognize and negotiate with unions, even the Massachusetts and New York boards—and the many other state arbitration boards that were modeled or remodeled on the same lines during the 1880s and 1890s—could not prevent strike waves. In various states, arbitration officials and labor leaders called in the late 1880s and early 1890s for additional, *compulsory* arbitration laws. But these failed to pass. And before long, responding to changes within the U.S. "state of courts and parties," mainstream labor leaders abandoned the quest for tougher provisions and enforcement of both the arbitration measures and many other early labor laws.

American labor's political prospects actually declined around the turn of the century, just as the prospects of British and European labor were increasing in democratizing parliamentary systems. At the close of the century, the "highly competitive pre-1896 party system was replaced by a regionally structured system of one-party supremacy with only scattered areas of serious electoral competition."[74] Far fewer competitive elections, along with such changes in state-level electoral laws as the Australian ballot and the advent of cumbersome procedures for personal voter registration, weaked the voter-mobilizing capacities of the established political parties at the very juncture in American history when social changes were loosening the local community ties that had nourished nineteenth-century parties.[75] In turn, less competitive elections and weaker party capacities brought declining rates of voter participation in all regions of the nation, not just in the South (where blacks were forcibly excluded from voting), but also in the Northeast and Midwest. Young, poor, and immigrant voters were less likely to be part of the regularly voting electorate. Because the established party in any given state was not as likely to face tight elections, dissident social movements and independent political parties had less leverage within the transformed electoral terrain; and so did broad alliances of unions and other popular organizations.

U.S. trade unions retained the greatest political leverage at the local level, where those unionists with the most narrowly circumscribed political and market goals could work out cozy relationships with parts of dominant Republican or Democratic party organizations.[76] Leaders of local craft unions—the kind that were becoming predominant in the U.S. labor movement through the AFL—had every reason to make deals with local political machines, who could offer them and their followers such particularistic benefits as public offices; jobs in the private enterprises that employed local workers; influence in cases decided before local or state judges; and regulatory breaks that were crucial, for example, to the construction trades. Above the local level, moreover, individual unions with specific goals used their alliances with local politicians to gain access to ad hoc bargaining within state legislatures.

Given all of the incentives for unions to become and remain enmeshed in particularistic ties to party factions, the national American Federation of Labor found it very difficult to wage any unified political campaign on labor's behalf.[77] In 1906, spurred by an Illinois court's use of the injunction against the Typographers' Union and inspired by British labor's electoral gains, AFL President Gompers called a conference to draw up a list of legislative demands—including relief from the Sherman Act, an anti-injunction law, an eight-hour day for government workers, and anti-immigration measures. Then, in the 1906 and 1908 elections, Gompers tried to mobilize AFL voters to elect representatives willing to support labor's priorities and defeat selected Congressmen holding key committee seats who had previously obstructed legislation on the injunction issue. But Gompers could not get unanimous support from other national union leaders in the AFL; his appeals for union contributions to a central fund for electoral and lobbying activities netted less than $10,000 in each election; and local union leaders failed to break their usual ties to local machines to further national AFL political objectives. Although some friends of labor did well in 1906, the "enemy" congressional leaders targeted by the AFL were reelected, and no favorable legislation ensued. Moreover, the 1908 presidential election brought a whopping victory for the antilabor Republican William Howard Taft—a victory fueled in part by strong, locally brokered labor votes for the Republicans across the industrial states. After 1908, Gompers and the national AFL fared somewhat better in national politics when the Democrat Woodrow Wilson became President and took some administrative and legislative steps favorable to the AFL's agenda. Organized labor supported Wilson's reelection in 1916, but in this and later elections the AFL could never reliably "deliver the vote" to its friends (or withold it from its enemies) in Congress and the Presidency. Not until the 1920s, after the Progressive tide had passed, did the AFL even develop continuous organizational mechanisms for participating in elections.

The AFL Recoils from a Court-Dominated State

U.S. trade unionists at the turn of the century not only suffered from adverse electoral shifts and lack of capacities for concerted political mobilization; more decisively, they became increasingly embittered about state repression, and wearied of pursuing labor's goals through governmental action in a "court-dominated" state.[78] American trade unions were profoundly threatened in their very organizational existence by the aggressive use of court injunctions against strikes and boycotts. These were wielded by judges who were alarmed at the growing power of unions and determined to take matters out of the hands of elected local and state authorities who might sympathize with striking unions. What is more, while British trade unionists were benefiting from legislative enactments gained through a system in which Parliament was supreme, the American trade union movement, operating in a polity with judicial supremacy over legislatures, repeatedly ran up against judicial vetoes of social legislation and of legislation guaranteeing union rights to organize and strike. In the words of the legal historian William Forbath, American "labor discovered that it was the courts that principally determined how labor legislation, once passed, would fare . . . By the turn of the century state and federal courts had invalidated roughly sixty labor laws. During the 1880's and 1890's courts were far more likely than not to strike down the very laws that labor sought most avidly," including laws proscribing discrimination against unions, hours limits and antisweating measures, and laws restricting labor injunctions. "Although both state and federal constitutional standards were somewhat liberalized after the turn of the century, by 1920 courts had struck down roughly three hundred labor laws."[79]

"For workers," Forbath concludes, "judicial review—the invalidation of labor laws under the language of 'liberty of contract' and 'property rights'—became both evidence and symbol of the intractability of the American state from the perspective of labor reform."[80] Bitter experiences with the courts could sour labor leaders on the very idea of working for change through elections and legislatures, as the experience of Samuel Gompers himself illustrates. In a chapter of his autobiography called "Learning Something of Legislation," Gompers told the story of his leadership of the New York Cigarmakers' Union in a lobbying drive during the early 1880s to outlaw sweated manufacturing in tenements. The New York legislature passed two versions of union-supported laws prohibiting the manufacture of cigars in tenement dwellings. Gompers's union celebrated the legislative victories, but soon learned that "[s]ecuring the enactment of a law does not mean the solution of the problem," when the New York Court of Appeals in *In re Jacobs, 1885* struck down the second statute (as it had the first) on free-contract grounds. "We found our work nullified," Gompers wrote. After that, the Cigarmakers rejected legislative action as useless and turned to "strikes and agitation" to secure the tenement ban through contracts with employers. In this case, as in many others during this period of judicial hostility toward union-supported legislation, a craft unionist concluded that the "power of the courts to pass upon constitutionality of law so complicates reform by legislation as to seriously restrict the effectiveness of that method."[81]

Repeated experiences with a court-dominated state around the turn of the century thus left indelible marks on the U.S. trade union movement—discouraging in a number of ways any concerted AFL support for the social insurance and general labor regulations advocated by the AALL and other associations of reformist professionals. Most basically, during the entire period from the 1890s through the 1920s, U.S. trade union leaders could hardly move on, as British unionists had done, from victories over judicial repression toward support for positive governmental social legislation, because the American trade unionists remained obsessed with freeing workers' associations from judicial repression. Anti-injunction bills dominated the AFL's legislative agendas; and trade union leaders sought alliances with business interests when they imagined these might help them get protection from the courts.[82]

Many AFL leaders turned into veritable lawyers and legal theorists, devising a liberal constitutionalist language of workers' "rights" as American citizens to associate and help themselves collectively "free from" domination by a paternalist state.[83] Just as capitalist corporations had been given by the courts rights analogous to those of individual American citizens, trade union theorists argued that unions should be protected in their use of strikes and collective bargaining to further workers' interests in the marketplace. This liberal, constitutionalist language, in turn, made it difficult for union leaders to turn around and advocate paternalist social legislation that would have placed workers as a class under the special protection of the state.

Disagreements among AFL unionists about the value of organizing an independent labor party or waging campaigns for governmental legislation on behalf of workers tended to be resolved in favor of those who argued that such "English-style" methods would be futile in the U.S. context, that it would be better—and quicker—for the unions to seek results through market actions alone. Thus during an 1894 AFL debate, Adolph Strasser of the Cigarmakers' Union countered those advocating a political program that included a demand for a legal eight-hour day. He dismissed the idea that the AFL should emulate the political tactics of the British unions, asking "Is it not a fact that in England there is no constitutional provision to stymie an eight-hour law?" For the United States, there "is one fact that can't be overlooked," Strasser declared. "You can't pass an eight hour day without changing the Constitution of the United States and the Constitution of every state in the Union . . . I am opposed to wasting our time declaring for legislation being enacted for a time . . . after we are all dead." Instead of pursing the eight-hour day by statute, Strassner maintained, AFL members would do better to emulate the achievements of the Cigarmakers and other crafts in "pass[ing] and enforc[ing] [their own] law without the government."[84] On this and other occasions of such internal AFL debates, those asking the unions to get involved in politics had trouble countering the "pure and simple" trade unionists, because judicial use of constitutional provisions to strike down U.S. prolabor laws was in fact such a frequent occurrence. "I sometimes wish I had been born in any other country than in the United States," replied an exasperated Henry Lloyd to Adolph Strasser in 1894, as the Socialists for whom Lloyd spoke went down to defeat in the AFL discussion. "I am sick and tired of listening to lawyers and laboring men like Mr. Strasser declaring everything we ask unconstitutional."[85] Interaction with a court-dominated state thus strengthened opponents to labor politics within the U.S. trade union movement, even as exactly the opposite was happening in Britain, where the advocates of political involvements by the TUC were bolstered by the relative immunity of parliamentary legislation from constitutional judicial review.

A Distrust of Administrative Bureaucratization

Finally, there was one other way in which experiences with a court-dominated state made many AFL leaders reluctant to support AALL drives for social insurance and general labor regulations. Many union leaders generalized from their experiences with one educated, professional elite—judges—to the experiences they potentially might have with "paternalist" labor reformers, if the latter ever got the chance to administer new social legislation. As Samuel Gompers explained to the 1899 AFL Convention:

> We have seen laws passed ostensibly in the interests of the people, and particularly in the interests of labor, construed by the courts to apply with particular severity upon labor. The Interstate Commerce Law, enacted with the avowed purpose of protecting the people from discrimination at the hands of transportation companies, has been utilized for no other purpose than to imprison the union men employed in transportation service. The so-called Sherman Anti-trust Law, ostensibly enacted to protect the people from unlawful combinations of capital, has simply resulted in the arrest and indictment of union workmen, because in their effort to protect their common interests, their action has been construed in restraint of trade. These two laws have been cunningly devised

by our antagonists . . . [and] foolishly acquiesced in by men believing themselves reformers.[86]

Sixteen years later in the *American Federationist,* Gompers still argued
that "enacting a law and securing the realization of the purpose the
law is aimed to secure are two vastly different matters."[87] If the AFL
could not even win legislative protections for unions, or be sure that
apparent victories for reformist social legislation would not be per-
verted by the courts, why risk giving further powers to professional
elites within government administration—such as regulatory powers
to set hours and wages, or power to determine which workers would
be eligible for insurance benefits, or power to collect taxes for "contributory" social insurance?

Labor leaders understood—and worried—that proposals for social
insurance and labor regulations were tied up with the aspirations of
the middle-class professionals to build and staff administrative agencies free from political control. Gompers repeatedly denounced the
bureaucratic aspirations of reformist professionals. In fact he quit
his membership in the AALL during a 1915 dispute over that body's
support for a bill to create an "omnibus" Industrial Commission in
New York State. Modeled on the Wisconsin Industrial Commission
of 1911 that the AALL so admired, this new bureaucracy would
replace a Department of Labor sympathetic to organized labor and
a Workmen's Compensation Commission to which unionists had
been appointed by the AFL's friends in the Tammany-dominated
Democratic Party.[88] In the eyes of the AALL, the change would
improve the efficient, expert administration of all New York labor
laws. But the AFL was worried about the loss of comfortable administrative arrangements and officials sympathetic to—and politically
influenceable by—the unions. As this incident illustrates, even when
U.S. trade unionists were willing to support public regulation, they
had a different conception from the AALL of how it should be
organized and situated within the polity. Union leaders preferred to
work through party politicians with whom they had already worked
out comfortable arrangements.

American labor federation leaders can be forgiven for not understanding that administrative professional elites—even administrators
relatively "autonomous" from political controls—would probably
have been much more helpful to unions than were judicial profes-

sional elites. Given the general weakness of public bureaucracies in the United States during this period, the American trade unionists rarely shared the experiences of their British, Continental European, and Australasian counterparts. After initial wariness, unionists in those countries learned that governmental administrators would bargain with unions about the implementation of social legislation, and would often seek to strengthen unions in relation to businesses as a way to "rationalize" labor markets and create conditions for labor peace and industrial efficiency. Except in a few states and particular policy domains, by contrast, American trade unionists before the 1930s almost never had the chance to bargain with, or share objectives with, strong public administrators. Instead, their expectations for what it would mean to have professional elites holding public power were generalized from the bitter experiences they actually were having with judges and lawyers in the courts.

The Exception That Proves the Rule

If the experiences of American trade unionists in the U.S. polity around the turn of the century discouraged the national AFL from supporting social insurance and general labor regulations, then how are we to understand the exception the national Federation made in endorsing federal old-age pension bills between 1909 and 1914? Here, too, an understanding of trade unionists' prior experiences in the U.S. polity can be very helpful.

It was surely not incidental that advocates of old-age pensions within the AFL, as well as the text of the AFL-endorsed "Old Age Home Guard" bill of 1909, drew explicit positive analogies to Civil War pensions, arguing that the "army of labor" should receive benefits similar to those going to the Union military veterans. In this particular social policy area, the AFL was not speculating about something new and unknown in the United States. The Federation was seeking to extend to its own members federally funded old-age benefits that were already going—in visibly honorable ways, without "contributory" taxes, and without many bureaucratic hassles—to many other American citizens from middle-class as well as working-class backgrounds. In the area of old-age pensions, a precedent for relatively universalistic, democratic social provision already existed in the U.S. polity, and the AFL simply wanted to have all of its members covered by noncontributory public pensions. It must have been very difficult for those leaders of the Miners' Union (including William Wilson) who were elected to Congress in 1906 on the Democratic ticket to watch the powerful Republican Party celebrate Civil War pensions in Pennsylvania and other mining states, without looking for analogous ways to help their Democratic Party constituents who were likely to have been born at the wrong time, or to have come to the United States too late, to be eligible for Civil War pensions. More generally, it must have been difficult for AFL leaders—preoccupied as they were with establishing wage earners' rights and respectability within U.S. democracy—not to consider their constituents equally worthy of the sorts of public pensions that were going to other deserving American citizens. As Gompers himself put it, if "the government will take men as soldiers to fight their battles, and, in consequence of injuries received, give them pensions, I think that a man who works from the earliest time that he can work is entitled to some consideration in his old age."[89]

The exact form of early AFL support for old-age pension legislation was influenced by the unions' experiences in the U.S. polity, as well as by the national Federation's organizational capacities and perceived political opportunities. Reflecting typical labor worries about U.S. politics, the 1909 "Old Age Home Guard" bill was justified through a legal "Brief" focused on getting around constitutional obstacles. It also contained careful wording to preclude any possible behavioral supervision of elderly workers by a government bureaucracy. Finally, too, this AFL-endorsed bill was introduced into the national Congress, and explicitly *not* pressed upon state legislatures. Of course, Representative Wilson was an AFL leader who was personally in a position to introduce the bill into the Congress, and the analogy to Civil War benefits cried out for fulfillment at the federal, not state, level of government. Yet Wilson also argued that this was the most expedient road to follow to avoid constitutional obstacles.

From the entirety of the AFL debates during the 1910s about national versus state legislative action on old-age pensions, one gets the sense that the national Federation leadership was profoundly reluctant to try to work through the state trade union federations. One resolution that the leadership shunted aside in 1916 called upon the AFL to disseminate a model bill to the state Federations, and then allocate resources to support state-level legislative lobbying. But, of course, the national leadership could hardly have felt positively about such an approach. International unions, not state federations, were the centers of power within the national AFL. Thus, if the national AFL leadership was to take electoral or legislative initiatives, it preferred to do so with Presidents of the United States, or in the Congress, or through bargaining with the leaders of other nationally organized associations. For organizational reasons, the national AFL leadership was not politically efficacious in the states. Nor did it wish to strengthen the hands of state federation leaders, who (as we are about to see) had very different attitudes toward political action from those of the craft union leaders who dominated the national AFL.

State Federations of Labor Favor Social Legislation

Although many national trade union leaders in the early-twentieth-century United States were wary of social legislation, leaders of subnational central labor bodies—especially the state federations of labor—were much more supportive of strong governmental initiatives to help both organized and unorganized workers. In his now-classic 1968 study of the California State Federation of Labor, Philip Taft argued that the "failure of European and American writers to recognize the significance of the state federation of labor as a political institution is perhaps the chief reason for their inability to understand American labor's political behavior . . . American organized labor has been very active in politics since its beginnings . . . [State] federations concentrated their political efforts in the state capitols, where they were largely successful."[90] Also writing in 1968, Andrew Thomson argued that the legislative agendas of the U.S. state labor federations resembled that of the early British TUC much more closely than the national AFL agenda ever did.[91] Following such pioneering analytic leads, U.S. labor historiography has placed more and more emphasis on the political doings of subnational labor federations. Perhaps the most important contemporary expert on the topic, Gary Fink, has gone so far as to declare that U.S. local and state central bodies have long "advocated a program of legislated social reform approximating the welfare or guarantor state."[92] Except in the area of minimum-wage laws for men, evidence in favor of Fink's assertion is not hard to find for the social policies of particular interest here: old-age pensions; protective labor regulations, and social insurance.

Old-Age Pensions

We have seen that the national Federation of Labor was an early supporter of federal noncontributory pensions for the needy aged, yet a bit slow and reluctant to support state-level legislative campaigns in this area. Not until 1929 did the national AFL unequivocally endorse a nationwide campaign for state-level old-age assistance.[93] State labor federations, however, endorsed such old-age pension bills from the 1910s onward. Christopher Anglim and Brian Gratton examined the convention proceedings of eighteen state labor federations during the 1910s and 1920s. They found no mention of (that is, neither support for nor opposition to) old-age pensions in the proceedings of the Idaho, Iowa, and Kentucky Federations of Labor. But they found clear-cut and often repeated endorsements of pension legislation in the proceedings of fifteen other state federations in all regions of the nation: California, Connecticut, Georgia, Illinois, Indiana, Maryland/District of Columbia, Massachusetts, Michigan, Minnesota, New York, Ohio, Oregon, Pennsylvania, Texas, and Wisconsin.[94] To be sure, most of the activity by state federations of labor on behalf of state-level old-age pensions came during the decade of the 1920s, after the Progressive Era was over. This labor activity proceeded for a time in close collaboration with a multiple-state campaign for county-option old-age pensions conducted by a widespread federated association, the Fraternal Order of Eagles. This was a social fraternity with both middle- and working-class members associated in many local clubs called "aeries."[95]

Some state federations of labor did begin to call for old-age pensions prior to the 1920s, however. According to Jill Quadagno, in "1911 the Arkansas state federation of labor, dominated by the only strong noncraft union, the United Mine Workers, became one of the first to adopt a resolution supporting Socialist congressman Victor Berger's . . . proposal to provide 'old age pensions for deserving men and women over sixty years old.'"[96] The Mine Workers were also active during the 1910s in supporting state-level investigations of old-age pensions in Illinois and Ohio (and the federations in these states officially endorsed pensions starting in 1921).[97] In 1918 the president of the Pennsylvania State Federation of Labor joined with the reformer Abraham Epstein and the Legislative Committee of the United Mine Workers "to begin planning a state pension campaign."[98] According to Gary Fink, the Missouri State Federation of Labor supported old-age pensions during the Progressive Era; and he also suggests early support for old-age pensions by the West Virginia and Washington State Federations.[99] In 1916, too, the Executive Council of the California State Federation of Labor unanimously endorsed an amendment to the state constitution authorizing the legislature to enact laws providing for old-age, unemployment, and sickness insurance.[100]

Perhaps the most thorough study has been done of the prolonged support for old-age pensions by the Massachussetts State Federation of Labor. A representative of Massachusetts organized labor, Arthur M. Huddell, dissented from the negative 1910 *Report of the Commission on Old Age Pensions*; Huddell called for the enactment of William Wilson's 1909 federal "Old Age Home Guard" proposal.[101] Subsequently, during "1916–17 and 1923–25 . . . [l]abor unions and their representatives led the proponents of pensions" in public hearings before the Massachusetts legislature, the General Court.[102] In the words of Anglim and Gratton:

> Between 1917 and 1930, the issue of old-age pensions was a particular topic of concern in Massachusetts State Federation convention proceedings . . . clearly among the top four labor interests during this period . . . The [state-level] bill which Massachusetts labor wanted was liberal in age qualifications, benefits, and means tests . . . The non-contributory feature, which the Massachusetts proposal shared with labor-backed bills in other states, was central to the proposal; the federation resisted any scheme to fund pensions which would directly tax the working class. In addition, the federation expressed deep antagonism toward the state Department of Public Welfare and its social workers . . . and demanded a new agency to distribute old age pensions, because these were not charity, but a "right" earned by the veterans of industrial toil.[103]

Labor Regulations and Social Insurance

In the area of protective labor regulations, we can note that state and local labor leaders often supported minimum-wage laws for women workers, yet they usually agreed with national AFL opposition to such laws for men, on the grounds that regulated minimum male wages could become maximum wages.[104] Meanwhile, as Gary Fink argues, statutes mandating eight-hour work days for all sorts of workers were "a generally accepted objective of the labor movement in all but the highest councils of the AFL." Fink cites indications of support at various times by central labor bodies in Milwaukee and Los Angeles, and in the states of California, Oklahoma, Colorado, New York, Connecticut, Minnesota, Illinois, Washington, Pennsylvania, Ohio, and Oregon.[105] Not only after it came under Socialist leadership in 1900, but from its founding in 1893, the Wisconsin State Federation of Labor called for an eight-hour statute.[106] Most prominently during the Progressive Era, the trade unionists in California, Oregon, and Washington campaigned on behalf of such statutes in public referenda in 1913; and the California and Washington Federations officially challenged the opposition of national AFL leaders to the legal eight-hour day at the 1914 AFL Convention.[107] In 1915, the Illinois State Federation of Labor endorsed the eight-hour day "by any means we can get it" and commissioned their delegate to the national AFL Convention to support the principle of a legislated eight-hour day.[108] The typical pattern was for subnational labor bodies to campaign first for legal hours limits for children, women, and particular male occupations, following up victories in these areas with campaigns for general eight-hour statutes. This meant that general eight-hour statutes never became a practical priority in many states during the early twentieth century.[109] Still, state federation leaders almost never echoed Samuel Gompers's doctrinaire statements in opposition to the legislated eight-hour day, and they tried to get such statutes whenever political conditions looked promising.

The sharpest divergence between national and state-level AFL stances came in the area of contributory social insurance. We have seen that the hostility of Gompers and other national AFL leaders to unemployment and health insurance prevailed throughout the 1910s and early 1920s, such that the Federation never did endorse such bills championed by the reformist social scientists of the AALL. But many state labor federations did endorse the early AALL-sponsored proposals for social insurance. The AALL launched its nationwide campaign for health insurance in 1916. In December 1918, as Figure 11 shows, the Association proudly announced "Prominent Labor Organizations Already on Record for Health Insurance," including eighteen state federations of labor and twenty-one international unions. Of these state labor federations, those in Missouri, Nebraska, New Jersey, Ohio, and Wisconsin endorsed health insurance in 1916; and those in Alabama, California, Connecticut, Illinois, and Minnesota also joined the movement relatively early, in 1917.[110] By 1920, a total of twenty-one state labor federations and twenty-nine national trade unions had endorsed health insurance proposals.[111] In New York State, where the health insurance movement came closest to legislative success, the state federation played a very strong role in 1918 and 1919, pressing the cause upon the legislature and distributing favorable propaganda.[112] The 1918 pamphlet spelling out the federation's endorsement of health insurance went "To the Officers of Unions" with the request right on its cover: "Please Give Contents of This Pamphlet the Widest Publicity Among Your Members."[113]

State labor federations were also early supporters of reformers' proposals for unemployment insurance. When the first unemployment insurance bill in U.S. history was introduced in 1916 by an AALL-affiliated group into the Massachusetts legislature, it carried the endorsement of the Massachusetts State Federation of Labor.[114] After the end of World War I, the Illinois State Federation of Labor helped to launch an independent labor-party initiative which, among other policies, endorsed British-style unemployment insurance of the sort the AALL proposed during the 1910s; and there were similar brief-lived labor-party initiatives supported by radical unionists in other states.[115] During the early 1920s, the Pennsylvania State Federation of Labor cooperated with the AALL in an attempt to get a different kind of unemployment compensation legislation.[116] And throughout the decade, the Wisconsin State Federation of Labor repeatedly lobbied for what eventually, in 1932, would become the nation's first unemployment-benefits law.[117]

In sum, although scholars still have much to learn about the legislative endorsements and achievements of state federations of labor in the early twentieth century, we can pull together what is known for the ten wealthiest large industrial states of 1910: California, Illinois, Indiana, Massachusetts, Michigan, New Jersey, New York, Ohio, Pennsylvania, and Wisconsin.[118] State federations of

Prominent Labor Organizations Already on Record for Health Insurance

State Federations

Alabama Federation of Labor, 1917
Arkansas Federation of Labor, 1918
California Federation of Labor, 1917
Colorado Federation of Labor, 1918
Connecticut Federation of Labor, 1917
Illinois Federation of Labor, 1917
Iowa Federation of Labor, 1918
Kansas Federation of Labor, 1918
Maryland-District of Columbia Federation of Labor, 1918
Minnesota Federation of Labor, 1917
Missouri Federation of Labor, 1916
Nebraska Federation of Labor, 1916
New Jersey Federation of Labor, 1916
New York Federation of Labor, 1918
Ohio Federation of Labor, 1916
Pennsylvania Federation of Labor, 1918
West Virginia Federation of Labor, 1918
Wisconsin Federation of Labor, 1916

Internationals

International Typographical Union, 1916.
International Union of Steam and Operating Engineers, 1916.
Spinners' International Union, 1916
United Textile Workers of America, 1916
Pulp, Sulphite and Paper Mill Workers of the U. S. and Canada, 1916
Glass Bottle Blowers' Association of the U. S. and Canada, 1917
International Brotherhood of Foundry Employees, 1917
International Glove Workers' Union of America, 1917
Brotherhood of Railway Carmen of America, 1917
Amalgamated Clothing Workers of America, 1918
Int'l Stereotypers' and Electrotypers' Union of North America, 1918
International Fur Workers' Union of the U. S. and Canada, 1918
National Brotherhood of Operative Potters, 1918
International Union of Mine, Mill and Smelter Workers, 1918
American Wire Weavers' Protective Association, 1918
Retail Clerks' International Protective Association, 1918
National Federation of Federal Employees, 1918
United Garment Workers of America, 1918
Int'l Wood Carvers' Association of North America, 1918
Brewery, Flour, Cereal and Soft Drink Workers of America, 1918
Broom and Whisk Makers' International Union, 1918

Other Organizations

National Women's Trade Union League, 1917
Southern Labor Congress, 1917
California Building Trades Council, 1918
Massachusetts Association of Letter Carriers, 1918
New Jersey Joint State Labor Legislative Board, 1918
New York Women's Trade Union League, 1918

Figure 11

Source: *American Labor Legislation Review* 8(4) (December 1918), p. 319.

labor in at least three of these states (California, Illinois, and Wisconsin) endorsed general hours laws. More striking, nine of these state federations are known to have endorsed old-age pensions during the 1910s or 1920s (and the tenth case, the New Jersey federation, was not included in Anglim and Gratton's study, so it may also have endorsed pensions). At least eight of these ten federations endorsed unemployment and/or health insurance. All ten of the labor federations in these large industrial states endorsed at least one of the new kinds of social spending policies of concern to us here; and at least seven of them endorsed both pensions and social insurance. And we have seen that many state federations of labor in smaller, less industrial states were also active in support of these measures.

Understanding the State Federations

Why did state federations of labor in the early twentieth century take more favorable stands toward social legislation than the national American Federation of Labor? Some scholars have suggested, simply, that state federations were in closer touch with popular working-class opinion. Philip Taft argues that the "behavior of workers and their organizations at the grass roots in their communities is a much better key to understanding American labor politics than the forensic efforts of Gompers and his coworkers."[119] In "a very literal sense," Gary Fink agrees, "local labor organizations were much more democratic than either the AFL or the various international union bureaucracies. If an old-age pension system seemed a reasonable and desirable reform to local union members, that interest was soon expressed in the meetings" of city centrals and state federations.[120] There is no doubt something to this, but we should beware of romanticizing as "more democratic" one set of labor organizations and leaders in contrast to another.

We can better understand the role of the state federations by locating them in the overall structure of the U.S. trade union movement in the early twentieth century. As Gary Fink explains,

disparate constituencies at different levels of organization encouraged differing outlooks. The AFL owed its origin and continued existence to the several international union bureaucracies that had

confederated at its formation . . . It was this constituency to which
the AFL leadership felt responsible. State and local central bodies,
on the other hand, served a much different clientele. Their support came primarily from individual union locals. Local central
bodies were voluntary associations of local trade unions; and that
association . . . was unlikely to be continued if the central body
did not serve the needs and reflect the desires of its affiliated local
unions.[121]

Because the national AFL was a confederation of nationally organized unions, mostly craft unions, it was understandably oriented
toward supporting the marketplace activities and internal leadership
hierarchies of those established unions. State federations, in contrast,
did not charter or control unions as market actors; and state federations could not require the affiliation of the unions in their jurisdiction. Instead, state federations were purely voluntary associations.
They tried to attract participation in annual conventions, as well as
financial contributions, from local unions. State federations thus had
an incentive to speak for interests perceived to be common to many
local unions and workers in their geographic jurisdiction. They also
had a somewhat greater interest than individual craft unions in
promoting the organization and social welfare of currently unorganized workers in their state.

State federations, furthermore, were founded and explicitly defined as politically specialized actors within the U.S. trade union
movement. "As has been true of other State organizations," an early
history of the Iowa State Federation of Labor explained, "the original
purpose . . . was to influence State and Federal legislation."[122] The
preamble to the Iowa federation's founding constitution declared in
1893:

> Recognizing the fact that the very instinct of self-preservation
> demands the closer unionism of all trades and labor organizations,
> in order that the equality of right and privilege may be obtained
> for wage workers, we, the representatives of the TRADES AND LABOR
> UNIONS OF IOWA, in convention assembled, do hereby unite our
> forces in this convention in the cause of Labor Emancipation, and
> call upon wage workers throughout the State to join with us in
> obtaining needed industrial and social reforms.[123]

As was the case with the founding of the British Trades Union
Congress, the "establishment of a [U.S. state labor] federation was

stimulated in some states—New York [1867], for example—by the threat of antilabor legislation."[124] In other places, such as Iowa, California (1901), Missouri (1891), and the Oklahoma Territory (1904), the creation of federations was spurred "by recognition of the need to strengthen the political force exerted by labor."[125]

Some state federations antedated, and others came after, the formation of the national AFL. Once the AFL was created, both already-established and subsequently founded state bodies became chartered groups, relegated to a limited place within the national Federation. The comprehensive 1919 AFL *Encyclopedia* was full of details about the national Federation, Samuel Gompers, other national AFL leaders, and the international unions, but only briefly mentioned the state federations. It described their functions as educating workers and seeking "state legislation favorable to labor."[126]

The national AFL did not let the state federations become important to its own decisionmaking. Under the AFL constitution, "each central body [that is, city central body or state federation] had only one delegate at annual conventions of the AFL. By contrast, national and international unions had one delegate for every four thousand members, and on rollcalls they cast one vote for every hundred members, while the representatives of the [city and state] central bodies still had only one vote. This constitutional arrangement had the effect of denying the labor organizations that were most influential on the local [and state] level the power in the national organization to which the size of their constituencies entitled them."[127] Thus, for example, when the 1914 AFL Convention voted on the issue of eight-hour statutes, the California and Washington state federations that argued so strongly in favor of endorsing such legislation had only one vote apiece, while the tiny International Union of Broom and Whisk Makers had seven votes. Overall in that convention, the 647 city centrals and 43 state federations had only 690 votes, while 110 international unions and 570 directly affiliated locals together had 20,495 votes![128]

State federations were nevertheless able to pursue their own priorities relatively free from central AFL control. These bodies were, in essence, labor's organizational counterparts to the state governments where most of the action on supralocal social policy was to be found in the late-nineteenth- and early-twentieth-century United States. Well-established state federations carried out a number of important governmentally related activities.[129] Following the mandates given to their officers at annual conventions attended by representatives of local unions, the federations maintained lobbying operations in state capitals, where federation representatives pursued the enactment of bills endorsed by organized labor, and formed ad hoc alliances with other groups to push through prolabor legislation. In addition, state federations waged court cases on behalf of union interests. And they monitored the implementation of labor laws, often intervening with attorneys general or labor bureaus or governors. Moreover, the best-organized and most politically active state federations engaged in extensive electioneering, keeping track of the voting records of legislators, endorsing candidates, and trying to educate union voters about candidates and issues. The California State Federation, for example, issued for each session of the California legislature comprehensive reports on "Labor Legislation" and on the "Labor Record of Senators and Assemblymen."[130]

State federations of labor might have been tempted to pursue only policy goals of narrowly defined interest to the local unions that supported them. But even to attain such goals, federation leaders had to work with available allies in each state—allies such as farmers' groups, women's associations, middle-class reform groups, party factions, or reformist professionals and civil administrators. Each kind of ally could pull state federations toward endorsements of certain kinds of social policy proposals—even if labor was not prepared to take the initiative, and even if the kind of proposal put forward was not exactly what unionized workers might have ideally preferred. Across many states, women's groups encouraged AFL leaders to work with them for women's hour laws, and sometimes persuaded state federations to support women's minimum wage regulations in the face of national AFL reluctance.[131] Reformist professional experts persuaded quite a few state federations to endorse proposals for health and unemployment insurance, overcoming worries about the taxes from workers that these would entail if implemented. Agrarian movements in peripheral states sometimes drew tiny local federations into alliances on behalf of a wide array of strong governmental measures, including labor regulations; this happened for example during the ascendancy of the Non-Partisan League in North Dakota.[132] And during the early to mid-1920s, state labor federations joined campaigns that were led by the cross-class Fraternal Order of Eagles on behalf of county-option old-age pensions for the very needy, even though the forces of organized labor usually preferred old-age pensions with state-level financial contributions and more generous eligibility provisions.[133]

The Limited Capacities of the State Federations

Because state-level politics was the central preoccupation of state federations of labor, and because of the intergroup alliances through which these labor organizations often defined and pursued legislative goals, it is not surprising that the state federations took a much more favorable stance toward positive governmental initiatives to help unions and workers than did the national AFL leadership. We have answered the question with which we started this section: why the national AFL and the state federations often differed about social legislation. We cannot, however, leap to the idea that state federations of labor were the prime force—let alone a very effective force— behind U.S. social policymaking in the early twentieth century. Even when they did enthusiastically endorse hour laws, or old-age pensions, or social insurance, there were severe limits on what even the largest and strongest state federations could accomplish politically on behalf of these measures. State federations were hampered by many of the same obstacles in the U.S. polity that we have already reviewed in the discussion of the national AFL: electoral demobilization after the 1890s; the absence of competing programmatic political parties; the weakness of governmental bureaucracies that might work with organized labor; and (in many states) the need to concentrate on defending unions' rights to organize and strike, as well as any gains in social legislation, through protracted and costly judicial proceedings. In addition, state federations of labor experienced difficulties from within the trade union movement itself when they tried to speak for the united political interests of unions and workers.

Whenever they endorsed social policies opposed by the national AFL leadership, state federations were hampered from above. We have already noted that western labor leaders blamed negative pronouncements from Samuel Gompers for helping to defeat 1913 referenda on eight-hour laws supported by the California, Oregon, and Washington State Federations of Labor. Nor did Gompers's attacks on social insurance help the cause of state-level labor proponents of health insurance, since the national AFL president's influence could help to divide labor's voice. Thus, during 1917–18 in California, despite "the approval of the state federation, many powerful groups, including the San Francisco Labor Council, were opposed to compulsory social insurance."[134] The editor of the San Francisco *Labor Clarion* echoed Gompers's arguments as he wrote and spoke in opposition to a constitutional amendment to allow health insurance which had been endorsed by the leadership of the state federation. In the end, rank-and-file workers in California heard, at best, a mixed message before they and other California voters overwhelmingly rejected the proposed amendment in a 1918 referendum.[135]

The difficulties state federation leaders faced when speaking for labor came from below as well as above. Even when explicit disagreements over given legislative proposals were not involved, there could be problems of resource mobilization and coordination of objectives analogous to those faced by AFL President Gompers when he launched the largely unsuccessful electoral initiative of 1906 that I discussed earlier. State AFL leaders had great difficulty persuading all or most of a state's workers and unions to work together in support of broad political programs. Many local unions never joined their state federations in the first place; the Iowa Federation around 1909, for example, included an estimated one-half of the union locals and 35 percent of the union workers in that state.[136] Certain large miners' locals were at odds with, and remained outside, the state federation in Iowa. Divisions might equally well occur within the ranks of unions that were officially enrolled in state federations. In Illinois, for example, the State Federation of Labor had chronic troubles raising money for its legislative committee in Springfield, while the "Chicago Federation of Labor frequently quarreled with the cautious state organization, . . . [and] the most influential Illinois unions—the four railroad brotherhoods and the United Mine Workers of America—conducted an independent lobby until 1905. Between 1885 and 1919, nearly 42 percent of the labor bills approved by the [Illinois] General Assembly benefited miners and railroad workers" and many of the rest were not the initiatives of unions at all.[137] In New York, similarly, the Workingmen's Federation never claimed more than one-third of the state's unions as affiliates, could not deliver unionists' votes for politicians or referenda it endorsed, and "never achieved the goal of becoming the sole representative of labor interests in the state. Despite the Federation's claims that . . . [a] multiplicity of labor lobbyists reduced the effectiveness of all, member organizations refused to give complete control over legislation to the state body—an example of the particularism which was also so prominent in the economic activities of the trade unions."[138]

Even at the level of the states, in sum, U.S. labor organizations did not provide any strong push toward a British-style paternalist welfare state, centered in labor regulations and social spending measures targeted on adult male workers and their dependents. Arguably, U.S. trade unionists did voice earlier and more consistent support than any other social force for noncontributory old-age pensions. But organized labor did not spearhead movements across the states in favor of gender-neutral wage and hour laws, or unemployment and health insurance. Usually, nonlabor political allies influenced organized labor's social policy agenda more readily than it influenced the agendas of its helpers, if any, in state-level legislative lobbying. This led to great diversity across the states of America's decentralized polity. What is more, no matter how their policy goals came to be defined, state labor federations were never strong enough to mobilize all or most of organized labor's resources on behalf of any legislative objective. At best, U.S. organized labor at either the national or the state level could be a junior partner in what had to be a multifaceted intergroup coalition if any legislation was to be pushed through in this period of American politics.

Conclusion

In Britain and other Western nations around the turn of the twentieth century, trade unions moved from initial wariness about labor regulations and workingmen's benefits to become strong supporters of the further expansion of nascent public protections for the working class. Elite reformers and trade unions increasingly worked together to build welfare states. In the United States, however, the unions did not consistently move toward greater support for public social provision. As reform-minded professionals placed more and more hope in new governmental policies as positive tools for realizing "the public interest," many national trade union leaders lost faith in what they perceived to be a court-dominated U.S. state hostile to the basic organizational interests of trade unions. These trade union leaders also came to resent the efforts of reformist intellectuals to enlist labor's support for "paternalist" social policies—especially those such as contributory social insurance and labor regulations that were seen as likely to enhance bureaucratic and fiscal demands on workers.

By the height of the Progressive Era, moreover, there were ironic differences between what U.S. trade union federations would and could do on behalf of social policies, and what the American Association of Labor Legislation would and could do. From 1909 to 1914, the national AFL was prepared to push for federal noncontributory old-age pensions. But this willingness on the part of American organized labor came just as the reformist professionals of the AALL were turning away from such old-age pensions, choosing instead to emphasize contributory unemployment and health insurance—measures to which the majority of the national AFL leadership remained firmly opposed throughout the 1910s.

To be sure, many state federations of labor did eventually become willing to support AALL proposals for social insurance. Yet such labor support for social insurance appeared at a level of government, the states, where the AALL was ill-prepared to operate. The AALL preferred to work through leadership consultations with other national associations, and it certainly expected organized American workers to follow its well-intentioned lead toward a paternalist welfare state. In practice, though, the AALL's most likely partners in the early-twentieth-century U.S. trade union movement were federations scattered across dozens of states, in most of which the AALL and other reformist professionals supportive of social insurance had little organized presence. What is more, neither the AALL nor the national or state AFL federations had much capacity to mobilize resources or bring political pressure to bear across many local communities and many individual legislative districts. As we shall see in Part III, this situation contrasted to what female professional reformers and widespread federated associations of women's clubs could accomplish during the 1910s and early 1920s on behalf of social legislation for mothers and women workers.

In the final analysis, however, we have to realize that the proponents of general labor regulations and social insurance for male workers might have succeeded without much support from AFL unions. Not only were U.S. unions in this period rarely decisive in any aspect of politics. In other Western nations around the turn of the century, unions were not necessarily initiators in drives for labor regulations and social insurance. Reformist intellectuals often influenced elite and middle-class opinion to see the desirablity of reforms for (rather than by) the workers. As a prelude to enticing unions into subsequent efforts to expand public social provision, reformers initially worked with political executives, bureaucrats, and political party leaders to devise and implement these measures "from above." More remains to be learned about why American advocates of new social protections for the "army of labor" could not imitate such successes by their turn-of-the-century counterparts in Europe, Australasia, and—especially—Great Britain.

It also remains to be seen exactly why the professionals of the AALL, and other groups in the reform-minded "public" of the Progessive period, did not join hands with the national and state-level labor federations of the AFL to press for publicly funded pensions for the needy elderly. We know that the United States already had such pensions for many elderly men and their dependents. And we have learned in this chapter that—just like the trade unions in Britain—U.S. trade unions wanted public old-age pensions, and would have welcomed cross-class support in campaigns to get them legislated. But during the 1910s American reformers, and the elite and middle-class public audiences to which they spoke, were reluctant to champion noncontributory old-age pensions. Why, we must wonder, did the reformist experts of the AALL miss a golden opportunity to realize their dream of leading "trade union men" in a national campaign for a basic component of the modern welfare state?

CHAPTER 5

Progressive Era Politics
and the Defeat of Social Policies
for Workingmen and the Elderly

Articulate advocates of labor regulations and social benefits for work-ingmen were politically active in the early-twentieth-century United States. Why did they have so little success in securing legislation—except in the particular area of compensation for industrial acci-dents? And why did the reformist professionals who championed modern forms of social provision initially deemphasize old-age pen-sions, thus missing an opportunity to join forces with the trade unions during the Progressive period?

The time has come to examine the ways in which U.S. govern-mental structures and the politics of the Progressive Era made it difficult to enact new social policies benefiting workingmen and the elderly. A sideways glance to Britain is a good place to begin. Prior understanding of this other nation—where liberal advocates of new social policies were very successful—will help us to highlight political patterns and governmental structures distinctive to U.S. social poli-tics in the early twentieth century. Comparative analysis is the best tool we have to reveal the institutions and societal conjunctures that constrain willful social actors—such as the early U.S. advocates of workingmen's insurance—to make history not as they please.

British Counterpoint: Political Conditions Favorable to Liberal Policy Innovations

Britain, like the United States, was an industrializing capitalist nation with entrenched liberal traditions; and the advocates of social insurance and labor regulations in that country in the early 1900s were socially and ideologically very similar to their American contemporaries. The labels "progressive" and "new liberal" have appropriately been applied both to the U.S. advocates of new labor laws in the AALL and to the reform-minded professionals and Liberal Party leaders who were the leading advocates of old-age pensions, unemployment and health insurance, and new protective labor laws and labor market regulations in early-twentieth-century Britain.[1] Like their U.S. counterparts, British progressive liberals reworked laissez-faire liberal values to emphasize ways in which positive governmental measures could foster individual well-being under industrialism.[2] Also like their American counterparts, the British reformers had a penchant for doing thorough social investigations as a prelude to drafting legislation that could be pressed upon political leaders as a "rational" approach to social reform in the national interest, rising above mere class considerations.

Yet, of course, there was a major difference: The British progressive liberals succeeded in creating a comprehensive welfare state centered on workingmen during the very period when Americans were failing to do so. In Britain, workmen's compensation (including benefits for industrial diseases) was enacted under Liberal Party auspices in 1906, followed by old-age pensions in 1908, public unemployment exchanges and minimum wage boards in 1909, and unemployment and health insurance in 1911. Between 1914 and 1920, minimum wage regulations and unemployment and health benefits were extended to more and more British industrial workers. By the 1920s, when the Liberals ceased to be a dominant party in British politics, the foundations had been laid for a comprehensive welfare state for workers and their dependents. In a preemptive move, Conservatives sponsored further extensions of benefits to the elderly and to widows of workers in 1925; more generally, Britain's Labour Party took over from the Liberals as the champion of the maintenance and extension of social benefits for workers and their dependents.[3]

To their good fortune, British progressive-liberal advocates of social insurance and labor regulations were operating just after the turn of the century in a unitary national polity with administrative, electoral, and political party arrangements that made it relatively easy for them to achieve legislative breakthroughs—via access to a few strategically placed bureaucratic sites and party leaders. Britain's polity in the nineteenth century started out as a liberal oligarchy, ruled by and for landlords and their commercial allies.[4] During the course of the century, this polity underwent several intertwined transformations, which—institutionally speaking—laid the basis for the Liberal welfare breakthroughs of 1906–1911. These transformations included the expansion of national administrative activities, especially in the realm of social-welfare policy; the reform of the civil service; the step-by-step partial democratization of the male parliamentary electorate in the 1830s and 1860s; and transformations in the modes of organization and electoral operation of the major political parties.

In British civil administration during the eighteenth and early nineteenth centuries, oligarchic patronage predominated and "the public services were the outdoor relief department of the aristocracy."[5] Industrialization and urbanization, along with the geopolitical exigencies of maintaining British imperial domains and coping with growing international economic competition, generated pressures for the British government to become more efficient and technically competent than patronage would allow.[6] But governmental change did not come automatically; reform advocates were initially frustrated by those with a vested interest in the existing system.[7] Finally, proposals for civil service reform succeeded politically in the 1870s. Prior changes in universities made them plausible as agencies for training and credentialing civil servants. Once it became clear that working-class political influence might grow as the electorate expanded, the landed and business groups and the existing governing elites of Britain came together in order to maintain the elite civil service on a new basis.[8]

Civil service reform in Britain did not automatically ensure that bureaucrats would subsequently become policy innovators. At both the Local Government Board (LGB) and the Home Office, two of the departments most concerned with questions of domestic social policy, there developed after 1870 a "general inertia and disinvolvement from reform," accompanied by a view of the civil service "as a source of income and status."[9] But the British state structure was not administratively monolithic in this period. The Board of Trade, a competing agency outside of the control of the LGB and the Home Office, was able during the 1880s and 1890s to develop independent capacities in the collection and use of labor statistics.[10] The Board's activities expanded rapidly, and it recruited a remarkable core of young, progressive-minded officials, eventually including William Beveridge, an expert on labor markets and issues of unemployment, who had gone from Oxford into settlement house activities, journalism, and unemployment relief work, before coming into government service under the Liberals in 1908.

Finally, and perhaps most important, civil service reform along with step-by-step electoral democratization had implications for the organization and operations of the political parties. With the credentialization of the civil service, the parties had to stop relying on elite patronage and develop new methods of raising funds and rewarding activists and new ways of winning votes in an expanding electorate. In the 1870s and 1880s, both the Liberal and Conservative parties created constituency organizations and at the same time began to formulate programs to appeal through activists to blocs of voters and financial subscribers.[11]

The administrative arrangements and party system in place in Britain by the early twentieth century facilitated the Liberal welfare breakthroughs of 1906 to 1911. From the 1890s onward, there was widespread elite and popular disgruntlement with the way members of the respectable working class who became impoverished owing to old age, ill health, or unemployment were handled by poor-law institutions. National politicians, Conservative and Liberal alike, became interested in reforming or replacing the New Poor Law of 1834 to deal better with the problems of the "worthy poor."[12] Some of their concerns were generated from administrative dilemmas within established relief programs, as well as by the threat to the whole edifice of local government finance posed by the rising and uneven costs of the poor law. Other concerns arose from the obvious political fact that the votes of working-class people—and the support of their organizations, the unions and friendly societies—had to be wooed by parties engaged in increasingly programmatic competition. The Liberals and the Conservatives fought tightly contested elections around the turn of the century.

During the 1890s, the voluntarist resistance of the British friendly societies to old-age pensions helped to delay new welfare breakthroughs; and then the Boer War of 1899–1902 provided political diversion and temporary financial excuses for avoiding new domestic expenditures.[13] But after the war, the Liberal welfare reforms—which bypassed the New Poor Law without abolishing or fundamentally reforming it—crystallized by two routes in the context I have outlined.[14] First, in the face of the cross-class campaign waged by the National Committee of Organized Labour on Old Age Pensions, the Liberals devised their noncontributory and need-based old-age pensions as a tool of programmatic competition with the Conservatives. The Liberals hoped to retain the loyalty of working-class voters and reinforce their party's alliance with the Labour Representation Committee. Secondly, after the passage of pension legislation, proposals for contributory unemployment and health insurance came through initiatives from Liberal Cabinet leaders allied with civil administrators at the Board of Trade. For unemployment and health insurance alike, intragovernmental professional elites with reformist intentions took the initiative in persuading both working-class and business interests to go along, convincing businesses and unions that social insurance could be implemented through the Board of Trade in ways that would not compromise their vital interests. Once this persuading was done and the Cabinet was set on its course, the discipline of the Liberal Party in Parliament ensured passage of the National Insurance Act, and there were no independent courts to which disgruntled parties could appeal.

Stepping back to put these policy departures in broader context, we must underline that the administration of new social spending as such was not fundamentally problematic for British elites in this period. The "corruption" of patronage politics was behind them, and disputes were now focused on levels and forms of spending, and especially on direct versus indirect taxation.[15] The Labour Party was not yet a major actor in British politics (though the Liberals were anxious to preempt this nascent force), and both Liberal and Conservative leaders were concerned to attract or retain working-class electoral support by devising new public programs. Parts of the British state bureaucracy had the capacities and the personnel to take the initiative in devising innovative social policies. In this context and conjuncture, effective regulatory interventions in labor markets looked feasible to informed British public opinion; and pensions and social insurance seemed appropriate to circumvent for the respectable working class the cruelties, inefficiencies, and costs of the New Poor Law of the nineteenth century. Such policies also seemed appropriate for appealing to—and, in the case of the social insurance measures, newly *taxing*—the working class, involving them more fully in the life of a united nation, yet under the hegemony of enlightened professional middle-class leadership.

The U.S. Polity in Transition: Obstacles to New Social Policies

However much they might want to imitate the social-policy innovations of the British Liberals, U.S. reformers had to operate in a much less favorable governmental and political context. In a non-parliamentary polity without strong civil service ministries, and lacking programmatically oriented political parties, there could not be any straightforward parallel to what happened with social benefits and labor regulations in Britain. In that country, strategically situated, high-level public officials like William Beveridge and his colleagues in the Board of Trade worked out firm compromises with organized interest groups, formulated new policies using existing administrative resources, and pressed those policies on political executives able to make legislatively binding decisions.

To be sure, active in the early U.S. movements for labor regulations and social insurance were many officials of fledgling state and federal bureaus of labor statistics, men like the pioneering labor statistician Carroll Wright, who had similar ideas and aspirations to those of their British counterparts in the Board of Trade.[16] But the American labor statistics officials could not proceed by capturing the ears of ministers and executives. On the rare occasions when they proposed successful policy innovations, officials of these bureaus entered into alliances with reformist voluntary associations—in order to educate public opinion, pressure legislators to enact new measures, and finally persuade governors to accept them. In short, American labor statistics officials operated as legislative lobbyists and educators of public opinion, in tandem with other progressives of the day. Labor statistics officials were among the founders and active leadership of the American Association for Labor Legislation.

More than the absence of British-style civil service institutions bedeviled the efforts of early U.S. advocates of labor regulations and workingmen's insurance, however. Reformers were also impeded by the special leverage of courts in U.S. politics, and by the public mood accompanying the governmental transformations the United States was undergoing around the turn of the century. Judicial opposition hobbled drives for broad hours and wage regulations that would have covered the entire working class. And the worries of the American public about "political corruption" and administrative ineffectiveness discouraged reformers from pursuing old-age pensions, while undercutting their campaigns for social insurance legislation.

The U.S. Courts and Social Legislation

When Professor Henry Farnam mentioned the "bugaboo of unconstitutionality" as an obstacle to new labor legislation in his 1910 presidential address to the AALL, he was pointing to something of which his listeners were already acutely aware: The United States had sovereign courts whose judges took an active role in shaping social legislation.[17] In Britain, there was no written constitution, and the sole apex of the legislative and judicial structure was the national Parliament. The appellate jurisdiction of courts culminated in the ten Law Lords of the House of Lords. These judges had the final word in the application of the common law, but they could not rule unconstitutional statutes passed by the Parliament as a whole, in which the House of Commons was effectively dominant. Parliament, moreover, could pass statutes to reverse judicial decisions it did not like. There was "for all practical purposes a single body of law, uniformly applied by all courts" in Britain.[18] By contrast, in the United States, there were separate federal and state-level court systems, linked only by the national Constitution and by a shared heritage of the Anglo-Saxon common law. From the early 1800s onward, moreover, higher courts in the American states and at the federal level effectively claimed the power of judicial review. Their justices could interpret parts of the written constitutions of the states and the nation to sustain or strike down executive actions or laws passed by majorities in the state legislatures or the national Congress. Judicial doctrines and their application were thus an important, independent factor to be taken into account by Americans who wanted to devise new kinds of laws in changing social and economic circumstances. Whereas British progressive liberals at the turn of the century could concentrate on politics affecting one nationally sovereign Parliament, their American counterparts had to worry about dozens of state legislatures and higher courts as well as about Congress and the federal Supreme Court.

Despite the complexity of the institutional situation they faced, however, leading U.S. reformers right at the turn of the century were relatively optimistic that they could quickly persuade judges to adapt rulings to changing social circumstances. Ironically, reformist professionals became—temporarily—optimistic about the courts just at the time when the national leadership of the U.S. trade union movement was despairing of making legislative progress in a "court-dominated" polity.

Writing in 1904 about "The Attitude of American Courts toward Restrictive Labor Laws," Henry Rogers Seager posed the issue unflinchingly: While "the Parliament of Great Britain has continuously expanded the labor code by adding each session some new regulation, the efforts in the same direction of American state legislatures have again and again been balked by the decision of the courts that their enactments were unconstitutional."[19] But then Seager proceeded to explore the doctrines used by the state courts to decide about the constitutionality of labor laws. Labor laws, he found, were struck down by judges who invoked constitutional prohibitions against "special" or "class" legislation, and by judges who reasoned that "freedom of contract" as a personal and a property right was protected by the "due process" provision of the Fourteenth Amendment to the federal Constitution and by similar provisions in all state constitutions. Yet American judges and courts did not invariably invoke these considerations to strike down new social legislation. Sometimes, Seager found, they invoked the "police power of the state" to allow the infringement of otherwise sancrosanct individual and property rights for the sake of protecting the morals, safety, and health of society as a whole. Arguing against the pessimistic conclusion that America's written constitutions and activist courts would necessarily obstruct new labor legislation, Seager maintained that a natural doctrinal tendency to broaden the scope of the police power would occur as judges became persuaded that the social abuses of industrialism were real, and that "workmen constitute a class in the community that needs special protection because specially exposed to unfair treatment by unscrupulous employers."[20] In support of this view, he invoked key judicial decisions that delighted and emboldened many American reformers at the turn of the century.

An 1896 Utah law limiting to eight hours a day the hours of workers in mines and smelters was immediately upheld by the state Supreme Court, and also by the U.S. Supreme Court in the 1898 decision *Holden v. Hardy*. Citing the dangers of long hours to the health of workers and acknowledging that "the proprietors of these [mining] establishments and their operators do not stand upon an equality," the U.S. Supreme Court justified Utah's right to interfere in free contracts, even over the protests of employees, as a valid excercise of the police power.[21] Subsequently, some state high courts, such as Colorado's, ignored this precedent. But quite a few others invoked it to justify protective laws for special groups of male workers—including not just miners but also street railway workers, as covered by a ten-hour Rhode Island statute passed and upheld by that state's Supreme Court in 1902, and bakers, as covered in a ten-hour New York statute passed in 1895 and upheld by the Court of Appeals in 1904. The New York high court cited not only the well-being of the bakery workers but also the fact that "the family of today is more dependent upon the baker for the necessaries of life than upon any other source of supply."[22]

These court decisions, argued Seager in his 1904 essay,

> open an indefinitely large field to the exercise of the police power in the regulation of hours of labor. If a limitation of hours to ten a day for bakers can be justified as a means of protecting the community's bread, manifestly a large number of trades may be subjected to similar restrictions . . . If the hours of those employed in mines and smelters may be limited to eight a day for the reason that longer hours are detrimental to health, what ground remains for opposing reasonable restrictions on hours of any employment? It is incontestable that excessive hours of work of any kind are injurious to health . . . May not any restriction on hours which is defensible on economic grounds be properly characterized as a reasonable health measure and therefore brought within the pale of the police power.[23]

The "conclusion to which I have been brought," declared Seager, is that "under the flexible provisions of our constitutions the question of the constitutionality of a restrictive labor law is inseparably connected with the question of the wisdom of such a law . . . If this view is correct no amendments to American constitutions will be needed to provide the country with as comprehensive labor codes as are found abroad. All that will be required is the conversion of American judges to belief in the beneficence of this species of legislation."[24]

Echoes of this optimism still reverberated in Farnam's 1910 presidential ddress to the AALL, with its vision of producing investigations and skillfully drafted laws that would be acceptable to "the trained minds of our courts."[25] Arguably, the reformist social scientists of the AALL placed so much emphasis on investigation and rational arguments about the public interest not just because they were professionally comfortable with this mission but also because they initially believed that the all-important lawyers and judges of the United States were open to straightforward persuasion about the societal need for, and the economic merits of, new kinds of industrial regulations and social legislation. Key founders of the AALL saw themselves as engaging in an intra-elite politics of factually informed discussion among reasonable professionals. They, as progressive social scientists, would quickly enlighten—and thereby persuade—the judges!

Matters did not proceed so smoothly, however. In 1905, the U.S. Supreme Court rendered a startling five-to-four decision in *Lochner v. New York*. Striking down the 1895 New York ten-hour law for bakers, and driving a doctrinal wedge between it and the 1896 Utah eight-hour law for miners, the Court declared:

> We think that there can be no fair doubt that the trade of a baker, in and of itself, is not an unhealthy one to that degree which would authorize the legislature to interfere with the right to labor, and with the right of free contract on the part of the individual, either as employer or employee . . . It might be safely affirmed that almost all occupations more or less affect the health. There must be more than the mere fact of the possible existence of some small amount of unhealthiness to warrant legislative interference with liberty . . . Statutes of the nature of that under review, limiting the hours in which grown and intelligent men may labor to earn their living, are mere meddlesome interferences with the rights of the individual.[26]

Reformers including Henry Seager initially hoped that *Lochner* would be a temporary aberration—which may account for the AALL's continuing optimism in its early years about the possibility of enlightening judges. But in fact this decision proved to be highly influential during most of the Progressive Era. In the words of the labor historian Elizabeth Brandeis, *Lochner* was the first decision "in which the United States Supreme Court held a statute to protect labor unconstitutional. It demonstrated that the court might outdo the state courts in construing the Fourteenth Amendment as forbidding such legislation . . . The effect of the Lochner decision was to circumscribe rather narrowly the occupations in which hours might be limited" for male workers.[27]

Bad as the *Lochner* decision was, state supreme courts were even more likely to render decisive blows against new social legislation, especially since their adverse decisions could not be appealed to the U.S. Supreme Court prior to 1914.[28] Although reformers understood that a number of state-level judiciaries such as those of Washington and Wisconsin were moving in a progressive direction, they complained bitterly about inconsistency across the states. "The very indefiniteness and uncertainty of this [constitutional] barrier," explained Seager, "depending as it does upon the variable opinions of the judges of our higher courts, makes it even more of an obstacle to intelligent law making."[29] Reformers perceived, as W. F. Dodd put it, that "the greater number of our state courts are illiberal and, under our present constitutional and judicial organization, are able to block needed social and industrial legislation."[30] Especially embittering were adverse decisions such as *Ives v. South Buffalo Railway.* In this 1911 case, the New York Court of Appeals (as the highest court in that state was called) struck down a popular compulsory workmen's compensation statute, citing the "due process" clauses of both the state and federal constitutions. The court denounced the 1909 law as "plainly revolutionary" and claimed that it would be an unconstitutional "taking of property" to modify the longstanding common-law precedent that "no man who was without fault or negligence could be held liable in damages for injuries sustained by another."[31] The *Ives* decision could not be appealed—although it could have been had the New York Court of Appeals ruled in favor of the statute.

By the height of the Progressive Era, therefore, the initial optimism of American labor law advocates about the likely adaptability of the courts had given way to palpable irritation—and their tactics had changed accordingly. In 1912, Seager called for changes in the judicial system, including "machinery for the easy amendment of state constitutions" to facilitate the reenactment of judicially invalidated labor laws "that have public opinion overwhelmingly behind them."[32] And in 1915, Seager denounced repeated instances in which "legislation that has had the well-nigh unanimous approval of students of economics and of social workers has been declared unconstitutional by our Court of Appeals." He argued to an audience at the New York City Club that the "point of view so frankly expressed in the Ives decision should warn us from expecting too great liberality of interpretation from judges trained and selected as our judges are trained and selected."[33]

No longer willing to trust in the reasonableness of American judges, Seager and others proposed on behalf of the AALL a comprehensive "social legislation amendment" to the New York State Constitution. "[B]road enough to enable the Legislature to pass any kind of social or protective legislation that is in actual operation in other countries or currently advocated by any considerable number of our citizens," the proposed amendment covered the entire AALL wish-list, including maximum hours and minimum wages for men and women to be administered by a commission; workmen's compensation; and contributory insurance against death, illness, old age, and unemployment.[34] Seager also wanted the new state constitution to include a provision that the Court of Appeals could not rule a law unconstitutional except by two-thirds majority. But the AALL could not persuade the New York Constitutional Convention to include anything more than a provision allowing for workmen's compensation legislation. Anyway, in November 1915, the people of New York voted overwhelmingly against the proposed new constitution—just as the people of California would in 1918 vote overwhelmingly against a constitutional amendment sponsored by the AALL to allow health insurance in that state.[35]

If worries about court declarations of unconstitutionality prompted the reformers of the AALL to shift tactics from intra-elite arguments toward campaigns to amend constitutions, those worries also affected their legislative efforts. Recently, the historian Melvin Urofsky has argued that progressive reformers were "delayed in the courts . . . [but] not blocked there."[36] Delays, however, could be decisive, given that campaigns for new social legislation during the 1910s either succeeded suddenly across many states at peak moments of publicity and public concern about a given problem, or else did not succeed at all. The campaign for health insurance in California was sidetracked, for example, by the need to fight first for an enabling amendment to the state constitution, a situation which gave opponents extra time and reasons to mobilize.[37] Moreover, Urofsky fails to take account of the ways reformers modified the content of their proposals, or even dropped policy goals altogether, in response to anticipated difficulties in the courts.[38]

Seager testified that the New York Wainwright Commission, which fashioned the 1909 workmen's compensation bill, gave "anxious thought to trying to draft an act that the Court of Appeals would uphold . . . Our act was maimed and twisted so that it might commend itself to the judges."[39] This sort of anticipatory modification was common for many state-level workmen's compensation proposals, and usually resulted in statutory concessions being made to propertied interests, in the hope that the courts would accept the laws once enacted. We also know that reformers saw possible difficulties about the constitutionality of old-age pensions, because of state-level provisions that forbade taxation and spending for anything but a clear "public purpose." Old-age pensions for the poor were considered the most likely to stand up to state constitutional tests, and this perception may have influenced the kinds of proposals reformers backed during the 1920s, when they finally began to promote this sort of social legislation.[40]

More important, during the Progressive Era the reformers of the AALL backed off altogether from pursuing maximum hour and minimum wage regulations applicable to all workers. The 1905 *Lochner* decision forced all progressive social reformers to deemphasize broad hours laws for male workers, and to concentrate instead on limits for narrowly circumscribed male occupations as well as on laws for women, as we shall see in Chapter 7. Minimum wages for men, moreover, seemed entirely unattainable. Clearly wishing that it could imitate the British Trade Boards Acts of 1909 and 1918, which allowed administrative regulation of wages for workers in unorganized industries, the AALL sponsored discussions on minimum wages and several of its leading members published articles on the topic.[41] But given the reasoning of the U.S. courts in protective labor law cases, the Association never dared to make general minimum wage regulations a legislative priority during the 1910s.

Speaking in 1915, the year he became president for the second time of the AALL, a chastened Seager appropriately summed up the effects of the courts on early U.S. advocates of social legislation. Not only did the courts set back or force the modification of positive proposals. In addition, the "fear that . . . legislation might be declared unconstitutional has been a constant bugaboo paralyzing the efforts of advocates of promising legislative experiments. If . . . American states are . . . behind progressive European countries in the field of social and labor legislation," he concluded, "it is chiefly because of this constitutional barrier."[42] Through frustrating experiences with the U.S. courts, Seager and the AALL had come a long way from their optimism of the very early 1900s about quickly convincing judges to accept new European-style social legislation. A decade later, the reformers were unavoidably faced with the task of persuading the broad American public, not just to press for new laws, but also to modify constitutional provisions that judges might use to strike them down.

The Struggle against Patronage Democracy and Public Wariness about Social Spending

When American advocates of social legislation tried to arouse broad public support for legislative proposals or constitutional revisions, they soon found out how difficult this could be. Part of the problem lay with the rationalist outlook and limited organizational capacities of the reformers themselves. As we learned in Chapter 3, the AALL was a tiny national association of experts, mostly professors, with a preference for talking with fellow professionals and interest-group leaders; and it was ill-prepared for grassroots mobilization across many local communities and legislative districts. In addition, as we learned in Chapter 4, the AALL was often at cross-purposes with the AFL on matters of social legislation. But the political difficulties faced by the AALL went deeper still. Across the United States during the Progressive period, the reform-minded middle-class public was not a very receptive audience for messages about new public spending for adult male wage earners.

When the international ferment over modern social insurance and pensions spread to Britain and the United States around the turn of the century, it caught these nations and their social and political elites at very different moments of political transformation. These were two liberal polities that had moved from patronage-dominated politics toward public bureaucratization at different phases of industrialization and democratization. Because Britain already had a reformed civil service, programmatically competing political parties, and legacies of centralized welfare administration to react against and build upon, modern social spending and labor regulations complemented the organizational dynamics of government and parties in that nation, and were not alarming to many within the elite and middle class. The United States, however, was embroiled in efforts to create regulatory agencies and policies free from the "political corruption" of party-dominated patronage democracy. At this juncture of American history, public social benefits aimed at masses of adult male citizens were not politically acceptable—and did not seem administratively feasible, either—to elite and middle-class public opinion. This was especially true for social-spending measures that closely resembled Civil War pensions, which epitomized "political corruption" for many reform-minded citizens.

Whatever its social-welfare achievements through the extension of Civil War pensions and other distributive benefits, the patronage democracy of the nineteenth-century United States was not ideally suited to coping with the governmental problems of a rapidly maturing industrial-capitalist economy and an increasingly differentiated and integrated national society. In one way or another, politically dissident Americans of various classes and outlooks were saying exactly this from the 1870s onward. "Populist" movements called for strict governmental regulation of railroads and financiers, along with more generous governmental supports for farmers (and sometimes tenants as well).[43] Movements of "labor"—which often appealed beyond wage-workers alone to include all who worked productively for a living—called for regulation of finance-capital and "monopoly" businesses, and advocated such social measures as expanded public education and regulation of working conditions.[44] Meanwhile, at the other end of the class spectrum, groups of patricians and professional people in New England and beyond pursued the Mugwump movement for better and more honest government.[45]

Like the British civil service reformers of the 1870s, the Mugwumps wanted public adminstration to be taken out of patronage politics. Determined advocates of a professional and meritocratic civil service, the Mugwumps hoped to take government out of the hands of party politicians and give it instead to socially respectable, educated people—like themselves. Yet the Mugwumps also had broader objectives; they wanted to make possible public policies that were consistent and nondistributive, policies to do such collectively beneficial things as provide efficient and reliable municipal public services for urban-dwelling property owners, or create a predictable regulatory environment for economic enterprises. The Mugwumps opposed populist or labor-oriented policies, yet they also opposed cutthroat capitalist competition and "corrupt" arrangments between businessmen and party politicians. Farmers, businessmen, and workers had to resolve their conflicts of interest consensually if anarchy, ruthless competition, and class conflicts were to be avoided in industrializing America. Administrative reforms and principled, nonpartisan politics were means for developing efficient consensual solutions in the public interest, the Mugwumps believed.

Despite the stresses placed upon it by industrialization, the nineteenth-century American "state of courts and parties" did not change quickly or in any smoothly functionalist manner. Patronage democracy actually reached its apogee in the late nineteenth century. Together with the courts, the regular parties defused threats of working-class radicalism; and the parties first absorbed and then destroyed the Populist challenge.[46] Party politicians, moreover, fended off the Mugwumps, co-opting some of their issues, including their civil service proposals when these could be used to shore up rather than replace the patronage system.[47] The reform proposals of the Mugwumps at first made only limited headway, because U.S. party politicians had secure roots in the fully democratized and tautly mobilized mass white-male electorate. In contrast to the situation in Britain, there was no impending threat of further electoral democratization to prod political party leaders as well as social elites into civil service reform.[48]

Only around the turn of the twentieth century did patronage democracy finally weaken as a coordinative system for the national polity as a whole.[49] The "Third party system," which had held sway from the 1870s through the 1890s, could not withstand the sudden imbalancing of electoral competition that occurred in the aftermath of the realigning election of 1896. Rather than closely balanced electoral competition, where either Democrats or Republicans could hope for spoils after every election, the post-1896 imbalance of the "Fourth party system" sharply favored the Republicans nationally and in most states of the East and Midwest. With less party competition in most areas, electoral participation declined—from an average of 81.6 percent outside the South in presidential elections between 1876 and 1892 to an average of 75.4 percent in similar elections between 1900 and 1916.[50] The ability of regular parties to mobilize and control voters was weakened in many states by the passage of laws making voter registration and elibility tougher, outlawing public voting and "straight" tickets, and establishing primary elections and popular referenda instead of party-controlled procedures for nominating candidates and enacting legislation. Lower-strata voters were more likely than middle-class citizens to abstain from voting after the 1890s, and less privileged voters also abstained disproportionately from primaries and special referenda. Meanwhile, as organized groups outside of regular party organizations intervened directly in politics, insurgent politicians within each party saw opportunities to challenge the party regulars by appealing to reform-oriented associations.[51]

These processes did not by any means eliminate patronage-oriented party organizations or fully eclipse the distributional styles of policymaking that were their primary stock in trade. Urban machines still flourished in many industrial cities; state party "bosses" held their own in many instances; and much of congressional politics still revolved around the tariff. But the U.S. governmental system as a whole became less integrated—across the levels of the federal system, and between legislative and executive functions—than it had been when the competing patronage parties were at their strongest. This happened at the same time as extralocal social and economic ties were increasing, allowing groups to associate directly for political ends without working through the established political parties. With the weakening of party organizations and the slacking off of party competition, fresh opportunities opened up to achieve innovative policies and to institutionalize new forms of politics and administration. The new opportunities were especially great where associations with reform objectives could gain influence not only with legislatures but also with the executive officials—mayors, governors, and Presidents—who were becoming more independent of party controls and assertive in relation to legislatures.

The Progressive Era thus arrived. In keeping with the phase of political transformation in which it emerged, the general mood of progressivism was infused with determination to root out "corrupt" forms of party patronage and machine democracy (which were, in fact, already weakened). As corruption was fought, "the public interest" could be quickly recognized, embodied in reform laws, and implemented by experts free from the divisions and corruptions of older-style politics.[52] Or so many people hoped, rather apocalyptically, during this time of reform ferment from about 1906 to 1920.

New uses of governmental authority, not just political reforms, were very much on public agendas during the Progressive Era. "Social progressivism" is the label some historians have given to movements in this period that worked not primarily for structural reforms in civil service and the parties (such reforms could readily gain the support of conservatives and business rationalizers), but mainly for new public measures to improve industrial working conditions, to help families and children, and to ensure better products, services, and environmental conditions for consumers.[53] The AALL was, of course, part of social progressivism, as were various other leagues or associations mainly peopled by upper-class and professional people sympathetic to the working class. In addition, groups of social workers and many kinds of women's associations figured prominently in the phenomenon of social progressivism.[54]

It will not do, however, to imagine social progressivism as a fixed collection of groups and associations pursuing a master legislative agenda of socioeconomic reform. Actually, particular coalitions of groups formed and reformed around changing specific issues.[55] And the pursuit of reforms through government was only one avenue of action for most individuals and organizations involved in progressive social reform. The period witnessed an outpouring of voluntary civic efforts for purposes of social betterment: to make cities more livable; to help the working classes and the "deserving" poor; to speed the assimilation of immigrants. Some of the more traditional, moralistic groups avoided politics. But most reform groups proceeded partly through voluntary efforts to deal directly with specific social problems, and partly by mobilizing support for new laws and government agencies, where it was believed that these might deal more effectively with given problems. Social progressives, therefore, combined voluntary and governmental tactics. As Robert Buroker's insightful study of the Illinois Immigrants' Protective League demonstrates, they could be very flexible in emphasizing one approach or another,

even moving back and forth as individuals or groups from civic
voluntary efforts to working through government agencies, as
changing circumstances warranted.[56]

When reform-minded groups in the Progressive Era did mobilize
politically, the main tactics they used were publicity about a specific
problem for consumers or workers, followed by agitation and lobbying for model laws to be passed across a number of states. State
legislatures were the sites of most social-policy debates during the
Progressive Era, because party and regional balances in the federal
Congress made it difficult to pass reforms other than economic
regulations.[57] Measures dealing with problems that could be widely
and simply dramatized in human terms were the socioeconomic
reform laws most likely to be enacted in the states. Broad and het-
erogeneous coalitions of support—including many social progressive
groups along with (at least some) other forces, such as urban machines, trade unions, progressive business associations, or farm
groups—were mobilized into the successful legislative campaigns. In
each state, conservatives invariably argued against reforms on the
ground that local taxes or business costs might rise while leaving
competitors in other states untouched. To defuse this issue of interstate competition, the social progressives simultaneously sought uniform laws, especially for adjacent states.[58] Dramatic publicity and
broad coalitions were essential because, in the absence of disciplined
programmatic parties, ad hoc and transpartisan sets of politicians in
numerous state legislatures had to be persuaded to act, ideally in a
kind of snowballing succession. If state legislatures could be induced
to imitate one another, this could turn U.S. federalism from a structure that impeded legal reforms into a framework that facilitated
sudden bursts of enactments through competitive emulation.

New social spending measures to benefit male wage earners or the
elderly did not fit the formula for legislative success in the Progressive Era, however. Such policies could not get support or acquiescence from broad coalitions including middle- and upper-class
groups. Reacting to policy legacies from the nineteenth century, such
people lacked confidence in the administrative capacities of government and opposed large-scale public spending programs that would
deliver benefits directly to individual voters. Throughout the Progressive Era, the common denominator of all reform remained the
struggle against political corruption. Upper- and middle-class people

doubted that social spending measures could be implemented honestly, and feared that they might well reinforce the hold over the electorate of patronage politicians.

Elite Fears about Public Pensions—Especially in Massachusetts

These fears were strongest and most openly expressed about non-contributory old-age pensions, which were perceived as governmental handouts very likely to recapitulate the political abuses that elites perceived in outdoor relief and post–Civil War pensions for Union veterans. Writing in the *Independent* in 1899, W. E. H. Lecky highlighted the analogy to outdoor relief and argued that old-age pensions would

> certainly introduce into our political life most dangerous and unhealthy influences . . . such a policy could hardly fail to pass into the arena and the competitions of party politics, and to bring in its train gross political corruption. Few well-wishers of the country could look forward with equanimity to a general election in which the increase or extension of the pension system was the main question at issue, and in which the majority, or at least a preponderating section of the electors had a direct, personal, money interest in the result.[59]

Others thought they saw a clear precedent for exactly this unedifying scenario in the nation's experience with Civil War pensions. Speaking back in 1889 at the time of an election involving the future of Civil War pensions, a leading Mugwump and the president of Harvard, Charles Eliot, had denounced the politicization of these benefits in a speech at the Bay State Club of Boston:

> I hold it to be a hideous wrong inflicted upon the republic that the pension system instituted for the benefit of soldiers and sailors of the United States has been prostituted and degraded . . . As things are, Gentlemen, one cannot tell whether a pensioner of the United States . . . is a disabled soldier or sailor or a perjured pauper who has foisted himself upon the public treasury. I say that to put the pension system of the United States in this condition is a crime. . . against Republican institutions.[60]

A year after President Eliot's speech, Edward Henry Hall devoted a whole Sunday sermon at the First Parish Church in Cambridge to denouncing Civil War pensions. While condemning unscrupulous politicians, Hall was especially upset about the degradation of the nation's patriotic citizen-soldiers through their dependency on (and unseemly demands for) pensions. He lamented that the "united endeavors of all the wisest philanthropists in all our cities to substitute self-support for beggary will be like sweeping back the waves of the ocean, so long as the nation itself is feeding a horde of hungry mendicants at the public table."[61] Echoes of Eliot's and Hall's revulsion against public pensions reverberated into the early twentieth century.

Indeed, much evidence for the pivotal state of Massachusetts points to the centrality of upper- and middle-class fears about the political corruptibility of pensions as a chief obstacle to new noncontributory old-age benefits. Except for elite opinion, other conditions favored the early adoption of British-style old-age pensions in Massachusetts. As the first state in the United States to industrialize and urbanize in forms and tempos close to those of England, Massachusetts was the pioneer state in economic regulation, labor statistics, and social legislation in the nineteenth century, often serving as the gateway for British-style reforms to pass into the United States. Moreover, this state was the home of America's counterpart to Charles Booth, the early British advocate of old-age pensions.[62] Edward Everett Hale, a Boston Unitarian minister and editor of the "magazine of organized charity," *Lend a Hand: A Record of Progress,* proposed in an 1890 address to the National Association of Life Companies that the state of Massachusetts devote the revenues from its annual poll-tax on all adult males over age 18 to fund a "universal life endowment" offering a "pension of one hundred dollars annually, paid to all men over eighty who have lived twenty-five years in the state, and to the wives of those who are married."[63] Pointing out that a "well-considered plan [that is, Booth's] for a general system of pensions for all the aged has been under discussion in England for several years," Hale argued that his proposed "endowment" would allow all of the "old taxpayers in Massachusetts" to "receive a pension . . . without regarding themselves as paupers."[64]

Over the next two decades, Hale continued to promote the pension idea.[65] In 1905–06, old-age pension bills were introduced in the Massachusetts legislature and received considerable support, as the

Boston Transcript commented that "the same policy is said to be receiving support from the new liberal Government in England."[66] In 1907, the Massachusetts legislature, the General Court, authorized the governor to establish "a commission . . . to investigate and consider the various systems of old age insurance or old age pensions, or annuities, proposed or in operation in this commonwealth or elsewhere, and report upon the advisability of establishing an old age insurance or pension system in the commonwealth."[67] During and after the life of this commission, finally, we have much evidence that both organized labor and the Massachusetts citizenry in general found the possibility of noncontributory old-age pensions very appealing.[68] In short, if a cross-state movement for the enactment of old-age pension laws *had* started in the early twentieth century United States, Massachusetts is surely where it would have begun.

But when it reported in 1910, the Massachusetts Commission on Old Age Pensions, Annuities and Insurance dealt a virtual death blow to what had previously been a growing movement toward this type of social provision in that state—as well as in other states whose reformers and officials tended to keep an eye on developments in Massachusetts. Entirely staffed by private citizens appointed by a conservative Republican governor, the Massachusetts Commission included one representative of organized labor, Arthur Huddell, who ultimately dissented from the arguments against noncontributory old-age pensions and endorsed the AFL's and William Kelley's "Old Age Home Guard" proposal pending in the national Congress.[69] Otherwise, the Commission was staffed by upper-class and professional people, including Mrs. M. R. Hodder and a representative of employers, along with its chairman, Magnus W. Alexander, a chief engineer at the General Electric Company; its executive secretary, F. Spencer Baldwin, an economics professor at Boston University; and Walter Greenough Chase, a prominent Boston physician.[70]

After analyzing considerable data on the elderly destitute, the Commission concluded that elder poverty was much less a problem in Massachusetts than in England, and that there were many charitable and relief measures already in place to deal with it. The Commission acknowledged that compulsory contributory old-age insurance might one day be necessary:

A system of State insurance thus grounded would be based on the principle of enforced obligation on the part of the individual to insure himself, and not on that of the recognized duty on the part of the State to pension all worthy citizens. The British and Australian pension systems are based on the latter principle, involving the doctrine that a citizen may claim a pension from the State as a civil right. That doctrine is distinctly un-American.[71]

But the Commission felt that compulsory insurance was not yet "expedient" and—perhaps sensing the greater popularity of non-contributory pensions—directed most of its fire against them. Vivid arguments against noncontributory pensions were summarized at length and often commented upon approvingly in its report:[72] Individual character would be "debilitated" and families would "disintegrate" if thrift were no longer rewarded. On this, the Commission cited testimony by Miss Alice L. Higgins, Secretary of the Associated Charities of Boston; she voiced views typical of Massachusetts charity and social workers, who maintained over several decades a staunch stand against any noncontributory "outdoor relief."[73] The Commission also argued that this sort of "class legislation" would "tax the rich for the benefit of the poor" and was of "extremely doubtful" constitutionality. Moreover, the "cost of noncontributory pensions would be enormous," because predicted reductions in the cost of poor relief would "not be forthcoming."

The Commission's worries about high costs were clearly spurred by its sense that the "political effects of any non-contributory pension system would be mischievous; it would open the door to political favoritism or various sorts. There would be constant political pressure to increase the amount of pensions, to lower the age limit, to make the administration laxer."[74] Significantly, the Commission was able to cite the testimony of John Graham Brooks, the leading social reformer and pioneering American student of workingmen's insurance.[75] At a hearing on November 27, 1908, Brooks criticized the 1908 British old-age pension act for giving "the local politicians a chance to call upon the vague sympathy of the community," and declared to the Commission:

I should say that the condition of our politics is the first difficulty in the way of the working of a pension scheme. I need not waste any breath on that. You know precisely what this is, and we have no end of illustrations of the way that we pension off all sorts of persons in the army; while there are a large number of deserving, there are many thousands who are not,—and pensions are given on account of politics. I do not see how we can save any pension system in this country from running into politics.[76]

Supporter of new social protections for workingmen that he was, Brooks was also part of the Massachusetts reform tradition stretching back through Charles Eliot's opposition to Civil War pensions. Non-contributory old-age pensions were too "political" for him to endorse; and the Commission obviously agreed.

As the 1907–1910 Commission deliberated, reformers were already attempting to cope with needs for old-age protection through the "Savings Bank Insurance Plan," which enjoyed broad support from unions, employers, social workers, and "other public-spirited citizens" as "Massachusetts' substitute for old age pensions."[77] This interesting (albeit ultimately ineffective) plan attacked the vested interest of insurance companies in their profits on life-insurance schemes, thus indicating a willingness on the part of Massachusetts reformers to oppose big business. But in order to avoid relying on government spending, the Savings Bank Insurance Act passed in 1907 mandated savings banks to market low-cost old-age or life insurance policies to Massachusetts citizens. The author of the savings bank scheme, Louis Brandeis, wanted to avoid public benefits because he believed that "our government does not now grapple successfully with the duties which its has assumed, and should not extend its operations at least until it does."[78] The Commission on Old Age Pensions, Annuities and Insurance cited the prior existence of this scheme as a primary reason against endorsing any other legislation in 1910: "Massachusetts is definitely committed . . . to an experiment with voluntary insurance under public administration . . . We are of the opinion, accordingly, that it would be premature and inconsistent to experiment with any non-contributory or compulsory scheme until the savings bank insurance system has been allowed ample opportunity to demonstrate its full effects."[79] Brandeis and the Commission were willing to ask the state to regulate, but not to spend.

During the life of the Commission on Old Age Pensions, "good government" reformers in Massachusetts were engaged through an investigatory Financial Commission in denouncing the extravagant practices of patronage politicians in Boston.[80] Indeed, Boston machine politicans, along with those in other Massachusetts towns, were very much in the practice of pursuing their own interests, and incidentally ameliorating social problems of unemployment, by dispensing jobs in government and on public works projects.[81] But reform-minded upper- and middle-class citizens did not approve. With dissent coming only from a labor representative, the 1909 Financial Commission Report censured Boston Mayor John F. ("Honey Fitz") Fitzgerald for expanding public employment, letting out public contracts without competitive bidding, and hiring patronage workers. The Financial Commission's solution was to propose strict controls on public spending.

Ethnic tensions between the Anglo-Saxon Protestant Massachusetts establishment and the predominantly Irish Catholic Boston lower strata obviously figured in such happenings, and one might wonder whether such ethnic conflicts account for U.S. versus British patterns of social policymaking.[82] Ethnic conflicts in politics were not simply primordial givens, however. They crystallized especially in struggles over the role of political patronage.[83] These struggles, rather than the more-often-cited ethnic divisions within the U.S. working class, are the primary mechanism by which ethnic variety in America adversely affected the prospects for modern social benefits programs. For we must keep in mind that floods of Irish poor also immigrated into industrializing England, creating sharp sociocultural tensions there as well, but without preventing the emergence of a modern welfare state in a British polity *not* racked with quarrels over patronage at the turn of the twentieth century.

The Public—and Reformers—Connect Pensions to Corruption

Not only in Massachusetts but across the nation during the early 1900s, noncontributory pensions took on bad connotations in public discourse. Magazines ran exposés of the corruption of Civil War pensions, especially when Congress was debating possible new liberalizations of pension rules, thus keeping negative images of what could happen with public pensions before the educated public.[84] In due course, even advocates of new forms of social provision for workingmen and the elderly realized that noncontributory old-age pensions could not be imported from Britain to the United States.

The magazine that pursued the antipension cause the most

doggedly was *The World's Work*, launched in 1900 as a "quality" magazine partially owned and editorially controlled by Walter Hines Page.[85] Page was from the South, a region whose leaders felt sharply disadvantaged by Civil War pensions; and he had formerly been editor of the *Forum,* which had published a spate of exposés of pension politics during the late 1880s and the 1890s.[86] *World's Work* was "a moderate success from the beginning, attaining a circulation of 100,000, with 50 to 100 pages of advertising per issue by 1907."[87] Optimistic about the future of large-scale American industry in the new century, and ambivalent about trade unions, the magazine was editorially friendly to both Theodore Roosevelt as a progressive Republican and Woodrow Wilson as a progressive Democrat. Along with other mildly reformist journals of opinion, *World's Work* both reflected and helped to constitute moderate public opinion. Abuses by business were sometimes criticized in its pages, but government corruption and extravagance were more often highlighted. And the "abuse against which *World's Work* waged its longest war was the 'padding' of pension rolls and the growth of the pension burden on the taxpayers."[88] The first article, criticizing "Our Enormous Pension Roll" appeared in 1904.[89] Then came not one, but two, blockbuster series of articles tracing the historical expansion of Civil War pensions, each series replete with illustrations, graphs, and colorful exposés of fraud and abuse in the bloated pension system. From October 1910 through March 1911, William Bayard Hale, the magazine's staff representative in Washington, DC, published six articles on "The Pension Carnival" whose individual titles nicely convey their message:[90]

"Staining a Nation's Honor-Roll With Pretense and Fraud: An Introduction to an Inquiry Why, Half a Century After the Civil War, We are Still Paying a Hundred and Fifty Millions a Year for Pensions."

"Rolling Up the Big Snowball: The Origin and Early Years of Pension Legislation—How the Nation's Natural Gratitude Was Capitalized By Sharp-Practice Lawyers and 'Protective'-Tariff Advocates."

"Capitalizing the Nation's Gratitude: Story of the Period of Accelerated Legislation—The High Tariff—Big Pension Alliance—How It Created Surpluses in the Treasury and Then Looted It."

"Favorite Frauds for Tricking the Treasury: Particular Cases of Masqueraders, Rogues, Perjurers, Fake-Veterans, and Bogus Widows in the Merry Game of Swindling the Government."

"The Growing National Scandal of the Private Pension Act: An Investigation of Typical Special Legislation by Congress—Absurd and Impudent Claims Passed by Political Influence—'Lame Duck' Senators and Representatives Busier Than Ever."

"'Correcting' Records of the Dishonorably Discharged: How Congress is Rewriting the History of the Great Struggle and Admitting Deserters, Embezzlers, Murderers, and Cowards to the Ranks of Heroes."

Lest any of its readers fail to get the point, *World's Work* followed up Hale's articles of 1910–11 with another set of three on "Pensions—Worse and More of Them" written by a former brigadier general in the Union army, Charles Francis Adams of 84 State Street, Boston. These articles portrayed the ever rising costs of Civil War pensions, detailed the machinations of legislators in making them ever more generous, and documented lurid cases of "fraud and abuse" by individual claimants. Adams's articles originally appeared from December 1911 through February 1912, and were subsequently reprinted in a pamphlet whose colorful title is illustrated in Figure 12.[91]

World's Work did not hesitate to make explicit the ways in which any new old-age pension legislation might be expected to repeat the abuses attributed to Civil War pensions. "Experience is uniform and invariable," argued Adams, "to the effect that every measure of indiscriminate public giving far exceeds, in its practical operation, any previous estimate made of the cost thereof. It proved so in the case of the British Old Age Pension act, the provisions of which were most general."[92] Even limited proposals for civil service retirement benefits had to be ruled out according to *World's Work:* "There are many arguments in favor of a pension for men and women who have given long and faithful service in the civil branches of Government. But no thoughtful man can favor such pensions in the light of our experience with military pensions. We have proved that the Government cannot be trusted with further responsibilities of this nature."[93] Ultimately, what worried *World's Work* most was not just

THE CIVIL-WAR PENSION LACK-OF-SYSTEM

A FOUR-THOUSAND-MILLION RECORD

OF LEGISLATIVE INCOMPETENCE

TENDING TO

GENERAL POLITICAL CORRUPTION

BY

CHARLES FRANCIS ADAMS

Reprinted from The World's Work

*"I want to say this, here and now, though I realize the
effect of my vote upon this question, that $50,000,000
a year is too big a price for the country to pay to bring me
back to Congress."* — Hon. WILLIAM HUGHES, M. C.—
Congressional Record, January 10, 1911, page 750.

Figure 12   Title page of "The Civil-War Pension Lack-of-System,"
by Charles Francis Adams, 1912

the proclivity of politicians to spend without limit; the magazine's editors also worried that universal public pensions would have broad popular appeal:

> So pervading is the effect of this long pension debauchery that this incredible thing happened: a petition to Congress to grant pensions to Confederate veterans received many signatures in an intelligent Southern community and was sent to Washington. The argument was that the Confederate veterans fought for a principle that they believed to be right.
>
> Such an incident might be dismissed as ludicrous or pathetic or imbecile; but it has this important significance: it shows that many people have come to regard pensions as a charity. If the Government gives out hundreds of millions to the deserving who fought for one principle why not to others who fought for another principle? Are we not living in a liberal age? Should charity be narrowly circumscribed?
>
> Thus it is possible that the poison of this demoralization may in time taint all public opinion and the Government come to be regarded as the great dispenser of alms.[94]

Walter Hines "Page claimed in 1913 that there had been 'a decided stiffening of courage and opinion' . . . [in opposition to further liberalizations of pensions] as a result of his magazine's articles."[95] Newspapers and other magazines echoed and amplified the exposés featured in *World's Work*.[96] "Sooner or later the country will have to smash the pension machine," declared a December 23, 1911, editorial in the *New York Evening Post* that cited Adams's articles.[97] The February 20, 1913, *Cleveland Plain Dealer* agreed that "Pension grabbers have Congress by the throat."[98] Similarly, the columnist Walter Lippmann cited William Bayard Hale articles in "Gratitude and Graft" for the August 1911 issue of *Everybody's Magazine*. "Whatever resentment there is in the country to-day on the subject of pensions," Lippmann concluded, "is directed against the notion that a recognition of service on the part of the nation should be used as a pork barrel by the unscrupulous . . . Perhaps some day we shall extend our notion of patriotism till it includes other kinds of service. What we resent is any extension of the notion to include private graft."[99]

In the context of the general crusade against political corruption waged by the polite media of the Progressive period, the articles in *World's Work* and other magazines about the abuses of Civil War pensions both expressed and reinforced the prejudice of educated public opinion against more universal noncontributory public old-age pensions.[100] Visible and highly emotional negative publicity about Civil War pensions during the Progressive period drowned out the scattered voices of labor leaders, certain reformers, and even an occasional businessman, who were prepared to see Civil War pensions as a positive precedent paving the way toward more universal old-age pensions.[101] The apparently overwhelming opposition of educated public opinion toward the legacies of Civil War pensions, and the general belief that noncontributory old-age pensions would be similarly politically corrupt, made even leading advocates of workingmen's benefits wary about uniting with the AFL to work for this potentially popular kind of public social protection.

For example, the University of Chicago sociologist and leading AALL member Charles Richmond Henderson wanted to believe that the logic of the Civil War pensions pointed toward more universal modern social provision. But Henderson was forced to acknowledge in his 1909 book *Industrial Insurance* that the "extravagance and abuses of the military pension system have probably awakened prejudice against workingmen's pensions."[102] Similarly, the AALL leader Henry Rogers Seager wrote favorably about Australasian and British-style old-age pensions in the early 1900s, but then backed away from making them central to the AALL's public campaign for workingmen's insurance.[103] Seager pointed out in his 1910 public lectures and book on *Social Insurance: A Program of Social Reform* that "Our experience with national military pensions has not predisposed us to favor national pensions of any description." Invoking the specter of what his listeners at the School of Philanthropy of the Charity Organization Society of New York surely knew had happened with Civil War pensions, Seager projected similar possibilities for public old-age pensions as he explained why they were not a good idea for the United States at that time: "Giving full weight to the fact that the number of aged persons is strictly limited, there is still the danger that, if we were once embarked on the policy of granting annuities out of the public treasury to private citizens, pressure would be brought to bear on Congress to lower the age limit and increase the annuity, and that this might lead to unwise extensions of policy in both directions."[104]

As the totality of Seager's remarks on old-age provision made clear, he was concerned that existing enterprise-level plans, run for loyal employees by a few private employers, failed to cover all employees and interfered with labor mobility. Even so, rather than risk politically motivated raids on the federal treasury by pensioners—the horror that had haunted Harvard's President Eliot—Seager cautiously concluded that it was necessary to keep hoping for the best in the evolution of private pension plans: "If corporation managers can be persuaded to substitute for their establishment pension plans systems that do not interfere with the mobility of labor, such full provision may be made through these systems . . . that government action, except to provide for public employees, will be unnecessary."[105]

Unlike the situation in turn-of-the-century England, in short, U.S. reformers, middle-class groups, and trade unionists could not come together in support of noncontributory old-age pensions as the first step toward a modern welfare state. Americans were split primarily along social class lines in their reaction to a previous policy—Civil War pensions—that everyone understood as similar to noncontributory old-age pensions. Given their opposition to patronage democracy, elites and the educated middle class tended to see Civil War pensions as an unsavory precedent to be avoided. At the same time, many labor leaders (and a very few reformers) regarded Civil War pensions as an honorable, democratic precedent that should to be extended to new categories of worthy citizens. A broad, cross-class political coalition for old-age pensions could not form in the United States during the critical 1910s. And even the reformers who advocated European-style social policies decided, for the time being, to direct their energies elsewhere.

Contributory Insurance and Doubts about Governmental Efficiency

It remains for us to understand what happened to state-level campaigns for social insurance in the United States. Except in the sensitive area of old-age pensions, Henry Seager's 1910 lectures on social insurance were a forceful call for positive governmental actions to promote the welfare of workingmen—fittingly enough for one who was a leading spokesman in the AALL's campaigns for contributory health and unemployment insurance. The evidence is clear-cut that the AALL and state-level investigatory commissions influenced by it deliberately deemphasized old-age pensions during the 1910s and chose to promote contributory social insurance instead.[106] Reformers clearly hoped that this kind of social legislation, which required the collection of tax "contributions" from workers as well as the disbursement of monies (and health services) to persons in their productive prime of life, would be more acceptable to elite and middle-class public opinion than were noncontributory old-age pensions.

Advocates of health insurance often argued that taxes collected from business and wage-earners would motivate both groups to "prevent" illness or unemployment; and they stressed the contributions social insurance would make to national efficiency.[107] Reformers were willing to endure the national AFL's hostility toward social insurance in the hope of appealing to fellow elites and public opinion with a vision of this allegedly more cost-efficient type of social provision. As the New Jersey Commission on Old Age, Insurance and Pensions explained in 1917 in terms that echoed standard arguments of the AALL:

> The Commission, originally authorized in 1911 to make investigations regarding the operation of pension, insurance and annuity systems, has collected much material relating to benefit systems of all kinds . . . In the course of its first studies of pension plans the Commission had its attention drawn to sickness as a factor in old age poverty . . . Obviously a reduction in the sickness problem would materially simplify the problem of old age poverty, in addition to saving for the State vast human resources now subject to the ravages of sickness. Moreover, health protection, which for some time has been regarded as the next logical step following the enactment of workmen's compensation laws and prevention of industrial accidents, has been raised by the war from a position deserving humanitarian consideration to one demanding action if we are to survive as a nation. We must have healthy armies in the field, we must have an efficient army of industrial workers behind the lines, and we must have healthy mothers and healthy babies to recruit our population. In this national emergency this Commission believes therefore that adequate health protection is of greater importance than measures designed merely to ease the often hard lot of those too old to do their bit with efficiency. Looking to the future, the Commission believes that sickness care and prevention will assure greater returns to the State in the

improved health and welfare of its citizens than a measure providing for care of the aged.[108]

By avoiding advocacy of potentially popular pensions for "those
too old to do their bit with efficiency," the AALL and other proponents of workingmen's benefits may have assuaged elite and middle-
class worries about the blatant corruption old-age pensions would
entail, but to little political avail. After the national American Federation of Labor failed to get support from the AALL on proposals
for federal old-age pensions, the AFL gave up on this idea around
1914. But simultaneously (as we saw in Chapter 4) the AFL refused
more explicitly than ever to cooperate with the AALL on social
insurance or labor regulations. More to the point, the AALL failed
to convince the public in general that health insurance was high-
priority reform legislation.

No doubt there are many reasons for the failure of state-level
campaigns for health insurance between 1916 and 1920, and in the
absence of contemporary public opinon polls we cannot be sure why
this proposed reform failed to generate sufficient support to urge
bills through legislatures and constitutional referenda. Nevertheless,
I think we can conclude that the reasons for the failure of health
insurance to gain broad public support lie deeper than the voluntarist values and fears about bureaucratic control often cited by
previous analysts as the chief reasons for the failure of this legislation.[109] To be sure, spokesmen for life insurance companies, for
some doctors, and for some parts of the trade union movement
invoked horrible specters of German-style bureaucratic oppression
as they argued against "compulsory" social insurance and in favor
of private initiatives.[110] Such arguments were magnified by the fact
that the United States was fighting a war with authoritarian Germany. But arguments against state controls were a feature of many
unsuccessful interest-group campaigns against social insurance in
Europe between the 1880s and the 1920s, and also of many unsuccessful arguments against other kinds of reform legislation in the
United States during the Progressive period. Such arguments would
not have been sufficient to stop health insurance—*if* there had been
broad and passionate public sentiment in favor of it in the United
States during the late 1910s.

That such sentiment did not develop was surely partly due to the
inability of the AALL and its allies to reach local communities and

ordinary Americans with vivid arguments in favor of health insurance. As I have already suggested, this failure was partly a by-product of the AALL's organizational structure and its penchant for rationalist discourse. It is hardly incidental that the one state in which health insurance came close to enactment, New York in 1919, was the state where both the State Federation of Labor and many women's groups, including the widespread New York Federation of Women's Clubs, became fully engaged in a passionate grassroots campaign for health insurance.[111] As Figure 13 illustrates, a cartoon reprinted from the *New York Telegram* at the front of the December 1918 issue of the *American Labor Legislation Review* acknowledged the centrality of women's groups in that state's health insurance drive by "progressive organizations." New York women's associations probably became involved because a strong Consumers' League and social settlement movement, both led by higher-educated women reformers, served as links between the "expert" world of the AALL and clubs of married women in hundreds of local communities across the state.[112] In most states, however, the AALL never got much further than stimulating favorable endorsements from state labor leaders and a few professional groups, and perhaps obtaining favorable recommendations for health insurance bills by public investigatory commissions. This was hardly enough to persuade state legislators to act.

Proponents of health insurance came up against another deep-rooted concern about U.S. government, in addition to the general fears about political corruption in any social spending program. The educated American public in the early twentieth century was not just worried that party politicians would spend too much on masses of voters if they got the chance; it was also worried that public programs could not be administered efficiently by municipal, state, and federal governments lacking strong civil services. This was stated by W. E. H. Lecky in 1899 as one argument against old-age pensions for the needy. "The question will naturally arise," he wrote,

> how it would be possible for the Government for ascertain the real means of the claimant for a pension, to discover whether he possesses private resources or savings so large as to disqualify him . . . Nothing . . . is more conspicuous in these schemes than the unlimited faith which seems to be felt in the power of the State to undertake any amount of administration, to multiply almost indefinitely its functions, its functionaries, and its responsibilities.

Greene, in New York (N. Y.) Telegram

A WOMAN'S WORK IS NEVER DONE

Following efforts for regulation of child labor, establishment of the living wage, and reduction of the working day, progressive organizations of all types are giving an increasingly prominent place on their programs to legislation for universal workmen's health insurance.

Figure 13

Source: *American Labor Legislation Review* 8(4) (December 1918), facing title page.

The danger of such a persuasion is very great. The State may easily be overweighted by the tasks that are thrown upon it, and, if so, its administration will be both inefficient and extremely costly.[113]

Almost two decades after Lecky's article, the U.S. Commissioner of Labor Statistics, Royal Meeker, gave a speech about "Social Insurance in the United States" to the National Conference of Social Work. A thoughtful supporter of many kinds of protections for workingmen, Meeker carefully worked his way through many arguments against health insurance, refuting most. But he ended up calling for private mutual insurance rather than public health insurance, because another "objection to social insurance is the incompetence of public officials which leads to extravagance in administration. There is unfortunately much truth in this allegation . . . [T]he public are unwilling to trust themselves to conduct insurance economically, efficiently and honestly."[114]

Even the leaders of the AALL, stalwart proponents of social insurance, appreciated that the public might like "efficient" reforms, but at the same time not believe that the U.S. government was efficient enough to administer them well. When Henry Seager gave his lectures on social insurance in 1910, he clearly understood the worries of the New York City audience of reform-minded, middle- and upper-class people to whom he was lecturing. He acknowledged that the

> characteristic common to most of the policies that I have advocated is that they call for vigorous governmental action. It is right here that we find the principal source of opposition to them in the United States . . . The truth is that our distrust of them is not due to the form of our government, or even to the size of our country, but to our distrust of government itself—a distrust which is partly inherited and partly the result of painful experience. We do not wish our cities, our states, nor our nation to undertake new and difficult functions, because we know that the functions they now take are too often ill performed.[115]

Seager conceded that the "next step toward introducing the program of social reform which I have outlined must be political reform" and he digressed to talk about a "housecleaning" campaign then going on in Albany to rid the state of "corrupt" legislators. Still, to Seager talking in 1910, an optimistic conclusion was warranted. "I believe," he declared to his audience, "that the fight for honest and efficient government is being won. And as it is won, we can safely impose on the government new and difficult functions . . . The argument that no new duties must be intrusted to the government because it fails in the duties it already has, seems to me no longer admissable."[116]

But when we realize that Seager was well toward the liberal, socially minded end of the Progressive Era's spectrum, we have to suspect that for many of his listeners (not to mention others who were not in such a reformist audience), the argument about governmental incapacities that Seager was trying to counter must still have been a very convincing reason *not* to support new measures of public social provision. Struggles against patronage politics—with its simultaneous links to business corruption and machine democracy—always remained paramount for middle- and upper-class Americans during the Progressive Era. Accordingly, the new governmental functions they were willing to support were those that could be safely entrusted to efficient, professional agencies carefully insulated from the "political" pressures toward "corruption" that any large-scale disbursements of public funds would necessarily bring. New regulatory policies were thus much more likely to succeed than new social spending measures.

Of course, a proposed new social spending measure might seem appropriate if noncorrupt, professionalized administrative agencies were already in existence—as was the case with mothers' pensions, whose administration during the 1910s (as we shall see in Chapter 8) was usually entrusted to juvenile courts. Also, to be sure, reformers could argue for the establishment of new administrative bodies along with the social policies they would putatively implement, as the AALL did in its drives for both health insurance and workers' compensation. But such arguments could backfire—arousing uncounterable, speculative fears about new forms of bureaucratic domination. Many private doctors seem to have responded in this way to the AALL's projections about the administration of health insurance. What is more, many members of the educated public must have perceived as pure pie-in-the-sky the promises of reformers that new administrative agencies could, without corruption or inefficiency, tax and spend to deliver health benefits to workers.

Reformers' hopeful projections about the honest and efficient "expert" administration of new social policies probably seemed plausible to the general public only if many groups already felt a compelling need for innovative governmental actions in a given policy area. As we are soon to see, many groups in the early-twentieth-century United States did feel such a need for new, reorganized governmental means to deal with industrial accidents. But few groups seem to have felt a compelling need for brand-new forms of governmental involvement in taxing and spending for workingmen's health benefits. And in the absence of such a felt compelling need, why take the chance that these benefits would be inefficiently administered, would entail unwelcome bureaucratic intrusions, or would bring new forms of political corruption in a democratic polity?

We can now sum up the messages of this section, which has explored Progressive Era politics in general along with specific obstacles to old-age pensions and social insurance. In clear contrast to contemporary Britain, the United States at the turn of the twentieth century was undergoing a transformation from party-dominated patronage democracy to interest-group-oriented, regulatory politics, a transformation that discouraged the inauguration of a modern paternalist welfare state. In this institutional setting and conjuncture of political change, American proponents of workingmen's insurance were unable to follow European-style routes for the implementation of new policy ideas from above. And they could not follow the route of successful Progressive reform campaigns, either. In the matter of health insurance, the reformers of the AALL could not convince broad coalitions of politically active groups to press new taxing and spending functions on state governments that palpably lacked already-established, efficient administrative capacities. And on the pivotal matter of noncontributory old-age pensions, where a cross-class coalition between reformers and trade unions might have been possible, most of the reformers of the 1910s could not even convince themselves. The precedent of Civil War pensions aroused too many fears, even among reformers, about what American politicians might do if they were handed a brand-new source of popular, democratic patronage—through social spending on masses of elderly voters.

The Success of (a Limited Kind of) Workmen's Compensation

It will not do to explain how America's governmental and political context in the early twentieth century frustrated prospects for old-age pensions and contributory insurance without at the same time explaining why it allowed the enactment of laws mandating businesses to compensate workers (and the survivors of workers who died) for industrial accidents. Between 1911 and 1913, twenty American states passed workmen's compensation laws that required regular compensations for industrial accidents, regardless of who caused them; and by 1920, forty-two states plus Alaska and Hawaii had such laws on the books.[117] "The enactment of accident compensation laws in state after state came with suprising rapidity," the labor historian Harry Weiss has written. "No other kind of labor legislation gained such general acceptance in so brief a period in this country."[118] We learned in Chapter 3 that the nationwide movement for workmen's compensation was endorsed by the the American Association for Labor Legislation, as what it expected to be the "first step" toward workingmen's insurance in the United States, soon to be followed by health insurance as the "next great step." The AALL used the same tactics in both campaigns, but obviously to very different political effect.

What the reformers of the AALL did not calculate was that contributory social insurance would have drawn the U.S. government as a taxer and spender into brand-new realms of social relations, whereas workmen's compensation legislation simply meant a *change in the form of longstanding governmental regulation* of the human consequences of industrial accidents. "In theory," as the historians Edward Berkowitz and Kim McQuaid have written, "passage of workers' compensation . . . marked a significant imposition of public control over private processes. In practice, . . . this public control had already existed in the form of the court system" within the nineteenth-century U.S. state of courts and parties.[119] Efforts by reformers to persuade U.S. governments to enact European-style workmen's compensation succeeded—up to a point—only after business, workers, and the educated public alike had became severely dissatisfied with America's preexisting governmental methods of dealing with industrial accidents.

Unpredictable Regulation by the Courts Leads to a Consensus for Reform

During the 1800s, workers injured in industrial accidents, as well as the survivors of workers killed on the job, turned to the courts if they wanted compensation; and the judicial reception of injured workers and their survivors shifted over time. In the very early phases of capitalist industrialization, Anglo-American common law was ambiguous about responsibility for many accidents.[120] Within tort law, the doctrine of *respondeat superior,* under which a principal was liable for the negligent acts of his agents, could potentially have been elaborated to hold enterprise owners responsible for injuries to their workmen that were attributable either to owners' negligence or to the negligent acts of other workmen. Instead, an 1837 English case called *Priestley v. Fowler* and an 1842 Massachusetts case called *Farwell v. Boston & Worcester Railroad Corporation* pushed the common-law response to industrial accidents in a very different direction. As Lawrence Friedman and Jack Ladinsky explain, judges who "placed their hopes of salvation on rapid economic growth," and who "were anxious to see that the tort system of accident compensation did not add to the problems of new industry," developed the "fellow-servant rule" as

> an instrument capable of relieving employers from almost all of the legal consequences of industrial injuries . . . Under this rule, a servant [that is, an employee] could not sue his master [employer] for injuries caused by the negligence of another employee. The consequences of this doctrine were far reaching. An employee retained the right to sue the employer for injuries, provided they were caused by the employer's personal misconduct. But the factory system and corporate ownership of industry made this right virtually meaningless.[121]

Along with the fellow-servant rule, two other common-law defenses were also available to employers hailed before the courts, as Melvin Urofsky explains.[122] "Contributory negligence" absolved the employer if the employee was "only minutely responsible for the accident." And that "led to the third defense, assumption of risk. If a laborer knew of dangers in the workplace, the law posited that the servant had bargained for a higher wage to compensate for the additional risk. Once having reached such an agreement, the worker 'assumed' the risk, and the employer could only be held liable if he had hidden or misled the worker about that risk." The doctrine of "assumption of risk" could even be stretched to absolve employers guilty of allowing obviously unsafe conditions to persist in their establishments.[123]

The "fellow-servant," "contributory negligence," and "assumption of risk" doctrines, taken together, shifted most of the cost of industrial accidents to unlucky individual workers and their families. When and where these doctrines held sway, injured workers who went to court usually did not make it past the judge to the (possibly) sympathetic ears of a jury of their peers. Judges simply threw their cases out of court, if the lawyers of the employers could show that one or more of the common-law defenses against liability applied.

But the doctrinal purity of the common-law defenses for employers eroded in the later nineteenth and early twentieth centuries. Sometimes the principles were modified by judges themselves. This happened, for example, in the state of Washington, where in 1902 a populist-minded Supreme Court—in an opinion written by Justice William H. ("Wild Horse Bill") White, a man with "little respect for judicial niceties"—ruled in *Green v. Western American Company* that, contrary to established judicial precedents, employers could not evade statutory safety rules by invoking "assumption of risk" arguments to blame workers.[124] The injured miner suing in this case was awarded damages. Less idiosyncratically, in Washington and other states over several decades,

> courts modified traditional employer defenses by making principled exceptions to them. One such exception was the "vice-principal" rule which maintained that an employer could not abrogate responsibility for an employee's injury caused by a foreman's negligence. A foreman, the doctrine held, acted as the agent—the "vice-principal"—of the employer and therefore could not be considered a "fellow servant" of the injured worker. The "common-employment" doctrine was another exception. If a conductor of a train negligently signaled the train to start moving before linemen had been warned and an injury occurred, then the railroad company could not escape responsibility by claiming that both the conductor and linemen were "fellow servants." Where the actual work of the two parties was utterly different they could not be considered fellow servants though they might have the same employer. Cases in which the "vice-principal" and the "common-employment" rules applied resulted in decisions favorable to the plaintiff.[125]

Overall, according to Friedman and Ladinsky, there "were scores of . . . 'exceptions' to the fellow-servant rule enunciated in one or more states."[126] As a Connecticut court explained as early as 1885, the "tendency in nearly all jurisdictions" was to "limit rather than en-large" the range of the fellow-servant rule.[127]

Legislatures as well as courts moved away from the strict medicine for injured workers of the common-law employer defenses. They passed various sorts of liability statutes. Urofsky tells us that as

> early as 1855 Georgia modified the fellow-servant rule, and by 1906 a sporadic but definite trend could be discerned. Seven states abolished the rule completely, and eighteen others modified it significantly . . . Nearly twenty states limited assumption of risk, and others restricted contributory negligence, often allowing re-covery under a theory of "proportional negligence" [in which an injured worker could get some damages if the employer or his agents shared in responsibility for the accident].[128]

Significantly, state legislatures could usually make their statutory revisions of the employer defenses stick with the courts, because the employer defenses were merely judicial interpretations of the com-mon law, not constitutional provisions. "Although courts followed a general rule that legislation annulling common law would be subject to close scrutiny, they also recognized that the legislature had the right, absent constitutional prohibitions, to amend or abrogate com-mon-law doctrine. Employers constantly claimed that such [liability] legislation violated due process or freedom of contract, but state courts consistently upheld the change in rules."[129]

As courts and legislatures chipped away at employer immunities under the common law, more and more injury suits were brought, and injured workers and survivors won higher proportions of them. There were growing numbers of potential plaintiffs, because "by the last quarter of the nineteenth century the number of industrial accidents had grown enormously. After 1900, it is estimated, 35,000 deaths and 2,000,000 injuries occurred every year in the United States. One quarter of the injuries produced disabilities lasting more than one week."[130] Having already lost life or employment, potential plaintiffs had little to lose by trying the courts, especially after lawyers became willing to take workers' cases on a contingent-fee basis. If lawyers and their clients could persuade judges to let cases go to jury trial—something that became easier to do as the principled employer defenses were eroded—then their chances of winning in the lower courts were good. "For example, in Wisconsin, of 307 personal injury cases involving workers that appeared before the state supreme court up to 1907, nearly two-thirds had been decided in favor of the worker in the lower courts."[131] And in a nationwide sample of 1,528 "appellate court cases tried between 1875 and 1905, juries [had] decided in favor of the employer in only 98 of 1043 cases. During this same period the number of workers' compensation cases rose from 92 to 736 per year."[132]

From the point of view of industrial employers, "doctrinal complexity and vacillation in the upper courts coupled with jury freedom in the lower courts" meant that the common-law defenses against liability for industrial accidents no longer worked well by the turn of the twentieth century.[133] At the very time "when American business, especially big business, was striving to rationalize and bureaucratize its operations," companies had to pay rising and wildly unpredictable amounts of legal costs of litigation and ever greater premiums for insurance against accident awards to injured workers.[134] "Private employer-liability insurance . . . [was] introduced in the United States in the 1880s, and premimums rose from about $200,000 in 1887 to more than $35,000,000 by 1912."[135] All of this happened, moreover, without satisfying most injured workers' demands for accident compensation. For even though the occasional lucky worker or his surviving family might win a big award in the courts, most workers or survivors either lost their suits—especially when employers appealed jury decisions to higher courts—or could not bring them in the first place. Winners of suits (or out-of-court settlements in anticipation of possible victories in litigation) also had to face uncertainty, and had to wait a long time for any compensation they won.

Between the 1880s and 1910, U.S. legal practices for dealing with industrial accidents were clearly under strain, and many groups—including business elites as well as organized labor and reformers—searched for new approaches. Meanwhile, muckrakers and social investigators spread to the general American public a vivid picture of the economic and human cost of industrial accidents, accompanied by analyses of the failings of the common-law system. Industrial accidents lent themselves to that combination of statistics and emotional human-interest stories that could best capture the public imagination on behalf of "efficient" reform in the Progressive period. "'If no nation in the world rivals the United States in the dash and energy of its business methods, no other nation is willing to pay the price in flesh and blood of citizens,' wrote Ellery Sedgwick in a famous [1904] article [in *Leslie's Monthly Magazine*] entitled 'The Land of Disasters,'" which argued that the U.S. rate of accidents was much higher than in Europe, and that many could be prevented.[136] In *Everybody's Magazine* in 1907, Arthur B. Reeve decried "the wanton slaughter of the toilers."[137] And the reformer-journalist William Hard declared in his 1910 book *Injured in the Course of Duty* that "Every accident (and especially every unpaid-for accident) hurts the *country* as well as the *individual*." Workers' compensation, he argued, would be a "National Economy" and a "Saving of Physical and Financial Strength for the World Struggle."[138]

The most influential study of industrial accidents during the Progressive period was unquestionably Crystal Eastman's *Work-Accidents and the Law*, a study financed between 1907 and 1910 by the Russell Sage Foundation as part of the comprehensive Pittsburgh Survey of working-class conditions.[139] Facing the title page of Eastman's data-packed book was a "Death Calendar in Industry for Allegheny County," Pennsylvania, with 526 crosses on days from July 1906 through June 1907, subtitled "Each cross stands for a man killed at work, or for one who died as a direct result of an injury received in the course of his work." This chart conveyed facts, and also had emotional punch. Using interviews and records, Eastman thoroughly investigated the causes of 1,000 fatal and nonfatal work accidents in Allegheny County, concluding that about two-thirds were not the fault of the men involved. Her study included accounts of the social consequences of accidents—most of them meagerly compensated or not compensated at all—for the families of injured and dead workers. It concluded with a suggestion that workmen's compensation might well be the way to correct the severe faults of the common-law employers' liability system, which Eastman, herself a lawyer, unequivocally summed up:

> The law in many of its principles is unjust; in operation it uses up time, money, and good will, to little purpose; it furnishes small incentive for the prevention of work-accidents; and leaves well-nigh the whole economic burden of work-accidents to be borne by the injured workman and his dependents, with consequent hardship and privation. It is to be condemned from the standpoints of justice, method, and practical utility.[140]

Here, then, was a situation amenable to broad support for new legislation, according to the usual script for progressive reforms.

Businessmen wanted relief from high and unpredictable costs; workers wanted quicker and more adequate compensation; and reformers and the educated public wanted an end to inefficiencies and unfairness. Accordingly, in a "brief but intense period of commission investigations," there were thirty state-level official examinations of the accident compensation issue between 1909 and 1913, and all of them condemned the system of employers' liability.[141] Reformers argued that an "efficient" and "rational" solution in "the public interest" would be laws requiring employers to pay fixed compensations to all injured workers, no matter what caused the accidents, in return for release from legal liability in the courts.

Although unions were reluctant to give up workers' rights to sue, they were eventually persuaded to support laws along these lines.[142] A prime example was the active participation of AFL unions and other labor organizations in the development of one of the first compensation laws in New York State during 1909 and 1910.[143] Increasingly convinced that even modified employer-liability rules were not allowing many workers to win compensation through the courts, the national AFL under Samuel Gompers took a strong interest in workmen's compensation from 1910 onward, and accepted it as a replacement for employers' liability in 1914.[144] In that year, the AFL also began agitation for significantly higher benefit levels and state insurance funds, and also sought to counter the practice of certain companies of subjecting workers to rigorous medical exams. Significantly, in the campaign for workmen's compensation, organized labor called upon women's clubs for support. The General Federation of Women's Clubs endorsed workmen's compensation at its 1910 Biennial Convention, after hearing AFL Vice President John Mitchell of the Mine Workers give a resounding account of "The Death Roll of Industry," as he praised the critical role of organized American women in achieving new social legislation.[145]

Many business groups were also involved in the movement for workmen's compensation. The otherwise arch-conservative Illinois Manufacturers' Association started to push for such legislation in 1909.[146] Speaking for progressive corporations, the National Civic Federation proposed a model bill for workmen's compensation in 1911.[147] And the National Association of Manufacturers, ordinarily opposed to all social legislation, endorsed workmen's compensation

at its 1911 Convention after a "1910 survey . . . of 13,000 businessmen showed that over 99 percent were in favor of automatic compensation as a way to reduce the waste and hostility engendered by
the common law and avoid having the problem 'settled for us with
a vengeance by the agitator and the demagogue.'"[148] According to
NAM, which was clearly worried about what kinds of laws would
replace the old employers' liability system, "the employer or insurance man who in the present day and age is obstructive or even
inactive in developing equitable workmen's compensation laws, and
above all in preventing accidents, is not a progressive or desirable
member of his class."[149]

The Enactment and Administration of Compensation Laws

Not surprisingly, state legislatures responded to the broad consensus
by enacting many workmen's compensation laws during the 1910s.
Although laws spread across most of the states with remarkable
speed, there was of course variation in how quickly state legislatures
acted on the new idea. One study has found that states "were quicker
to adopt legislation when [industrial] productivity and work-accident
litigation were high and when non-agricultural workers outnum-
bered agricultural ones."[150] Of course, the specific provisions of laws
also varied across the states. The important patterns of such statutory
variation have not been systematically analyzed, but available historical case studies suggest that much depended upon varying balances
of power and effort among business groups, labor organizations,
and reform associations. The "consensus for reform" that existed in
this policy area did not extend to the specific provisions of the laws—
which often accommodated the preferences of the industries dominant in each state, and occasionally met the demands of strong labor
movements.[151]

What the consensus around 1910 about the inadequacies of the
existing common-law system did do, however, was to create a sense
across most of the U.S. states that some sort of compromise should
be worked out, in order to give the new workmen's compensation
legislation a try. When the AALL took up the cause of workmen's
compensation legislation from 1909 onward, it obviously positioned
itself on promising terrain and joined armies of interest groups and
reformers already in the field of battle for a viable public policy

substitute to the legislatively amended common-law system of industrial-accident regulation. This is not to suggest that the AALL's contributions were not important, only that they helped to crystallize compromises in favor of workmen's compensation laws that were already in the making.

As with other kinds of labor policy, the courts had to be persuaded to accept this new kind of legislation—a fact which was highlighted for reformers by the jolting *Ives* decision by the New York Court of Appeals in 1911. This was a unanimous ruling that overturned that state's pioneering compulsory workmen's compensation act of 1910.[152] For two years after *Ives,* the AALL was engaged in New York state debates leading to a constitutional amendment and new workmen's compensation legislation in 1913. In addition, the AALL watched with concern as many other states sought to avoid constitutional difficulties by allowing all kinds of insurance options, including self-insurance, and by passing "optional" laws, which allowed businesses to opt out of workmen's compensation if they were willing to accept diminished common-law defenses. Not many businesses actually took this option, but optional state workmen's compensation systems usually kept benefits to injured workers low in order to discourage businesses from opting out.[153]

Given judicial diversity, not all legislatures or high courts followed the precedent of the *Ives* decision. Washington state, for example, created a compulsory state fund for workmen's compensation in 1911, and its Supreme Court quickly validated this law with reasoning opposite to that of the New York Court of Appeals.[154] Subsequently, in 1917, the U.S. Supreme Court found constitutional all three types of workmen's compensation schemes then in existence: those using private insurance, mutual funds, and state-administered insurance.[155] Probably, many state high courts and the U.S. Supreme Court found it easier to accept workmen's compensation than other kinds of social legislation for two reasons. First, government was already involved in this realm, so constitutional prohibitions about interference in free contracts may not have seemed as pressing to many judges. Secondly, prior to the enactment of workmen's compensation, the courts had been increasingly overwhelmed by industrial-accident cases, making it harder for them to deal adequately with other kinds of disputes, including kinds that may have been doctrinally more interesting to appellate court judges.[156] Like others in turn-of-the-century America, many judges may therefore have been quite happy to move the handling of industrial accidents onto a new, more rationalized regulatory basis.

In significant contrast to what it would do at the start of the health insurance campaign in 1915–16, the AALL did not at first promote an official "model bill" for workmen's compensation—probably because it joined rather than launched an already widespread movement when it officially began to promote workmen's compensation statutes in 1909. But a few years later, at the Association's 1913 Conference on Social Insurance, Professor William Willoughby complained that "No consistent or measurably complete [workmen's compensation] program has been adopted by any state. Legislatures are merely feeling their way step by step."[157] To counteract this disorderly pattern, the Committee on Social Insurance published in 1914 a pamphlet called *Standards for Workmen's Compensation Laws*. This set forth "a set of standards or minimum requirements for adequate legislation which could be used to evaluate the twenty-four state laws which had been passed."[158] The AALL's standards included calls for compensation of two-thirds of the lost wages of injured workers and 35 percent of wages to widows (plus more for dependent children); medical attendance of injured workers; creation of special boards or commissions to implement workers' compensation instead of the courts; and coverage of occupational diseases within workmen's compensation. Before long, moreover, the AALL was calling upon states to make workmen's compensation compulsory, not voluntary, and to substitute state-run insurance schemes for self-insurance or the use of private insurance carriers.

Although it had some success over the next decade in pushing new or improved state laws toward the standards it set in 1914–1918, the AALL never achieved anything close to universal acceptance of its prescriptions. Not heeded were the Association's recommendations for uniform benefits and generous compensation standards across the states. Not heeded either were various recommendations that would have pushed workmen's compensation in the direction of broad public provision rather than piecemeal regulation of private practices. "The AALL wanted coverage under the law to be universal, yet many states excluded casual, farm, or domestic workers. The association favored strict insurance regulations to put the force of law behind an employer's obligation to compensate his injured employees . . . [but] state laws offered a wide variety of insurance arrangements, including, in many states, the right of the employer to insure himself."[159] Despite the AALL's preference for state insurance funds, private insurance companies often continued to hold sway. As illustrated by Figure 14, only one-third of the states had established some sort of "state fund" by 1920.

A final shortfall of the workmen's compensation laws in relation to AALL recommendations was no doubt the most portentous for the future. In the words of the historians Berkowitz and McQuaid, the AALL "recommended that benefits to meet an accident's cost should include medical, surgical, and hospital expenses, and two-thirds of an employee's wages." But "most states failed to meet this standard; instead, they followed New Jersey's lead and adopted a schedule that equated the loss of a particular part of the body with a certain number of weeks of compensation payments."[160] As a result, corporations and insurance companies had strong incentives to try to keep the publicly regulated "body parts" schedule of compensations as niggardly as possible. These powerful capitalists had no incentive to support proposals for public disability insurance or public health insurance. In England, Germany, and other early welfare states, support—or at least acquiescence—for these "next steps" in workingmen's social insurance often came from employers looking for ways to avoid paying costs for health care and lost wages to injured workers covered in terms like those the AALL had advocated.[161] As matters turned out in the United States, the vast majority of the state-level workmen's compensation laws passed during the Progressive Era would undercut rather than promote momentum toward additional forms of public social benefits.

Overall, as we have seen, workmen's compensation laws of the 1910s represented a *reworking* of the American polity's way of handling problems already under public jurisdiction. Other kinds of workingmen's insurance—such as the unemployment and health insurance also advocated by the AALL—would have required brand-new extensions of governmental jurisdiction, along with new taxes and the empowerment of agencies to disburse payments to clients. In contrast, workmen's compensation promised no greater costs and supposedly more predictable benefits to everyone involved, without increasing the intervention of the state as taxer and spender. For many members of the reform-minded public who were worried

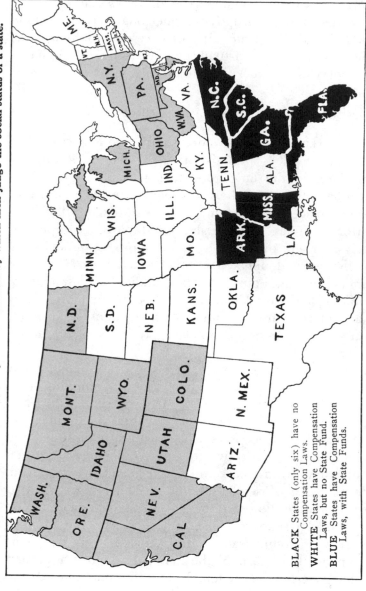

"A compensation law is in these days one of the tests by which men judge the social status of a state."

BLACK States (only six) have no Compensation Laws.
WHITE States have Compensation Laws, but no State Fund.
BLUE States have Compensation Laws, with State Funds.

WORKMEN'S COMPENSATION LAWS IN THE UNITED STATES

FIVE-SIXTHS OF THE MAP IS NOW COVERED. WITHIN THE PAST TEN YEARS 42 OF THE 48 STATES, IN ADDITION TO PORTO RICO AND THE TWO TERRITORIES OF ALASKA AND HAWAII, HAVE ADOPTED COMPENSATION LAWS.

Figure 14

Source: *American Labor Legislation Review* 10(1) (March 1920), p. 6.

about political corruption, as well as for conservative forces also worried about preserving private wealth, workmen's compensation measures were the only acceptable part of the social insurance agenda. Consequently, these proposals alone could garner the kind of cross-class and multiple-group support necessary for new social legislation to be enacted across virtually all of the states in the changing American polity of the early twentieth century.

The Limits of Administrative Statebuilding

Proponents of workingmen's insurance simultaneously worked to create new realms of public administration in America. Reformers were convinced that it did little good to pass new laws—such as workmen's compensation—and then see them ineffectively enforced. They wanted to replace the nineteenth-century system, in which laws were not enforced unless individual injured parties complained through public attorneys and the courts, with more continuous legal enforcement by expert-dominated regulatory agencies.[162] What is more, reformers sometimes pursued "statebuilding" well in advance of laws mandating new social benefits or labor regulations. They hoped that new or reorganized realms of expert-dominated public adminstration would pave the way for later advances in substantive social legislation.

Indeed, U.S. supporters of workingmen's insurance conceivably might have been very successful as statebuilders, even when they couldn't get new benefits enacted. If, as I have argued, the early twentieth century in the United States was a time when elites and the middle-class public were preoccupied with structural political reforms and relatively unreceptive to new public spending, then perhaps a solid administrative basis could have been laid to underpin the future development of regulations and social insurance. As matters unfolded historically, however, the most substantial statebuilding occurred in particular states in close connection with the administration of workmen's compensation. But reformers failed to reorganize and expand those parts of the national administration and the federal-state governmental system dealing with public health and the functioning of labor markets. Such efforts came to grief on the shoals of preexisting administrative fragmentation, executive-legislative conflicts, and localist resistance to "bureaucratic interference" from Washington, DC—all enduring features of U.S. governmental arrangements.

Commissions to Implement State Labor Laws

The AALL's statebuilding efforts were most successful in completing a transition from courts to regulatory commissions as the arenas of decisionmaking about workmen's compensation awards. During the early years of workmen's compensation enactments over one-third of the states that passed such laws "failed to provide any formal institutions to administer workers' compensation laws and, as a result, the laws remained the province of the courts."[163] The AALL was very critical of this approach, however, and in 1915 it published an evaluation of New Jersey's initial workmen's compensation system, highlighting the inadequacies of court administration.[164] From early in its workmen's compensation campaign, moreover, the AALL advocated the implementation of workmen's compensation and other labor laws by several-person regulatory commissions that could work out specific rules and ensure prompt settlement of claims.[165]

Because implementation of workmen's compensation through the courts was truly cumbersome, repeating many of the problems that had caused business and labor to favor workmen's compensation in the first place, the AALL had considerable success in its campaign for administration by commissions instead. By 1920, "34 of 45 states with workmen's compensation laws administered those laws through industrial commissions"; and by 1933, forty-four states had boards or commissions to administer their laws, while seven still left enforcement to the courts.[166] As the transition to administrative enforcement occurred, the AALL along with the federal Bureau of Labor Statistics encouraged the state commissioners to meet regularly and "coordinate" their states' approaches to labor legislation. Such coordination never went as far as promoting anything like uniformity. A highly uneven "state-by-state approach to disability" was in fact accommodated and frozen within the federal system from the Progressive Era onward.[167] Yet new realms of public administration with an interest in industrial matters were established in most of the states, along with the workmen's compensation systems themselves.

Still, as we learned in Chapter 3, the AALL and fellow advocates of new labor laws wanted something more than just new regulatory agencies to administer workmen's compensation. They wanted the often scattered agencies involved with administering separate labor laws in each state to be consolidated and given additional powers to investigate social conditions and recommend new labor laws. Actual developments within the state of Wisconsin were the model for the "omnibus industrial commissions" advocated by the AALL. As John R. Commons explained in a 1913 article:

> Instead of creating a commission to administer the compensation law, and then leaving the factory inspector to enforce the safety laws, as other states have done, the Wisconsin legislature of 1911 . . . proceeded to abolish the old bureau of factory inspection, as well as the industrial accident board, which it had just created, and to merge the two into a new administrative and investigating board, to be known as the Industrial Commission . . . As a matter of economy to the state and convenience to employers, as well as recognition of the wide scope of administrative investigation, all of the departments dealing with employes [sic] and employment were consolidated under the same commission. These include the state employment offices, the board of arbitration, child labor, street trades, truancy, women's hours of labor, apprenticeship, etc.[168]

So broad was the rule-making discretion granted to the Wisconsin Industrial Commission that it could develop workplace safety rules in close conjunction with workmen's compensation, urging employers to prevent accidents and thus lower their compensation insurance premiums. What is more, the Commission was able to do studies and develop rationales for new kinds of social legislation. Throughout the 1920s and until the enactment of the nation's first unemployment insurance law in 1932, the Wisconsin Industrial Commission was a consistent advocate of a "preventionist" variety of unemployment compensation modeled closely on its favorite policy, workmen's compensation. To various degrees, the Commission also made the administration of other kinds of labor laws conform with the practices it developed for safety and workmen's compensation. Thus, in many ways the Wisconsin Commission fulfilled the hopes of AALL advocates of omnibus industrial commissions. It unified the administration of labor law and proved an effective governmental force for further public regulation.[169]

But Wisconsin was not a typical American state.[170] From the nineteenth century its industrial inspection system was stronger than those of virtually all other states, and Wisconsin experienced general civil service reform by early in the twentieth century.[171] Progressive Republicans and moderate Socialists were, together, uniquely powerful in this state's politics. And Wisconsin had America's most influential "academic-administrative" complex, with a major research-oriented state university right in its capital city, Madison, and a strong Legislative Reference Bureau creating ties between legislators and academics.[172] Not incidentally, the Wisconsin Industrial Commission was created within this unique concatenation of institutional and political circumstances; and the Commission flourished because of their continuation.

Despite the urgings of the AALL, only a handful of other U.S. states established omnibus industrial commissions, although more than a dozen did combine safety regulation with the administration of workmen's compensation during the 1910s, and nine more followed suit by 1930.[173] Even when states created omnibus commissions on paper, these often did not function the same way as Wisconsin's commission. In New York state, for example, a broad commission created in 1915 always remained more enmeshed in divided, partisan politics, and more detached from academics and legislators, than did its Wisconsin counterpart; and the New York commission never became as influential in further legislative developments in that state.[174] Central as it was to the AALL's plan for administrative statebuilding across the forty-eight states, the institution of the omnibus industrial commission remained primarily a vision realized in Wisconsin. Consequently, it was a source of variation rather than uniformity in social policy for the nation's future. More generally, the U.S. states expanded their corps of factory inspectors and other kinds of labor-law administrators during the early twentieth century, but often kept them scattered in various specialized bureaus with modest budgets and powers of enforcement, and even more modest capacities for conducting independent investigations or recommending new legislation.[175]

Roads toward administrative rationalization and the increase of expert influence in social politics lay through Washington, DC, in addition to the state capitals. Along with other reformers, the American advocates of workingmen's insurance traveled these roads, too—but did not get as far as they did in spreading workmen's compensation commissions across the states.

The Quest for a National Health Department

One telling example was the failure of what the medical historian Manfred Waserman calls the "quest for a national health department in the Progressive Era."[176] This effort would seem to have had a decent chance of success. After the yellow fever epidemic of 1878, Congress chartered a temporary National Board of Health. Although this was discontinued in 1883, the precedent did indicate the potential nationwide concern with issues of public health. As Figure 15 illustrates, moreover, the Progressive Era brought to a crescendo concern about "social efficiency," prompting calls for the extension of federal government efforts from animals, as aided by the Department of Agriculture, to people, who would be helped by a new Bureau or Department of Public Health. The early-twentieth-century campaign for a national bureau or department of public health was endorsed by many reform associations and by the General Federation of Women's Clubs.[177] From 1908 through the 1910s, this effort was spearheaded by the "Committee of One Hundred on National Health," which included prominent physicians, professors, politicians, and social reformers.[178] The Committee was chaired by Yale Professor Irving Fisher, who also played a leading role in the AALL's campaign for health insurance.

The campaign for a national health bureau got sympathy from Presidents Theodore Roosevelt and William Howard Taft, and was to some degree endorsed by all three political parties in 1912. But it did not succeed. The Committee of One Hundred did not conduct a grassroots campaign, and it failed to generate anywhere near as much publicity in favor of a national bureau as opponents generated against it. States' rights advocates and assorted groups concerned about the close involvement of the American Medical Association with any new agency fought against creating a "national health trust." Yet perhaps the most significant cause of the campaign's failure was the confusion of the reformers themselves over whether they wanted a Cabinet-level department or just a bureau, as well as their inability to convince the heads of existing federal agencies with public health

A STARTLING INNOVATION

Chester White—Hello, Doc, who are you?
Dr. Sprayem—I'm the new Secretary of Public Health
Chester White—Hog or cattle?
Dr. Sprayem—Just people!
Chester White—My, but this government is getting progressive.

Figure 15

Source: *Minneapolis Journal,* January 3, 1908. Reproduced here from Manfred Waserman, "The Quest for a National Health Department in the Progressive Era," *Bulletin of the History of Medicine* 49 (1975), p. 354.

mandates that they should all acquiesce in the "reorganization" of their domains into one grand federal agency. In 1912, social reformers and women's groups succeeded in convincing Congress and President Taft to create the federal Children's Bureau as a tiny, brand-new, fact-finding body.[179] This effort had enthusiastic grassroots support, and also benefited from the fact that existing federal agencies (though some wanted to claim the new functions for themselves) did not see the Children's Bureau as an effort to reorganize their existing activities under new leadership. In contrast, the campaign for a national public health agency was a reorganization drive as well as an attempt to enhance the expert capacities of the federal government to investigate conditions and coordinate programs affecting the nation's public health. Existing federal officials energetically opposed this reorganization effort in Congress. Particularly consequential was the reluctance of the Surgeon General, head of of the nation's longest-lived public health agency, the Public Health and Marine Hospital Service.

In the end, various bills, including those submitted by Senator Robert L. Owen of Oklahoma to establish a new national Department of Public Health, were deflected or defeated in Congress between 1908 and World War I. The nation was left with a consolidated Public Health Service, but without an omnibus health agency. Since the reformers had hoped that a new federal agency would stimulate and coordinate state and local health efforts and lay the evidentiary basis for new programs, the failure of this statebuilding effort certainly weakened the plausibility of the AALL campaign during 1916–1920 for public health insurance in the United States. Arguably, this failure also reverberated throughout twentieth-century American history, weakening public jurisdiction in the health field in many ways. The federal cabinet-level Department of Health, Education, and Welfare was not established until 1953.

Public Employment Offices as a Basis for Unemployment Insurance?

A more poignant shortfall of progressive efforts at statebuilding for social insurance came in the realm of public employment offices—poignant because it apparently came close to success through the short-lived existence of the United States Employment Service during World War I. During the 1910s, as we have seen, AALL reformers modeled their aspirations for public measures to combat unemployment on the achievements of the British Liberals and Board of Trade. Inspired by the arguments of William Beveridge in *Unemployment: A Problem of Industry,* both British and American progressive liberals believed that labor markets could be "regularized" if a network of public employment offices spread information about shifting job opportunities to all willing workers.[180] Many of the unemployed could quickly be put back to work in this way, reformers argued. Equally important, unemployed workers could be given benefits through employment service offices, because, by coming to these offices in the first place, the workers would have proved their willingness to accept jobs if available, thus obviating any worry that unemployment benefits would lead to shirking. In Britain, it was not incidental that the Liberals and the Board of Trade first created a nationwide network of public employment offices through the Employment Exchanges Act of 1909. Only after this was in place did the British reformers move on to enact unemployment insurance in 1911.[181]

Not surprisingly, the unemployment remedies put forward during the recession of 1913–1915 by the AALL and by the Massachusetts Committee on Unemployment imitated the British by explicitly joining proposals for public works and unemployment insurance with advocacy of public employment offices.[182] After the recession ended and prospects for other employment-related measures faded, the AALL continued to discuss and agitate for such offices. The establishment of free, public employment offices under municipal, state, and federal auspices was deemed critical by labor law advocates, not only as a first step toward insurance, but also because many state high courts and (from 1917) the U.S. Supreme Court were striking down laws that prohibited or strongly regulated business-run, for-profit employment agencies.[183] Only if a strong public employment service could be built up in the United States would the labor market be "rationalized," as the reformers saw it.

Members of the AALL and other reformist professionals debated alternative ways of organizing public employment offices. Some authors of articles on this subject, and some speakers at AALL forums, advocated relatively centralized systems similar to the British or the Canadian. But as late as the first months of U.S. involvement in World War I, the preponderance of U.S. expert opinion seemed to favor varying degrees of federal "coordination" of local and state employment offices. In 1915, AALL Secretary John Andrews called for the creation of federal employment bureaus to "supplement and assist" local and state bureaus.[184] Early in 1917, William Leiserson put forth a fascinating proposal for a "federal reserve board for the unemployed."[185] Drawing clever analogies to another system of federal regulation already established to smooth out "fluctuations" in the national economy, and noting that there "has been much loose talk about the federal government establishing employment offices, like post offices, throughout the country, or making the post offices do the work of employment bureaus," Leiserson argued that no

> federal labor exchange system can be successful that ignores the existence of state and municipal employment offices. There are now about one hundred of them in more than half the states, and some of them have reached a high degree of efficiency and influence in their communities. For the federal government to duplicate their work or to try to compete with them would seem most unwise . . . The Federal Reserve Board did not establish new local banks. It welded the existing banking institutions into one national organization. It is just this sort of a labor exchange system that must be constructed out of the existing employment offices.[186]

As the nation's leading student of employment services and labor market rationalization, Leiserson was America's counterpart to Britain's William Beveridge, whose arguments about administrative "regularization" of the labor market he repeatedly cited.[187] Yet Leiserson proposed a federal board to regulate, subsidize, and expertly advise local and state employment offices, because he understood that any attempt to establish a centralized labor market administration would run against the grain of American politics. At an AALL forum held in late 1917, former AALL President Henry Seager echoed many of Leiserson's ideas as he argued against proponents of a centralized federal system and in favor of federal coordination of city and state labor exchanges.[188]

But events soon overtook the better judgment of reformers about how to organize employment services in the United States. Within months of U.S. entry into World War I in mid-1917, President Wilson undertook "emergency" measures of national mobilization for total war.[189] Reformers flocked to Washington, DC, along with American business leaders. The crisis appeared to create sudden opportunities for national statebuilding in policy areas that, only a little while before, had seemed amenable only to coordination of decentralized initiatives. Management of the nation's industrial labor supply was one of many areas in which new public initiatives seemed possible and essential. Although problems of this sort were tackled relatively late in the overall war mobilization effort, the creation of a national United States Employment Service (USES) occurred with amazing speed.[190]

Prior to 1918, the federal government's minimal involvement in the management of labor supply was centered in the Bureau of Immigration, reflecting its origins as "a service for the placement of immigrants on farms."[191] After World War I broke out in Europe in 1914, the Secretary of Labor mandated this original employment bureau to disseminate job information more generally, not just to immigrants. But this "service was handicapped . . . by small appropriations, by its subordinate position in another bureau, and by the fact that many of its employees were immigration officials, whose main line of work was not labor placement."[192] The really big changes came after the United States mobilized economically to support its own military efforts in World War I. In January 1918, the Secretary of Labor separated the U.S. Employment Service from the Bureau of Immigration. Soon the USES was given, on presidential authority, an initial appropriation of $2 million, with more to follow; and it "began developing cooperation with all state and municipal systems and opening new offices at the rate of almost 100 a month."[193] In August 1918, the USES was assigned an official monopoly on the allocation of unskilled laborers to U.S. industries. At the height of its wartime operations, the USES had over 4,000 employees and directly operated 854 offices in all states across the nation.[194] Some 1,890,593 workers were placed in jobs during 1918.[195] The USES began to distribute the *U.S. Employment Service Bulletin* and created five major administrative divisions in Washington: Control, Field Organization, Clearance, Personnel, and Information.[196] As the end of the war approached, moreover, USES officials and allied reformers, including the AALL, devised all sorts of plans calling for the USES, once put on a regular footing by Congress, to devote its widespread organization and expertise to the management of a smooth industrial demobilization and the prevention of unemployment in peacetime.[197]

Such hopes for a postwar Employment Service were not to be realized. For the United States, a late entrant into the conflict, World

War I ended suddenly, just months after the country reached its peak of war mobilization. Before the Armistice, at a time when politicians and voters knew the war was ending, the 1918 congressional elections brought the Republicans to power, reflecting unease in the country over the bureaucratic intrusions of war mobilization.[198] This election deprived Democratic President Wilson of the authority to shape international or domestic transitions to peacetime. Any prospect that many of the "emergency" executive agencies created during the war would carry over into postwar U.S. governance disappeared. Congress quickly dismantled the emergency federal agencies, including the the USES.

Like other wartime agencies, the USES suffered from the suddenness with which it had thrown together new operations, often without appropriate personnel or well-thought-out policies. Its often inefficient performance had given business, labor, and local governments alike reasons for complaints to Congress. But chiefly, the USES suffered the inevitable discontents that accompanied a sudden shift from labor shortage to economic contraction and labor glut. Business, above all, no longer wanted its services, and many capitalists feared that USES policies respecting the rights of union workers would undercut postwar anti-union drives. In a survey conducted in early 1920, thirty-seven out of sixty employers' associations opposed the continued existence of the USES, often echoing the view of the the Pittsburgh Employers' Association that "the United States Employment Service is the most effective promoter of unionism in the United States."[199] Only two employers' associations claimed to favor the continued operation of the USES, while twenty-one took no position.

The wartime USES spent nearly $6 million in fiscal 1919, and the President requested $4,600,000 for 1920. But Congress allocated only $400,000 for 1920, and cut the budget to $225,000 for 1921, with the same for 1922.[200] The rump federal agency had to disband its field offices and resort thenceforth to requesting voluntary submissions of data from private corportions and from the dwindling numbers of state and municipal employment offices that remained open without federal aid. Throughout the 1920s, Congress continued to starve the USES for resources and block efforts to create national or federal systems of public employment offices. Moreover, in the absence of effective stimulus and coordination from Washington, during "the twenties public employment services gradually shrank to insignificance except in a few states. Where in 1920 there were 269 public employment offices scattered in 41 states, by the end of 1930 there were only 151 in some 24 states. Several states reported only one office each, and many offices had but a single employee."[201] At the advent of the Depression, the United States was the only major industrial nation that lacked a nationwide employment agency.[202] Obviously, the absence of administrative and data-collection capabilities undercut possibilities for many public interventions in U.S. labor markets, including the provision of insurance benefits to unemployed workers during the 1920s or the early 1930s.

This outcome was an especially bitter one for U.S. reformers to accept, because the wartime nationalization and expansion of the USES had—very fleetingly—given them a heady vision of a publicly "regularized" national labor market, and a commitment to an administrative system that could have been used to promote and implement social insurance. The advocates of workingmen's insurance in the United States learned to their chagrin that a modern war, fought very quickly on an "emergency" basis by a government accustomed to divided powers and federal decentralization, was not a promising conjuncture for sustainable centralized statebuilding. On the contrary, emergency wartime extensions of executive power only spurred decentralizing and privatist reactions against public administration and social provision after the brief war was over.

Conclusion

Isaac Max Rubinow's characterization of workingmen's insurance as "a well-defined effort of the organized state to come to the assistance of the wage-earner and furnish him something he individually is quite unable to obtain for himself" nicely captured the logic of this set of reforms as they were understood and acted upon in Britain, the rest of Europe, and Australasia between 1880 and 1920.[203] In the pioneering welfare states, previously existing administrative bureaucracies could be used to implement new social spending programs and labor regulations, either directly or in superordinate collaboration with interest groups or local governmental bodies. In Europe, moreover, the new policy ideas came along at a time when the incorporation into national politics of workers who had not formerly been full citizens was at issue. Under these conditions, social insurance advocates in Europe could capture the ears of government executives and political party leaders. Reformers' ideas about social insurance either grew out of or could readily be adapted to practical administrative experience, and they seemed appropriate to both appease and politically control working-class citizens.

But the governmental and political contexts within which American carriers of social insurance ideas had to operate around the turn of the century were strikingly different from those of Europe and Australasia. The American working class had long since been enrolled by nonprogrammatic, patronage-oriented parties into a democratic electoral system. The United States had sovereign and assertive courts, able to deflect many of the legislative innovations that did occur, especially regulations applicable to adult male workers, who were deemed freely contracting subjects under the common law. The American polity, furthermore, lacked at national, state, and local levels the sorts of penetrating, autonomous administrative organs whose ministers and civil servants figured so importantly in the adoption and implementation of regulations and social benfits elsewhere. Even the national crisis of World War I was not sufficient to alter the decentralized and divided arrangments of this federal and congressionally centered state.

Proposals for new social spending on behalf of workingmen, finally, ran against the grain of governmental reform in the Progressive Era. The middle and upper classes were preoccupied with battles against patronage and corruption, and they were not about to support new social benefits that might lubricate ties between politicians and the populace. Thus America's patronage democracy facilitated the expansion of Civil War benefits in the late nineteenth century, but these benefits were not to serve as an "entering wedge" for an American welfare state protecting the "army of labor." In the early twentieth century, elite and middle-class determination to change the political practices and distributive social policies of patronage democracy discouraged the United States from joining other Western nations on the road to more universal social provision for workers and their dependents, including the elderly. Legacies from a pioneering democratic past obstructed possibilities for paternalist social democracy in the American future.

PART III

Foundations for a Maternalist Welfare State?

In order to secure legislation it is almost necessary to have a strong moral sentiment favorable to it. This sentiment is largely a matter of education, and the club women should be the teachers. Enlist the citizen in behalf of the measure, interest the press, and marshall the eloquence of the pulpit and the bar. Through the public school, the church, the newspaper, and the bar, the members of a community may be brought to see the justice of any measure you propose. Then when your Representative and Senator chosen to represent you in your State assemblies and legislatures and your member of the National Congress propose your measures for enactment into law, they will do so assured that they have with them not only the consciousness of a just cause but also the satisfying consciousness of a united constituency.

Mrs. Samuel Forter,
General Federation of Women's Clubs, 1906

The mother is not only the heart of the home, she must be the heart of the world . . . Let mothers have the opportunity and privilege of performing their God-given work as they should, and the whole body politic will feel new life, new aspirations, new conceptions of the relative value of things.

Child-Welfare Magazine, April 1919

Let us be our sisters' keepers.

Employed womanhood must be protected in order to foster the motherhood of the race.

Slogans used by California women's groups in
the referendum campaign for enforcement
of the minimum wage law, 1913

State aid [to widowed mothers] . . . is an advance, as showing the policy of the nation, to conserve its children and its homes, and in recognizing the mother as a factor in that campaign, for the welfare of all.

Mrs. Clara Cahill Park, 1913

The Children's Bureau . . . is the result of the belief, on the part of many individuals and associations interested in the protection and betterment of children, that the Federal Government should aid in that service . . . Fifty years ago the field of the Department of Agriculture was defined as "all information concerning agriculture." In the same way the field of the Children's Bureau is now defined as "all matters pertaining to the welfare of children and child life." It is obvious that the bureau is to be a center of information useful to all the children of America, to ascertain and to popularize just standards for their life and development.

Julia Lathrop,
Chief of the Children's Bureau, 1913

The passage of the Maternity and Infancy Bill marks an epoch in the history of the nation. Equality of opportunity for life will be made possible for all women . . . Hundreds of thousands of children will be blessed by a mother's care, who in the past have been orphans. Hundreds of thousands of homes will be protected by the saving of the mother's life. The influence on child welfare resulting from this law is beyond measure.

Child-Welfare Magazine, September 1921

Pioneering European and Australasian welfare states were doubly paternalist. Elite males, bureaucrats and national political leaders, established regulations or social benefits *for* members of the working class—that is, programs designed "in the best interest" of workers, rather than just along the lines their organizations requested. What is more, the "breadwinning" male wage earner was the core beneficiary envisaged in these programs; if benefits went to his dependents, they did so on account of his labor-force participation and level of earnings. Even when certain benefits such as non-contributory old-age pensions went directly to females, the image of the respectable working-class family normally headed by a male earner was the ideal policymakers had in mind. Such pensions were not sufficient to support an elderly person entirely on his or her own, and simply served to make it easier for other family members to keep that person in a household.[1] Early pensions, social insurance, and labor regulations were intended, in short, to keep respectable working-class families headed by male breadwinners away from the indignities of poor relief.

In the United States, advocates of labor legislation followed this paternalist model as well as they could. The illustrations in Figures 16 and 17 appeared in the programmatic booklet *Labor Problems and Labor Legislation* issued by the American Association for Labor Legislation. The first portrays a working*man* sheltering his wife, children, and elderly mother under an umbrella labeled "health insurance," protecting his family from sickness and the ensuing destitution to which uninsured workers and their dependents were vulnerable.[2] This illustration nicely captured the features of the AALL's proposed health insurance bills, which, following the 1911 British precedent, pegged benefits to wage earners' contributions. Throughout the AALL booklet, ideal types of "labor legislation" were portrayed as benefiting male wage earners and their dependents. In the vision of the Association, American men wanted "work not alms," and they needed social insurance for themselves and their families, as well as safe working conditions and limited working hours. Figure 17 shows that the "Cycle of the Working Day" the AALL had in mind was very much geared to the male worker-citizen,

"PROTECTED!"

This workingman's family is ready for the inevitable "rainy day" caused by sickness.

Figure 16

Source: John B. Andrews, *Labor Problems and Labor Legislation* (New York: American Association for Labor Legislation, 1922), p. 116.

CYCLE of the WORKING DAY

Eight hours for work!
Eight hours for sleep!
Eight hours for home and citizenship!

Figure 17

Source: John B. Andrews, *Labor Problems and Labor Legislation* (New York: American Association for Labor Legislation, 1922), p. 48.

who would ideally spend eight hours at his job, eight hours sleeping, and eight hours in a leisurely and intelligent home life. Someone else at home would presumably do the housework and tend the children while the male worker rested and read his newspaper, but she was not portrayed in the AALL's ideal "working day."

Early American advocates of paternalist labor legislation were not very successful, however. In the previous chapter, I argued that during the Progressive Era a reaction against nineteenth-century patronage democracy and the open-ended social spending associated with it in the minds of middle- and upper-class Americans, created obstacles to new types of social spending for workingmen and the elderly. The absence of established civil service bureaucracies rendered contributory social insurance measures less credible than they were in Britain. And the U.S. courts placed special roadblocks in the way of attempts to legislate maximum hours and minimum wages for adult male workers.

Yet while very little paternalist labor legislation was passed in the early-twentieth-century United States, the story was different when it came to what might be called maternalist legislation. Most U.S. states enacted new or tightened restrictions on women's hours of employment, and many states also passed minimum-wage laws and special safety regulations for women.[3] Such labor laws were premised on the idea that women workers needed extraordinary protection as actual or potential mothers. Most U.S. states also passed laws enabling localities to provide "pensions" to needy mothers who had to raise children without the wages of a male breadwinner. In 1912, the U.S. federal government established a Children's Bureau headed and staffed by female reformist professionals who aimed to look after the needs of American infants and mothers; and by 1921, the Children's Bureau had successfully spearheaded a campaign for the first explicitly welfare-oriented program of grants-in-aid to the states. The Sheppard-Towner Infancy and Maternity Protection Act mandated the creation of federally subsidized clinics to disseminate health-care advice to mothers before and after the birth of their babies.

Why did such maternalist measures succeed during the Progressive Era, even as the first efforts to launch a paternalist American welfare state mostly came to naught? The answer to this question—and, indeed, the key to many other progressive reforms focused on

consumer products, family welfare, and urban living conditions—
lies in the heights of social organization, ideological self-consciousness, and political mobilization achieved by American middle-class
women around the turn of the twentieth century. As we have seen,
conditions in the industrializing United States did not facilitate class-
conscious political organization by industrial workers; and U.S. governmental institutions gave little sway to bureaucrats who might
speak in "the public interest." At the same time, however, conditions
did favor a certain kind of women's gender consciousness. Social
circumstances and political arrangements in the turn-of-the-century
United States facilitated middle-class women's consciousness and mobilization, and encouraged women to make collective and hegemonic
demands—that is, demands not only for themselves but also on
behalf of the entire society—to a degree highly unusual for any
broad category of people in American politics.

During the nineteenth century, both a sharply gender-based division of labor and Protestant evangelism encouraged American
middle-class women to form voluntary associations to deal with matters of social welfare as well as their own well-being. In addition, the
rapid expansion of higher education in the late-nineteenth-century
United States brought an internationally uprecedented opening of
doors to women, some of whom ended up providing a high order
of politically engaged intellectual leadership to the broad mass of
middle-class women.

Even as such conditions favored the organization and civic engagement of American women, females were barred from electoral
and party politics in the world's first mass democracy for males
(except in some localities and territories or states from the late
nineteenth century onward). Operating largely without votes,
women became civically involved in a polity where plenty of "space"
was available for new forces who favored collective as opposed to
distributive, patronage-oriented policies. Outside of the formal political institutions of patronage democracy, yet in many ways in parallel to them, female voluntary federations increasingly pursued legislation that American women boldly claimed was in the moral best
interest of society as a whole. Maternal values were projected from
homes and local communities onto the agendas of state and national
politics. Eventually, many women's voluntary associations demanded
the vote not so much as an "equal right" for women, but primarily

as an instrument for achieving their "unselfish" policy goals—policies that the women meanwhile pursued through public agitation and legislative lobbying.

The Progressive Era was the time when the nationwide political mobilization of American middle-class women reached its height, when women agitated for maternalist social measures as a way to protect children and mothers and at the same time address the inequities and inefficiencies of an industrial and urban society. Organized womanhood brought greater and more effective pressures to bear on behalf of such social policies than the AALL and the trade unions brought to bear on behalf of labor legislation focused on male breadwinners. Among women, intellectual leaders and grassroots community organizations worked together effectively.

But it wasn't just a matter of social pressure by women. At the height of their voluntary mobilization along organizational lines that neatly paralleled the local-state-national layers of U.S. federal political institutions, women in the Progressive Era were also favored by the changing structures and routines of American politics. For a time, women's mode of politics—public education and lobbying through widespread associations—was ideally suited to pressuring legislatures to pass bills along nonpartisan lines, to getting around obstacles from the courts, and to taking the place of absent administrative bureaucracies. What is more, because they were, relatively speaking, in a structurally and culturally favored position, organized American women could attract certain elite male allies and set the agendas of progressive social politics very much in terms of their own ideals for mothers, families, and the community.

Ironically, this situation prevailed only as long as women were collectively mobilized for styles of politics that did not depend primarily on voting. As we shall later see, after the franchise was fully won, politically active American women faced the same choices and obstacles "within the system" as other U.S. citizens. This happened even as male-dominated bureaucratic and professional arrangements gained new predominance in U.S. civic life, and even as changes in gender ideals undercut middle-class women's proclivities for gender-wide separate organization. By the mid-1920s, women's will and capacities to achieve further maternalist policies diminished, just as powerful backlashes developed against policy gains that had already been achieved. Ultimately, with the emergence of new social insurance measures during the New Deal, the maternalist policies surviving from the Progressive Era were reworked in unforeseen ways—to become in due course subordinate and marginal parts of nationwide social provision in the United States.

The next chapter examines the roots and characteristics of American women's reform efforts during the Progressive Era. This discussion of feminine civic action in Chapter 6 lays the basis for Chapters 7, 8, and 9, which analyze, in turn, protective labor legislation for women workers, mothers' pensions, and the Children's Bureau and Sheppard-Towner Act.

Expanding the Separate Sphere:
Women's Civic Action
and Political Reforms
in the Early Twentieth Century

The situation of women in the industrializing United States, from the early to late 1900s, was paradoxical. On the one hand, a sharp division of labor—and an even more rigid cultural orthodoxy—confined American women to a narrower sphere of activities, more thoroughly separate from male activities than before or after this century of basic capitalist development. On the other hand, American women developed the largest and most assertive "woman movements" in the world.[1] Those movements, in turn, set the stage for the maternalist social policy breakthroughs of the Progressive Era, so it is important to understand how they grew in the social and political conditions of the nineteenth century.

Women in the Industrializing United States:
Separation and the Growth of Gender Consciousness

Women in Colonial and early Republican America were expected to be pious believers and obedient helpmates, yet their lives were intertwined with those of men in a wide range of economic and social activities.[2] In towns and villages, on farms and in small shops and artisanal enterprises, family life and economic activities went on together, often under the same roof. Community politics took place through informal discussions, meetings, petitionings, and occasional demonstrations—all activities in which women could participate, even though they were excluded from voting or holding public office.[3] In fact, most nonelite men were also excluded from such formal political practices, so community politics did not seem solely structured around gender divisions. Women shared many political advantages—or disadvantages—with fathers, husbands, and brothers of the same social location.

Fundamental changes in gender roles came with the growth of capitalist commerce and industry. After 1810, the transportation revolution linked towns to cities and agricultural hinterlands to urban markets; the resulting commercial growth spurred the migration of sons and daughters to seek new opportunities. Market competition intensified, wage labor spread, and family enterprises often broke apart. These economic transformations were accompanied by the emergence of a new division of labor between the genders. In the words of the social historian Carroll Smith-Rosenberg:

> The divorce of home and work, task differentiation, and, by the 1840s and the 1850s, the introduction of mechanization altered the easy flow of time. Recreation and work became binary opposites. So did public and private space. Women, of course, experienced this division more intensely than men . . . When work left the home, men freely followed it into the agora, to countinghouses and factories. Women, in contrast, found themselves confined within an increasingly isolated domesticity.[4]

In precept if not always in practice, the confinement was especially intense for middle-class married women. "Woman, in the cult of True Womanhood presented by the women's magazines, gift annuals and religious literature of the nineteenth century, was the hostage in the home."[5] Men were presumed to be preoccupied with the self-interested pursuits of money-making and party politics, forced to make their way out in the cold, hard, competitive public world. Meanwhile, naturally selfless women were in charge of the private space of the home. Women were expected to abstain from premarital sex, marry male breadwinners, and work to maintain restful, cultured domiciles. Above all, they were expected to be loving, full-time mothers, devoted to raising their children to be Godfearing, solid citizens. Women's patriotism was best expressed, in this view, through the principles they inculcated in their children.

Indeed, after the suffrage was extended to all white men, and once mass-based parties were organized in the Jackson era, formal "politics" became as strictly a male sphere as home life was a female sphere. This was true not only because women were excluded from voting but more importantly because rituals of male fraternalism were central during "the party period" of U.S. governance.[6] At the grassroots, partisan supporters associated in Democratic, Whig, or Republican clubs. The party faithful staged marches and parades replete with military trappings as "officers" mobilized the "rank-and-file" for electoral "battles." Campaigns "culminated in elections held in saloons, barber shops, and other places largely associated with men."[7] Voting rights and party loyalties tied men together across class lines—so much so that partisan political participation was part of the very definition of American manhood. Thus, when elite civil service reformers emerged after the Civil War as independent critics of the dominant patronage parties, they were often ridiculed as unmanly. "Most of all, reformers were seen as politically impotent. Men whose loyalty to a party was questionable were referred to, for example, as the 'third sex' of American politics, 'man-milliners,' and 'Miss-Nancys.'"[8]

Similarly, those few nineteenth-century women who demanded rights to participate equally with men in the marketplace or the electoral polity were deemed not real women by the ideologists of True Womanhood. Also morally condemned were "fallen women" who practiced extramarital sex and the men who, it was supposed, tempted or forced such women into evil. "If anyone, male or female, dared to tamper with the complex of virtues which made up True Womanhood, he was damned immediately as an enemy of God, of civilization and of the Republic. It was a fearful obligation, a solemn reponsibility, which the nineteenth-century woman had—to uphold the pillars of the temple with her frail white hand."[9] Actual and aspiring middle-class ladies were judged, and judged themselves, according to the vision of True Womanhood, and many wives of skilled workers seem to have embraced ideals of domesticity as well.[10] Conceived in stark opposition to the aggressiveness, striving, and all-too-frequent selfishness of masculine identity in the public worlds of commerce and politics, True Womanhood made the pursuit of virtue in a separate sphere centered on the home the touchstone of feminine identity.

The Growth of Women's Organizations

Yet even the most proper ladies in nineteenth-century America were not confined to the privacy of the home, despite the fact that their special virtues were deemed to be most fully expressed there. One aspect of community life—church activity—was understood in feminine terms from the inception of the cult of True Womanhood, because women were deemed naturally more pious than men. What is more, according to the cult of True Womanhood, the "appropriate field of development for women was caretaking and nurturing inside *and outside* the home."[11] As supposedly unique embodiments of morality and warmth, virtual ministering angels, who else but women in the community could be expected to succor the poor and educate the wayward? Ironically, the "very perfection of True Womanhood . . . carried within itself the seeds of its own destruction," as Barbara Welter has aptly put it.[12] This set of ideals simultaneously encouraged nineteenth-century American women to stay at home—and to become involved in those civic affairs that had to do with religion, morality, and (as we would say today) social welfare.

American women responded with enthusiasm to the civic possibilities contained within their gender's ideally assigned sphere. We know this because throughout the nineteenth century elite and middle-class women, sometimes joined by working-class women, built organizations to promote feminine virtues. Women built these associations for their own edification and also to elevate others and work for the good of the entire society. Antebellum women's associations sometimes pursued reforms on a nondenominational basis, without stressing religious conversion. For example, the women of the Providence Employment Society considered the welfare of female workers "peculiarly their province" and fought for "*fair wages for women's work,*" devoting themselves "to aiding self-supporting seamstresses, providing employment, relief, and vocational education."[13] But this type of organization seems to have flourished only among elite women in cities.[14] More typical were the religiously based organizations sustained by middle-strata women in—and across—many localities.

During the early nineteenth century, transformations within Protestant denominations "feminized" much of American religion, as ministers addressed increasingly female congregations by softening harsh doctrines of predestination and placing greater emphasis on God's love and possibilities for Christian redemption for sinners.[15] In this doctrinal climate, many women congregants expressed their piousness not only through individual devotion and attempts to guide their families according to biblical precepts. They also organized community groups to pray and read the Bible, support missionaries, and minister to unfortunates.

Religious enthusiasm could also lead women well beyond such routinized, orthodox activities. During the "Second Great Awakening" that swept across much of the nation from the 1820s through the 1840s, revivalist preachers exhorted their followers, disproportionately women, to proselytize others and reform the world.

> Women's religious activities multiplied. Female revival converts formed Holy Bands to assist the evangelist in his revival efforts. They gathered with him at dawn to help plan the day's revival strategies. They posted bills in public places urging attendance at revival meetings, pressured merchants to close their shops and hold prayer services, buttonholed sinful men and prayed with them. Although "merely women," they led prayer vigils in their homes that extended far into the night. These women for the most part were married, respected members of respectable communities. Yet, transformed by millennial zeal, they disregarded virtually every restraint upon women's behavior. They self-righteously commanded sacred space as their own. They boldly carried Christ's message to the streets, even into the new urban slums.[16]

The movement to abolish slavery was also launched as part of this evangelical tide, and during the 1830s about a hundred women's societies became active in the cause. "More than half of the signatures on the great petitions that forced Congress to take up the slavery question were women's" and "most of these were obtained by female circulators."[17] To attack the evils of slavery, a few daring women even began to speak in public to mixed-sex groups.

Another crusade spawned by the Second Awakening was still more woman-dominated. The American Female Moral Reform Society was founded in New York City and eventually spread to include 445 auxiliary associations of women, mostly in greater New England.[18] This remarkable body employed only women on its staff and aimed to reform prostitutes, to ostracize their male clients, and—most important—to reform the sexual mores of American men in general. Men were understood as "the initiators in virtually every case of adultery or fornication—and the source, therefore, of that widespread immorality which endangered America's spiritual life and delayed the promised millennium."[19] "The Moral Reform Society," concludes Smith-Rosenberg, "was based on the assertion of female moral superiority and the right and ability of women to reshape male behavior. No longer did women have to remain passive and isolated within the structuring presence of husband or father."[20] The "Society's 'final solution'—the right to control the mores of men— provided a logical emotional redress for the feelings of passivity the Cult of True Womanhood enjoined on Victorian matrons."[21]

The antebellum years were not the only ones to witness this sort of civic assertiveness by organized American women. Decades later, the transdenominational Women's Christian Temperance Union (WCTU) again expressed the grievances of middle-class American women against men, and expressed women's will to reform society on moral lines congruent with their maternal and domestic values. As the historian Ruth Bordin explains, native-born middle-class American women (including some blacks and Native Americans) joined the WCTU "in numbers that far surpassed their participation in any other women's organization in the nineteenth century and that made the WCTU the first women's mass movement."[22] Although the WCTU built on church-based networks, it was an organization in which women, not male preachers, were in charge of meetings and rituals. Significantly, too, organized temperance activities in the late-nineteenth-century United States were much more female-dominated than contemporary temperance activities in England.

The WCTU got its start in the wake of a revival-spawned crusade against drinking and saloons. "Throughout the winter of 1873 and 1874 a grass-roots women's temperance crusade swept through Ohio, the Midwest and parts of the East. Thousands of women marched in the streets, prayed in saloons, and organized their own temperance societies in hundreds of towns and cities."[23] When it became obvious that one-shot demonstrations could gain only temporary results—because the saloons reopened after the women stopped praying in them—the WCTU was formed as a translocal federation of women's temperance groups. By 1879, Frances Willard of Illinois, who advocated opening local elections to women under the slogan of the "Home Protection Ballot," became president and guided the WCTU toward aggressive efforts to press for prohibition of alcohol through legal as well as voluntary means.[24] The WCTU expanded from 27,000 members in over a thousand locals in twenty-four states in 1879, to over 168,000 dues-paying members in some

7,000 locals in every state of the union around the turn of the century.[25] Tellingly, the spreading WCTU departed from the practice of earlier local women's groups by organizing along the lines of established state political districts, setting a pattern that would be recapitulated by later women's federations.[26]

The WCTU adopted a "do-everything policy" to fight evils associated with male irresponsibility and immigrant cultural intrusions. As the organization's motto declared, "Woman will bless and brighten every place she enters, and will enter every place."[27] Wide-ranging in their efforts, departments of the WCTU fought against prostitution, campaigned for female wardens and police matrons, worked for temperance propaganda in the schools, ran day nurseries for working mothers, and even supported labor reforms that might sustain respectable working-class homes.[28] In due course, the WCTU endorsed the goal of female suffrage on the ground that, as Willard argued, the "home was once almost a world apart in which the outside state interfered but little . . . Now that kingdom has been invaded . . . woman, the dethroned queen, demands and has a right to demand that her position of equal authority in the home be recognized in the state." Besides, Willard queried rhetorically, "Who has so great a stake in the Government as the Nation's motherhood?"[29] The WCTU, writes Barbara Epstein, "pushed the women's culture of its time to its limits," turning women's subordination in a separate sphere into a resource for seeking political reforms for the good of the nation as a whole.[30]

By the turn of the century, the WCTU was no longer growing rapidly, and it refocused its program on more narrowly temperance-related goals after the death of Frances Willard in 1898. Ironically, this happened as leadership in the temperance cause was partially passing to the Anti-Saloon League, and as younger women were gravitating to suffrage organizations or to federations of literary and civic women's clubs.[31]

For all its dynamism from the 1870s to the 1890s, the WCTU was far from the only route through which American women became involved in community affairs during the later nineteenth century. During the Civil War, women worked side by side with male agents in the many branches of the the Sanitary Commission that brought many northern elite women into public service on behalf of soldiers, veterans, and their families.[32] After the war, many of these women remained active in orthodox social-welfare policymaking through charity associations and appointive governmental boards.[33] Other women, a tiny radical minority, responded to the frustration of not being included when the vote was extended to male ex-slaves by becoming full-fledged equal-rights feminists, devoted to the struggle for the suffrage and other opportunities for women to gain full access to education, property, and careers.[34] Still other women, another small minority, joined associations to aid female wage-workers. Notable examples of such groups were the Women's Educational and Industrial Unions, founded in Boston in 1877 and in Buffalo, New York, in 1885.[35]

Probably the largest proportion of American women between the 1870s and the early 1900s confined their community participation, beyond church attendance, to clubs promoting what was known as "self culture," where women listened to invited lecturers or—more important—themselves gave reports and engaged in discussions about books and intellectual topics. The culture club movement of the nineteenth century got its formal start in 1868, when Sororis was founded by career women in New York City and the New England Woman's Club was founded by elite reformers in Boston. As other local literary clubs spread throughout the United States in the 1870s and 1880s, however, most shied away from careerist and reform causes. Married matrons in cities and towns constituted the bulk of members and officers in these clubs.[36] Such women were usually not pursuing paid careers at the time of their club participation, although a goodly number may have gone to college and worked as schoolteachers before marriage. In the words of the historian Karen Blair, cultural clubs "provided an exchange among women and an opportunity to refine the educations they had begun as schoolgirls, but had abandoned for marriage and family . . . clubs enabled women to become so closely associated with culture that they expropriated the previously male world of literature and the arts as their own, feeling they possessed a special humanistic sensitivity which provided an alternative to the acquisitive and competitive goals of men in an industrializing America."[37]

The General Federation of Women's Clubs

In due course, the originally inwardly oriented and locally based literary clubs became nationally organized and civicly assertive, following the route of predecessor women's associations, especially the WCTU, in parlaying women's separate sphere into translocal political power. After 1890, local literary and other special-purpose women's clubs coalesced into a national network, the General Federation of Women's Clubs (GFWC). The initiator of the General Federation, Jane Cunningham Croly, had established Sorosis in 1868, and then unsuccessfully advocated a national "Woman's Parliament" that would have worked for female-inspired social reforms without suffrage and involvement in the male electoral system.[38] In some ways, the GFWC realized this old dream in a new way. The General Federation was launched in New York City in April 1890, "to bring into communication with each other the various women's clubs throughout the world, in order that they may compare methods of work and become mutually helpful."[39] Following the usual pattern for widespread associations in the United States, state federations of women's clubs also sprang up starting in the 1890s, and soon affiliated with the General Federation. As Table 6 reveals, women's club federations spread into less industrial and urban states of the United States much more quickly than one might expect if only internal socioeconomic forces were at work. Elite and middle-class women in states such as Kansas, Texas, and Montana were in touch with eastern ideas, and they organized federations and parallel club activities as ways to "civilize" their states and communities.[40] Rural Maine actually established the first state federation in 1892. Federations of Women's Clubs operated in thirty-four states by 1900 and had spread to all forty-eight states by 1911. Overall, by 1910 the entire General Federation boasted over one million members in affiliated clubs across the nation.[41]

The GFWC thus became a three-tiered network of organization and social communication. At the center was the the General Federation, which staged huge and elaborate Biennial Conventions in various cities across the nation, published an official journal, and held regular meetings of elected national officers. It also maintained a national office and in due course sponsored standing committees ("departments") focused on Art, Civil Service Reform, Education, Home Economics, Pure Food, Forestry, Library Extension, Public Health, Industrial and Child Labor, Legislation, and other concerns. From the early 1900s on, articles on such topics and more appeared regularly in the General Federation's official journals. To give just one example, the typically wide-ranging November 1907 issue of the

Table 6.   Dates of organization of state Federations of Women's
Clubs

Maine 1892	North Dakota 1897
Iowa 1893	Arkansas 1897
Utah 1893	Connecticut 1897
Massachusetts 1894	Delaware 1897
Kentucky 1894	Florida 1897
Illinois 1894	Oklahoma 1897
Ohio 1894	Texas 1899
New Jersey 1894	South Carolina 1899
New York 1894	Maryland 1900
Nebraska 1894	California 1900
Minnesota 1895	South Dakota 1900
District of Columbia 1895	Oregon 1901
Michigan 1895	Arizona 1902
Colorado 1895	Louisiana 1902
Pennsylvania 1895	North Carolina 1902
Rhode Island 1895	Montana 1904
Georgia 1895	West Virginia 1904
Kansas 1895	Mississippi 1904
New Hampshire 1895	Wyoming 1904
Missouri 1895	Idaho 1905
Tennessee 1896	Indiana 1906
Vermont 1896	Alabama 1907
Washington 1896	Virginia 1907
Wisconsin 1896	Nevada 1910
	New Mexico 1911

Sources: Mary I. Wood, *The History of the General Federation of Womens' Clubs* (New York: General Federation of Women's Clubs, 1912), p. 353; and Sallie Southall Cotten, *History of the North Carolina Federation of Women's Clubs, 1901–1925* (Raleigh, NC: Edwards and Broughton Printing Co., 1925), p. 8.

Federation Bulletin: A Magazine for Club Women included articles on "Wisconsin's Child Labor Law," "Legislative Reforms in North Carolina," "What Civil Service Reform Means for Women," "A Place for Literature in the Club, "Arts and Crafts in the Home," "Women and Children in the Industrial World," and reports from Federation departments concerned with literature, forestry, and issues of health.[42] In turn, state federations held annual conventions and typically maintained specialized committee structures parallel to those of the national federation. Finally, at the base of the network were thousands of clubs, congregating women in virtually every town or city in America for weekly, biweekly, or monthly meetings about cultural, and civic matters.

As Karen Blair explains, the "enormous federation network facilitated the transmission of national policy to local and state federations and, from there, to all clubwomen."[43] After the crystallization of the network in the 1890s, local women's clubs gave more weight to social reform initiatives devised by national federation leaders, by the professional experts that GFWC officers regularly consulted and brought to speak at conventions, and by the specialized departments of the national and state federations. An example of a large, active, multidepartmental urban club that clearly paralleled the national federation was the Chicago Woman's Club; in 1913 this club "had committees on civics, public baths, social hygiene, permanent school extension, child labor, minimum wage, public schools as social centers, playgrounds, [and] civil service in public institutions."[44] More telling is the testimony of the historian of Texas white women's clubs that

the organization of the state federation [in 1899] served to encourage many individual clubs to take up involvement in the public sphere . . . Within one year a network was created through which individual clubs learned of the accomplishments and projects of other clubs, both in Texas and throughout the nation. Individual clubs joined the new state federation and, soon after, evinced a new sense of confidence and a dose of healthy competition . . . [with the ideals that] had become the order of the day in the club world of the Northeast and Midwest. The act of federation seemed to signal to Texas clubs that it was time to broaden their horizons.[45]

Clubwomen made the transition from cultural to reform activities not by abandoning the Victorian conception of women's special domestic sphere but by extending it into what came to be called "municipal housekeeping." In the words of Rheta Childe Dorr, the author of a 1910 book about clubwomen in politics entitled *What Eight Million Women Want:* "Woman's place is in the home. This is a platitude which no woman will ever dissent from . . . But Home is not contained within the four walls of an individual home. Home is the community. The city full of people is the Family. The public school is the real Nursery. And badly do the Home and the Family and the Nursery need their mother."[46] As Mrs. T. J. Bowlker further explained in an article on "Woman's Home-Making Function Applied to the Municipality," which appeared in a special 1912 issue of *The American City* devoted to the civic activities of women's clubs: "Our work is founded on the belief that woman has a special function in developing the welfare of humanity which man cannot perform. The function consists in her power to make, of any place in which she may happen to live, a *home* for all those who come there. Women must now learn to make of their cities great community homes for all the people."[47]

Having decided that "all clubs, as bodies of trained housekeepers, should consider themselves guardians of the civic housekeeping of their respective communities,"[48] many turn-of-the-century women's clubs initially devoted themselves to effecting improvements in libraries and schools, institutions close to women's proper concerns with culture and education.[49] Problems of consumption—such as the need for pure milk and clean meat—also represented a logical concern for organized women, as did the need to clean up the urban environment. In due course, many clubs and clubwomen also felt justified in promoting far-reaching social reforms, including measures to benefit working-class families. Thus the New Hampshire Federation of Women's Clubs maintained that the "increase of ideal homes must mean the decrease of many of the evils which we club women are trying to correct, such as illiteracy, intemperance, divorce, child labor, juvenile criminals, feeble minded children, tuberculosis, and many others, in fact, the millennium awaits only the perfect home."[50] A similar vision was put forward by Rheta Childe Dorr. Once "men and women divide the work of governing and administering, each according to his special capacities and natural abilities," she wrote, the city

> will be like a great, well-ordered, comfortable, sanitary household. Everything will be as clean as in a good home. Every one, as in a family, will have enough to eat, clothes to wear, and a good bed to sleep on. There will be no slums, no sweat shops, no sad women and children toiling in tenement rooms. There will be no babies dying because of an impure milk supply. There will be no "lung blocks" poisoning human beings that landlords may pile up sordid profits. No painted girls, with hunger gnawing their empty stomachs, will walk in the shadows. All the family will be taken care of, taught to take care of themselves, protected in their daily tasks, sheltered in their homes.[51]

Compelling as it was, "municipal housekeeping" was not the only ideological rubric that could justify the extension of proper women's involvement from the home into the community and nation. As Sheila Rothman has written, the "Progressive Era witnessed the triumph of a new ideal for womanhood . . . [a]ppropriately labeled 'educated motherhood'."[52] Based on the belief that children needed insightful guidance at each stage of development, this ideal "at once transformed the character of private and public duties and altered the tasks of mothers and the obligations of legislators."[53] Mothers needed training and expert guidance to perform their duties effectively. Public policies needed to be devised to improve schools, to adapt institutions like the courts to deal with the special needs of juveniles, and—above all—to allow children to stay with their mothers. Even less privileged mothers, it was felt, should be allowed to devote their time to childrearing, rather than be forced to do menial wage-work.

The National Congress of Mothers

In quintessential American fashion, the ideal of educated motherhood was promoted by voluntary associations, of which the most prominent was the National Congress of Mothers. The Congress was to become in 1924 the "PTA," or "National Congress of Parents and Teachers," a change of name that reflected its evolution by then into a virtual adjunct of the nation's public school system. But at its founding in 1897, and on into the Progressive Era, the National Congress of Mothers was an elite maternalist organization, one which many school officials initially opposed for fear that it might meddle in their domain.[54] Indeed, the fledgling Congress was devoted "to carry[ing] the mother-love and mother-thought into all that concerns or touches childhood in Home, School, Church, State or Legislation."[55] Although efforts to organize parent-teacher associations, rather than just mothers' clubs, became systematic from 1908 onward, the National Congress for some years still placed major emphasis on understanding and improving not just public education but all aspects of government's role in relation to marriage and children.[56]

The National Congress of Mothers was conceived by Mrs. Alice McLellan Birney, the wife of a Washington, DC, lawyer. As she later recounted in a personal notebook, when her "last little daughter" was born in January 1895, she and her husband

> had been living in Washington not quite two years, and I was impressed . . . with the great number of conventions and assemblages of all kinds and for all purposes held at the national capital . . . I asked myself . . . "How can the mothers be educated and the *nation* made to recognize the supreme importance of the child?" Congress was in session at this time, and I knew how its doings were telegraphed to all parts of the earth and how eagerly such messages were read . . . and then like a flash came the thought: Why not have a National Congress of Mothers . . . ?[57]

In contrast to the gradual, bottom-up growth of the General Federation of Women's Clubs, the National Congress of Mothers was rapidly organized from the top down. During 1895 and 1896, Mrs. Birney shared her idea with supporters of the kindergarten movement at a Chautauqua summer camp session, as well as with Mrs. Phoebe Apperson Hearst, the socially prominent benefactress from the Hearst clan of businessmen, statemen, and newspapermen.[58] Then Mrs. Birney and her associates sought out "in each of various localities, the name of one 'woman of position,' a key person to whom correspondence about the Mothers' Congress might be directed."[59] To such contacts, as well as to already-established women's associations, went the "Official Call to the first National Congress of Mothers" to be held February 17–19, 1897. Washington, DC, was "selected as the most fitting place for such an assemblage because the movement is one of national importance."[60]

The focus of the National Congress was to be on developing and spreading maternal influence throughout society, not on directly furthering women's rights. At the opening convention, Mrs. Birney stressed that "This is in no sense a sex movement." She noted that many contemporaries were placing stress on opportunities for women, "yet how, I ask, can we divorce the woman question from the child question?"[61] Still, the Congress of Mothers took a strong stand on the empowerment of mothers through education and organization. As Mrs. Helen H. Gardner put it:

> Subject mothers never did, and subject mothers never will, produce a race of free, well-poised, liberty-loving, justice-practicing children . . . The race which is born of mothers who are harassed,

bullied, subordinated, or made the victims of blind passion or power, or of mothers who are simply too pretty and self-debased to feel their subject status, cannot fail to continue to give the horrible spectacles we have always had of war, of crime, of vice, of trickery, of double-dealing, of pretense, of lying, of arrogance, of subserviency, of incompetence, of brutality, and, alas! of insanity, idiocy, and disease added to a fearful and unnecessary mortality . . .

If you have a daughter who is finer and truer, more capable and noble, more intellectual and able than the rest, she is the one whose education and development as an individual should be carried to the highest reach, not simply because she is to be a writer or speaker or teacher . . . but because it may also be her pleasure and province to be the wife and mother in a real and true and inspiring home life . . .

When our republic has such mothers . . . the question of women in the other professions will have adjusted itself. When woman is developed and free to choose, capacity will find its level and outlet. Ignorance will cease to be looked upon as beautiful in either sex.[62]

What is more, women were to be the leaders of the new maternal movement, because, as Mrs. Birney pointed out, "Men have a thousand imperative outside interests and pursuits, while nature has set her seal upon woman as the caretaker of the child; therefore it is natural that woman should lead in awakening mankind to a sense of the responsibilities resting upon the race to provide each new-born soul with an environment which will foster its highest development."[63] Those women the leaders of the National Congress had in mind were not only actual mothers of young children but also "women whose children are grown, and who, by the experience of life, have gained the judgement and knowledge so valuable in the broad and varied fields of the world's work." As Congress President Mrs. Frederic Schoff explained,

when the birds have flown from the nest, the mother-work may still go on, reaching out to better conditions for other children. It may be in providing day nurseries, vacation schools, playgrounds, and kindergartens, manual and domestic science. It may be in forming mothers' circles and awakening in the busy mother an appreciation of all that motherhood means. It may be in working for laws regulating child labor, juvenile courts and probation, pure food, divorce and marriage, compulsory education . . . It may be in providing wholesome, hygienic homes through tenement house inspection, visiting nurses, schools for the defective and backward, homes for the homeless, help for the erring. It may be in fighting against any evil that menaces the security and sacredness of the home and undermines the moral tone of society . . . [T]he women of today may effect a greater uplift in physical and moral life than has ever been felt. The Mothers' Congress, Guardian of the Children of the Nation! Is there any woman who will not enlist under that banner?[64]

The National Congress convened yearly national conventions, and staged a major "international" convention every three years. Congress conventions were often held in Washington, DC (1897, 1898, 1899, 1902, 1905, 1908, and 1911), but also convened in other cities around the country (Des Moines, Iowa, in 1900; Columbus, Ohio, in 1901; Detroit in 1903; St. Louis in 1904; Los Angeles, deferred because of the earthquake in 1906, held in 1907; New Orleans in 1909; and Denver in 1910). The Congress grew steadily, first by co-opting or helping to create local clubs, then by stimulating state "branches" with affiliated local clubs. During the first five years, eight states were officially organized. By 1910, twenty-one states were organized and the Congress had 50,000 dues-paying members; and by 1920, when its second president, Mrs. Schoff, stepped down, the Congress was organized in thirty-seven states and had 190,000 members.[65]

Although the National Congress of Mothers did not at first become anywhere near as large or as geographically extensive as the General Federation of Women's Clubs, its social influence was nevertheless considerable. Because of its top-down organization, its early members were often elite women active in other organizations (including the GFWC) and well connected in their communities and nationally. As a 1907 pamplet explained the "Influence of the Congress," the work "extends from the homes of the wealthiest and most cultured to the homes of the poorest and the lowliest, and the help it gives is eagerly sought by thousands of mothers. It is applying the best thought of earnest, intelligent men and women to the problems of child-care throughout the land."[66] This no doubt claimed too much about the involvement of poor women in the National Congress of Mothers, but for the early 1900s it was accurate in saying that many wealthy women were involved.

Male politicians, moreover, gave the Congress much publicly visible approval, perhaps because of its social prominence and perhaps also because they liked its ideas about women's sphere. Its founding conference in 1897 included a gala reception at the White House; and state and federal officials, elected and appointed, regularly spoke at subsequent conventions. Before, during, and after his presidency, Theodore Roosevelt was especially supportive of the Congress of Mothers. At the First International Congress in America for the Welfare of the Child, organized by the Congress in March 1908 (see Figure 18), President Roosevelt spoke (not for the first time), characteristically assuring the assembled delegates that "there is no other society which I am quite as glad to receive as this. This is the one body that I put even ahead of the veterans of the Civil War; because when all is said and done it is the mother, and the mother only, who is a better citizen even than the soldier who fights for his country."[67] The President went on to attack the woman "who shirks her duty as wife and mother" and declared that the "mother is the one supreme asset of national life; she is more important by far than the successful statesman or businessman or artist or scientist."[68] Roosevelt waxed eloquent about the selfless dedication of women as mothers and homemakers, yet he also understood that the members of his audience had extradomestic concerns. He called upon them to agitate publicly for a series of municipal reforms as well as new state laws outlawing child labor. "The field of your activities," he acknowledged, "is so very wide that it would be useless for me to attempt to enumerate the various subjects of which you will and ought to treat."[69]

Concerns with municipal housekeeping and educated motherhood could indeed take turn-of-the-century women deeply into progressive politics. Reform efforts needed only to be justified as somehow connected to moral and healthy homes—something readily done for any proposed policies having to do with consumption, health and safety, children, mothers, or urban order. Understandably, too, participation in efforts to obtain such new public policies might eventually lead elite and middle-class women (many of whom were not convinced before the early 1900s) to advocate full female enfranchisement. Although the National Congress of Mothers avoided taking a stand on suffrage, the WCTU gave a degree of endorsement to the woman's suffrage cause in 1881, and the GFWC fully endorsed

The National Congress of Mothers

Earnestly invites you to participate in the

First International Congress

to be held in

Washington, D. C.
March 10-17, 1908

Subject of Consideration

The Welfare of the Child

President Roosevelt opens International Congress by welcoming delegates at White House and giving address

President Roosevelt says:

"I take the heartiest interest in your First International Congress to deal with the welfare of the children.

"I am delighted that you have planned to bring the representatives of the nations together to confer upon such a subject.

"What I can personally do to help you will, of course, be done.

"I shall hope to welcome your delegates at the White House, and there to greet them, and to express to them my deep realization of the importance of their work and my profound sympathy with it."

Governors of Every State in the Union are Appointing Delegates to this Congress

---

The
National Congress of Mothers of the United States

has been studying the needs of childhood for the past ten years, and through its local circles and annual conferences has endeavored to unify the best thought of the nation on the wisest measures to be adopted to secure the highest physical, mental and moral development of the coming race.

With the purpose of stimulating world-wide interest in these subjects, this International Congress has been called.

Figure 18 Program for the First International Congress of Mothers, 1908

Source: Phoebe Apperson Hearst Papers (72/204 c), The Bancroft Library, University of California, Berkeley.

Suggested Topics

---

helps to Parents	Child Study; Physical, Mental, Spiritual.
Moral Training	In the Home; the Sunday School; the Day School.

Education

- Compulsory Education.
- Stimulation of Parental Responsibility; Parent-Teacher Associations.
- The School Curriculum; Physical Exercises.
- Manual Training; Household Economies.
- Industrial Schools.
- Coeducation.

Provision for the helpless and Defective

- The Deaf; the Blind.
- The Epileptic and Insane.
- The Mentally Deficient and Dependent.

Preventive and Protective Agencies

- Playgrounds; Public Baths.
- Day Nurseries.
- Libraries; Boys' and Girls' Clubs.

Treatment of Erring Children

- Causes of Delinquency, Truancy, Vagrancy, Theft, Immorality.
- Placing out in Homes.
- Juvenile Courts; Probation.
- Reformatories.

Legislation

- Special Schools; Regulation of Child Labor.
- Protection of the Home and the Child.
- Marriage and Divorce.
- Tenement Laws.
- Pure Food Laws.
- Juvenile Courts.
- Establishing Parks and Playgrounds.

What is your city, state or nation doing to raise the standards of care and guardianship of children?

suffrage in 1914.[70] When these associations predominantly composed of married women endorsed female suffrage, they did so not
simply for reasons of equality in the abstract, but as another tool
that women might use to promote the home-protective, environmental, and child-centered reforms for which they had already been
agitating for many years. As Rheta Childe Dorr put it in 1910: "To
the anxious inquiry, What will women do with their votes? the answer
is simple. They will do, or try to do, precisely what they do, or try
to do, without votes . . . Social legislation alone interests women . . .
Without votes, without precedents, and without very much money
. . . [t]he organized non-voting women of this country have devoted
themselves for years to precisely these objects."[71] Indeed, the widespread, gender-specific associations of the turn of the century were
very successful "at extending woman's influence into the public realm
by building upon the concept of separate spheres."[72] This happened
well before the achievement of full women's suffrage in the United
States, allowing women to influence profoundly the legislative agendas of the Progressive Era. It remained to be seen what, if anything,
the suffrage would add.

Educated Women as Reform Leaders

The potential influence of women upon progressive reforms lay not
only with widespread associations of married ladies. Highly educated
career women, mostly single—women such as Jane Addams, Florence Kelley, Lillian Wald, Edith Abbott, Julia Lathrop, and Alice
Hamilton—were also to play a crucial part in the achievement of
maternalist social policies.[73] The extent and character of higher education for American women, and the special nature of the social
settlement movement in the turn-of-the-century United States, help
to explain the influence of these female intellectuals and reform
activists.

Women in American Higher Education

Despite the ideology of domesticity, the United States led the world
in offering higher education to women in its decentralized and fast-
growing system of colleges and universities. Access was granted to
women because a few philanthropists believed in educating them,

because competing institutions of higher learning vied to attract students, and—above all—because educated women were badly needed to staff the public schools that became one of the bulwarks of American mass democracy.[74] Women students attended eastern women's colleges such as Mount Holyoke (founded 1837), Vassar (1865), Smith (1875), Wellesley (1875), and Bryn Mawr (1885); and there were also various "female seminaries" across and beyond the East.[75] Other women students became "co-eds" in formally equal but actually primarily separate sectors of universities and liberal arts colleges. Oberlin College in Ohio was the first to accept women, starting in 1837.[76] Similarly, most of the early coeducational universities were outside the East, even though some eastern universities eventually became coeducational during the nineteenth century (including the pioneering Cornell University in 1872). "The eight state universities open to women in 1870 were, in the order of accepting women, Iowa, Wisconsin, Kansas, Indiana, Minnesota, Missouri, Michigan, and California."[77] Yet so strong were the forces working toward access for women that by 1890 only 37 percent of American institutions of higher learning were still closed to them.[78]

At both the women's colleges and the coeducational institutions the numbers enrolled mounted rapidly (although not all women stayed for B.A. degrees, because they could become teachers with fewer years of higher education). By 1870, some 11,000 women constituted over one-fifth of all American students in institutions of higher learning; and by 1880, some 40,000 women constituted a third of enrollees. Women's share increased to about 37 percent in 1900, with 85,000 enrolled, and rose to nearly half at the early-twentieth-century peak in 1920, when some 283,000 women were in institutions of higher learning.[79] Even so, of course, only a small proportion of all American women (or for that matter, men) attended college in this era. Less than 2 percent of women aged 18–21 were enrolled in 1880; and by 1910 the proportion of the relevant cohort in college was still under 4 percent.[80]

We can gain some perspective on American's women's considerable educational achievements by noting that contemporary British women lagged far behind. In 1880, when women were already a major presence in U.S. higher education, "only London University granted degrees to women scholars. The handful of the students in the women's colleges of Cambridge and Oxford (less than 200 in

1882) took the same examinations given to men, but were not allowed to receive degrees until after World War I."[81] Around 1890, America's "Smith College alone had more women students than Oxford and Cambridge."[82] And according to a list compiled by the Women's Institute, the total number of British women enrolled in all women's colleges in 1897 was still only 784—a minuscule number compared to the tens of thousands of American women then enrolled.[83]

Attendance at a college or university did not in and of itself breed intellectuality or a commitment to social reform among American women (any more than among men). Most institutions of higher learning purposefully educated their female students to become cultivated ladies and good mothers; and indeed many women graduates, such as the alumnae of Grinnell College in Iowa, seem to have moved smoothly into the late Victorian world of marriage, motherhood, and participation in women's literary clubs.[84] Those higher-educated women who took jobs went overwhelmingly into school-teaching, and some worked only for a few years before marriage.[85] Nevertheless, the sheer extent of female higher education produced, over time, large numbers of educated American women, spread across the country, who could appreciate reform efforts justified in terms of both feminine values and the need for greater "professional expertise" in politics. This mattered, even if most educated women simply served as rank-and-file supporters of reform through such bodies as the American Association of Collegiate Alumnae (later the American Association of University Women) and the General Federation of Women's Clubs.

Higher education for women also led a critical minority to become leading reformers by way of the social settlement movement. Significantly, from "the 1870s through the 1920s, between 40 and 60 percent of women college graduates did not marry, at a time when only 10 percent of all American women did not."[86] And among those who obtained Ph.D.'s between 1877 and 1924, fully 75 percent remained single.[87] From the ranks of the mostly unmarried women in the earliest cohorts of the higher-educated, including the elite few with graduate degrees, came the founders of many "social settlements" in American cities. According to John Rousmaniere's study of the women who formed the College Settlement Association between 1889 and 1894, the most persistent of these pioneering settlers in New York, Boston, and Philadelphia were graduates of particular women's colleges—Vassar, Smith, Wellesley, and Bryn Mawr—whose philosophies of education were distinctive.[88] Vassar, one of the earliest women's colleges, "differed from other women's colleges and seminaries in picturing its alumnae serving in other places than the home."[89] Similarly, at Smith and Wellesley, two new colleges founded in the mid-seventies, "intellectual discipline received more emphasis than . . . [Victorian feminine] accomplishments," while at another newer school, Bryn Mawr, the educators believed that "Only marriage and sexual needs—which the truly disciplined woman could control—stood between the educated female and high achievement."[90] These "schools constantly impressed on the students their uniqueness and superiority to other young women."[91]

Certain of America's many higher educational institutions thus fostered an unusual sense of independence and determination in an elite minority of women. These independent women were not 1960s-style feminists but, in Rousmaniere's term, "cultural hybrids," for they retained a Victorian sense of the uniqueness and special moral mission of women, and they also believed in mutual commitment among women. Carroll Smith-Rosenberg has made some insightful comments about "the more adventurous and determined" of the college-educated women who "experimented with alternative life styles and institutions":

> Like their mothers, they formed separatist organizations of women to deal with new problems of an industrial and urbanized world. Unlike their mothers, they used these single-sex institutions to sustain a life lived permanently outside the bourgeois home . . . [W]hile rejecting the patriarchal family and their mothers' domestic lives . . [they] did not repudiate the traditional world of female love or the concept of the female family.[92]

Some of the women Smith-Rosenberg is talking about remained as faculty members in the women's colleges. Others founded or joined social settlements in which women were the core, long-term residents. "The settlement house represented their home, their fellow women residents, their family."[93]

Women in Social Settlements

Social settlements were, as Allen Davis has aptly written, "spearheads for reform."[94] Located in poor urban neighborhoods and aiming "to bring men and women of education in to closer relations with the laboring classes for their mutual benefit," the social settlements were both homes and outreach institutions.[95] For a few months or many years, settlements served as homes for higher-educated young adults from elite and middle-class backgrounds, allowing them to experience and often systematically investigate urban social conditions. The settlements also dispensed educational and social services to surrounding working-class residents, and got involved in politics on their behalf. They organized social and instructional clubs, ran day nurseries, agitated for better city services, and—over time—pursued new social legislation on behalf of the less privileged.

Settlement houses were a British innovation. The first one, Toynbee Hall in the East End of London, was founded by Canon Samuel Barnett and Henrietta Barnett in 1884, and by 1911 there were forty-six settlements in British cities.[96] Some British settlements were staffed by college women, but none of these became a leading center of reform; women were attracted to them as routes toward specialized types of charity work and, in due course, social work.[97] The more prominent British settlements, and especially Toynbee Hall, were mostly staffed by male graduates of Oxford and Cambridge, who spent a few years engaged in social investigation and urban reform en route to careers in journalism, the universities, or the civil service. Nearly a quarter of the men who resided at Toynbee Hall between 1884 and 1914 went on to become civil servants, and the proportion taking this career path increased with time.[98] In due course, four men who became prime ministers had close connections to Toynbee Hall.[99] As one observer commented sarcastically, "men who went in training under the Barnetts . . . could always be sure of government and municipal appointments . . . [They] discovered the advancement of their own interests and the interests of the poor were best served by leaving East London to stew in its own juice while they became members of parliament, cabinet ministers, civil servants."[100]

A telling instance was William Beveridge, who became the Board of Trade official behind the Liberal plans for social insurance in 1911. After graduating from Oxford, Beveridge became subwarden of Toynbee Hall in 1903, writing to reassure his parents that "Toynbee Hall is not a cul de sac. It is known among men of position."[101] While at the settlement, Beveridge did economic research, served on private and public bodies dealing with unemployment in London, and became a regular writer on social issues for the *Morning Post* prior to joining the newspaper's regular staff.[102] All of this, of course, was a prelude to Beveridge's achievement of many important national governmental assignments during a lifetime of shaping the British welfare state.[103]

The early social settlements in the United States were directly modeled on Toynbee Hall. They were established in major cities of the East and Midwest after their founders were inspired by personal visits to the Barnetts' domain in Whitechapel, and they imitated Toynbee Hall's instructional activities and college-like living quarters.[104] Nevertheless, the American social settlement movement ultimately differed in important ways from its British counterpart. In the first place, the American movement became much larger. There were fewer than fifty British settlements by 1910, because Britain was a relatively small country, and because settlements became less attractive to educated young people once the Liberal welfare state and the Labour Party were launched. Meanwhile, the U.S. settlements proliferated at an accelerating pace. "In 1891 there were six settlements in the United States; in 1897 there were seventy-four. By 1900 the number jumped to over one hundred settlements, to over two hundred, five years later, and by 1910 there were more than four hundred."[105] Social settlements in the United States remained for quite some time a prime outlet for the aspirations of idealistic, higher-educated young people who wished to find public solutions to the problems of urban, industrial capitalism.

Not only was the U.S. settlement movement larger and more persistent than the British, its philosophy was more democratic. British settlers worked closely with charity organizations and had a definite air of upper-class superiority and noblesse oblige toward the poor. The American settlers, in contrast, initially broke with charity organizations and presumed that they would not just teach but also learn valuable lessons from the U.S. urban poor, who were mostly ethnic immigrants.[106] The American settlers aimed to blur class lines by helping their neighbors to achieve full participation in American democracy and social life.

Some of the most decisive contrasts between the British and American settlement movements had to do with their gender dynamics and the ways in which the divergent national political contexts interacted with the career trajectories of men and women. If Canon Barnett and William Beveridge, leaders of Toynbee Hall in the British capital of London, were exemplary and highly influential leaders of the British settlement movement, it is not incidental that Jane Addams, founder and long-term resident of Hull House in the midwestern U.S. city of Chicago, is the best known American settlement leader.[107] There were, of course, male settlement leaders in the United States, including Robert Woods in Boston and Graham Taylor in Chicago. But women were more important than men in the U.S. settlements, and women were much more influential in the United States than in Britain, for several reasons.

Women settlers predominated numerically in the U.S. movement. Between 1886 and 1917, 60 percent of American social settlement residents were women.[108] However, the sheer persistence of U.S. women settlers might well have been (and in some cases surely was) associated with marginality, and in any event the simple numerical preponderance of women did not set the U.S. settlement movement apart from the British.[109] More important, higher-educated, unmarried women were the most persistent American settlers, the ones who gave houses and the movement staying power over time. While the median number of years spent by all residents of U.S. social settlements was three, unmarried women spent a median of ten years in the settlements, and many remained for their entire adult lifetimes.[110] In contrast, after spending a short time in the settlements during their twenties, male residents usually married and moved on to other careers.

Perhaps most telling, the United States had many successful mixed-gender settlements in which women were leaders. Britain had only six mixed-gender settlements in 1913, and these were not considered to work well.[111] As a contemporary observer of English settlements wrote:

> Theoretically the mixed Settlement might appear to be the ideal, for only in common work can men and women embrace the whole life of their poor neighbours with their understanding and assistance. In practice, however, many difficulties present themselves . . . If the mixed Settlement is, as a rule, not desirable, yet an effort is made as far as possible to ensure its advantages by attracting women as helpers to Men's Settlements, while the Women's Settlements suitably limit their field of work to their own powers . . . In

a certain respect a peculiar position is occupied by several Women's Settlements, which stand in entire dependence on the clergy . . . or form a branch of a Men's Settlement.[112]

Meanwhile, American women were dominant figures in numerous mixed settlements—a pattern which struck British observers. Thus, after "visiting mixed settlements in America, Henrietta Barnett remarked, 'Candour compels me to state that with few exceptions in the settlements I visited, the grey mare was the better horse of the pair.'"[113] Similarly, Beatrice Webb's *American Diary* recorded about Hull House in Chicago that "the residents consist, in the main, of strong-minded energetic women, bustling about their various enterprises and professions, interspersed with earnest-faced self-subordinating and mild-mannered men who slide from room to room apologetically."[114] Nor was the situation at Hull House idiosyncratic. According to one student of U.S. social settlements, "men and women shared leadership positions in the first eight major settlements, [and] the vast majority of the later leaders . . . were women."[115]

Finally, in sharp contrast to the situation in Britain, certain American women in both mixed-gender and female settlements became highly influential reformers and public figures—that is, leaders outside as well as within the settlements. The balance of opportunities offered to male and female reformers in the British versus the U.S. polity can help us to understand why the American women settlers could become so prominent. Whereas British male graduates of Oxford and Cambridge could use settlement work as a predictable and quite direct route to elite careers in political parties and the civil service, such opportunities were not usually or predictably available to American male college graduates who went into settlement work. For those American male residents who did not stay over the long term in the settlements, careers in the ministry, journalism, social work, or academia were the likely destinations. Such careers did not afford the national prestige and connections that certain British male settlers quickly achieved; and the kinds of men destined for such careers were probably, on the whole, less ambitious and overweening than the British male settlers. In sum, American male settlers lacked the outside connections and career prospects that might have made it possible for them to dominate the U.S. social settlements—or to use social settlements as effectively as British males did as proving grounds for paternalist welfare-state reforms. With Liberal Party connections and a Board of Trade position available to him, Britain's William Beveridge could, with the help of a short sojourn at Toynbee Hall, accomplish policy breakthroughs for social insurance the likes of which were out of reach for America's male social settlement leader Robert Woods (or any other male social reform leader in the United States at that time).

Yet for American women, the social settlements allowed more scope than settlements did either for American men or for British women. The British women either operated in sex-segregated environments or else were treated as "helpers" in male-led settlements. They faced a situation in which their male counterparts, sporting Oxford and Cambridge degrees that the women could not obtain, were predictably headed for elite establishment careers, including positions of political and bureaucratic authority. Understandably, therefore, British male settlers preempted the leadership of the settlements and became identified with the most publicly visible efforts at social reform, leaving the women to pursue locally centered social work activities.[116] In the United States, meanwhile, there were many highly educated women with the training and ambition to undertake professional careers in universities and politics, yet most such career opportunities were closed to them.[117] University professoriats discriminated against women, and so did the political parties in a polity where patronage predominated and women could not vote in national elections. The United States also lacked a professionalized national civil service, and even if one had existed it would surely have relegated women to subordinate positions, as did the contemporary British civil service.[118] In a way, American women were advantaged by the fact that much governmental "bureaucratization" in this period occurred through the creation of particular agencies by local and state governments. Although work in such agencies rarely added up to the equivalent of civil-service careers, higher-educated women were often appointed, at least temporarily, to labor bureaus, or factory inspectorates, or local social-welfare agencies.

In this situation, certain American settlement houses—such as Hull House in Chicago and Henry Street in New York—became settings from which talented women could create and pursue an alternative kind of wide-ranging career, combining social research, public education, civic activism, and intermittent periods of official service. American men were not in a position to preempt all of the possibilities along this line, and the kinds of institutions that in Britain increasingly took up the relevant "civic space," as we might label it—institutions such as expert career bureaucracies, programmatic political parties, and in due course the "welfare state" itself—simply did not exist to the same extent in the United States. Through the settlements, intellectual American women at the turn of the twentieth century had considerable scope to pursue long-term careers as reformers, supporting one another, and cooperating with some male co-workers without being crowded out by a dominant male social policy establishment.[119]

Women reformers based in the U.S. settlements became key leaders in campaigns for maternalist social policies.[120] Jane Addams, head of Hull House, and Florence Kelley, who lived there from 1891 to 1899, teamed up to press the fight for child labor reform and women's hours laws in Illinois and across the nation. After an early success for women's hour regulations in Illinois, Florence Kelley served as Illinois State Factory Inspector, and she used Hull House as a base for further public organizing after the initial women's hour legislation was judicially overturned. Kelley moved in 1899 to Henry Street Settlement in New York, where she became executive secretary of the National Consumers' League and an activist in the National Child Labor Committee, continuing the fight for legislation regulating women's work and child labor. These were causes that also inspired leadership from Sophonisba Breckinridge and Grace Abbott, other residents of Hull House, from Cornelia Bradford of Jersey City's Whittier House, from Lucile Eaves of San Francisco's South Park Settlement, and many others. Activities on behalf of women workers were pushed forward through the Women's Trade Union League by Jane Addams along with Mary McDowell of the University of Chicago Settlement, Helena Dudley of Denison House in Boston, Vida Scudder of College Settlement in New York, Mary Kingsbury Simkhovitch of Greenwich House in New York, and Lillian Wald, head of the Henry Street Settlement in New York. Wald led the campaign to establish the New York City Bureau of Child Hygiene, which operated under the motto "Better mothers, better babies, and better homes." Joined by Florence Kelley, Jane Addams and others,

Wald also lobbied successfully for the establishment of the federal Children's Bureau in 1912, and the Bureau's first chief was Julia Lathrop, a former resident of Hull House and a pioneer in establishing the juvenile court system. Mary Simkhovitch, Lillian Wald, Jane Addams, Florence Kelley, Grace and Edith Abbott, and Julia Lathrop were all early supporters of mothers' pension legislation. Women settlement leaders also lobbied energetically for the Sheppard-Towner Act of 1921, which was modeled on the New York City Bureau of Child Hygiene and other local efforts to aid mothers and children.

Finally, one may speculate that many male reformers connected to the American settlement movement were themselves affected by the presence of the strong women leaders. Not only did such male reformers often learn to defer to female leaders such as Jane Addams, they may also have come to think in more female-centered ways about basic issues of social policy. An especially telling instance was William Hard, a journalist who (as we shall see in Chapter 8) played a leading role in the campaign for mothers' pension legislation, giving many speeches and writing an influential series of articles in a leading women's magazine. Hard was for a time the "head worker" (as the leader was called) at the Northwestern University Settlement, and he also lived for a time at Hull House. Mary McDowell described him in a letter to Lillian Wald as "brilliant, honest, and independent—not a socialist—but a true Social Democrat, one of my best friends—is devoted to 'Lady Jane' [Addams] and Julia Lathrop."[121] Here, obviously, was a male reformer strongly tied to leading settlement women, and it is hard to believe that his views were not powerfully affected by his associations with them.

Building Reform Coalitions

American social settlement people could not pursue reforms through programmatic parties and national bureaucracies as the British social policy establishment did. Instead, the Americans were builders of eclectic political coalitions capable of civic education and legislative lobbying. Settlement leaders were especially adept at knitting together coalitions, on the one hand across classes, and on the other hand among women in the middle and upper classes. A bit can be said about the organizational links and ideological affinities through which settlement leaders built each kind of coalition.

American social settlement leaders enjoyed, for one thing, friendly relations with leaders of organized labor; and they established especially strong ties with organizers of working women. While British elite reformers were able to ally with male trade unions in support of new social policies, American social settlement leaders worked more extensively for, and with, female unionists and workers, especially when social legislation was at issue. In the early-twentieth-century United States, there was no consistently strong cross-class alliance in support of social legislation for male workers because, as we have already seen, the elite reformers of the American Association of Labor Legislation were reluctant to press for old-age pensions during the 1910s, while national leaders in the American Federation of Labor would not accept the contributory social insurance and the wages and hours measures that the AALL preferred to emphasize. At the same time, ties between female American wage earners and reformers were readily forged, because women workers, largely unskilled and terribly exploited, were not of much interest to the American Federation of Labor. The Federation's units were primarily based in skilled trades dominated by male, native-born or earlier-immigrant workers; and its leaders believed that women should be in the home, supported by adequate male family wages, not competing with men for scarce employment opportunities.[122] Thus women workers needed support from middle- and upper-class allies.

Women trade unionists got such help through the Women's Trade Union League (WTUL), which was founded in 1903 (with the AFL's nominal blessing) by an alliance of women's trade union organizers, settlement house leaders, some upper-class matrons active in charity work.[123] It was "not by coincidence that branches were first opened in the three cities"—New York, Boston, and Chicago—"where the settlement movement was most strongly established."[124] Much of the initiative was taken by settlement house people, because "from the beginning most settlement workers found neighborhood working women more desperately in need of support [than male workers] and more willing to accept their aid."[125] The WTUL provided critical resources, including money and strike support, for women workers attempting to unionize. And to help make up for the weakness of women workers in labor markets and trade unions, the WTUL agitated for new laws to limit their hours of work, improve their wages, and regulate working conditions that might threaten women's health.[126] It also brought working women into alliances on behalf of female suffrage.[127]

Significantly, the American WTUL was more devoted to legislative causes, especially to the fights for protective laws and women's suffrage, than was its British counterpart.[128] Operating in a national setting where unions were steadily gaining organizational and political strength, the British WTUL actively guided female unions into the national labor confederation. Indeed, in 1921 the British WTUL dissolved and became instead the women's section of the Trades Union Congress. Meanwhile, the American WTUL persisted as a basically gender-based and fully cross-class organization devoted to legislation and the cause of women's suffrage, as well as to unionization. For American WTUL members, the rhetoric of "sisterhood" was more meaningful than the language of class.

Another small gender-based policy organization was the National Consumers' League (NCL), which involved many upper-class as well as middle-class women in economic boycotts and legislative struggles on behalf of working women.[129] Some prominent male academics and reformers were titular officers of the NCL, but they often failed to show up for meetings, and the organization was clearly both run and energized by women. The NCL—which had no British counterpart—was founded during the 1890s by Mrs. Josephine Shaw Lowell, Mrs. Frederick (Maud) Nathan, and other elite women who came together to agitate for better working conditions for shop girls.[130] Although the Consumers' League membership never grew beyond several thousand nationwide, the organization did claim sixty-four local leagues in twenty states in 1905. After that, the number of states organized dropped, with fifteen states still claiming one or more local leagues by 1917.[131] Members of the Consumers' Leagues were well connected socially in their states and communities and thus often strategically placed to agitate for legislative reforms. Moreover, the NCL took the bold step of hiring the remarkable socialist reformer and social settlement resident Florence Kelley as its executive secretary.[132] Under her politically principled and technically expert leadership, the National League became a persistent and remarkably effective advocate of child labor legislation as well as protectionist legislation for women wage-workers.[133] Thus, even more than the WTUL, the National Consumers' League was a pure embodiment of gender politics around a social-democractic agenda, for it engaged women career-reformers from the settlements, along with upper- and middle-class matrons, on behalf of reforms deemed beneficial for working-class women and their children.

The WTUL was a cross-class organization, and both the WTUL and the NCL were dedicated to helping working women. Still, these groups were relatively small, staff-led organizations. Women's politics did so well in the early-twentieth-century United States because settlement leaders did much more than operate through and in alliance with such staff-led organizations. Settlement leaders also worked cooperatively on many political issues with the larger and more widespread associations of elite and middle-class married women, especially the General Federation of Women's Clubs. As we shall see again and again in the next three chapters, leading settlement house reformers were members of—and, at times, committee chairs in—the national women's federations. And these professional reformers repeatedly wrote articles for women's magazines and spoke on behalf of new social legislation at women's conventions.

Such cooperation between social settlement leaders and organized married women was possible during the Progressive Era in large part because the two sides of this partnership shared beliefs about women's roles in society and about the morally justifiable need for reforms in industrializing America. Although women leaders from the social settlement movement were often unmarried and childless, they thought of themselves as "public mothers."[134] They believed that mothers and children were especially worthy of public help. Moreover, many of them believed that women had special proclivities for moral decisionmaking and civic activity; thus women were the logical ones to lead the nation toward new social policies.[135] Along with many of their male co-workers in the ranks of progressive reformers, unmarried, higher-educated social settlers shared these ideas about woman's special qualities with the far larger numbers of women in the turn-of-the-century United States who were married, committed to motherhood, and not pursuing paid careers.

In sum, intellectual women from the settlement movement ended up working in close political cooperation with organized American middle-class womanhood on reform issues understood to be part of women's special spheres of concern. Some higher-educated women developed expertise and tactical political wisdom on issues affecting women and children in the industrializing United States. And because these reformist intellectuals shared maternalist values with noncareerist married women, they could readily communicate with the nationwide women's federations. The organizational and ideological ties that allowed women intellectuals to work so cooperatively with locally rooted women's clubs stand in clear contrast to the absence of such links between the mostly male expert advocates of paternalist social programs in the American Association for Labor Legislation and the male-dominated trade unions of the American Federation of Labor. During a period when intellectuals and workers' organizations could not work together to launch a paternalist U.S. welfare state, intellectuals and grassroots women's groups were able to cooperate to extend motherly concerns into new public programs claimed to be for the good of the entire nation.

Women's Politics in the Progressive Era

For many years, historians tried to find the "true progressives," sifting through the biographies of one group of (mostly male) reformers after another, and placing one economic interest group after another under the historical microscope.[136] Historians have not managed to find the essence of progressivism in this way, however; and no wonder. The Progressive Era was a kaleidoscopic array of diverse movements, each engaging a different coalition of groups, and justified by its own reading of the central progressive values of efficiency, democracy, and bureaucracy.[137] Equally important, women's politics played a much more central role in progressivism than most historians have heretofore acknowledged. Only recently have women's historians developed the arguments rehearsed in the previous section about the remarkable civic capacities of American women toward the end of the era of "separate spheres" for the sexes. A few of these scholars have, in turn, begun to reconceptualize progressivism on the basis of the new women's historiography.[138] Even so, there has not yet been enough analysis of the ways in which women's civic capacities intersected with changing U.S. political structures in the early twentieth century.

The Feminine Version of Civil Service Reform

The leitmotif of U.S. politics during the early twentieth century was the effort to overcome the "corruption" of patronage democracy, replacing it with efficient and responsible government in the public interest. Thus it should not come as a surprise that civicly active women were ideologically and organizationally crucial to many progressive movements. Before 1920, with a few state and local exceptions, American women could not vote in a polity where all men could. They were not implicated in the organizational routines and male fraternal rituals of existing political parties and elections. Both settlement workers and national women's associations were vocal critics of political party bosses, of distributive policies that they saw as "corruption," and of narrowly partisan public policy choices. Settlement reformers and women's associations alike were dedicated advocates of civil service reform. Yet—as with their calls for the suffrage—these female forces advocated structural reforms only in close connection with actual new policies to improve daily life for municipal residents, consumers, and workers, especially women and child laborers. What is more, women active in reform causes during the Progressive Era were more likely than their male counterparts to favor the expansion of the public sector through reform, rather than its contraction in deference to business preferences for low taxes and business-oriented government.[139]

Immersed in the problems of urban neighborhoods and poor people, settlement workers inevitably found themselves in competition with party machines. They joined civic reform efforts and campaigned for reform mayors in major cities.[140] In turn, the competition between settlements and urban bosses could lead settlement leaders to sharp insights about the functions of bossism and the need for structural political reforms in close conjuction with improved social policies. Thus, after Hull House's unsuccessful efforts to unseat Johnny Powers, boss of Chicago's seventeenth ward, Jane Addams wrote about the ties of patronage and loyalty that developed when bosses met concrete, individual needs for poor urban residents.[141] Effective political reform, she argued, could make headway against the boss, "against this big manifestation of human friendliness, this stalking survival of village kindness," only when reformers find out what needs, which the alderman [that is, party boss] supplies, are legitimate ones which the city itself could undertake in counter-distinction to those which pander to the lower instincts of the constituency. A mother who eats her Christmas turkey in a reverent spirit of thankfulness to the alderman who gave it to her, might be gradually brought to a genuine sense of appreciation and gratitude to the city which supplies her little children with a Kindergarten, or, to the Board of Health which properly placarded a case of scarlet-fever next door and spared her sleepless nights and wearing anxiety, as well as the money paid with such difficulty to the doctor and druggist. The man who in his emotional grati- tude almost kneels before his political friend who gets his boy out of jail, might be made to see the kindness and good sense of the city authorities who provided the boy with a playground and read- ing room where he might spend his hours of idleness and rest- lessness, and through which his temptations to petty crime might be averted . . . The voter who is eager to serve his alderman at all times, because the tenure of his job is dependent upon aldermanic favor, might find great relief and pleasure in working for the city in which his place was secured by a well-administered civil service law.[142]

Settlement people also supported civil service reforms for the entire nation. In her 1916 speech to the General Federation of Women's Clubs on "The Common Sense of Civil Service," Julia Lathrop defined the civil service as

all the publicly paid service which does not belong to the military branch of Government . . . embracing all those appointive positions which have some elected intermediary power between them and the ultimate voter. In this sense the civil service may be said to begin with the Chief Justice of the United States and to include every school officer and to reach to the last street sweeper, espe- cially note that it includes every branch of the Inspection Service.[143]

Over the last generation, Lathrop pointed out, Americans had "se- cured the passage of an unexampled number of State and Federal laws, all increasingly placing in the hands of civil servants work of utmost social importance." But unfortunately Americans were re- adier to pass laws than to ensure their honest and efficient admin- istration. "Consider," Lathrop urged her audience, "how absolutely the effectiveness of factory, housing, sanitation and food laws depend upon the skill and good will of those who may be grouped as inspectors . . . [Moreover, the] highest degree of character and training and fitness is needed even in the less conspicuous positions for the sick, the dependent, the delinquent, and for every branch of the educational system."[144] Thus Lathrop called on clubwomen to work not only for merit-based civil service appointments but also for training programs for future appointees and—most important—for the divorce of civil service appointments from "politics" and the institution of "nonpartisan methods" for the nomination and election of officials. Only such steps, Lathrop concluded, could ensure "the promotion of the welfare of all the citizens and . . . the securing of equality of opportunity for 'All the Children of All the People.' Is not this the Common Sense of Civil Service?"[145]

Along with the leaders of the settlement house movement, the national women's federations developed a vision of honest civil servants administering maternalist regulations and social policies. The National Congress of Mothers never took up civil service reform as a general cause, but it did seek new governmental structures—staffed with officials possessing "motherly" qualities—in social policy areas directly related to child welfare. The Congress was not reluctant to make demands of the state. "We are stateswomen," Mrs. G. H. Robertson told fellow Congress members. "Any woman interested in social problems and anxious to unravel them, any woman who feels that around her there are conditions that she wishes to improve is a stateswoman."[146] Mrs. Robertson argued that "our government should be maternal, some may prefer to call it paternal, there is no difference. The state is a parent, and, as a wise and gentle and kind and loving parent, should beam down on each child alike . . . We, the mothers of the land, should go in a body and make the appeal for what we wish; then stand aside and rejoice as we see our desires expressed—just gifts given by a loving Father, received equally by the children."[147] Thus the Congress applauded the creation of the Children's Bureau under Julia Lathrop's direction.[148] And it repeatedly pushed for new public health bureaus and measures for "baby saving" and "care of mothers."[149]

The Congress also lobbied persistently—and ultimately successfully—for the creation of the "Home Education Division" of the U.S. Bureau of Education, a federal government agency that would directly embody the Congress's own mission.[150] Indeed, when this new division was established in 1913, the Congress's president, Mrs. Frederic Schoff, was appointed its director; she held the post gratis and the Congress paid for the services of a secretary as well as covering the cost of literature distributed to over 13,000 mothers by the division. In essence, a federal bureau simply rendered official certain of the voluntary educational functions of the National Congress, and helped it to extend its local organizational reach. This delighted the Congress, which clearly believed it was optimal for the federal government to operate through organized mothers to help private homes and parents raise their children more effectively. As President Schoff reported to the Congress in 1914, "no other [government] department could cover home education and child nurture as can the Bureau of Education; and no other organization stands exclusively for the education of parents except the National Congress of Mothers. The combination is therefore very valuable on both sides."[151]

When matters went beyond the offical but unpaid co-optation of its own personnel and activities to direct action by government employees, the Congress's views about good government come through most clearly in its rhetoric and efforts on behalf of juvenile courts and probation systems. From the time of its national conventions in 1899 and 1900, the Congress of Mothers developed a keen interest in juvenile courts, with special judges and probation officers, as public instruments for the supervision and reform of wayward children and their families.[152] Progressive reformers outside the Congress originated this innovation in criminal structures and procedures, starting in the state of Illinois.[153] But once the Congress adopted the idea it regularly heard addresses (and read articles in its official magazine) by prominent juvenile court judges such as Ben B. Lindsey of Denver and E. E. Porterfield of Kansas City; and Congress members worked assiduously for the spread of juvenile courts and probation systems across all of the states.[154]

Not only did the National Congress of Mothers work for the creation of juvenile courts, it took a continuing interest in how they were run and staffed. The Congress recommended that "a committee of mothers attend every session of a juvenile court to offer such help as may be needed."[155] And it remained ever vigilant against hints of "political" corruption. "The probation system, unless properly administered, becomes a menace instead of a protection," declared an official resolution passed in 1911; "therefore the National Congress of Mothers recommends the establishment of State probation commissions in every State, whose duty it shall be to devise such measures as will ensure the employment of probation officers qualified to develop the highest ideals in the children under their care, and *which shall not be subject to political control.*"[156] The Congress, moreover, had definite ideas about the types of people who should work for the juvenile court system. "The problem which the Juvenile Court faces is one of moral education . . ." declared Congress President Schoff. "There is no magic power in the law unless it is administered by those who are qualified by sympathetic knowledge of child nature . . . Probation work must be done only by those who have the ability and love and patience in character building and in teaching home-making to parents. *Whenever possible, the service of kindergartners and good mothers must be enlisted as Probation Officers,* as they are qualified to develop the better nature of the child."[157] In short, if the National Congress of Mothers had its way, probation systems across the land would be kept strictly out of "politics" and staffed by good-hearted mothers, ready to work for the salvation of the nation's children.

Going beyond the efforts of the National Congress of Mothers, the General Federation of Women's Clubs took up the overall cause of civil service reform, establishing a standing committee of this title in 1902.[158] Thereafter, civil service reform became a growing and ramifying concern of both the national Federation and the state affiliates, which regularly reported helping to achieve new laws in this area.[159] Women's distinctive responsibilities, it was felt, justified clubwomen's efforts in this area. "Civil service reform," declared a resolution passed at the Federation's 1908 Biennial, "is really a moral, rather than a political reform, and as such, should commend itself to the women of the country, who have ever been the conservers of morality."[160] The details of this gendered opposition of morality to "politics" were spelled out by Mrs. Sarah S. Platt Decker at the 1910 Biennial. "How," she asked, "shall the mother combat the influence of the saloon, the street, and especially the fealty to party politics which treats all offices as political rewards for the faithful, and considers not at all the value of an honest, conscientious, well trained office holder who happens to belong to the other political faith[?] . . . Men in authority are beset by their friends and adherents for political preferment." The way out of this situation, Mrs. Platt Decker argued, lay in substituting civil servants for party hacks. "Party fealty must be abandoned as a theory too antiquated for modern times . . . Mere politicians will not do; we must have thoughtful, honest, intelligent men and women whose term of office shall expire only when they have ceased to be the right person for the right place. This is Civil Service Reform."[161]

Social policies were at issue along with basic morality in the view of Federation supporters of civil service reform. At the 1912 Biennial, Mrs. Imogen B. Oakley, head of the Civil Service Reform Department, reviewed the history of the GFWC's efforts since 1902, explaining that "as the work of our clubs for social and economic betterment expanded and developed, it was suddenly revealed to us that the Civil Service is really not a political, but a domestic institution."[162] Mrs. Oakley pointed to new tasks that reformed government might undertake, especially at the subnational level where women's clubs were most engaged:

> The Civil Service of states and cities exists for the sole purpose of ensuring the comfort, health and well-being of the people. We depend upon the civil service for the sanitation of our houses; the paving and cleaning of our streets; the quality of our drinking water; the purity of our foods; the efficiency of our schools; the decency and public morality of our communities. None of these things is political; they are all domestic, and in so far as the civil service has become political and partisan, it has been removed just so far from its proper functions.[163]

Speaking right after Mrs. Oakley, Mrs. John Theodore Tabor echoed that "Politicians want things for their friends without thought of competency for the position or the good of the country . . . Let us then care in our hearts for our cities and for our country and use the power which is ours for the advancement of Civil Service reform, which is civic patriotism in its broadest sense." "Factory laws, child labor laws and pure food laws," she maintained, "will never be enforced without trained and efficient inspectors."[164]

At the 1914 Biennial, Mrs. Oakley proudly reported "a total of thirty-nine states [that is, state federations of women's clubs] engaged in an effort to put *their* civil servants beyond the reach of partisan politics," and then, in a detailed rendition of "The Domestic Side of

Civil Service Reform," reflected that when "a standing committee on Civil Service Reform was first appointed . . . some conservative clubs felt doubtful of the wisdom of this policy. 'The Civil Service will lead us into politics,' they said. That was in 1902. In this year of grace, 1914, even our most conservative members know that the path of Civil Service Reform leads straight into our homes."[165] In sum, we see that the General Federation of Women's Clubs rationalized its concern with civil service reform by reference to traditional moral values of domesticity. This allowed clubwomen to develop a distinctively feminine version of the overall progressive effort to substitute an "honest" and "efficient" civil service for the "corrupt" party politics of U.S. patronage democracy. Clubwomen could also support the growth of differentially female professions in such areas as social work, public health, and labor law administration.

A Politics of Public Education

While antiparty attitudes and a devotion to civil service reform put women activists in tune with the political logic of progressivism, these hardly explain their positive contributions to social policymaking as such. Civicly active women not only criticized party politics, they also got around it—and they did so without the aid of already-existing civil service bureaucracies. Starting with nineteenth-century moral crusades and reaching a crescendo during the Progressive Era, American women devised ways of making political demands felt outside of party meetings, or elections, or standing bureaucracies.

At crucial times, prominent women from the national associations joined leading professional reformers in directly lobbying legislators and formally testified at legislative hearings.[166] Clubwomen also engaged in broad letter-writing campaigns when important social legislation was being considered by legislatures. Such activities were especially important in creating simultaneous pressure on legislators from many localities in a given state, and on legislatures in many different states at roughly the same time. The national women's federations tended to target a few key issues in a given year, and became increasingly adept at instructing state organizations and, through them, individual clubs and members in effective tactics for pressuring legislators through visits or letters.[167] State women's federations also set legislative priorities of their own, and pursued them in similar ways.

It would be overly simple, though, to treat women's politics in the early twentieth century merely as astute interest-group lobbying. More fundamentally, women's politics had to do with moral education—by which I mean not only a politics of supporting certain kinds of instruction in the schools (although this was a major theme of women's efforts). I mean that associated women repeatedly sought to learn about public issues and then proceeded to use moralistic publicity and talk to reshape public opinion and the opinions of well-placed male citizens as well as officials. Thus, after calling upon women to support the establishment of "departments for women and children" in the labor bureaus of every state, Mrs. Perry Starkweather of Minnesota told an audience at the 1910 GFWC Biennial, "Ladies, we can do much if we will but try. Men make laws. Women, just such women as you, are all the time writing the greater higher law—the law stronger an [sic] mightier than any written upon the book—the law of Public Opinion . . . Get information as to the truth of conditions and then spread abroad the knowledge you have gained. None of you realize your own influence. Here within the sound of my voice is influence enough to overturn or build up a kingdom."[168] And as Mrs. Imogen Oakley summarized the women's strategy of politics at the conclusion to her (previously cited) 1914 speech on civil service reform, "'Congress is not the place to begin reforms. Washington is not the place' . . . Let us examine into the iniquities of the spoils system, let us familiarize ourselves with the merit system and its great possibilities for good—and then—let us go home and talk."[169]

At their recurrent national conventions, and then in local communities across the land, associated women channeled incalculable energies into informing themselves about the key social issues of the day. Women's associations started into a legislative campaign by gathering information about an issue, compiling reports, and listening to experts. Speaking at the 1910 Biennial of the GFWC on "The Influence of Women on Legislation," Nanette B. Paul, LL.B., took the need for careful study of the functions of the law as her primary theme. "We, as women, can no longer rule by the heart alone. We must add the influence of the head."[170] A few years later at the Legislative Conference of the 1914 Biennial, Miss Josephine Schain, chairman of the Legislative Committee of the Minnesota Federation, recommended that a "careful investigation should be made before any measure is endorsed . . . It may take longer to thoroughly investigate before action is taken but in the end it means more efficient work."[171] Indeed, the process of investigation was often orchestrated by state federation leaders who had been inspired by speeches and resolutions at the national conventions. Back at home, they would contact local clubs and arrange for the dissemination of informational literature and speeches on a given topic, often borrowing resources from the national federation offices and from other state organizations that had already gotten involved in the particular issue.[172] Nor was the effect of such activity merely to spread information. As Jane Addams astutely observed, it was "the great function of the women's clubs . . . to create community of feeling and thought about the world and the way it works—what Professor [William] James used to call 'likemindedness' which is so essential in any effort toward concerted action . . . [T]he soil was prepared in which a sound public opinion might be nurtured."[173]

After educating themselves, associated women set out not only to lobby legislators but also to dramatize problems in their own communities. The process could, quite literally, begin at home, where civicly aware ladies might lobby their husbands. Writing in 1907 in the GFWC's organ, *The Federation Woman*, Miss Anna L. Clark spelled out how this was to be done:

> Through what I have been pleased to call "A Wife's Hour," when the shades are drawn, the children in bed or busy with their own occupations, the wife then gives to the man of the household a few facts she may have gleaned from her investigation during the time the man has been busy creating the leisure by which the wife has been able to find out things that have escaped the notice of the occupied man. Thus, quietly and persuasively, through definite facts, not emotions or intuitions, this husband of a wife who is living for a purpose, is converted into a sure enough "Man of Wrath," who may become just as much a knight to correct abuses as one of the olden time, when he received so proudly the colors from his lady-love for valiant deeds in her behalf. Through this means, as well as through direct and concerted measures of organized womanhood in clubs, many evils may be corrected.[174]

When action shifted from drawing rooms to local communities, the tactics clubwomen might use were listed by Mrs. Leota W. Keil, a Michigan Federation official reporting at the 1910 Biennial on a campaign for civil service reforms:

> To circulate literature.
> To place literature in libraries.
> To place primers in schools . . .
> To try to interest churches to take up the agitation . . .
> To influence newspapers to agitate the subject . . .[175]

Mrs. Keil felt that her state's locals had achieved considerable success with these tactics. "Education," she declared, "is the weapon which will kill out the 'Lions' of 'Indifference' and 'Ignorance' and even 'Partisanship.'"[176] As evidence of newly aroused public opinion in Michigan, she especially cited the recent development that "Many leading papers in the state are showing friendliness toward the movement."[177]

Indeed, by the height of the Progressive Era, the General Federation of Women's Clubs was well aware of how much newspapers could do to publicize its views on social issues and new legislation. Back in the early 1890s, when the Federation was forming, attitudes toward the press were unfriendly; according to the Federation's official historian, "some of the most able women advocated the exclusive club and strongly objected to the presence of newspaper reporters at club meetings, as well as to printed newspaper reports of their deliberations."[178] But such attitudes soon changed. At the Fourth Biennial in 1898, an entire "session was devoted to the press, and well-known newspaper women discussed the Relation of Women to the Press; the Club and the Press; the Club and the Newspaper; Cooperation of the Press with the Altruistic Movements of the Times. These addresses were given by women to whom words were easy weapons, and did much toward placing the press in the right light before the women to whom the printed page was a mysterious and unknowable factor in civilization."[179] At the Fifth Biennial, too, there was a "session devoted to the influence and value of the press . . . an indication of the continual alertness of the minds of the club-women regarding the most powerful instrument for the formation of public opinion in the modern world, the newspaper."[180] Thus the Federation developed a positive attitude toward press publicity.

Attempts to use the press became routine parts of Federation strategies for molding public opinion and promoting reform legis-

lation. At the 1908 Biennial, the Federation noted in a formal resolution that "Publicity is essential to the growth of a strong and
powerful national organization," and recommended "to State presidents an increased, and more systematic method of press work . . .
placed so far as possible in charge of a responsible clubwoman."[181]
From then on, at Biennial after Biennial, state federations proudly
reported on the close relations they had achieved with the press. For
example, Mrs. Henry B. Fall, president of the Texas Federation,
reported to the 1914 GFWC Biennial that while the Texas Educational "Committee has concentrated its work on compulsory education laws in the state, active support has been given by clubs all over
the state in getting discussions of compulsory education before the
public. Literature and information were furnished to a large number
desiring information. The Education Committee and club members
were active in having facts and data published in the newspapers.
Sixty papers were kind enough to give space for such articles."[182]

Perhaps because a member of the Hearst newspaper family was
one of its founders, and also because of its top-down inception, the
National Congress of Mothers courted press coverage from the very
start, seeing it as a way to encourage the spread of mothers' clubs.[183]
At its very first national convention, the Congress resolved that "we
ask our officers to continue national headquarters at Washington,
D.C., from which a Press Committee shall send out each month, to
all newspapers agreeing to publish them regularly, articles germane
to our objects and information relative to the progress of our
work."[184] Before long, the Congress saw the press as a readily ma-
nipulated tool for arousing public opinion in favor of social improvements. "The Press the Greatest Ally of the Congress," declared a
headline in the October 1908 issue of the *National Congress of Mothers
Magazine*.[185] "The [National] Press Committee," explained Mrs. Edgar A. Hall, chairman of the Illinois Press Committee,

> has found that the leading newspapers are cheerfully disposed to
> unite their great powers with those of the Congress in promoting
> such interests of childhood as are vital to the present happiness
> and well-being of the child and vital to his future citizenship. Let
> us consider the bigness of just one big newspaper as an extension
> agent. The editor of a great newspaper of Chicago testified in
> court that he buys 15,000 tons of news print paper a year . . . This
> paper is read by 130,000 people daily, and its Sunday circulation

is 200,000 . . . Can you imagine a more economical system of
extension work or a more far-reaching extension agent? . . .

The living voice of a speaker on any subject may reach his
tens or his hundreds, but when reproduced by the public press
his audience is increased by an invisible host of countless thousands . . .

The Press Committee would recommend that each club in membership appoint its press committee, whose duty it shall be to
collect, compile and forward to the leading local newspaper such
news as shall result to the advantage of the work of the Congress
in conserving the welfare of the child. Also that the chairmen of
such committees shall be ex-officio members of the State Press
Committee, in just the same way that the Press Committee chairmen of the several States are ex-officio members of the National
Press Committee . . . By perfecting the plan under which we are
now working we should be prepared to give definite and tangible
proofs that the press is the most economical and most powerful of
all agencies in the extension work of the Congress of Mothers.

Nor did the Congress confine its media work only to newspapers;
it also cultivated relations with magazines, which at times went so far
as to directly promote the organization. The *Ladies Home Journal*, for
example, published "Why Not Become an Organized Mother!" an
article that gave rise to "over 100 requests for further information
. . . many enclosing fee for individual membership" in the Congress.[186] The *Ladies Home Journal* was one of the top-ranked national
women's magazines; it commanded top advertising rates and had an
annual circulation of about one and three-quarters of a million copies
in 1914.[187]

Over the years, the National Congress of Mothers became astutely
self-conscious about its media tactics. Thus, at the Third International Congress on the Welfare of the Child in 1914, Anna Steese
Richardson, chairman of the Congress's Department of Child Hygiene, spoke about not just "*any* kind of publicity,—but the kind of
publicity that works," and her remarks were later reproduced in full
in *Child-Welfare Magazine*.[188] Taking for granted that Congress people would be working with the press, Richardson advised her listeners and readers on the types of newspapers to target and the types
of stories to write. Because "our publicity must have a general appeal—not class appeal," Richardson told Congress people to avoid
both "the ultra-conservative newspaper representing the moneyed

interests" and "the yellow journal, whose appeal is purely sensational and directed to what is commonly known as the . . . laboring element" and to aim instead for publicity in "the well-balanced, fair, unprejudiced paper . . . [with] appeal for the mass of readers in all walks of life."[189]

Richardson further advised Congress people to avoid preachy articles in favor of those with dramatic story ideas and "personal appeal, in order to get past the editor, to go under the skin of the political powers and to arouse the parents to action."[190] "You can pretty generally count on getting a response if you knock at the door of the great American heart" and "you can reach the great American public more quickly by pointing out something they should have—that they are not getting—than by telling them what is good for the community."[191] Lastly, Richardson astutely emphasized that articles should do more than just report the opinions and activities of the mothers themselves:

> Names count in publicity. Americans are not snobs but they worship success . . . [I]f you say that Dr. James Smith, the most successful oculist in your city, acting for the Mothers' Club, has investigated certain conditions and found that the eyesight of two of three hundred children is endangered by those conditions,—everybody is going to say—Something Must Be Done . . . If, in addition to the protest of Dr. James Smith, you can offer the protest of the heaviest tax-payer in your community, the most important clergyman and the leading educator, and a woman whose personal magnetism attracts other women,—the desirabity of your article is increased just so much.[192]

The Political Uses of Moral Rhetoric

What are we to make of the just-surveyed educational tactics used by women during the Progessive Era? We should not dismiss them as mere window dressing for weakness, nor underestimate their political effectiveness. In the actual political conditions of the early-twentieth-century United States, women's educational tactics—ranging from conversations with husbands to the orchestration of local and national publicity for selected causes—probably served as the quickest route to legal reforms. As we learned in the last chapter, during this period of U.S. politics new social policies could not readily be implemented from the "top down" by bureaucrats and programmatic party leaders. Instead, broad, transpartisan coalitions of groups—and ultimately legislators—had to be assembled for each particular issue. Coalitions of women's groups and their allies could very effectively do precisely this, mostly through *concerted, likeminded talk*. In the jargon of today's political science, women's groups were good at the art of "agenda setting" in politics.[193] Women's talk could reach into many cities and towns across the United States, because women's clubs were so widely federated, and because many of the those active in women's clubs were socially well connected. As the historian William O'Neill has observed:

> Clubwomen, either through marriage or in their own right, were influential members of their communities. They had access to the power structure and, while they did not vote, they had male friends and relatives who did. Thus, because it was impossible to measure their actual potency, wise politicians conceded some power to club-women for safety's sake. Clubwomen did not ask for a great deal, but when they wanted something badly it was prudent to assume that their frustration might have unpleasant consequences.[194]

The maternalist *rhetoric* used by politically active women was surprisingly effective with civic leaders and legislators. Women's rhetoric appeared to rise above narrowly partisan considerations. Symbols of motherhood and domesticity were invoked, resonating with deeply engrained notions of selfless morality, notions held by women and men alike in this era of "separate spheres" for the genders. Women had so long been regarded as guardians of morality that when they spoke with apparently unanimous conviction about the lofty purposes to be served by new social policies, their demands were hard for legislators to ignore. This was especially the case when organizationally weighty women's groups advocated new measures on behalf of children, and for the sake of women as actual or potential mothers. True, women's advocacy might not be automatically heeded if measures were at stake that interfered with powerful interests within the wage-labor process. But even when trade unions or business groups felt threatened (for example, by minimum-wage proposals), women's groups could at least gain a public hearing for their maternalist arguments.

Not only did maternalist political rhetoric have a compelling effect on legislators and public opinion during the Progressive Era, it also persuaded many judges at the state and federal level to accept as constitutional certain protective labor laws that they might otherwise have struck down as excessively paternalist, invoking the constitutional norms of due process and freedom of contract.

As we learned in the last chapter, many state courts and the U.S. Supreme Court discouraged male workers from looking to government for legislative solutions to workplace problems; in the late nineteenth and early twentieth centuries, American courts were hostile to the rights of unions, and they repeatedly struck down state laws limiting hours of work for broad categories of adult male workers. The only protective laws for male workers allowed to stand by the courts were statutes about public works employment, where the state was a party to the contract, and hours laws narrowly targeted on especially dangerous occupations, like mining, or on industries where there were compelling public safety concerns, such as the railroads.[195] Thus, a few narrowly circumscribed male occupations could look to government for a bit of protection, but industrial workers as a broad class could not. During the Progressive Era, however, the courts evolved a very different stand on laws protecting women workers—initially through their consideration of various state laws that limited the number of hours women could work per day.

Leading American judges became convinced that women wage-workers could be seen as a separate class deserving of special public protection because of the health requirements of their actual or potential roles as mothers. Although the highest courts of Illinois and New York did not at first accept this approach, the Pennsylvania Supreme Court clearly stated the rationale for this view in a 1900 decision upholding a twelve-hour law for females and minors.[196] "Surely an act which prevents the mothers of our race from being tempted to endanger their life and health by exhaustive employment," wrote Pennsylvania's Justice Gray, "can be condemned by none save those who expect to profit by it . . . If such legislation savors of paternalism, it is in its least objectionable form in that it cares for those who from their own necessities . . . may be prompted or required to jeopardize their health . . . [and hence] the interests of the state itself."[197] The Pennsylvania court maintained that the state could legitimately use its police powers to modify contracts when such fundamental considerations of health and public well-being were involved. Using similar reasoning, the Nebraska Supreme Court upheld a women's hour law in 1902; and in that same year, the Washington Supreme Court became the first to uphold a ten-hour limit for women workers, followed by the Oregon Supreme Court in 1906.[198]

An appeal of the Oregon decision allowed the U.S. Supreme Court to render its most famous decision in favor of legal protection for women workers. Recall that in 1905, the Supreme Court had dealt a crushing blow to the hopes of reformers advocating broader protection for male workers, by ruling in *Lochner v. New York* that hours could not be limited for bakers. According to the majority opinion in that case, "Statutes of the nature of that under review, limiting the hours in which grown and intelligent men may labor to earn their living, are mere meddlesome interferences with the rights of the individual."[199] But the Supreme Court took a very different view in its unanimous 1908 ruling in favor of Oregon's ten-hour law covering women. In this case, the judges saw not individuals whose rights were being infringed, but mothers who needed protection. In the unmistakable words of Mr. Justice Brewer's opinion,

> That woman's physical structure and the performance of maternal functions place her at a disadvantage in the struggle for subsistence is obvious. This is especially true when the burdens of motherhood are upon her. Even when they are not, by abundant testimony of the medical fraternity continuance for a long time on her feet at work, repeating this from day to day, tends to injurious effects on the body, and, as healthy mothers are essential to vigorous offspring, the physical well-being of woman becomes an object of public interest and care in order to preserve the strength and vigor of the race . . .
>
> Differentiated by these matters from the other sex, she is properly placed in a class by herself, and legislation designed for her protection may be sustained, even when like legislation is not necessary for men, and could not be sustained.[200]

Where did American judges of the early twentieth century get these ideas about women's special nature and needs? As we shall see in more detail in the next chapter, "expert" arguments about women's physical being and special needs were pressed upon the courts in briefs specially prepared by well-organized reformers. Yet it would be too simple to believe that the judges simply acceded to expert opinions from doctors and social scientists, for in other cases they demonstrated an ability to ignore or legally controvert such "evidence." Surely the judges of the Progressive Era were also responding to the general climate of public opinion about women's separate—and special—roles as mothers. Courts are profoundly rhetorical institutions bound to be affected by moral understandings deeply embedded in categories of political discourse. Thus, as Mr. Justice Brewer saw it, the expert opinions presented to the Supreme Court in *Muller v. Oregon* were

> significant of a widespread belief that woman's physical structure, and the function she performs in consequence thereof, justify special legislation restricting or qualifying the conditions under which she should be permitted to toil. Constitutional questions, it is true, are not settled by even a consensus of present public opinion . . . At the same time, when a question of fact is debated and debatable, and the extent to which a special constitutional limitation goes is affected by the truth in respect to that fact, a widespread and long continued belief concerning it is worthy of consideration. We take judicial cognizance of all matters of general knowledge.[201]

In short, the justices of the Supreme Court, who unanimously decided in 1908 to treat women workers as a special class deserving public protection, were strongly affected by contemporary public understandings of gender differences. We can hypothesize, I think, that the justices saw women as mothers especially worthy of help from innovative public policies because organized American women had taught civic leaders—and the educated public in general—to think in this way. If governmental paternalism was still suspect, governmental maternalism had become much more acceptable by the Progressive Era, even to crusty judges still largely wedded to individualistic doctrines of free contract.

Conclusion

During the early twentieth century, federated U.S. women's clubs and their reformer allies carried on their civic activities in a country that lacked strong, autonomous public bureaucracies. Not only were women's groups at the height of their own organizational prowess and ideological self-confidence, they could also credibly claim to be the broadest force of the day working for the public interest. This helped to persuade legislators to act, especially when all that were at issue (it sometimes seemed) were measures that had to with women's moral concerns, and not so much with matters of institutionalized male self-interest. When women seemed to be asking for forms of help for children and mothers that would not apparently severely disadvantage established political, business, or labor interests, then legislators might act quite rapidly. Furthermore, state and federal court judges were also more likely to allow laws to stand if they were specifically targeted on women understood as mothers.

All of these considerations gave proponents of maternalist social policies an advantage in defining what the public interest meant—in legislative campaigns that involved widespread publicity and lobbying and, when necessary, legal arguments to defend legislative victories. Women's political agitation was well suited to overcoming the structural obstacles that the early-twentieth-century U.S. polity placed in the way of advocates of new social policies. There was, for a time, an especially good fit between what politically active American women wanted and could do, and what the changing U.S. state structure could accommodate.

Drawing on what we have learned about the political capacities and proclivities of many women in the turn-of-the-century United States, we are now in a good position to analyze three relatively successful efforts to achieve maternalist social policies: the campaigns on behalf of state-level laws regulating hours and minimum wages for women workers; the movement for state-level laws allowing mothers' pensions; and the campaigns to establish the U.S. Children's Bureau and then to expand its mission to include health education for all American mothers. The following three chapters will take up each of these sets of maternalist policies in turn.

CHAPTER 7

Safeguarding the "Mothers of the Race": Protective Legislation for Women Workers

The idea of using government regulations to set limits on the exploitation of wage workers gained early popularity with Americans. Legislation mandating ever shorter working days for all laborers was a recurrent demand of worker movements during the nineteenth century.[1] And by the turn of the new century in the United States as elsewhere, social reformers advocated regulations about hours, safety conditions, and minimum wages as ideal ways to ameliorate class conflict and protect workers, including those too weak to organize trade unions. Nevertheless, protective laws covering adult male workers made little headway, for reasons we have already explored. U.S. judges applied doctrines of due process and freedom of contract to nullify many protective regulations covering male workers. And by the second decade of the twentieth century, cross-class coalitions rarely lobbied legislatures on behalf of protective laws for men, because the leaders of the American Federation of Labor preferred direct economic bargaining by organized skilled workers as the way to achieve shorter hours and higher wages. Given these unpropitious judicial and political conditions, no general minimum wage laws for male workers were enacted in the early-twentieth-century United States, and "hour legislation covering adult men was fragmentary in character . . . Most of it was narrowly limited in scope to special occupations for which legal protection was especially needed or especially easy to secure."[2]

For American workers of the female gender, however, the story was quite different. The political forces in favor of special protective laws for women gathered momentum from the 1890s until the early 1920s; and by the 1910s the courts had given their imprimatur to women's hour laws and were not yet an overt obstacle to minimum wage laws. Thus forty-one states passed women's hour laws by 1921, with most new or improved laws coming between 1909 and 1917; and many states also passed prohibitions on night work for women and regulations prohibiting them from working in specified unsafe occupations or conditions.[3] Minimum wage laws for women made more limited headway, but legislative developments were neverthe-less signficant between 1912 and 1923, when the Supreme Court reversed an earlier decision and found these measures unconstitu-tional. Altogether, fifteen states plus the District of Columbia enacted minimum wage laws for women during this period, with all but one of these enactments coming between 1912 and 1919.[4] Finally, in 1920, Congress passed legislation to establish a federal Women's Bureau, making permanent what had earlier been an emergency wartime agency. From its beginnings in 1918, the Women's Bureau gathered data on the conditions faced by female wage earners and generally promoted the cause of protective labor legislation for women.[5]

This chapter will explore the role of organized labor, women's groups, and other forces in state-level campaigns for women's hour and minimum wage regulations during the early twentieth century. As we shall see, broad coalitions cutting across classes and genders led the movements for hour laws, while certain women's organiza-tions were more often on their own in leading campaigns for mini-mum wage measures. For both hours restrictions and minimum wages, however, appeals to legislators and the public were made with reference to the special vulnerablities of women workers. Women, it was argued, were marginal participants in labor markets, too weak to fend for themselves in bargaining with employers. And they were especially deserving of public protection as actual or potential moth-ers. Business enterprises, turn-of-the-century Americans were told— above all by politically active women's groups—should not be allowed to exploit the gender whose established, sacred function was the nurturance of children and the home.

Organized Labor and Women Cooperate
for Women's Hour Laws

Laws restricting women's hours of work came earlier, easier, and more steadily in the U.S. political system than any other category of social legislation for adult workers. During the last third of the nineteenth century, Massachusetts and a few other industrializing states enacted loose (and essentially unenforceable) limitations on the hours that women (as well as minors) could work; and some state courts accepted these laws as valid exercises of governmental "police power" as applied to weak categories of workers whose health and morals required extra protection.[6] Despite these early developments, the curtain on the modern drama of U.S. protective legislation for women can properly be said to have gone up in Illinois during the 1890s. For it was in this state that the legislature passed in 1893 a really strong law mandating an eight-hour day for women workers, and establishing an administrative inspection mechanism through which officials, including women factory inspectors, would police recalcitrant employers. It was also in Illinois that the issue of the constitutionality of protective laws was sharply posed in 1895, when the Illinois Supreme Court's decision in *Ritchie v. People* struck down the 1893 eight-hour law.

Events in Illinois foretold the future for many other campaigns across the nation on behalf of women's hour legislation. Organized labor, women trade unionists, settlement-based reformers, and women's associations all became involved in the struggle.[7] Initial public agitation on behalf of an eight-hour day for women, as well as for a variety of legislative reforms for children, came from the Illinois Women's Alliance, organized in the 1880s by Elizabeth Morgan, leader of the Ladies Federal Labor Union. Under the motto "Justice to Children, Loyalty to Women," the Alliance brought together women trade unionists, the Chicago labor federation, and a large number of elite and middle-class women's associations, including the Woodlawn Branch of the Women's Christian Temperance Union, the Women's Press Association, and the Ladies of the Grand Army of the Republic. In the early 1890s, when the Alliance was faltering, Florence Kelley, newly arrived at Hull House, arranged for an Illinois legislative commission to look into women's sweatshop labor.

Working through personal contacts and through connections already institutionalized at Hull House, Kelley and Jane Addams revitalized and extended the cross-class coalition that Morgan had originally established. "Before the passage of the law could be secured," Addams later recalled, "it was necessary to appeal to all elements of the community, and a little group of us addressed the open meetings of trades-unions and of benefit societies, church organizations, and social clubs literally every evening for three months . . . The Hull-House residents that winter had their first experience in lobbying . . . and we insisted that well-known Chicago women should accompany this first little group of Settlement folk who with trades-unionists moved upon the state capitol in behalf of factory legislation."[8]

Cross-class and women's organizing in Illinois paid off nicely, at first. Florence Kelley prepared a draft of the Factory and Inspection Act, which passed the General Assembly in June 1893. Reformist Governor John P. Atgeld appointed Kelley the new State Factory Inspector. Drawing again on broad support from women and trade unionists associated with Hull House, Kelley vigorously enforced the new law—until it was abrogated two years later by the challenge to its constitutionality mounted by the newly formed Illinois Manufacturers' Association.

Under the U.S. Judiciary Act as it stood before 1914, the Illinois Supreme Court's decision in *Ritchie v. People* could not be appealed to the U.S. Supreme Court, so it stymied the movement for protective laws in Illinois. This decision also discouraged administrators from vigorously enforcing laws elsewhere for fear of generating court appeals, and it may have delayed political movements for new laws in some other states. Yet, especially back at the turn of the century, the U.S. states varied considerably in political culture and in their constitutions and traditions of judicial interpretation. An adverse court decision in one state could not entirely stop parallel legal changes elsewhere. From 1896 until 1908 (the year in which the U.S. Supreme Court found women's hour statutes constitutional), eight state legislatures passed new women's hour laws and five others improved existing laws.[9] Some of the innovations occurred in states like Massachusetts where courts had already accepted such laws, but during this period four more state supreme courts, three of them outside the East (in Nebraska, Oregon, and Washington), also accepted women's hour laws as constitutional.[10] In the state of Washington, for example, this outcome was virtually foreordained by the fact that judges were elected in a strongly prolabor state, and by the fact that the state's constitution had been drawn up—under the influence the Knights of Labor and the Populists—to include an explicit mandate for governmental intervention to promote social welfare.[11]

Perhaps even more important than the trickle of new women's hour laws that passed between 1896 and 1908, during this same period a political basis was laid for rapid legislative progress after the Supreme Court's favorable ruling in 1908. A veritable flood of new legislation was to come soon after *Muller v. Orgeon.* "From 1909 through 1917, 19 states and the District of Columbia enacted women's hour laws for the first time; and 20 more affected substantial improvements in existing laws by decreasing the legal maximum or widening the scope."[12] Most of the new legislation, moreover, came in those years immediately following 1908 when significant numbers of state legislatures were in session, and especially in 1911 and 1913.[13]

Officials and Experts as Policy Advocates

What were the political forces at work across the nation to promote laws restricting women's hours of work? One force, although not the most significant, was situated within government itself. Both before and after 1908, officials of certain state governments—particularly members of bureaus of labor statistics, factory inspectors, and labor commissioners—took the lead in fighting for restrictions of women's hours. Sometimes, as happened in Massachusetts and California, bureaus of labor statistics completed investigations that revealed conditions crying out for reform, or gathered facts that helped labor and reform groups make the case for a pending piece of legislation.[14] Factory inspectors were, however, more likely than mere statistics-gatherers to take activist stances. In states where there were already industrial regulations, such officials charged with enforcement readily learned of conditions requiring new laws or tougher sanctions. Interestingly, some of the inspectors charged with implementing early child labor laws eventually concluded that they could not succeed until the work hours of women were also restricted. Limits on the hours of adult women, these officials felt, would discourage minor females from lying about their age, and would also allow mothers to supervise their children at home after work.[15] And conditions inside each state's factories were not the only considerations that impelled administrators toward supporting further legislation. After 1887, the International Association of Factory Inspectors, dedicated to promoting uniformity of labor laws, helped to familiarize officials in one state with innovations in other states and nations.[16]

Factory inspectors suggested legal extensions to legislators or to civic groups or public commissions. In Massachusetts, for example, "During the eighties and nineties the factory inspectors . . . through their director, the chief of the district police, were instrumental in securing amendments to the existing labor laws, making evasion less easy," but after 1890 the Massachusetts officials adopted an "impartial" stance and tried to avoid open advocacy of new types of laws.[17] Meanwhile, in New York, "practically all the legislation that, prior to 1900, clarified and extended the 60-hour-week law of 1886 was initiated by factory inspectors." And after 1901, when a department of labor with a commissioner was created to supervise the New York inspectors, most commissioners continued to take "an active interest in securing labor legislation for women workers . . . Many of the laws passed . . . [in New York during the Progressive Era were] suggested by labor-department officials and later taken up and pushed by organized labor or by one or more of the social and civic organizations interested in securing improvements in the working conditions of women."[18] New York, moreover, was a state where public investigatory commissions played a very important role in early-twentieth-century labor-law innovations, and state labor-law administrators worked closely with such commissions.[19]

Labor-law experts outside of government also promoted new protective laws for women workers. After its founding in 1906, the American Association for Labor Legislation (AALL) supported laws for women in lieu of the general regulations covering all workers that its leaders clearly preferred.[20] Had the judicial and legislative climate been more favorable to general protective laws for all workers, the AALL probably would have placed greater emphasis on wage and hour measures, and probably would have kept the relevant activities in the hands of its dominant male professional elite, as it did for measures such as workplace safety and workmen's compensation laws. For women's protective legislation, though, the AALL simply published occasional summaries of legislative progress, and also set up a special Committee on Woman's Work—a body consisting mostly of women, including wives of male AALL members—through which it lent support to the initiatives of female-dominated reform associations such as the National Consumers' League and the National Women's Trade Union League.[21]

Indeed, whatever their contributions in particular states, neither government officials nor the labor law experts of the AALL were the most important proponents of women's hour laws in the early twentieth century. The key supporters were organized trade unionists as well as local and national women's associations. In particular states, one group or another might take the lead in drafting legislation and pressing it upon the legislature, but alliances of *both* labor and women's groups were involved in most states. Taking labor and women in turn, we can analyze their goals and activities and note the kinds of political resources each brought to the cause.

Organized Labor Presses for Women's Hour Laws

Organized labor—including leaders of established male federations and organizers of emerging women's unions—provided steady pressure for legal restrictions on women's hours of work. For some union leaders and male workers, no doubt, protective laws were a way to express Victorian notions that women should ideally stay at home, and these laws were also devices to make women workers less competitive with men.[22] The desire to undercut female competition was not, however, the primary reason for organized labor's support of women's hour laws; this was more prominent as the motive behind scattered laws that completely prohibited women from working at certain jobs previously dominated by skilled craftsmen, or else so closely regulated women's activities as to in effect prevent them from taking the jobs in question.[23] Hours limits for women are better understood as part of a broader aspiration by, and for, virtually all American workers. Until 1914, the American Federation of Labor (AFL) accepted legislation mandating an eight-hour workday for all or any workers—and especially for particular groups, including women, who were viewed as unlikely to make gains simply through union action. Not until after women's hour statutes were in existence in most states did the national Federation actually begin to oppose further hour laws—on the grounds that they might undercut the efforts of unionized skilled workers to attain, by contract, better hours than even an eight-hour legal minimum.[24] Yet even after the national Federation took this position in 1914 and 1915, many state federations and particular unions continued to support legalized hours restrictions, just as they had done earlier.

State-level AFL leaders tended to be more responsive than the national leaders to precariously organized industries, in which legislation might encourage or reinforce union efforts to shorten the working day.[25] Union leaders in industries that had already gained legal restrictions wanted to extend them to other industries.[26] And male workers and unions in certain female-dominated industries hoped that shorter hours for everyone might come as a by-product of new laws covering women. Labor leaders in Massachusetts, for example, long fought for general hours restrictions for all workers. Eventually, they focused their efforts on the state's dominant textile industry, in which unions were relatively weak, and ended up pushing for limits solely on the hours of women and children in the textile industry. It was easier to convince the public and legislators to accept such laws, and, in any event, "women and minors . . . made up such a large proportion of the working force that if . . . [a limited working] day were established for them it would apply automatically to the men."[27]

Organizers and supporters of fledgling women's unions also worked to get state or municipal labor federations actively involved in campaigns for women's hour laws—as did Elizabeth Morgan of the Ladies Federal Labor Union in Illinois during the late 1880s, as did the "union women and wives of trade-unionists" of the Women's Union Label League in California in 1910, and as did the "female trade union representatives of the Laundry Workers Union of Toledo" in Ohio between 1909 and 1911.[28] The Women's Trade Union League (WTUL) also persuaded certain leaders of organized labor to work for protective legislation, especially in the eastern states where immigrant women made up a large proportion of the female labor force and were likely to be perceived by male unionists as "unfair" competitors, undercutting wage levels. Of course, the female advocates of hours laws had their own point of view. Arguing that their constituents could not rely on unions alone and needed positive state protection, the leaders of the WTUL, including many women trade unionists, placed ever stronger emphasis on protective legislation for women workers (even as the national leadership of the AFL viewed legal approaches to workplace issues with less and less favor).[29]

Not only did union leaders in the states usually favor women's hour bills; in a few states where labor groups had great leverage in legislatures or with progressive governors, they actually spurred the passage of laws virtually unaided. In highly industrialized and urbanized Massachusetts, for example, textiles was the dominant industry and, according to Clara Beyer:

> the concentration of the industry in certain cities gave the textile workers a political strength out of proportion to their numbers. In many cases, legislators from the textile centers were officials of the textile unions. From such advantageous position as chairmen of the labor committees of both houses, these union leaders were powerful factors in the legislative fights for the hours laws . . . [Consequently] [t]o the constant agitation carried on by the labor movement of Massachusetts, and in later years by its affiliated body, the Women's Trade Union League, is to be ascribed the passage of practically all the legislation shortening the hours of work of women in factories and mechanical establishments in that State.[30]

Similarly in California, the pioneering 1911 women's hour law—which covered a very broad range of industries and occupations, and limited work to a then unprecedented eight hours per day and forty-eight hours per week—was almost entirely attributable to the San Francisco Labor Council, at that time a key component of Governor Hiram Johnson's dominant progressive political coalition.[31]

In other states labor could not go it alone, but took the lead in forging broader alliances favoring women's hour laws. In Washington state, organized labor was an important part of a dominant populist-progressive coalition that also included farmers and women's groups, and this coalition put through, first, a ten-hour law for women workers passed in 1901, and then an eight-hour law passed in 1911.[32] In Ohio, the Executive Committee of the State Federation of Labor, soliciting additional "support from women's organizations across the state," introduced a women's hour bill into the legislature in 1909, and reintroduced it until it passed in 1911.[33] Finally, in New

York state, it was the Workingmen's Federation (the state AFL affiliate), rather than elite reformers, that pressed between 1901 and 1910 for reduced hours for women workers. But organized labor in New York did not enjoy the political leverage to proceed without allies. The major legislative breakthroughs on women's hours and other protective legislation did not occur in New York until after the Triangle Shirtwaist fire of March 25, 1911. After that event, organized labor was able to work more closely with elite reformers, including the leaders of women's groups, to influence the state commission set up to investigate conditions and propose new laws.[34]

The Consumers' League at the Vanguard of Organized Women

If organized labor was one of the mainstays of the multifarious state-level campaigns for women's hour laws, the other was organized women. Across the nation during the late nineteenth and early twentieth centuries, major women's associations educated public opinion on the perils of female wage drudgery and aroused widespread, cross-class support for new or improved hour laws.

To be sure, not all women's associations became active on protective legislation for women workers. The National Congress of Mothers virtually never mentioned industrial regulations beyond the child labor laws that it strongly supported. The Illinois and Texas state branches of the Congress of Mothers did support hour laws in 1919, and by that time the national leaders were supporting the federal Women's Bureau, which promoted hour and wage laws for women workers.[35] At the height of the Progressive Era, however, there is reason to believe that the national leaders of the Congress of Mothers actually opposed regulations for women workers, because the "President's Desk" section of the May 1914 issue of *Child-Welfare Magazine*, under the headline "Women's Freedom Restricted," reprinted an editorial from the Philadelphia *Public Ledger* called "Legislating Women Out of a Livelihood." This editorial bemoaned that women selling subway tickets were thrown out of work after the Legislature restricted women's hours and made it "cheaper to employ man labor . . . Here is a concrete result of too much paternalism."[36]

In contrast to the National Congress of Mothers, though, other elite and middle-class women's associations repeatedly drew analogies between "dependent" child and women laborers, and strongly supported protective laws as in the best interest of economically marginal women wage-workers, who would otherwise be cruelly exploited by long hours and low wages. Above all, both the National Consumers' League (NCL) and the General Federation of Women's Clubs (GFWC) made hour laws for women workers a high priority for investigation, education, and political action. Inspired by their links to educated women reformers from the social settlements, each of these national associations contributed in crucial ways to the widespread achievement and improvement of women's hour laws during the first two decades of the twentieth century.

The National Consumers' League, of course, veritably embodied an alliance between social settlement reformers and activist matrons, because when the local leagues of New York City, Brooklyn, Syracuse, Philadelphia, Boston, and Chicago came together to form the National League in 1899, they hired Florence Kelley as executive secretary. She became and remained the whirlwind center of activity in the National League, with each year's annnual report detailing her amazing travels to spread Consumers' Leagues to new cities and states, and to energize a huge range of reformist, religious, and women's associations in support of the League's agenda. During 1899–1900, for example, Kelley—despite having to take off two months from public speaking to recover from "a severe case of diphtheria contracted during a visit to Cleveland"—reported travels to ten states and the District of Columbia to address fifty-four organizations, including a federal government commission, three national associations, eight state associations, six different colleges and universities, and thirty-six individual organizations.[37] Kelley's efforts only escalated in succeeding years, so that by 1914–15 she reported addressing ninety-eight organizations spread across nineteen states and the District of Columbia![38]

Given Kelley's centrality, the NCL understandably added agitation on behalf of child labor laws and women's protective legislation to its original emphasis on voluntary consumer boycotts of "unethical" merchants and manufacturers. The changes of emphasis came gradually, however, as Kelley sequentially introduced new themes from the top, and as constituent leagues gained organizational experience and learned the limits of purely voluntary action.[39] According to the NCL's Annual Reports, child labor laws became a priority around 1903 to 1905, and legislation to restrict women's hours became a major preoccupation after 1908. In early 1912, the NCL put out a pamplet called "The Long Day," which is reproduced in Figure 19.

THE LONG DAY

TO FIGHT AGAINST THE
LONG DAY

THE NATIONAL CONSUMERS' LEAGUE was organized a dozen years ago.

It has, ever since, called attention to the Christmas cruelties.

That the workers may be relieved from overpowering fatigue and exhaustion, it urges Early Christmas Shopping.

It has, at all seasons, made consumers feel their responsibility for the length of the working day of sales-girls and others, seen and unseen, who serve the public.

Just as the shoppers can get any commodities which they desire, so they can relieve the strain and suffering caused by overtime, worked in their behalf.

It has been the pioneer in urging the value, as a health and efficiency measure, of the summer half holiday for workers in stores and factories.

It has granted to manufacturers the use of its label for your convenience, so that you can be sure that the garments you wear are not the products of sweat-shops, of child labor, or of excessive hours of labor on the part of women and girls.

The label is the only known device for freeing our consciences from a share in the evils of the sweating system.

It has made a powerful plea, for the alleviation on rational, scientific grounds, of human misery, through the publication of Miss Josephine Goldmark's studies of fatigue in her book, "Fatigue and Efficiency."

This book affords a powerful argument for the most advanced position yet taken by the Federal Supreme Court with respect to governmental control over health conditions in industry.

It has helped to obtain, within the last two years, in sixteen states, the passage of laws or of amendments to laws, to protect wage-earning women from over-work.

It has co-operated in the legal defense of such laws in four important cases.

In Oregon when the Supreme Court of the United States upheld, for the first time in its history, the constitutionality of a ten-hours law for women.

In Illinois where, in 1909, the favorable decision of the Court, sustaining the ten-hours day, freed from overstrain over 30,000 women who had been working more than ten hours a day.

In Ohio when the ten-hours day and the fifty-four hours week were sustained.

In Illinois, in 1911, when the extension of the ten-hours law to occupations not previously included in the law, was upheld.

Every case which the National Consumers' League has helped to defend has been won.

It has done all of this on an income of less than $10,000 a year.

IT HAS LEFT UNDONE MUCH THAT IT WOULD HAVE DONE IF THE FINANCIAL SUPPORT HAD BEEN EQUAL TO THE NEED.

Figure 19

Source: Pamphlet from the National Consumers' League. Schlesinger Library, Radcliffe College, Vertical Files, National Consumers' League #2. Photo by Lewis Hine.

This pamphlet indicated how important the struggle for women's hour laws had become to the organization's self-presentation. "Within the last two years," it claimed, the League "has helped to obtain . . . in sixteen states, the passage of laws or of amendments to laws, to protect wage-earning women from over-work."[40]

"While the National Consumers' League does not initiate legislation for working women in the separate states," explained Josephine Goldmark, Secretary of the Committee on Legislation and Legal Defense of Labor Laws, in 1917, "it has assisted the state and local leagues in securing the passage of many laws by sending representatives to hearings, furnishing printed matter, statistics and expert advice, particularly with reference to the form of bills."[41] As this indicates, the role of the Consumers' League in passing hours limitations for women workers in the various states depended on the strength and orientation of its local organizations. According to information that I have pieced together and summarized in Table 7, Consumers' Leagues definitely or very probably supported legislative drives to regulate women's hours in fifteen states plus the District of Columbia between 1891 and 1920. Not surprisingly, the list of states where this occurred includes twelve of the fourteen states where Consumers' Leagues were officially in existence in both the years 1905 and 1912 (see Figure 20 below), a reasonable measure of the durability of state leagues.[42] The list of states where Consumers' League were active on behalf of women's hour laws also includes all but two of the seventeen states where leagues were officially organized in 1912—along with California, whose league existed for some years after 1902, but then passed out of existence once the California Industrial Commission was established under the leadership of clubwoman Katherine Philips Edson.[43] The state Leagues that did *not* work for women's hour laws were either those such as Colorado's that existed for only a few years or those such as Indiana's and Tennessee's that apparently did not move beyond sponsoring voluntary consumer boycotts in one city.[44]

As one might expect, the state Consumers' Leagues that worked most consistently for innovations or improvements in women's hour laws were the northeastern leagues, especially those of New York, Pennsylvania, Massachusetts, Connecticut, and New Jersey.[45] These leagues were the earliest to organize; they often had local organizations in several cities and employed paid executive secretaries to

Table 7. Supporters of new and improved hour laws for women workers, 1900–1920

Year and state	Evidence of support from		
	Consumers' Leagues	Federations of Women's Clubs	Others
1900			
Massachusetts	yes		WEIU; SFL; women trade unionists; other women's clubs
1901			
WASHINGTON			SFL
1902			
Rhode Island	yes		
1903			
COLORADO			
OREGON	yes	yes	
1907			
Connecticut	yes		unions
MICHIGAN	yes	probably	unions
New Hampshire			
Oregon	yes		
TENNESSEE	yes	yes	
1908			
Louisiana			
Massachusetts			textile unions
Rhode Island	yes		
1909			
ILLINOIS	yes	probably	social settlement people; WTUL; women unionists
Maine	yes	probably	
Michigan			
MINNESOTA			
MISSOURI	yes	yes	WTUL; AALL
1911			
CALIFORNIA		yes	WCTU; Women's Union Labor League; unions
Illinois	probably	yes	
Massachusetts	yes		WTUL; WEIU; unions

(continued)

Table 7 (continued)

	Evidence of support from		
Year and state	Consumers' Leagues	Federations of Women's Clubs	Others
Missouri	probably	yes	
OHIO	yes		SFL took the lead
UTAH		yes	
Washington		yes	SFL
Wisconsin	yes	probably	
1912			
KENTUCKY	yes	yes	
MARYLAND	yes	yes	
New Jersey	yes	yes	
New York	yes	yes	SFL; WTUL
VERMONT			
Virginia			
1913			
ARIZONA		yes	
California	yes	yes	WCTU
Colorado		probably	Judge Ben Lindsey referendum
Connecticut	yes		
DELAWARE	yes	yes	
IDAHO		yes	
Illinois	probably		
Massachusetts	yes		WTUL; WEIU; SFL; other women's groups
MONTANA		probably	
Nebraska			Bureau of Labor and Industrial Statistics
New Hampshire			
New York	yes		
Ohio			
Oregon	yes		
Pennsylvania	yes		
Rhode Island	yes		
South Dakota			
Tennessee			
TEXAS			
Washington		yes	SFL
Wisconsin	probably	probably	

Table 7   *(continued)*

Year and state	Evidence of support from		
	Consumers' Leagues	Federations of Women's Clubs	Others
1914			
DISTRICT OF COLUMBIA	yes	yes	
MISSISSIPPI			
New York	yes		
1915			
ARKANSAS			
KANSAS		yes	
Maine			
NORTH CAROLINA			
OKLAHOMA		yes	
Texas			
Wyoming		yes	
1917			
Kansas			
Montana			League of Good Government Clubs (formerly women's suffragists)
NEVADA			
Ohio			
Vermont			
1918			
New York	yes	yes	other women's groups
1919			
Kansas			
Massachusetts	yes	yes	WTUL; SFL; WEIU; suffragists; women workers
Minnesota			
North Dakota			Non-Partisan League w/SFL support
Utah			

Note: ALL CAPS = First law or one replacing a law found unconstitutional
AALL = American Labor Legislation Association
SFL = State Federation of Labor
WCTU = Women's Christian Temperance Union
WEIU = Women's Educational and Industrial Union
WTUL = Women's Trade Union League

(continued)

Table 7   (continued)

Sources: Florence P. Smith, *Chronological Development of Labor Legislation for Women in the United States,* rev. Dec. 1931, Bulletin no. 66, pt. 2, Women's Bureau, U.S. Department of Labor (Washington: U.S. Government Printing Office, 1932); Elizabeth Brandeis, "Women's Hour Legislation," ch. 3 in *Labor Legislation,* in vol. 3 of *History of Labor in the United States, 1896–1932,* by John R. Commons and associates (New York: Macmillan, 1935); "State Reports" in the *Official Reports* of Biennial Conventions of the GFWC, for 1904, 1906, 1908, 1910, 1912, 1914, 1916, 1918, 1920, and 1922; *National Consumers' League [Annual] Reports* for 1900, 1903, 1904, 1905, 1909, 1910, 1911, 1912, and 1914–1916–1916; Maud Nathan, *The Story of an Epoch-Making Movement* (Garden City, NY: Doubleday, Page, and Co., 1926), appendix G, "Reports of the State Consumers' Leagues"; Louis L. Athey, "The Consumers' Leagues and Social Reform, 1890–1923" (Ph.D. diss., University of Delaware, 1965), chs. 2 and 6; Jacob Andrew Lieberman, "Their Sisters' Keepers: The Women's Hours and Wages Movement in the United States, 1890–1925" (Ph.D. diss., Columbia University, 1971), ch. 3; Clara M. Beyer, *History of Labor Legislation for Women in Three States,* Bulletin no. 66, pt. 1, Women's Bureau, U.S. Department of Labor (Washington: Government Printing Office, 1929); Dennis Irven Harrison, "The Consumers' League of Ohio: Women and Reform, 1909–1937" (Ph.D. diss., Case Western Reserve University, 1975), p. 42; Joseph Frederick Tripp, "Progressive Labor Laws in Washington State, 1900–1925)" (Ph.D., diss., University of Washington, 1973), chs. 1 and 4; Joseph Candela, "The Struggle to Limit the Hours and Raise the Wages of Working Women in Illinois, 1893–1917," *Social Science Review* 53(1) (March 1979): 15–34; *A Record of Twenty-Five Years of the California Federation of Womens' Clubs, 1900–1925,* vol. 1, comp. Mary S. Gibson (pamphlet in the holdings of the Bancroft Library, University of California, Berkeley), p. 181; Gertrude Schmidt, "History of Labor Legislation in Wisconsin" (Ph.D. diss., University of Wisconsin, 1933), ch. 6; Bureau of Labor and Industrial Statistics of Nebraska, *Fourteenth Biennial Report, 1913–14* (Lincoln, NE: Claflin Printing Co., 1914), p. 7; June O. Underwood, "Civilizing Kansas: Women's Organizations, 1880–1920," *Kansas History* 7(4) (Winter 1984–85), pp. 302, 304; Ida H. Harper, ed., *History of Woman Suffrage,* vol. 6 (New York: Source Book Press, 1970; orig. 1922), p. 367; and Jeanette Rankin, Speech on Woman's Responsibility in the State of Montana, delivered at State Federation of Women's Clubs on June 4, 1914, *Montana Progressive* [Helena], June 4, 1914, p. 3.

initiate and coordinate statewide activities from their central offices. Such early-organized and strongly rooted northeastern Leagues at first promoted hours restrictions for women in mercantile establishments and then extended their interest to women workers in manufacturing. They also consistently monitored the enforcement of whatever state laws were on the books. Yet not all of the Leagues organized early in industrial states were active campaigners for social legislation. During the early 1900s, for example, the Ohio League merely followed the lead of the state Federation of Labor on matters of industrial legislation; the Ohio League moved into leadership on social legislation only during the 1920s, just as other state Leagues became less active.[46]

Smaller Leagues outside the industrial Northeast and Midwest could also play key roles in obtaining protective laws. From the time of its founding in 1903, the Oregon League worked for a full range of protective laws for women workers as well as for other social legislation.[47] And the border-state Leagues of Maryland and Kentucky were surprisingly effective, as explained by Josephine Goldmark in the 1912 Annual Report of the National Consumers' League:

> During the first three months of 1912 four of the eleven legislatures in session enacted important measures regulating women's hours of work: Kentucky, Maryland, New Jersey and New York. It may well be a source of legitimate pride to the National Consumers' League that the efforts to secure these new laws have been most effectively supported . . . by the Consumers' Leagues in those four states. In the two southern states, Kentucky and Maryland, this legislation is practically new. Kentucky has never before limited the employment of women, and in Maryland, an earlier ten hour law, which was supposed to embrace all employes [sic] of cotton and woolen mills, has always remained a dead-letter . . .
>
> The enactment of the Kentucky law was preceded by the investigations of a commission appointed by Governor Willson in March, 1911, at the request of the Consumers' League of Kentucky. The president of the Consumers' League, Mrs. R. P. Halleck, acted as secretary of the commission . . . In spite of the lack of official funds and the short time at its disposal, the commission was able to show conditions of employment in Kentucky which called imperatively for relief . . .
>
> The new Maryland statute was enacted after a campaign of unusual vigor and efficiency led by the Ten Hour Committee of the Maryland Consumers' League.[48]

It would be mistaken, however, to consider the Consumers' Leagues as the weightiest feminine force pressing for state-level protective laws for women workers in the Progressive Era. After all, as Figure 20 illustrates, the Leagues had a persistent organizational presence, with state and city leagues in just over one-quarter of the U.S. states. Consumers' Leagues were strongest in major cities of the industrial East and Midwest.[49] In the West, the only persistently active League was the one centered in Portland, Oregon; and successful Leagues never flourished any farther south than Baltimore, Maryland, and Louisville, Kentucky. The affiliates of the National

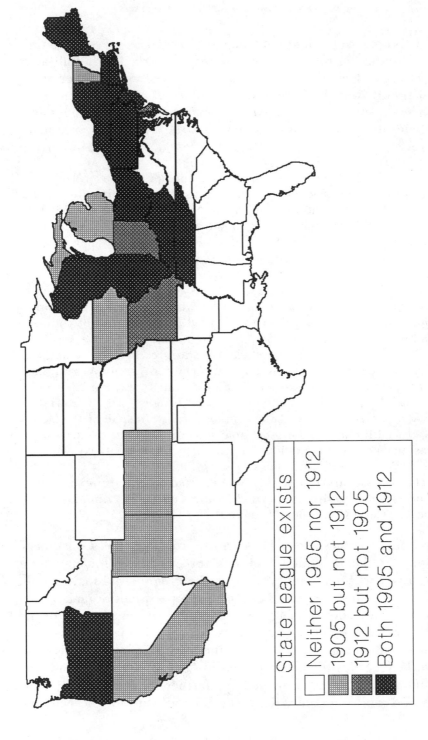

State league exists

☐ Neither 1905 nor 1912

▨ 1905 but not 1912

▩ 1912 but not 1905

■ Both 1905 and 1912

Figure 20 Consumers' Leagues by state

Source: *Annual Reports of the National Consumers' League.*

Consumers' League, in short, never achieved the nationwide spread of the General Federation of Women's Clubs, which had state federations and local clubs in all forty-eight states in 1912. Because the NCL's geographical reach was limited, and because its individual membership never exceeded several thousand people—mostly elite married women in major cities, plus some token male university professors and scattered students in women's colleges and schools—the NCL could hardly equal the legislative lobbying potential of other contemporary women's federations. Other federations, and especially the GFWC, not only had many more members than the NCL but also included local units disproportionately more likely to be situated in rural states and in smaller cities and towns. Indeed, the Consumers' Leagues often promoted legislation primarily by working with and through other associations, including the Federations of Women's Clubs, with which the Consumers' Leagues had an intimate and symbiotic relationship in many areas.[50]

While working with others on behalf of new state laws, the Consumers' League—and especially its national staff—increasingly placed emphasis on defending protective labor laws, once passed, before the courts. As Kelley reflected in 1915, "the defense of labor laws" was "the field which the league . . . made peculiarly its own" starting in 1907.[51] Over succeeding years into the mid-1930s, the NCL sponsored some fifteen legal briefs in support of labor laws challenged before the courts.[52]

Outlook and resources alike urged the NCL in this direction. Herself trained as a lawyer, Florence Kelley had already learned the hard way in Illinois during the 1890s that, after years of political struggle, progressive legislative enactments could be undone in the courts by the stroke of a judicial pen. Thus she well understood the importance of defending the hour laws for women passed in other states in the early 1900s. Many of these laws were at risk, Kelley knew, when the Oregon Consumers' League notified her of laundryman Curt Muller's appeal to the United States Supreme Court of the Oregon Supreme Court's 1906 decision upholding the Oregon ten-hour law.[53] The main resources the NCL national staff could bring to bear on any problem were social connections, small flows of money, and capacities for investigation and publicity—in short, resources ideally suited to the preparation and coordination of arguments before the courts. Thus with but short notice, the National

Consumers' League staff in November 1907 approached Louis Brandeis, a well-known reformist lawyer who was a friend of Kelley's and the brother-in-law of NCL staffer Josephine Goldmark, asking him to take on gratis the advocacy of the cause of the Oregon State Industrial Commission in defending the ten-hour law before the Supreme Court. The NCL also turned Goldmark's time and talents to the mobilization of research data for use in the brief Brandeis would present to the Court.

Brandeis's famous brief contained two pages of legal argument backed up by over a hundred pages of facts and expert opinion about the fatigue and illness that long hours of labor could cause, particularly in women.[54] The goal of Brandeis and the League was to persuade the Supreme Court to differentiate between *Muller* and *Lochner v. New York,* the 1905 case in which the Court had struck down hours limits for male bakers on the grounds that there were no special considerations of unhealthy work conditions for bakers as opposed to miners. To do this, they argued before the Court that industrial overwork was especially damaging for women workers as actual or potential mothers, thus justifying the use of police powers by the state to modify market contracts. Ideally, Kelley, Goldmark, and Brandeis would have preferred to argue on behalf of legally limited hours for all workers regardless of gender; we know this because in 1916–17 the National Consumers' League actually made such an argument in *Bunting v. Oregon.*[55] But in 1908, the only available opportunity seemed to be to persuade the Supreme Court that women workers were unusually vulnerable employees rather than regular workers, like bakers, who should take their chances in unfettered labor markets as freely contracting individuals. Thus women's biological vulnerabilities were highlighted in the "facts" and expert opinions that Goldmark mobilized for Brandeis, even though most of them were gleaned from European sources that had often advocated protection for workers in general.

The Supreme Court's 1908 decision to uphold hour laws for women in *Muller v. Oregon* both regenerated and reoriented the National Consumers' League. For the League's New York–based staff this "epoch-making event," as Florence Kelley described it in her report to the NCL National Council, came at a time when the growth of local and state leagues was past its peak, and just as the impossibilities of carrying out comprehensive investigations of industrial conditions by local voluntary action were becoming acutely obvious.[56] At this crucial juncture, the "success of this work," said an editorial about the Brandeis brief and the Supreme Court decision in the March 21, 1908, edition of *Outlook* magazine, "has convinced the National Consumers' League that there is a new field of service for it."[57] Thus the National Council amended the Consumers' League bylaws to rename Josephine Goldmark's "Committee on Legislation" the "Committee on Legislation and on the Legal Defense of Labor Laws" and to extend its official functions accordingly.[58] And new resources arrived, as the Russell Sage Foundation gave Goldmark and the NCL a grant to finance the distribution of copies of the Brandeis brief and to support further research on "the nature of fatigue" and "strain" in industry, particularly as reflected in "the greater morbidity of women." These funds allowed Goldmark and Brandeis to prepare further briefs, most immediately for the defense of a new ten-hour law before the Illinois Supreme Court in 1910. They also allowed Goldmark to prepare a 1912 Russell Sage book on *Fatigue and Efficiency,* pulling together the research she had done for the major NCL-sponsored briefs.[59]

After the 1908 judicial victory, in the words of the historian Louis Athey, "the Brandeis brief' became a major vehicle in the emergence of the National Consumers' League as an important reform organization in the Progressive era."[60]

A steady demand for copies of the brief from lawyers, reform organizations, colleges, universities and state enforcement commissions in every part of the country poured into the National Consumers' League office in New York City. One of the earliest publications distributed by the American Association for Labor Legislation to its members was the "remarkable brief" prepared by the National Consumers' League . . . [whose leaders were delighted] to serve as a "clearing house for information and center for effective cooperative effort." Certainly, the victory in the Oregon case and the wide dissemination of the brief based upon the "living facts" of industrial America increased the importance of the Consumers' Leagues and encouraged League personnel to a more vigorous reform effort on behalf of a legal maximum workday for women.[61]

The 1908 Oregon victory also reenergized the nationwide movement for new and improved state laws to limits the hours of working

women, contributing to the burst of new enactments after 1908
summarized in Table 7. "Encouraged by this decision," Kelley told
the NCF Council, "Consumers' Leagues and other organizations in
. . . [many] states . . . have renewed the effort to establish a legal
maximum working day."[62] Of the legal victories that soon came, the
most gratifying to Kelley was the Illinois ten-hour law passed in 1909
and upheld by the Illinois Supreme Court in 1910 in reponse to a
brief argued by Brandeis with the help of the Consumers' League.
Exulting in this 1910 reversal of *Ritchie v. Illinois* of (1895), Kelley
declared:

> If the National Consumers' League had done no other useful thing
> besides its contribution towards this decision, our eleven years of
> existence would be justified by this alone. For the thousands of
> women and girls in Illinois whose fatigue will at once be reduced
> are by no means the only beneficiaries of this work. All their
> innumerable successors will profit by it. But this is not all. The old
> decision has been for fifteen years a baneful influence in every
> industrial state in the Republic, always raising the question
> whether, after all, it was wise to spend energy in trying to get
> legislation of this character when the courts were likely to hold it
> contrary to the state if not the federal constitution. This mildewing
> influence is now at an end, and we can go forward with new hope
> and assurance . . . [to extend hours laws for women] in every state,
> and to all industries in the census period 1910–1920.[63]

As Kelley correctly understood, by intervening in key court decisions about the constitutionality of protective laws for women, the
National Consumers' League had parlayed scarce resources into
victories that could reenergize forces at work across many individual
states, including forces in those places where the League had little
or no local presence.

The General Federation Spreads the Agitation Nationwide

Already active in the struggle for women's hour laws, another major
women's association, the huge, nation-spanning General Federation
of Women's Clubs, was among the forces reinvigorated by the Consumers' League victory in *Muller v. Oregon*. The General Federation
had gotten into industrial matters, including protective laws for
women workers, early and from the top down. During the Illinois

eight-hours campaign of the early 1890s, Jane Addams later recalled, "The national, or to use its formal name, The General Federation of Women's Clubs, had been organized in Chicago only the year before this legislation was secured. The Federation was then timid in regard to all legislation because it was anxious not to frighten its new membership, although its second president, Mrs. Henrotin, was most untiring in her attempts to secure this [1893] law."[64] By 1895, moreover, Mrs. Henrotin was urging upon the Federation that "Departments of civics and social economics should be a part of all club work and study classes . . . The social life of the place, whether city or country, should be enlarged and the tone elevated, for the woman's club is the most democratic of institutions, and therefore a strong social factor."[65] At the Fourth Biennial in 1898, this new orientation became more focused:

> The program of Friday afternoon was a distinct departure from the ordinary, educational, literary or artistic club program. The chairman . . . had chosen the general subject, The Industrial Problem as it affects Women and Children, and she presented one of the most prominent social workers in London at that time, Mrs. Sidney Webb, who contrasted English and American conditions, and with unequivocal force drove home to the women in her audience their duty and responsibility for the conditions under which the women of America toil. Mrs. Webb was followed by Mrs. Corinne S. Brown of Chicago, Miss Helena Dudley [a social settlement worker] of Boston, and others, each one of which presented some telling phase of the economic and industrial problems confronting the nation. The subjects were presented as matters of vital interest to the General Federation, matters which could not be ignored and must not be thrust aside.[66]

And they were not thrust aside. The 1898 Biennial held unanimously "that women of larger opportunities should stand for the toilers who cannot help themselves" and passed a number of resolutions, including a resolution against child labor and a remarkably progressive injunction that "in mill, factory, workshop, laundry, and mercantile establishment, the maximum working day for women and children shall not exceed eight hours, or forty-eight hours per week."[67] In addition, the Biennial took organizational steps to carry out an industrial program, by resolving:

That each club in this Federation shall appoint a standing committee whose especial duty it shall be to inquire into the labor conditions of women and children in that particular locality. That each state federation shall appoint a similar committee to investigate its state labor laws and those relating to sanitation and protection for women and children. That it also shall be the duty of these committees to influence and secure enforcement of labor ordinances and state laws of this character . . . also that the General Federation shall appoint a . . . Committee on Legislation for Women and Children.[68]

After the 1898 Biennial, a circular was sent out, along with a letter from the Federation's president, urging each club to take up work on behalf of working women and children.[69]

Over the following two decades, GFWC Biennials often passed resolutions calling for protective labor legislation for children and women, and also calling for the appointment of female officials to enforce laws and further study the conditions of women workers.[70] The rationale for these activities remained as the chairman of the Industrial and Child Labor Committee put it in her report to the Tenth Biennial in 1910: "Millions of women are in the industries. They are frequently almost as helpless as the children in obtaining redress from oppression, or in securing improved surrounding and better pay. Club women should be constantly urged to have in mind the needs of their industrial sisters, and to bend energy and influence to the improvements of conditions under which they toil."[71]

To educate clubwomen on topics related to child and female workers in industry, women reformers from the social settlements sometimes served as chairs of the Federation's standing committees on industrial matters; for example, between 1900 and 1902 Florence Kelley led the Committee on the Industrial Problem as It Affects Women and Children.[72] In addition, Federation Biennials regularly included presentations by social settlement leaders, such as Jane Addams's 1902 address on women and children in factories and 1906 discussion of her work at Hull House, Mary McDowell's 1906 "account of her work in behalf of a bill in Congress to authorize the Secretary of Commerce and Labor to investigate and report upon the social, moral, educational, and physical conditions of child laborers in the United States" (a bill the Federation resolved to support right after her talk), and Florence Kelley's 1916 speech advocating the establishment of a "Woman's Division" in the U.S. Department of Labor (which the Federation also resolved that year to support).[73]

Similarly, at the 1910 Biennial, the assembled delegates heard the State Factory Inspector of Ohio, Miss Ella Haas,

> plead with the mothers of this audience this morning, or with any woman who has influence with the employers of labor, to use your influence which God has given you for the protection and for the preservation of the womanhood of our country . . .
>
> I know there are women in this audience that are the wives, mothers, or sisters of some of some of the best manufacturers of our country . . . [P]lead with your husbands or your brothers, that the women who are helping to make the business, who are creating the money going into your bank account, are worthy of being more than numbers, for these women will be the mothers of the next generation and their children must be the voters of this country. They are going to have their influence wherever they go regardless how poor they are . . .
>
> The men are drawing the women out of the homes into the industries. Now, I say, every employer of labor in the United States owes the women that he takes into these institutions, such conditions that they can go out, and, without any shame, face the world, saying, "I am a pure woman when I leave this institution."
>
> Ninety percent of our wage-earning women have not one hour left in which to prepare for wifehood, or motherhood.
>
> I am advocating an eight-hour day from my own experience. I know that . . . when I was working ten hours . . . I was not fit to go into any man's home and be the proper wife or mother of that home. Do you want your daughter to be robbed of that God-given privilege? Now think of the other mother.[74]

The General Federation's support for protective labor legislation involved more than such exhortation from the national level. To limit the working hours of women, many state federations and local clubs soon became active in educating the public and pressing legislatures for new laws. As early as the 1908 Biennial, the president of the Michigan Federation reported that "Some important laws were enacted for the benefit of working women and children, which I have not the time to name, drawing from the Commissioner of Labor, a hearty letter of commendation for the assistance of clubwomen and a request for its continuance."[75] And the Wisconsin Federation reported that "Our foremost work last year centered upon the problem of child and woman labor, the latter having increased in our state 31 percent since 1903."[76] Most notably, the women of the Oregon Federation bragged at the 1908 Biennial that "We did active work in securing the ten hour law for women which has made Oregon famous, and as club women, we here return thanks to Justice Brewer for the decision [the 1908 U.S. Supreme Court decision in *Muller v. Oregon*] that affects all women workers throughout the land."[77] At the 1910 Biennial, the Washington State Federation added its claims to the list of pioneering legislative steps: "The office of female labor commissioner has been created and is now filled by a competent woman; the Eight Hour Labor bill for women has passed . . . [and] other bills of value to women and children are being prepared for legislation."[78]

After 1910, reports of state-level activities multiplied. At the 1912 Biennial, the Federations of Idaho, Illinois, Kentucky, Maryland, Missouri, New Jersey, New York, and Utah all reported specific activities on behalf of women's hour laws, and many other state federations reported in more general terms that they had worked (as the Pennslyvania report put it) "for the bettering of child labor laws and for the protection of women workers."[79] At the 1914 Biennial, the Federations of Arizona, Delaware, the District of Columbia, Idaho (again), and Pennsylvania reported specific efforts for women's hour laws, and the Maryland Federation reported that it had prevented adverse amendments to a women's hour law passed earlier.[80] And at the 1916 Biennial, the clubwomen of Oklahoma and Wyoming added their claims to the accumulation of state federations that had acted on behalf of legal limits to women's working days.[81]

As Table 7 reveals, the nationally reported efforts of state Federations of Women's Clubs on behalf of women's hour laws paralleled the nationwide spread of these laws after 1908. State federations were definitely or probably active in promoting thirteen of the nineteen new women's hour laws that passed between 1909 and 1917. Federated clubwomen also worked for major legal improvements in many other states. Moreover, the information in this table is certainly only partial, for in most cases I have not been able to supplement it with more detailed data from state-level reports. Thus the table indicates only some of the contributions of organized clubwomen in working for women's hour laws across the U.S. states. Note in particular that Federations promoted women's hour statutes in a number of western states, such as Arizona, Idaho, Oklahoma, and Utah, where Consumers' Leagues did not exist at the times the laws passed. In many other states, meanwhile, the Federations worked closely with the urban-based Consumers' Leagues, helping to spread the message much farther into many towns and legislative districts.

With the imperfect data at hand, there is no way to specify the relative impact of women's groups as opposed to other forces pushing toward the enactment of new and improved women's hour laws during the Progressive Era. Nevertheless, the evidence I have been able to gather reveals that the efforts of women's organizations were extensive and sustained. It is hard to imagine these laws spreading so quickly across the United States without the victories of the National Consumers' League in the courts and the efforts at public education and legislative lobbying mounted by alliances of womens' groups before and after the watershed judicial decisions. In many states, of course, the efforts of organized women and those of organized labor went hand in hand to promote the same end: legal limits to the hours that female workers, the "mothers of the race," could toil in factories, stores, and service establishments. Despite opposition or footdragging from business groups and other conservatives, the alliances that advocated this sort of regulatory protection for women workers eventually prevailed to some degree in all but four U.S. states.

The Limited Success of the Campaign for Minimum Wage Laws

Hour laws for women were supported by trade unionists as well as elite and middle-class reformers, and these laws were enacted in the United States over many decades prior to the burst of new and improved legislation at the height of the Progressive Era. In contrast, no minimum wage statute appeared before the 1912 Massachusetts law, and the national movement for similar measures remained almost exclusively the affair of reformers and women's groups. Remarkably, even though both business organizations and state Federations of Labor opposed minimum wage statutes in most places, the proponents were able to get specific proposals onto the public agenda in many states. As Table 8 shows, laws were eventually passed

Table 8. Supporters of minimum wage laws for women workers, 1912–1923

Year and state	Evidence of support from		
	Consumers' Leagues	Federations of Women's Clubs	Others
1912			
Massachusetts			WTUL; WEIU; branch of the AALL
California	NCF staff consulted	yes	Katherine Edson; State Legislative Council of Women; WCTU
Colorado		probably	
Minnesota	member of NCF National Board	probably	Father Ryan; some labor support
Nebraska			Committee of Ladies in Omaha; Lincoln YWCA; Bureau of Labor and Industrial Statistics
Oregon	yes	probably	Branch of the AALL
Utah		yes	
Washington		yes	State Federation of Labor; churches
Wisconsin	yes	yes	Professor John Commons; Milwaukee Federation of Churches
1915			
Arkansas		yes	
Kansas		yes	Progressives; State Labor Inspector; Topeka Council of Mothers
1917			
Arizona		yes	

Table 8   (continued)

| Year and state | Evidence of support from | | |
	Consumers' Leagues	Federations of Women's Clubs	Others
1918			
District of Columbia	yes		
1919			
North Dakota			Non-Partisan League; State Federation of Labor
Texas	yes		State Federation of Labor; Congress of Mothers
1923			
South Dakota			

Note: AALL = American Association for Labor Legislation
WCTU = Women's Christian Temperance Union
WEIU = Women's Educational and Industrial Union
WTUL = Women's Trade Union League
YWCA = Young Women's Christian Association

Sources: Brandeis, "Minimum Wage Legislation," ch. 4 in *Labor Legislation;* Nathan, *Epoch-Making Movement,* appendix G; *NCL [Annual] Reports* for 1909, 1910, 1911, 1912, and 1914–1915–1916; "State Reports" in the *Official Reports* of GFWC Biennials for 1910, 1912, 1914, 1916, 1918, 1920, and 1922; Athey, "Consumers' Leagues and Social Reform," ch. 7; Lieberman, "Their Sisters' Keepers," ch. 7; Beyer, *Labor Legislation for Women*; Tripp, "Labor Laws in Washington," ch. 4; Schmidt, "Labor Legislation in Wisconsin," ch. 7; *Twenty-Five Years of California Federation of Women's Clubs,* pp. 186, 191–92; Bureau of Labor and Industrial Statistics of Nebraska, *Thirteenth Biennial Report, 1911–12* (Lincoln, NE: Claflin Printing Co., 1912), p. 69; Report of the Nebraska Special Investigation Committee on the Wages of Working Girls, *Proceedings of the Thirty-Third Session of the Nebraska House of Representatives* (Lincoln, NE: Jacob North and Co., 1913), p. 970; "Start Probe on Working Girls' Wages," *Lincoln Daily Star,* Feb. 12, 1913, p. 4; Robert L. Morlan, *Political Prairie Fire: The Nonpartisan League, 1915–1922* (Minneapolis: University of Minnesota Press, 1955), p. 65; Underwood, "Civilizing Kansas," pp. 302, 304; Kansas Report in "State News," *Child-Welfare Magazine* 9(5) (Jan. 1915), p. 168; W. M. W. Splawn, "A Review of the Minimum Wage Theory and Practice with Special Reference to Texas," *Southwestern Political Science Quarterly* 1(4) (March 1921), p. 347n; Texas Report in "State News," *Child-Welfare Magazine* 13(10–11) (June–July 1919), p. 320; and Minutes of the 1917 Convention of the Arizona Federation of Women's Clubs (Rena Mathews Papers, Ms 125, Arizona State Historical Society).

in fifteen states plus the District of Columbia—with eight of these legislative breakthroughs occurring suddenly in 1913. Indeed, from the vantage point of that year, it looked as if minimum wage laws for women, like hour laws, would soon sweep across almost all of the U.S. states. But this was not to be, as the Progressive Era's movement for minimum wage laws remained narrowly based and hampered by an uncertain judicial climate. Given the obstacles, it is testimony to the efficacy of women's politics that minimum wage laws made as much headway as they did.

The Consumers' League Raises the Issue

Proposals for minimum wage laws arose in the United States through the efforts of the leaders of the National Consumers' League.[82] In 1907, the NCL Council voted "to investigate wages and the standard of living of self-supporting women throughout the country."[83] In addition to local efforts, Sue Ainslie Clark of the national staff worked on this investigation for two years, eventually producing an official report as well as vivid material for muckraking articles in national magazines. The articles included "Why Working Girls Fall into Temptation" in the November 1909 issue of the *Ladies Home Journal*, "Man's Inhumanity to Woman" by Ida Tarbell in the February 1910 issue of *American Magazine*, and "Working-Girls' Budgets" by Edith Wyatt in the February 1911 issue of *Mc'Clure's*.[84] The Consumers' League report and the related magazine articles coincided with other nationally visible investigations of the low wages and strained budgets of working girls and women—such as the Russell Sage Foundation's *Women and the Trades* published as part of the "Pittsburgh Survey" in 1909, and the U.S. Department of Commerce and Labor's nineteen-volume study of the condition of women and child laborers throughout the country published in 1910–11.[85] As Josephine Goldmark would later put it, the results of such investigations "aroused public horror at the low wages of women workers. American complacency was seriously shaken."[86] Reform organizations like the National Consumers' League had already learned from experience that voluntary pressures alone would not be enough to induce businessmen to raise the wages of unskilled and unorganized workers, so demands for legislative solutions became a logicial next step.[87]

There were also transnational influences at work. In 1908, Florence Kelley and the U.S. League's First Vice President Mrs. Frederick [Maud] Nathan attended the first International Conference of Consumers' Leagues at Geneva, Switzerland. Among the topics discussed there were the experience of New Zealand and Australia with minimum wage boards, and the plans of English reformers that were soon to bear fruit in the Trade Boards Act of 1909.[88] After their return to the United States, Kelley and Nathan obtained from the 1909 Annual Meeting of the Council a resolution "That the National Consumers' League recommends that state and local leagues study the subject of minimum wage boards with a view to a legislative campaign in 1910, and that the President be authorized to appoint a special committee of the National League to further this object."[89] The League's "Special Committee on Minimum Wage Boards" included Miss Emily Balch of Wellesley College, who during 1909–1910 drew up a bill modeled on the English Trade Boards Act, and Reverend John A. Ryan of Minnesota's St. Paul Seminary, who did a great deal to publicize the minimum wage ideal in that state and in national circles of Catholic labor reformers.[90] The committee soon came to be chaired by Professor Arthur N. Holcombe of the Harvard Department of Economics. Along with the other academics on the committee—Professors Henry Rogers Seager of Columbia University and Herbert E. Mills of Vassar College, and Mr. A. B. Wolfe of Oberlin College—Holcombe developed and disseminated intellectual rationales for public regulations to set floors under the wages of unskilled and unorganized workers.[91] A burst of articles offering such rationales appeared in many magazines and professional journals during the 1910s.[92]

Very rapidly, the minimum wage became a priority for leading progressive reform groups. The Women's Trade Union League (WTUL) included demands for a minimum wage in a legislative program adopted at its 1909 biennial convention and also in the comprehensive "Programmme of Legislative Measures to be introduced into the various State Legislatures by the Local Leagues or in co-operation with other organizations" endorsed at its 1911 Convention.[93] In March 1910 the National Consumers' League made the minimum wage part of its ten-year program.[94] In May of the same year, Florence Kelley spoke on "The Case for the Minimum Wage" at the annual meeting of the National Conference of Charities and

Corrections, which was at that point under the leadership of reform-minded settlement house workers and their allies in the social work profession. These were the same reformers who were soon to write the social legislation planks of the 1912 Progressive Party platform, including one calling for "minimum wage standards for working women to provide a 'living wage' in all industrial occupations."[95]

Efforts by state Consumers' Leagues and their allies quickly led to pioneering minimum wage laws for women in Massachusetts, Oregon, and Wisconsin. The Massachusetts campaign was kicked off when Florence Kelley made a speech to the state branch of the WTUL in December 1910.[96] Within months, the WTUL convened a committee of reform groups to petition the General Court (the Massachusetts state legislature) to appoint an investigatory commission. Besides the Consumers' League and the WTUL, this alliance included the Massachusetts Child Labor Committee, the Women's Educational and Industrial Union, the Central Labor Union of Boston (affiliated with the State Federation of Labor), and the Massachusetts branch of the AALL. The General Court established a commission essentially run and funded by these groups, but also including a lawyer to represent the concerns of employers. The commission investigated women workers' wages and recommended a minimum wage law modeled on British precedent, except that it would apply only to women. In 1912 the Massachusetts legislature passed the recommended bill virtually unanimously, but only after amending it in one crucial respect that dismayed reformers as much as it mollified alarmed employers: Publicity was substituted for legal enforcement as the method for getting employers to raise low wages.

The next year in Oregon and Wisconsin, however, industrial commissions—including representatives or advisors from employers and organized labor—gained the legal power actually to order higher wages for women workers. In Oregon, the Consumers' League led the way in pushing for this outcome along with the American Association for Labor Legislation and a Catholic priest, Father E. V. O'Hara, who subsequently became chairman of the new Oregon Industrial Commission.[97] In Wisconsin, the Consumers' League worked on behalf of the minimum wage in alliance with the state Industrial Commission, Professor John Commons, and the state's Progressive Republicans, who endorsed the minimum wage and took control of the governorship and legislature in the 1912 election.[98]

Buoyed by these early triumphs, state and local branches of the Consumers' League eventually agitated for investigatory commissions and minimum wage bills virtually everywhere that the organization had a presence. Some of these campaigns came at the height of the Progressive Era, simultaneous with the first League initiatives; others were launched in the late teens and went on into the 1920s. Overall, according to the information I have been able to pull together, state Leagues agitated for minimum wages in Connecticut, Delaware, Illinois, Maryland, Massachusetts, Missouri, New Jersey, New York, Ohio, Oregon, Pennsylvania, and Wisconsin; and metropolitan leagues were also active in the District of Columbia and Austin, Texas.[99] Of those state Leagues in existence in 1912, only the small Leagues of Indiana, Maine, and Tennessee, as well as the Rhode Island League, which was probably discouraged by overwhelming industrial oppposition, seem not to have engaged in any agitation for legal minimum wages.[100]

Why Women Rather Than All Workers?

Why did the Consumers' League and other elite reform organizations such as the AALL and the WTUL agitate for minimum wage laws applicable only to adult women laborers rather than to adult males as well? This question is pertinent given that the Australian, New Zealand, and English minimum wage boards all covered low-wage male as well as female workers.[101] It is even more pertinent given that American reformers, including the members of the NCL's Special Committee on Minimum Wage Boards, normally argued for minimum wages in gender-neutral terms and adhered to a vision of what minimum wages might accomplish that obviously encompassed protection for male workers.[102] In Florence Kelley's stirring words:

> The advocates of minimum-wage boards are animated by the hope that the boards may produce far-reaching indirect effects. Thus child labor can be more effectively minimized and school life prolonged, when unskilled fathers attain a living wage for the maintenance of their families, and when minors must be paid a reasonable wage and can no longer be had for a song. Tuberculosis can be warded off when wage-workers can more universally afford a nutritious dietary, and the tuberculosis crusade may thus become a less hopeless undertaking. Those cases of insanity which arise

from worry over insufficient wages combined with physical deple-
tion due to a too low standard of living may reasonably be expected
to diminish when wages are rationalized. And the same reasoning
applies in great measure to alcoholism among wage-earners. The
social evil can be combated when honest labor enables girls—as in
tens of thousands of cases it now fails to do—to earn an honest
living and enjoy a share of decent recreation. The blunt weapon
of the strike for better wages is supplanted when the joint intelli-
gence of the interested parties is brought to bear for their own
benefit and that of the public.

In brief, the hope is cherished that through the extension of
wage boards industry can be made increasingly to pay its own way
in the form of living wages.[103]

In accord with this almost millennial vision, Kelley herself wanted
general minimum wage laws that would reinforce "the American
tradition that men support their families, the wives throughout life
and the children at least until the fourteenth birthday." Writing in
the *Journal of Political Economy* just as the nationwide U.S. movement
for minimum wage statutes was getting under way, she lamented
that the 1912 "Massachusetts law . . . does not face the question:
Why is the man no longer the breadwinner? It does not contribute
toward conserving the family and the home with the man as its
economic support. This is important because, as the Massachusetts
law is the first one in this country, other states may incline to accept
it as their model, in place of the more comprehensive Australian
and English laws."[104]

Indeed, minimum wage laws opened the prospect not just of
limiting participation in the paid workforce, as hour laws did, but
of legally mandating higher-than-market-level incomes for employees. Whenever such a possibility arose in this historical period, virtually all American professional reformers, men and women alike,
felt that the ideal goal should be a legally supported "family wage"
plus additional social benefits generous enough to allow married
men to support their families, allowing married women, especially
mothers, to remain at home.[105] Thus when it came to regulating
family standards, which was a major preoccupation of reformers in
the Progressive period, laws limiting work hours for women and
laws shoring up women's wages were not analogous. Hours restrictions would help safeguard women's primary role as wife and

mother, while minimum wages might actually pull women out of homes, especially if—as Kelley feared—the wages of male breadwinners were not kept high enough to support families. To be true to their ideals, therefore, virtually all the reformers of the Progressive Era should have agitated for legal minimum wages for men as well as women workers.

Yet the reformers led by the National Consumers' League ended up agitating for legal minimum wages targeted specifically on women. This happened for several important practical reasons. Not just ideological preferences for a gender-based familial division of labor, but also preexisting policies and structures in U.S. politics, affected the goals and tactics of reformers.

In the first place, as Kelley explained in commenting on the pioneering Massachusetts campaign, the "restriction of its field to women and minors was in accordance with the Massachusetts tradition of making laws especially in interest of the health and welfare of women."[106] It was easier for reformers to get the public and legislators to go along with this politically established approach. Yet there was also a logic of administrative intervention in markets at work, a logic affecting the preferences of the reformers themselves. One public intervention tends to beget further ones targeted on the same group, because otherwise market forces can undermine the purposes of the earlier intervention. In this instance, supporters of legal restrictions on hours for women's employment—restrictions which had already made considerable headway in the United States when the minimum wage movement was launched—felt that further legal protections were needed to keep women employees from suffering outright losses in their wages when their hours of work were cut back. As the advocate for mostly unorganized wage-earning women, the WTUL felt strongly about the mutually reinforcing logic of hour laws, minimum wage laws, and other legislative remedies for the weak bargaining position of women workers.[107] Other reformers also accepted this logic as did Oregon's Judge Cleeton, who reasoned that "the laws fixing maximum hours of labor and minimum wages are complements, the minimum wage law being necessary in some instances to make the maximum hours law effective."[108]

The prior existence of regulations about child and female workers also meant that in certain states there were statisticians, factory inspectors, and other labor-law administrators well situated to under-

take official investigations into the conditions faced by women workers, and these officials might also be in a position to advocate new
minimum wage laws, working in cooperation with reform associations. Thus, in California, Katherine Philips Edson, "then associated
with the state Bureau of Labor Statistics brought to the attention of
Hiram Johnson, the Progressive governor of the state, the low wages
being paid to women workers as shown by studies made by that
bureau. Impressed with the need for state action, the governor asked
Mrs. Edson to have a bill drafted," and she proceeded to do so in
conjuction with women's groups.[109] Similarly, in Kansas a law was
passed in 1913 requiring the appointment of a female deputy factory
inspector to "have charge of the enforcement of all laws relating to
the health, sanitary conditions, hours of labor, and all other laws
affecting the employment of female wage earners."[110] Accordingly,

> Miss Linna E. Bresette was appointed as woman factory inspector
> and devoted her entire time to inspection of factories and work-
> shops where women or children were employed. During 1913 she
> conducted an investigation under the direction of Labor Commis-
> sioner O'Brien. She visited 365 establishments in which a total of
> 19,854 women were employed, and found that 34 percent of the
> women employed received less than $6 per week; 21 percent
> worked 10 hours or more per day; and more than 50 percent
> worked 54 hours per week or longer. Almost universally the
> women who have to work the longest hours receive the lowest
> wage. A great many married women are employed in the industrial
> world, many of them from necessity. A large percentage of the
> married women are mothers supporting or assisting in the support
> of a family.[111]

Two years later, in 1915, the Kansas legislature, urged on by progressives and women's associations, passed a minimum wage law for
women and set up an Industrial Welfare Commission to enforce this
and other measures. The rationale given for the new measures stated
that it "is the opinion of the legislators of Kansas that inadequate
wages, long-continued hours and unsanitary conditions of labor exercise a pernicious effect on the health and welfare of women and
children," suggesting that Miss Bresette's studies had contributed to
the extension of protective regulations for women in Kansas.[112]

Another consideration cited by Florence Kelley as a reason for
tailoring minimum wages to women was "the hope that the courts

might be more likely to sustain a new application of state intervention if it were confined to women."[113] Indeed, the anticipated stance of the courts was crucial. As the National Consumers' League took up the minimum wage cause in 1909–1910, it was flush with the victory of the Brandeis-Goldmark brief in *Muller v. Oregon*. Likewise, after September 1913, when Oregon's pioneering minimum wage statute came under challenge in the state and federal courts, the Consumers' League once again mobilized the Brandeis-Goldmark team to make an analogous argument about the value of legal wage floors for protecting women. After Louis Brandeis was elevated to the Supreme Court in 1916, the same line of argument was carried forward by the NCL-sponsored team of Goldmark and Felix Frankfurter.[114] As the chairman of the Oregon Industrial Welfare Commission explained the stance the NCL developed in conjunction with Oregon officials to argue in favor of the minimum wage statute: "The principle on which the act is based is that the welfare of women must take precedence over any commercial consideration. The mothers of the future generation should not be sacrificed to industrial gain."[115] The Consumers' League had already used this approach successfully to defend women's hour laws before the courts, and then had used the legal victories to spur a nation wide campaign for futher legislative victories. It hoped to repeat the performance with minimum wage laws. In short, in the turn-of-the-century U.S. polity, where the courts had great influence over social legislation, the gender-specific rationale seemed essential to meet the proclivities of judges, whatever might have been the ideally greater merits of minimum wages for all workers, including male breadwinners.

Finally, too, there was the important matter of political coalition-building. The National Consumers' League and other tiny associations of professional reformers badly needed allies and a receptive audience from the broad middle-class public if legislative campaigns for minimum wages were to hold any prospect of success in most places. Allies and a favorable audience were needed in part because the obstacles to passage of these bills were greater than for hour laws. Business organizations and other conservative forces feared that government might actually order extra expenditures on wages, and this was perceived—not only by businessmen, but also by many legislators and judges—as more intrusive than were statutes limiting who might be employed and for how long. "When the National

Association of Manufacturers reviewed this new species of reform, it wondered when an end would come to the 'fetish' of 'fantastic and grotesque legislation' . . . [This legislation] would only encourage the prolific growth of bureaucratic boards. Furthermore, once women were guaranteed a minimum wage, men would demand the same. All labor would then come within the grip of the state. Common sense demanded the rejection of this 'pure socialism.'"[116]

Opposition from Organized Labor

Whatever the fears of business, however, the national leadership of the American Federation of Labor was also adamantly opposed to minimum wage laws, especially for men, fearing that they would become ceilings rather than floors and would frustrate union organizing and bargain efforts.[117] National AFL opposition to minimum wage measures was stronger than the opposition to hour laws, because the AFL did not have to deal with a deeply rooted working-class tradition in favor of legally regulated wages (while it did have to deal with such a tradition on the question of the legally limited working day). Moreover, Samuel Gompers and other national AFL leaders were especially hostile to the Australian- and English-style minimum wage boards of which the progressive reformers were so enamored, because the AFL leaders worried that these boards might become bureaucratic instruments for wage-setting and labor arbitration as a substitute for collective bargaining.

Of course, as ever, not all state federations went along with the position of the national AFL leaders. Certain state federations—such as those operating as junior partners within populist reform alliances, or those taking stands at especially reformist conjunctures in nonindustrial states—actually played leading roles in working for minimum wage laws applicable to women workers. Thus the Washington State Federation of Labor joined with its usual partners in reform, women's groups, church groups, and farmers' groups, to put through that state's minimum wage law in 1913.[118] The Texas State Federation of Labor, eventually joined by the Consumers' League of Austin and the Texas Congress of Mothers, agitated for minimum wage bills from 1911 until the Texas law passed in 1919.[119] And the tiny North Dakota State Federation of Labor, a supporting player in the farmer-based Non-Partisan League, consistently advocated minimum wage as well as hour laws for women workers. These were enacted along with dozens of other measures, many much more radical, after the Non-Partisan League swept the governorship and both houses of the legislature in the 1918 election.[120] Even in highly industrialized states, the labor federations might be persuaded to support female minimum wages by trade union women or the Women's Trade Union League. This happened in Massachusetts. And the Illinois Federation of Labor joined that state's—ultimately unsuccessful—campaign for minimum wages, because trade union women pressured the men and, as explained by "Victor A. Olander, secretary-treasurer of the Illinois State Federation . . . women were 'the best judges of what is for their own interests.'"[121]

But even if particular state federations might break with the national AFL leadership to lend support to minimum wage laws for women, few of them would have strayed so far as to support across-the-board minimum wage laws including adult men. Thus the advocates of minimum wages mollified labor opposition and picked up occasional supporters from the ranks of organized labor by focusing their advocacy on laws for women in particular. They also made it easier for third parties tied to the skilled labor unions, such as Catholic labor reformers, to work for minimum wages. And in a few states, such as Oregon and Washington, where proportionately fewer women were employed than in the eastern industrial states, the proponents of minimum wages for women actually avoided strong business opposition as well.[122]

Mobilizing Women's Groups and Public Opinion

Most important, by focusing the campaign on women, proponents of minimum wage laws maximized the possibilities for appealing to churches and women's groups, the morally minded sectors of the middle-class public. Publicity in favor of minimum wage bills often stressed that young female workers could not earn "decent" livings, or avoid falling into sin, on the pitifully low wages paid by sweating businesses. In Illinois, for example, attention was drawn to the issue of women's low wages when the investigators of the Chicago Vice Commission of 1911 "concluded that the low returns of respectable labor were a contributing cause of prostitution."[123] Well beyond Illinois, minimum wages were seen as a way to help prevent female immorality. As a contemporary student of the progressive movement explained in 1915, the "agitation in this country for the fixing of a minimum wage had its origin in a belief that has become widespread in recent years, that there is a close connection between immorality and the poor wages which young working girls receive."[124] Arguments connecting legally supported wages with women's virtue rolled easily off the tongues of Catholic priests, Protestant ministers, and leaders of the Women's Christian Temperance Union. And these were forces that figured prominently in the successful coalitions behind minimum wage laws in California, Minnesota, Oregon, Washington, Wisconsin, Kansas, and no doubt other states too.[125] Moreover, in this respect as well as others, the special focus on women's well-being facilitated the involvment of Federations of Women's Clubs in state-level campaigns for minimum wage laws.

In contrast to what happened with women's hour laws and mothers' pensions, the Biennial Conventions of the General Federation of Women's Clubs never officially endorsed minimum wage laws as a national goal. But the nationally assembled clubwomen did hear a discussion of the state-by-state movement for female minimum wages in the "Greetings from the National Consumers' League" presented to the 1912 Biennial by Mrs. Frederick [Maud] Nathan, and in the "Report of the Department of Industrial and Social Conditions" presented at the 1914 Biennial.[126] More to the point, we know from the state reports to the national Biennials, as well as from other sources, that State Federations of Women's Clubs definitely worked actively in favor of the minimum wage laws passed in 1913 in California, Utah, Washington, and Wisconsin, as well as those passed in 1915 in Arkansas and Kansas.[127] State Federations of Womens Clubs also reported efforts on behalf of minimum wages for women in Maryland, Michigan, Idaho, and Montana.[128] Significantly, the reach of the Women's Club Federations extended much further into rural and western states than did that of the National Consumers' League. Thus the alliance of the two organizations magnified reform influence, as the Consumers' League Vice President Mrs. Nathan vividly explained in her remarks to the 1912 GFWC Biennial:

[T]he League realizes that the Federation of Women's Clubs is one of the most potent forces for uplift in our country. It is the embodiment of enlightened and progressive womanhood . . . The National Consumers' League, I believe, as one of its founders and also as one of the old club women in the Federation, has revolutionized or spread the work among many of the federated clubs . . . [T]he social conscience of the club women has been aroused . . . Through this awakened conscience there has been a wonderful impetus that has been sweeping a great wave of social reform throughout our country from the Atlantic to the Pacific Coast . . . [T]hrough the Federated Clubs and the National Consumers' League, I dare say that through public sentiment, through legislation, and through Supreme Court decisions, we are maintaining that supreme fact that the conservation of the human race is paramount to mere material increase of wealth.[129]

Altogether, as indicated by Table 8, one or more women's groups—including the Federations of Women's Clubs, the Consumers' Leagues, the Women's Christian Temperance Union, the Congress of Mothers, the Women's Educational and Industrial Union, and the Women's Trade Union League—were definitely active in the campaigns for minimum wage laws in ten of the fifteen states plus the District of Columbia that passed them. And women's groups were probably active in some or all of the remaining five states; information is simply too sketchy to be sure. Along with other parts of the public at large, women's groups could actually carry the day for a minimum wage law even when both business and organized labor were opposed.

The most telling example of this was the campaign for the minimum wage in California led by Katherine Philips Edson, an officer in the State Federation of Women's Clubs.[130] Normally, the forces of organized labor concentrated around San Francisco could call the shots in labor legislation; and both male and female trade unionists in California were vocally opposed to a minimum wage law for women. The initial California law passed in 1913 after being endorsed by the WCTU and the California State Federation of Women's Clubs, partly because at that point both organized labor and business groups were preoccupied with other legislative battles. Yet, according to labor historian Clara Beyer:

It was after the law was passed that the opposition came. Both labor and the employers became excited. The California constitution offered them a chance to discredit the law and render it practically ineffective, and they made the most of their opportunity . . .

The enabling act [for the original 1913 law] was submitted to the people [in a referendum] at the general election of November, 1914. Each side had ample opportunity to prepare its case and present it. Labor carried on an active campaign through the labor press and on the public platform against the measure. The Los Angeles and San Francisco Chambers of Commerce, the California Merchants and Manufacturers' Association, and various other business organizations assailed the measure.[131]

Among business groups, only the California Retail Dry Goods Association supported the minimum wage measure. Otherwise, a campaign of public education had to be waged without reliance on major economic interests. "The Progressive Party, which was then the dominant party in the State, made the amendment one of its major issues," and it surely also helped that women had gained the right to vote in California in 1911.[132] Yet, above all, the organized women of California waged the kind of moralistic educational effort at which women in this period excelled. "The State Federation of Women's Clubs, with Mrs. Edson as chairman of the section on industrial relations, had been thoroughly aroused to support this legislation" and the "Women's Christian Temperance Union also was active with its membership and in church circles." "Club women adopted slogans, such as 'Let us be our sisters' keepers' and 'Employed womanhood must be protected in order to foster the motherhood of the race.'"[133] With the focus on a women's issue defined in moral terms, the associated women decisively defeated both business and labor. "After a wide educational campaign the people [of California] were called upon to vote. The amendment [favoring minimum wage enforcement] carried by 379,311 to 295,109."[134]

Of course, minimum wage laws for women did not sweep across the entire nation, as their proponents had hoped. State and local Consumers' Leagues made unsuccessful efforts to pass minimum wage statutes in many states. Overall, Consumers' League efforts failed in many more states—in Connecticut, Delaware, Illinois, Kentucky, Maryland, Missouri, New Jersey, New York, Ohio, and Pennsylvania—than in the three states plus the District of Columbia where they succeeded. Why did Consumers' League leadership fail to spark successful campaigns for minimum wages in so many states? Lack of activity on behalf of minimum wages by the other, more broadly based and geographically widespread women's associations may have been a factor in many of the states where League efforts fell short (except Maryland, where the Federation of Women's Clubs did join the struggle). Significantly, as can be seen by comparing Tables 7, 8, and 9, State Federations of Women's Clubs reported to the national level much more involvement in the Progressive Era campaigns for women's hour laws and mothers' pensions than in the campaign for minimum wage laws for women. As far as we can tell from the claims their officers made at the national Biennial Conventions of the GFWC, the state Federations do not seem to have adopted the cause of minimum wages in many key states.

An equally important factor, surely, was that the states which refused to pass proposed minimum wage bills were much more highly industrialized than those that did pass such laws. In the more industrialized states, strong opposition from business organizations—and usually from the AFL unions as well—had a telling effect on legislators.[135] In the eastern and midwestern industrial states that refused to pass minimum wage bills, states such as New York and Illinois, the conditions that allowed proponents to prevail over business and labor opposition in California—namely, Progressive political hegemony, women's suffrage, and intensively mobilized women's associations—were simply not present, either singly or together. Comparing the campaigns for women's hour laws with the campaigns for minimum wage laws, we can speculate that the former faced less intense opposition in the major industrial states, and at the same time enjoyed broader support across the nation from women's groups and from organized labor. Hours bills were therefore less dependent for successful enactment than were minimum wage bills on especially propitious political conjunctures, such as the 1912–1915 peak of Progressive electoral politics, or the upsurge of reformism that occurred in some states at the end of World War I in 1918–1919.

Institutionalizing the Protective Impulse

World War I provided an opening for groups advocating protective laws for women workers to achieve a related bureaucratic goal, the establishment of a separate agency within the federal government devoted to investigating the conditions of women workers and advocating their welfare. This agency would build upon, and increasingly coordinate its efforts with, the various state-level bureaus and commissions that were established during the 1910s and 1920s to enforce laws, investigate conditions, and protect the interests of women (or, sometimes, women together with child) laborers.[136] When the "Woman in Industry Service" was established within the U.S. Department of Labor in 1918, this rewarded—at least temporarily—lobbying efforts that had been under way for some years.

Back in 1906 and 1907, women's groups and organized labor had together pressed the U.S. Department of Commerce and Labor to undertake comprehensive investigations of the conditions of women and child laborers. Two years of investigation yielded nineteen volumes of reports. "The conditions revealed were worse than imagined, and the experiment showed a need for continuing investigations."[137] But efforts to do such studies through the existing federal Bureau of Labor Statistics were unsuccessful and by "1916 the Secretary of Labor, William B. Wilson, favored the reorganization of the Women's Division [of the Bureau of Labor Statistics] into a separate unit."[138] The 1916 national convention of the American Federation of Labor refused to support this proposal, but it was enthusiastically backed by the National Women's Trade Union League, the General Federation of Women's Clubs, the Young Women's Christian Assocation, the Children's Bureau—and of course by the National Consumers' League.[139] "A governmental investigative body similar to the Children's Bureau [which had been established in 1912] was . . . considered a necessity by the National Consumers' League," explains the historian Louis Athey. Thus an "active letter-writing and lobbying campaign, coordinated by Miss Zip S. Falk, Executive Secretary of the Consumers' League of the District of Columbia, was conducted during 1916–1917."[140]

In 1916, Wilson's proposal was "buried in apathy" upon its arrival in Congress, but America's subsequent mobilization for World War I "focused attention upon the industrial woman."[141] The sudden demand for more workers and increased labor time drew more women into the workforce, and simultaneously put in jeopardy previous statutory and voluntary efforts to protect working women against exploitation. What is more, the war emergency allowed the establishment of "emergency" agencies. Thus, at the Secretary of Labor's initiative, and with a congressional appropriation of $150,000, the Woman in Industry Service was established on July 1, 1918, and charged to use investigation and persuasion, but not legal coercion, to "develop in the industries of the country policies and methods which will result in the most effective use of women's services in production for the war, while at the same time preventing their employment under injurious conditions."[142] "Symbolic of the connection between laboring women and middle-class reformers" that lay behind the Service's creation, the newly appointed director was Mary Van Kleeck, a graduate of Smith College and a social worker, who had been formerly connected with the National Consumers' League and the Russell Sage Foundation; and the assistant director (who would later head the Women's Bureau) was Mary Anderson of the International Boot and Shoe Workers Union.[143] Right after its inception, the Woman in Industry Service got involved in recruiting women for wartime work; and it also drew up recommended "Standards Governing Employment of Women in Industry" that reflected the current highest standards of protective labor legislation. These standards stressed safe working conditions, eight-hour days and forty-eight-hour weeks, and minimum wages that were equal between the sexes and adequate to "cover the cost of living for dependents."[144]

World War I came to an end only four months after the establishment of the Woman in Industry Service, jeopardizing its continuation. Dependent upon year-to-year appropriations by a Congress that was in a mood to slash budgets and eliminate emergency bureaus, the Service needed to be transformed into a permanent agency if it was to survive.[145] In their very first Annual Report, submitted in June 1919, the Service's leaders offered an explicit rationale for this:

> Women in industry in 1910 constituted more than 21 per cent of the total number of persons gainfully employed in the United States. It is not only their importance in numbers, but the special problems of their employment affecting industry on the one hand and family life and child welfare on the other which necessitates special provision by the Federal Government for a clearing house of policies and facts relating to their position in industry . . .
> The problems of women following the war are likely to be more

crucial than at any time during the past . . . [I]t is hoped that the Women's Bureau will be permanently established by legislation as a part of the Department of Labor, and that its resources will be enlarged in order to make possible more comprehensive work.[146]

Predictably, women's groups mobilized to lobby on behalf of this plan for the creation of a permanent Women's Bureau. This goal aroused not just the women's groups that had been active earlier in support of protective labor laws, but others as well, now including the National Congress of Mothers.[147]

Because World War I had brought women's nation wide mobilization to a peak, and because women were becoming voters, Congress acceded to the demand for a permanent Women's Bureau. The enabling legislation was passed in June 1920. Although the Bureau's initial appropriation and the salaries mandated for its women employees were low, Congress did respond to the lobbying of women's groups during the early 1920s by raising its budget slightly (until 1925).[148] In any event, the advocates of special public protection for women workers achieved an important bureaucratic victory simply by establishing the Women's Bureau on a continuing basis after the end of the wartime emergency. This achievement by women's groups contrasts to the failure of reformers to preserve the United States Employment Service after World War I.

Through the 1920s, the Women's Bureau furthered the ideals of the progressive reformers who had worked for its creation, struggling as best it could with limited resources and authority. Often working in cooperation with state agencies and voluntary associations, the Bureau did investigations and put out a steady stream of of publications on such topics as "A Physiological Basis for the Shorter Day for Women" (1921), "The Share of Wage-Earning Women in Family Support" (1923), "Women in Missouri Industries" (1924)—one of many such studies for individual states—and "The Effects of Labor Legislation on the Employment Opportunities of Women" (1928).[149] As exemplified by this last study, the Bureau avidly defended protective labor laws against charges from equal-rights feminists as well as conservatives that these laws hurt rather than helped wage-earning women.[150] Overall, the Women's Bureau

advanced the collection of information which had been left to social workers and the Consumers' League in previous decades, and it advocated a set of industrial standards closely aligned with those of the National Women's Trade Union League. This included equal pay, six-day week, eight-hour day, no night work for women, minimum wage, prohibition of women from certain industries shown to be more dangerous for women than for men, improved working conditions, and the appointment of qualified women to positions of authority in state departments of labor.[151]

The Women's Bureau could not, however, directly bring about legislative innovations; nor could it administer laws or sustain them from reverals in the courts. Like the progressive forces that had created it, the Bureau was dependent for the realization of its mission—the legal protection of women workers—on shifting political and judicial climates. Because the Women's Bureau had no federal spending program or laws to administer, it could not readily advance further than did protective laws and administrative innovations in the various states.

Conclusion: The Courts Turn against Minimum Wages

During the Progressive Era, reformers and women's organizations working for both women's hour laws and minimum wage statutes argued that "employed womanhood must be protected in order to foster the motherhood of the race." We have learned, too, that hour laws were supported by broader political alliances than those that fought for minimum wages. Yet an important contrast needs to be drawn between the unequivocally favorable judicial climate for women's hour laws after *Muller v. Oregon* in 1908 and the much more uncertain judicial climate that prevailed for minimum wage measures from 1914 onward—a climate which became fatal to minimum wage laws in 1923. This contrast explains why, ultimately, the movement for minimum wages was completely stopped, and then reversed, leaving protective legislation for women workers focused solely on restrictions of full female participation in the wage labor force. Starting around 1920, equal-rights feminists were very critical of such restrictive effects of protective labor legislation. But it is important to remember that vanguard progressive groups such as the Consumers' League and the Women's Trade Union League had originally intended not only to limit the working hours but also to to improve the incomes of women employees. The reformers had also hoped to use protective laws for women as an entering wedge for legally guaranteed improvements for all workers.

As we have already seen, the Consumers' League was able to take full *political* advantage of the Supreme Court's unambiguous 1908 endorsement of women's hours statutes in *Muller v. Oregon,* using this victory to spur legislative efforts in many states. Subsequent to the *Muller* decision, moreover, additional decisions by state and federal courts reaffirmed the validity of women's hour laws. Favorable judicial decisions helped to sustain political momentum until virtually all state legislatures had passed new or improved women's hour statutes. Most of these new hour laws came during the Progressive Era, but some innovations and administrative improvements continued during the 1920s.[152]

The situation was very different for minimum wage laws, however. By 1914, the 1913 Oregon minimum wage statute was under full challenge in the courts. It survived review by the Oregon Supreme Court in *Stettler v. O'Hara,* 1914, when the Court, to the delight of reformers, affirmed that "Every argument put forth to sustain the maximum hours law or upon which it was established applies equally in favor of the constitutionality of the minimum wage law as also in the police power of the state, and as a regulation tending to guard the public morals and the public health."[153] Yet the 1914 Oregon decision was immediately appealed to the Supreme Court.[154] And there the case became bogged down, with no decision rendered for three long years, during which the Consumers' League and its allies had to contend with the political effects of uncertainty about what the Court would say. Then, when the Supreme Court did decide *Stettler v. O'Hara* in 1917, it divided right down the middle (with recently appointed Justice Brandeis staying out), four in favor and four against upholding the constitutionality of Oregon's minimum wage law. Technically speaking, this upheld the constitutionality of the law, and reformers tried to put the best face on this outcome to encourage further state legislation. But such a divided Supreme Court decision encouraged further constitutional challenges, and the District of Columbia's 1918 minimum wage law was in due course appealed to the Supreme Court. For various reasons, this appeal again took many years to be decided, prolonging the uncertainty. Only a few more states passed minimum wage laws in the interim between 1917 and 1923.

Finally, in 1923, the Supreme Court—with four justices different from those in 1917, and Justice Brandeis again not participating—ruled in *Adkins v. Children's Hospital* by five to three against the constitutionality of the District of Columbia's minimum wage statute. This decision applied by extension against other minimum wage statutes that might be construed as similar to the D.C. law. In the majority opinion, Justice Sutherland cited favorably the precedent of *Lochner v. New York,* 1905. In the words of the labor historian Elizabeth Brandeis, Justice Sutherland "recognized that in *Muller v. Oregon* and subsequent cases hour legislation for women had been distinguished from the ten-hour law for bakers held invalid in the Lochner case, but he contended that the physical difference between the sexes which justified a different rule as to hours did not warrant a different rule as to wages . . . All the other statutes [upheld by the Court] dealt, he said, 'with incidents of the employment having no necessary effect on the heart of the contract, that is, the amount of wages paid and received.'"[155] Justice Sutherland also pointed to the Nineteenth Amendment granting women the suffrage, arging that this reflected women's elevated status and indicated that it was no longer necessary to have "restrictions on their liberty of contract which could not lawfully be imposed on men."[156] After years of politically debilitating uncertainty, therefore, the U.S. Supreme Court accepted the laissez-faire, business-oriented argument that minimum wage regulations—even for the "mothers of the race"—went too far in infringing on rights of free contract.

Reformers could not agree on an effective strategy for countering the Supreme Court's decision in *Adkins.* After 1923, the Consumers' League maneuvered to defend certain existing minimum wage laws, such as California's and Wisconsin's, from the negative effects of the *Adkins* precedent.[157] But further political efforts—either efforts rigorously to enforce existing minimum wage regulations or efforts to pass new state laws—came to naught during the 1920s. Until the New Deal, hopes faded for using governmental power to put floors under workers' incomes. The practical strategy of the progressive reformers, the strategy of working first for laws supporting the incomes of women workers, fell apart. It was undone, ironically, by the very courts it had originally been designed to propitiate.

CHAPTER 8

An Unusual Victory for Public Benefits: The "Wildfire Spread" of Mothers' Pensions

During the Progressive Era, proposals for pensions and social insurance to benefit male workers ran up against insuperable obstacles, as we learned in Chapter 5. Political parties and the U.S. state structure did not make it easy to enact such proposals; and elite and middle-class public opinion was strongly biased against new social spending measures that might possibly recapitulate the "corruption" of Civil War pensions. Yet if the Progressive Era was generally not the right time for new social spending measures in the United States, mothers' pensions constitute an obvious exception. Enacted very suddenly by twenty state legislatures in 1911–1913 and by forty states before 1920, mothers' pensions—or "widows' pensions" as they were sometimes called—authorized local governmental authorities to make regular payments directly to impoverished mothers (and occasionally other caretakers) of dependent children. Mothers' pension payments were meant to cover at least part of the cost of raising such children in their own private homes, so that they would not have to be placed in foster homes or institutions such as orphanages.[1]

Why were mothers' pensions enacted across most of the states during the Progressive Era? This question deserves a more precise answer than it has yet received. The best available account is Mark Leff's descriptively excellent article "Consensus for Reform," which presents mothers' pensions as a proposal that spread easily after it was raised at the 1909 Conference on the Care of Dependent Children, held in Washington, DC. The conference was convened by President Roosevelt with an appeal that the widowed mother be helped through public or private relief to "keep her own home and keep the child in it."[2] This gathering helped to crystallize a growing consensus among child welfare experts that children should be kept with their mothers whenever possible, rather than being placed in the orphanages that Catholics supported, or the foster homes that Protestant reformers tended to favor.[3] But despite this consensus, the 1909 Conference was also careful to endorse only private, not public, relief for widowed mothers. The relevant Conference resolution said:

> Home life is the highest and finest product of civilization. It is the great molding force of mind and character. Children should not be deprived of it except for urgent and compelling reasons. Children of parents of worthy character, suffering from temporary misfortune and children of reasonably efficient and deserving mothers who are without the support of the normal breadwinner, should, as a rule, be kept with their parents, such aid being given as may be necessary to maintain suitable homes for the rearing of the children. This aid should be given by such methods and from such sources as may be determined by the general relief policy of each community, *preferably in the form of private charity*, rather than of public relief. Except in unusual circumstances, the home should not be broken up, for reasons of poverty, but only for considerations of inefficiency or immorality.[4]

The idea of *government-provided* mothers' pensions was not unanimously accepted once it came onto the public agenda.[5] Opposition from business, and from economically conservative forces generally, may well have been less of a factor in the case of mothers' pensions than it was for hour and minimum wage laws. Mothers' pensions purported to save public monies that might otherwise be spent on institutionalized fatherless children; and they did not directly affect the terms of contracts between employers and employees. Nevertheless, in intense debates from 1911 to 1915, proposals for these new public benefits were fiercely opposed by most charitable groups, and by peak associations speaking for charities, such as the National Conference of Charities and Corrections and the Russell Sage Foundation. Only a handful of charity leaders, mostly affiliated with Jewish associations, broke ranks to endorse mothers' pensions.[6] The mainstream charity groups were defending their own private, voluntary measures for helping widows and children. "Public relief for mothers," a contemporary analyst noted, "strikes at the very vitals of private philanthropy which makes its most effective appeals for funds for dependent widows."[7] Moreover, the charity workers were maintaining the elite American tradition, entrenched since the 1870s and 1880s, of strong opposition to public spending for any "outdoor relief"—that is, assistance to the poor outside of institutions.[8]

In the fight against mothers' pensions, prominent charity officials such as Mary Richmond explicitly invoked Civil War pensions as a negative precedent. In Richmond's words, "the mixture and confusion of the two ideas of service pensions and relief grants will make nothing but trouble. It is a confusion that has cost our country dear already. The same mixture of motive appears again and again in the records of soldiers' pension legislation—now it is payment of a debt, and again it is charity; now the pension roll is a 'roll of honor,' and again it is a thing that must be kept private because the veterans are sensitive about its publication."[9] Drawing in detail on graphs and arguments from William Glasson, Richmond then proceeded to tell the story of politically fueled, ever rising expenditures for Civil War pensions, suggesting that the same thing would happen again should the United States institute the principle of public pensions for mothers.[10] Concerned with possibilities for political corruption, she did not consider the difference between the cross-class male constituency helped by Civil War pensions and the impoverished female constituency that would benefit from mothers' pensions; the former consitutency was much easier to mobilize politically and far more appealing as an object of public largesse than the latter would ever prove to be after public benefits for dependent mothers were instituted.

Despite opposition from charity groups, mothers' pension bills were widely enacted. After a few years delay, such a bill was passed even in New York state, where the private charitable establishment had its headquarters. If we want to know why this happened, we must attend to the role of women's politics. When reform proposals such as old age pensions and social insurance were at issue, strong interest-group opposition and the invocation of general elite and middle-class fears about the likely "political corruption" of social spending were enough to stall forward momentum toward legislative enactments. Tellingly, this was true even for proposals to pension the needy elderly, which had many apparent similarities to mothers' pensions. Exactly like mothers' pensions, early proposals for old-age pensions called for state-level enabling statutes that would leave decisions about funding and implementation to localities; and the proponents of old-age pensions also argued that they would save public monies otherwise spent on institutions (that is, poor houses). Also like mothers' pensions, old-age pensions would have avoided direct interventions in contractual relations between employers and employees. Despite all these similarities, however, mothers' pensions were enacted during the 1910s, while proposals for old-age pensions were derailed by fears about instituting new kinds of public social spending. Part of the difference, no doubt, is that old-age pensions would have gone to male voters. Yet we have seen that mothers' pensions also aroused fears about possible political corruption. For mothers' pensions, such fears were ultimately overcome, because much more positive momentum was quickly generated for them than for old-age pensions. And that momentum was created by elite and middle-class women's clubs across the United States.

"Perhaps more women have agreed on the wisdom of mothers' pensions than on any other single piece of social legislation," noted a contemporary observer, Mary Ritter Beard.[11] Leaders of women's federations were willing to counter opposition to mothers' pensions from the charity "experts." In the words of Mrs. Clara Cahill Park, vice president of the Massachusetts Mothers' Congress (written in rebuttal to a critique of mothers' pensions by Dr. Edward Devine, secretary of the Charity Organization Society and director of the New York School of Philanthropy),

> perhaps it is not surprising that a plain mother may still go on thinking that such aid is in reality preventative in that it reaches the affairs of the home at a crisis, and tides them over without loss of self-respect. You see, mothers, in spite of the sociologists, feel themselves, for once, on their own ground in this matter; and in possession of all their faculties, will continue to think that, as far as children are concerned, not they, but the learned doctors, are in the amateur class . . . [F]rom the mere fact of being able to gain more aid for more mothers by state subsidies the idea seems to them of value. They [mothers], and perhaps they only, can also feel the importance of preserving self-respect as an asset, to be saved by the new attitude of the states . . . State aid, to my mind, is an advance, as showing the policy of the nation, to conserve its

children and its homes, and in recognizing the mother as a factor
in that campaign, for the welfare of all.[12]

Armed with such confidence that they were the true experts on
family issues, leaders of women's voluntary groups enjoyed a strong
rhetorical advantage in public debate. They could invoke positive
symbols and feelings about motherhood in support of the new social
spending they advocated. And they could draw positive, not negative, analogies to pensions for veteran soldiers, arguing that both
soldiers and mothers served the Nation. Equally if not more important were the organizational resources that women's associations
could bring to bear and the structural leverage they could generate
on a policy issue that required action by dozens of state legislatures.
Because the reach of the women's federations stretched from national to state and local levels, they were able to spread the word
among active women quickly, and put simultaneous pressure on
many state legislatures, ensuring the rapid enactment of mothers'
pensions across the nation.

What Was Done by Officials, Reformers, Politicians, and Organized Labor?

The very first mothers' pension laws were engineered, quite literally,
by a few reformist juvenile court judges who wanted governmentally
appropriated funds to help keep poor children in school and not at
work. The judges also wanted relief from the unpleasant duty of
taking inadequately supervised "delinquent" children away from the
custody of impoverished working widows. During the winter of
1910–11, Judge E. E. Porterfield of the Juvenile Court of Kansas
City persuaded the Missouri legislature to pass a law that applied
only to Jackson County (where Kansas City is located). This measure
allowed the award of "allowances" to any widow (or, as soon
amended, wife of an inmate of the state insane asylum) who was "in
the judgement of the Juvenile Court . . . a proper person, morally,
physically, and mentally, for the bringing up of her children."[13] A
few months later in Illinois, the "Funds to Parents" act was passed
as a brief amendment to enabling legislation for the juvenile courts.
Juvenile Court Judge Merrit W. Pinckney "engineered its passage
quietly without informing or consulting representatives of the city's
social agencies until after it was approved by the legislature."[14] After

the relatively liberal Illinois law did become widely known, it aroused considerable concern about corruption and indiscriminate relief. Within a year it was amended to become narrowly applicable only to widows, not to other guardians, and only to citizens, not to recent immigrants.[15]

In addition to Judges Porterfield and Pinckney, a few other juvenile court judges promoted mothers' pension bills. But they had to gain broad public support to overcome opposition and inertia, as did Judge Ben Lindsey in orchestrating a two-to-one referendum victory for the Colorado Mothers' Pension Act of 1912.[16] Indeed, had the initiative continued to rest only with scattered individual judges, mothers' pensions would not have become a nationwide legislative movement. Opponents in the private charity world were mobilized against mothers' pensions by 1912; and many of the usual elite supporters of progressive social reforms sat out this particular campaign. Even among juvenile court judges, many did not favor mothers' pensions.[17]

Reformist professionals interested in progressive social legislation were divided and reluctant to accept or push for mothers' pensions. Agreeing with charity officials, many labor legislation experts who advocated social insurance lacked enthusiasm for mothers' pensions—on the grounds that they smacked of refurbished poor relief. To be sure, despite reservations, Isaac Max Rubinow was one social insurance advocate who did cautiously accept mothers' pensions "as a step towards, if not yet quite a measure of, social insurance."[18] Rubinow's attitude is not surprising, given his broad-minded view of public social provision. But many others in the social insurance movement placed much greater stress than did Rubinow on strictly contributory programs designed to benefit (and tax) wage earners. Tellingly, therefore, at the first American Conference on Social Insurance sponsored by the AALL in June 1913 in Chicago, the featured talk on mothers' pensions was given by the charity official Edward T. Devine, a leading opponent of such legislation who was also a member of the AALL's Committee on Social Insurance. In his presentation, Devine argued that widows should be aided either by contributory social insurance covering industrial-worker husbands or, failing that, by private charities, concerned neighbors, and improved public poor relief. He denounced mothers' pensions as "not in harmony with the principles of social insurance . . . but merely a revamped and in the long run unworkable form of public outdoor relief . . . having no claim to the name of pension and no place in a rational scheme of social legislation."[19] Probably because it could not get argreement among its leaders on this issue, the American Association for Labor Legislation did *not* make mothers' pensions one of its legislative priorities, and did not enter state-level campaigns to enact these bills.

A number of prominent social settlement women, including Mary Simkhovitch, Lillian Wald, Jane Addams, Florence Kelley, Julia Lathrop, and Edith and Grace Abbott, broke ranks with most charity people and social insurance advocates to give early support to mothers' pensions.[20] The endorsement of these visible and active female reformers was certainly important in legitimating this new public benefit for mothers and children. But their efforts on behalf of this particular reform were noticeably more limited than their efforts on behalf of child labor legislation, protective laws for women workers, and child and maternal health programs. And even if their activities had been much more extensive, a few social settlement women based in big cities and small national organizations could not—alone—have accomplished nationwide legislative victories for mothers' pensions.

Two other groups that endorsed mothers' pensions but cannot be credited with the nationwide legislative enactments are the Fraternal Order of Eagles and the American Federation of Labor. Himself a member of the Eagles, Judge Porterfield of Kansas City had the support of this cross-class male fraternity in pressing the Missouri legislature in 1911 to authorize mothers' pensions for his county. The Eagles subsequently campaigned for mothers' pensions in some other states, but they never made them as important a priority as they did old-age pensions during the 1920s and 1930s.[21] As for the AFL, at its Thirty-First Annual Convention in November 1911, among dozens of resolutions introduced and methodically discussed by the assembled union men was Resolution number 172 from the Hatters Delegation, whose reasoning is worthy of consideration. In the words of the Hatters:

Whereas, Owing to the death or disability of the husband and father, many women are left with dependent children to provide for; and

Whereas, This condition compels such women to enter the industrial world handicapped by their necessities which very often force them to work for less than others in order to support their children, thereby injuring their sisters and brothers in the economic struggle as they are often compelled to do work that should be done by men; and

Whereas, This deprives the children of such women of a mother's care, and denies the mother herself, to a large extent the pleasure of her children's society; therefore, be it

Resolved, That we, the representatives of the American Federation of Labor in Convention assembled, are of the opinion that in all such cases, the National Government should assume the support of the mother and children until it will become possible for them to become self-supporting; therefore, be it

Resolved, That we hold this policy to be in line with the best principles of trade unionism. For years we have been trying, and to large extent, succeeded in having laws passed by legislatures prohibiting the employment in factories of children of tender years and putting them in school where they properly belong; we should develop this policy a little further and take the mothers out of the economic struggle and put them where they properly belong, in the home. A law of this kind would lift a nightmare from the minds of millions of men. Every man with children would know that in case of his death, his family would be provided for by this great fraternal principle; and in our opinion if union labor is to be true to itself it will take this matter up with the same spirit and determination we have shown in the child labor prohibition. Nothing we could think of would bring home more forcibly to the minds of our non-union brothers how thoroughly in accord with the best interests of labor in general are the principles of trade unionism. It would bring this fact home to others than the working class. Lawyers, doctors, clergymen and others who might die poor would have their families provided for under this law. The adoption of this principle would place union labor on a higher moral plane than ever before, and would draw increased attention to us, and to our high purposes, with the result that we would be supported as we were never supported before in our noble mission to elevate mankind.[22]

This resolution is fascinating for its invocation of organized labor's concern to further fraternal principles across class lines—and, indeed, the AFL enjoyed friendly relations with the Fraternal Order of Eagles.[23] Unmistakably, too, the AFL resolution invoked the interests of skilled trade unionists in keeping women and children out of labor markets, as well as the interests of wage-earner husbands and fathers in public provision for their families if the male breadwinners should die.

The 1911 AFL Convention unanimously adopted the principle of the Hatters' resolution, directing that mothers' pensions should be incorporated by the AFL Executive Council into the old-age pension legislation that the Federation then had pending in the U.S. Congress. We can conclude from this episode that AFL unionists liked the idea of mothers' pensions, and did not oppose them as they often did oppose contributory insurance for male workers. But of course the U.S. Congress never acted on mothers' pensions (any more than it did on the AFL's proposal for old-age pensions through the "National Old Age Home Guard"). And there is no evidence that many state Federations of Labor actively lobbied for mothers' pensions in the forty-some legislatures where the issue was actually decided.

Nor were party politicians, even reformist ones, the ones who led the way toward mothers' pensions—except in particular states like Wisconsin, where progressive Republicans were responsible for the 1913 mothers' pension law, or Ohio, where a Democratic governor with progressive sympathies promoted the 1913 legislation.[24] Across the nation, according to Mark Leff, politicians "remained followers rather than molders of public opinion."[25] Even the national Progressive Party hung back. Probably reflecting the wariness of many of its supporters from the ranks of charitable workers, the Progressive Party failed to endorse mothers' pensions in its 1912 platform, a document that did explicitly call for workmen's compensation, social insurance, and protective regulations for women workers.[26] This accurately signals that a somewhat distinctive constellation of forces—not exactly the same as the constellations supporting *either* labor legislation for workingmen *or* hour and wage laws, the other state-level maternalist policies of the Progressive Era—spearheaded the drive for mothers' pensions after 1911.

Women's Magazines and the *Delineator's* Campaign

The ideological ground was prepared for the rapid, nationwide spread of mothers' pension enactments during the 1910s, not so much by the 1909 White House conference of child welfare experts as by values and ideas propagated by magazines and newspapers—and particularly by one major magazine for women, the *Delineator*. Home life and motherhood were values celebrated and reinforced by mass-circulation women's magazines that reached millions of middle-class readers during the early 1900s. These magazines were distributed across the entire United States, including through the mail to many small towns and farms. So commercially successful were these rapidly expanding magazines that their editors enjoyed during the pre–World War I period a great deal of leverage in relation to advertisers (room to maneuver that the editors would lose in the 1920s, when the advertisers gained the upper hand).[27] One of the uses that women's magazine editors made of their discretion was to sponsor campaigns for social reform causes. To promote these campaigns, they sometimes sought to work with the General Federation of Women's Clubs and other women's groups, because it was their general policy to cultivate friendly relations with women's clubs as a method of boosting subscriptions and circulation.

During 1912 and 1913, one women's magazine, the *Delineator*, published a series of articles about the legal rights of married women, a series that culminated in a campaign specifically for mothers' pension legislation. Its large covers and pages richly adorned with color sketches of beautifully attired ladies, the *Delineator* was a fashion magazine published by the Butterick Publishing Company, distributor of Butterick sewing patterns. By the turn of the century, the magazine included literary selections and sections on current social issues, along with articles about fashions and home life. With a circulation through the mail of about one million in 1912, the *Delineator* was the third largest of the "big six" women's magazines; and it was also sold alongside Butterick sewing patterns in stores around the United States.[28]

Well before it took up the specific cause of mothers' pensions, the *Delineator* had well-established routines for arousing women readers on behalf of charitable causes and legal reforms. From 1907 to 1909, it sponsored a well-known "Child Rescue Campaign," devoted to finding foster homes for orphans who would otherwise go to institutions.[29] "For the Child that Needs a Home and the Home that Needs a Child" was the motto of the campaign, which featured regular articles with photographs and stories about individual childen awaiting foster care.[30] In addition to doing this series, the editors of the *Delineator,* James West and the well-known author Theodore Dreiser, established a "Child-Rescue League" and worked with many prominent leaders across the nation, including settlement house workers, wives of reformist governors, and many officers of the General Federation of Women's Clubs.[31] Furthermore, Dreiser and West were the key promoters of the 1909 White House Conference on the Care of Dependent Children, which (as we have seen) proclaimed that home care rather than institutional care was best for all children.[32]

Yet the *Delineator's* specific decision to take up the mothers' pension cause came after Dreiser and West had left the magazine, and depended very much on the reformist views of the journalist William Hard, who took over the magazine's policy-oriented column in 1911, transforming its emphasis from children's rights toward the legal rights of married women and mothers.[33] William Hard, of course, was the former Chicago social settlement worker who was a good friend of Jane Addams and Julia Lathrop.[34] Under the recurrent motto "With All My Worldly Goods I Thee Endow," Hard started a series in October 1911 with the question "Yes, But Does He?" The first article had an illustration of a trusting-looking young bride in a sweeping gown. In this and subsequent installments, Hard proceeded to "explore the sea which rises round the Island of Security on which our young bride stands."[35] Hard wrote about rules that might consign most of a deceased husband's property to relatives other than his wife, and examined patriarchal custody laws that allowed husbands to take even small children away from their mothers.[36] Encouraging readers to write to him about examples of women's suffering and the nature of laws in their states, Hard claimed that he received and answered thousands of letters; and he published selected letters with commentary in his column.[37]

In a more directly political move, Hard also used the pages of the *Delineator* to launch "The Home League," which readers were invited to join as a way of receiving regular information about legislation pending in various states and ways that women could lobby on behalf of improvements. "Real Work Begins," declared Hard's column in the April 1912 issue of the *Delineator,* "To Secure Better Laws for the Home You Are Invited to Join the New Organization."[38] In his description of the Home League, Hard explained that its members need not be magazine subscribers, but should commit themselves to writing letters to their state legislators and bringing up potential legal reforms for discussion in "clubs and societies and circles and granges to which you may belong." He also explained that *"It is not at all necessary that we should be in favor of the suffrage in order to be in favor of the increase of women's powers in their homes."* In a subsequent column, he elaborated:

> Deeper than suffrage, and coming out of the growth of the modern woman toward mental independence—a growth in which suffrage is merely one incident, though a big one—is the question which the modern woman has long been asking, the question which this department of *The Delineator* asks every month.
>
> How can Love, Marriage and the Home, through laws regulating the marriage contract, through laws establishing the equal control of children, through laws protecting the wife's property and earnings, through laws preventing non-support and desertion by the husband and father, through laws guaranteeing to the widow a fair and sure proportion of the family's possessions—how, in these ways and in other ways, too, can Love, Marriage and the Home be so safeguarded by the State that Motherhood, the greatest of all works, shall be the most secure?[39]

In short, Hard hoped to activate women politically around the established ideals of domesticity and motherhood, without running aground on the shoals of then-current disputes between those opposing and those favoring formal votes for women.

In due course, William Hard incorporated the cause of mothers' pensions into his established series about laws affecting women. In August 1912, the *Delineator* launched its campaign for mothers' pensions with an article entitled "Four Counties That Prefer Mothers to Orphan Asylums" (Figure 21).[40] This piece described the new mothers' pension laws of Missouri and Illinois and less official practices of mothers' aid in California and Wisconsin, and told the human-interest story of one Mary Ellen McKay, widow of an ironworker killed in a construction accident and mother of seven children. An illustration graphically conveyed the essence of Mrs. McKay's situation as, surrounded by fearful children, she sat in a courtroom before a judge who was about to commit her offspring to various institutions. The caption read: "Woman, you stand convicted of sickness, hunger, wretchedness and want. What have you to plead that sen-

FOUR COUNTIES THAT PREFER MOTHERS
TO ORPHAN ASYLUMS

BY MARY O'CONNOR NEWELL

EDITOR'S NOTE:—Every year man puts asunder those whom God, with bonds even more sacred than those of matrimony, has joined together. Every year thousands of American children are torn from their mothers to be given to strangers. Not because those mothers are bad. Only because, through no fault of their own, they are poor.

At the Southern Woman and Child Labor Conference at Memphis in 1910, Mrs. Henrietta C. Cosgrove, a mine-owner, of Joplin, Missouri, suggested "Pensions for Mothers." Next January in many legislatures—why not in the legislature of your own State?—there will be introduced "Pensions for Mothers" bills.

Mrs. Newell, who has seen the new idea in operation in Chicago, tells you about it in this article in a way that will make you see it with your heart as with your eyes.

IF MARY ELLEN McKAY had never given up her twelve dollars a week job as forewoman in a stocking factory to marry Patrick Casey, ironworker,—

And if both had not followed the Creator's decree and the State's behest to multiply and fill the land,—

And if Pat Casey had not died from falling from the girders of the magnificent new Bluestone Hotel, ten days after accepting a three-hundred-dollar final settlement from the company,—

It's ten chances to one that Mary Ellen Casey would not have been haled before the judge of the county court to face inquiry why her brood of seven should not, according to statutes written and provided, be scattered to the four corners of the earth.

"Woman, you stand convicted of sickness, hunger, wretchedness and want," said the judge to her, in effect if not in so many words. "You are charged with being unable to support your children. What have you to plead that sentence of breaking up your home be not passed upon you, and your children's rearing and companionship given to others?"

"Judge—your honor," Mary begins—they always say it that way in court, a hopeless "Judge," a pause, then with upward quaver, "Your honor," lest seeming lack of deference be accounted against them—"I do the best I can. I work when I can get work, but between the worriment and the sickness I can't make ends meet. With just a little help, a few dollars a month, judge—your honor——"

"The complaint reads that while you are down-town scrubbing floors the children are roaming the streets," continues the judge. "They don't go to school, they are ill-nourished and almost naked, and the oldest boy has been in trouble with the police."

"Judge, they are good children. They do fine, considering I'm so little home to look after them. Johnny was only playing when the stone went through the window. The boy meant no harm. Don't take the children away from me, judge—your honor—they are all I've got to live for, before God, your honor."

Splitting Up the Family

THE testimony of the policeman or probation officer only emphasizes the truth of her story and the inefficiency of the woman, torn between the need of her at home and the hardships of her new work. The last penny of the family's money spent, the neighbors' aid exhausted, county rations insufficient, steps must be taken, the officer says, to put the children where they will be sure of enough to eat and wear and some schooling.

Again the judge's voice:

"The Court orders Johnny to Gloomwood, Mary to Knollsite, Agnes to St. Eleanor's, Jane to the Girls' Industrial, William to the Parental, Thomas to St. John's and the baby to the Infant Welfare," these places being chosen only with reference to a slip on his desk telling how many children each overcrowded institution will accept.

It's all over in a minute, and the corridor's intervening wall smothers the mother's protests and chalk-white Johnny's cries of "You let my mother alone—darn you—don't you touch my mother," as he beats with small clenched fists upon the legs of the big bailiff who is half-leading, half-dragging his mother.

Then and there for all time came to an end the Casey family, which might have been the Smith family, or the Schlagheimer family, or the Soblitzky family. The State makes no provision for keeping the members of one family together.

The reassembly of the family unit, once it has been split into fragments, has proved an almost insurmountable difficulty to many a philanthropic agency.

How the Substitute for Home Works

THAT night little Johnny Casey, who, as we intimated, might have been Johnny Anybody of any nationality, with bruised and broken little heart wept out his grief and loneliness into the sheets—nice, clean, sanitary sheets—of Gloomwood, the big barracks where they housed a hundred other children like Johnny, and

"Woman, you stand convicted of sickness, hunger, wretchedness and want. What have you to plead that sentence of breaking up your home be not passed upon you?"

taught them to get up, and sit down, and walk, and eat and work, in exact time and with the same number of motions, and tried to make them good in the hardest way ever invented by anybody for any one, let alone little boys and girls.

This was what Johnny got in exchange for the care of a real mother when everything was going as best it could in the big barracks, when teachers were all God-sent, and politicians were not palming off weevily flour, wormy bacon and sandy sugar on the county's wards.

Nothing came to fill the place of mother, unless he was a determined little Johnny, when something that resented, hated, schemed to get even, was born in the vacant space, and then he was called an incorrigible little Johnny, and got his secondary education, very likely, in a reform school, and was graduated into prison.

But most of these little Johnnies—and Marys, too—were tongue-tied, reserved little folk, never got into anybody's way, never did anything good or bad.

It cost the State an average of not less than ten dollars a month apiece for twelve months of twelve years and more to "educate" these little Johnnies and Marys into mute, unquestioning obedience.

Let out into the world, these Johnnies and Marys had a hard time of it. People complained that they had no push, enterprise, resistance, generosity. They even found them unloving and indifferent—just think, of it!—those little children that had wept such tears those first nights into the nice, clean, sanitary sheets of institutions!

One day that disconcerting person who is always fussing over statistics came along.

"Hang uniformity!" he said. "Uniformity isn't for children. Makes sticks and clods of them. What every child needs is a mother and the freedom of a home. One home-reared boy has more get-up-and-get in him than a dozen institution products."

He said worse than that. "Tell me the name of the institution, and I'll tell you the delinquency to which the child leans," he said.

Straightway society went to Gloomwood and Knollsite and the other institutions and took as many little Johnny and Mary Caseys and Johnny and Mary Smiths out of them as it could, to "board out" in families.

Society found many Mrs. Joneses, who might be, for all society cared at first, Mrs. Casey's and Mrs. Smith's next-door neighbors. It boarded Johnny Casey and Mary Casey, and Johnny Smith and Mary Smith, with these various Mrs. Joneses, still paying as much as ten dollars a month for the Johnnies and fifteen dollars a month for the Marys. It was costing the State right along seventy dollars a month at least to take care of the family of Mary Ellen Casey.

In the meantime, Mary Ellen, back at the stocking factory, was making six dollars a week at piece-work. She didn't earn as much as she used to, for Mary Ellen's hand had lost its cunning at the stocking-machine. All it was good at now was blessing and guiding little children—and there were no children now for Mary Ellen to guide.

Tolerant, well-meaning and just Mrs. Joneses, who wanted little children to board, were hard to find. When found, most of them demanded little Mary Smiths, not little Johnnies.

Boys are such a trial to raise, you know. Everybody finds them so but angels and mothers, and you never heard of angels taking children to board, did you?

Boarding Them in Their Own Homes

ABOUT the time institutions fell back on the cottage plan, or boarding out the children in families, the peripatetic person with the pencil bobbed up again.

He said: "Why not board the Casey children with Mrs. Casey, and the Smith children with Mrs. Smith? You have been running around in a circle trying to find the right environment for the dependent child. Why not close the circle by giving the children back to the mothers, and help the mothers to make them into good citizens?"

"Stuff and nonsense! Sentimentality! Purest bosh!" snorted the conservative taxpayer, whose personal experience had given him no reason to question the old-fashioned way of dealing with dependent children.

The peripatetic person with the pencil didn't explain the situation as at first he thought he would. He saw it was not the ripe time to announce that children are the business of society even more than of parents, or

To Join

THE HOME LEAGUE

*write to William Hard
care of The Delineator
Butterick Building, New York*

Figure 21

Source: *The Delineator*, August 1912, p. 85.

tence of breaking up your home not be passed upon you?" An Editor's Note preceding this article commented: "Every year man puts asunder those whom God, with bonds even more sacred than those of matrimony, has joined together. Every year thousands of American children are torn from their mothers to be given to strangers. Not because those mothers are bad. Only because, through no fault of their own, they are poor . . . Next January in many legislatures—why not in the legislature in your own State?—there will be introduced 'Pensions for Mothers' bills." And another Editor's Note at the end of the article commented: "The German way is ideally best. but we can't have it here till we have a universally compulsory insurance system. Which is a thing we can not bring about for many years to come. In the meantime we can, and must have 'Mothers' Pensions.'"[41]

In the September 1912 issue of the *Delineator,* Hard called women to action. "Help the 'Widow's Pension' Idea in Your State," he urged his readers in an article describing efforts in six states. "See how the idea grows? Is it going to sprout in your State? Are you going to tell some neighbor about it, or some club president, or some legislator? Whether you start helping it now or not, if you are a member of The Home League, I will tell you when it appears in the legislature of your State, and I will tell you how you can help it through the legislature into the statute-books."[42]

The *Delineator*'s campaign for mothers' pensions was persistent and emotionally engaging. In December 1912, the magazine editorialized on the first page about "Our Christmas Wish for Women: That Every Decent Mother in America Could Have Her Babies With Her" (Figure 22):

> And it need not be a vain wish, in the years to come, if you will only let your mother-love spread itself just a little way outside your own door . . .
>
> Women's clubs, clubs of loving and hopeful women, in Massachusetts and in California, and in many States in between, are working hard to get laws which will give to the mother the money which is now being given to the institutions in which her children are *imprisoned.*
>
> Set the children free! Let them go back to their mothers! And let the mothers earn their living from the State by doing the most useful thing they could possibly do—bring up their children![43]

Vol. LXXX

THE DELINEATOR

No. 6

GEORGE BARR BAKER, *Managing Editor*

OUR CHRISTMAS WISH FOR WOMEN:

That Every Decent Mother in America Could Have Her Babies With Her

THAT is all. But is it not enough? You who are rich; you who are well off; you who think you are poor yet have your children under your own roof, to work for, to see, to hear, to touch; is it not enough for one wish?

And it need not be a vain wish, in the years to come, if you will only let your mother-love spread itself just a little way outside your own door. The way is plain, and could be made easy.

Just read this letter, which came from Brooklyn and has been translated quite literally:

"I have read your article in THE DELINEATOR and thank you in the name of the public and especially in the name of women and children. The next generation will thank you, my good sir; and if there is a world beyond, you can rest in peace, for it is the truth, as the Scriptures say: 'Love thy neighbor as thyself,' especially the innocent children. Believe me, good sir, I have suffered this martyrdom and know what it means to separate from one's children, for whom a mother is willing to sacrifice her life. This only a mother can feel, especially when she sees how indifferently they are treated by the attendants of the homes. I have two boys of three and one years respectively, that are at present in a home, and every time I visit them my heart aches. At night I imagine I hear them call me. But why must I tell you of my sleepless nights? Dear sir, is there no possible way that a respectable woman can have her children with her? For it may take years before your most beautiful idea can be realized. If you know of any possible way to fulfil my wish, please let me know. I am looking for a position as caretaker or janitress or any other honest position in the country, but I wish to have my children with me. I am healthy, thirty-four years old and understand any kind of work. I think that there is at least one more opening for us in the big city. Do you not think so too, dear sir?"

The case is typical. Like the woman in our August number, she stands "convicted of sickness, hunger, wretchedness and want."

Her children have been taken from her, and are being boarded at the public expense.

Why are they not being boarded with her?

It has been proved in Kansas City and in Chicago that it costs less to board children with their mothers than in institutions.

If this can be done in Kansas City and in Chicago, why not in New York and Boston?

And if in New York and Boston, why not everywhere?

Women's clubs, clubs of loving and hopeful women, in Massachusetts and in California, and in many States in between, are working hard to get laws which will give to the mother the money which is now being given to the institutions in which her children are *imprisoned*.

Set the children free! Let them go back to their mothers! And let the mothers earn their living from the State by doing the most useful thing they could possibly do—bring up their children!

That's what the club women we mentioned are working toward. And THE DELINEATOR is helping them do it. And we are going to succeed. We tell the story of it all in our next month's issue.

To our own readers, whether club women or not, we say:

If one million of you wrote in to us and joined The Home League and so told us of your willingness to write a letter of appeal to your State legislator from your district—if you did just that—we could, in two years, make our Christmas wish a reality in every State in the Union

Just look back to the top of the page and read that Christmas wish again. Is it worth one letter from you?

Here is another way to help: If you believe in the cause we fight for, and won't assist in the spreading of our gospel, why not use THE DELINEATOR as a Christmas present? You can send in a subscription, giving name and address of a friend. We will then send the friend a handsome Christmas card, on which will be stated the fact that with your holiday greeting goes a year of good reading, practical helps, and the news of a propaganda for the care of mothers and children.

Figure 22

Source: The Delineator, December 1912. Courtesy of the Trustees of the Boston Public Library.

The magazine's January 1913 issue featured "Motherless Children of Living Mothers" (Figure 23), telling the story of a New York widow who had been forced by poverty to commit her four children to a Catholic orphanage. Above the title of the feature story appeared the photographs of seven prominent officials, reformers, and clubwomen from around the nation who were working for mothers' pensions in their states.[44] The February issue included a broad overview of "1913 Styles in Laws: The New Models Now Being Shown to Women Customers in Our State Capitol Buildings at the Opening of the Annual Legislative Season."[45] The March issue celebrated the 1913 year's "Victory Number One" for mothers' pensions in Philadelphia.[46] And the April issue contained "Financing Motherhood," dramatizing more American cases and surveying European schemes for helping widows and orphans in straitened circumstances, and declaring: "In Order to Make Full Use of the Love of Mothers, the World is Forging a Chain of Practical Devices of which 'Widows' Pensions' is Only One Link" (Figure 24).[47] Rounding out its major efforts to publicize mothers' pensions, the *Delineator* financed a lecturer who toured women's clubs in Massachusetts, and the magazine's staff compiled a twenty-page pamphlet providing full technical details on legislation and proposals throughout the nation.[48]

During the crucial 1912–1914 period when many state legislatures were taking up the pension idea, other women's magazines and print media paralleled or followed the lead of the *Delineator* by running articles favorable to this new legislation. With a circulation of about 375,000, *Good Housekeeping* advocated "Pensioning the Widow and the Fatherless"; and with a circulation of over 2 million, *Collier's* discussed "A First Step Toward the Endowment of Motherhood."[49] Indeed, reports the historian Mark Leff, the "new idea found quick acceptance throughout the spectrum of Progressive magazines," and the "Scripps-McRae and Hearst chains both conducted editorial campaigns for widows' pensions, as did a number of locally based papers."[50]

Organized Women and the Spread of Mothers' Pensions

It would be a mistake, however, to envisage the nationwide mothers' pension movement simply as a media-orchestrated mobilization of scattered individual women. That would overlook the more impor-

"With all my worldly goods I thee endow"

Judge E. E. Porterfield
Of Missouri. Judge Porterfield was one of the principal promoters of the first real "widows' pension" law in the United States.

Mr. David F. Tilley
Mr. Tilley is a member of the Massachusetts "widows' pensions" commission (of which Prof. Robert F. Foerster, of Harvard University, is chairman) and is also a member of the State Board of Charities.

Miss Helen M. Winslow
Miss Winslow, on behalf of The Delineator, has lectured on the subject of "widows' pensions" before sixty women's clubs in Massachusetts.

Mrs. William Grant Brown
President of the New York City Federation of Women's Clubs, which has 80,000 members. Mrs. Brown is one of the most active leaders in the movement for a "widows' pension" law in New York State.

Mrs. Clara Cahill Park
The existence of the Massachusetts Commission to Study the Question of the Support of Dependent Minor Children of Widowed Mothers is largely due to the efforts of Mrs. Park.

Mr. Frank S. Shankland
Iowa legislator. Having heard of "widows' pensions," Mr. Shankland energetically started in to get a "widows' pension" law for Iowa.

Judge Ben B. Lindsey
Judge Lindsey drew up the "Mothers' Compensation Act" which was presented to the voters of Colorado last November under the initiative and referendum law.

MOTHERLESS CHILDREN
OF LIVING MOTHERS

There are Many Thousands of Them in the United States. Let us Give Them Back to their Mothers. Three Cities have Shown Us How. The Delineator, in a practical way, is assisting in this Reconstruction of Homes. Will you? You can.

BY WILLIAM HARD

Figure 23

Source: *The Delineator*, January 1913, p. 19. Courtesy of the Trustees of the Boston Public Library

"With all my worldly goods I thee endow"

FINANCING MOTHERHOOD

In Order to Make Full Use of the Love of Mothers, the World is Forging
a Chain of Practical Devices of which "Widows'
Pensions" is Only One Link

BY WILLIAM HARD

Figure 24
Source: The Delineator, April 1913, p. 263. Courtesy of the Trustees of the Boston Public Library.

tant educational and lobbying intiatives undertaken by the large women's federations, whose advocacy for the new benefits reached into most if not all states of the nation. The *Delineator*'s articles themselves influenced women's *groups* as well as individual female readers.[51] What is more, certain initiatives by women's groups on behalf of mothers' pensions started *before* William Hard began his campaign in the *Delineator,* and may actually have helped to inspire it. The references in the magazine's December 1912 editorial to ongoing efforts by clubwomen in California and Massachusetts suggest as much.[52] The *Delineator* had a tradition of pursuing social reforms in close cooperation with the General Federation of Women's Clubs; and Hard's series on legal reforms for women, including his discussions of mothers' pensions, made repeated references to current efforts by state federations and other women's clubs, such as the National Congress of Mothers.[53] As we shall soon see, the Mothers' Congress endorsed mothers' pensions well before Hard wrote his articles in the *Delineator.* And one of the national leaders of the Mothers' Congress was Phoebe Hearst, whose family owned the nationwide Hearst newspaper chain that editorialized on behalf of mothers' pensions. Given all of these indications that women's groups mattered as much or more than the print media, we need to explore in turn the contributions of the General Federation and the Mothers' Congress to the nationwide drive for mothers' pension laws.

Support from the General Federation of Women's Clubs

At the national level, the General Federation of Women's Clubs discussed and endorsed legal reforms for women, including mothers' pensions, during its 1912 Biennial in San Francisco. In the portion of the convention organized by the Federation's Department on Industrial and Social Conditions, Miss Mary Wood argued for mothers' pensions in her address on "The Legal Side of Industrial Betterment"—drawing, interestingly enough, a positive analogy to soldiers' benefits.

> One of the causes of pauperism among women is to be found in the large proportion of women who are left widows with families of small children . . . Such widows should receive from the state, a pension sufficient to enable each to look after children and home.

This pension would relieve the stigma of pauperism—felt under existing Charity relief . . . The woman who produces citizens and soldiers should be placed in a class with the disabled soldier, during the period she is unable to earn for herself and children.[54]

William Hard also addressed the Biennial on "The State and the Home," summarizing the various legal disadvantages faced by married women and widows and calling upon clubwomen to work for a series of legislative reforms.[55] Although Hard did not explicitly discuss mothers' pensions, the Biennial officially adopted a resolution that encompassed this reform along with others he had discussed. "*Resolved,*" said the General Federation,

that among the continuous interests of organized women, in these times when the home is shaken by economic changes, there should be a progressive legislative policy for the greater honor and greater stability of home life. Such a policy should include laws delivering the married woman from all legal disabilities not equally imposed on the married man; laws dealing effectively with the great and growing evils of non-support and desertion of children by their fathers; laws granting to the mother equal rights with the father in relation to their children; and laws adequately protecting the widow against unnecessary impoverishment at her husband's death. We believe that the function of motherhood should bring to a woman increased security rather than increased insecurity and that the legislative policy above outlined, in safeguarding motherhood, safeguards the race.[56]

By 1912, clearly, mothers' pensions appeared as potential publicly funded benefits for needy women in their capacity as mothers. Significantly, however, much of the perceived need for such benefits had arisen earlier in the context of child labor reforms, designed to protect the welfare of poor children.[57] Certain groups within the General Federation, along with Consumers' Leagues, local charitable groups, and associations favoring child labor reforms, had for some years been involved with voluntary, private measures—often called "widows' scholarships"—that were, in a sense, forerunners to mothers' pensions. Reformers who worked from the early 1900s on behalf of tough child labor laws and compulsory schooling often found that impoverished widows felt deprived of the wages their children might earn. Thus reform groups sometimes tried to offer the privately funded "scholarships" to replace the wages the child might have earned or to cover the poor family's expenses while the widow's children went to school rather than into the factory.

During 1903, women within the National Consumers' League (NCL) and the Illinois Consumers' League promoted the establishment of widows' scholarships, working through the GFWC's Committee on the Industrial Question as It Affects Women and Children, which was chaired by Mrs. Frederick [Maud] Nathan, vice president of the National Consumers' League, and also through the Federation's Committee on Child Labor, which was chaired by Jane Addams.[58] A circular advocating widows' scholarships was drafted by the Illinois Consumers' League and State Federation of Women's Clubs, and then recommended by Jane Addams to the national Federation, which ultimately sent a version of it out to local women's clubs across the nation.[59] As Florence Kelley observed in the 1903 Annual Report of the National Consumers' League, if this "method of caring for dependent families . . . should be generally taken up in the hundreds of manufacturing centers represented in the General Federation of Women's Clubs, and in the 53 centers where Leagues exist, the child-labor problem would be on the way toward a prompt solution. For the fear of injuring the widowed mother has been a serious obstacle to the proper legislation for the protection of the orphan child."[60]

In practice, of course, nothing so sweeping developed. Widows' scholarships were funded in the early 1900s on a small scale in scattered localities, by such groups as the Illinois Consumers' League in partnership with the Bureau of Charities, the Public Education Association and child labor committees in Philadelphia, the New York City Child Labor Committee, the Associated Charities of Minneapolis, the Inter-Church Child Labor Committee of Grand Rapids, Michigan, and the Los Angeles District Federation of Women's Clubs.[61] Obviously, these private efforts were far from sufficient to meet the needs of dependent mothers and children, but they probably did help to lay a groundwork for the later transition to public legislation. This transition started even before the label "mothers' pensions" took hold: At the 1910 Biennial of the General Federation of Women's Clubs, the Michigan Federation reported that "at the coming session of our Legislature, [we] will introduce a bill of our own entitled 'An Act to Provide for the Pensioning of Indigent Children of School Age.'"[62]

As always in the relatively decentralized General Federation of Women's Clubs, state Federations became the key promoters of mothers' pensions once they became a legislative issue. Table 9 summarizes the evidence for this. At the 1912 and subsequent Biennials, a dozen state Federations proudly reported specific activities on behalf of mothers' pension laws; and I have discovered from other sources that at least eleven more state Federations also supported mothers' pension legislation. Already in June 1912, the Massachusetts Federation reported to the GFWC Biennial its support for that state's recently appointed "commission to study the conditions of widowed mothers with minor children"; and the Washington Federation listed "Pension for Mothers" as one of the bills to be "presented to our Legislature next winter."[63] At the 1914 GFWC Biennial, the Michigan and Utah Federations claimed to have helped pass mothers' pension laws in their states, and the Florida Federation reported the initiation of study classes on the subject.[64] In 1916 there were similar claims of effective support for new mothers' pension laws from the state Federations in Kansas, Maryland, Missouri (where the county measure was extended statewide), Nevada, Oklahoma, and Wyoming.[65] That year, too, the Florida Federation proudly claimed to have supported a law to create a new state commission to study the need for mothers' pensions—with "two club women appointed" to serve on it.[66] After the 1916 Biennial, state Federations stopped reporting activities on behalf of mothers' pensions, perhaps because the Federations' efforts really were concentrated into just four years, and perhaps because the coming of World War I precipitated a change of focus in what the state presidents discussed in their necessarily brief reports to the national Biennials. I suspect that both reasons hold to some degree: after 1915 (a peak year along with 1913 for legislation), there was less state-level activity on behalf of mothers' pensions, and in all probability less of what did happen was reported to the national level of the General Federation.[67]

Leadership and Persistence from the National Congress of Mothers

The National Congress of Mothers did at least as much as the Federations of Women's Clubs to spur the enactment of mothers'

Table 9. Women's voluntary associations
and the spread of state-level mothers' pension enactments

Year of enactment and state	Activities undertaken by		
	Federation of Women's Clubs (or member clubs)	Congress of Mothers (or member clubs)	Other women's groups
1911			
Illinois*	[yes]	[yes]	
1913			
California	yes	yes	State Legislative Council of Women (53 groups)
Colorado	yes		
Idaho		yes	
Iowa		yes	
Massachusetts	yes	yes	
Michigan	yes		
Minnesota	yes		
Nebraska			
New Hampshire	yes		
New Jersey*		[yes]	
Nevada	yes		
Ohio	yes		Consumers' League
Oregon		yes	
Pennsylvania	yes		Mothers' Pension League of Allegheny County
South Dakota	yes		
Utah	yes		
Washington	yes		
Wisconsin	yes		
1914			
Arizona*			
1915			
Kansas	yes	yes	Women's Christian Temperance Union
Montana			League of Good Government Clubs
New York	yes		
North Dakota*			
Oklahoma	yes		
Tennessee	yes	yes	Women's Christian Temperance Union

Table 9   *(continued)*

Year of enactment and state	Activities undertaken by		
	Federation of Women's Clubs (or member clubs)	Congress of Mothers (or member clubs)	Other women's groups
West Virginia	yes		
Wyoming	yes		
1916			
Maryland	yes	yes	
1917			
Arkansas			
Delaware		yes	Consumers' League
Maine		yes	
Missouri	yes	yes	Consumers' League
(state-wide law)			
Texas		yes	
Vermont	yes		
1918			
Virginia			
1919			
Connecticut		yes	
Florida	yes		
Indiana		yes	
1920			
Louisiana			
Laws passed in 1920s			
North Carolina (1923)			
Rhode Island (1923)			
Kentucky (1928)			
Mississippi (1928)		yes	
Laws passed in early 1930s			
Alabama (1931)			
New Mexico (1931)			
States without laws in 1935			
Georgia*			
South Carolina			

* Please read the special explanation about this state in Appendix 2, "Sources for Table 9 and Figure 27."

Note: Brackets indicate that the known endorsements came after initial legislation was passed.

pensions. The efforts of the National Congress did not reach into as many states as those of the Federations of Women's Clubs. This is partially explained by the fact that, as Figure 25 shows, state branches of the Mothers' Congress existed in only twenty-two states by 1911 (and still in only thirty-six states as late as 1920). Meanwhile, Federations of Women's Clubs were organized in all forty-eight states by 1911.[68] Yet the advocacy of the National Congress of Mothers for mothers' pensions was not confined to a few years; it persisted until these laws were enacted almost everywhere, as one can see by scanning Table 9. In my view, this association of elite and middle-class married ladies deserves much of the credit for transforming an idea initially sponsored by a few juvenile court judges into a national social movement and legislative reality. Welfare historians argue that the mothers' pension movement had no coordinating national organizational center; but to a man and woman they have overlooked the priority and clarity, as well as the consistency, of the National Congress's efforts. Early in 1911—soon after the Kansas City measure was enacted, before the pioneering Illinois law was passed, and over a year before William Hard and the *Delineator* took up the cause—the National Congress of Mothers formally endorsed mothers' pensions and nationally dramatized strong maternalist and social-justice arguments on their behalf. As the organization's president would later correctly claim, "the movement for mothers' pensions was inaugurated by the Congress" in 1911. "At that time no other organization had taken up the subject, and many actively opposed it."[69]

Mothers' pensions were a logical, ideologically comfortable cause for the National Congress of Mothers. From its inception, this organization had celebrated the special importance of mother-love for the proper nurture of children, and had concerned itself with the fate of orphans and poor children as well as the offspring of intact and economically secure families. In this context, at the First International Congress in America for the Welfare of the Child in 1908, the members of the National Congress listened to Edwin D. Solenberger of the Children's Aid Society of Philadelphia advocate "school scholarships" in terms that foreshadowed the rationales that would soon be offered for mothers' pensions. "In considering the kind of children to be placed out," Solenberger declared to the the assembled delegates:

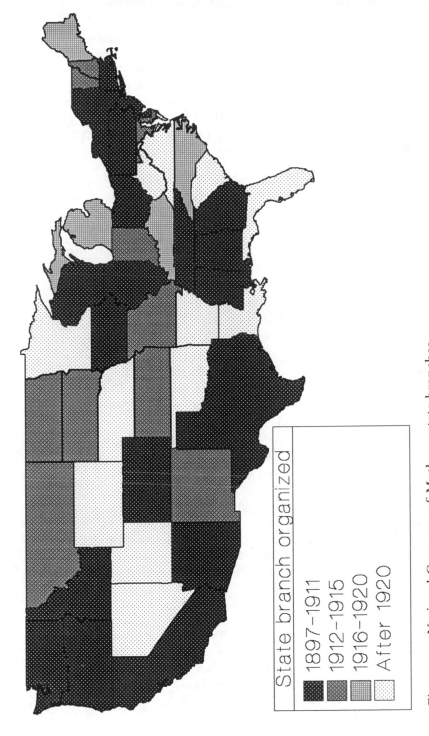

Figure 25 National Congress of Mothers: state branches

Source: Golden Jubilee History, 1897–1947 (Chicago: National Congress of Parents and Teachers, 1947), p. 199.

State branch organized

1897–1911
1912–1915
1916–1920
After 1920

> I wish to enter a protest against breaking up families unnecessarily. I do not believe that children should be taken under ordinary circumstances from a good mother merely because of poverty . . . If she has been left a widow or has been deserted and is unable to bring up her family it is far wiser to provide enough relief to enable her to keep her children. We should make a clear distinction between pecuniary incapacity and moral incapacity. A good mother is a splendid asset to society.[70]

Over many years, too, the Congress developed intimate working relations with juvenile courts and their judges and probation officers. Thus, once public funding for mothers' pensions began to be advocated by reformist judges like Porterfield and Lindsey, it was easy the members of the Congress to appreciate the practical importance of such monies as a tool in the hands of juvenile court judges anxious to keep families intact and help widows supervise their children.[71]

The opening speech in the campaign the National Congress waged for mothers' pension legislation occurred in late April 1911 at the Second International Congress on Child Welfare. The assembled delegates heard a remarkable address on "The State's Duty to Fatherless Children," published some months later as an article in *Child-Welfare Magazine*.[72] The speaker was Mrs. G. Harris Robertson, President of the Tennessee Congress of Mothers, "whose work among mothers and children had emphasized the crying need for . . . recognition of motherhood."[73] She could hardly have been more eloquent as she spoke to the ladies and friends of the National Congress of Mothers gathered in Washington, DC:

> My dear friends of the states and other nations: I have been asked to speak to you of a type of home which is a blot upon the name of civilization . . . This semblance of a home that I speak of is a broken family circle, shattered by loss of father, the breadwinner—the home of the helpless widow burdened with little children . . .
>
> These homes cannot *even be considered* a local care, for they dot and tarnish every community . . . And until measures are drafted for their betterment, they should be thorns in the flesh of every thinking citizen . . . [W]e cannot afford to let a mother, one who has divided her body by creating other lives for the good of the state, one who has contributed to citizenship, be classed as a pauper, a dependent. She must be given value received by her nation, and stand as one honored.[74]

How do we help?, Mrs. Robertson queried rhetorically. Neither private charity nor workmen's compensation are "far-reaching enough . . . These things done for the few mean next to nothing."[75] She argued instead for "a national commission and appropriation" to provide regular and liberal sums to needy mothers, along with an "advisor and friend" who would "supervise and [make] suggest[ions] . . . to the lonely mother."[76]

Quite remarkably, Mrs. Robertson also advocated that "our provision include the deserted wife, and the mother who has never been a wife . . . To-day let us honor the *mother* wherever found—if she has given a citizen to the nation, then the nation owes something to her."[77] Mrs. Robertson squarely identified the issue as poverty and, in conclusion, spoke directly to the possible political fears of her more conservative listeners:

> Think what a dreadful thing it is to tear the children from the natural mother on account of *poverty*. A good mother, a loving mother, who must submit to seeing her children carried to public institutions or leave them, while she works at a factory or mill, to wander in the streets . . . By not providing for the fatherless homes we are forcing criminals upon our state, we are stifling the possibilities of many children by crushing out of the mother the joy she should feel in the high vocation of motherhood.
>
> Do not rise up in indignation to call this Socialism—it is the sanest of statesmanship. If our public mind is maternal, loving and generous, wanting to save and develop all, our Government will express this sentiment . . . We need no [*sic*, not] fear to create idleness by this most just provision . . . [E]very step we make toward establishing government along these lines means an advance toward the Kingdom of Peace.[78]

"The appeal was so convincing," the president of the National Congress later recounted about Mrs. Robertson's address, "that the National Congress of Mothers unanimously recommended that its State Branches should make it their work for the coming year."[79] With no equivocation about preferring private instead of public relief, the relevant 1911 resolution declared:

> *Resolved:* That it is the sense of this Congress that families should, if possible, be held together. That the mother is the best caretaker for her children. That when necessary to prevent the breaking up of the home the State should provide a certain sum for the support

of the children instead of taking them from her and placing them elsewhere at the expense of the State. And

Be it Further Resolved: That each branch of this Congress, located in the several States, be urged to assist in securing such legislation as will accomplish this result.[80]

After 1911, the Congress of Mothers worked for the enactment of mothers' pensions in many states. The next international convention in 1914 reiterated the endorsement of mothers' pension legislation.[81] Officers of the Mothers' Congress testified, wrote letters, and published articles on behalf of relevant bills.[82] The Congress's official journal, *Child-Welfare Magazine,* regularly included feature stories on mothers' pensions, as well as accounts of particular bills and the efforts of state branches to secure their enactment. Such stories and reports appeared in the magazine in January, May, June, October, and December 1912; in January, February, March, May, June, August, October, and November 1913; in February, May, and December 1914; in January, February, March, April, May, June, July, November, and December 1915; in January, March, April, May, and December 1916; in April, May, June, July, and September 1917; in November and December 1918; in January, March, April, May, September, and November 1919; and in January and June 1920. Significantly, these pieces in *Child-Welfare Magazine* continued long after the 1912–13 peak of interest in mothers' pensions, ensuring that the subject remained on the agenda for members of the Mothers' Congress. Features about mothers' pensions also appeared in publications of the state branches.[83]

Advocacy articles in *Child-Welfare Magazine* carried such titles as "Putting Motherhood on the State Pay-Roll" and "A Recognition of Motherhood—The Mothers' Pension."[84] They argued that "this recognition of motherhood is not charity. It is justice to childhood[,] economy to the state, and given for service rendered just as the soldier service is recognized. Charity has nothing to do with it. The mothers are not to be classed with paupers for no court would grant the pension to mothers who come under that category."[85] Interestingly, one article on "A Wider Pension Move" reiterated Mrs. Robertson's call for aid to unmarried mothers, concluding "Let us work for a Mother's Pension, not a Widow's Pension."[86]

Although the National Congress of Mothers was a more centralized and less ramified association than the General Federation of Women's Clubs, state branches of the Mothers' Congress were important promoters of mothers' pension legislation. The editors of *Child-Welfare Magazine* claimed that every state branch of the Mothers' Congress took up the issue.[87] This may have been true, yet the state and local affiliates of the Congress that definitely engaged in legislative advocacy during the 1910s were located in California, Connecticut, Idaho, Illinois, Indiana, Iowa, Kansas, Maine, Maryland, Massachusetts, Mississippi, Missouri, New Jersey, Oregon, Tennessee, and Texas.[88] As Table 9 suggests, Congress branches were often active in states where the Federated Clubs do not appear to have been very involved. Of course, cooperation occurred in many states between the Federation and the Congress; but there may also have been some deliberate or de facto trade-offs, with the Federation taking the lead in some states and the Congress in others.

In some states, grand alliances of different women's groups promoted mothers' pensions; and in others special ad hoc groups appear to have played a crucial role in coordinating women's support for mothers' pension legislation. In Tennessee, the 1915 "Bill for the Partial Support of Certain Poor Women" was co-sponsored by the Women's Christian Temperance Union, the Federation of Women's Clubs, and the Congress of Mothers.[89] In Pennsylvania, a group of young women organized the Mothers' Pension League of Allegheny County to push for the mothers' pension law that passed in 1913.[90] And by 1912 in California, a group called the California League for the Protection of Motherhood was campaigning for mothers' pensions along with the California State Federation of Women's Clubs, the California Congress of Mothers, the Women's Christian Temperance Union, and forty-nine other women's groups in an umbrella lobbying organization, the California State Legislative Council of Women.[91] Although no doubt a small group within this impressive galaxy of California women's organizations, the League for the Protection of Motherhood had prominent "patronesses" from the ranks of elite married women active in other women's organizations. And it is of special interest because it advocated mothers' pensions in conjunction with maternity benefits for working women and health care for all poor women and children. The organization's letterhead proclaimed that it was "Organized for the Purpose of Securing Legislation":

1st—Forbidding the employment of working women five weeks before and five weeks after confinement.

2nd—Providing for the payment by the State, to employed mothers, of a pension amounting to 50% of their wages, during their enforced idleness as above.

3rd—Providing for the payment to widowed mothers, or mothers of dependent children, of the pro rata per child now paid by the State to institutions for the support of such orphaned or dependent children.

4th—Affording free hospital facilities for dependent mothers and infants.[92]

The program of this California League was certainly much broader than the support of widows who remained outside of the paid labor force; it wanted to help mothers whether or not they worked for wages.

When it came to actually achieving mothers' pension legislation, how did women's groups proceed within the states? We have some indications, especially from nuts-and-bolts articles that appeared in *Child-Welfare Magazine.* In Massachusetts, Mrs. Clara Cahill Park, vice president of the state's branch of the Congress of Mothers, successfully worked for a state investigatory commission and was appointed to serve as its secretary. She helped guide the commission to a positive recommendation and, later, mobilized Massachusetts women's organizations in support of the commission's position.[93] We noted above that something similar happened in Florida, where the Federation of Women's Clubs worked for the creation of a public commission with representatives from its own ranks.

As for states where no official commission was appointed prior to the enactment of mothers' pensions, the Oregon Congress reported in the greatest detail on its activities, providing a glimpse of how events may have transpired in other states, although probably not with comparable organization or intensity of effort in most cases. According to the secretary of the Oregon Congress's Committee on Widows' Pensions:

At the Child-Welfare Conference held in Portland, Oregon, November, 1911, Mrs. G. H. Robertson's address, "What the State Owes to its Fatherless Children," was read, and during the discussion that followed, a motion carried that the Oregon Congress of

Mothers prepare a Widows' Pension Bill to be presented to the next Legislature. The President . . . named a special committee . . . to proceed toward enactment of such Legislation . . .

After securing all obtainable data from the various states that have pension laws, suggestions were asked from our Juvenile Court, our Child Labor Commissioner, and our Charity Board, and from this mass of information the committee improvised a bill . . . Copies of the bill were sent to every Grange and to every club in the State, asking for their endorsement; also, to every newspaper in the State with letters asking them to give the bill publicity. In most cases it was received with approval and splendid support. As soon after the election. . . as the names of the Legislators were secured by the committee, a copy of the bill with a letter of appeal was sent to each one.

Then ninety petitions were prepared and sent to co-workers in various counties, asking them to have them filled with signatures of voters requesting their senators and representatives to support the measure . . .

Wherever possible personal calls were made upon members of the legislature by the committee, and where this was not possible letters were written asking for further suggestions. After receiving these suggestions, some amendments were made to the original draft.

The committee has been greatly aided by the splendid article [*sic*] in *The Child-Welfare Magazine* and "The Delineator" and by the helpful suggestions received from Judge Ben Lindsey, Judge Porterfield, of Kansas City, . . . Judge Wilbur D. Curtis, of Los Angeles . . . [the] Juvenile Protective Association of Chicago, and the Mothers' Congress of Idaho and of Washington.

Some idea of the work done may be realized when I say that over one thousand letters and over 2500 pages of typewritten matter were sent out over the State, and this, with seventeen days of personal work done by different members of the committee at the State Capital, which is fifty miles distant from our home city, was done at a total cost of less than $100 to the Congress, and how well the work was done I leave for you to glean from the fact that the bill has passed both houses *just as presented* with only one dissenting vote, and to-day, February 8, 1913, was signed by Governor West.[94]

"Mothers'-pension provisions," as Mark Leff points out, "usually carried by near unanimous tallies; opposition successes depended upon preventing the bills from coming to a vote."[95] But such obstruc-

tionist tactics rarely succeeded for long in the face of public education and agitation by proponents of mothers' pensions, who could
wholeheartedly wield a rhetoric of sacred motherhood that was hard
for others to gainsay. So resonant was this rhetoric with the mores
of the day, that legislators might echo it directly in their speeches
justifying mothers' pensions—as did an Indiana Representative who
reportedly declared: "We make an awful mistake when we assume
. . . that we can add or take away from a mother's love . . . It is a
jeweled diadem placed upon the brow of a finite creature that the
world may honor and obey . . . [I]t is cherished as life's chiefest
beatitude, wielding empire over the domain of human tenderness."[96]

Explaining Policy Diffusion across the States

By 1920, over three-quarters of the states had acted positively on
mothers' pensions, and four more states plus the District of Columbia
passed such legislation during the next decade, before the onset of
the Great Depression and the New Deal. We can probe more deeply
into the patterns by which mothers' pensions spread so widely and
quickly across the states. In a 1973 article about the diffusion of
legislative innovations across U.S. states, the political scientist Virginia Gray noted that the timing of adoption of mothers' aid laws
did *not* fit the usual pattern of a gradual cumulation of innovations
as various potential adopters interact with, and learn from, one
another.[97] Instead, after two adoptions occurred in 1911, mothers'
pensions were very suddenly adopted by eighteen states in 1913,
with nine more innovations quickly following in 1914 and 1915 and
eleven more between 1916 and 1920. As a little-known sociologist,
Ada Davis, pointed out in an article published in 1930, "Aside from
the central section of the country, where laws were passed mostly
between 1917 and 1919, and the absence of any laws in the block of
states in the [Deep] South [that is, South Carolina, Alabama, and
Georgia], there seems to be no dependence upon geographical location in the matter of the time the laws appeared."[98] Davis maintained that a nationwide "movement" was responsible for the rapid
spread of these laws "independently of spatial limitations or relations." Table 10 and Figure 26 suggest that Davis was basically correct, although virtually all of the western states, including the Rocky
Mountain states, did enact mothers' pensions by 1915.

Table 10.   Enactment of mothers' pension laws by time period and region

Time period	Region			
	East	Midwest	West	South
1911–13	Massachusetts New Hampshire New Jersey Pennsylvania	Illinois Iowa Michigan Minnesota Nebraska Ohio South Dakota Wisconsin	California Colorado Idaho Nevada Oregon Utah Washington	
1914–15	New York	Kansas North Dakota West Virginia	Arizona Montana Wyoming	Oklahoma Tennessee
1916–17	Delaware Maine Maryland Vermont	Missouri		Arkansas Texas
1918–20	Connecticut	Indiana		Florida Louisiana Virginia
1923–28	Rhode Island (1923)			Kentucky (1928) Mississippi (1928) North Carolina (1923)
1931–34			New Mexico (1931)	Alabama (1931)
After 1935				Georgia South Carolina

What explains the tempos and patterns (mapped in Figure 26) by which mothers' pension enactments spread across the United States? A statistical study that I have done with several collaborators indicates that the timing of state-level enactments of mothers' pensions was not at all a byproduct of economic modernization.[99] Although political scientists have argued that more urbanized, more industrial-

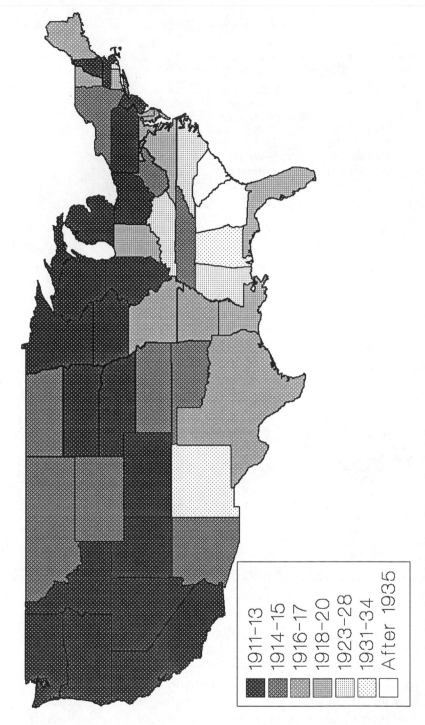

Figure 26 Mothers' pension laws: dates of enactment

ized, and wealthier U.S. states are likely to adopt new kinds of legislation more quickly than other states, this pattern does not hold for mothers' pension enactments.[100] Instead, the literacy of state populations was by far the most important general predictor of which states would enact mothers' pensions sooner than others. Many smaller, less industrial, and less urban states—including the Rocky Mountain states—had relatively high literacy rates in 1910, and were also among the earliest enactors of mothers' pensions even though these states were not usually among the earliest to adopt new kinds of laws. Of course, literacy rates are a very general variable, and we need to probe further to figure out exactly what political and social processes were at work in the various states.

Was electoral politics perhaps decisive? Virginia Gray argues that "Progressive influence," which she links to the Progressive Party's fortunes in state-level elections just before 1913, was responsible for the large wave of early adoptions in that year.[101] Her findings are not as compelling as they might be, because she merely contrasts the eighteen adopters of 1913 to all twenty-eight states that eventually adopted after 1913, including those that waited until the 1930s. If one examines the percentage of presidential votes that went to the Progressive Party in 1912 in each state, one finds that only half of the eighteen states that adopted mothers' pensions in 1913 were more than two percentage points above the national average, while four out of nine (44 percent) of the 1914 and 1915 adopters were also more than two percentage points above the national average for the Progressive presidential vote.[102] This is not a very big contrast. The real dividing line falls between 1915 and 1916. Only two of the fifteen adopters between 1916 and 1928 were "progressive" states by this measure, and they both enacted mothers' pensions in 1917. We can tentatively conclude that from 1912 through 1915 votes for the Progressive Party may well have clustered in states where mothers' pensions (along with other social reforms) were more readily enacted. Yet at most we are talking about a facilitating contextual influence, because the national Progressive Party did not make mothers' pensions an explicit legislative priority, and only rarely did Progressives actually win elections at any level. More typically, where they mattered at all, Progressives prompted changes within the major parties, especially the Republicans. In Wisconsin, to give perhaps the strongest example of this kind of influence, progressively oriented

Republicans listed mothers' pensions in their 1912 platform and enacted them in 1913.[103]

More generally, the states that adopted mothers' pensions relatively early—whether we define "early" as 1913 alone, or also consider 1914 and 1915—were diverse on many potentially relevant electoral-political measures. These states included Progressive strongholds and places where the Progressive Party did very poorly; states where Republicans of various stripes were dominant; and states that granted women's suffrage early, along with states that delayed women's suffrage, in many cases until the national Constitutional amendment in 1920. In our statistical study, there turned out to be significant tendencies for earlier enactments of mothers' pensions to be associated with more competitive and participatory state elections; with weaker Democrats and stronger Republicans; with higher percentages of presidential votes cast during the 1910s for all reformist third parties (including the Progressive, Socialist, Prohibition, and Farmer-Labor parties); and with the fact that a state granted women's suffrage at some point before the Nineteenth Amendment in 1920. But none of these variables referring to the patterns of electoral politics in the states proved to be as powerful in predicting earlier mothers' pension enactments as the other key variables I am about to discuss.

"If it is to the advantage of the measure to be nonpartisan," argued Ada Davis in her evaluation of the movement that spread mothers' pensions across the United States, "then we find that the method of proceeding is by the development of an effective lobby with its dependence on agitation and . . . publicity."[104] "[A]dvocates of such measures were particularly anxious and worked hard to keep the issue from becoming a party issue."[105] We know that supporters of mothers' pensions did not usually try to link them to partisan party programs, and that such laws usually passed state legislatures by large bipartisan majorities. Likewise, we have seen that supporters of mothers' pensions tried to keep them separate from the matter of women's suffrage. This was wise, because it enhanced women's ability to influence legislative outcomes in the many states that were still resistant to the suffrage, and it allowed women regardless of their attitudes about suffrage to work together to affect the views of the public and of legislators of many political persuasions. "[E]ven if the parties lost no votes," Davis observed, "they could not afford to lose the good will of the women who are capable of affecting political affairs by other methods than by voting. 'They are able to talk'."[106] "Mothers' pension laws," concludes Ada Davis, ". . . passed because of strong emotional public opinion in their favor; because of effective lobbying; and because of the number and strength of organizations whose appeals to legislators, of whatever party, could not be ignored."[107] "Most effective in their influence were the organizations working from outside upon legislators," and Davis identifies the press and women's clubs as the ones who waged the campaigns to shape public opinion in favor of mothers' pensions.[108]

The qualitative and quantitative evidence I have gathered suggests that Davis's interpretation accounts for both the temporal patterns and the extent of the enactments of mothers' pensions during the Progressive Era. The sudden burst of mothers' pension legislation in 1913, cutting across a diverse range of states, corresponded to the *Delineator*'s advocacy in late 1912 and 1913. It also followed soon after the National Congress of Mothers launched its campaign for mothers' pensions in 1911 (bearing in mind that practically no state legislatures met in 1912), and came soon after the General Federation of Women's Clubs endorsed and publicized mothers' pensions and other legal reforms for women at its 1912 Biennial. The fact that literacy was strongly associated with the priority of enactments makes sense when we consider that the presence of more people able to read could well have facilitated the communication of ideas about mothers' pensions through newspapers, women's magazines, and networks of women's clubs. Many less industrial and urban states—including many western states that enacted mothers' pensions early—were among those with highly literate populations in 1910 as well as higher densities of women's clubs per capita.

After 1913, women's groups continued to press for mothers' pensions in the states that had not yet passed them. In the words of Mary Ritter Beard (probably written in late 1913), "Mothers' pension laws now exist in seventeen states, the great majority of which passed the laws within the last year, a year in which women have been their busiest at urging this legislation . . . In all the states where home assistance has been secured for dependent mothers, women have agitated and lobbied for this measure. In states which do not yet have such legislation, women's clubs and organizations have this legislation as one of their demands."[109] The National Congress of

Mothers and the General Federation of Women's Clubs were ideal federal networks, able to communicate legislative models and arguments for mothers' pensions to state and local groups in a position to organize effective lobbying in a variety of states with diverse socioeconomic and political characteristics. Overall, as Table 9 (above) shows, state affiliates of the Congress of Mothers and the Federation of Women's Clubs—as well as other women's groups, such as the State Legislative Council of Women in California, the Consumers' League of Ohio, and the Mothers' Pension League of Allegheny County, Pennsylvania—were active in promoting mothers' pension in sixteen (or 89 percent) of the eighteen states that adopted mothers' pensions in 1913. And women's groups were active prior to the initial legislation in at least thirty-two (or 80 percent) of the forty states that enacted mothers' pensions between 1911 and 1920.

Figure 27 graphically presents the information in Table 9, all that I have been able to discover about the presence and timing of one or more women's groups' endorsements of mothers' pensions in each state. In our statistical study, the variable corresponding to Figure 27 was by far the most powerful predictor in multiple regression models of the timing of state enactments of mothers' pensions. Where and when organized women took up the cause, they virtually always succeeded—although in some states it took longer than in others. Moreover, the failure of women's organizations in certain states to endorse mothers' pensions was definitely associated with the failure of those states to enact mothers' pensions until very late (or not at all prior to 1935).

Characteristics of states, as well as related endorsement decisions by women's clubs, probably explain why some states had the debate over mothers' pensions earlier than others (with earlier debates usually followed by earlier enactments). Our statistical study revealed that the prior public policies and wage-labor-force characteristics of the various states in 1910 influenced how quickly they enacted mothers' pension laws after that. States with stricter child labor laws and higher levels of per capita expenditures on public schools in 1910 tended to enact mothers' pensions sooner. This makes sense, because such states were already committed to keeping children out of the wage-labor force; therefore groups within those states were likely to view mothers' pensions as a logical next policy step, a way to give widowed mothers the wherewithal to keep their children in school,

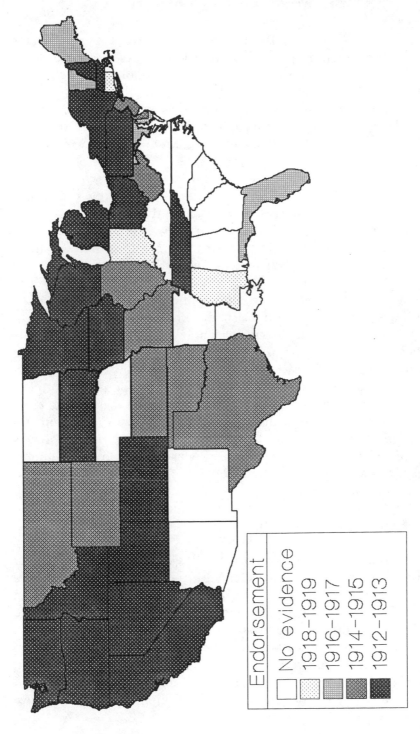

Figure 27 Endorsements of mothers' pensions by women's groups
Sources: See Appendix 2.

living at home, and away from wage labor.[110] What is more, states with relatively high proportions of females over age ten engaged in wage labor, and states with relatively high proportions of child laborers in manufacturing, were likely to enact mothers' pensions late or not at all. In such states, widows and fatherless children were more likely to be surviving through wage-labor; and there may well have been entrenched economic interests who wanted to keep it that way.

All in all, of course, those states with lower public school expenditures and weaker child labor laws, and with more women and children working for wages, were mostly the same states where women's groups either did not take up the cause of mothers' pensions or else had to struggle for many years before the legislature responded.[111] The latter was the case in Mississippi, where the Congress of Mothers endorsed mothers' pensions in 1919, but the law did not pass until 1928. Again, these patterns make good sense. In such states as Georgia, South Carolina, Rhode Island, New Mexico, and Mississippi, women's groups probably considered improvements in the public schools or in child labor laws to be more pressing priorities than mothers' pensions. Women's groups in these and other laggard states were often weaker organizationally than elsewhere, and they invariably faced political and socioeconomic environments unfriendly to many kinds of social reform. Thus women's groups in the laggard states had to orient their energies to reforms that seemed more basic than mothers' pensions. Meanwhile, in most other U.S. states—including many not-so-urban urban and industrial states with lots of educated people—women's groups were strong and could concentrate on supplementing already-enacted public policies about children with the new pensions that would help widowed mothers keep their families intact.

In sum, if the "'Widows' Pensions' idea . . . spread more rapidly than any other humanitarian idea" during the Progressive Era, we can reasonably conclude that this did not occur just because of an automatic consensus.[112] It happened in significant part through the deliberate, organized, state-by-state efforts of associations of (mostly) married women, who worked in conjunction with a few key reformers—particularly with reformist juvenile court judges and with William Hard, the former social settlement resident much influenced by Jane Addams, who became a journalist willing to pursue legislative reforms through writing for women's magazines. This was the coalition that brought about an exception to the usual reluctance of middle-class public opinion during the Progressive Era to countenance public social spending. This coalition used women's pre-suffrage political styles to make claims for poor widows on behalf of values traditionally associated with the feminine domestic sphere of more privileged women. Consequently, adult women as widowed mothers became in most states the legitimate recipients of public monetary benefits not defined as poor relief. Even though mothers' pension laws were merely state-level enabling statutes, their enactment was a meaningful victory for organized U.S. women during the 1910s. This victory was all the more telling because it occurred at a time in the history of the United States when—given the weaknesses of bureaucratic and class politics, and reformers' reactions against political "corruption"—adult males could not become legitimate beneficiaries of public social spending for workers.

Early Mothers' Pensions in Practice: Intended and Unintended Results

The women's groups and social reformers who led the original campaigns for public aid for needy mothers had a vision of what these new laws were supposed to accomplish. According to that vision, widowed mothers, and perhaps other mothers who lacked the economic support of male breadwinners, were to be enabled to keep their children out of institutions. While avoiding low-wage drudgery, they were to be given regular money to sustain good homes for their families. To be sure, public aid would go only to mothers deemed—after careful investigation—to be able and willing to keep good homes. Yet for such worthy impoverished mothers, public aid was intended to be honorable and adequate, a predictable salary of sorts for public service, and certainly not a demeaning form of charity or poor relief. As the Illinois Congress of Mothers explained, the "pension removes the mother and her children from the disgrace of charity relief and places her in the class of public servants similar to army officers and school teachers."[113]

Only some aspects of this original vision were realized, while others were actually contradicted, as mothers' pensions were put into effect during the 1910s and 1920s. Of course any detailed analysis of the implementation of mothers' pensions in this period would have to deal with many different local patterns, because legal provisions varied across the states, the financing and administration of mothers' pensions were left almost entirely to thousands of local communities, and practical administrative discretion extended right down to the varied handling of applications for assistance from individual women. Even if the data were available, this is not the right place to do a full analysis of such variations. But keeping their existence in mind, we can reach some overall conclusions about what happened to the original vision as mothers' pensions were put into practice across the United States.

In one sense the hopes of the proponents of mothers' pensions were realized, because many needy mothers and children were helped by these laws. A 1931 study by the federal Children's Bureau estimated that about 45,800 families were receiving mothers' aid grants in 1921 or 1922, a number which more than doubled to about 93,600 families (with about 253,300 children) in 1931.[114] Prior to the existence of mothers' pensions in their local communities, these families would have faced fewer and less pleasant options: voluntary or legally enforced placement of the children in orphanages or foster homes; child labor or the mother's full-time wage-labor to help sustain the family; or greater dependence on irregular, small sums from outdoor public relief or private charity. A study of mothers' pension recipients in Chicago showed that they did better than when previously dependent on private charity; and another study suggested that some widows even got more income from public aid than they had received from their husbands when the latter were alive.[115] Critics of early mothers' pensions argue (with some justification) that they slapped "social controls" on poor, often immigrant women. But it is well to remember that the families helped by mothers' pensions hardly faced good options before such public aid was made available. Indeed, husbandless mothers were often subjected to the most extreme form of public control, legally mandated breakup of the family unit. Many poor women must have thought that public aid was better than their other alternatives, because "wherever widows' pensions were introduced there was a flood of applications."[116] For many impoverished mother-headed families in the early-twentieth-century United States, we can conclude along with Muriel and Ralph Pumphrey that mothers' pensions "substituted new, more constructive sets of social controls for the older, more punitive and destructive ones, permanently reducing the number of institutionalized children."[117]

To be sure, some kinds of needy mothers and their children tended to be helped much more than others with equal or greater material need. The original laws emphasized widows as expected recipients, and sometimes mentioned other categories of legitimate recipients, such as women whose husbands were mentally or physically incapacitated or incarcerated in asylums or prisons. Some early laws named many kinds of beneficiaries, or else were worded broadly enough to include deserted wives, divorced women, or unwed mothers; and over time there was a tendency for laws to be amended to include more categories of mothers. Nevertheless, by 1931, there were still only ten states that allowed localities to grant aid to all kinds of needy mothers.[118] And across all the states, local administrative practices were usually more restrictive than the governing statutory provisions.[119] Consequently, in 1931 over 80 percent of those receiving mothers' pensions were widows; very small proportions of clients were deserted mothers or divorced mothers, while only fifty-five beneficiaries in the entire country were unmarried mothers.[120]

Originally just one state, and still only three states in 1931, explicitly allowed unmarried mothers to receive aid.[121] Legislators and mothers' aid administrators were also reluctant to help deserted or divorced women, for fear of encouraging husbands to leave their families. As the prestigious 1914 *Report of the New York State Commission on Relief for Widowed Mothers* explained in the course of making an eloquent brief for generous public aid to mothers whose husbands were dead, "adequate relief" strictly for widows "cannot in any way increase the number of worthy families in distress[,] as can easily be the case with other mothers whose husbands are living. To pension desertion or illegitimacy would, undoubtedly, have the effect of putting a premium on these crimes against society."[122] Significantly, the New York State Commission approached the issue of eligibility for mothers' pensions in a much less inclusive spirit than did Mrs. Robertson in the 1911 address to the National Congress of Mothers that I quoted above.

Mothers' pension laws included behavioral as well as categorical criteria for public aid recipients. Potential recipients, including those in the blameless category of widows, could get help only if they were personally "worthy"—for example, not drunkards, not living with male partners out of wedlock, not neglecting their children. Written right into the laws were criteria for investigating the moral as well as the economic status of women who applied for mothers' pensions.[123] Maine's law, for example, stipulated that an investigation had to show that a potential recipient was "a fit and capable person to bring up her children, and whether the inmates and surroundings of her household are such as to render it suitable for her children to reside at home."[124] Lengthy and intrusively detailed applications often had to be filled out.[125] And once accepted for pensions, clients were supervised while receiving aid, not only to establish that they continued to be in economic need, but also to ensure that they were meeting acceptable standards as mothers and homemakers. In jurisdictions that had adequate supervisory personnel, social workers visited mothers every month (and sometimes even more frequently); and mothers were required to keep regular "household budgets" to prove they were managing their grants efficiently.[126]

The existence of behavioral as well as economic criteria for mothers' pensions led to a great irony: many of the private charity officials and social workers who were originally opposed to the enactment of mothers' pension laws ended up taking over their implementation. The original mothers' pension laws more often designated juvenile courts than public welfare agencies as the administering agencies; yet there was a tendency during the 1920s for county welfare agencies to take over this function.[127] And even if juvenile courts or nonwelfare public agencies were nominally in charge, they hired social workers to run proper-home investigations and supervise clients, or else delegated such activities to private charity groups. As Muriel and Ralph Pumphrey conclude, mothers' pension administrators "became captives of the very organizations that had fought most vigorously against publicly administered pensions."[128]

The women's groups that campaigned for mothers' pensions envisaged a continuation under more fiscally generous and socially honorable conditions of the charitable traditions of "friendly visiting."[129] The lonely widow, they believed, would welcome regular visits by a public aid worker, preferably a female, who would not only check up on her mothering but also help her with practical problems such as contacting city agencies, arranging for health examinations, dealing with schoolteachers, and so forth. There is anecdotal evidence that social workers often did these kinds of things, and that many mothers indeed welcomed such help.[130] "Raising a family alone is almost more than a woman can do," said one mothers' aid recipient. "I should never have been able to bear it if it had not been for the help of Miss A and Miss B."[131]

But at the same time, scholars who regard mothers' pensions as social control have been able to point to other kinds of anecdotes showing that standards for clients could sometimes be arbitrary impositions of Protestant middle-class norms. In urbanized localities, about 40 to 60 percent of the those receiving mothers' pensions were foreign-born immigrants.[132] Such women were sometimes required to apply for citizenship as a condition of receiving aid, and social workers might use cultural criteria of "Americanism" in evaluating their applications or judging their continued eligibility for assistance.[133] Women could be penalized not only for neglect or mistreatment of their children but also for inability to prove their marriages, for using a language other than English in the home, for refusing to remove relatives deemed unsavory from their homes, for living in improper houses or neighborhoods, or for failing to maintain sufficiently clean and orderly homes.[134] Obviously, ethnocentric as well as class biases could enter into judgments by social workers and officials.

What is more, mothers' aid clients could be forced to forswear relatively lucrative full-time wage-labor in favor of poorly paid part-time work, so that they could remain at home with their children. Thus, according to the *Second Annual Report of the State Public Welfare Commission* in Rhode Island,

> [W]here it was found that a mother was away from home all day at work in a mill or a factory she was advised to give up this work and return to the job of caring for and training her own children. Other work of a less confining nature such as jewelry work at home, sewing, cleaning by the hour, and part-time work in lunchrooms was secured for these mothers . . . All this in an effort to build for the State the best possible type of citizen.[135]

Extremely needy mothers (including widows) who did not meet the moral and behavioral criteria enshrined in their states' laws or in their localities' administrative cultures could have their applications for pensions denied. And mothers' aid recipients who went astray by those criteria could be suddenly removed from the rolls. In some instances, moreover, mothers with needy children voluntarily avoided mothers' pensions, or left the rolls, or were denied continued benefits, because they refused to accept restrictions on the jobs they could take to make ends meet.[136] Case Record no. 973 of the St. Louis Board of Children's Guardians records one such instance:

> This case has been anything but satisfactory. Mrs.—— was granted an allowance of $35.00 in August 1922, for the care of her five children. Of course, she was obliged to supplement and being an ignorant woman, factory work was all that was available. This suits her type and temperament exactly. She hates house work, does not care properly for the children when at home, but is a good factory worker. Therefore, after two years of futile effort to improve the care and condition of the children by keeping the mother more at home, we gave it up.[137]

In a sense, there is nothing really surprising in these patterns. Most of those who originally campaigned for mothers' pensions were strong believers in the sanctity of the normative middle-class family, with a male breadwinner and a married female homemaker and mother. Believing that impoverished mothers as well as materially secure mothers should be allowed to take care of their children and their homes, the proponents of mothers' pensions wanted the new laws and their implementation to symbolize and reinforce community support for what they sincerely believed were universal family norms. A few—like Mrs. Robertson, who spoke to the National Congress of Mothers in 1911—were even willing to place the emphasis on helping all mothers, including unmarried ones. Yet hardly any supporters of mothers' pensions, before or after the 1910s, would have endorsed the notion of payments going automatically to needy mothers regardless of their personal conduct or their ability and willingness to provide a wholesome home life for their children. In the apt words of the historian David Rothman, to those active in social reform causes during the Progressive Era, "all Americans were to enter the ranks of the middle class. The melting-pot metaphor implied not only an amalgam of immigrants into a common mold, but an amalgam of classes into a common mold."[138]

We should keep in mind, nevertheless, that official criteria of moral deservingness were legally written into early U.S. public benefits for men, as well as into mothers' pension laws. Thus the 1890 Dependent Pension Act stipulated that Civil War pensions would go to Union veterans who had served ninety days or more and been "honorably discharged therefrom," and who had later become incapacitated for manual labor through "a mental or physical disability of a permanent character, not the result of their own vicious habits."[139] Similarly, all early U.S. proposals for old-age pensions, as well as the local-option laws that passed in a few states prior to the 1930s, contained stipulations that the recipients had to be of good character—just as did the pioneering national old-age pensions enacted in Denmark in 1891 and in Britain in 1908. In short, when governments in either the United States or elsewhere around the turn of the twentieth century gave out public benefits to citizens, they typically claimed the right to make moral judgments about the recipients.[140] This was true for both men and women, not just for female beneficiaries of mothers' pensions, as some feminist scholars have argued.[141]

But if the original supporters of mothers' pensions accepted categorical and behavioral rules defining which husbandless mothers were "worthy" of public aid, they certainly did *not* want large numbers of eligible mothers to go without grants; nor did they want aid recipients to receive so little that they could not primarily devote themselves to homemaking and motherhood. Yet this is exactly what happened as mothers' pension laws were implemented, for two main reasons.

First, early mothers' pension laws allowed localities (usually counties) to decide for themselves whether to establish and fund programs; and only a minority of states became involved over the course of the 1910s and 1920s in funding or supervising local programs.[142] Given so much local discretion, western, urban-midwestern, and urban-northeastern localities were much more likely than southern and some (but not all) rural localities to set up mothers' pensions, and were also more likely to devote funds to them.[143] The Children's Bureau's 1931 study revealed that only 3 percent of all U.S. mothers' pension recipients were Negroes—even though many local jurisdictions in the North had percentages of Negro beneficiaries that equaled or exceeded that group's proportion of the population.[144] Nationwide, the primary reason for the severe underrepresentation of black families, as well as the reason for the exclusion of many poor rural whites from mothers' pensions, was the absence of any program in many rural counties, or else the token presence of a program with practically no funds to dispense. Figure 28 gives the numbers of families aided per 10,000 population in the various states in 1931, dramatizing how geographically uneven was the practical availability of mothers' pensions. (Within-state variations are not presented here, although they were also very great. What is more, the numbers in Figure 28 are based only on the local jurisdictions that actually had programs; they do not include the population of counties that had not established programs at all by 1931.) Many very needy mother-led families were obviously left without public aid. In the mid-1920s, Emma Lundberg estimated that less than one-third of the needy American children "for whom aid should be granted" were actually benefiting from mothers' pensions; and she admitted that she was not including in this calculation many other children of "permanently disabled" families.[145]

Second, severe underfunding of mothers' pensions was a problem across the entire nation, even in relatively generously funded programs, and even in the twenty-nine states that by 1931 had programs set up in three-quarters or more of their local jurisdictions.[146] Funding levels for mothers' pensions did tend to rise over the 1910s and 1920s, and more and more states contributed funds to local programs.[147] But funding never came anywhere close to meeting the needs of eligible persons or actual recipients—even at statutorily defined levels, which were themselves pitifully inadequate to the real needs of families.[148] Figure 29 shows the overall pattern of average grants across the states in 1931. At that time, average monthly mothers' pension grants ranged from $4.33 a month in Arkansas to $69.31 a month in Massachusetts; and the median grant was $21.78 a month.[149] In 1930, the mothers' aid committee of the White House Conference on Child Health and Protection concluded that "adequate grants in large urban centers will probably average $60 or more," yet only eight cities altogether, six of which were in Massachusetts, were providing grants averaging this much.[150]

Administrators of mothers' pensions proceeded in the face of inadequate funds in various ways. Sometimes they spread available funds very thin, giving tiny grants to as many eligible mothers and children as possible. This was a common pattern in nonurban areas

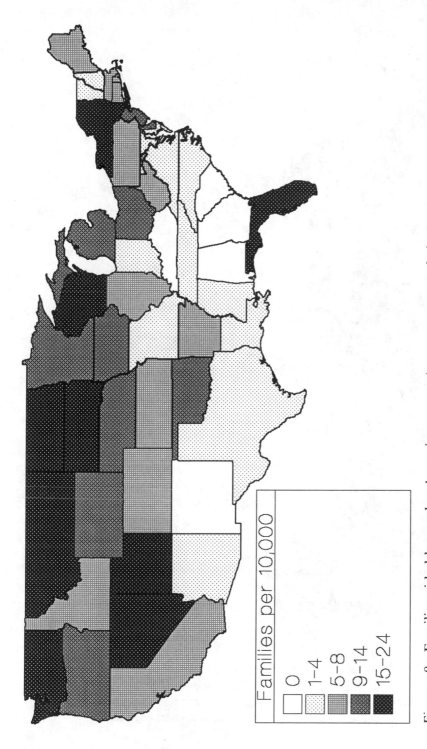

Figure 28 Families aided by mothers' pensions, 1931 (per 10,000 population)

Source: Children's Bureau, U.S. Department of Labor, *Mothers' Aid, 1931*, publication no. 220 (Washington: Government Printing Office, 1933), p. 19.

Families per 10,000

0
1–4
5–8
9–14
15–24

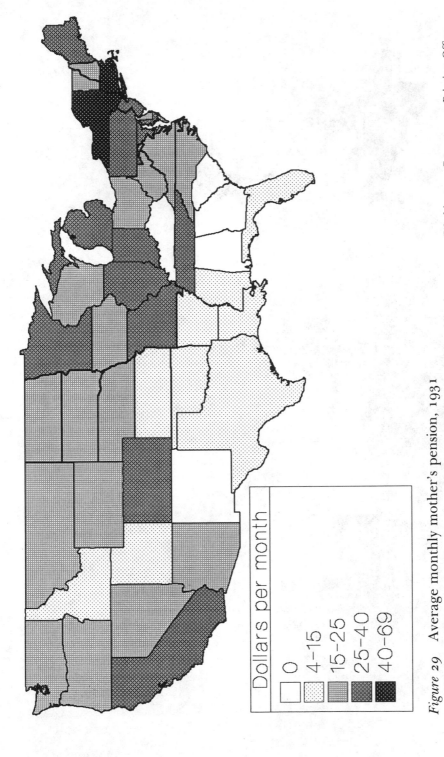

Figure 29 Average monthly mother's pension, 1931

Source: Children's Bureau, U.S. Department of Labor, *Mothers' Aid, 1931*, publication no. 220 (Washington: Government Printing Office, 1933). p. 17.

where large staffs were not available for administration and supervision, and it could result in grants that were no better than traditional poor relief.[151] But in certain urban areas, where administrators and social workers wanted to maintain "high standards," another tactic was adopted. When funds were inadequate to provide for all eligible families at the statutory levels for mothers' pensions, "there was a definite tendency . . . to limit the number of families accepted for care, in order that allowances for families should not fall below an amount necessary to assure normal and satisfactory development of children for whom the public had accepted responsibility."[152] Thus, for example, in 1922, 73 mothers were receiving relatively high levels of assistance from the mothers' pension program in Denver, Colorado; but 82 other eligible mothers in that city were relegated to the waiting list.[153] That same year, 477 families in Pittsburgh (Allegheny County) Pennsylvania, were receiving mothers' aid, while another 425 families were on the waiting list; and 477 families in Cincinnati (Hamilton County), Ohio, were receiving aid, while another 500 were on the waiting list.[154] In 1925, according to a student of mothers' pensions in Philadelphia, an approved widow had to wait two years for assistance, no matter how needy she was.[155]

Urban agencies using the triage tactic had every incentive to apply moral and behavioral standards with a vengeance, so as to ensure that families actually given mothers' pensions looked good by community standards. San Francisco actually went so far as to establish a two-tier system, in which the most respectable widows received relatively generous aid from the Widows' Pension Bureau, while other needy mothers who might have been statutorily eligible for pensions were given less generous aid and relegated to much closer supervision by other agencies.[156] Other jurisdictions accomplished the same result less formally. Thus shortages of funds led to the tightening of surveillance over "high-type" widows and—above all—to the drawing of firm lines between "high-types" and "pauper types" of needy mothers.[157] Inadequate funds, handled by social service workers who were trying to demonstrate the worth of their programs to a skeptical and tight-fisted public, inevitably made mothers' pension programs more and more like traditional poor relief or charity, with their burdensome and demeaning regulations and investigations. Ironically, this happened even though the intention of mothers' aid administrators was to separate their programs and clienteles from poor relief.

So severe, finally, was the funding problem for mothers' pensions that even the most respectable widows receiving regular grants in the most generous places were unlikely to be able to make ends meet for their families without doing wage labor on the side. It goes without saying that an even greater need for supplementary income prevailed for the vast majority of mothers' aid recipients, who were getting grants ranging around the median of $21.78 a month in 1931. Studies of urban mothers' aid recipients in the 1920s consistently showed that half to two-thirds of them were also doing wage-labor.[158] In 1926, to give a specific example, a study by the Mothers' Assistance Fund Division of the Pennsylvania Department of Welfare revealed that only 39 percent of the family incomes of 2,404 mothers' aid recipients came from their grants. Wage-earnings of mothers provided another 21 percent; and earnings of children fourteen and above another 27 percent.[159] Fifty-nine percent of the mothers were engaged in kinds of wage-work that the investigator deemed "undesirable." As Emma Lundberg commented:

> This study shows the way[s] in which shortcomings of the grants had to be compensated for—premature employment of children who should have continued in school, poorly paid home work by mothers, employment of mothers away from home when they were needed there for the proper care and protection of the children, work that was beyond the physical strength of the mother, housing conditions below proper standards for health, and other injuries to home life brought about by lack of a few dollars a week or month that nullified the benefits derived from the public money expended for the family.[160]

Indeed, mothers' pensions in practice truly boomeranged on the intentions of their orginial supporters by pushing poor women into marginal wage-labor markets. Pensions were nowhere near enough to support full-time motherhood, even in frugal homes. And aid recipients were usually prohibited from doing better-paid, full-time labor. Thus the poor women who got inadequate mothers' aid were prodded into such low-wage drudgery as taking in washing at home, part-time work as a housecleaner, or home-based production day-work such as lacemaking or sewing buttons on clothing.[161] This was certainly not the outcome envisaged by most of the upper- and middle-class ladies who campaigned for mothers' pensions—understood as "salaries" for needy women who would "serve the state by giving all their time to rearing good citizens."[162] "The mother of young children," the originators of mothers' pensions believed, does "better service to the community and one more worthy of pecuniary remuneration when she stays at home and minds her children than when she goes out charing and leaves them to the chances of the street or to the care of a neighbor."[163]

I am arguing, in short, that many of the ills accompanying the implementation of mothers' pensions, ills to which feminist and other critics have pointed, were directly or indirectly traceable to the severe underfunding of these programs. But why *were* mothers' pensions so poorly funded? Much of the explanation surely lay in the gap between the political requisites of the original nationwide movement for mothers' pension laws and the very different conditions for the drawn-out and varied, locality-by-locality, state-by-state struggles necessary to improve statutes, administration, and levels of funding after the mothers' aid programs were set up. Widespread federated associations like the General Federation of Women's Clubs and the National Congress of Mothers were ideally suited to spread the word about, and coordinate, the campaigns of the 1910s for state-level enabling statutes. But when it came to waging the battles over the funding of mothers' pensions, individual local and state women's clubs were much more on their own, battling uphill against well-entrenched business, agricultural, and other conservative interests determined to keep taxes low in the localities and states.

The style of politics practiced by women's groups in the early twentieth century—a style that emphasized dramatizing morally pressing issues, educating public opinion, and agitating for legislation—was better suited to passing new laws or creating new regulatory agencies than to raising resources for them over the long run. Nevertheless, women's groups did not simply fight for mothers' pension laws and then forget about the matter. In her detailed research on Chicago between 1900 and 1930, Joanne Goodwin has found that the Chicago Woman's Club, the Illinois Federation of Women's Clubs, and the Illinois Congress of Mothers worked during the later 1910s and the 1920s for legislation to expand eligibility and funding for their state's mothers' pension program.[164] Similarly, from the mid-1910s, the official organ of the National Congress of Mothers, *Child-Welfare Magazine*, published recurrent descriptions of efforts to obtain higher county and state appropriations for mothers' pensions. These articles often expressed frustration about the inadequacy of public appropriations to meet the evident needs of poor widows and their children.[165] Yet such struggles by the Mothers' Congresses and other groups for improved funding were inevitably coordinated only at local or state levels, not across the entire nation. And as the struggles proved often unsuccessful, one gets the impression that upper- and middle-class women's groups gradually lost interest in mothers' pensions. After the early 1920s, there are hardly any mentions of mothers' pensions in *Child-Welfare Magazine* or in the proceedings of the Biennial Conventions of the General Federation of Women's Clubs. As Emma Lundberg reflected in 1928, "When the law was safely on the statute books the interest of the public in the humanitarian principle was overshadowed by a desire for economy." Consequently, she pointed out, most "of the improvements that have come in the laws governing the amount and application of aid and in the provision of increased appropriations to make the laws effective have come about through the combined efforts of those directly concerned with the administration [of mothers' aid] and the social agencies that face the results of the absence of this form of prevention of child dependency."[166] By the late 1920s, in other words, the politics of improving mothers' pensions had become mostly the affair of local social workers and charity groups, not the concern of broad alliances of reformers and nation-spanning women's federations.

Following a pattern typical for social policies targeted on very poor people, the clients of mothers' pensions were too busy with struggles of daily life, and too morally cowed, to demand higher funding for these programs. Until the Great Depression overwhelmed the system-as-usual and created possibilities for new national-level subsidies, the major advocates of more public funding for mothers' aid were the mostly female and low-paid social service workers, who could barely gain the attention of state legislatures and county officials. What is more, broad political alliances cutting across social classes never came together to campaign for the expansion of these public aid programs for poor mothers. There was nothing comparable to the alliances that had pushed for the expansion of Civil War pensions in the late nineteenth century. Therefore, it is hardly surprising that early U.S. mothers' pension programs were persistently starved for adequate funds.

The original proponents of mothers' pensions—above all the ladies of the National Congress of Mothers and the General Federation of Women's Clubs—said that they saw these public benefits as a way of "honoring motherhood." We should, I think, take them at their word. These upper- and middle-class women were trying to embrace as sisters, as fellow mothers, the impoverished widows who would be helped by mothers' pensions. The originators of mothers' pension laws intended to include needy mothers in the same moral universe as themselves, providing them with regular and nondemeaning material assistance to make it possible for them to realize a version of the same basic ideals of homemaking and motherhood to which the ladies themselves aspired. But the organized elite and middle-class women who helped to spur the rapid spread of mothers' pension statutes during the 1910s did not have the political clout to achieve adequate levels of funding once the locally varied programs were established. And once mothers' pensions were put into practice, they became the concern of bureaucrats and social workers, most of whom did not see their clients as part of the same moral universe as themselves. As this happened, women's voluntary associations tended to lose interest. The moralistic, educational style of politics best practiced by those associations was, in any event, not as well suited to persistent struggles over fiscal and administrative expansion as it had been to the dramatic campaigns of the 1910s through which mothers' pensions were enacted.

The aspiration to a moral unity for all American mothers that lay behind the launching of mothers' pensions did not survive as these pioneering modern public welfare benefits were implemented. During the later 1910s and the 1920s, the starvation of early mothers' aid programs for public funds ensured that gaps between worthy and unworthy, and between givers and receivers, would become ever more entrenched in the practices of mothers' pensions. These same gaps eventually became entrenched as well in the American public's perception of mothers' pensions, turning them into the forerunners of demeaning "welfare" rather than the honorable salaries for mothers that their original supporters had envisaged.

CHAPTER 9

Statebuilding for Mothers and Babies: The Children's Bureau and the Sheppard-Towner Act

During the Progressive Era, reformers not only sought to establish new social insurance benefits; they also fought to build new public agencies, including a national health department and a national employment service. But as we saw in Chapter 5, such statebuilding efforts fell short. Efforts to consolidate all federal agencies dealing with medical and sanitary issues into one cabinet-level Department of Health were defeated between 1910 and 1912. The United States Employment Service was set up as an emergency agency during the war, but it was quickly denationalized afterward. The rump federal bureau was starved for funds during the 1920s, as state and municipal employment services disappeared or went their own way. The late establishment and early demise of the USES was indicative of the poor prospects for workingmen's insurance in the early-twentieth-century United States.

In telling contrast to the failures experienced by early U.S. advocates of a paternalist social insurance regime, the statebuilding efforts of American advocates of maternalist social policies fared much better during the Progressive Era and for some years into the 1920s. Several federal agencies were established and controlled by women interested in maternalist social welfare measures. The Home Education Division of the Bureau of Education was created at the behest of the National Congress of Mothers in 1911.[1] Following years of agitation by many women's organizations, the Women's Bureau was launched as a wartime agency in 1918, and was made permanent by new legislation in 1920.[2] Another new agency created in response

480

to the urgings of women's organizations was the Bureau of Home Economics, founded in 1923 during a reorganization of the U.S. Department of Agriculture.[3] Yet by far the most important success for maternalist statebuilders commenced in 1912, at the height of the domestic reform period and well before the wartime emergency on which most other reformers rode to federal power. In that year, maternalist welfare advocates succeeded in establishing the Children's Bureau as a federal agency grandly charged to "investigate and report . . . upon all matters pertaining to the welfare of children and child life among all classes of our people."[4]

Although the Children's Bureau started with a paltry budget of $25,640 and a tiny staff of fifteen, by the third year of its operations in 1915, Congress had increased its budget to $164,640 and its staff to seventy-six—leaps of more than six-fold and five-fold, respectively, in these critical components of state formation.[5] Moreover, the Children's Bureau was soon to extend its reach into states and localities, and enlarge the scope of its activities to include the promotion of new programs and the administration of large federal grants. In 1921—just as many wartime social agencies such as the USES were being dismantled or defunded by Congress—the Children's Bureau was put in charge of administering America's first explicit federal social welfare legislation, the "Federal Act for the Promotion of the Welfare and Hygiene of Maternity and Infancy," commonly known as the Sheppard-Towner Act. The Bureau was given over one million dollars of funds annually for five years, mostly to disburse to cooperating states; and by 1922 its own budget had increased almost sixty-fold since 1913.[6] During the following seven years of administering Sheppard-Towner, the Bureau coordinated a nationwide program that distributed "over twenty-two million pieces of literature, conducted 183,252 health conferences, established 2,978 permanent prenatal centers, and visited over three million homes."[7] "Women from every geographic region, social class, and educational background wrote to the Bureau as many as 125,000 letters a year," and by 1929 the Bureau "estimated that one-half of U.S. babies had benefited from the government's childrearing information."[8]

Remarkable statebuilding successes during a period otherwise inimical to U.S. welfare state formation, the Children's Bureau and the Sheppard-Towner Act were the joint political achievements of women reformers and widespread associations of married women.

The political and ideological processes were similar—but not identical—to those that brought mothers' pensions across virtually all of the states during the 1910s. As my account in the previous chapter made clear, federations of married women's clubs lobbied in and across the states for mothers' pensions; and the National Congress of Mothers highlighted these laws as a top priority. Professional women reformers based in the social settlements endorsed mothers' pensions, but did not make them a top priority. In contrast, as this chapter will show, leading women reformers from the social settlements explicitly mobilized local and national women's clubs into campaigns to establish the federal Children's Bureau and expand its mission. These statebuilding campaigns led by female reformist professionals would not have succeeded, however, without the vitality of the vast locally rooted women's federations already engaged in child welfare work and other civic activities. Especially from 1900 to the mid-1920s, federations of women's voluntary associations enjoyed political leverage within U.S. federalism that was entirely unavailable to higher-educated reformist professionals—except when the latter cooperated with the voluntary federations on terms influenced by the federations' own outlooks and organizational structures.[9]

The Creation of the Children's Bureau

To be sure, women reformers led the way toward the establishment of the Children's Bureau inside the federal government. As a student of the matter has insightfully written, it

> is not accidental that originators for the idea of the Bureau and its first two chiefs, Julia Lathrop and Grace Abbott, had all cut their social welfare teeth in the social settlement movement . . . the Children's Bureau and the settlements had a good deal in common. The two organizations acted as clearinghouses for information and experimental stations, and both emphasized a multiple approach to solving child welfare problems . . . People trained in the settlement's clearinghouse ideal had a natural affinity for experiment and social reform and they were not content with piecemeal attempts to improve the lives of children. Consequently, the Bureau was . . . something like a national settlement with a specialty in children.[10]

Legend has it that the idea of a federal bureau to deal with child welfare crystallized at a breakfast discussion in 1903 between Florence Kelley and Lillian Wald (public health nurse and the founder of New York's Henry Street Settlement, where she and Kelley both lived). As Robyn Muncy tells the story, Kelley opened

> a letter that asked why nothing was done about the high summertime death rate among children . . . As Wald mused that she knew no source of information on variable death rates among children, Kelley read aloud an article from the morning paper, which announced that the federal government was sending the Secretary of Agriculture to investigate damage inflicted by the boll weevil in southern cotton fields. Wald is purported to have retorted: "If the Government can have a department to take such an interest in what is happening to the cotton crop, why can't it have a bureau to look after the nation's child crop?"[11]

In fact, both women had been thinking along these lines for some time. And Kelley went on to offer a specific proposal for a national commission to gather facts on child welfare in her 1905 book, *Some Ethical Gains through Legislation,* which was based on lectures she had given some years earlier.[12]

Persuading Congress and the President

After the idea was born, legislative proposals for a federal bureau were devised and pushed by the National Child Labor Committee, in which Kelley was a leading light.[13] This ensured a public hearing for a proposed federal bureau, but also aroused the ire of opponents of child labor laws, who managed to keep bills from coming to a vote in Congress. The 1909 White House Conference on the Care of Dependent Children formally endorsed a proposal for a federal children's bureau and culminated in a favorable message to Congress by outgoing President Roosevelt, followed by testimony at congressional hearings by eighteen prominent reformers.[14] The White House Conference not only gave the proposal for a children's bureau wide publicity; it also helped to reposition it as a fact-gathering project on behalf of "child-caring work" and "the needs of children throughout the United States," thus softening fears that it would merely be a bureaucracy to advocate new child labor laws.[15] Despite

the ensuing enhanced support from national reform leaders, however, bills to establish the Children's Bureau were kept from coming
to full congressional vote for three years after the 1909 Conference—until a bill previously passed by the Senate was finally passed
by the House on April 2, 1912, and signed by President Taft on
April 8.[16]

Some opposition to the Bureau's creation came from legislators
fearful of child labor reforms. Yet in the crucial House vote of 177
in favor and 17 against, more Representatives failed to vote than the
combined total of those who voted for or against—indicating either
that many Representatives thought the measure insignificant or that
they were mildly opposed but did not want to say so on the record.[17]
President Taft had not been enthusiastic about the Children's Bureau, either, preferring the idea of a federal bureau of public health.
But once the Congress acted, he accepted the Bureau, possibly (as
one of his biographers would have it) because his aunt liked the
measure, or possibly because Taft was about to face a tough struggle
for reelection in a progressive political climate.[18]

Public agitation by women's organizations over the course of several years was surely a factor in the 1912 congressional vote and in
President Taft's acceptance of the new federal bureau. Under Florence Kelley's guidance, Consumers' Leagues had taken up the
cause.[19] More important, the widespread women's federations also
got involved. At its First International Congress on the Welfare of
the Child in 1908, the National Congress of Mothers declared that
"the time has come when every nation through a special department
should provide data concerning infants, which may be used by
Boards of Health and mothers everywhere," and at its Second International Congress in 1911, the Congress specifically endorsed the
establishment of the Children's Bureau.[20]

In closer touch with the settlement house movement, the General
Federation of Women's Clubs offered even earlier and stronger
support for the proposed children's bureau. At its 1906 Biennial,
the General Federation heard two leaders of the National Child
Labor Committee give addresses in which they urged support for
pending legislation to create a Children's Bureau. In one of these
addresses, Samuel McCune Lindsay explained:

> The bill now pending in Congress to create such a [Children's]
> bureau will become law, I believe, only if you women want it

earnestly enough to work for it, but this will not be enough to get it. You must endorse it over and over again, you must write personally over and over again to Senators and Representatives, seeing them when they return home from Washington.

Write "Children's Bureau" on your program for work and discussion next fall in every club here represented, and when the next Congress assembles in December, we will have a National Children's Bureau, and half the battle will be won.[21]

Lindsay was over-optimistic, of course; the battle dragged on for several more years. The General Federation cooperated with the National Child Labor Committee in efforts to secure congressional passage of the relevant bills. At its 1908 Biennial, the Federation passed a resolution in favor of the establishment of a children's bureau, to be headed by a woman.[22] And at the 1910 Biennial, Mrs. Ellen Spencer Mussey of the Legislative Committee reported that the General Federation's

President, Mrs. Moore, wrote officially to many Senators in behalf of the measure and assured them of the interest women have in getting authoritative information on all that concerns the welfare of children. While the Bill was before the Senate Committee on Education and Labor, I had occasion to appeal for assistance to several State Presidents and I wish now to publicly thank the President of the State Federation of Indiana and the President of the State Federation of Pennsylvania for their effective and timely work in behalf of this measure.[23]

Indeed, the all-important state federations and local clubs became quite involved in this campaign. For example, at an important conjuncture, just after the U.S. Senate had passed a bill to establish the Children's Bureau and while similar legislation was pending in the U.S. House, the California State Federation of Women's Clubs sent letters of support to the Representatives.[24] Similarly, in reports to the 1912 GFWC Biennial (which was held soon after the enabling legislation for the Children's Bureau had been signed into law) a number of state federations emphasized their lobbying activities on behalf of the bureau—including the Kentucky Federation, which boasted of sending "postal telegrams to our Congressmen."[25] The 1912 Biennial also featured a plenary lecture by the new chief of the Children's Bureau, Julia Lathrop. The nationally assembled delegates celebrated the creation of the new federal agency and passed a resolution thanking President Taft for appointing a woman to head it.[26]

Weaving Ties between the Bureau and Local Communities

The relationship between the Children's Bureau and associated American women continued and deepened after April 1912—and this relationship was critical for the expansion of the Bureau's budget and activities. Without the further activation of locally associated women, building upon their preexisting organizational capacities and their moral convictions about women's responsibilities for the well-being of all children and mothers, the tiny new agency could never have expanded as it did over the next decade into a coordinator of far-flung social programs and the core of a potential maternalist welfare state.

Despite the key role the National Child Labor Committee had played in lobbying for the new Bureau, not to mention for her appointment as its first chief, Julia Lathrop chose not to stress child labor issues as the agency's initial priority. This was an astute decision that enabled the fledgling Bureau to avoid doing battle with already-aroused business foes.[27] Instead, Lathrop selected infant mortality and, a few years later, maternal mortality, as early matters on which to gather new data and publicize information. In time, these issues would bring the Bureau into perilous conflict with the Public Health Service and the American Medical Association. But in the early years they allowed the Bureau to highlight broad socioeconomically rooted welfare concerns around topics not already effectively claimed by competing power centers.

Perhaps even more important, these concerns, so clearly part of women's special moral sphere, allowed Lathrop to engage the imagination of the rank-and-file members of women's organizations, extending the Bureau's reach into local communities—much as farmers' voluntary organizations worked with representatives of the U.S. Department of Agriculture (USDA) and (after 1914) with the Extension Service to extend data-gathering and information-dissemination into local areas. Indeed, Julia Lathrop repeatedly invoked parallels between the USDA and the Children's Bureau, and not only for rhetorical purposes. It is fascinating that Lathrop modeled aspects of her statebuilding work for women and children on this unusually well-articulated part of the otherwise weak U.S. federal administration of the early twentieth century.[28] She understood well the need to link a federal agency staffed with a few experts into networks of private as well as public organizations in the states and localities. Not only would this approach extend the organizational reach of the Bureau, it would also give it a means to lobby Congress effectively for increased appropriations, just as the USDA's networks were able to do.[29]

Soon after she was confirmed as the Children's Bureau's first chief, Lathrop traveled at her own expense to San Francisco to address the 1912 Biennial of the General Federation of Women's Clubs. "Where else could the Bureau more reasonably look for cooperation," she asked the assembled members and delegates, "than to this Federation nearly a million strong?" Lathrop discussed the administrative, political, and ideological advantages that cooperation from clubwomen could bring to her tiny bureau:

> What other association can offer such widespread help? What other force exists, loving pure culture, yet loving more, pure humanity, embracing all parties and all creeds in its practical program of social betterment, at work in hundreds of towns, and with apparently unlimited power of growth?
>
> These associations . . . represent as was constantly admitted during the long debate [over the creation of the Bureau] in Congress, the most influential and the wisest views in this country on the care and protection of children. If the Bureau can continue to have your aid, it cannot fail of usefulness and it will escape a danger which has been repeatedly mentioned; namely the possibility that a Federal Bureau will relieve local bodies and volunteer associations of the sense of responsibility . . . A distant office in Washington, filled with Government employees, whose business it is to know about children, to gather and classify facts about them, instead of doing things for them, must make a constant effort to avoid academic faults . . . [It is in order for this] Bureau to be vital, co-operative, serving the needs of the whole country and stimulating rather than dulling the sense of personal responsibility and the functions of states and cities and counties, that I am here tonight.[30]

In the rest of her detailed and inspirational address to the Biennial, Lathrop explained the Bureau's organization and initial appointments, taking care to stress that they followed strict civil service merit principles.[31] She also promised to gather expert information and disseminate it publicly in popular form. Above all, Lathrop argued for the value of studying the causes of infant mortality and, as a step toward that end as well as toward realizing other child welfare goals, maintained the need to obtain improved "birth registration" statistics all across the United States. Finally, Lathrop thanked the General Federation for a resolution it had passed that morning asking the Bureau to prepare "material to be used in securing proper registration of births and deaths in the large part of the United States where such records are neglected"—a resolution Lathrop and the Federation president ("my old friend, Mrs. Moore") had no doubt discussed in advance, since it furthered one of the Bureau's very first official projects.[32]

Nowadays, an official might go out from Washington, DC, and make a speech such as Lathrop's, only to revert upon his return to the capital to bureaucratic procedures well insulated from local action. But even though Lathrop constantly stressed that her Bureau's work was "purely statistical," she held to the social-progressive view— a view in turn rooted in preprofessional nineteenth-century social science—"that no legislation can be secured, no legislation when secured can be made effective, without the steady conscious push of a convinced public opinion, and the statistics of wisely conducted inquiries form the indisputable basis of facts which will at once convince and inspire public opinion."[33] The "theory on which the Bureau was created," Lathrop explained, was "that if the Government can investigate and report, the conscience and power of local communities can be depended upon for local action."[34] Not only in order to augment her tiny official resources for "securing actual data of current value," therefore, but also in order to stimulate "general interest in better legislation and enforcement" at the state and local levels, Lathrop fully involved locally organized women in the major projects of the Children's Bureau.[35]

From 1913 onward, the Children's Bureau mobilized organized women to perform "tests" of the accuracy of birth registration statistics. The purpose here was "to popularize a knowledge of the value of birth registration" and encourage improvements in the accuracy of local statistics-gathering.[36] Julia Lathrop understood that she was calling upon voluntary groups of American women to achieve what the bureaucracies of European states were doing for military purposes. "There is one expedient," she told the 1912 General Federation Biennial,

> the sternest, hatefulest in all the world, by which we can secure at once faultless birth registration. It is the expedient which makes registration imperative in the great countries of Europe. This expedient is the establishment of a conscription and standing army. God forbid that this country should ever count its children to that cruel and wasteful end . . . Are not human lives in a civilization of peace each in turn to be dignified by such public record as shall preserve each precious link in the human chain?[37]

Responding to Lathrop's maternalist arguments for a function usually performed by paternalist and militarist state bureaucracies, many women's groups got involved in the Bureau's campaign for improved birth statistics, including the General Federation of Women's Clubs, the National Congress of Mothers, the Association of Collegiate Alumnae, and even local chapters of the genealogy-minded Daughters of the American Revolution.[38] As Lathrop explained the process in her *Third Annual Report:*

> Members of the [local women's] committees receive copies of the standard birth-certificate blank, and after having carefully filled them out for a certain number of babies in their neighborhoods they then compare these records with those in the local registrar's office so as to discover in each instance whether the births have been registered and whether the record is properly filled out. The certificates are then sent to the Children's Bureau for tabulation.[39]

During the 1914 test, the Bureau reported corresponding with 1,500 individual clubwomen in seventeen states, and during 1915 it claimed to have received reports by 222 communities in twenty-four states.[40] The statistical results were summed up by Lathrop, along with the political dividends that came from the Bureau's interactions with local groups:

> Up to July 1, 1915, 12,865 certificates have been returned to this bureau, of which 9,450 are for registered births and 3,415 for unregistered births . . . [T]he proportion of births found duly registered in the different localities varies from approximately 100 to 14 percent.
>
> In some States the test was made to help the passage of the uniform vital statistics law. This was true in Florida, where committee members made a house-to-house canvass in 30 cities . . .

This canvass . . . gave a strong impetus to the passage of the excellent vital statistics law secured in the Florida legislative session of 1914–15.

The public authorities charged with the investigation of births in several States have appealed to the Children's Bureau to organize the birth-registration test in their states, because of the publicity and good will thus secured . . . [E]very city which secures independently a good ordinance is a center showing the urgent need for a good State law for vital statistics . . .

If we may judge by the increasing numbers of the volunteers reporting on these committees, it is safe to say that the interest is growing in the test and in the better vital statistics, to aid which it was begun.[41]

The Children's Bureau continued for some years to pursue the involvement of local communities and women's groups in the birth registration tests, and steady progress was made in persuading local and state authorities to collect reliable statistics.[42]

Simultaneously with the birth registration project, the Children's Bureau pursued field investigations of infant mortality in selected local communities, starting with Johnstown, Pennsylvania. These investigations were more genuinely statistical, yet also involved crucial components of local mobilization. Women's clubs were asked to help draw up complete lists of babies born in a given year, who could be traced through the first year of life; the babies' mothers were then interviewed by female agents from the Bureau. Moreover, after each local survey was completed, its results were in turn used to stimulate local improvements. Thus, following the publication of the results of the Johnstown study, Lathrop proudly reported that the

files of the Johnstown press, the reports of the city health officer, the statements of clubs and individuals show a remarkable and sustained interest expressed in many forms [sic, reforms], among which may be mentioned the securing of infant-welfare nurses, an improved milk supply, a baby-welfare station, and renewed effort for a complete sewerage system . . . The understanding shown by the people and press of Johnstown indicates that there is a clear view of the ceaseless work required to secure permanent reduction of infant mortality.[43]

In due course, the Bureau in Washington compiled the locally gathered statistics to argue that infant mortality was directly related to low incomes for many working-class fathers, as well as to the unfortunate necessity for mothers in impoverished families to take ill-paid and tiring jobs outside the home.[44] The statistics of the Children's Bureau revealed that mothers of infants were likely to work outside the home only when the fathers' earnings were very small. Like other social progressives, the leaders of the Bureau refused to celebrate women's wage-work and felt that, ideally, mothers and infants should be supported by an adequate family wage paid to husbands. Eventually, the Bureau's annual reports featured graphic presentations of these "sociological" findings about the fundamentally economic causes of America's high infant mortality rates, as illustrated in Figures 30 and 31.

Predictably, the Children's Bureau began to arouse opposition as soon as the implications of its work became clear. Some officials in the Census Bureau and in public health departments worried that their bureaucratic domains were being invaded or their activities held up for public criticism; and business-oriented conservatives cared not at all for the Bureau's propensity to link the deaths of infants to low wages for working-class fathers.[45] Indeed, from 1914 onward, Bureau officials had to fend off the possibility that Congress would fail to grant its budget requests. Yet in the face of recurrent threats to its resource base, the Bureau could rely not just on fellow reformist professionals but also on its widespread ties to locally organized groups.

Portent of others to come, the first budget battle occurred in the spring of 1914, after the House Appropriations Committee voted not to recommend an increased appropriation that Lathrop had requested for fiscal 1914–15. Working with fellow social settlement women and with Owen Lovejoy of the National Child Labor Committee (NCLC), Lathrop soon got the word out through the *Ladies Home Journal* and other magazines and newspapers, and got in touch with leaders of the AFL and the women's federations. In turn, the NCLC contacted its state committee secretaries; the GFWC contacted the state federations; and word spread among social settlements and local social work agencies.[46] The result is reported by Dorothy Bradbury, a later in-house chronicler of the Children's Bureau: "[M]embers of Congress began to receive letters of protest from all over the country. Friends of the Bureau wrote and spoke in its behalf. Women's clubs, parent-teacher associations [that is, the Mothers' Congress], state child labor committees rallied to its support. Many newspapers and magazines carried articles endorsing the in-

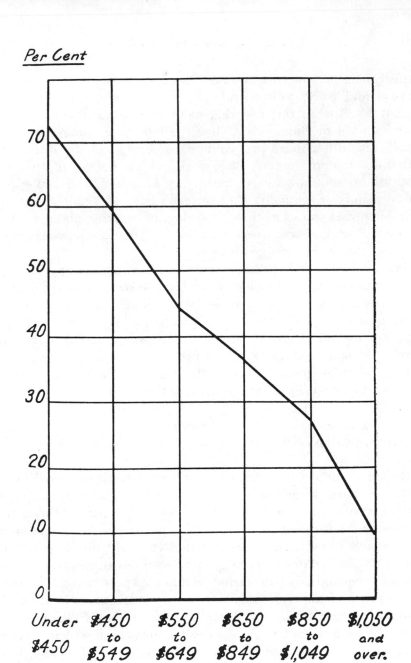

Figure 30 "Per Cent of Mothers Gainfully Employed in Manchester, N.H., During Year Following Baby's Birth When Fathers Earned Specified Amounts"

Source: *Fifth Annual Report of the Chief, Children's Bureau*, 1917, p. 17.

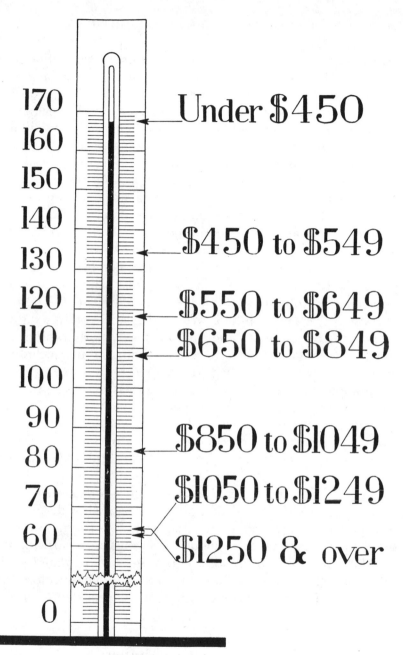

170

160

150

140

130

120

110

100

90

80

70

60

0

Under $450

$450 to $549

$550 to $649

$650 to $849

$850 to $1049

$1050 to $1249

$1250 & over

As wages decrease the baby death rate rises.

Figure 31 "Infant mortality rates [per 1000 births] according to father's earnings. Combined figures for eight cities"
Source: *Sixth Annual Report of the Chief, Children's Bureau*, 1918, p. 11.

creased appropriation for the Bureau."[47] Lathrop's use of tactics that exactly paralleled what the USDA did through farmers' associations quickly paid off. Congress reversed the decision of the Appropriations Committee, and voted exactly the increases in budget and staff that Lathrop had requested for 1914–15. Similar efforts still had to be mounted during subsequent congressional reviews of proposed appropriations, however. Thus the Bureau's far-flung social ties remained vital to its survival and expansion as a federal agency.

The Children's Bureau found ingenious ways to keep local communities working for improved infant and maternal health. Following up its statistical work on infant mortality, the Bureau joined with the General Federation of Women's Clubs—which Lathrop described as "an organization of more than 2,000,000 women representing clubs in every State, in Alaska, and in the island possessions"[48]—to sponsor "Baby Week" in March 1916. To "address the constructive side of infant care" and reach "not only individual parents but communities," the Bureau worked with local groups to sponsor "meetings, exhibits, conferences with parents, including examinations of well babies, flags distributed by Boy Scouts or other organizations to every house where there is a baby; processions, plays, tableaus, school children's essays" and more.[49] In its *Fourth Annual Report,* the Bureau claimed to have communicated with over 4,000 local communities and received actual reports of Baby Week activities from 2,083; and the report proudly displayed a map of the United States with a dot for each community where events were reported.[50] Not surprisingly, the GFWC and the National Congress of Mothers were both involved in stimulating such widespread local participation.[51] State organizations in both associations proudly reported to the national level about the enthusiastic participation of local clubs in 1916 Baby Week events.[52] In May 1917 another Baby Week was held, again with support from the nationwide women's federations, although this time with a bit less reported local participation.[53]

A Federal Program to Save Mothers and Babies

Not content with sporadic mobilizations, Julia Lathrop lost little time in attempting to translate enthusiasm for Baby Weeks into support for a major new federal welfare program to be administered by her agency. "Breaking out of its mandate to investigate and report, the Children's Bureau assumed a positive role in formulating and lobbying for a legislative child welfare reform."[54] Presaging the Sheppard-Towner Act, Lathrop outlined in her 1917 *Fifth Annual Report* a proposed nationwide program for "the public protection of maternity and infancy with federal aid."[55] Although the new program was intended to build upon the local energies tapped by earlier Children's Bureau projects, it also aimed to break new ground. As Lathrop explained in a talk at the 1916 GFWC Biennial about the "Education of Mothers as a Problem of Democracy," studies by the Children's Bureau had demonstrated "a close connection between infant mortality and the ill health and death of mothers . . . Here is a double need for the education of mothers which women themselves must make clear and demand."[56] Bureau investigations had also revealed that mothers and babies in America's rural areas frequently suffered from lack of access to basic health information and obstetrical services.[57] In a way that was politically astute as well as empirically justifiable, the proposed new program was therefore designed to encompass rural areas as well as the urban centers that typically were the targets and supporters of social reforms during the Progressive Era.

To explain what she had in mind, Lathrop invoked the model of the Smith-Lever Act, which authorized the U.S. Department of Agriculture to distribute matching funds to the states for extension work by county agents. She suggested that the federal government could similarly stimulate continuing state and local efforts to educate mothers about their own and their babies' health needs. States would have a powerful financial inducement to accept the program, because they would receive federal funds to enhance their own maternal and infant health education programs. And Congress would have an inducement to enact the program, because of its broad appeal across rural and urban areas. "Respecting traditional values and institutions in the United States, the . . . [proposed program] straddled the boundary between a comprehensive national health program, on the one side, and localism and voluntarism on the other."[58]

During the time that Lathrop launched the campaign for a new federal program to promote maternal health education, she decided not to put the full weight of the Children's Bureau behind the 1916–1919 drive of the American Association for Labor Legislation for public health insurance—despite the fact that such insurance would have included maternity benefits to help many needy working women and wives of industrial workers. As the historian Richard Meckel argues, tactical expediency may have been at work; the Children's Bureau could hardly afford to become too closely identified with the AALL's sputtering drive, just as the AALL was alienating the organized medical profession and arousing outcries against "un-American" attempts to import "bureaucratic paternalism" from Germany. Yet of equal importance, argues Meckel, was "the serious doubt . . . [shared by] Lathrop and others in the bureau . . . that an essentially urban industrial social insurance could adequately deal with the reality of infant mortality in America . . . [T]he bureau by 1917 was exhibiting an acute awareness that most Americans lived outside of large cities and industrial centers and therefore had no access to the maternal and infant health programs thus far established."[59] I would add that Lathrop's preference for maternal education over industrial social insurance was surely related to her belief that widespread local women's groups could and should be mobilized for the implementation of federal programs to help all mothers and babies, including those not tied to wage-earning men. There was, in short, a good fit between the new social policy the Children's Bureau chose to push and the values and organizational capacities of the voluntary women's federations with which it was so fruitfully interconnected.

Lathrop's plan for a federal maternal and infant health program was not immediately introduced into Congress, however, because the country was preoccupied with fighting World War I. During the conflict, the Children's Bureau continued its activation of local women in officially endorsed voluntary efforts. Astutely avoiding any condemnation of the war effort, and placing the stress on conserving and enhancing human resources, the Bureau worked with the Women's Committee of the Council of National Defense. "This war-spawned organization, representing a large proportion of the nation's women's groups, was composed of seventeen thousand local units organized under the State Councils of Defense and totalling approximately eleven million women."[60] Together, the Bureau and the Women's Committee sponsored the "Year of the Child" starting in April 1918, followed by a May 1919 White House Conference on Standards of Child Welfare.[61] The Children's Year campaign allocated to each state a "quota" of infant lives to be saved during the campaign, and the 1919 Conference capped off this year-long effort by seeking to establish and publicize a comprehensive set of standards for infant and child welfare in America.[62]

Amid these efforts during and right after the war, Bureau leaders, seconded by prominent reformer allies, agitated on behalf of the proposed new federal legislation to fund permanent infant and maternity health programs on a nationwide basis. To explain why new federal efforts were needed, the Bureau published information about America's appallingly high rates of infant and maternal mortality, using catchy graphics, such as the "thermometers" in Figures 32 and 33 that appeared in its *Eighth Annual Report* in 1920, to illustrate the poor international standing of the United States. Bureau leaders also explained the proposed program to groups across the nation. "Writing for and speaking to a wide variety of lay and professional organizations . . . Miss Lathrop slowly but surely built a wide-spread public interest in her plan."[63] Obviously, women's groups were well prepared to hear this message, because they had already been involved in the local efforts stimulated by the Children's Bureau. As Mrs. Brown of the GFWC would later put it in testimony for Sheppard-Towner before Congress, "the women of this country trust the Children's Bureau. It has . . . become known in every state and city. It has established cooperation with state health authorities and with countless agencies working for children. Women's clubs and committees are accustomed to cooperating on health campaigns under its guidance."[64] Appealing to fundamental moral values that everyone agreed were appropriate for women to espouse, even during a war, the Children's Bureau and women's groups could talk— to one another and to the broader public—about Lathrop's proposed federal program. They discussed it as a much-needed measure to protect the well-being of babies and mothers.

Getting the Program through Congress

Lathrop's plan was first submitted to Congress in a July 1918 bill sponsored by the nation's first Congresswoman, Jeannette Rankin of Montana. Various other versions of the measure were also introduced in 1918, 1919, and 1920, and it eventually converged on the "Sheppard-Towner" version, sponsored by Democratic Senator Mor-

MATERNAL MORTALITY RATES

per 1000 births
Latest available figures up to 1917

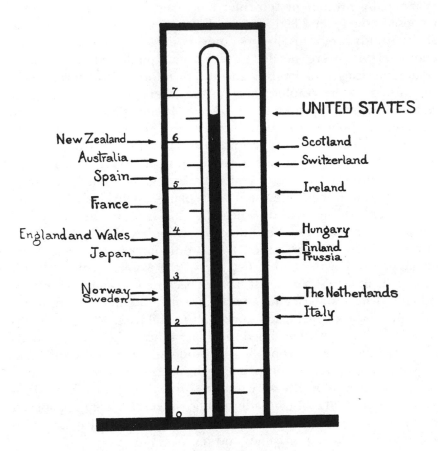

The United States lost over 23,000 women in 1918 from childbirth. We have a higher maternal death rate than any other of the principal countries.

CHILDREN'S BUREAU, U.S. DEPARTMENT OF LABOR.

Figure 32
Source: *Eighth Annual Report of the Chief, Children's Bureau, 1920, p. 9.*

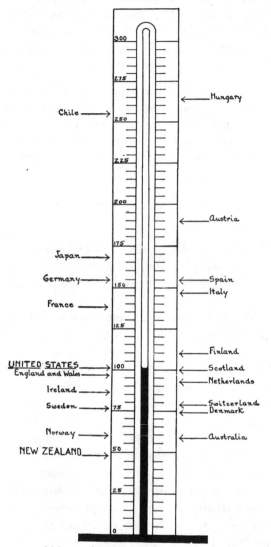

INFANT MORTALITY THERMOMETER

DEATHS UNDER 1 YEAR OF AGE PER 1,000 BIRTHS

Within the first year after birth, the United States loses 1 in 10 of all babies born. It ranks eleventh among the principal countries of the world. New Zealand loses fewer babies than any other country.

Rates are for latest available years up to 1918.

CHILDREN'S BUREAU, U.S. DEPARTMENT OF LABOR.

Figure 33

Source: Eighth Annual Report of the Chief, Children's Bureau, 1920, p. 10.

ris Sheppard of Texas, a well-known supporter of prohibition and women's suffrage, and by Republican Representative Horace Mann Towner of Iowa.[65] Significantly, the measures debated in Congress carried an explanatory clause stressing that "the act is not a charity." As the historian Louis Covotsos recounts:

> An earlier draft had limited the act's application to those unable to pay. Lathrop explained, however, that "further study seemed to show that this would result in charity rather than a measure designed to be in large part educational. The bill is designed to emphasize public responsibility for the protection of life just as already through our public schools we recognize public responsibility in the education of children." If the services of the bill were not open to all, Lathrop cautioned, "the services would degenerate into poor relief."[66]

Committee hearings and reports recurred during several sessions, before Congress finally passed the Sheppard-Towner bill by large margins. President Harding signed it into law on November 23, 1921.[67]

We may well wonder why the measure ever passed. After all, this innovative federal welfare undertaking slipped through during a period of intense conservative reaction against "meddling" by the national government in state and local affairs. Republicans swept the U.S. presidential and congressional elections of 1920. Congress, heeding outcries by business interests and by people prepared to engage in vicious red-baiting, quickly discontinued "emergency" federal agencies which reformers had hoped to make permanent after the war. Along with other reformer-dominated federal agencies, the Children's Bureau had its share of determined enemies, so that Sheppard-Towner was roundly denounced during the congressional debates by antisuffrage groups, by defenders of states' rights, by some medical groups, and by forces trying to protect the bureaucratic prerogatives of the Public Health Service.[68] Proponents of the legislation were accused of trying to foist on the American people "paternalistic" or "socialistic" measures from Europe, since some members of Congress sensed that reformers had broader hopes for the development of an American welfare state. As Representative Frank L. Greene explained:

> Back of this unpretentious, simple looking bill today are the agencies that for a long time have been persistently and insidiously

working to incorporate into our American system of public policy
. . . Government supervision of mothers; Government care and
maintenance of infants; Government control of education; Government control of training for vocations; Government regulation
of employment, the hours, holidays, wages, accident insurance and
all; Government insurance against unemployment; Government
old-age pension.[69]

What is more, the women who led the Children's Bureau were
ridiculed in Congress. Senator James Reed of Missouri led the way,
declaring: "It is now proposed to turn the control of the mothers of
the land over to a few single ladies holding government jobs at
Washington . . . We would better reverse the proposition and provide
for a committee of mothers to take charge of the old maids and
teach them how to acquire a husband and have babies of their
own."[70]

Several factors account for Sheppard-Towner's success in the face
of such opposition, even during a period when other federal programs died or suffered sharp reverses. For one thing, the Children's
Bureau was, ironically, fortunate that it had not already achieved
something like Sheppard-Towner as an emergency measure during
World War I. Emergency programs that were established for the
duration of the war had time to arouse opposition, energizing interest groups that could press Congress to dismantle them in 1919 and
1920. Potentially, Sheppard-Towner faced opposition especially
from medical doctors associated locally, at state levels, and nationally
in the growing American Medical Association. But even though some
local medical groups along with the AMA's official journal and the
Illinois State Medical Association voiced considerable opposition to
Sheppard-Towner during 1920, the national AMA did not take an
official oppositional stance until a few months after the initial legislation passed.[71] The AMA's opposition was to become more intense
and effective over time, as local doctors learned (in part, from Sheppard-Towner centers) about the value of preventive care for mothers
and infants, and as they actually had to deal with competition from
programs funded by Sheppard-Towner.[72] Had Sheppard-Towner
already existed throughout the war, locally rooted and nationally
coordinated opposition to it might have built up more fully by 1921,
as comparable opposition did for many other reform measures that
became "emergency programs" at the start of the war.

Not only did the proposed Sheppard-Towner program escape

opposition it might have faced as the war ended; it also benefited from the buildup of well-organized support, rooted in thousands of localities across the nation and reaching into the halls of Congress. Professional reformers, charity organizations, churches, and labor unions all were involved in the campaign. So were leading national women's magazines, including the *Woman's Home Companion, McCall's,* the *Ladies Home Journal,* and above all *Good Housekeeping* under the editorship of W. F. Bigelow.[73] Yet the pressure for Sheppard-Towner came especially from women's associations, whose members resonated with the arguments about the need to protect babies and mothers that the Children's Bureau had articulated so clearly. Naturally, Florence Kelley was an early, passionate, and persistent advocate of the proposed federal program; and the National Consumers' League endorsed it.[74]

Offering a broader base of support, the General Federation of Women's Clubs also strongly supported Sheppard-Towner. At its Fourteenth Biennial Convention in May 1918, the Federation declared

> *Whereas,* it has been shown that the deaths of mothers from causes incident to maternity and the deaths of young children are largely preventable, and
>
> *Whereas,* the inevitable losses of war are an additional reason for stopping avoidable waste of life, therefore be it
>
> *Resolved:* That the General Federation of Women's Clubs approve the plan for Federal aid for the public protection of maternity and infancy set forth in the Fifth Annual Report of the Children's Bureau of the Department of Labor, and urge the prompt enactment by Congress of a measure to that end.[75]

And two years later at its Fifteenth Biennial, the General Federation called upon Congress for "speedy passage" of the by-then-pending Sheppard-Towner bill.[76]

By now organized across thirty-seven states, the National Congress of Mothers pushed for the enactment of Sheppard-Towner as well. In December 1919, *Child-Welfare Magazine* announced the introduction of Sheppard's bill by declaring: "Federal Maternity Bill Gives Aid to Welfare Work: States to go Fifty-Fifty on Giving to Mothers and Children Same Care as to Their Farm Animals."[77] Thereafter the leaders of the Congress repeatedly urged their members to take action, using announcements in *Child-Welfare Magazine* to spread the word and point the way.[78] In addition, the president of the National Congress, Mrs. Milton Higgins, joined other heads of women's groups in testifying in Washington. She not only supported the establishment of the maternal and infant health program but also defended the Children's Bureau as its administrator, despite the fact that the Mothers' Congress enjoyed especially close ties to one of the potential bureaucratic rivals, the Education Bureau.[79]

All in all, according to Dorothy Bradbury, a huge array of women's groups joined along with the Consumers' League, the General Federation, and the Mothers' Congress in the feminine chorus of support for Sheppard-Towner. Among "the many other organizations endorsing the measure" were:

> . . .
> Women's National Democratic Committee
> Women's National Republican Committee
> Association of Collegiate Alumnae
> National Women's Christian Temperance Union
> Council of Jewish Women
> National Board of Young Women's Christian Association
> Continental Congress of the
>   Daughters of the American Revolution
> National Association of Deans of Women
> National Federation of Business and Professional Women
> . . .
> National Organization for Public Health Nursing
> National Child Welfare Association
> National Council of Women
> Service Star Legion
> American Child Hygiene Association
> National Women's Trade Union League
> Superintendant's Department of the
>   National Educational Association
> Women's Press Club
> League of American Pen Women.[80]

Women's groups did much more than endorse Sheppard-Towner; they also coordinated efforts across all levels of the polity. Some flavor of this can be discerned in the instructions given in the "President's Desk" section of the official magazine of the National Congress of Mothers in February 1920:

Maternity and Infancy Bill, U.S. Senate.

Every woman must be interested in helping secure the passage of the above important measure . . .

Petitions will be sent to organizations in the National Congress of Mothers and Parent-Teacher Associations. It is earnestly desired that women will take them, secure as many signatures as possible and return them to the address given on them.

They will be arranged by states, and presented to the Senate. Which state will get the largest number of signers? . . .

Copies of the bill have been sent to all presidents of State Branches. Publicity through your local papers will help in education of public opinion . . .

Only by this expression will Congress know that women approve the bill and want it made law.[81]

Three months after issuing this appeal, *Child-Welfare Magazine* followed it up with an inquiry:

Have you sent in a petition to your Senator and Congressman to support the Sheppard bill, S.3259[?] Babies have a right to live. Mothers have a right to such instruction as will save infant lives. The country needs every life. It will take several generations to make up for the losses of human life in the war. Never has there been greater need for saving life.

Mothers can save 200,000 lives of babies every year if Congress helps them by passing this bill.

Use the petition given on the last page of [this] magazine . . . [82]

In efforts such as this one by the National Congress of Mothers, *Good Housekeeping* magazine aided women's groups by supplying petitions for the Sheppard-Towner bill.[83] So strong was locally organized women's interest in Sheppard-Towner that thirty-four state governors ended up publicly supporting the legislation.[84]

In November 1920, after consulting with ten major women's associations with over 10 million members, leaders of the recently created National League of Women Voters (a reorganization of the National American Woman Suffrage Association), set up the Women's Joint Congressional Committee (WJCC) designed to promote legislative goals important to women.[85] The WJCC made enactment of the Sheppard-Towner bill its first priority and "lobbied vigorously while the constituent organizations drummed up grass-roots support through meetings, leaflets, and newsletters, causing members of Congress to receive a deluge of letters and telegrams. One Senator's secretary reported, 'I think every woman in my state has written to the Senator.'"[86] As the historian J. Stanley Lemons explains:

> Delegations trooped to Washington to see their representatives and President Harding. In the final weeks before passage the WJCC subcommittee conducted interviews with congressmen at the rate of fifty per day . . . Senator Kenyon, a strong backer of the bill, confirmed the effectiveness of the lobby: "If the members could have voted on that measure secretly in their cloak rooms it would have been killed as emphatically as it was finally passed in the open under the pressure of the Joint Congressional Committee of Women."[87]

Seeking to explain why legislation so distasteful to many doctors had passed anyway, the *Journal of the American Medical Association* pointed out that "the women's lobby for the bill was 'one of the strongest that has ever been seen in Washington.'"[88]

The coordinated lobbying of women's organizations on behalf of Sheppard-Towner came at a supremely propitious political conjuncture. The "Act for the Promotion of the Welfare and Hygiene of Maternity and Infancy" passed overwhelmingly in late 1921, and the appropriation to fund it was approved the following year. These measures came to congressional votes *just after* American women were fully enfranchised, yet *before* actual patterns of female voting in national elections had become clear. In the words of Stanley Lemons, the "principal force moving Congress was fear of being punished at the polls. The women's vote was an unknown quantity at the time. For years suffragists had promised to clean house when they got the vote, and they claimed that women would be issue-oriented rather than party-oriented. Politicians feared that women voters would cast a bloc vote or remain aloof from the regular parties" if they did not get the Sheppard-Towner welfare measure that virtually all women's groups supported with such intense moral conviction.[89]

At the climactic moment when female suffrage was achieved, it seemed to many, prosuffragists and antisuffragists alike, that the values of women's formerly separate sphere might now reshape the public realm. Before too many years, these fears about American women becoming a political "gender for themselves" would prove unfounded. But in 1921, the potential of concerted action by millions of new female voters spurred politicians to accede to Sheppard-Towner. It sensitized them to the temporary moral consensus that the Children's Bureau and women's associations had created in favor of an expanded maternalist welfare effort by the federal government. The nation as a whole, argued the women who led the fight for Sheppard-Towner, would gain from this expansion of the resources of the Children's Bureau, an official embodiment of organized mother love reaching throughout the civic community.

Institutionalizing a New Program and a Long-Standing Vision of an Expanded Feminine Sphere

After the enactment of the federal enabling legislation for Sheppard-Towner, the Children's Bureau faced the challenge of working out relationships with the dozens of U.S. states that had to be involved in the implementation of the new program. The Bureau was now headed by Grace Abbott, longtime friend and professional associate of Julia Lathrop, former director of the Illinois Immigrants' Protective League, and former resident of Hull House.[90] Drawing on her previous experience as administrator for the Children's Bureau of the 1916 federal child labor law, Abbott was anxious to work cooperatively with state officials, encouraging the states to develop various programs suited to their needs as they saw them.[91] Indeed, even though governors could initially accept temporary federal matching funds on behalf of their states, federal funding could not continue unless each state legislature officially agreed to set up and partially fund a public Sheppard-Towner program in that state. "By the end of the fiscal year 1922, all but six states had accepted the provisions of the act," and eventually all but three states—Illinois, Connecticut, and Massachusetts—joined the federal program.[92] The state of Massachusetts actually mounted a constitutional appeal against the Sheppard-Towner Act. But the Children's Bureau ensured that the U.S. Solicitor General was prepared to support the program in court and the Supreme Court brushed aside the challenge.[93] The matching-grant principle featured in Sheppard-Towner had previously been used in other federal programs.

With the blessing of the Bureau, many women's groups, including the Federations of Women's Clubs and Leagues of Women Voters, were active in persuading state legislatures to establish Sheppard-Towner programs.[94] Grace Abbott addressed the Sixteenth Biennial Convention of the General Federation of Women's Clubs in June 1922 on "The Responsibility of Club Women in Promoting the Welfare of Children." Reminding the assembled clubwomen that "the Children's Bureau had its beginning in the desire of the Child Welfare Divisions of clubs all over the country to see their work put on a national basis, with national and official recognition of its fundamental importance," Abbott spoke about the steps involved in state-level implementation of Sheppard-Towner and suggested approaches local clubwomen might use to influence state-level efforts, stressing, however, that there "can be no single model plan because conditions differ so widely in our forty-eight states."[95] Also with the encouragement of the Children's Bureau, clubwomen concerned themselves with the administration of the new programs under Sheppard-Towner after they were set up. The Minnesota State Federation, for example, reported to the Sixteenth Biennial that "Our Federation is represented in the administration of the Sheppard-Towner Act, for which Minnesota now has money available. We have at least two women on our state Board of Control."[96] As Mrs. Ira Couch Wood summarized the situation for the delegates to the Biennial:

> It will now be the duty of the women in each state to see that adequate programs are developed for the expenditure of the Federal and state appropriations under this [Sheppard-Towner] act. The reports from the various states show that many club women are alive to the possibilities of benefit to mothers and babies through this new legislation, and it is strongly recommended that women continue to show their deep interest until they are officially recognized on all the State Boards created under this act, and are appointed on all Advisory Committees.[97]

Once states opted into the Sheppard-Towner system of matching subsidies, the 1921 act had the effect of reinforcing and spreading a nationwide system of "permanent administrative units that would promote child welfare reforms."[98] As the historian Sheila Rothman explains this important structural point:

> To receive federal funds, a state had not only to approve matching funds, but also to establish a state agency that would coordinate its health programs with the Children's Bureau. And this agency had to be a separate unit, a Bureau of Child Hygiene or Division of Child Welfare, within the state Department of Health. Its concern for children could not be diluted with any other responsibility. Further, this agency had to spawn county agencies, mini-departments of child hygiene to administer the funds. All of this was intended to bring into being a powerful and pervasive network of governmental bodies whose *exclusive* concern was child welfare.[99]

Sheppard-Towner, meanwhile, gave the Children's Bureau in Washington, DC, a greatly expanded public mission along with the influence over substantial resources to be disbursed to the states. Although the final 1921 legislation forced the Bureau to share administrative powers with representatives of other agencies, including the Commissioner of Education and the Surgeon General from the Public Health Service, cooperative patterns were soon established that left the Bureau's Maternity and Infant-Hygiene Division in charge of Sheppard-Towner's practical implementation.[100] The 1921 legislation also eliminated explicit mention of some of the Bureau's goals—such as the preference for rural areas, and the requirement that women be appointed to official positions—yet the Sheppard-Towner program ended up evolving as the Bureau had originally hoped.

Central Children's Bureau personnel devoted to implementing the act were kept to a minimum; only nine officials were involved as late as 1926: three physicians, three nurses, and three clerks.[101] Nevertheless, under Sheppard-Towner's authority, the Bureau carried through special studies on maternal and infant-welfare issues, some at its own initiative, and others requested by the states.[102] Building upon practices established well before Sheppard-Towner, yet now coordinating them where possible with the new state and local programs, the Bureau also circulated millions of pieces of informational literature, above all copies of the pamphlets *Infant Care* and *Prenatal Care*, and carried on an extensive correspondence with hundreds of thousands of mothers who wrote to Washington asking for information and advice.[103] While allowing state-to-state variation in program design, the leadership of the Children's Bureau was able to push all states toward improving official birth statistics as a way of developing the knowledge base necessary for designing sound Sheppard-Towner programs and channeling resources toward places where infant and maternal mortality rates were highest.[104] Finally, of course, states across the nation had an incentive to set up widespread infant and maternal health programs, because they were spurred by the women's federations and encouraged by the carrot of the federal subsidies administered by the Bureau.

The upshot was that many Sheppard-Towner programs did place a priority on delivering public health information and services to small towns and rural areas.[105] "Prenatal and child health conferences conducted by a physician and a nurse reached many women in thousands of counties. They were held wherever space was available—in churches, schoolrooms, grocery stores, or homes."[106] Public health nurses funded by Sheppard-Towner, or added on by states and localities responding to the stimulus of the federal program, soon excelled at reaching mothers and babies in remote areas, extending to them practical advice that had already become available in urban centers.[107] From time to time, too, states called upon the Bureau to send out its "Child Welfare Special":

> a truck compactly equipped as a child health center which had been used by the bureau for rural demonstrations since 1919. For example in 1922 thousands of preschool and school-age children in the small towns and rural counties of Tennessee and Oklahoma received attention and physical examinations in the "Child-Welfare Special," brought in at the request of the state health officer. The attention which it attracted all along the route added to the educational value. Some states adopted the model and sent their own mobile clinic to tour the countryside.[108]

All in all, the historian Richard Meckel tells us, the enhancement of activities "was particularly noteworthy in southern and western states. Prior to Sheppard-Towner, maternal, infant, and early childhood health programs in those states had been all but nonexistent. By 1925, however, many of these states had appropriated sufficient funds to allow them to receive near or all of the federal matching grants available to them." The southern states that fully utilized

Sheppard-Towner funds included ones such as Alabama and Georgia that had not enacted mothers' pensions or protective labor laws. Meckel also points out that

> at least some of this [Sheppard-Towner] work was reaching nonwhites, who had been virtually ignored up to this time. Minnesota and Nebraska targeted their Native American populations for special attention. New Mexico, Arizona, and Texas employed Spanish-speaking nurses to give lecture-demonstrations and make home visits within the Hispanic community. And the South, although keeping its programs segregated, for the first time made an effort to extend public health services to blacks.[109]

In the final analysis, too, women provided much of the official and professional personnel for agencies subsidized fully or partially by Sheppard-Towner, even as voluntary women's groups provided organized support from the citizenry. In Washington, DC, the Children's Bureau was led and primarily peopled by female officials. Out in the states, not only were women appointed to advisory committees, female professionals also led most of the bureaus and divisions that directed state Sheppard-Towner programs, especially at the beginning. And women provided virtually all of the paid and volunteer services that directly reached pregnant women, babies, and small children in local communities.[110] As Sheila Rothman writes, "Sheppard-Towner essentially relied on the skills of women trained in the scientific care of children and female-led community reform campaigns to reduce infant and maternal mortality."[111]

"Sheppard-Towner . . . made public health nurses the mainstay of the program," employing 812 of them by 1926.[112] They "were the ones who gave hygienic advice, who encouraged breast-feeding, who gave routine care to expectant mothers, and who instructed the midwives" in the many state programs to improve and supervise midwife services.[113] Their "work in education and disease prevention made the public health nurse[s] the ideal staff member[s]" in the nearly 3,000 prenatal centers as well as the many other grassroots programs run through Sheppard-Towner.[114] Public health nurses were social workers of sorts as well as medical practitioners, whose "training frequently came through courses offered in schools of social welfare"; and such nurses typically served "on the staff of a settlement house, a municipal department of child hygiene, or a public school," rather than in hospitals.[115]

Working along with the public health nurses, "physicians . . . performed the straightforward medical tasks in Sheppard-Towner clinics," while a "few full-time physicians assumed administrative responsibilities, generally heading state programs, and part-time and even volunteer physicians conducted health conferences."[116] The physicians who became involved in Sheppard-Towner tended to be women, reflecting the proclivity of women doctors "to practice social medicine in a public setting." Women in the medical profession of the early-twentieth-century United States faced strong obstacles if they attempted to build private practices. At the same time, many women physicians felt "a special commitment to the field of preventive health," a commitment they shared with other educated women in the ranks of Progressive Era reformers and with the members of the women's federations of the day. "Accordingly, female medical societies were affiliated both with local medical societies and with the General Federation of Women's Clubs. And women physicians often led community campaigns to improve child health care."[117] "Being women as well as physicians," Dr. Florence Brown Sherborn, president of the Iowa Society of Medical Women, had explained in the *Women's Medical Journal* at the height of the Progressive Era, "we share with our sex in the actual and potential motherhood of the race. Being woman we make common cause with all women as it is shown in our present affiliation with federate clubs, etc. And being women and mothers, our first and closest and dearest interest is the child."[118] Not suprisingly, the Children's Bureau, state child welfare agencies, and local Sheppard-Towner projects all found it easy to draw upon the talents of professional women who shared such an outlook.

The Sheppard-Towner program, as Sheila Rothman has so ably argued, embodied a feminine vision of public preventive health care that had been worked out by social settlement reformers, by women professionals, and by civically engaged clubwomen. This vision drew upon the cultural resources of the "separate sphere" of nineteenth-century American women, yet extended what was once domestic action into a new understanding of governmental action for societal welfare. Sheppard-Towner expanded the responsibility of the state, giving authoritative backing and federal resources to a function—education of mothers in hygienic health practices—that educated and organized American women had come to understand as a female responsibility in the community as well as the home. Women, along with many others in the Progressive Era and the early 1920s, believed that doctors were responsible for curing illnesses, while communities led by women should take active steps to prevent illnesses, especially for the sake of mothers and babies. In the words of the Child Welfare Committee of the National League of Women Voters: "Prenatal and maternity care means more than good obstetrics; it means normal family life, freedom of the mother from industrial labor before and after childbirth, ability to nurse the child, above all, education in standards of care so that women and their husbands will demand good obstetrics and will no longer run the risk of . . . preventable tragedies."[119] "Medicine in other words was only a small part of a campaign for health," and health itself was to be grounded in the well-being of entire families and communities.[120] Through the Sheppard-Towner programs—which spread services to impoverished rural areas, yet were open to all American mothers and children—the Children's Bureau put this maternalist vision of social welfare into effect.

The Defeat of Sheppard-Towner

So well established were Sheppard-Towner activities by 1926 that local and state staff members, officials of the Children's Bureau, and supportive women's associations across the United States anticipated that it would be easy to persuade Congress to renew the federal appropriation, which was scheduled to run out in 1927. At first, things went smoothly.[121] At the suggestion of the Secretary of Labor in the Coolidge administration, Representative James S. Parker introduced a bill authorizing an extension of funds from 1927 to 1929. After brief committee hearings and a favorable recommendation, the House of Representatives passed this bill by a margin of 218 to 44 votes on April 5, 1926. "Perhaps because it was popular with their constituents and with the various county and municipal officials in their districts, the members of the House discounted opposition arguments and overwhelmingly approved the extension."[122] But then conservative forces, "fresh from having recently beaten another progressive proposal—the federal child labor amendment," manuevered to stop the bill in the Senate.[123]

Arguing against extension were the same kinds of groups that had opposed the enactment of Sheppard-Towner back in 1921: defenders of the prerogatives of localities and states; formerly antisuffragist women's groups; and above all organized private physicians, now speaking through the full force of the American Medical Association, whose House of Delegates had from 1922 onward condemned Sheppard-Towner as "an imported socialistic scheme" of "state medicine."[124] During the 1926 debate, the AMA fully mobilized against Sheppard-Towner. The *Journal of the American Medical Association* asked all physicians to protest the extension in letters to the President; the AMA sent oppositional pamphlets to all Representatives and Senators; and the AMA leadership sent telegrams opposing Sheppard-Towner to the President, the Vice President, and certain interested Senators.[125] Indeed, by 1926, the opponents to Sheppard-Towner were highly mobilized and determined; and they were operating in a generally conservative political climate, presided over by President Calvin Coolidge, who had been elected by a landslide in 1924. Coolidge endorsed more funds for Sheppard-Towner, but only for an interim period during which he expected the states to prepare themselves for a full takeover of its programs.

Inside the Senate, the Committee on Education and Labor reduced the proposed funding extension for Sheppard-Towner to only one year (reflecting the view held by a minority of all Senators that this "successful" federal matching program should be handed over to the states). Meanwhile, a few ultraconservative Senators gave voice to extremist attacks on Sheppard-Towner and to attacks on the integrity of the mostly female officials who ran its programs.[126] These Senators wanted immediate repeal of Sheppard-Towner, and they conducted a running filibuster that could not be broken, forcing the renewal bill up against the January 1927 deadline of the end of the brief second session of the 69th Congress. Extension of Sheppard-Towner monies had to be approved in that session if state legislatures meeting early in 1927 were to be in a position to vote matching funds to continue existing programs.

Faced with the dilemma of what to do at this critical juncture, Senator Sheppard consulted the chief backers of the two-year extension, Grace Abbott of the Children's Bureau and the leaders of the Women's Committee for the Extension of the Maternity and Infancy Act (a committee of the Women's Joint Congressional Caucus). Reluctantly, the supporters of Sheppard-Towner inside and outside the Senate agreed to an amendment to the funding extension bill that secured the acquiescence of the program's opponents. The amendment said that after a continuation of federal funding from 1927 to 1929, the Sheppard-Towner Act itself would be removed from the books, thus terminating the program altogether. Grace Abbott, Florence Kelley, and the leaders of the Women's Committee accepted this compromise as a way to keep funds flowing, and because, as Kelley rationalized, it "seems inconceivable that the next Congress could be as bad as this one. I don't believe it can."[127] Opponents of Sheppard-Towner were jubilant at having forced its imminent demise. The amended extension bill quickly passed the Senate, and the House concurred. On January 22, 1927, President Coolidge signed "the virtual repealer bill," and some months later he made clear that he welcomed the withdrawal of the federal government from this and other "state-aid projects."[128]

Before and after Sheppard-Towner actually expired on June 30, 1929, many attempts were made to undo the decision of January 1927. Between 1928 and 1932, some fourteen bills were introduced proposing to give new life, in one way or another, to federally coordinated and funded maternity and infancy health programs.[129] The Children's Bureau and the organized women "rallied behind a bill which was more liberal than Sheppard-Towner. It specified that the money would be spent in cooperation with the states, but did not require either acceptance by the state legislatures or matching funds. The federal money was to be apportioned on the basis of need, not population."[130] Needless to say, the forces of opposition importuned even more strongly against proposals such as this. Meanwhile, the new President, Herbert Hoover, proved to be no friend of the Children's Bureau.[131] Sensitive to advice from medical experts and advised by the Secretary of the Interior, a close friend who was an M.D., Hoover favored amalgamation of all federal health programs within the Public Health Service, something proposed in one way or another by many of the bills introduced into Congress between 1928 and 1932. President Hoover froze the Children's Bureau out of planning for the 1930 White House Conference on Child Health and Protection, which ended up recommending in favor of new programs to be run by the Public Health Service.

The Children's Bureau managed to rally its allies to forestall any takeover by the male- and medical-dominated Public Health Service. But the result was a stalemate, which meant no continuation of federal involvement in maternity and infancy health programs after 1929. At first, to be sure, many of the states maintained such programs on their own, although only "sixteen states appropriated enough money to exceed or equal the previous total."[132] Then, as the deepening Depression brought economic and relief issues to the fore, state-level funding shrank, and a number of states dropped maternity and infancy programs altogether. The Children's Bureau was not in the position it might have been had Sheppard-Towner programs survived to respond to the family needs created by the Depression. Arguably, too, the Bureau would have had much greater say in the social policy debates of the New Deal had it retained after 1929 the influence across the country and inside the Executive Branch that administration of this "first federal social-welfare program" had once given it.

The foregoing paragraphs have recounted the ending of Sheppard-Towner in a "miasma of controversy, frustration, and defeat."[133] But we still need to understand why this demise occurred. What changes took place between the contested launching of Sheppard-Towner in 1921 and 1922 and its strangulation through congressional stalemate and presidential tepidness between 1927 and 1932?

One set of changes has been ably analyzed by Sheila Rothman. In her words:

> Leaders of the American medical profession successfully expanded the domain of the private doctor to encompass the role of women and the responsibility of the state. In essence, they helped to incorporate the services offered by the public clinics into the practice of the private physician. During the 1920s, it became appropriate and desirable for the first time for a private doctor to offer preventive health services and to give advice on personal hygiene . . . [Thus the] defeat of Sheppard-Towner marked the end of female expertise in the field of health care and, at the same time, shifted the provision of preventive health services from the public to the private sector. Women trained in hygiene working in state-supported clinics gave way to physicians engaged in private practice.[134]

Already by the late 1910s, to be sure, the American Medical Association, reflecting the outlook of many local and state associations of doctors, had become determined to oppose any strong federal role in the provision of basic medical services in the United States, promoting instead the fee-for-service relationship of private physicians to their individually recruited patients. The national AMA's hostile stance toward Sheppard-Towner grew out of its ideological opposition to anything that smacked of "state medicine." Yet, as Rothman argues, local doctors did not at first have a clear alternative to offer to the Sheppard-Towner clinics, because doctors were accustomed to treating only very sick patients. The custom of regular, preventive health-care visits to doctors' offices by well patients, including pregnant women and infants and children, had not yet been established. Then, during the 1920s, the AMA took many steps to persuade and instruct doctors about the virtues of providing preventive health care in their own offices.

Ironically, too, the Sheppard-Towner programs themselves helped to educate their own medical competition. Specialist doctors were regularly incorporated into Sheppard-Towner conferences, including some who later sought to make enhanced claims for the medical oversight of pregnancy.[135] Sheppard-Towner clinics also fostered ties with local general practitioners, in effect suggesting to many of them the value of incorporating preventive maternity and infancy health services into their private practices. The result of all these changes in medical practices and claims, as Rothman explains, was to put the organized medical profession into a stronger and stronger position to claim to the federal government that "private doctors were the appropriate and the exclusive guardians of *all* matters of health—including, of course, the reduction of infant and maternal mortality rates."[136] Certain groups of women doctors and of physicians especially concerned with public health were the only dissenters from the growing certainty of organized doctors that they could handle all of the health needs of Americans through private practices and organizations. But by the mid-1920s women and public health doctors (often the same people) were thoroughly marginalized within the power structures of the American Medical Association.[137]

Rothman's explanation for the demise of Sheppard-Towner is ingenious. Because the AMA was a widespread federated association, its local and state associations of private physicians, increasingly confident that they could do better what Sheppard-Towner clinics were trying to do, certainly could pressure congressional representatives against the program's extension, even as women's clubs were press-

ing for its continuation. Yet it is not clear how much grassroots
pressure actually was exerted by doctors in 1926–27.[138] Besides, at
that point Sheppard-Towner still had a strong actual majority in the
House, as well as a potential two-thirds majority in the Senate (if an
up or down vote could have been obtained).[139] Thus, to my mind,
Rothman's argument makes better sense of why the various efforts
between 1928 and 1932 to restart Sheppard-Towner were so divided
and inimical to continued control of federal maternal and infant
health services by the Children's Bureau. Private doctors gained the
ear of President Hoover after his election in 1928. And they worked
closely with the Public Health Service inside the federal government,
supporting its efforts to take away from the Children's Bureau the
administration of any further health programs for mothers and
infants that the federal government might fund.

Not surprisingly, the 1930 White House Conference controlled by
the Public Health Service concluded, first, that "the experience of
municipal health departments has demonstrated conclusively that
programs for the improvement of the health of the mother and
child can be conducted successfully only as part of the general program of a well-organized health department" and, second, that
"some activities now included in the program of most health departments can be transferred gradually to the general practitioner
of medicine. In the interests of child health, insofar as practical, the
family physician should become a practitioner of preventive as well
as curative medicine."[140] Influenced by this definition of the ideal
situation, President Hoover and his key advisors were unwilling to
promote the straightforward rechartering of Sheppard-Towner.
And even though the Children's Bureau and organized women could
block the Hoover administration's effort to pass bills favoring the
Public Health Service, they could not push through Congress a
renewal (or enhancement) of Sheppard-Towner without President
Hoover's support.

If the growing hegemony of "medical expertise" inside (and connected to) the executive branch helps to make sense of the stalemated
struggles over the federal health role during Herbert Hoover's presidency, this factor does not offer a fully satisfactory explanation for
the contrasting fate of Sheppard-Towner in Congress in 1926–27
versus 1921. Both the Harding and the Coolidge administrations,
after all, nominally supported Sheppard-Towner bills. And even if

the forces opposed to Sheppard-Towner were more determined in 1926, they were not much different from the opposition back in 1921. At both legislative junctures, moreover, opponents could only command minorities of votes in Congress. This suggests that changes from the early to the late 1920s affected not only forces working against Sheppard-Towner but also those working in the program's favor. Let us inquire a bit further into this possibility.

At the outset we should note that organized American women, the chief proponents of Sheppard-Towner in 1921, certainly did *not* abandon the program in 1926–27 (or afterward). Julia Lathrop's original insistence on establishing Sheppard-Towner as a nominally universal program, open to all mothers and babies and not just targeted on the poor, paid off in the continued enthusiasm and dogged loyalty of virtually all upper- and middle-class women's as-sociations—loyalty both toward the federal maternity and infancy health education effort and toward the female-led Children's Bureau as its administrator.[141] There was no sharp falling off of organized women's support for Sheppard-Towner, as occurred with mothers' pensions during the 1920s. To be sure, one small and exclusive women's group, the Daughters of the American Revolution, did switch sides between 1921 and 1927, accepting the red-baiting at-tacks launched against Sheppard-Towner by the ultraconservative Woman Patriots.[142] But otherwise there was remarkable continuity of organized women's support, and new groups joined the cause as well. The Women's Committee for the Extension of the Maternity and Infancy Act was composed of representatives of the "National Board of the Young Woman's Christian Association; National Coun-cil of Jewish Women; National Consumers' League; National Asso-ciation of Colored Women; National Council of Women; General Federation of Women's Clubs; National League of Women Voters; American Association of University Women; National Women's Trade Union League; National Congress of Parent-Teachers; and Women's Christian Temperance Union."[143] The leaders of all these organizations signed letters sent to every Senator during the critical 1926–27 debate on Sheppard-Towner's extension.[144] Hundreds of thousands of organizational units and millions of women were en-compassed by this array of organizations. If push had really come to shove about Sheppard-Towner, presumably these supporters could have mobilized a combination of the new female voting power and the traditional capacity of women's voluntary groups to engage in moralistic agitation of public opinion in states, communities, and congressional districts across the land.

Maybe not. There certainly is some evidence that general-interest women's voluntary groups, especially those old stalwarts of grass-roots maternalist politics, the General Federation of Women's Clubs and the National Congress of Parent-Teacher Associations (PTA), had lost much of their political energy and broad sense of social concern by the mid-1920s. To be sure, the PTA had grown significantly from the 1910s into the 1920s, and it was organized across forty-seven states by 1926.[145] But as the very name "PTA" signifies ("Congress of Mothers" was dropped in 1924), this widespread federated association had evolved into an adjunct of local school systems.[146] More strictly a middle-class association closely tied to the concerns of professional educators, the new PTA was no longer trying to "carry Mother Thought" into all realms of society and public policy, as the motto of the earlier Mothers' Congress had declared. Meanwhile, the General Federation of Women's Clubs was, from the middle of the 1920s, deemphasizing social concerns and turning back toward its original preoccupation with literary programs and "cultural uplift."[147] In 1926 and 1928, there were also internal challenges to the strong role the GFWC's leaders had taken in legislative lobbying through the Women's Joint Congressional Committee.[148] During the 1920s, many married women seem to have turned inward toward private family life, as sexuality and marriage were redefined in "companionate" terms, and as childrearing became culturally understood as a demanding maternal role.[149] Meanwhile, in the public sphere, specialized groups of women professionals were expanding, no doubt reducing the total sum of female commitment going into broad-spectrum associations such as the General Federation of Women's Clubs.[150]

Despite these tendencies, one can argue that an all-out fight over the continuation of Sheppard-Towner in 1926–27 could still have aroused nationwide efforts by women's voluntary organizations, simultaneously capturing the attention of large numbers of women voters. Arguably, such a fight might even have helped to keep middle-class American women engaged with broad social and political concerns. The impact of political battles on social outlooks should never be underestimated; the latter are not simply primordial givens outside of political processes.

But in this instance, we can never know for sure, because push never did come to shove about Sheppard-Towner. As we have seen, Grace Abbott and the leaders of the Women's Committee for the Extension of the Maternity and Infancy Act struck (what from their point of view was) a deal with the devil, agreeing to trade the statutory death of Sheppard-Towner in 1929 for two more years of fiscal and bureaucratic continuity after 1927. These national leaders of the organized women's coalition in American politics chose not to go to a full test of their political strength against the forces that wanted to kill Sheppard-Towner. They could have chosen to let a full-blown crisis develop in 1927, turning to grassroots mobilization to pressure the Senate into a straightforward vote on continuing the Sheppard-Towner program. Had this course of action been taken, and had the proponents of Sheppard-Towner won a victory, as they might well have done, subsequent renewals of Sheppard-Towner funding certainly would have been easier to get through Congress. And the Children's Bureau would have been in a much stronger position going into the Hoover administration, the Great Depression, and the New Deal.

Forces of bureaucratic inertia may be enough to explain why the supporters of Sheppard-Towner did not turn to grassroots mobilization and a full-scale political battle in 1927. In my view, Grace Abbott was always more prone than Julia Lathrop to deal with political problems through administrative negotiations with state-level officials and other federal officeholders; I do not believe that she ever understood as well as Lathrop the importance of combining the Children's Bureau's central initiatives with local voluntary mobilizations. But, of course, personal proclivities were not the only factors at work, since the changing personalities fitted the evolving structural realities. Precisely because of the initial successes of Sheppard-Towner, by the mid-1920s the Children's Bureau sat atop a vast federal network of professional agencies. Both Grace Abbott and the directors of the state Sheppard-Towner programs (who were heavily involved in lobbying Congress during 1926–27) were desperate to keep the already-established organizations and projects going. Understandably, the disproportionately female professional employees of Sheppard-Towner programs had a vital stake in such continuity. Already marginal in their public health professions, these women would have been out of work at least temporarily during 1927—if Sheppard-Towner supporters had allowed a full-blown crisis to develop in order to mobilize local voluntary groups of elite and middle-class married women to pressure Congress. What is more, like all leaders of nationally focused "corporatist" groups, the leaders of the Women's Committee (and of its parent organization, the Women's Joint Congressional Committee) probably found it easier to strike a back-room compromise than to turn back to their member organizations for political support. And the overall political climate in 1926–27, more conservative than that in 1921, encouraged Sheppard-Towner supporters to acquiesce in a deal.

Indeed, I wonder whether a lack of confidence about what organized American women could accomplish politically was not also at work here. Historians of Sheppard-Towner all agree that the original 1921 legislation achieved presidential and congressional support at a unique juncture, just after the Nineteenth Amendment had given all American women the right to vote, yet before it was clear how little immediate difference women's voting would make in the U.S. electoral and legislative landscape. Historians also agree that, by 1926–27, politicians understood that women were not going to vote as a bloc. As Joseph Chepaitis puts it, "the power of the women organized in behalf of the act was now vulnerable and no longer an overestimated force courted by both the legislative and executive branches; the women were forced to capitulate to the filibusters and compromise."[151] I doubt that the women were actually "forced" to capitulate. But we can speculate that the leaders of the Children's Bureau and the various women's organizations may themselves have been susceptible to the same doubts about female political prowess that affected politicians and legislators by the mid-1920s. If women's political prowess was overestimated in 1921, it was probably *underestimated* by both politicians and women's leaders in 1926–27. Consequently, the supporters of the extension of Sheppard-Towner may have given in too quickly, agreeing to a "compromise" whose terms were worse than necessary for their cause, and further undercutting American women's distinctive political capacities in the process. Their decision was understandable, but perhaps more a matter of choice and judgment than historians have recognized.

In the final analysis, however, we need to keep in mind that, whatever the tactical decisions of its supporters, Sheppard-Towner was politically vulnerable in the later 1920s, because the 1921 legislation had not established any permanent entitlement to its services;

nor had that legislation set up Sheppard-Towner as a program with automatically renewed appropriations. After five years, Sheppard-Towner was subject to the annual appropriations process, and thus vulnerable to short-term shifts and maneuvers in Congress. The broad political support that follows from a universalistic program constituency is clearly not the only factor affecting the fate of social policies. In contrast to mothers' pensions, Sheppard-Towner had such support, and so it flourished and expanded—but only for a time. Entitlement status, or automatically renewable appropriations, have also been important in ensuring the longevity of social policies throughout U.S. history. The most succesful measures, such as Civil War pensions and the Social Security old-age insurance system launched in 1935, have been those that ensured entitlements to cross-class categories of beneficiaries. The Sheppard-Towner program for mothers and infants might have joined this select policy company, had it enjoyed not only the cross-class support of American women but also the kind of legislative charter that would have freed it from the vagaries of congressional politics during the 1920s.

The Children's Bureau and the Potential for a Maternalist Welfare State

Looking back at the maternalist social policies achieved by the distinct, yet intertwined, campaigns on behalf of protective legislation for women workers, mothers' pensions, the establishment of the Children's Bureau, and the expansion of that agency's activities through Sheppard-Towner, we can discern the faint outlines of a broader institutional and ideological achievement. During the Progressive Era and the early 1920s, a nascent maternal welfare state began to come together in the United States, emerging in the space left open by the absence of civil bureaucracies and a strong working-class movement (the forces that were creating paternalist welfare states in other nations). Through regulations, public benefits, and services focused particularly on mothers and their children, the nascent maternalist welfare state sought to use public powers to promote the well-being of all American families. Women officials disproportionately staffed the government agencies charged with implementing these programs. And the new governmental functions were normatively justified as a universalization of mother love.

The Children's Bureau developed by the early 1920s into something close to the central directorate of this possible maternalist welfare state. This happened in several ways. Had the broadest hopes of its leaders been realized, the Bureau would have continued to expand maternal and infant health programs as efforts in civic education and community engagement, not just the personalized provision of medical or other professional services. Given its successful albeit short-lived experience in enforcing the Keating-Owen child labor legislation of 1916, the Bureau certainly would also have been able and willing to enforce strong federal child labor laws, along with generously funded programs for children with special needs.[152] What is more, the Bureau gathered and disseminated information about mothers' pensions, frequently noting that they were not being adequately funded by the states; so we can surmise that Bureau officials would gladly have provided federal coordination for more generously funded mothers' pensions, preventing them from deteriorating into a stigmatized type of public assistance inadequate to the needs of children and their mothers.[153] Finally, and most sweepingly, judging from the Bureau's studies and its reactions to economic depressions, it might well have promoted national health and maternity insurance, a minimum wage for all workers, and unemployment programs—all in the name of helping children and their families.[154]

"From its founding in 1912 until the passage of the Social Security Act of 1935," Lela Costin has correctly pointed out, "the Children's Bureau not only served the interests of children but was the central federal source . . . for authoritative information on families and their social and economic characteristics and needs."[155] This was a comfortable role for the Bureau, for its vision of children's welfare, like the vision of the social settlement movement from which its founders sprang, was always linked to a broad understanding of the need for socioeconomic security for all families. As Lillian Wald of the New York City Bureau of Child Hygiene, the prototype for the Children's Bureau and Sheppard-Towner, put it: "Control of child life, is more of a socio-economic than a medical problem . . . [It is] a question of environmental adjustment, industrial opportunities, living wage and civic cooperation."[156]

The social settlement leaders and elite and middle-class married women who worked hardest to achieve the Children's Bureau along with the other maternalist social policies of the Progressive Era operated with moral conceptions, and also with modes of nonelectoral politics, grounded in nineteenth-century America's system of "separate spheres" for males and females. In their eyes, the less-privileged American families whose security was especially to be furthered by new public policies were, ideally, families with a sharp division of labor between wage-earning husbands and domestically oriented mothers. From the perspective of later "feminist" thinking, which emphasizes the potential similarity of men's and women's activities, this idealization of separate spheres for the genders does not look progressive.[157] Thus it has been hard for many later observers to discern the possibilities for a generous and caring American welfare state inherent in the maternalist policy breakthroughs of the Progressive Era and the early 1920s.

Still, those possibilities existed and flourished—until they met defeats and setbacks from the middle to late 1920s. Had the possibilities for a maternalist American welfare state ever been fully realized, there would have been a very different system of public social provision in the United States from the one elaborated through Civil War benefits in the late nineteenth century, and also a very different system from the one the nation would eventually build around the Social Security Act's program of contributory old-age insurance. A maternalist American welfare state, as promoted and partially realized by the distinctive women's politics of the Progressive Era, would have done much more than earlier or later U.S. systems of social provision to help children rather than the elderly, to benefit women directly rather than through the wage-earning capacities of husbands, and to buffer families from the full impact of participation in capitalist labor markets. No doubt, such a maternalist welfare state would have had its problems and limitations. But it would also have approximated ideals that have been marginalized in alternative systems of public social provision, in the United States and elsewhere.

America's First Modern Social Policies and Their Legacies

The story of modern social provision in the United States does not, as many people suppose, begin with the Social Security Act of 1935. Nor was America merely a laggard on a universally traveled road toward "the modern welfare state." From the late nineteenth century onward, the United States took a journey with marked twists and turns, exploring several different paths as its national and state governments devised public regulations and social spending to buffer many citizens against material want, market dislocations, and family crises. Between the 1870s and the 1920s, the paths explored in U.S. social policy were especially distinctive. In an era when many industrializing Western nations were launching fledgling paternalist welfare states for workers—that is, sets of regulations and benefits devised by male bureaucrats and politicians for the good of male wage earners and their dependents—the United States sought to help not workers but soldiers and mothers.

From the 1870s through the turn of the century, the U.S. federal government and many states expanded costly pensions and custodial institutions to aid veteran soldiers of the Union army and their dependents. This was the first phase of modern social provision in the United States, when many disabled, elderly, and dependent Americans were helped more generously than in the fledgling foreign welfare states of the day. During the early 1900s, proposals for general old-age pensions, health and unemployment insurance, and labor regulations covering adult male workers were rebuffed by U.S. legislatures and courts, ensuring that the United States would *not*

smoothly transform Civil War benefits into a welfare state for the
"army of labor." During the same period, however, the federal government and forty-some states did enact social spending, labor regulations, and health education programs to help American mothers
and children along with women workers who might become mothers.

Indeed, as the Civil War system of social provision faded away
with the passing of the part of the generation it sought to honor,
the United States briefly looked as if it would fashion an internationally distinctive maternalist welfare state. Largely administered by
female professionals, this system of social provision tried to ensure
public protection for mothers and children regardless of their ties
to wage earners. A fully developed maternalist welfare state might
have gradually expanded help to all American families, primarily by
bolstering the security of children and mothers. Many social policies
pointing in this direction were instituted by the U.S. states and
federal government during the 1910s and early 1920s. But some of
these measures, such as mothers' pensions and protective labor laws
for women workers, were flawed, and also failed to be implemented
as their sponsors had hoped. Others, such as minimum wage laws
and the federal Sheppard-Towner program, were clipped off by the
Supreme Court and Congress during the 1920s.

Thus the United States stopped short and turned back from its
route toward a possible maternalist welfare state. With the coming
of the Great Depression and the New Deal of the 1930s, the nation
would take new paths. Earlier experiences with Civil War benefits
and maternalist policies of course influenced the Social Security Act
and subsequent U.S. social policymaking. But from the 1930s onward, new political actors, policy proposals, and principles of legitimation for public social provision came to the fore. The United
States would no longer so exclusively focus its social policies on
veteran soldiers or on actual or prospective mothers, as it distinctively
did between the 1870s and the 1920s.

The Value of a Polity-Centered Perspective

We can understand *why* the United States has elaborated distinctive
sorts of social policies at different phases of its history only by situ-
ating the politics of social policymaking within a broader, organizationally grounded analysis of American political development. Social

policies in the United States (and elsewhere) have not developed simply in tandem with capitalist industrialization or urbanization; and they have not been straightforward responses to the demands that emerging social classes place upon governments. Governmental institutions, electoral rules, political parties, and prior public policies—all of these, and their transformations over time, create many of the limits and opportunities within which social policies are devised and changed by politically involved actors over the course of a nation's history. There are a number of analytically distinct ways in which this happens, as we have seen.

The organizational arrangements of national states and political party systems influence the policy initiatives undertaken by politicians and officials. Acting in pursuit of their career interests, and engaged in conflicts or alliances with one another, political leaders try to use existing governmental and party organizations to devise and implement policies that will attract support from various social groups. Conforming to the needs and capacities of the organizations within which they must maneuver, officials and politicians often evolve distinctive policies that are not only responses to the demands of social groups. Prime examples from U.S. politics in the late nineteenth century are Republican Party stands on protective tariffs and Civil War pensions. The early U.S. state featured electoral rights for males of all classes, strong legislatures, minimal bureaucracies, and competitive, patronage-oriented political parties. After the Civil War and Reconstruction, the Republicans faced tight competition from the Democrats and needed to hold together complex cross-class and cross-regional coalitions in the North. Republican politicans and governmental officials discovered that expanded Civil War benefits, along with minutely adjusted protective tariffs that simultaneously raised revenues to pay for generous benefits, could be used to distribute rewards at strategic times to the right combinations of party supporters. This process culminated in the creation of America's internationally precocious system of public social support for many disabled and aged men and their dependents.

The institutional arrangements and electoral rules of a national state and party system affect which of the society's groups become involved in politics, and when. Given that certain social groups do become politically active, moreover, some of them achieve more political leverage than others. Much of the reason has to do with the "fit," or lack thereof, between a nation's governmental institutions at a given time and the goals and organizational capacities of the various groups and alliances that seek to influence policymaking. A few examples will remind us of usefulness of these analytic principles.

In the process of expanding Civil War benefits during the late nineteenth century, Republicans fostered the rapid growth of a supportive organized social group, the Grand Army of the Republic (GAR). Governmental openness to demands for distributive benefits encouraged the reorientation of GAR goals toward support for pensions and tariffs; and the GAR in turn achieved many legislative successes when pursuing such demands. "Old soldiers," especially Union veterans, became organizationally and ideologically central to the politics of late-nineteenth-century America.

Around the turn of the twentieth century, U.S. social politics stood out in cross-national terms because it was more focused on solidarities of (male or female) gender than on solidarities of economic class position. Compared to many other industrializing Western nations of the day, including Britain, the United States did not experience much of a social-democratic politics of working-class consciousness, or a politics featuring appeals by elites to working-class political goals. At the same time, U.S. politics gave great play to gendered nationwide associations—not only to the male political parties, the Grand Army of the Republic, and other federations of men who were fraternally associated across class lines, but also to widespread federations of elite, middle-class, and some working-class women. Huge maternalist associations, organized as local clubs tied into state and national federations, sought to extend into civic life and public policymaking the caring values of the separate "domestic sphere" culturally ascribed to the female gender during that time.

An understanding of nineteenth-century U.S. political institutions and the changes they were undergoing around 1900 helps us to understand the gendered social identities that figured so prominently in the nation's social politics, as well as the remarkable leverage achieved by the maternalist women's federations at a time when most American women could not yet vote. During the course of the nineteenth and early twentieth centuries, the politics of many industrializing nations focused on the struggles of (especially) working-class men to gain access to governmental and electoral systems from which they were formally excluded. Meanwhile, in the United

States, virtually all adult white men of all classes (and for a time after the Civil War, black men as well) were formally fully included as citizens and voters in the world's first mass democracy. Nineteeth-century U.S. political parties, and many organized groups tied to them, functioned as cross-class male fraternal bodies, in effect making it difficult for classes, including emerging wage earners, to achieve separate political class-consciousness and organization. Ethnic and religious identities were, however, often the building blocks of local male solidarities.

Meanwhile, American women of all social strata were excluded from formal electoral participation, thus also encouraging the political consciousness and solidarity of their gender. Without either governmental bureaucracies or an established church, the U.S. federal polity left plenty of room for voluntary associations. And American women were, by international standards, very highly educated, well prepared to participate in community life. As alternatives to participation in formal electoral and party politics, many American women, especially middle-class women, established local voluntary associations for religious, charitable, and welfare purposes. By the late 1900s, certain of these were knit together into huge nation-spanning federations, networks that paralleled the local-state-national structure of U.S. parties and government. And as this knitting-together occurred, American women increasingly thought of themselves as uniquely moral political actors who had the duty to "mother the nation." Achieving a remarkable kind of maternalist political consciousness at a time when U.S. industrial workers were not very politically class-conscious, American women used their clubs and federations to engage in "municipal housekeeping," and to propose new public social policies to help mothers, children, and families. Organized American women also believed that their moral and educational styles of political practice could help to "clean up" political "corruption" in the United States.

Of course these would-be mothers of the nation did not enjoy the right to vote in most states until 1920 or a few years before, so their calls for maternalist legislation might well have been in vain. Significantly, however, even as many American women built up voluntary associations parallel to, and in tension with, the male-dominated organizations of U.S. federal patronage democracy, that system reached its limits and began to falter. The fraternal political parties of nineteenth-century democracy were internally weakened as elections became less intensively competitive after the 1890s, and as movements for electoral and bureaucratic reform proliferated. In a nation where executives and legislatures were not linked by parliamentary discipline, and where autonomous, professional civil services were not established, this weakening of major, patronage-oriented political parties left open considerable civic space. Into that widening space stepped women's groups prepared to set agendas of public debate and legislative deliberation for the early twentieth century.

Because the women's groups were organized into geographically widespread federated associations, they had much more ability than other groups of the day—such as urban professional associations, or trade unions of male industrial wage earners—simultaneously to influence politics at local, state, and national levels. Working with higher-educated female professionals, the nationwide women's federations could spread a policy idea quickly—from New York or Chicago or Washington, DC, across the forty-eight states and right down into local communities, the districts that were the homes of representatives to state legislatures and to the U.S. Congress. In a period generally marked by reform movements against party "corruption" and in favor of educational and professional styles of politics, U.S. maternalist voluntary associations could use publicity, lobbying, and moral and emotional rhetoric to persuade Congress or dozens of state legislatures to vote along relatively nonpartisan lines for new social policies.

It was also fortunate that women's groups above all wanted new benefits and regulations for mothers, children, and women workers. Around the turn of the twentieth century, U.S. state and federal courts repeatedly used their powers of constitutional review to strike down laws intended to shield unions, regulate the working conditions of men, or otherwise regulate the market economy. But especially during the 1910s and very early 1920s, when maternalist women's associations were at their most effective in shaping public opionion and influencing legislatures to act, the state and federal courts, right up to the U.S. Supreme Court, were willing to accept laws aiming to protect mothers and women workers. In the case of the protective labor laws for women workers, the courts recognized that these interfered with rights of "free contract" between employers and employees in the marketplace. Yet the courts acquiesced where only women workers were concerned, on the grounds that female wage earners were actual or potential mothers—just as the women's groups of the day argued.

All in all, the kinds of organizational and rhetorical capacities that widespread maternalist associations of women could bring to bear in U.S. social politics in the early twentieth century had a suprisingly good "fit" to the points of legislative and judicial leverage available at the time—as the federal state of courts and parties was undergoing an uneven and fragmentary transformation into a partially bureaucratic, interest-group-oriented system of governance.

A final sort of insight is also built into the polity-centered framework used in this book: Policies not only flow from prior institutions and politics; they also reshape institutions and politics, making some future developments more likely, and hindering the possibilities for others. Surely it is fitting to conclude by reflecting in such terms on the legacies left by each of the first three great phases of modern U.S. social provision—the expansion of Civil War benefits, the failure of early proposals for workingmen's insurance and general old-age pensions, and the proliferation of many maternalist social policies for mothers and women workers. Let us remind ourselves of the links tying the expansion of Civil War benefits to the later failure of workingmen's insurance, and tying both of these to the efflorescence of policies for mothers and women workers. Yet let us not stop there. However briefly and speculatively, I can also point to some broader legacies and lessons of each of the major phases of early modern social provision.

Successes, Failures, and Lessons for the Future

Civil War benefits were among the politically most successful social policies ever devised in the United States. Expanded very significantly right at the beginning of the country's modern national history—during an era that most historians claim was dominated by limited government and rugged individualism—these policies signaled the potential for honorable, cross-class and cross-racial social provision to flourish in American democracy.

Fueled by the close electoral competition of late-nineteenth-century parties firmly rooted in the cross-class male electorate of the

North, the expansion of federal pensions for Union veterans and survivors was also reinforced over time by the cooperation of the Republican Party, the locally rooted and broadly federated Grand Army of the Republic, and the U.S. Bureau of Pensions (an agency that had, for its time, remarkable clerical capacities). Within the same northern political context, moreover, the federal and many state governments established custodial institutions for needy veterans, while state and local governments gave supplemental benefits to impoverished veterans and survivors outside of traditional poor relief. Because all who received Civil War benefits were said to have "earned" them through their own efforts (or those of their husbands and fathers), the inclusion in the same system of public care of African-Americans, native-born whites, and ethnic whites was accepted by northern Americans, even in an era of open racism and ethnic bigotry. What is more, given the supportive democratic electoral context and the eligibility of all socioeconomic classes of veterans and survivors for Civil War benefits, those disabled and elderly men, widows, orphans, and other dependents who accepted the benefits were made to feel worthy. These beneficiaries did not feel demeaned as if they were accepting "charity" or "welfare." And they were not ill-regarded by their fellow citizens.

This remarkable combination of political and ideological supports that nourished the expansion of Civil War benefits ensured their survival as long as the relevant generation lived. Growing numbers of elite and middle-class political reformers—men such as Harvard President Charles Eliot and his Mugwump fellows and progressive heirs—fiercely denounced generous Civil War benefits as the epitome of democratic "corruption." But these critics were not able to roll back the governmental protections for the Civil War generation.

The protests of Eliot and his friends were not entirely in vain, however. Their broadsides against democratic patronage parties and the "horrors" of social spending for the masses helped to ensure that Civil War benefits would become an obstacle rather than an entering wedge for more general old-age pensions and workingmen's insurance in the United States. To be sure, some trade unionists and a few reformist professionals looked for veterans' pensions to be extended smoothly into pensions for all needy elderly Americans, and into social insurance for the "army of industry." But during early 1900s, most reform-minded Americans firmly opposed major new forms of public social spending. They were afraid that such spending might reinforce the grip of party politicans on popular support, or strain the dubious administrative capacities of U.S. governments that were not bureaucratized or staffed by educated professionals.

After the Civil War generation died out, and even after early proposals for old-age pensions and workingmen's insurance had been soundly defeated, Civil War benefits left behind among U.S. reformers a permanent legacy of worry about open-ended public spending, especially for military veterans but also for other social groups. After World War I and World War II, policy intellectuals deliberately avoided direct cash payments to veterans, favoring limited contributory social insurance after World War I, and educational and housing loans after World War II.[1] Memories of Civil War pensions, moreover, helped to shore up the determination of New Deal policymakers to emphasize *contributory* forms of unemployment and old-age insurance in the Social Security Act of 1935. Even in the midst of a national depression, the retirement insurance program of Social Security actually started collecting payroll taxes from employers and employees well before it paid out the first small checks to elderly beneficiaries![2]

As for the legacies of the second phase of modern U.S. social policymaking, the failure during the Progressive Era of most proposals for workingmen's social benefits was a permanently defining moment in U.S. politics. This failure undercut prospects for the growth of unions, and hurt possibilities for political alliances or a labor party oriented to expanding public social provision. Along with other important factors, it ensured that the United States would never become a working-class-oriented social democracy and blocked the development of a European-style welfare state.[3]

Meanwhile, the tiny victories achieved by early advocates of social insurance in state-level campaigns for workers' compensation helped to set the stage for future social insurance politics in the United States. From the 1920s, the "policy action" shifted especially to the state of Wisconsin, where important breakthroughs of administrative state-building were associated with that state's regulatory approach to workmen's compensation. Expert ideas about social insurance after the 1910s tended to build on the very limited successes that reformers had achieved during the Progressive Era, giving up on the broader European-style conceptions of partially tax-financed workingmen's insurance that had failed before 1920. When the New Deal came, therefore, "Wisconsin experts" were uniquely well-positioned to be called to Washington, DC. Their prior political and administrative experiences greatly influenced the formulation and implementation of the Social Security Act, ensuring that it did not resemble the early European welfare states for workers.[4] Besides, even though the cross-class contributory retirement insurance program established in 1935 was destined to expand as fully and become as politically entrenched within U.S. democracy as the Civil War benefits of old, the Wisconsin experts, true progressive reformers that they were, ensured that this program did not recapitulate the open-ended public spending from general revenues characteristic of Civil War pensions.

Finally, let us consider the legacies of the maternalist phase of U.S. social policymaking, the phase that proceeded in tandem with the failure of workingmen's insurance. The legacies of maternalism are important, and at the same time inextricably complex and ambivalent. Since the 1920s the places and self-conceptions of women in American families, workplaces, society, and government have changed. These changes have inevitably affected what has happened to social policies surviving from the maternalist phase. The changes also influence how those of us who are now feminists look back on the values and goals of early-twentieth-century American women's organizations.

U.S. social policies for mothers and women workers enacted during the 1910s and early 1920s never quite crystallized into a full-fledged maternalist welfare state, as we have learned. The maternally oriented women's federations that originally pressed for and sustained these policies weakened or changed from the mid-1920s onward. At the same time, various kinds of women's organizations contended among themselves over the merits of alternative political strategies, now that U.S. women had the vote. Organized women increasingly disagreed about the virtues of such previously enacted maternalist measures as protective labor laws for women workers; and the value of such regulations was in any event badly undercut once the Supreme Court ruled out minimum wages as an accompaniment to restricted working hours for women.

Keystone of the fledgling maternalist welfare state, the federal

Sheppard-Towner program was throttled and killed by Congress after 1926. Of course, certain states continued to promote infant and maternal health, and a chastened, medically dominated version of Sheppard-Towner was revived in 1935. But the Children's Bureau was greatly weakened by the loss of Sheppard-Towner in the late 1920s. Even as women's groups were changing in the larger society, the Bureau's momentum as a preeminent planner of social provision in the United States was undercut just before the Depression and the New Deal suddenly opened new vistas for federal public policy.

Increasingly viewing themselves in professionally defined terms rather than as part of an omnibus "woman movement," U.S. female advocates for public social provision arguably went on the defensive after the mid-1920s. Seeking (perhaps not always wisely) to preserve separate sectors of policy for U.S. mothers and children, female administrators and policy intellectuals worked from a position of relative marginality—certainly from a more marginal position than they would have enjoyed if the Children's Bureau had remained on course with an expanding Sheppard-Towner program. And certainly from a weaker position than if female professionals had remained as strongly tied to vital local voluntary groups across the nation as Julia Lathrop, Jane Addams, and many others were during the early 1900s. The era of the all-encompassing "woman movement" was over in American politics, and with it the centrality of maternalist social programs. From the 1930s to the 1960s, as the United States created nationwide social insurance and public assistance programs, separately administered benefits and protections for women, mothers, and children often survived, yet they were subordinated and pushed to the side.

For example, mothers' pensions were incorporated into the public assistance provisions of the Social Security Act of 1935; the states would henceforth receive partial subsidies if they offered these benefits. Yet even as the new federal monies were provided, the federal supervision of Aid to Dependent Children (later to become Aid to Families with Dependent Children) was taken away from the Children's Bureau and lodged in the Social Security Board, a male-dominated agency that consistently built up contributory insurance and downplayed the development of noncontributory public assistance programs, including ADC/AFDC.[5] From 1939 onward, moreover, many "worthy widows" and their children—those originally intended to be the chief beneficiaries of mothers' pensions—were transferred into the survivors' insurance program of Social Security. This left ADC/AFDC, where states and localities remained virtually sovereign under loose federal supervision, as a nationally uneven and chronically underfunded public assistance program of last resort. Its clients increasingly became very impoverished families in which mothers were divorced, or not married, or widows of men without histories of wage earning in occupations covered by social insurance.[6]

Contrary to the hopes of many women reformers and maternalist groups active in the early 1900s, therefore, the female-oriented parts of U.S. social provision after the 1920s were confined to often demeaning and ungenerous "welfare" for the poor alone, rather than contributing to the creation of honorable and adequate support for the less privileged, in conjunction with public benefits and services universally available to all American mothers, children, and families. The direct legacies of maternalist social policies in the United States thus involve the working out of unfortunate unintended consequences, reinforced by the political marginalization of female administrators, social workers, and surviving maternalist programs in the era of Social Security.

But it would be a mistake to end on such a downbeat note. Although early-twentieth-century advocates of maternalist social policies were in many ways defeated, and certainly prevented from realizing their best goals and hopes, they left positive legacies, too. Certain of their aims and political methods remain relevant for today, pointing to enduring challenges and possibilities for U.S. social policymaking—as well as for the contemporary U.S. feminist movement.

The enduring challenge of maternalism for U.S. social provision continues to be clearly articulated. To hear the voice of the leaders of the Children's Bureau in present guise, one need only listen to such contemporary national advocacy groups as the Children's Defense Fund and the National Forum on the Future of Children and Families. The leaders of these groups, many of whom are articulate, higher-educated female professionals, argue with detailed data and high moral passion that mothers, children, and families are not at all adequately served by public social benefits and services as they exist in the United States today. Like Julia Lathrop during the Progressive Era debates over health insurance, the modern maternalists tell us that social insurance programs geared only to stably employed wage earners overlook the needs of many women and children. As the United States in the 1990s enters a period of intense debate about health care reform, with public discussion emphasizing needs for universal insurance coverage and "cost containment" in medical care, these present-day advocates of maternalist ideas repeatedly remind us that separate, community-based maternal and child health programs will be needed along with financial insurance for medical treatment.[7] Echoing the philosophy behind Sheppard-Towner, they believe that health care for mothers, children, and families cannot rest on biomedical interventions alone. Preventative health education, community-based social services, active outreach to the less privileged, and medical care—all must go together.

But to whom, and for whom, are today's advocates of maternalist ideals for American social policy speaking? Like most members of what Hugh Heclo calls "issue networks" in U.S. politics today, these fine people are professionals working for various public agencies, foundations, universities, and public-interest lobbying associations.[8] Most of them work in Washington, DC, New York City, or major university centers across the country. Using specialized discourse, they talk mostly to one another—and to the staffs of legislative committees charged with overseeing very specific public programs that they want to defend, expand, or incrementally improve to better help children, mothers, and families. Most of the people the policy specialists and advocates are trying to help are underprivileged Americans; and most of the public programs that they try to create, defend, or improve are poverty programs.

Unlike the higher-educated women professionals who figured so strongly in U.S. maternalist social policymaking during the 1910s and early 1920s, today's U.S. advocates for mothers and children are *not* supported by federations that regularly reach from the great urban centers down into local communities across the entire nation. Nor do they work or speak as part of an encompassing movement of virtually all politically active American women. The contemporary era of U.S. women's politics is marked, on the one hand, by feminist movements stressing the goals of abortion, professional access, and equality within the paid labor force for women who want to be fully equal competitors with men, and on the other hand by right-wing organizations appealing to "homemakers" with claims that governments should not "interfere" with families.[9]

In this setting, it is not possible for advocates of say, new health programs for poor mothers and babies to deploy a political rhetoric of "honoring motherhood." Around the turn of the twentieth century, perhaps, such a rhetoric could symbolically and relatively unproblematically connect many elite, professional, middle-class, and poor American women. It could tie appeals for the welfare of all of America's children to appeals for honoring all of the nation's mothers—actual mothers, prospective mothers, and even higher-educated single professionals who were "public mothers." But in the United States today no such unproblematic connections of womanhood and motherhood, or of private and public mothering, are remotely possible—not even in flights of moralism or rhetorical fancy.

Of course this is just as well. None of us who live as women participating fully in work and politics along with family would, for a moment, want to return to the days when higher-educated American women felt they had to choose between careers and marriage and childbearing. We would not want to be excluded from academic and many other professional careers, as the women of the social settlements were. We would not want to be left without rights to vote and hold all elected and appointed public offices. And the nation would be much worse off if we were.

Still, contemporary U.S. feminists can learn some positive lessons from early-twentieth-century women who, in the face of all such restrictions and exclusions, found ways to create encompassing and geographically far-flung women's organizations. These widespread federated associations nurtured political conversations far less specialized than those that go on among contemporary American advocates of social policy, and conversations considerably less elitist that those carried on today among middle-class American feminists. Contemporary feminists may also be able to learn lessons from the maternalists of old who, in their self-conceptions and public rhetoric, stressed solidarity between privileged and less privileged women, and honor for values of caring and nurturance.

To be sure, many feminists in the United States today recognize that women have a special stake in a society that honors and publicly supports caring for the vulnerable, even as it celebrates individual equality in the competitive search for excellence. Yet paying lip service to the ideal of a caring society will not be enough. To help realize it, both individual and organized feminists may have to place a higher priority on policy goals that can bring Americans together across lines of ideology, class, race, and gender. In order to contribute to broad political alliances, feminist organizations may well have to moderate priorities that are legitimate for upper-middle-class career women, but not so important (or even acceptable) to other Americans. Such decisions will be difficult, because American women today are profoundly divided by class, work, and family commitments, as well as by ideologies.[10] Clashes among differently situated women over matters such as abortion serve, along with divisions of class and race, to undercut possibilities for an improved welfare state from which all American families and communities would benefit.

The United States is never going to have a European-style welfare state, propelled by bureaucrats, programmatic party leaders, and strong trade unions. But the possibility remains that America might develop strong, universal social programs designed to help working single-parent and two-parent families live well and raise their children.[11] American feminist groups could be only part of broad, democratic political alliances to create and sustain such family security progams; but they could be a vital part. Hopeful scenarios for contemporary American social politics will become more likely, it seems to me, if feminists can learn to recapitulate in contemporary ways some of the best ideas and methods once used by the proponents of maternalist social policies. Feminists must work in organizations and networks that tie them to others in very different social circumstances. They must also articulate values and political goals that speak to the well-being of all American families. If feminists can find better ways to do these things, organized women will again be at the forefront of the development of social provision in the United States.

Percentages of the Elderly in the States and the District of Columbia Receiving Civil War Pensions in 1910

State	Number of pensioners	Adjusted pensioners*	Population 65 and older	Percentage of pensioners
Alabama	3,707	2,780	65,000	4.3
Arizona	897	673	6,000	11.2
Arkansas	10,691	8,018	45,000	17.8
California	28,762	21,572	125,000	17.3
Colorado	9,400	7,050	27,000	26.1
Connecticut	11,531	8,648	60,000	14.4
Delaware	2,629	1,972	10,000	19.7
D.C.	8,532	6,399	17,000	37.6
Florida	4,244	3,183	22,000	14.5
Georgia	3,410	2,558	81,000	3.2
Idaho	2,479	1,859	9,000	20.7
Illinois	63,788	47,841	243,000	19.7
Indiana	56,416	42,312	149,000	28.4
Iowa	32,596	24,447	125,000	19.6
Kansas	35,506	26,794	88,000	30.4
Kentucky	24,398	18,299	94,000	19.5
Louisiana	6,368	4,776	50,000	9.6
Maine	16,577	12,433	61,000	20.4
Maryland	12,400	9,300	61,000	15.3
Massachusetts	38,904	28,178	175,000	16.7
Michigan	38,444	28,833	157,000	18.4
Minnesota	15,199	11,399	86,000	13.3
Mississippi	4,682	3,512	54,000	6.5
Missouri	45,873	34,405	150,000	22.9
Montana	2,408	1,806	9,000	20.1
Nebraska	15,182	11,387	51,000	22.3
Nevada	453	340	3,000	11.3
New Hampshire	7,384	5,538	34,000	16.3
New Jersey	21,384	16,038	107,000	15.0
New Mexico	2,240	1,680	10,000	16.8
New York	78,227	58,670	418,000	14.0
North Carolina	4,005	3,004	78,000	3.9
North Dakota	2,241	1,681	13,000	12.9
Ohio	89,227	66,920	262,000	25.5
Oklahoma	13,097	9,823	41,000	24.0

State	Number of pensioners	Adjusted pensioners*	Population 65 and older	Percentage of pensioners
Oregon	8,101	6,076	28,000	21.7
Pennsylvania	89,828	67,371	326,000	20.7
Rhode Island	5,208	3,906	25,000	15.6
South Carolina	1,974	1,481	44,000	3.1
South Dakota	4,863	3,647	19,000	19.2
Tennessee	18,478	13,858	83,000	16.7
Texas	9,177	6,883	111,000	6.2
Utah	1,106	830	12,000	6.9
Vermont	7,487	5,615	29,000	19.4
Virginia	8,652	6,489	85,000	7.6
Washington	11,213	8,410	37,000	22.7
West Virginia	11,930	8,948	42,000	21.3
Wisconsin	23,528	17,646	119,000	14.8
Wyoming	1,043	782	3,000	26.1

* I estimate that 93.7 percent of military pensioners in 1910 were Civil War pensioners; and as explained in note 115 to Chapter 2, I estimate that 80 percent of all pensioners were 65 or older. Thus I adjusted the total pensioners in 1910 by 75 percent to estimate the elderly Civil War pensioners in that year.

Sources: Report of the Commissioners of Pensions, in the *Reports of the Department of the Interior for the Fiscal Year Ended June 30, 1910,* vol. 1 (Washington: Government Printing Office, 1911), pp. 146, 168; and *Historical Statistics of the United States: Colonial Times to 1970,* Bicentennial ed., pt. 1 (Washington: Bureau of the Census, 1975), pp. 24–37, series A209.

Endorsements of Mothers' Pensions by Women's Groups: Sources for Table 9 and Figure 27

Alabama

No evidence of endorsements in *Official Reports* of GFWC Biennials or in *Child-Welfare Magazine.*

Arizona

No evidence of endorsements in *Official Reports* of GFWC Biennials, in *Child-Welfare Magazine,* or in a search done for me of records in the state. "An act providing for an old age and mothers' pension and making appropriation therefor" passed by popular referendum in November 1914, following an initiative petition. This legislation was ruled unconstitutional in 1916, but the mothers' pension provision must have been reenacted, because Arizona continued to have these benefits.

Arkansas

No evidence of endorsements in *Official Reports* of the GFWC Biennials. No Mothers' Congress in state until 1925.

California

Endorsements in 1912–13 by the California Federation of Women's Clubs, the California Congress of Mothers, and 51 other women's groups in the State Legislative Council of Women. *A Record of Twenty-five Years of the California State Federation of Women's Clubs, 1900–1925,* vol. 1, comp. Mary S. Gibson. (California State Federation of Women's Clubs, 1927; in the holdings of the Bancroft Library, University of California at Berkeley), pp. 186, 194–95, 197–99.

Colorado

Sponsored in 1912–13 by the Colorado Federation of Women's Clubs, as indicated in a speech prepared by Mrs. Sarah Platt Decker of Colorado. *Official Report of the Eleventh Biennial, GFWC* (1912), p. 362.

Connecticut

Endorsed in March 1919, by a Mothers' Congress club, the New Haven Women's Club, whose president represented the club's position at a hearing at the state legislature. *Child-Welfare Magazine* 13(8) (April 1919), pp. 238–39. The state branch of the Mothers' Congress had "under consideration" by early 1915 a "Mothers' Pension law modeled after the best of those state laws"; see ibid. 9(6) (Feb. 1915), p. 206. It seems likely that the Connecticut state branch officially endorsed mothers' pensions sometime between 1915 and 1919, but I have found no firm evidence of this.

Delaware

A proposal was sponsored by the Delaware Congress of Mothers at its October 1914 annual convention, when "Mrs. Chas. Gilpin of Philadelphia, Pa., explained Mothers' Pensions in Pennsylvania . . . [and the] Convention passed a resolution calling upon all the Associations in Delaware to work for the passage of such an act in Delaware." *Child-Welfare Magazine* 9(6) (Feb. 1915), p. 207. The bill that eventually passed was apparently cosponsored by the Mothers' Congress and the Delaware Consumers' League in ca. 1916–17. According to Maud Nathan, *The Story of an Epoch-Making Movement* (Garden City, NY: Doubleday, Page, and Co., 1926), appendix G, "Reports of State Consumers' Leagues," p. 154, "A mothers' pension bill, introduced by another organization, was found to be extremely faulty, and the League was permitted to redraft the measure, whereupon the two organizations cooperated and secured its passage."

Florida

At the 1914 GFWC Biennial, the Legislative Committee of the Florida State Federation of Women's Clubs was reported to be urging "study" of mothers' pensions; and at the 1916 Biennial the State Federation claimed to have persuaded the legislature to create a public commission "to study the need for mother's pensions. Two club women appointed." *Official Report of the Twelfth Biennial, GFWC* (1914), p. 320; and *Official Report of the Thirteenth Biennial, GFWC* (1914), p. 186. I also consulted Lucy Worthington Blackman, *The Florida Federation of Women's Clubs, 1895–1939* (Jacksonville, FL: Southern Historical Publishing Associates, 1939), but there is no direct mention of mothers' pensions.

Georgia

No evidence of organizational endorsements in *Official Reports* of GFWC Biennials or in *Child-Welfare Magazine*. There was a bit of female activity in Georgia, however. A 1919 Georgia Mothers' Congress report eulogized a branch official, Mrs. Walton H. Wiggs, who died that year: "For the past two years she has had two bills before the Legislature, one to make provision for the Defective and Delinquent child and the other to secure the passage of the Mother's Pension Law. Others may reap what she has sown, for she passed on before the gathering of the harvest; but to this noble woman is due the honor of sowing the seed of these two important movements in Georgia." But there is no evidence that the Georgia Branch or any of its member clubs ever endorsed mothers' pensions, either before or after Mrs. Wiggs's brief efforts. And this woman was not the branch president; she was the chairman of the Extension Committee. *Child-Welfare Magazine* 13(7) (March 1919), p. 201; and 14(1) (Sept. 1919), p. 23.

Idaho

Sponsored in ca. 1912–13 by the Idaho Congress of Mothers. *Child-Welfare Magazine* 7(10) (June 1913), p. 388; and 8(3) (Nov. 1913), p. 104.

Illinois

The 1911 law was sponsored by a Chicago juvenile court judge. However, one could argue that
women's groups had already established the
model for this legislation. During 1903, the Illinois Consumers' League and the Illinois Federation of Women's Clubs proposed clear forerunners of mothers' pensions called "widows'
scholarships" to the GFWC. Subsequently, the Illinois Consumers' League worked with the Bureau of Charities and other women's groups to
fund such scholarships. On these pre-1911 developments, see "Report of the Secretary," *NCL
Fourth Annual Report* (1903), pp. 19–20; Mrs.
A. O. Granger, "The Work of the General Federation of Women's Clubs Against Child Labor,"
Annals 25 (May 1905), pp. 516–17; and John
Clayton Drew, "Child Labor and Child Welfare:
The Origins and Uneven Development of the
American Welfare State" (Ph.D. diss., Cornell
University, 1987), pp. 103–04. From 1915 into
the 1920s, women's groups including the Chicago
Woman's Club, the Illinois Federation of Wom-
en's Clubs, and the Illinois Congress of Mothers
worked for extensions of eligibility and increased
funding for mothers' pensions. Personal letter of
January 2, 1990, from Joanne Goodwin, based
on "Gender, Politics, and Welfare Reform, Chicago 1900–1930" (Ph.D. diss., University of Michigan, 1991). For a resolution by the Illinois Congress of Mothers calling for the extension of
mothers' pensions to all counties in the state, see
Child-Welfare Magazine 9(11) (July 1915), p. 383.

Indiana

A bill was sponsored during 1918–19 by the Indiana Congress of Mothers, which apparently
tried to work with the Indiana Federation of Labor, another group sponsoring a bill. *Child-Welfare Magazine* 13(3) (Nov. 1918), p. 80; 13(5) (Jan.
1919), p. 138; 13(8) (April 1919), p. 240; and

14(10) (June 1920), p. 315. The last of these references speaks of hoping to get a bill through when the legislature meets "this winter." The Indiana legislature met in 1919 and enacted mothers' pensions, so I believe that this report must have been written many months before it was published.

Iowa — Endorsed in 1912 by the Sixth Biennial of the Iowa Congress of Mothers. "*Resolved:* Believing in the conservation of the home and that poverty alone should not deprive a mother otherwise competent of the care of her own child, or the child of an opportunity for a normal home life; the Iowa Congress of Mothers endorse the Mother's pension bill." *Child-Welfare Magazine* 7(4) (Dec. 1912), p. 142.

Kansas — Endorsed ca. 1914–15 by the Kansas Federation of Women's Clubs and by the Kansas Congress of Mothers and its member group, the Topeka Council of Mothers. *Official Report of the Thirteenth Biennial, GFWC* (1916), p. 198; and *Child-Welfare Magazine* 9(5) (Jan. 1915), p. 168; 11(11) (July 1917), p. 323. The WCTU and the Progressives were also supporters of mothers' pensions in Kansas. Robert Sherman LaForte, *Leaders of Reform: Progressive Republicans in Kansas, 1900–1916* (Lawrence: University Press of Kansas, 1974), pp. 220–21, 231, 241.

Kentucky — No evidence of endorsements in *Official Reports* of GFWC Biennials or in *Child-Welfare Magazine*.

Louisiana — No evidence of endorsements in *Official Reports* of GFWC Biennials. No Congress of Mothers branch until 1923.

Maine — Sponsored during 1916–17 by the Maine Congress of Mothers. *Child-Welfare Magazine* 11(6) (Feb. 1917), p. 182; 11(10) (June 1917), p. 302;

and 11(11) (July 1917), p. 324. Earlier the Maine
Branch had reported, "We have no Mothers' Pen-
sion Law, and have made no attempt to get one."
Ibid. 8(11) (July 1914), p. 465.

Maryland

Endorsed in March 1916 by the Maryland Congress of Mothers. *A History of the Maryland Congress of Parents and Teachers* (Baltimore: Maryland
Congress of Parents and Teachers, 1965), p. 9.
Apparently not fully endorsed by the Maryland
Federation of Women's Clubs, but supported by
"individual clubs in different parts of the state."
Official Report of the Thirteenth Biennial, GFWC
(1916), p. 205.

Massachusetts

Both the Massachusetts Mothers' Congress and
the Massachusetts Federation of Women's Clubs
sponsored the establishment of a 1912 state commission to study mothers' pensions. Clara Cahill
Park of the Mothers' Congress served on the
commission and guided it toward recommending
the 1913 legislation. Clara Cahill Park, "Widows'
Pension in Massachusetts," *Child-Welfare Magazine*
6(10) (June 1912), pp. 343–46; and *Official Report
of the Eleventh Biennial, GFWC* (1912), p. 491. According to the *Delineator* 81(2) (Feb. 1913), p. 86,
"Mrs. Snow Rick—Chairman of the legislative
committee of the Massachusetts State Federation
of Women's Clubs; strongly favors and energetically supports the campaign in Massachusetts for
allowances out of public funds to widows to enable them to keep their children with them and
to bring the up in their own homes."

Michigan

Endorsed in 1913 (or earlier) by the Michigan
Federation of Women's Clubs, which had previously introduced a bill entitled "An Act to Provide for the Pensioning of Indigent Children of
School Age." *Official Report of the Tenth Biennial,*

GFWC (1910), p. 319; and *Official Report of the Twelfth Biennial, GFWC* (1914), p. 293.

Minnesota

Endorsed in 1913 by the Minnesota Federation of Women's Clubs. *Official Report of the Twelfth Biennial, GFWC* (1914), p. 286.

Mississippi

Endorsed in ca. 1919 by the Mississippi Congress of Mothers. *Child-Welfare Magazine* 13(8) (April 1919); p. 242.

Missouri

A juvenile court judge sponsored legislation for Kansas City only in 1911. Statewide mothers' pensions were sponsored by the Missouri Children's Code Commission in 1915–16. The Missouri Federation of Women's Clubs endorsed the Commission's legislative program, and the president of the Missouri Congress of Mothers served on it. Peter Romanofsky, "'The Public Is Aroused': The Missouri Children's Code Commission," *Missouri Historical Review* 68 (1974), pp. 207–09; and *Child-Welfare Magazine* 10(3) (Nov. 1915), p. 105. See also *Child-Welfare Magazine* 13(6) (Feb. 1919), p. 163. The Consumers' League of Missouri also "assisted in getting the Juvenile Court Bill and the Mother's Pension Bill passed. Members of the Social Legislation Commission representing various organizations active in the legislative campaign agreed that these laws could not have been passed but for the effective work of the Consumers' League." Maud Nathan, *The Story of an Epoch-Making Movement* (Garden City, NY: Doubleday, Page, and Co., 1926), appendix G, pp. 178–79.

Montana

Supported in 1915 by the Montana League of Good Government Clubs, formerly the Montana suffrage organization (and subsequently the League of Women Voters). Ida H. Harper, editor, *History of Woman Suffrage,* vol. 6 (New York:

Source Book Press, 1970; orig. 1922), p. 367; and Ronald Schaffer, "The Montana Woman Suffrage Campaign, 1911–14," *Pacific Northwest Quarterly* 55(1) (Jan. 1964), pp. 13–15.

Nebraska

No evidence of endorsements in *Official Reports* of the GFWC Biennials, or in *History of Nebraska Federation of Women's Clubs,* comp. Cora Beels (held in the State Archives, Nebraska State Historical Society, MS260, Nebraska Federation of Women's Clubs). An address was given to the 1914 Nebraska Federation Convention entitled "Laws Pertaining to Women," but the content is not available. The Nebraska Congress of Mothers was not established until 1922. There are two other hints: George Elliott Howard of the University of Nebraska wrote about and advocated "state endowment of motherhood" in "Social Control of the Domestic Relations," *American Journal of Sociology* 26 (May 1911): 812–13. And according to the Bureau of Labor and Industrial Statistics, *Fifteenth Biennial Report, 1915–16* (Lincoln: State of Nebraska, 1916), p. 42, the "legislature of 1913 passed a mothers' pension law pattered after the law then in force applicable to Cook county, Illinois." It is possible that Nebraska's 1913 law passed through simple official imitation of what nearby Illinois had done in 1911.

Nevada

Endorsed in 1913 by the Nevada Federation of Women's Clubs. *Official Report of the Thirteenth Biennial, GFWC* (1916), p. 215. No Mothers' Congress was established in Nevada; the Parent and Teachers' Association was founded in 1940.

New Hampshire

Endorsed in 1912–13 by the New Hampshire Federation of Women's Clubs. *A History of the New Hampshire Federation of Women's Clubs, 1895–1940,* comp. Federation Committee (Bristol, NH: Musgrove Printing House, 1941), pp. 49–50.

New Jersey

The situation in this state is complicated. Mrs. Buttenheim of the New Jersey Federation of Women's Clubs actually *opposed* the 1913 New Jersey mothers' pension law. Along with representatives of New Jersey charity groups, she was a member of a committee of a January 1913 "Child Saving Conference" that sent a resolution to the governor saying the "time is not ripe" for such legislation. [*Trenton*] *Evening True American* 78(18) (Jan. 21, 1913). However, no mention of mothers' pensions or of the Child Saving Conference appears in the New Jersey reports to GFWC Biennials, or in *A History of the New Jersey State Federation of Women's Clubs, 1894–1958* (Caldwell, NJ: Progress Publishing Co., 1958). The New Jersey Congress of Mothers definitely endorsed mothers' pensions starting in November 1914; see *Child-Welfare Magazine* 9(5) (Jan. 1915): 178–80. It is not clear whether the New Jersey Congress supported the original law passed in 1913. It is possible that that measure was not considered a true mothers' pension law; and that the Congress undertook in 1914 to sponsor what it considered a better measure. In New Jersey, an official state welfare agency, the Board of Children's Guardians, was involved in granting outdoor mothers' aid both before and after the 1913 legislation, which it did not like. See James Leiby, *Charity and Correction in New Jersey: A History of State Welfare Institutions* (New Brunswick, NJ: Rutgers University Press, 1967), pp. 92–96, 355–56. It is possible that some or all of the women's organizations in New Jersey were allied with this agency, but I have not been able to pin down the full story with the sources available to me.

New Mexico

No evidence of endorsements in *Official Reports* of GFWC Biennials or in *Child-Welfare Magazine*.

New York   Mrs. William Grant Brown, president of the very large New York City Federation of Women's Clubs, was described as "one of the most active leaders in the movement for a 'widows' pension' in New York State," in the *Delineator* 81(1) (Jan. 1913), p. 19. Liberal social workers and social settlement people were also strong advocates of mothers' pensions in this state.

North Carolina No evidence of endorsements in *Official Reports* of GFWC Biennials, in *Child-Welfare Magazine,* or in Sallie Southall Cotten, *History of the North Carolina Federation of Women's Clubs, 1901–1925* (Raleigh, NC: Edwards and Broughton Printing Co., 1925).

North Dakota No evidence of endorsements in *Official Reports* of GFWC Biennials or in *Child-Welfare Magazine.* The North Dakota Non-Partisan League, a radical agrarian movement, came to power in 1915 and enacted many legislative reforms.

Ohio   Endorsed in 1912 by the Ohio Federation of Women's Clubs, and in 1913 by the Ohio Consumers' League. *History of the Ohio Federation of Women's Clubs for the First Thirty Years, 1894–1924,* comp. Annie Laws (Cincinnati: Ebbert and Richardson Co., 1924), p. 248; and Dennis Irven Harrison, "The Consumers' League of Ohio: Women and Reform, 1909–1937" (Ph.D. diss., Case Western Reserve University, 1975), p. 42.

Oklahoma   Sponsored in 1915 by the Oklahoma Federation of Women's Clubs. *Official Report of the Thirteenth Biennial, GFWC* (1916), p. 224.

Oregon   Sponsored in 1912–13 by the Oregon Congress of Mothers. Elizabeth Hayhurst, "How Pensions for Widows Were Won in Oregon," *Child-Welfare Magazine* 7(7) (March 1913): 248–49; and 7(12) (Aug. 1913), pp. 459–60.

Pennsylvania   Sponsored in 1913 by the Mothers' Pension
                League of Allegheny County, and by the Penn-
                sylvania State Federation of Women's Clubs. Roy
                Lubove, *The Struggle for Social Security* (Pitts-
                burgh: University of Pittsburgh Press, 1986; orig.
                1968), p. 101; and Ada J. Davis, "The Evolution
                of the Institution of Mothers' Pensions in the
                United States," *American Journal of Sociology* 35
                (1930), p. 583.

Rhode Island   No evidence of endorsements in *Official Reports*
                of GFWC Biennials or in *Child-Welfare Magazine.*

South Carolina No evidence of endorsements in *Official Reports*
                of GFWC Biennials or in *Child-Welfare Magazine.*

South Dakota   Endorsed in 1913 by the South Dakota Federa-
                tion of Women's Clubs. *Official Report of the
                Twelfth Biennial, GFWC* (1914), p. 328.

Tennessee   The president of the Tennessee branch of the
                Mothers' Congress, Mrs. G. Harris Robertson,
                delivered the address that launched the national
                mothers' pension campaign at the International
                Congress of Mothers, Washington, DC, April 25,
                1911; rpt. in *Child-Welfare Magazine* 6(5) (Jan.
                1912): 156–60. Mrs. Robertson subsequently
                pursued the idea in Tennessee; ibid. 7(9) (May
                1913), p. 332. In due course, the 1915 law was
                supported by the Tennessee Federation of Wom-
                en's Clubs and the Tennessee Women's Christian
                Temperance Union, in addition to the Tennessee
                Congress of Mothers. Mabel Brown Ellis, "Moth-
                ers' Pensions," ch. 8 in *Child Welfare in Tennessee,*
                An Inquiry by the National Child Labor Com-
                mittee for the Tennessee Child Welfare Commis-
                sion (Nashville: Department of Public Instruc-
                tion, State of Tennessee, 1920), p. 511; *Child-
                Welfare Magazine* 9(9) (May 1915), p. 286; 10(4)
                (Dec. 1915), p. 145; 11(9) (May 1917), p. 274;
                and 11(11) (July 1917), p. 325.

Texas

Endorsed in 1915 by the Texas Congress of Mothers. "The congress selected for its next legislative measure 'Public Aid for Needy Mothers.' The committee which has been investigating conditions affecting the dependent child, rendered a report which called forth this action." *Child-Welfare Magazine* 10(5) (Jan. 1916), p. 183; 11(4) (Dec. 1916), pp. 105, 131; and 11(11) (July 1917), p. 326. The Texas Federation of Women's Clubs does not seem to have concerned itself with mothers' pensions; there is no mention of them in the very thorough study by Megan Seaholm, "Earnest Women: The White Woman's Club Movement in Progressive Era Texas, 1880–1920" (Ph.D. diss., Rice University, 1968).

Utah

Endorsed in 1913 by the Utah Federation of Women's Clubs. *Official Report of the Twelfth Biennial, GFWC* (1914), p. 282.

Vermont

Endorsed in 1916 by the Vermont Federation of Women's Clubs. Minutes of the Executive Board Meeting, November 8 and 9, 1916, in Secretary's Report, 1907–1921, Vermont Federation of Women's Clubs, Doc. Box 142, Vermont Historical Society Library, Montpelier, VT.

Virginia

No evidence of endorsements in *Official Reports* of GFWC Biennials. No Mothers' Congress in Virginia until 1921.

Washington

Sponsored in 1912–13 by the Washington Federation of Women's Clubs. Listed in advance as a bill "to be presented to our Legislature next winter." *Official Report of the Eleventh Biennial, GFWC* (1912), p. 538.

West Virginia

The Chester Women's Club of Hancock, West Virginia, "helped to promote the establishment of a Mother's Pension Fund," probably in 1915. *A History of the West Virginia Federation of Women's*

Clubs, a member of the General Federation of Women's Clubs, 1904–1982, comp. Mrs. Henry W. Bassel, Jr. (Charleston, WV: West Virginia Federation of Women's Clubs, 1982), p. 135.

Wisconsin — Endorsed "in principle" in 1912 by the Wisconsin Federation of Women's Clubs; and in 1913 a federation committee proposed to "throw our influence" behind legislation resulting from an investigation then under way by the state Board of Control. *Proceedings of the Sixteenth Annual Convention, Janesville, Wisconsin, October 8–10, 1912*, p. xxix; and "Report of the Committee on Industrial and Social Conditions," *Proceedings of the Seventeenth Annual Convention, Sheboygan, Wisconsin, October 22–24, 1913*, p. 55.

Wyoming — Endorsed in 1915 by the Wyoming Federation of Women's Clubs. *Official Report of the Thirteenth Biennial, GFWC* (1916), p. 244.

Introduction: Understanding the Origins of Modern Social Provision in the United States

1. Quoted in Donald M. McMurry, "The Political Significance of the Pension Question, 1885–1897," *Mississippi Valley Historical Review* 9 (1922), pp. 34–35.
2. About 35 percent of northern men 65 and over were federal military pensioners. See note 123 to Chapter 2.
3. Charles Richmond Henderson, *Industrial Insurance in the United States* (Chicago: University of Chicago Press, 1909), pp. 273, 277.
4. Mrs. Imogen B. Oakley, "The More Civic Work, the Less Need of Philanthropy," *American City* 6(6) (June 1912), p. 805. Oakley cited a French observer of American life who "Knew of no civic clubs of women in France . . . because the city authorities take care of all these matters—as they should."
5. Mrs. G. H. Robertson, "The State's Duty to Fatherless Children," *Child-Welfare Magazine* 6(5) (Jan. 1912), p. 160.
6. The "big bang" phrase comes from Christopher Leman, "Patterns of Policy Development: Social Security in the United States and Canada," *Public Policy* 25 (1977): 261–91.
7. This paragraph and the next draw especially from Peter Flora and Jens Alber, "Modernization, Democratization and the Development of Welfare States in Western Europe," pp. 37–80 in *The Development of Welfare States in Europe and America,* ed. P. Flora and A. Heidenheimer (New Brunswick, NJ: Transaction Press, 1981); Francis G. Castles, *The Working Class and Welfare: Reflections on the Political Development of the Welfare State in Australia and New Zealand, 1880–1980* (London and Boston: Allen and Unwin, 1985); James M. Malloy, *The Politics of Social Security in Brazil* (Pittsburgh: University of Pittsburgh Press, 1979); and I. M. Rubinow, *Social Insurance* (New York: Henry Holt, 1913).

8. Peter Flora and Arnold J. Heidenheimer, "The Historical Core and Changing Boundaries of the Welfare State," in *The Development of Welfare States in Europe and America,* pp. 18–19.

9. On the British reforms and their rationale, see Derek Fraser, *The Evolution of the British Welfare State,* 2nd ed. (London: Macmillan, 1984), ch. 9; José Harris, *William Beveridge: A Biography* (Oxford: Oxford University Press, 1977), chs. 16–17; and Norman Furniss and Timothy Tilton, *The Case for the Welfare State* (Bloomington: Indiana University Press, 1977), ch. 5.

10. Francis G. Castles, *The Social Democratic Image of Society* (London: Routledge and Kegan Paul, 1978); Gösta Esping-Andersen, *Politics Against Markets: The Social Democratic Road to Power* (Princeton, NJ: Princeton University Press, 1985); and Furniss and Tilton, *Case for the Welfare State,* ch. 6.

11. Further elaboration of the points in this and the next paragraph can be found in Margaret Weir, Ann Shola Orloff, and Theda Skocpol, eds., *The Politics of Social Policy in the United States* (Princeton, NJ: Princeton University Press, 1988); and in Edwin Amenta and Theda Skocpol, "Taking Exception: Explaining the Distinctiveness of American Public Policies in the Last Century," pp. 292–333 in *The Comparative History of Public Policy,* ed. Francis G. Castles (Oxford: Polity Press, 1989).

12. For examples, see Flora and Heidenheimer, *Development of Welfare States;* and citations in notes 20 and 56 below.

13. Roy Lubove, *The Struggle for Social Security, 1900–1935,* 2nd ed. (Pittsburgh: University of Pittsburgh Press, 1986; orig. 1968). See also Daniel Nelson, *Unemployment Insurance: The American Experience, 1915–1935* (Madison: University of Wisconsin Press, 1969).

14. Daniel Levine, *Poverty and Society: The Growth of the American Welfare State in International Comparison* (New Brunswick, NJ: Rutgers University Press, 1988), p. 283 and ch. 18.

15. James T. Patterson, *America's Struggle Against Poverty, 1900–1980* (Cambridge, MA: Harvard University Press, 1981).

16. Michael B. Katz, *In the Shadow of the Poorhouse: A Social History of Welfare in America* (New York: Basic Books, 1986). Part I of this book deals with "The Poorhouse Era" of the nineteenth century and, as Katz explains (pp. xii–xiii), "Part II covers the great era of corporate capital from roughly the 1890s through the 1930s, when replacements for the failed earlier nineteenth-century policies, especially poorhouses and scientific charity, became urgent and the impotence of state and local governments before the great problems of dependency became unmistakable. Its focus is the creation of what I have called the semi-

welfare state, whose structure was completed by the New Deal." The book also has a Part III, which is mainly about the emergence and fate of the War on Poverty.

17. Along with many others, this factual point will be documented in a later chapter. References are not given here for statements that summarize arguments substantiated in later chapters.

18. Kathryn Kish Sklar, "Florence Kelley and the Integration of 'Women's Sphere' into American Politics, 1890–1921" (paper presented at the Annual Meeting of the Organization of American Historians, New York, April 1986), p. 17.

19. Harold Wilensky, *The Welfare State and Equality* (Berkeley and Los Angeles: University of California Press, 1975), p. 24, echoing Harold Wilensky and Charles N. Lebeaux, *Industrial Society and Social Welfare* (New York: Russell Sage Foundation, 1958), p. 230.

20. See Phillips Cutright, "Political Structure, Economic Development, and National Social Security Programs," *American Journal of Sociology* 70 (1965): 537–50; and Ramesh Mishra, "Welfare and Industrial Man: A Study of Welfare in Western Industrial Societies in Relation to the Hypothesis of Convergence," *Sociological Review* 21 (1973): 535–60.

21. See F. L. Pryor, *Public Expenditures in Communist and Capitalist Nations* (London: George Allen and Unwin, 1968); and Wilensky, *Welfare State and Equality*. Some proponents of logic of industrialism ideas maintain that policies and expenditure patterns converge only up to a point, after which sociocultural variations persist among very rich countries; see Wilensky as well as Robert W. Jackman, *Politics and Social Equality: A Comparative Analysis* (New York: Wiley, 1975), and John B. Williamson and J. J. Fleming, "Convergence Theory and the Social Welfare Sector: A Cross-National Analysis," *International Journal of Comparative Sociology* 18 (1977): 242–53.

22. The highly aggregated dependent variables include total years of "program experience," as in Cutright, "National Social Security Programs," and broad categories of national social expenditure, as in Wilensky, *Welfare State and Equality*, and many others.

23. Flora and Alber in "Modernization, Democratization, and the Development of Welfare States" demonstrate that levels of industrialization fail to predict the timing of the adoption of social insurance programs by 12 European nations between the 1880s and the 1920s. And David Collier and Richard Messick in "Prerequisites versus Diffusion: Testing Alternative Explanations of Social Security Adoption," *American Political Science Review* 69 (1975): 1299–1315. find that neither levels nor significant thresholds of industrialization explain the timing of social insurance program adoptions in 59 nations between the 1880s

and the 1960s. On the matter of expenditure growth, Francis Castles examines the expansion of public social expenditures in 18 democratic capitalist nations during the 1960s and 1970s in "The Impact of Parties on Public Expenditures" in *The Impact of Parties,* ed. Francis G. Castles (Beverly Hills, CA: Sage Publications, 1982), pp. 61–70. He finds that neither economic level nor economic growth can account for recent divergences in national expenditure patterns. Furthermore, both John Stephens in *The Transition from Capitalism to Socialism* (London: Macmillan, 1979), ch. 4, and John Myles in *Old Age in the Welfare State: The Political Economy of Public Pensions* (Boston: Little, Brown, 1984), pp. 94–97, adduce evidence against Wilensky's pivotal argument in *Welfare State and Equality* that national social expenditures are significantly determined by the proportions of aged in the population.

24. See Collier and Messick, "Prerequisites versus Diffusion," p. 1309.

25. The best evidence we have on who received pensions comes from the analysis of county-level data for Ohio, 1886–1890, by Heywood Sanders, "Paying for the 'Bloody Shirt': The Politics of Civil War Pensions," in *Political Benefits,* ed. Barry Rundquist (Lexington, MA: D. C. Heath, 1980), pp. 150–54. Sanders concludes (p. 152) that "generally, pensions were distributed to predominantly rural, Anglo-Saxon areas, with high population stability." Urban Cuyahoga County, including Cleveland with its high post–Civil War immigrant population, had the lowest per capita county rate of pension receipt (five per thousand). Sanders found that an "index of urbanism, percent of families in homes rather than on farms," had a significant negative correlation with county-level rates of pension receipt. Nevertheless, there is some indication in Sanders's data that smaller cities, such as Dayton, Ohio, were sites of high rates of pension receipt. Small and medium cities may have had higher native-born (and early-immigrant) populations, and they may have served as nodes of communiciation among veterans, including those living on nearby farms, encouraging them to apply for benefits.

26. This argument is developed and documented in Ann Shola Orloff and Theda Skocpol, "Why Not Equal Protection?: Explaining the Politics of Public Social Spending in Britain, 1900–1911, and the United States, 1880s-1920," *American Sociological Review* 49 (Dec. 1984), pp. 732–33, 736, 743–44.

27. See, for example, the discussions in Edwin Amenta, Elisabeth S. Clemens, Jefren Olsen, Sunita Parikh, and Theda Skocpol, "The Political Origins of Unemployment Insurance in Five American States," *Studies in American Political Development* 2 (1987): 137–82; Keith L. Bryant, Jr., "Kate Bernard, Organized Labor, and Social Justice in Oklahoma

During the Progressive Era," *Journal of Southern History* 35 (1969): 145–64; Robert Morlan, *Political Prairie Fire: The Nonpartisan League, 1915–1922* (Minneapolis: University of Minnesota Press, 1955); Joseph Frederick Tripp, "Progressive Labor Laws in Washington State (1900–1925)" (Ph.D. diss., University of Washington, 1973); and Richard M. Vallely, *Radicalism in the States: The Minnesota Farmer-Labor Party and the American Political Economy* (Chicago: University of Chicago Press, 1989).

28. Louis Hartz, *The Liberal Tradition in America* (New York: Harcourt Brace, 1955).

29. Louis Hartz, *The Founding of New Societies* (New York: Harcourt, Brace and World, 1964).

30. Gaston Rimlinger, *Welfare Policy and Industrialization in Europe, America, and Russia* (New York: Wiley, 1971).

31. Levine, *Poverty and Society,* p. 23. In Levine's view (p. 11), "Nations perceive reality in their own way and act according to those perceptions' relation to their own history."

32. Lubove, *Struggle for Social Security,* p. 2.

33. Anthony King, "Ideas, Institutions, and the Policies of Governments: A Comparative Analysis: Part III," *British Journal of Political Science* 3(4) (1973), p. 418; emphasis in the original removed. The entire article spans 3(3): 291–313 and 3(4): 409–423.

34. Both Rimlinger, *Welfare Policy and Industrialization,* and Levine, *Poverty and Society,* emphasize this comparison.

35. In addition to the authors already cited, see Kirstin Grønbjerg, David Street, and Gerald D. Suttles, *Poverty and Social Change* (Chicago: University of Chicago Press, 1978), pp. 5–6. Actually, there is no necessary relation between economic laissez-faire and minimalist social provision. Under its regime of "free trade" Britain in the nineteenth century was more closely wedded to laissez-faire economic policies than was the United States, and when the British Liberals proposed pensions and social insurance after 1906, they did so partly in order to *maintain* free trade by heading off Conservative proposals for new protective tariffs on British industries. See H. V. Emy, "The Impact of Financial Policy on English Party Politics before 1914," *Historical Journal* 15 (1972): 103–31.

36. See Arnold J. Heidenheimer, "The Politics of Public Education, Health and Welfare in the USA and Western Europe: How Growth and Reform Potentials Have Differed," *British Journal of Political Science* 3(3) (July 1973): 315–40.

37. King, "Ideas and Policies," pp. 419–20.

38. For futher discussion and documentation see Theda Skocpol,

"Brother Can You Spare a Job? Work and Welfare in the United States," pp. 192–213 in *The Nature of Work,* ed. Kai Erikson and Steven Peter Vallas (New Haven: Yale University Press, 1990).

39. Overviews of the arguments of the charitable societies appear in Lubove, *Struggle for Social Security,* pp. 101–106. For telling examples, see Mary Richmond, "Motherhood and Pensions," *Survey* 29(22) (March 1, 1913): 774–80; and Edward T. Devine, "Pensions for Mothers," *American Labor Legislation Review* 3(2) (June 1913): 191–201.

40. Robert Shalhope, "Toward a Republican Synthesis: The Emergence of an Understanding of Republicanism in American Historiography," *William and Mary Quarterly* 29(1), 3rd ser. (Jan. 1972), p. 70. The key works that crystallized the new synthesis were Bernard Bailyn, *The Ideological Origins of the American Revolution* (Cambridge, MA: Harvard University Press, 1967); and Gordon S. Wood, *the Creation of the American Republic, 1776–1787* (Chapel Hill: University of North Carolina Press, 1969).

41. James T. Kloppenberg, "The Virtues of Liberalism: Christianity, Republicanism, and Ethics in Early American Political Discourse," *Journal of American History* 74(1) (June 1987); p. 27. For another recent assessment, see the Special Issue on "Republicanism in the History and Historiography of the United States," *American Quarterly* 37(4) (Fall 1985).

42. Kloppenberg, "Virtues of Liberalism," p. 30.

43. Sean Wilentz, "On Class and Politics in Jacksonian America," in *The Promise of American History,* ed. Stanley I. Kutler and Stanley N. Katz, vol. 4(4) of *Reviews in American History* (Baltimore: Johns Hopkins University Press, 1982), p. 55.

44. Mustafa Emirbayer, "Moral Education in America, 1830–1990: A Contribution to the Sociology of Moral Culture" (Ph.D. diss., Harvard University, 1990), ch. 3.

45. Stuart Charles McConnell, "A Social History of the Grand Army of the Republic, 1867–1900" (Ph.D. diss., Johns Hopkins University, 1987), pp. 379–402.

46. Among the key works are Paul G. Faler, *Mechanics and Manufacturers in the Early Industrial Revolution* (Albany: State University of New York Press, 1981); Sean Wilentz, *Chants Democratic: New York City and the Rise of the American Working Class, 1788–1850* (New York: Oxford University Press, 1984); Alan Dawley, *Class and Community: The Industrial Revolution in Lynn* (Cambridge, MA: Harvard University Press, 1976); and Leon Fink, *Workingmen's Democracy: The Knights of Labor and American Politics* (Urbana: University of Illinois Press, 1983). For overviews, see Sean Wilentz, "Against Exceptionalism: Class Con-

sciousness and the American Labor Movement, 1790–1920," *International Labor and Working Class History*, no. 26 (Fall 1984): 1–24; and Leon Fink, "The New Labor History and the Powers of Historical Pessimism: Consensus, Hegemony, and the Case of the Knights of Labor," *Journal of American History* 75(1) (June 1988): 115–36.

47. Wilentz, "Against Exceptionalism," pp. 14–15.

48. Fink, *Workingmen's Democracy*, p. 228 and passim.

49. Tripp, "Labor Laws in Washington State."

50. An excellent overview appears in Paula Baker, "The Domestication of Politics: Women and American Political Society, 1780–1920," *American Historical Review* 85(3) (June 1984): 620–47.

51. For some key works, see Linda K. Kerber, *Women of the Republic: Intellect and Ideology in Revolutionary America* (Chapel Hill: University of North Carolina Press, 1980); Nancy F. Cott, *The Bonds of Womanhood: Woman's Sphere in New England, 1790–1835* (New Haven: Yale University Press, 1975); Barbara Berg, *The Remembered Gate: Origins of American Feminism* (New York: Oxford University Press, 1978); Karen J. Blair, *The Clubwoman as Feminist: True Womanhood Redefined, 1868–1914* (New York: Holmes and Meier, 1980); Ruth Bordin, *Woman and Temperance: The Quest for Power and Liberty, 1873–1900* (Philadelphia: Temple University Press, 1981); and Barbara Leslie Epstein, *The Politics of Domesticity: Women, Evangelism, and Temperance in Nineteenth-Century America* (Middletown, CT: Wesleyan University Press, 1981).

52. Rheta Childe Dorr, *What Eight Million Women Want* (New York: Kraus Reprint, 1971; orig. 1910), p. 327.

53. The phrase "social housekeeping" comes from Mary P. Ryan, *Womanhood in America: From Colonial Time to the Present*, 3rd ed. (New York: Franklin Watts, 1983), esp. pp. 198–210.

54. Michael Freeden, *The New Liberalism: An Ideology of Social Reform* (Oxford: Clarendon Press, 1978).

55. On parallel developments in Britain and the United States, see Kenneth O. Morgan, "The Future at Work: Anglo-American Progressivism, 1870–1917," pp. 245–71 in *Contrast and Connection: Bicentennial Essays in Anglo-American History*, ed. H. C. Allen and Roger Thompson (Columbus: Ohio University Press, 1976); and Charles L. Mowat, "Social Legislation in Britain and the United States in the Early Twentieth Century: A Problem in the History of Ideas," pp. 81–96 in *Historical Studies: Papers Read before the Irish Conference of Historians*, vol. 7, ed. J. C. Beckett (New York: Barnes and Noble, 1969). See also the recent major study by James T. Kloppenberg, *Uncertain Victory: Social Democracy and Progressivism in European and American Thought, 1870–1920* (New York: Oxford University Press, 1986).

56. Michael Shalev, "The Social Democratic Model and Beyond: Two Generations of Comparative Research on the Welfare State," *Comparative Social Research* 6 (1983): 315–51. Examples of recent research in this tradition include Lars Björn, "Labor Parties, Economic Growth, and Redistribution in Five Capitalist Democracies," *Comparative Social Research* 2 (1979): 93–128; Castles, *Social Democratic Image of Society;* Castles, "The Impact of Parties on Public Expenditures"; Esping-Andersen, *Politics Against Markets;* Gösta Esping-Andersen, *The Three Worlds of Welfare Capitalism* (Princeton, NJ: Princeton University Press, 1990); Bruce Headey, "Trade Unions and National Wage Policies," *Journal of Politics* 32 (1970): 407–39; Bruce Headey, *Housing Policy in the Developed Economy: The United Kingdom, Sweden, and the United States* (London: Croom Helm, 1978); Walter Korpi, *The Democratic Class Struggle* (Boston: Routledge and Kegan Paul, 1983); Andrew Martin, *The Politics of Economic Policy in the United States: A Tentative View from a Comparative Perspective,* Professional Paper in Comparative Politics 01–040 (Beverly Hills, CA: Sage Publications, 1973); John Myles, *Old Age in the Welfare State* (Boston: Little, Brown, 1984); and John Stephens, *The Transition from Capitalism to Socialism* (London: Macmillan, 1979).

57. Stephens, *From Capitalism to Socialism,* p. 89. See also Korpi, *Democratic Class Struggle.*

58. See Walter Korpi's discussion of the ideal-typical "institutional" welfare state in "Social Policy and Distributional Conflict in the Capitalist Democracies: A Preliminary Framework," *West European Politics* 3 (1980): 296–315.

59. Shalev, "Social Democratic Model," p. 11.

60. Hugh Heclo, *Modern Social Politics in Britain and Sweden* (New Haven: Yale University Press, 1974). Jens Alber, "Governmental Responses to the Challenge of Unemployment: The Development of Unemployment Insurance in Western Europe," pp. 151–83 in *The Development of Welfare States in Europe and America,* ed. Flora and Heidenheimer; and Flora and Alber, "Modernization, Democratization, and the Development of Welfare States."

61. See Castles, *Social Democratic Image of Society;* Esping-Andersen, *Politics Against Markets,* chs. 2–3; and Margaret Weir and Theda Skocpol, "State Structures and Possibilities for 'Keynesian' Responses to the Great Depression in Sweden, Britain, and the United States," in *Bringing the State Back In,* ed. Peter B. Evans, Dietrich Rueschemeyer, and Theda Skocpol (Cambridge and New York: Cambridge University Press, 1985), esp. pp. 141–48.

62. This is a major theme in Jill Quadagno, *The Transformation of Old Age*

Security: Class and Politics in the American Welfare State (Chicago: University of Chicago Press, 1988).

63. On the centrality of ethnic and racial collective identities in U.S. social politics, see Ira Katznelson, *City Trenches: Urban Politics and the Patterning of Class in the United States* (New York: Pantheon, 1981).

64. Practitioners of this basic genre (who nevertheless vary widely in the ways they specify intracapitalist splits and connect them to policy outcomes) include Edward Berkowitz and Kim McQuaid, *Creating the Welfare State,* 2nd ed., rev. and expanded (New York: Praeger, 1988); G. William Domhoff, *The Higher Circles* (New York: Random House, 1970); Thomas Ferguson, "From Normalcy to New Deal: Industrial Structure, Party Competition, and American Public Policy in the Great Depression," *International Organization* 38 (1984): 41–93; Quadagno, *Transformation of Old Age Security;* Ronald Radosh, "The Myth of the New Deal," in *The New Leviathan,* ed. Ronald Radosh and Murray N. Rothbard (New York: E. P. Dutton, 1972); and James Weinstein, *The Corporate Ideal in the Liberal State, 1900–1918* (Boston: Beacon Press, 1968). A more cultural interpretation appears in R. Jeffrey Lustig, *Corporate Liberalism: The Origins of Modern American Political Theory, 1890–1920* (Berkeley: University of California Press, 1982). Quadagno's argument is the most comparatively informed of all these studies; but even she does not do a full cross-national causal analysis to test propositions about the role of business interests in shaping national social policies.

65. Quadagno, *Transformation of Old Age Security,* pp. 29–47.

66. In my opinion, this is the strong suit of the sophisticated history by Berkowitz and McQuaid, *Creating the Welfare State.*

67. Understandably, much of the argument between welfare capitalist theorists and those who take positions similar to the one presented here has been played out on the empirical terrain of the Social Security Act of 1935. For some relevant arguments and counter-arguments, see Theda Skocpol and John Ikenberry, "The Political Formation of the American Welfare State in Historical and Comparative Perspective," *Comparative Social Research* 6 (1983), pp. 128–31 and n. 15; Jill S. Quadagno, "Welfare Capitalism and the Social Security Act of 1935," *American Sociological Review (ASR)* 49 (1984): 632–47; Theda Skocpol and Edwin Amenta, "Did Capitalists Shape Social Security?" *ASR* 50(4) (1985): 572–75; G. William Domhoff, "Corporate Liberal Theory and the Social Security Act," *Politics and Society* 15 (1986/87): 297–330; J. Craig Jenkins and Barbara G. Brents, "Social Protest, Hegemonic Competition, and Social Reform: A Political Struggle Interpretation of the Origins of the American Welfare State," *ASR* 54

(1989): 891–909; and Edwin Amenta and Sunita Parikh, "Capitalists Did Not Want the Social Security Act: A Critique of the Capitalist Dominance Thesis," *ASR* 56 (1991): 124–29.

68. See especially the works by Domhoff and Radosh cited in notes 64 and 67, along with Guy Alchon, *The Invisible Hand of Planning: Capitalism, Social Science and the State in the 1920s* (Princeton, NJ: Princeton University Press, 1985); Loren Baritz, *Servants of Power* (Middletown, CT: Wesleyan University Press, 1960); David Eakins, "Policy Planning for the Establishment," in *A New History of Leviathan*, ed. Radosh and Rothbard; and Jenkins and Brents, "Hegemonic Competition and Social Reform."

69. See, for example, the telling instance described in Steven J. Diner, *A City and Its Universities: Public Policy in Chicago, 1892–1919* (Chapel Hill: University of North Carolina Press, 1980), pp. 123–27. Kenneth Finegold also demonstrates business limits on policy-oriented progressive social scientists in "Progressivism, Electoral Change, and Public Policy: Reform Outcomes in New York, Cleveland, and Chicago" (Ph.D. diss., Harvard University, 1985), chs. 2 and 4 on New York and Chicago.

70. See Finegold, ibid., ch. 3 on the institutional conditions that allowed social analysts to help shape pro–working class social policies in Cleveland. See also the analysis of the American Association for Labor Legislation during the Progressive Era in Chapter 3 below.

71. A somewhat different and somewhat overlapping discussion of the literature appears in Linda Gordon's "The New Feminist Scholarship on the Welfare State," the introduction to her valuable edited collection, *Women, the State, and Welfare* (Madison: University of Wisconsin Press, 1990). See also an earlier article by Gordon, "What Does Welfare Regulate? A Review Essay on the Writings of Frances Fox Piven and Richard A. Cloward," *Social Research* 55(4) (Winter 1988): 609–30. Gordon's theoretical frame of reference for gender scholarship on social policy especially highlights interactions between mostly female social-welfare professionals and their mostly female clients. Consequently, her perspective is most useful for guiding the study of policy implementation and ongoing modifications of established lines of policy.

72. Eileen Boris and Peter Bardaglio, "The Transformation of Patriarchy: The Historic Role of the State," in *Families, Politics, and Public Policy: A Feminist Dialogue on Women and the State*, ed. Irene Diamond (New York: Longman, 1983), pp. 72–73.

73. Mimi Abramovitz, *Regulating the Lives of Women: Social Welfare Policy from Colonial Times to the Present* (Boston: South End Press, 1988), p. 4.

74. See Alice Kessler-Harris, *Out to Work: A History of Wage-Earning Women in the United States* (Oxford: Oxford University Press, 1981), ch. 5; and Heidi Hartmann, "Capitalism, Patriarchy, and Job Segregation by Sex," *Signs* 1(3, pt. 2) (Spring 1976). pp. 159–67.

75. See Carol Brown, "Mothers, Fathers, and Children: From Private to Public Patriarchy," pp. 239–67 in *Women and Revolution: A Discussion of the Unhappy Marriage of Marxism and Feminism,* ed. Lydia Sargent (Boston: South End Press, 1981); Nancy Folbre, "The Pauperization of Motherhood: Patriarchy and Public Policy in the United States," *Review of Radical Political Economics* 16 (Winter 1984): 72–88; Janet Marie Wedel, "The Origins of State Patriarchy During the Progressive Era: A Sociological Study of the Mothers' Aid Movement" (Ph.D. diss., Washington University, St. Louis, 1975), ch. 9; Libba Gage Moore, "Mothers' Pensions: The Origins of the Relationship between Women and the Welfare State" (Ph.D. diss., University of Massachusetts, 1986); and Barbara Nelson, "The Gender, Race, and Class Origins of Early Welfare Policy and the Welfare State: A Comparison of Workmen's Compensation and Mothers' Aid," pp. 413–35 in *Women, Politics, and Change,* ed. Louise A. Tilly and Patricia Gurin (New York: Russell Sage Foundation, 1990).

76. Abramovitz, *Regulating the Lives of Women,* ch. 6.

77. Ann Vandepol, "Dependent Children, Child Custody, and the Mothers' Pensions: The Transformation of State-Family Relations in the Early 20th Century," *Social Problems* 29(3) (Feb. 1982): 221–35.

78. For an extreme example, see Gwendolyn Mink, "The Lady and the Tramp: Gender, Race, and the Origins of the American Welfare State," pp. 92–122 in *Women, the State, and Welfare,* ed. Gordon. Mink traces social policies for mothers in this period to a vague, overarching sense of "race anxiety." She pays little analytical attention to variations. And much of her evidence consists of quotations using the word "race." Many quotes from female reformers and women's groups are taken out of context, and Mink often misunderstands the use of the word "race." Sometimes in this historical period it was, as she suggests, used to refer to whites versus nonwhites, or northwestern versus southeastern Europeans; but at other times it was used to refer to the human race, or all citizens, or all of humankind. Women reformers often used the word in these senses when they spoke of mothers' responsibility for furthering the well-being of "the race."

79. Paula Baker, "The Domestication of Politics: Women and American Political Society, 1780–1920," *American Historical Review* 89 (June 1984): 620–47.

80. Kathryn Kish Sklar, "Explaining the Power of Women's Political Cul-

ture in the Creation of the American Welfare State, 1890–1930,"
forthcoming in *Gender and the Origins of Welfare States in Western Europe
and North America* ed. Seth Koven and Sonya Michel (New York: Routledge, 1992).

81. For some excellent examples, see Jane Jenson, "Gender and Reproduction: Or, Babies and the State," *Studies in Political Economy* 20
(Summer 1986): 9–46; Desley Deacon, "Politicizing Gender," *Genders*
6 (Fall 1989): 1–19; Susan Pedersen, "Social Policy and the Reconstruction of the Family in Britain and France, 1900–1945" (Ph.D. diss.,
Harvard University, 1989); and Elisabeth Clemens, "Redefining the
Public Realm: Progressive Coalitions and Political Culture in the
American States, 1890–1915" (Ph.D. diss., University of Chicago,
1990).

82. *American Historical Review* 95(4) (October 1990): 1067–1108.

83. U.S.–Britain contrasts are featured in Sklar, "Explaining the Power of
Women's Political Culture," and in Theda Skocpol and Gretchen Ritter, "Gender and the Origins of Modern Social Policies in Britain and
the United States," *Studies in American Political Development* 5(1) (Spring
1991): 36–93. Koven and Michel are more inclined to stress similarities
between the U.S. and Britain in part because they primarily focus on
explaining local public health policies, whereas I place more emphasis
on labor regulations and social spending policies.

84. Desley Deacon, "Reply to 'Re-Politicizing Gender,'" *Genders* 11 (Summer 1991). Along with Deacon (who focuses on comparisons among
Australian states and between Australia and the United States), Lee
Ann Banaszak is doing pathbreaking work on the institutional contexts
within which women's movements have developed and had varying
political effects. See her articles "Gaining Access to the Political System: The Case of the Swiss and American Women's Suffrage Movements" (paper presented at the Annual Meeting of the Midwest Political Science Association, Chicago, April 1990), and "Federalism and
the Tactics of the Swiss and American Women's Suffrage Movements:
How State Institutions Affect Political Movements" (paper presented
at the Annual Meeting of the American Political Science Association,
San Francisco, September 1990).

85. See Jenson, "Babies and the State"; and Mary Ruggie, *The State and
Working Women: A Comparative Study of Britain and Sweden* (Princeton,
NJ: Princeton University Press, 1984).

86. See esp. Richard Titmuss, "War and Social Policy," pp. 75–87 in his
Essays on the Welfare State (London: Allen and Unwin, 1978).

87. Without reaching very conclusive results, the recent quantitative literature has focused on possible "trade-offs" between military and

social expenditures in the Cold War era of "small wars." See Wilensky, *Welfare State and Equality,* ch. 4; Bruce M. Russett, "Defense Expenditures and National Well-Being," *American Political Science Review* 76 (1982): 767–77; and Larry J. Griffin, Joel A. Devine, and Michael Wallace, "On the Economic and Political Determinants of Welfare Spending in the Post-War Era," *Politics and Society* 13 (1983): 331–72.

88. A start toward taking state formation seriously has been made by Flora and Alber in "Modernization, Democratization, and the Development of Welfare States." But the American case is not included in their article, which would require analytical reworking if it were.

89. The position I advocate here resembles the one put forward by Charles Tilly in *Big Structures, Large Processes, Huge Comparisons* (New York: Russell Sage Foundation, 1984), chs. 1–4.

90. I am indebted to Peter Hall for suggesting the label "structured polity approach." I am using this label rather than "state-centered," because the latter has too often be taken to mean "bureaucratic determinism," which I have never advocated. Equally important, I want to emphasize that several aspects of politics and state-society interactions are included in my analytical frame of reference. For further theoretical discussion, see *Bringing the State Back In,* ed. Evans, Rueschemeyer, and Skocpol. In political science, the kind of approach I am using is often called "the new institutionalism." See James G. March and Johan P. Olsen, "The New Institutionalism: Organizational Factors in Political Life," *American Political Science Review* 78 (1984): 734–49.

91. This discussion of political culture in relation to historical patterns of state formation draws especially upon J. P. Nettl, "The State as a Conceptual Variable," *World Politics* 20 (1968): 559–92; and Kenneth Dyson, *The State Tradition in Western Europe: A Study of an Idea and an Institution* (New York: Oxford University Press, 1980).

92. I draw this conception of the state from Max Weber and Otto Hintze. See Weber, *Economy and Society,* ed. Guenther Roth and Claus Wittich (New York: Bedminster Press, 1968; orig. 1922), vol. 2, ch. 9, and vol. 3, chs. 10–13; and *The Historical Essays of Otto Hintze,* ed. Felix Gilbert (New York: Oxford University Press, 1975; orig. 1897–1932).

93. See Charles Tilly, ed., *The Formation of National States in Western Europe* (Princeton, NJ: Princeton University Press, 1975).

94. On U.S. state formation in contrast to European see J. Rogers Hollingsworth, "The United States," pp. 163–96 in *Crises of Political Development in Europe and the United States,* ed. Raymond Grew (Princeton: Princeton, NJ: University Press, 1978); Samuel P. Huntington, *Political Order in Changing Societies* (New Haven: Yale University Press, 1968), ch. 2; Seymour Martin Lipset, *The First New Nation* (New York: Basic

Books, 1963); Stephen Skowronek, *Building a New American State: The Expansion of National Administrative Capacities, 1877–1920* (Cambridge and New York: Cambridge University Press, 1982), pt. 1.

95. Northern and southern battle deaths during the Civil War totaled 610,222 (or 17,093 per million of the national population), compared to 126,000 U.S. battle deaths (1,313 per million) in World War I, and 408,300 U.S. battle deaths (3,141 per million) in World War II. Over one-third of northern American males then 15 to 44 years old, and up to half of the southern white males, fought in the Civil War. And of course this was the only modern U.S. war that ever entailed great destruction of property on the American mainland.

For discussion of why the Civil War did not have a permanently centralizing effect on the U.S. state, see Eric L. McKitrick, "Party Politics and the Union and Confederate War Efforts," pp. 117–51 in *The American Party Systems,* 2nd ed., ed. William Nisbet Chambers and Walter Dean Burnham (New York: Oxford University Press, 1975); William G. Shade, "'Revolutions Can Go Backwards': The American Civil War and the Problem of Political Development," *Social Science Quarterly* 55(3) (Dec. 1974): 753–67; Morton Keller, *Affairs of State* (Cambridge, MA: Harvard University Press, 1977), pt. 1; and Richard Franklin Bensel, *Yankee Leviathan: The Origins of Central State Authority in America, 1859–1877* (Cambridge and New York: Cambridge University Press, 1990).

96. See Robert D. Cuff, *The War Industries Board: Business-Government Relations during World War I* (Baltimore: Johns Hopkins Univerity Press, 1973); and Harold G. Vatter, *The U.S. Economy in World War II* (New York: Columbia University Press, 1985).

97. John F. Witte, *The Politics and Development of the Federal Income Tax* (Madison: University of Wisconsin Press, 1985), ch. 7.

98. The phrase "state of courts and parties" comes from Skowronek, *Building a New American State,* ch. 2.

99. Richard L. McCormick, "The Party Period and Public Policy: An Exploratory Hypothesis," *Journal of American History* 66 (1979): 279–98.

100. Martin Schiesl, *The Politics of Efficiency: Municipal Administration and Reform in America: 1880–1920* (Berkeley: University of California Press, 1977); and Robert H. Wiebe, *The Search for Order, 1877–1920* (New York: Hill and Wang, 1967).

101. Skowronek, *Building a New American State,* pt. 3 and epilogue; and Barry Karl, *The Uneasy State* (Chicago: University of Chicago Press, 1983).

102. On the parties in relation to the polity as a whole, see Martin Shefter,

"Party, Bureaucracy, and Political Change in the United States," pp. 211–65 in *Political Parties: Development and Decay,* ed. Louis Maisel and Joseph Cooper (Beverly Hills, CA: Sage, 1978); *The American Party Systems,* ed. Chambers and Burnham; and David R. Mayhew, *Placing Parties in American Politics* (Princeton, NJ: Princeton University Press, 1986).

103. On Congress in the U.S. state structure of this century, see esp. Morris P. Fiorina, *Congress: Keystone of the Washington Establishment* (New Haven: Yale University Press, 1977); Samuel P. Huntington, "Congressional Responses to the Twentieth Century," pp. 6–38 in *The Congress and America's Future,* 2nd ed., American Assembly, Columbia University (Englewood Cliffs, NJ: Prentice-Hall, 1973); Morton Grodzins, "American Political Parties and the American System," *Western Political Quarterly* 13 (1960): 974–98; and Richard Polenberg, *War and Society: The United States, 1941–1945* (Philadelphia: Lippincott, 1972).

104. Skowronek, *Building a New American State.*

105. See Shefter, "Party, Bureaucracy, and Political Change"; and Martin Shefter, "Party and Patronage: Germany, England and Italy," *Politics and Society* 7 (1977): 403–51.

106. This argument is developed in Ira Katznelson, *City Trenches: Urban Politics and the Patterning of Class in the United States* (New York: Pantheon, 1981).

107. See Willam E. Forbath, *Law and the Shaping of the American Labor Movement* (Cambridge, MA: Harvard University Press, 1991).

108. Richard Oestreicher, "Urban Working-Class Political Behavior and Theories of American Electoral Politics, 1870–1940," *Journal of American History* 74(4) (March 1988), p. 1269.

109. Robert H. Salisbury, "Why No Corporatism in America?" pp. 213–30 in *Trends toward Corporatist Intermediation,* ed. Philippe C. Schmitter and Gerhard Lehmbruch (Beverly Hills, CA: Sage, 1979); and Graham K. Wilson, "Why Is There No Corporatism in the United States?" pp. 219–36 in *Patterns of Corporatist Policy-Making* ed. Gerhard Lehmbruch and Philippe C. Schmitter (Beverly Hills, CA: Sage, 1982).

110. This point is emphasized and its implications are explored in Baker, "Domestication of Politics."

111. For this point I am indebted to Sklar, "Explaining the Power of Women's Political Culture."

112. David Vogel, "Why Businessmen Distrust Their State: The Political Consciousness of American Corporate Executives," *British Journal of Political Science* 8 (1978): 45–78.

113. For examples in various policy areas, see Susan S. Fainstein and Norman I. Fainstein, "National Policy and Urban Development," *Social*

Problems 26 (1978): 125–46; Ira Katznelson and Kenneth Prewitt, "Constitutionalism, Class, and the Limits of Choice in U.S. Foreign Policy," pp. 25–40 in *Capitalism and the State in U.S.–Latin American Relations,* ed. Richard Fagen (Stanford, CA: Stanford University Press, 1979); Steven Kelman, *Regulating America, Regulating Sweden* (Cambridge, MA: MIT Press, 1981); Theda Skocpol and Kenneth Finegold, "State Capacity and Economic Intervention in the Early New Deal," *Political Science Quarterly* 97 (1982): 255–78; and David Vogel, "The 'New' Social Regulation in Historical and Comparative Perspective," pp. 155–86 in *Regulation in Perspective,* ed. Thomas K. McCraw (Cambridge, MA: Harvard Business School/Harvard University Press, 1981).

114. In an exemplary way, "political opportunity structures" and group "resource mobilization" are jointly analyzed in Edwin Amenta and Yvonne Zylan, "It Happened Here: Political Opportunity, the New Institutionalism, and the Townsend Movement," *American Sociological Review* 56 (1991): 250–65.

115. David Brian Robertson, "The Bias of American Federalism: The Limits of Welfare-State Development in the Progressive Era," *Journal of Policy History* 1(3) (1989): 261–91. A similar argument is made in William Graebner, "Federalism in the Progressive Era: A Structural Interpretation of Reform," *Journal of American History* 64(2) (Sept. 1977): 331–57.

116. Robert Asher, "Business and Workers' Welfare in the Progressive Era: Workmen's Compensation Reform in Massachusetts, 1880–1911," *Business History Review* 43 (1969), pp. 473–74. This overriding of business arguments in 1911 reversed an earlier Massachusetts decision in 1904. As explained by Charles Richmond Henderson in "Industrial Insurance I: The Extent and Nature of the Demand for a Social Policy of Workingmen's Insurance," *American Journal of Sociology* 7(4) (Jan. 1907), p. 484, a "bill brought before the Legislature of Massachusetts in 1904 to introduce the British Compensation Act of 1897 was defeated by the claim of the manufacturers that the indemnities required of them would cripple them in competing with manufacturers of other states."

117. Robertson, "Bias of Federalism," pp. 283–84, characterizes the American Federation of Labor as a "loose, state-based confederation" composed of "state and local units." I strongly disagree. As explained in Chapter 4 below, state federations of labor were not at all important constituent units within the national AFL, and there were no geographically defined local units. In contrast, state and local units were very important within the American Medical Association (which Rob-

ertson mistakenly treats as organizationally analogous to the AFL) and also within the great U.S. women's federations of the day.

118. A classic analysis that explores political class consciousness in terms of the relationships of intellectuals to labor organizations is Selig Perlman, *The Theory of the Labor Movement* (New York: August M. Kelley, 1970; orig. 1928).

119. Policy developments have been analyzed in these terms in Esping-Andersen, *Politics Against Markets;* and in Headey, *Housing Policy in the Developed Economy.* For an overview of studies dealing in various ways with policy feedbacks, see Theda Skocpol and Edwin Amenta, "States and Social Policies," *Annual Review of Sociology* 12 (1986): 149–51.

120. This is a central theme in Heclo, *Modern Social Politics.*

Introduction to Part I

1. Richard Franklin Bensel, *Sectionalism and American Political Development, 1880–1980* (Madison: University of Wisconsin Press, 1984), p. 67. Bensel computed his percentages from the *1936 Annual Report of the Secretary of the Treasury on the State of the Finances* (Washington: Government Printing Office, 1937), table 5, pp. 362–63.

2. In 1910 there were 562,615 invalid Civil War pensioners on the rolls, receiving $106,433,465, and the national population of males 65 and over was 1,985,976. The sources for these figures are *Report of the Commissioner of Pensions,* included in *Reports of the Department of the Interior for the Fiscal Year Ended June 30, 1910,* vol. 1 (Washington: Government Printing Office, 1911), pp. 146, 149; and U.S. Bureau of the Census, *Historical Statistics of the United States,* Bicentennial ed., pt. 1. (Washington: Government Printing Office, 1975), p. 15, series A 133.

3. *Report of the Commissioner of Pensions* (1910), p. 272.

4. Judith Gladys Cetina, "A History of Veterans' Homes in the United States, 1811–1930" (Ph.D. diss., Case Western Reserve University, 1977), ch. 3–7.

1. Patronage Democracy and Distributive Public Policies in the Nineteenth Century

1. The "compound" phrase comes from Harry N. Scheiber, "Federalism and the Constitution: The Original Understanding," pp. 85–98 in *American Law and the Constitutional Order: Historical Perspectives,* ed. Lawrence M. Friedman and Harry N. Scheiber (Cambridge, MA: Harvard University Press, 1978).

2. Samuel P. Huntington, *Political Order in Changing Societies* (New Haven: Yale University Press, 1968), p. 110.

3. Gordon S. Wood, "Interests and Disinterestedness in the Making of the Constitution," pp. 69–109 in *Beyond Confederation: Origins of the Constitution and American National Identity,* ed. Richard Beeman, Stephen Botein, and Edward C. Carter II (Chapel Hill: University of North Carolina Press, 1987).

4. John M. Murrin, "A Roof without Walls: The Dilemma of American National Identity," in *Beyond Confederation,* ed. Beeman, Botein, and Carter, pp. 346–47.

5. Insightful discussions of American attributions of sovereignty in comparative perspective appear in J. P. Nettl, "The State as a Conceptual Variable," *World Politics* 20 (1968): 559–92; and Ira Katznelson and Kenneth Prewitt, "Constitutionalism, Class, and the Limits of Choice in U.S. Foreign Policy," pp. 25–40 in *Capitalism and the State in U.S.– Latin American Relations,* ed. Richard Fagen (Stanford, CA: Stanford University Press, 1979).

6. Murrin, "Roof without Walls."

7. William G. Shade, "'Revolutions Can Go Backwards': The American Civil War and the Problem of Political Development," *Social Science Quarterly* 55(3) (Dec. 1974): 753–67; and Richard Franklin Bensel, *Yankee Leviathan: The Origins of Central State Authority in America, 1859– 1877* (Cambridge and New York: Cambridge University Press, 1990).

8. A. F. Pollard, *Factors in American History* (New York: Macmillan, 1925), pp. 31–33. A comparative study that approaches "the state" through European political culture is Kenneth Dyson, *The State Tradition in Western Europe: A Study of an Idea and an Institution* (New York: Oxford University Press, 1980).

9. Stephen Skowronek, *Building a New American State: The Expansion of National Administrative Capacities, 1877–1920* (Cambridge and New York: Cambridge University Press, 1982), pp. 19, 24.

10. Ibid., p. 19.

11. Ibid., p. 24. Skowronek takes the characterization of a state as "officials in action" from John R. Commons, *The Legal Foundations of Capitalism* (Madison: University of Wisconsin Press, 1968; orig. 1924), p. 123.

12. Ibid., p. 27.

13. Alexis de Tocqueville, *Democracy in America,* trans. George Lawrence, ed. J. P. Mayer (Garden City, NY: Anchor Books, 1969; orig. 1850, 13th ed.), p. 270. See also Tocqueville's discussion of "The Judicial Power in the United States and its Effect on Political Society" in vol. 1, ch. 6.

14. On the reworking of English common law in the wake of the American

Revolution, see William E. Nelson, *Americanization of the Common Law: The Impact of Legal Change on Massachusetts Society, 1760–1830* (Cambridge, MA: Harvard University Press, 1975). On challenges to judicial discretion, see Charles M. Cook, *The American Codification Movement: A Study of Ante-bellum Legal Reform* (Greenwood, CT: JAI Press, 1981); and Maxwell Bloomfield, "Lawyers and Public Criticism: Challenge and Response in Nineteenth-Century America," *American Journal of Legal History* 15(4) (Oct. 1971): 269–77.

15. Morton Keller, *Affairs of State: Public Life in Late Nineteenth-Century America* (Cambridge, MA: Harvard University Press, 1977), p. 362.

16. Works on this topic are Morton Horwitz, *The Transformation of American Law, 1780–1860* (Cambridge, MA: Harvard University Press, 1977); and Willard Hurst, *The Legitimacy of the Business Corporation in the Law of the United States, 1780–1970* (Charlottesville: University Press of Virginia, 1970). See also Harry N. Scheiber, "Federalism and the American Economic Order, 1789–1910," *Law and Society Review* 10 (Fall 1975): 57–118.

17. Keller, *Affairs of State*, pp. 355–56, 360–61; and William E. Nelson, *The Roots of American Bureaucracy, 1830–1900* (Cambridge, MA: Harvard University Press, 1982), pp. 133–55.

18. Arnold Paul, *Conservative Crisis and the Rule of Law: Attitudes of Bar and Bench, 1887–1895* (Gloucester, MA: Peter Smith, 1976), pp. 2, xv.

19. See Victoria Hattam, *Labor Visions and State Power: The Origins of Business Unionism in the United States* (Princeton, NJ: Princeton University Press, 1992); and William E. Forbath, *Law and the Shaping of the American Labor Movement* (Cambridge, MA: Harvard University Press, 1991).

20. Keller, *Affairs of State*, pp. 369–70.

21. This point is made by Skowronek, *Building a New American State*, pp. 28–29.

22. On rapid turnover in mid-nineteenth-century legislatures, see Nelson W. Polsby, "The Institutionalization of the U.S. House of Representatives," *American Political Science Review* 57 (March 1968): 146–47; and the research of L. Ray Gunn as discussed in Gerald N. Grob, "The Political System and Social Policy in the Nineteenth Century," *Mid-America: An Historical Review* 58(1) (Jan. 1976), p. 14, n. 16.

23. Hugh Heclo, *Modern Social Politics in Britain and Sweden* (New Haven: Yale University Press, 1974), pp. 304–07.

24. On late-nineteenth-century legal professionalization, see Keller, *Affairs of State*, pp. 349–53; and Nelson, *Roots of American Bureaucracy*, pp. 145–48.

25. Richard L. McCormick, *The Party Period and Public Policy: American*

Politics from the Age of Jackson to the Progressive Era (New York: Oxford University Press, 1986). McCormick's seminal essay, "The Party Period and Public Policy: An Exploratory Hypothesis" was first published in the *Journal of American History* in 1979 and is reprinted here. As will become evident, I agree with—and rely heavily upon—McCormick's characterization of party-policy linkages, although not with his rather vague account of the ultimate sociocultural causes of nineteenth-century parties and distributive policy patterns.

26. From President George Washington's "Farewell Address," as quoted in Michael Wallace, "Changing Concepts of Party in the United States: New York, 1815–1828," *American Historical Review* 74 (Dec. 1968), p. 473. Both Wallace and Wood, "Interests and Distinterestedness," present the Founders' views on parties and governance. Also helpful is Ralph Ketcham, *Presidents Above Party: The First American Presidency, 1789–1829,* published for the Institute of Early American History (Chapel Hill: University of North Carolina Press, 1987).

27. Tocqueville, *Democracy in America,* p. 173. In the following chapter (vol. 1, pt. 2, ch. 2) on "Parties in the United States," Tocqueville contrasts the "principled" "great parties," the Federalists and Republicans of the 1790s through the 1820s, with the emerging factious and faithless "small parties" of the Jacksonian era. Mostly, this is a nostalgic chapter, significant for Tocqueville's correct perception that a whole style of "aristocratic" republican governance was passing irrevocably from the American scene.

28. James Bryce, *The American Commonwealth,* 3rd ed., rev., vol. 2, (New York: Macmillan, 1895), p. 5. Bryce first toured the country in the 1870s and the first edition of his book appeared in 1888.

29. Ibid., p. 3.

30. Ibid., vol. 1 (New York: Macmillan, 1893), p. 6.

31. Ibid.

32. The "regime of notables" characterization comes from Martin Shefter, "Party, Bureaucracy, and Political Change in the United States," in *Political Parties: Development and Decay,* ed. Louis Maisel and Joseph Cooper (Beverly Hills, CA: Sage Publications, 1978), pp. 214–18. See also Ronald P. Formisano, "Deferential-Participant Politics: The Early Republic's Political Culture, 1789–1840," *American Political Science Review* 68 (June 1974): 473–87; and Formisano, "Federalists and Republicans: Parties, Yes—System, No," pp. 33–76 in Paul Kleppner et al., *The Evolution of American Electoral Systems* (Westport, CT: Greenwood Press, 1981).

33. Richard P. McCormick, *The Second American Party System: Party Formation in the Jacksonian Era* (New York: Norton, 1966), esp. pp. 28–

29, 343–56. On suffrage eligibility, see also Paul Kleppner, *Who Voted? The Dynamics of Electoral Turnout, 1870–1980* (New York: Praeger, 1982), pp. 7–8.

34. This paragraph and the next rely on McCormick, *Second American Party System.*

35. "Two-partyism" is discussed by McCormick, *Party Period and Public Policy,* p. 162.

36. William E. Gienapp argues that the North remained in many ways a regional political culture. See his "'Politics Seemed to Enter into Everything': Political Culture in the North, 1840–1860," pp. 14–69 in *Essays on American Antebellum Politics, 1840–1860,* ed. William E. Gienapp et al. (College Station: Texas A&M University Press, 1982); and *The Origins of the Republican Party, 1852–1856* (New York: Oxford University Press, 1987).

37. George Rogers Taylor, *The Transportation Revolution, 1815–1860* (New York: Rinehart, 1951).

38. Robert H. Wiebe, *The Opening of American Society* (New York: Vintage Books, 1985).

39. Shefter, "Party, Bureaucracy, and Political Change," p. 221.

40. Michael Wallace, "Changing Concepts of Party in the United States: New York, 1815–1828," *American Historical Review* 74 (Dec. 1968): 453–91; and McCormick, *Second Party System.*

41. Wallace, "Changing Concepts," pp. 465, 469. The "constituent" label for American political parties comes from Theodore Lowi, "Party, Policy, and Constitution in America," pp. 238–76 in *The American Party Systems: Stages of Political Development,* ed. William Nisbet Chambers and Walter Dean Burnham, 2nd ed. (New York: Oxford University Press, 1975).

42. McCormick, *Second American Party System;* Gienapp, "Political Culture in the North," pp. 51–52; Keller, *Affairs of State,* pp. 241–42; Michael E. McGerr, *The Decline of Popular Politics: The American North, 1865–1928* (New York: Oxford University Press, 1986), pp. 22–29; and Richard Jensen, "Armies, Admen, and Crusaders: Types of Presidential Election Campaigns," *History Teacher* 2 (1969): 33–50.

43. Amy Bridges, *A City in the Republic: Antebellum New York and the Origins of Machine Politics* (New York: Cambridge University Press, 1984).

44. Martin Shefter, "The Emergence of the Political Machine: An Alternative View," pp. 14–44 in *Theoretical Perspectives in Urban Politics,* ed. Willis Hawley and Michael Lipsky (Englewood Cliffs, NJ: Prentice-Hall, 1976).

45. Matthew Crenson, *The Federal Machine: Beginnings of Bureaucracy in Jacksonian America* (Baltimore: Johns Hopkins University Press, 1975).

46. Richard John made this point to me in a personal communication. He analyzes the origins of the spoils system in "Managing the Mails: The Postal System, Public Policy, and American Political Culture, 1823–1836" (Ph.D. diss., Harvard University, 1989).

47. Shefter, "Party, Bureaucracy, and Political Change," pp. 218–29; Peter D. Levine, *The Behavior of State Legislative Parties in the Jacksonian Era: New Jersey, 1829–1844* (Cranbury, NJ: Associated University Presses, 1977), chs. 4 and 8; and John M. Dobson, *Politics in the Gilded Age* (New York: Praeger, 1972), ch. 1. To see how the management of patronage worked in two different settings and phases, see Seymour Mandelbaum, *Boss Tweed's New York* (New York: Wiley, 1965); and James A. Kehl, *Boss Rule in the Gilded Age: Matt Quay of Pennsylvania* (Pittsburgh: University of Pittsburgh Press, 1981).

48. Dobson, *Politics in the Gilded Age,* p. 27.

49. Kleppner, *Who Voted?,* p. 32, table 3.1.

50. Walter Dean Burnham, "The Changing Shape of the American Political Universe," *American Political Science Review* 59(1) (March 1965): 7–28.

51. For comparative-historical perspectives on suffrage extension, modes of party operation, and working-class political orientations, see Reinhard Bendix, *Nation-Building and Citizenship* (New York: Wiley, 1964); Martin Shefter, "Party and Patronage: Germany, England, and Italy," *Politics and Society* 7 (1977): 403–51; Ira Katznelson, "Working-Class Formation and the State: Nineteenth-Century England in American Perspective," pp. 257–84 in *Bringing the State Back In,* ed. Peter B. Evans, Dietrich Rueschemeyer, and Theda Skocpol (Cambridge and New York: Cambridge University Press, 1985); and Ira Katznelson and Aristide R. Zolberg, eds., *Working-Class Formation: Nineteenth-Century Patterns in Western Europe and the United States* (Princeton, NJ: Princeton University Press, 1986).

52. See Sean Wilentz, "Society, Politics, and the Market Revolution, 1815–1848," pp. 51–71 in *The New American History,* ed. Eric Foner for the American Historical Association (Philadelphia: Temple University Press, 1990).

53. Eric Foner, *Free Soil, Free Labor, Free Men: The Ideology of the Republican Party before the Civil War* (New York: Oxford University Press, 1970); and George H. Mayer, *The Republican Party, 1854–1966,* 2nd ed. (New York: Oxford University Press, 1967), chs. 6–7.

54. Amy Bridges, "Becoming American: The Working Classes in the United States before the Civil War," in *Working-Class Formation,* p. 182.; Martin Shefter, "Trade Unions and Political Machines: The Organization and Disorganization of the American Working Class in the Late

Nineteenth Century," in ibid., pp. 210, 222, 243. Together, these two essays are outstanding overviews of U.S. working-class formation in the nineteenth century, and I rely heavily on them. See also Ira Katznelson, *City Trenches: Urban Politics and the Patterning of Class in the United States* (New York: Pantheon, 1981); and Alan Dawley and Paul Faler, "Working-Class Culture and Politics in the Industrial Revolution: Sources of Loyalism and Rebellion," *Journal of Social History* 9(4) (June 1976): 466–80.

55. Richard Oestreicher, "Urban Working-Class Political Behavior and Theories of American Electoral Politics, 1870–1940," *Journal of American History* 74(4) (March 1988), p. 1272.

56. Shefter, "Trade Unions and Political Machines," esp. pp. 198, 211, 267–68.

57. Herbert G. Gutman, "Class, Status, and Community: Power in Nineteenth Century American Industrial Cities," pp. 234–60 in his *Work, Culture and Society in Industrializing America* (New York: Vintage Books, 1977).

58. Oestreicher, "Urban Working-Class Political Behavior," p. 1272.

59. Both Bridges and Shefter make this point and give many examples of regular parties picking up policies from labor parties or responding to demands by locally organized unions.

60. McGerr, *Decline of Popular Politics*, pp. 22–23.

61. Ibid., pp. 23, 26. On the pre–Civil War roots of these electoral practices, see the fascinating study by Jean H. Baker, *Affairs of Party: The Political Culture of Northern Democrats in the Mid-Nineteenth Century* (Ithaca: Cornell University Press, 1982), esp. pp. 287–304.

62. McGerr documents this in *Decline of Popular Politics*, ch. 2.

63. This conclusion is now solidly grounded in quantitative analyses of past elections. Major empirical studies include Lee Benson, *The Concept of Jacksonian Democracy: New York as a Test Case* (Princeton, NJ: Princeton University Press, 1961); Richard Jensen, *The Winning of the Midwest: Social and Political Conflict, 1896–1896* (Chicago: University of Chicago Press, 1971); and Paul Kleppner, *The Cross of Culture: A Social Analysis of Midwestern Politics, 1850–1900* (New York: Free Press, 1970). An especially nuanced study, Richard Jensen's "The Religious and Occupational Roots of Party Identification: Illinois and Indiana in the 1870s," *Civil War History* 16 (Dec. 1970): 325–43, has shown joint occupational and ethnoreligious effects, but with the latter predominating. Overviews of the ethno cultural literature are to be found in Robert P. Swierenga, "Ethnocultural Political Analysis: A New Approach to American Ethnic Studies," *Journal of American Studies* 5 (April 1971): 59–79; Samuel T. McSeveney, "Ethnic Groups, Ethnic

Conflicts, and Recent Quantitative Research in American Political History," *International Migration Review* 7 (Spring 1973): 14–33; and Richard P. McCormick, "Ethno-Cultural Interpretations of Nineteenth-Century American Voting Behavior," *Political Science Quarterly* 89 (June 1974): 351–77.

64. Competitive imperatives could produce highly particular oppositions, such as the conflict among native-born residents of New York's Rockland County between the Democratic-affiliated "Dutch," whose ancestors had first settled in New York, and the Republican-affiliated "Yankees," who had migrated into New York from New England. McCormick, "Ethno-Cultural Interpretations," pp. 40–41, discusses this finding from Benson, *Concept of Jacksonian Democracy*, pp. 293–304.

65. See Jensen, *Winning of the Midwest*, ch. 3, "Pietists and Liturgicals"; and Paul Kleppner, *The Third Electoral System, 1853–1892: Parties, Voters, and Political Cultures* (Chapel Hill: University of North Carolina Press, 1979), ch. 5, "Political Confessionalism."

66. Roger E. Wyman, "Wisconsin Ethnic Groups and the Election of 1890," *Wisconsin Magazine of History* 51 (Summer 1968): 269–93.

67. Richard L. McCormick, "The Party Period and Public Policy: An Exploratory Hypothesis," *Journal of American History* 66(2) (Sept. 1979); pp. 283–84.

68. Ibid., p. 285.

69. Theodore J. Lowi, "American Business, Public Policy, Case-Studies, and Political Theory," *World Politics* 16 (July 1964): 677–715. See also Lowi, "Four Systems of Policy, Politics, and Choice," *Public Administration Review* 32 (July/Aug. 1972): 298–310, in which he adds a "constituent" type of policy having to do with the basic (re)design of political institutions.

70. Gerald N. Grob, "The Political System and Social Policy in the Nineteenth Century: Legacy of the Revolution," *Mid-America* 58(1) (Jan. 1976), p. 12, n. 12.

71. Dobson, *Politics in the Gilded Age*, p. 33.

72. Kehl, *Boss Rule in the Gilded Age*.

73. Leonard D. White, *The Republican Era: 1869–1901, A Study in Administrative History* (New York: Macmillan, 1958); and Mayer, *Republican Party*, pp. 17–18.

74. Mayer, *Republican Party*, p. 17.

75. Skowronek, *Building a New American State*, p. 23; Grob, "Political System and Social Policy"; and White, *Republican Era*, pp. 45–48.

76. Skowronek, *Building a New American State*, p. 23.

77. McCormick, "Party Period and Public Policy," p. 286.

78. Grob, "Political System and Social Policy," pp. 12–16.
79. Levine, *State Legislative Parties,* pp. 52–54; White, *Republican Era,* p. 70 and ch. 4 generally; and Keller, *Affairs of State,* p. 321.
80. McCormick, "Party Period and Public Policy," p. 286.
81. For a recent pertinent example see Jill Quadagno, *The Transformation of Old Age Security: Class and Politics in the American Welfare State* (Chicago: University of Chicago Press, 1988), pp. 36–47.
82. Bridges, *City in the Republic,* pp. 27–29; and James L. Huston, "A Political Response to Industrialism: The Republican Embrace of Protectionist Labor Doctrines," *Journal of American History* 70(1) (June 1983): 35–57.
83. Bridges, "Becoming American," p. 187; Susan E. Hirsch, *The Roots of the American Working Class: The Industrialization of Crafts in Newark, 1800–1860* (Philadelphia: University of Pennsylvania Press, 1978), pp. 120–23; and Shefter, "Trade Unions and Political Machines," pp. 250–51.
84. S. Walter Poulshock, "Pennsylvania and the Politics of the Tariff, 1880–1888," *Pennsylvania History* 29 (July 1962); p. 298; the following quotes come from pp. 299–300.
85. Ibid., p. 300.
86. Richard P. McCormick, *The Second Party System* (New York: Norton, 1966), p. 354.
87. See Shade, "'Revolutions Can Go Backwards'"; and Eric Foner, *Reconstruction: America's Unfinished Revolution, 1863–1877* (New York: Harper and Row, 1988).
88. This is a central argument in Quadagno, *Transformation of Old Age Security.*
89. Ira Katznelson and Margaret Weir, *Schooling for All: Class, Race, and the Decline of the Democratic Ideal* (New York: Basic Books, 1985).
90. Arnold J. Heidenheimer, "Education and Social Security Entitlements in Europe and America," pp. 269–304 in *The Development of Welfare States in Europe and America,* ed. Peter Flora and Arnold J. Heidenheimer (New Brunswick, NJ: Transaction Books, 1981); and Richard Rubinson, "Class Formation, Politics, and Institutions: Schooling in the United States," *American Journal of Sociology* 92(3) (Nov. 1986): 519–48.
91. For cross-national statistics, see Rubinson, "Class Formation," p. 522, table 1.
92. This is a central point in John W. Meyer, David Tyack, Joane Nagel, and Audi Gordon, "Public Education as Nation-Building in America: Enrollments and Bureaucratization in the American States, 1870–1930," *American Journal of Sociology* 85(3) (Nov. 1979): 591–613. As

Katznelson and Weir argue in *Schooling for All,* pp. 47–48, the temporal extent of school attendance over the course of the year probably did expand in relation to industrialization, but this is a different issue from the founding of schools in the first place.

93. Rubinson, "Class Formation," effectively criticizes theories that attribute patterns of U.S. education either to "class impositions" by capitalists seeking to discipline workers or to a well-organized industrial working class imposing its preferences for free, unstratified schooling. Nevertheless, much evidence of workers' support for schools appears in Bridges, "Becoming American"; Katznelson and Weir, *Schooling for All;* and Paul E. Peterson, *The Politics of School Reform, 1870–1940* (Chicago: University of Chicago Press, 1985).

94. Meyer et al., "Public Education as Nation-Building," pp. 599–600; David Tyack and Elisabeth Hansot, *Managers of Virtue: Public School Leadership in America, 1820–1920* (New York: Basic Books, 1982), pp. 44–56; and Carl F. Kaestle, *Pillars of the Republic: Common Schools and American Society, 1780–1860* (New York: Hill and Wang, 1983), ch. 5.

95. This argument is well developed by Katznelson and Weir, *Schooling for All,* ch. 2.

96. The phrase "participatory localism" comes from ibid.; and my argument also draws upon Heidenheimer, "Education and Social Security Entitlements," as well as Eric L. McKitrick and Stanley Elkins, "Institutions in Motion," *American Quarterly* 12(2) (Summer 1960): 188–97.

97. Peterson, *Politics of School Reform,* p. 9.

98. Tyack and Hansot, *Managers of Virtue,* pp. 30–31; and Levine, *State Legislative Parties,* pp. 186–90.

99. The worldviews of the common school reformers and their relation to party politics are explored in Mustafa Emirbayer, "Moral Education in America, 1830–1990: A Contribution to the Sociology of Moral Culture" (Ph.D. diss., Harvard University, 1990), ch. 3.

100. Tyack and Hansot, *Managers of Virtue,* pp. 59–62, 72–83, 100–103; Keller, *Affairs of State,* pp. 133–36, 138–42; and John Pratt, "Boss Tweed's Public Welfare Program," *New York Historical Society Quarterly* 45(4) (Oct. 1961); pp. 400–404.

101. Walter I. Trattner, "The Federal Government and Social Welfare in Early Nineteenth-Century America," in *Compassion and Responsibility: Readings in the History of Social Welfare Policy in the United States,* ed. Frank R. Breul and Steven J. Diner (Chicago: University of Chicago Press, 1980), p. 166, n. 3.

102. As quoted in Leonard P. Curry, *Blueprint for Modern America: Nonmi-*

litary Legislation of the First Civil War Congress (Nashville, TN: Vanderbilt University Press, 1968), pp. 110; see "The Land-Grant College Act," pp. 108–115.

103. Pratt, "Boss Tweed's Public Welfare Program."

104. This point is ably made and documented by Peterson, *Politics of School Reform*, pp. 44–50, drawing especially on a case study of late-nineteenth-century San Francisco. Overall, I rely on Peterson's nuanced discussion of the effects of political parties on educational expansion and reforms.

105. Steven P. Erie, *Rainbow's End: Irish-Americans and the Dilemmas of Urban Machine Politics, 1840–1985* (Berkeley and Los Angeles: University of California Press, 1988), pp. 45–57.

106. See the discussion of the rhetoric of San Francisco Boss Christopher Buckley in Peterson, *Politics of School Reform*, p. 47; see also pp. 89–92, 203–204.

107. Raymond A. Mohl, "Three Centuries of American Public Welfare: 1600–1932," *Current History* 65 (July 1973), pp. 6–7; and Charles R. Lee, "Public Relief and the Massachusetts Community, 1620–1715," *New England Quarterly* 55 (4) (1982): 564–85.

108. Benjamin J. Klebaner, "Poverty and Its Relief in American Thought, 1815–61," *Social Service Review* 38 (Dec. 1964): 382–99; and Michael B. Katz, *In the Shadow of the Poorhouse: A Social History of Welfare in America* (New York: Basic Books, 1986), p. 16.

109. Katz, *Shadow of the Poorhouse*, chs. 1 and 2.

110. See esp. David J. Rothman, *The Discovery of the Asylum: Social Order and Disorder in the New Republic* (Boston: Little, Brown, 1971).

111. Trattner, "Federal Government and Social Welfare," p. 160.

112. Ibid., pp. 163–64.

113. Pratt, "Boss Tweed's Public Welfare Program," p. 408.

114. Ibid., pp. 408–11.

115. Kehl, *Boss Rule in the Gilded Age*, pp. 62–63.

116. Seaton W. Manning, "The Tragedy of the Ten-Million-Acre Bill," *Social Service Review* 36 (March 1962): 44–50.

117. As quoted in ibid., p. 46.

118. Ibid., pp. 48–49.

119. See notes 102 and 112.

120. Manning, "Tragedy of the Ten-Million-Acre Bill," p. 48.

121. Grob, "Political System and Social Policy in the Nineteenth Century," *Mid-America*, pp. 18–19; and William R. Brock, *Investigation and Responsibility: Public Responsibility in the United States, 1865–1900* (Cambridge and New York: Cambridge University Press, 1984).

122. Jeremy P. Felt, *Hostages of Fortune: Child Labor Reform in New York State* (Syracuse: Syracuse University Press, 1965), chs. 1 and 2. Felt labels the period 1886–1902 the era of "legislation without enforcement."

123. See Frank Dekker Watson, *The Charity Organization Movement in the United States* (New York: Macmillan, 1922); Katz, *Shadow of the Poorhouse*, ch. 3; Marvin E. Gettleman, "Charity and Social Classes in the United States, 1874–1900," *American Journal of Economics and Sociology* 22(2) (April 1963): 313–29 and 22(3) (July 1963): 417–26; and Robert H. Bremner, "'Scientific Philanthropy,' 1873–93," *Social Service Review* 30 (June 1956): 168–73.

124. E. L. Godkin, "The City and the Country," *Nation* 25 (Nov. 29, 1877), p. 328, as quoted in McGerr, *Decline of Popular Politics*, p. 48.

125. For the distinctions between eastern and western party-patronage regimes, see Martin Shefter, "Regional Receptivity to Reform: The Legacy of the Progressive Era," *Political Science Quarterly* 98 (1983): 459–83.

126. Erie, *Rainbow's End*, p. 3. (The phrase "in the air" comes from Lincoln Steffens.) One of the many valuable findings in *Rainbow's End* is that nascent urban Democratic machines became more entrenched and centralized in times and places where they could get resources from the federal or state governments. This happened especially when machine-friendly Democrats controlled executives and legislatures.

127. I have drawn these examples, among many others, from the following accounts of grassroots machine dealings with urban residents: William L. Riordan, *Plunkitt of Tammany Hall* (New York: E. P. Dutton, 1963; orig. 1905); Alexander B. Callow, Jr., *The Tweed Ring* (New York: Oxford University Press, 1966), ch. 10; Lyle W. Dorsett, *The Pendergast Machine* (Lincoln: University of Nebraska Press, 1968), chs. 1 and 2; and Alex Keyssar, *Out of Work: The First Century of Unemployment in Massachusetts* (Cambridge and New York: Cambridge University Press, 1986), p. 261.

128. Riordan, *Plunkitt of Tammany Hall*, pp. 27–28.

129. When he repeatedly stresses that nineteenth-century Irish machines did not have enough resources to buy many voters, Erie seems at times to be interpreting matters too individualistically. See *Rainbow's End*, chs. 1 and 2.

130. Riordan, *Plunkitt of Tammany Hall*, p. 28.

131. Mary Kingsbury Simkhovitch, "Friendship and Politics," *Political Science Quarterly* 17(2) (June 1902), p. 195.

132. Ibid., pp. 195, 199.

133. Riordan, *Plunkitt of Tammany Hall*, p. 28.

134. Erie, *Rainbow's End*, stresses that the Irish machines hoarded oppor-

tunities for fellow Irishmen. He disputes some scholars who have argued that the machines spread allocations among all ethnic groups in their constituencies, suggesting that symbolic rewards and minor in-kind benefits were more likely to go to subordinate, later-arriving ethnic groups.

135. Ibid., pp. 57–66. Plunkitt discussed sources of patronage jobs both inside and outside of government, including jobs with private contractors available when the party was out of power. See "Reciprocity in Patronage," in Riordan, *Plunkitt of Tammany Hall,* pp. 37–40.

136. Erie, *Rainbow's End,* pp. 57–66, 85–91, 238–46.

137. Keyssar, *Out of Work,* p. 261.

138. Erie, *Rainbow's End,* ch. 2, discusses the fiscal restraints many "mature" machines adopted in the late nineteenth century (although he shows that they still found ways to expand regular patronage jobs under their control, even when overall public spending did not rise). For machine cities' responses to the downturn of the mid-1850s, see Bridges, *City in the Republic,* pp. 113–24. For machine cities' responses to demands for public works in the downturns of 1873–1878 and 1893–1897, see Mohl, "Three Centuries of American Public Welfare," p. 10; and Leah Hannah Feder, *Unemployment Relief in Periods of Depression* (New York: Russell Sage Foundation, 1936), pp. 185–88. See also Keyssar, *Out of Work,* pp. 261–62.

139. Bridges, *City in the Republic,* pp. 116, 123; Herbert G. Gutman, "The Failure of the Movement by the Unemployed for Public Works in 1873," *Political Science Quarterly* 80(2) (June 1965): 254–76; and Keyssar, *Out of Work,* pp. 211–12, 223–24.

140. Simkhovitch, "Friendship and Politics," p. 190.

141. Ibid., p. 194.

142. This is a main thesis of Erie, *Rainbow's End.* Documentation of the extent and nature of unemployment appears in Keyssar, *Out of Work.*

143. Keyssar, *Out of Work,* p. 261–62 and ch. 9 generally.

144. As Mayer, *Republican Party,* p. 17, notes: "The eagerness of local citizens to become postmasters had nothing to do with pay scales . . . The position could bring indirect [mobility] advantages . . . By locating the post office in his store, a postmaster could count on extra business from people who came to pick up their mail. As the first one in a rural community to receive news, the postmaster controlled a priceless commodity. Quite often, if he was not already an editor at the time of his appointment, he tried to buy a paper soon after. From there it was an easy step to the printing business, which in turn gave him the inside track on contracts for government notices and party ballots."

145. On the "passion for office-seeking" in late-nineteenth-century America, see White, *Republican Era,* pp. 5–8.

2. *Public Aid for the Worthy Many:*
   The Expansion of Benefits for Veterans of the Civil War

1. I. M. Rubinow, *Social Insurance, With Special Reference to American Conditions* (New York: Arno Press, 1969; orig. 1913), p. 404. One history of U.S. social welfare that *does* include military pensions is June Axinn and Herman Levin, *Social Welfare: A History of the American Response to Need* (New York: Harper and Row, 1975).
2. R. Ernest Dupuy and Trevor N. Dupuy, *The Encyclopedia of Military History from 3500 B.C. to the Present,* 2nd rev. ed. (New York: Harper and Row, 1986), p. 820.
3. Eugene C. Murdock, *One Million Men: The Civil War Draft in the North* (Madison: State Historical Society of Wisconsin, 1971), ch. 1; and James W. Geary, *We Need Men: The Union Draft in the Civil War* (DeKalb: Northern Illinois University Press, 1991).
4. U.S. Bureau of the Census, *Historical Statistics of the United States, Colonial Times to 1970,* Bicentennial ed. (Washington: Government Printing Office, 1975), pt. 2, p. 1140, series Y 856.
5. The 37 percent figure was estimated as follows, from *Historical Statistics,* pt. 1, pp. 22–23, series A 172–194: I added the 1860 population "15–24" and "25–44" for the Northeast, North Central, and West regions; then I multiplied by the proportion of males (51.36%) in the total populations of these regions in 1860. Then I divided the 2,213,000 who served on the Union side of the Civil War by the estimated 5,903,832 men aged 15–44 who lived in the nonsouthern regions in 1860.
6. Arthur Marwick, *War and Society in the Twentieth Century* (London: Macmillan, 1974), p. 61.
7. *Historical Statistics,* pt. 2, p. 1140, series Y 879–882.
8. I divided the northern mortal casualties by a total population figure of 20,310,000 outside the South obtained from *Historical Statistics,* pt. 1, p. 22, series A 172–194. Battle deaths in proportion to population for World Wars I and II come from J. David Singer and Melvin Small, *The Wages of War, 1816–1965: A Statistical Handbook* (New York: John Wiley and Sons, 1972), p. 260.
9. *Historical Statistics,* pt. 2, p. 1140, series Y.
10. Isser Woloch, *The French Veteran from the Revolution to the Restoration* (Chapel Hill: University of North Carolina Press, 1979), pp. 206, 209–10, 308, and ch. 7 generally.

11. Ibid.; and also Isser Woloch, "War-Widows Pensions: Social Policy in Revolutionary and Napoleonic France," *Societas* 6(4) (Autumn 1976): 235–54.

12. Woloch, *French Veteran*, pp. 101–109; and Woloch, "War-Widows Pensions," pp. 244–51.

13. Woloch, *French Veteran*, pp. 206–207.

14. See the report prepared for the U.S. Sanitary Commission during the Civil War: Stephen H. Perkins, *Report on the Pension Systems and Invalid Hospitals of France, Prussia, Austria, Russia and Italy, with Some Suggestions upon the Best Means of Disposing of Our Disabled Soldiers*, Sanitary Commission no. 67 (New York: William C. Bryant and Co., Printers, 1863).

15. This paragraph is based on William H. Glasson, *Federal Military Pensions in the United States* (New York: Oxford University Press, 1918), chs. 2 and 3 (specifically pp. 94–95); and John P. Resch, "Federal Welfare for Revolutionary War Veterans," *Social Service Review* 56(2) (June 1982): 171–95.

16. Eric Foner, *Free Soil, Free Labor, Free Men: The Ideology of the Republican Party before the Civil War* (New York: Oxford University Press, 1970).

17. John William Oliver, "History of Civil War Military Pensions, 1861–1885," *Bulletin of the University of Wisconsin*, no. 844, History Series, no. 1 (1917), pp. 5–6.

18. Glasson, *Federal Military Pensions*, pp. 124–25.

19. As quoted in Oliver, "History of Civil War Military Pensions," pp. 9–10, from House Exec. Doc., 38th Congress, 2nd Session, 1864–65, vol. 5, p. 11.

20. As quoted in Glasson, *Federal Military Pensions*, p. 125.

21. Oliver, "History of Civil War Military Pensions," p. 9.

22. Glasson, *Federal Military Pensions*, p. 126.

23. Ibid., pp. 129–38; see esp. the table on p. 133.

24. Ibid., p. 138.

25. This paragraph draws upon ibid., pp. 126–28, 138–42; and Oliver, "History of Civil War Military Pensions," pp. 10, 21–22.

26. Glasson, *Federal Military Pensions*, p. 124.

27. Ibid., p. 273.

28. As quoted in Oliver, "History of Civil War Military Pensions," p. 39.

29. Glasson, *Federal Military Pensions*, pp. 148–49.

30. I calculated an acceptance rate of 72 percent (and a rejection rate of 28 percent) from figures presented for the years 1861 and after in the *Annual Report of the Commissioner of Pensions for 1888* (Washington: Government Printing Office, 1888), p. 35, table 6. The number of applications filed is calculated for the years 1861–1875, and the number accepted is calculated for 1861–1876, in the conviction that many

applications filed in 1875 may have been processed during 1876. Interestingly, the 28 percent rejection rate for 1861–1875 was considerably lower than the rejection rate of about 38 percent for the entire period from 1861–1888. Presumably, applications in the period during and right after the Civil War were more likely to be corroborated by hard evidence of death or disability.

31. For the war's "mortal casualties" of 364,511 see note 8; for the 106,669 recipients of pensions for "widows and dependents" in 1875, see Glasson, *Federal Military Pensions,* p. 144. I divided the latter number by the former, to get a take-up rate of 29.3 percent. But actually, this percentage must be low, because about 100,000 more men died between 1864 and 1870, most presumably due to causes traceable to the war, and their relatives would have had time to apply for pensions before 1875. If these are included, the take-up rate for dependents' pensions in 1875 becomes 23 percent.

32. I arrived at a percentage of 15.4 by dividing the number of wounded survivors of the Civil War (for which see note 9) by the number of "union veterans in civil life" in 1865 given in Table 20. Of course, this is only a rough estimate, because some of the wounded surely died during 1864–65, and others of the orig. wounded who later recovered may have remained in the regular military after the end of the war.

33. U.S. Bureau of Pensions, *Laws of the United States Governing the Granting of Army and Navy Pensions* (Washington: Government Printing Office, 1925), p. 43.

34. James Q. Wilson, "The Rise of the Bureaucratic State," *Public Interest,* no. 41 (Fall 1975), pp. 88–89.

35. Mary Dearing, *Veterans in Politics: The Story of the G.A.R.* (Baton Rouge: Louisiana State University Press, 1952), pp. 397–401.

36. On the situation of the Grand Army in the 1870s, see Robert B. Beath, *History of the Grand Army of the Republic* (New York: Bryan, Taylor, and Co., 1888); Dearing, *Veterans in Politics,* ch. 6; Frank H. Heck, *The Civil War Veteran in Minnesota Life and Politics* (Oxford, OH: Mississippi Valley Press, 1941), pp. 11–12 and ch. 2 generally; Edward Noyes, "The Ohio G.A.R. and Politics from 1866 to 1900," *Ohio State Archaeological and Historical Quarterly* 55 (1946), pp. 80–81; and George J. Lankevich, "The Grand Army of the Republic in New York State, 1865–1898" (Ph.D. diss., Columbia University, 1967), chs. 4–6.

37. Stuart Charles McConnell, "A Social History of the Grand Army of the Republic, 1867–1900" (Ph.D. diss., Johns Hopkins University, 1987), pp. 368–79; Elmer Edward Noyes, "A History of the Grand Army of the Republic in Ohio from 1866 to 1900" (Ph.D. diss., Ohio State University, 1945), pp. 79–89; and Lankevich, "Grand Army in New York State," pp. 142–56.

38. Wallace Evan Davies, *Patriotism on Parade: The Story of Veterans' and Hereditary Organizations in America, 1783–1900* (Cambridge, MA: Harvard University Press, 1955), pp. 36, 160; and Stuart McConnell, "Who Joined the Grand Army? Three Case Studies in the Construction of Union Veteranhood, 1866–1900," in *Toward a Social History of the American Civil War: Exploratory Essays,* ed. Maris A. Vinovskis (Cambridge and New York: Cambridge University Press, 1990), p. 141. McConnell reports a slightly higher GAR membership figure for 1890 (427,981) than does Heck, *Civil War Veteran in Minnesota,* p. 257 (409,489). I adjusted the percentage from McConnell, because Heck's figure cross-checks with the number officially given in *Journal of the Twenty-fifth National Encampment, Grand Army of the Republic* (Rutland, VT: Tuttle Company, 1891), p. 66.

39. Although advocates of straight service pensions managed to get the National Encampments of the GAR to endorse that option in 1888 and 1890, key national GAR leaders preferred the more "moderate" disability-service pension that was actually enacted in 1890. Thus, during 1889, the GAR's national Pension Committee supported the introduction of both types of bills in the respective houses of Congress. See McConnell, "Social History of the Grand Army of the Republic," p. 377, and Lankevich, "Grand Army in New York State," pp. 235–37.

40. See William H. Glasson, "The South and Service Pension Laws," *South Atlantic Quarterly* 1 (Oct. 1902): 351–60.

41. Richard Franklin Bensel, *Sectionalism and American Political Development, 1880–1980* (Madison: University of Wisconsin Press, 1984), ch. 3.

42. Jill S. Quadagno, *The Transformation of Old Age Security: Class and Politics in the American Welfare State* (Chicago: University of Chicago Press, 1988), pp. 36–47.

43. Glasson, *Federal Military Pensions,* pp. 163, 166–73. In fact, because of the worries over costs, when the appropriations for the Act were made, some new provisions were added to limit somewhat the amounts of arrears paid to successful applicants (see pp. 172–73).

44. Lemon's suggestion appeared in his newspaper, the *National Tribune,* Feb. 1879, pp. 12–13. Subsequent issues show his advocacy of tariffs and the use of customs revenues to pay for ever more generous pensions.

45. Glasson, *Federal Military Pensions,* p. 175.

46. *Historical Statistics,* pt. 1, p. 165, series D 735–738.

47. From Hayes's December 14, 1881, letter to William Henry Smith, as quoted in Glasson, *Federal Military Pensions,* p. 164.

48. Oliver, "History of Civil War Military Pensions," pp. 51–52.

49. Ibid., p. 53.

50. These facts come from Glasson, *Federal Military Pensions,* pp. 156–57.
51. For example, the attorneys had been forced to accept statutory limits on their fees for handling pension applications.
52. On this point, see Dearing, *Veterans in Politics,* pp. 243–47.
53. This paragraph is based on Oliver, "History of Civil War Military Pensions," pp. 53–56.
54. As quoted in ibid., p. 67.
55. Eugene V. Smalley, "The United States Pension Office," *Century Magazine* 28 (n. s., vol. 6) (1884); p. 428.
56. Robert McElroy, *Grover Cleveland: The Man and the Statesman* (New York: Harper and Brothers, 1923), p. 190.
57. The quoted phrase is from "The Course of a Claim Through the Bureau," in *Report of the Secretary of the Interior for the Fiscal Year Ending June 30, 1891* (Washington: Government Printing Office, 1891), p. 70. See also the accounts of the application process in Smalley, "United States Pension Office," p. 430; the Dec. 15, 1883, letter of instructions to local examining surgeons from the Pension Office–Medical Division, Department of the Interior (a pamphlet in the holdings of the Harvard College Library); and *A Treatise on the Practice of the Pension Bureau Governing the Adjudication of Army and Navy Pensions* (Washington: Government Printing Office, 1898).
58. Leonard D. White, *The Republican Era: 1869–1901. A Study in Administrative History* (New York: Macmillan, 1958), pp. 211–14; and Smalley, "United States Pension Office."
59. The mission and early procedures of this division of the Bureau can be glimpsed in *General Instructions to Special Examiners of the United States Pension Office* (Washington: Government Printing Office, 1882).
60. Glasson, *Federal Military Pensions,* p. 165.
61. Oliver, "History of Civil War Military Pensions," pp. 43–44.
62. Ibid., pp. 44–45.
63. Ibid., pp. 83–86.
64. Green B. Raum, "Pensions and Patriotism," *North American Review* 153 (1891); p. 211. Raum was engaging in a bit of rhetorical exaggeration. See the description of the New South Wales (Australian) Department of Public Works, 12,000–15,000 strong as of the 1880s, in Desley Deacon, *Managing Gender* (Melbourne: Oxford University Press, 1989), p. 104.
65. Smalley, "United States Pension Office," p. 430.
66. On reinterpretations across administrations, see *Decisions of the Department of the Interior in Cases Relating to Pension Claims and to the Laws of the United States Granting and Governing Pensions,* vol. 4, ed. George Baber of the Board of Pension Appeals (Washington: Government

Printing Office, 1891). The editorial preface to this volume states (p. iii) that it is intended to highlight disagreements about legal interpretation with the previous administration of Democratic President Grover Cleveland, differences flowing "from a spirit of larger liberality exercised by the present administration [of Republican President Benjamin Harrison] in applying the pension system to those entitled to its benefits."

67. Heywood T. Sanders, "Paying for the 'Bloody Shirt': The Politics of Civil War Pensions," in *Political Benefits,* ed. Barry S. Rundquist (Lexington, MA: Lexington Books, D. C. Heath, 1980), p. 146.

68. White, *Republican Era,* p. 72.

69. Robert M. La Follette, *La Follette's Autobiography: A Personal Narrative of Political Experiences,* with a foreword by Allan Nevins (Madison: University of Wisconsin Press, 1968; orig. 1911), pp. 37–38. For other instances of particular congressional representatives who took pride in helping pension applicants, see Heck, *Civil War Veteran in Minnesota,* pp. 185–90.

70. White, *Republican Era,* p. 75.

71. I base this conclusion on a memorandum prepared by Edwin Amenta, who used statistics available in the 1890, 1900, and 1910 Annual Reports of the Commissioners of Pensions.

72. Glasson, *Federal Military Pensions,* p. 280.

73. Morton Keller, *Affairs of State: Public Life in Late Nineteenth-Century America* (Cambridge, MA: Harvard University Press, 1977), p. 311.

74. White, *Republican Era,* p. 76.

75. Glasson, *Federal Military Pensions,* pp. 275–76.

76. Oliver, "History of Civil War Military Pensions," p. 77, discussing the testimony of Pension Bureau officials before Congress, published in *House Committee Reports,* 46th Congress, 3rd Session, no. 387, p. 389.

77. Oliver, "History of Civil War Military Pensions," p. 107. My account of Dudley's activities draws on ibid., pp. 105–117, and Sanders, "Politics of Pensions," pp. 146–50.

78. Oliver, "History of Civil War Military Pensions," pp. 111–12, citing *House Report,* 48th Congress, 2nd Session, vol. 3, no. 2683, pp. 6–9.

79. Oliver, "History of Civil War Military Pensions," pp. 112, 117.

80. Sanders, "Politics of Pensions," p. 150.

81. According to Glasson, *Federal Military Pensions,* p. 224, President Cleveland's Commissioner of Pensions, John C. Black, attempted to use the Bureau to aid the Democrats in 1888, especially in Indiana.

82. Sanders, "Politics of Pensions," pp. 147–50; quotation on p. 150.

83. Donald Bruce Johnson, *National Party Platforms,* vol. 1: *1840–1956,* rev. ed. (Urbana: University of Illinois Press, 1978), p. 82.

84. Keller, *Affairs of State,* p. 381.
85. See R. Hal Williams, "'Dry Bones and Dead Language': The Democratic Party," pp. 129–48 in *The Gilded Age,* rev. and enlarged ed., ed. H. Wayne Morgan (Syracuse: Syracuse University Press, 1970). See also the Democratic Party platforms of this period in Johnson, *National Party Platforms,* vol. 1, pp. 56–57 (1880), 65–68 (1884), and 76–78 (1888).
86. See Allan Nevins, *Grover Cleveland: A Study in Courage* (New York: Dodd, Mead, 1944).
87. See Lewis Gould, "The Republican Search for a National Majority," pp. 171–87 in *The Gilded Age,* ed. Morgan; and (a contemporary party statement) *The Republican Party: Its History, Principles, and Policies,* ed. John D. Long (n.p., 1888).
88. Glasson, *Federal Military Pensions,* pp. 204–05.
89. See Bensel, *Sectionalism and American Political Development,* p. 68, map 3.1, and pp. 62–73.
90. We do not have good data on the precise social characteristics of pensioners, but suggestive findings along these lines appear in Sanders, "Politics," pp. 151–52.
91. My account of the events leading up to the election of Harrison in 1888 draws upon Dearing, *Veterans in Politics,* pp. 364–89; Glasson, *Federal Military Pensions,* pp. 204–25; and Donald McMurry, "The Political Significance of the Pension Question, 1885–1897," *Mississippi Valley Historical Review* 9(1) (June 1922): 19–36. The 10 percent figure comes from McConnell, "Social History of the Grand Army of the Republic," p. 15.
92. Glasson, *Federal Military Pensions,* p. 278; and McMurry, "Political Significance," pp. 28–29.
93. The GAR membership figure comes from Heck, *Civil War Veteran in Minnesota,* appendix A, p. 356.
94. See the 1888 Republican platform in Johnson, *National Party Platforms,* vol. 1, pp. 79–83.
95. Quoted in Dearing, *Veterans in Politics,* pp. 382–83.
96. Glasson, *Federal Military Pensions,* p. 225.
97. Sanders, "Politics of Pensions," pp. 150–54.
98. Donald L. McMurry, "The Bureau of Pensions during the Administration of President Harrison," *Mississippi Valley Historical Review* 13(3) (Dec. 1926): 343–64.
99. William Barlow, "U.S. Commissioner of Pensions Green B. Raum of Illinois," *Journal of the Illinois State Historical Society* 60(3) (Autumn 1967): 297–313. For Raum's own point of view, see his "Pensions and Patriotism," *North American Review* 153 (1891): 205–14.

100. Bureau of Pensions, *Laws of the United States Governing Pensions*, p. 38.
101. Quoted in Glasson, *Federal Military Pensions*, p. 233.
102. McMurry, "Pension Question," pp. 35–36.
103. Bureau of Pensions, *Laws of the United States Governing Pensions*, p. 43.
104. Rubinow, *Social Insurance*, chs. 1 and 2; and Peter Flora and Jens Alber, "Modernization, Democratization, and the Development of Welfare States in Western Europe," pp. 37–80 in *The Development of Welfare States in Europe and America*, ed. Peter Flora and Arnold J. Heidenheimer (New Brunswick, NJ: Transaction Books, 1981).
105. Peter A. Kohler and Hans F. Zacher, *The Evolution of Social Insurance, 1881–1981* (New York: St. Martin's Press, 1982), pp. 28–33 (Germany), and 182–87, 89–90, 216–217 (Britain).
106. Ibid., p. 28.
107. Flora and Heidenheimer, eds., *The Development of Welfare States*, p. 76, table 2.9.
108. Gerhard A. Ritter, *Social Welfare in Germany and Britain: Origins and Development*, trans. Kim Traynor (Leamington Spa, Britain, and New York: Berg Publishers, 1986), p. 191, table 3.
109. P. R. Kaim-Caudle, *Comparative Social Policy and Social Security: A Ten-Country Study* (New York: Dunellen, 1973), pp. 147–48 (Denmark) and 166–68 (Britain).
110. A special feature of the Danish system was that old-age assistance could be paid "in kind" as well as in monetary benefits, at the discretion of local authorities. "In the early part of the twentieth century about a quarter of pensioners received only payments in kind" (ibid., p. 148).
111. Rubinow, *Social Insurance*, p. 378.
112. Ritter, *Social Welfare*, pp. 177, 193; and Kaim-Caudle, *Comparative Social Policy*, p. 167.
113. I refer to "Civil War pensions" and pensioners because the vast majority of U.S. pensioners in 1910 (94 percent) were attributable to the Civil War. It is often not feasible to separate out pensioners from other wars; thus they are sometimes included in the calculations and tables to follow. Wherever possible, though, I make adjustments in figures, especially in order to pinpoint pensioners aged 65 and over, whom I estimate made up 80 percent of all military pensioners in 1910.
114. See Table 2, which (for 1910) does use figures for Civil War veterans and pensioners alone. I assume that virtually all Civil War veterans were 65 or older in 1910, because they were almost all between 15 and 45 at the time of their military service between 1861 and 1865. At entry into the army, the original Union soldiers clustered especially in the age categories of 18 and 21, with many in between and far fewer below 18 or above 21. See the discussion of soldiers' ages in Bell

Irvin Wiley, *The Life of Billy Yank: The Common Soldier of the Union* (Baton Rouge: Louisiana State University Press, 1952; reissued 1978), pp. 296–303. Union soldiers who were 18 in 1863, and who survived until 1910, would have been 65 years old, so it seems safe to assume that only a tiny proportion of veterans could have been under 65 in 1910 and still have served long enough (at least ninety days) prior to April 1865 to qualify for pensions.

115. These estimates, which include a few thousand old men and women pensioned for wars prior to the Civil War, are based on data from *Report of the Commissioner of Pensions,* in the *Reports of the Department of the Interior for the Fiscal Year Ended June 30, 1910,* vol. 1 (Washington: Government Printing Office, 1911), p. 146; and *Historical Statistics,* pt. 1, p. 15, series A 133. I arrived at my estimate of the total number of "old men" on the military pension rolls in 1910 by taking the total number of invalid pensioners in the 1910 report; subtracting the invalids from the War with Spain and the regular establishment rolls, on the grounds that many of them may have been below 65 years old; and then adding the "fathers" listed on the dependents' roll, on the grounds that virtually all of them must have been old men. I arrived at my estimate of the total number of "old women" by adding together the following numbers from the dependents' list in 1910: one Revolutionary War daughter; all "mothers"; and half of all "widows" listed for the Civil War and Regular Army categories; all widows for wars prior to the Civil War; and all Civil War nurses. I omitted widows for the War with Spain on the grounds that most may have been below 65 years old. Overall, I estimate that 80 percent of all pensioners in 1910 were over 65 years old; the rest were children and younger adults.

116. Kohler and Zacher, *Evolution of Social Insurance,* p. 29.

117. Ibid., p. 42.

118. Ibid., p. 40.

119. This percentage is calculated from data in the 1910 *Report of the Commissioner of Pensions,* pp. 149–50. All military pensioners, not just Civil War pensioners, are included in this estimate.

120. Ibid., p. 171.

121. Ibid., pp. 169–72; compare exhibits 7 and 8.

122. Rubinow, *Social Insurance,* p. 409.

123. Data for these estimates come from the 1910 *Commissioner of Pensions Report,* p. 168, with 62.87 percent of all pensioners in every state assumed to be old men; and from *Historical Statistics,* pt. 1, p. 23, series A 172–194, which gives data on people 65 and over in each region. Using the ratio of old men to all old people in series A 119–134, I

simply divided the regional numbers by half to obtain estimates for men 65 and over.

124. Sanders, "Politics of Pensions," pp. 151–52.

125. Wiley, *Life of Billy Yank,* pp. 307–09. Wiley estimates that three-fourths of the Union soldiers were native Americans; among the foreign-born, Germans were most numerous, followed by Irish. See also Ella Lonn, *Foreigners in the Union Army and Navy* (Baton Rouge: Louisiana State University Press, 1951). Unfortunately, there is currently no way to tell precisely whether natives among the Union veterans were more likely than foreign-born veterans to become pensioners in later years, although evidence given below on the tendency for pensioners to appear sooner and in greater numbers in Republican states suggests that probably natives did do better in the pension system.

126. James W. Geary, *We Need Men: The Union Draft in the Civil War* (DeKalb: Northern Illinois University Press, 1991), pp. 105–08.

127. See the reasoning in Rubinow, *Social Insurance,* pp. 407–09.

128. These statistics come from Wiley, *Life of Billy Yank,* pp. 312–13; and Dudley Taylor Cornish, *The Sable Arm: Negro Troops in the Union Army, 1861–1865* (New York: Longmans, Green, 1956), pp. 288–89. A somewhat higher estimate of 189,000 blacks serving in the Civil War comes from Maris Vinovskis in *Toward a Social History of the American Civil War* (Cambridge and New York: Cambridge University Press, 1990), p. 9.

Vinovskis's important lead essay in this edited volume, "Have Social Historians Lost the Civil War? Some Preliminary Demographic Speculations," orig. appeared in the *Journal of American History* 76 (1) (June 1989): 34–58. This article was published well after the statistical work for this ch. was completed. Vinovskis and I use different data sources and arrive at somewhat different estimates on key points about the demographics of Civil War pensions. But we both acknowledge that all estimates are inherently inexact. And our estimates on all key points are reassuringly similar.

129. My guesses about free black veterans from the North are based on dissertion research using Civil War pension records in progress by Earl F. Mulderink III, Ph.D. candidate in history at the University of Wisconsin, Madison. Some of Mulderink's research was shared with me in personal communications, and some was reported in a paper delivered at the 1988 Annual Meeting of the American Studies Association, entitled "'We Want a Country': New Bedford's Irish-American and Afro-American Communities during the Civil War Era." New Bedford "contained the highest proportion of black citizens of any New England urban area between 1850 and 1880, including a large

percentage of ex-slaves who migrated there before the war." The city was also "home to a substantial number of African-American soldiers who gained national fame in the 'brave black regiment,' the Fifty-fourth Massachusetts Volunteer Infantry, the first official regiment of northern black soldiers" (p. 2). Mulderink showed me summaries of African-American pension applications that were documented in regular ways (e.g., with official marriage certificates and other public municipal records). He reported his impression that African-American veterans were treated similarly in the pension application process to white Americans including the Irish-Americans from New Bedford. A true community, New Bedford's well-respected African-American soldiers helped comrades and their survivors to document pension applications—although Mulderink's article (pp. 5–7) also documents an instance in which African-American witnesses disagreed over the moral status of a soldier's widow who applied for a pension.

130. The absence of formal racism in the Pension Bureau was not just a procedural matter. According to the *Annual Report of the Commissioner of Pensions to the Secretary of the Interior for the Fiscal Year Ended June 30, 1903* (Washington: Government Printing Office, 1903), p. 43, some 79 "colored" men and 5 "colored" women constituted 84 out of 1,714—or about 5 percent—of the employees of the Pension Bureau that year. These black employees may well have been mostly veteran soldiers (who consituted 29 percent of all Bureau employees, and a majority of the employees over 50 years old), but there is no way to tell for sure from the commissioner's statistics (see pp. 42–43).

131. I base this on *General Instructions to Special Examiners of the United States Pension Office,* esp. the section on "Colored Claimants: Widows and Dependent Relatives," pp. 23–25. Some special suspicions of black applicants are noted here ("In some cases it will be found, upon a careful examination, that the claimant was in no way related to the soldier, but has been picked up by interested parties to represent the widow or some other relative"); yet similar suspicions are expressed elsewhere in the pamphlet, especially about widow applicants. Moreover, the section on "Colored Claimants" outlines special techniques for interviewing former fellow slaves and former owners to establish the accuracy of pension applications from relatives of black veterans. This suggests not bad will on the part of Pension Bureau Special Examiners, but that the absence of formal records (e.g., of slave marriages) could hurt or delay the chances for pension applications from blacks. Special Examiners only looked into cases that the Bureau found especially problematic or dubious, often those based only on personal testimony and lacking formal documentation.

132. William H. Glasson, "The South and the Service Pension Laws," *South Atlantic Quarterly* 1 (Oct. 1902): 351–60.

133. Judith Gladys Cetina, "A History of Veterans' Homes in the United States, 1811–1930" (Ph.D. diss., Case Western Reserve University, 1977), pp. 235–54, 274.

134. William H. Glasson, "The South's Care for Her Confederate Veterans," *American Monthly Review of Reviews* 36(1) (July 1907): 40–47. See also M. B. Morton, "Federal and Confederate Pensions Contrasted," *Forum* 16 (Sept. 1893): 68–74. Morton concluded that less than 5 percent of Confederates were pensioned for an average of $38.50 a year, at a time when about 30 percent of federal veterans were pensioned for an average of $165 a year.

135. My estimates here are *very rough*. I assumed that about 812,119 Confederate veterans were still alive in 1865, using Glasson's estimate ("South's Care," p. 42) of 1,082,119 Confederate enrollments, minus an estimate of as many as 270,000 casualties from battle and disease, taken from Samuel Eliot Morison, Henry Steele Commager, and William E. Leuchtenburg, *A Concise History of the American Republic* (New York: Oxford University Press, 1977), p. 290. Then I assumed that Confederate veterans survived at the same rate as Union veterans from 1865 to 1905. Finally, I did the best I could at estimating invalid pensioners in the Confederate states, using Glasson's (pp. 44–47) very uneven data for 1906. I guess that there were about 62,000 Confederate veterans pensioned in 1906, which amounts to about 17 percent of the veterans still living in 1905. Thus my conclusion that less than 20 percent of Confederate veterans were pensioned. Whether or not this figure is precisely correct, it is obvious that the proportion of Confederates pensioned was far, far less than the proportion of Union veterans pensioned in the early twentieth century.

136. To arrive at this estimate, I used Glasson's ("South's Care," p. 42) estimate of 1,082,119 Confederate enrollments, along with census data on age groups in the South adjusted by 51 percent for males and 63 percent for whites. These data came from *Historical Statistics of the United States*, pt. 1, pp. 22–23, series A 172–194.

137. Using data from Glasson, "South's Care," pp. 45–47, on numbers of Confederate pensioners per state in 1906, I arrived at the following *very rough* proportions of those 65 and older pensioned around 1910: Alabama 16 percent; Arkansas 11 percent; Florida 10 percent; Georgia 13 percent; Louisiana 3 percent; Mississippi 10 percent; North Carolina 13 percent; South Carolina 12 percent; Tennessee 4 percent; Texas 5 percent; and Virginia 12 percent. These percentages can be

added to the percentages of elderly federal pensioners in the southern states given in Appendix 1.

138. The data reported here are from Glasson, "South's Care," p. 45.

139. *Annual Report of the Commissioner of Pensions to the Secretary of the Interior for the Fiscal Year Ended June 30, 1906* (Washington: Government Printing Office, 1906), p. 5. The average for all types of federal pensions that year was $138.18.

140. Cetina, "History of Veterans' Homes," chs. 4 and 5. See also Bureau of the Census, Department of Commerce, *Benevolent Institutions* (Washington: Government Printing Office, 1910).

141. Ibid., Cetina, "History of Veterans' Homes," pp. 281–85.

142. Ibid., p. 171.

143. Ibid., pp. 402–08.

144. Ibid., ch. 7 and pp. 264–65; and Bureau of the Census, *Benevolent Institutions* (1910).

145. Cetina, "History of Veterans' Homes," p. 188.

146. The number of asylum clients comes from Bureau of the Census, *Benevolent Institutions* (1910), and I divided by the total number of elderly Union veterans in 1910, estimated by adding the numbers for all states and the District of Columbia given in Appendix 1.

147. Captain J. H. Woodnorth, "Pensions and State Soldiers' Homes," pp. 285–90 in *Proceedings of the National Conference of Charities and Correction*, 23rd Annual Session, Grand Rapids, Michigan, June 4–10, 1896 (Boston: George H. Ellis, 1896).

148. Numbers in Confederate homes come from Bureau of the Census, *Benevolent Institutions* (1910), and I divided by an estimate of surviving Confederate veterans reached by the method described in note 135 above.

149. Anne E. Geddes, *Trends in Relief Expenditures, 1910–1935*, Works Progress Administration Research Monograph no. 10 (Washington: Government Printing Office, 1937), p. 3.

150. I divided the total number of old people aided by local, state, and federal benefits as shown in Table 4, by the number of Massachusetts people 65 and over in 1915—189,047—as given in Bureau of Statistics, Commonwealth of Massachusetts, *Report of a Special Inquiry Relative to Aged and Dependent Persons in Massachusetts, 1915* (Boston: R. F. Foerster, 1916), p. 5. This generated a figure of 28 percent, which I reduced by 4 percent on the conservative assumption that as many as half of the federal pensioners were also receiving aid in Massachusetts.

151. Ibid., p. 6. No breakdowns of nativity for pensioners specifically are available.

152. Ibid., p. 6 and pp. 26, 28, tables 12 and 13.

153. For examples, see James Garfield's remarks as reported in Oliver, "History of Civil War Pensions," p. 42; Smalley, "United States Pension Office," p. 430; Charles Francis Adams, "A Civil-War Pension Lack-of-System" (a pamphlet reprinted from a series that appeared in *The World's Work* in 1912), p. 45; and "The Pension Bureau's 'Investigation' of Itself," *World's Work* 23(3) (Jan. 1912): 253–55.

154. Oliver, "History of Civil War Military Pensions," pp. 40–41.

155. For claims allowed from 1861 to 1876, see *Annual Report of the Commissioner of Pensions for 1888,* p. 35, table 6.

156. *Report of the Commissioner of Pensions to the Secretary of the Interior for the Year Ended June 30, 1893* (Washington: Government Printing Office, 1893), p. 8.

157. Ibid., p. 25, table 1.

158. See, for example, William Bayard Hale, "The Pension Carnival," a series of six articles in *World's Work* 20(6) (Oct. 1910) through 21(5) (March 1911). In his first article, "Staining a Nation's Honor-Roll with Pretense and Fraud," Hale featured (pp. 13491–503) the cases of deserters who later got pensions, along with the case of a Negro veteran from Philadelphia caught collecting five pensions, and several cases of widows who married veterans long after the war and later collected benefits after their deaths.

159. John DeWitt Warner, "Half a Million Dollars a Day for Pensions," *Forum* 15 (June 1893), p. 445.

160. Hale, "The Pension Carnival, III: Capitalizing the Nation's Gratitude," *World's Work* 21(2) (Dec. 1910), p. 13737.

161. Sanders, "Politics of Pensions," pp. 150–54.

162. Preliminary statistical results from a pooled time-series analysis of the determinants of numbers of pensions across the states in 1870, 1880, 1890, 1900, 1910, and 1920 were presented in Theda Skocpol, John Sutton, Ann Shola Orloff, Edwin Amenta, and Bruce G. Carruthers, "A Precocious Welfare State? Civil War Benefits in the United States, 1870s–1920s" (paper presented at the Annual Meeting of the American Sociological Association, Chicago, Aug. 19, 1987).

163. Johnson, *National Party Platforms,* vol. 1: *1840–1956,* p. 82.

164. Raum, "Pensions and Patriotism," p. 211.

165. Cetina, "History of Veterans' Homes," p. 218.

166. Mass. Bureau of Statistics, *Report of a Special Inquiry,* p. 30.

167. "A Soldier's View," letter from Frank Bell, *Century Magazine* 42(5) (n.s., vol. 20) (Sept. 1891), p. 791. Bell was responding to a critique of the pension system prepared for "The Sociological Group" of Massachusetts reformers. See William M. Sloane, "Pensions and Socialism," *Century Magazine* 42(2) (June 1891): 179–88.

Introduction to Part II

1. Charles Richmond Henderson, "Industrial Insurance XI: Protective Legislation," *American Journal of Sociology* 9(2) (Sept. 1908), p. 199.
2. For a sense of the interrelations progressive reformers saw between social insurance and labor regulations, see John R. Commons and John B. Andrews, *Principles of Labor Legislation* (New York: Harper and Brothers, 1916); Charles Richmond Henderson, *Industrial Insurance in the United States* (Chicago: University of Chicago Press, 1909); Henry R. Seager, *Labor and Other Economic Essays,* ed. Charles A. Gulick, Jr. (New York: Harper and Brothers, 1931); and the successive numbers of the *American Labor Legislation Review (ALLR)* during the 1910s. A discussion of progressive fascination with New Zealand's arbitration system appears in Peter J. Coleman, *Progressivism and the World of Reform: New Zealand and the Origins of the American Welfare State* (Lawrence: University Press of Kansas, 1987).
3. The text of this bill appears in *Report of the Commission on Old Age Pensions, Annuities and Insurance,* January 1910, Massachusetts House doc. no. 1400 (Boston: Wright and Potter, State Printers, 1910), pp. 339–40.
4. Henderson, *Industrial Insurance,* p. 286.
5. Ibid., pp. 308–09.
6. Lee Welling Squier, *Old Age Dependency in the United States* (New York: Macmillan, 1912), pp. 331–32.
7. Ibid., p. 336.
8. I. M. Rubinow, *Social Insurance, With Special Reference to American Conditions* (New York: Arno Press, 1969; orig. 1913), p. 409.
9. Elizabeth Brandeis, *Labor Legislation,* in vol. 3 of *History of Labor in the United States, 1896–1932,* by John R. Commons and associates (New York: Macmillan, 1935), p. 614. The territory of Alaska passed a law in 1915; and laws were passed in Arizona in 1914 and in Pennsylvania in 1923, but soon declared unconstitutional. In 1929, one state, California, finally enacted a mandatory, partially state-funded system of pensions for the needy elderly. The year 1929 marked the point at which dozens of states began to consider and enact old-age pension bills.
10. Ibid., chs. 5–7.

3. Reformist Professionals as Advocates of Workingmen's Insurance

1. Hugh Heclo, *Modern Social Politics in Britain and Sweden* (New Haven: Yale University Press, 1974), p. 305.

2. See ibid.; Gerhard A. Ritter, *Social Welfare in Germany and Britain: Origins and Development,* trans. Kim Traynor (Leamington Spa, Britain, and New York: Berg, 1986); Stein Kuhnle, "The Growth of Social Insurance Programs in Scandinavia: Outside Influences and Internal Forces," pp. 125–50 in *The Development of Welfare States in Europe and America,* ed. Peter Flora and Arnold J. Heidenheimer (New Brunswick, NJ: Transaction Books, 1981); James M. Malloy, *The Politics of Social Security in Brazil* (Pittsburgh: University of Pittsburgh Press, 1979), ch. 2; Peter J. Coleman, *Progressivism and the World of Reform: New Zealand and the Origins of the American Welfare State* (Lawrence: University Press of Kansas, 1987), ch. 2, "The Mission of New Zealand Democracy"; and Desley Deacon, *Managing Gender: The State, the New Middle Class and Women Workers, 1830–1930* (Melbourne: Oxford University Press Australia, 1989).

3. On the Americans' fascination with foreign models, see Gertrude Almy Schlichter, "European Backgrounds of American Reform, 1880–1915" (Ph.D. diss., University of Illinois, Urbana, 1960); Coleman, *Progressivism and the World of Reform.*

4. One of the books in the table, *Workingmen's Insurance in Europe,* was co-authored, and I have included biographical information only for the senior author, Lee K. Frankel.

5. I found no information on Frank Lewis beyond what can be deduced from his book, so some of these generalizations do not include him. Nor was his book referred to by the other authors, each of whom normally discussed the others.

6. One woman who did an investigation of social insurance was Professor Katherine Coman of Wellesley College (whose father was an abolitionist teacher, farmer, and lawyer in Ohio). At the request of Jane Addams and the American Association for Labor Legislation (AALL), Coman traveled in Europe during 1913–14, from whence she reported findings in line with AALL policy favoring contributory social insurance over noncontributory benefits. Entitled "Social Insurance: Where Europe Leads the Way," Coman's articles appeared in the *Survey* as follows: "Old Age and Invalidity Insurance in Sweden," 31(11) (Dec. 13, 1913): 318–19; "Thirty Years of Old Age Pensions in Denmark," 31(16) (Jan. 17, 1913): 463–65, 481; "The Problem of Old Age Pensions in England," 31(21) (Feb. 21, 1914): 640–42; "Unemployment, a World Problem, and the Congress at Ghent," 31(22) (Feb. 28, 1914): 667–71; "Insurance Against Unemployment in Norway and Denmark," 31(24) (March 14, 1914): 742–44; and "Great Britain's Experiment in Compulsory Unemployment Insurance," 31(26) (March 28, 1914): 799–802. I considered including Coman in Table 5, but decided against it for several reasons. Her articles did

not add up to a coherent book-like project, and they came later than any other research/publication included in the table. Most important, Coman's investigation was not part of a sustained interest in (or advocacy for) public social insurance. Perhaps it might have become so, and perhaps she would have written a book, if she had not been dying of cancer during her trip to Europe. She died in January 1915, soon after returning to the United States. For touching biographies of Coman and her companion-lover, see Judith Schwartz, "Yellow Clover: Katherine Lee Bates and Katherine Coman," *Frontiers* 4(1) (1979): 60–67.

7. Sadly, Jews were not given regular university appointments according to their merits during this period of U.S. history; if they had been, the brilliant Isaac Max Rubinow's career would no doubt have taken a different course, toward the highest positions in elite universities and national professional associations. More generally, on the formative years of the U.S. social sciences, see Thomas L. Haskell, *The Emergence of Professional Social Science: The American Social Science Association and the Nineteenth-Century Crisis of Authority* (Urbana: University of Illinois Press, 1977).

8. John Graham Brooks, *Compulsory Insurance in Germany, Including an Appendix Relating to Compulsory Insurance in Other Countries in Europe,* 4th Special Report of the Commissioner of Labor, Carroll D. Wright (Washington: Government Printing Office, 1893). See p. 10 for Wright's explanation of why he commissioned Brooks to do the study.

9. For background on Wright and labor statistics bureaus, see James Leiby, *Carroll Wright and Labor Reform: The Origins of Labor Statistics* (Cambridge, MA: Harvard University Press, 1960); S. N. D. North, "The Life and Work of Carroll Davidson Wright," *American Statistical Association,* n.s. 9(86) (June 1909): 447–66; and William R. Brock, *Investigation and Responsibility: Public Responsibility in the United States, 1865–1900* (Cambridge and New York: Cambridge University Press, 1984), ch. 6.

10. William Franklin Willoughby, *Workingmen's Insurance* (New York and London: Thomas Y. Crowell, 1898).

11. The original citations are Charles Richmond Henderson, *Industrial Insurance in the United States* (Chicago: University of Chicago Press, 1909; London: T. Fisher Unwin, 1909); Frank W. Lewis, *State Insurance* (Boston and New York: Houghton Mifflin, 1909); Henry Rogers Seager, *Social Insurance: A Program of Reform* (New York: Macmillan, 1910); Lee K. Frankel and Miles M. Dawson, *Workingmen's Insurance in Europe* (New York: Charities Publication Committee, Russell Sage Foundation, 1910); and Isaac Max Rubinow, *Social Insurance, With*

Special Reference to American Conditions (New York: Henry Holt, 1913). Rubinow's book was reprinted by Arno Press in 1969, and my citations are to that edition.

12. Isaac Max Rubinow et al., *Workmen's Insurance and Compensation Systems in Europe*, 2 vols., 24th Annual Report of the U.S. Commissioner of Labor (Washington: Government Printing Office, 1911). I have not included this here as a separate study, because Rubinow drew extensively upon it for his 1913 book.

13. Brooks, *Compulsory Insurance*, p. 293.

14. Ibid., p. 288.

15. Ibid., p. 292.

16. Willoughby, *Workingmen's Insurance*, pp. 330–60.

17. Henderson, *Industrial Insurance*, pp. 312–13; and Lewis, *State Insurance*, pp. 171–78.

18. Frankel and Dawson, *Workingmen's Insurance in Europe*, pp. 395–405. Frankel was the least favorably inclined toward "state compulsion" of any of the early experts on social insurance. Although he joined and remained a member of the AALL throughout the Progressive period, he would in 1917 chair a committee of the National Civic Federation that issued a report opposing the AALL's proposal for compulsory health insurance. See "Compulsory Health Insurance: Statement Issued by Social Insurance Department, The National Civic Federation" (New York: National Civic Federation, 1917). This pamphlet is included in the Harvard College Library's "Industrial and Social Insurance, U.S.: Miscellaneous Pamphlets, 1917–1922."

19. Similarly, twelve years after the publication of his pioneering study of workingmen's insurance, Brooks remained wary about the possibilities of recapitulating German policies in the United States. In 1905, he reported to the National Conference of Charities and Corrections that "the line of progress is steadily toward some adaptation of the German method," but that at least ten *more* years of "experience" with European precedents and of public education in the United States would be needed before workingmen's insurance could be transplanted here. As the chief obstacle, Brooks cited "the general condition of politics and civil service. The German success, such as it is, has been absolutely owing to a strictly competent and independent administration. They *barely* succeed as it is. With an administration like that which has controlled our army pensions, what would become of industrial insurance? One-fifth of the looseness and extravagance that have characterized that history would wreck any conceivable scheme of industrial insurance in a year." See Brooks, "Report on Workingmen's Insurance," *Proceedings of the National Conference of Charities and Cor-*

rections, Thirty-Second Annual Session, Portland, Oregon, 1905, pp. 453–54. Brooks's testimony along the same lines to the pivotal 1907–1910 Massachusetts Commission on Old Age Pensions is discussed below in Chapter 5.

20. Frankel and Dawson, *Workingmen's Insurance in Europe*, p. 395.
21. Ibid., p. 405.
22. Rubinow, *Social Insurance*, p. 26. See also pp. 13–27, 189, 309–10, 473–501.
23. Brooks, *Workingmen's Insurance*, pp. 20–21, 22, 24.
24. Ibid., p. 20.
25. Frankel and Dawson, *Workingmen's Insurance in Europe*, pp. 401–02.
26. Henderson, *Industrial Insurance*, p. 310.
27. Rubinow, *Social Insurance*, p. 11.
28. Ibid., p. 500.
29. Ibid.
30. Seager, *Social Insurance*, p. 5.
31. Ibid., pp. 161–62.
32. Mary O. Furner, *Advocacy and Objectivity: A Crisis in the Professionalization of American Social Science, 1865–1905* (Lexington: University Press of Kentucky, 1975), pp. 48–49; and Jurgen Herbst, *The German Historical School in American Scholarship: A Study in the Transfer of Culture* (Ithaca, NY: Cornell University Press, 1965). See also Seager's discussion of the ideas of the German and Austrian economists with whom he studied in "Economics at Berlin and Vienna," esp. pp. 9–10 on the state's role in promoting reforms. This essay was written when Seager was 23 and is reprinted in his *Labor and Other Economic Essays,* ed. Charles A. Gulick, Jr. (New York: Harper and Brothers, 1931), pp. 1–29.
33. "Report of the Organization of the American Economic Association," by Richard T. Ely, Secretary, *Publications of the American Economic Association* 1(1) (March 1886), p. 6.
34. Both the German and domestic religious roots of early social scientists' ethical orientations are discussed in Robert M. Crunden, *Ministers of Reform: The Progressives' Achievement in American Civilization, 1889–1920* (Urbana: University of Illinois Press, 1984), pp. 68–71 and ch. 3 generally. The Protestant religious roots of Henderson's thinking come across especially clearly in an earlier book, *The Social Spirit in America* (Meadville, PA: Flood and Vincent, the Chautauqua-Century Press, 1897).
35. Leadership for reforms affecting female wage-earners was mostly left by the AALL to its "sister" reform association, the National Consumers' League (NCL). The AALL and the NCL supported each other's

initiatives, however, and many men and women reformers were members of both associations.

36. Overviews of the AALL's origins and development appear in Lloyd F. Pierce, "The Activities of the American Association for Labor Legislation in Behalf of Social Security and Protective Labor Legislation" (Ph.D. diss., University of Wisconsin, 1953), ch. 1; and Richard Martin Lyon, "The American Association for Labor Legislation and the Fight for Workmen's Compensation Laws, 1906–1942" (Master's diss., Cornell University, 1952), ch. 3.

37. Pierce, "Activities of the AALL," pp. 5–6; and Lyon, "AALL Fight," p. 41.

38. Pierce, "Activities of the AALL," p. 9.

39. Ibid., pp. 12–13.

40. Ibid., pp. 12, 19.

41. Ibid., pp. 16–17.

42. Henry W. Farnam, "Practical Methods in Labor Legislation," *American Labor Legislation Review (ALLR)* 1(1) (Jan. 1911), p. 5.

43. Pierce, "Activities of the AALL," p. 15.

44. Farnam, "Practical Methods," p. 7.

45. Ibid., p. 14.

46. See "Legislative Program for 1913," back cover of the *Survey* 29(1) (Jan. 11, 1913).

47. Thus, according to various numbers of the *ALLR*, during the AALL's sixth annual meeting in 1912 in Boston, there was a joint session with the American Economic Association on "The Minimum Wage." In 1916, President Henry Seager's address on "American Labor Legislation" at the ninth annual meeting in Washington, DC, was delivered in a joint session with the American Political Science Association; and in 1917, President Irving Fisher's address on "The Need for Health Insurance" at the tenth annual meeting in Columbus, Ohio, was delivered in a joint session with the American Economic Association, the American Sociological Society, and the American Statistical Association.

48. See especially the proceedings of the first American Conference on Social Insurance, sponsored by the AALL in Chicago, June 6–7, 1913, *ALLR* 3(2) (June 1913).

49. I. M. Rubinow, "20,000 Miles Over the Land: A Survey of the Spreading Health Insurance Movement," *Survey* 37(22) (March 3, 1917), p. 632. No indication is given of the nonresponse rates among members of the two professional associations, and the figures are not disaggregated for social workers versus economists. As illustration of the obvious truth of his proposition, Rubinow cited the movements

for child labor laws and for protections of women in industry. But, as we shall see in Chapters 6 and 7, these movements drew on support from local women's clubs throughout the land, and they relied on a moralistic women's style of progressive politics that was significantly different from the top-down, rationalist style of the AALL.

50. I. M. Rubinow, "Health Insurance: The Spread of the Movement," *Survey* 36(16) (July 15, 1916), p. 408. A list of fourteen organizations that set up committees to consider health insurance appears in Odin W. Anderson, "Health Insurance in the United States, 1910–1920," *Journal of the History of Medicine and Allied Sciences* 5(4) (1950), p. 369.

51. See *ALLR* 6 (1916), pp. 155–236; 8 (1918), pp. 321–31; 9 (1919), pp. 173–78, 252–74.

52. Ronald L. Numbers, *Almost Persuaded: American Physicians and Compulsory Health Insurance, 1912–1920* (Baltimore: Johns Hopkins University Press, 1978).

53. Compare the quotes in "Brief for Health Insurance," *ALLR* 6(2) (June 1916), p. 180, and in *ALLR* 7(1) (March 1917), p. 11, with *ALLR* 7(4) (Dec. 1917), p. 694, and also with the speech by the NAM president in *Proceedings of the Conference on Social Insurance Called by the International Association of Industrial Accident Boards and Commissions, Washington D.C., December 5 to 9, 1916,* in the *Bulletin of the United States Bureau of Labor Statistics* 212 (1917) (Washington: Government Printing Office, 1917), pp. 849–54, and with the participation of a NAM representative in the preparation of the 1917 pamphlet, "Compulsory Health Insurance: Statement Issued by Social Insurance Department, The National Civic Federation," included in the Harvard College Library's "Industrial and Social Insurance, U.S.: Miscellaneous Pamphlets, 1917–1922."

54. Rubinow, "20,000 Miles," p. 631.

55. Pierce, "Activities of the AALL," pp. 154–59.

56. Arthur J. Visaltear, "Compulsory Health Insurance in California, 1915–18," *Journal of the History of Medical and the Allied Sciences* 24 (1969): 151–82.

57. Anderson, "Health Insurance in the United States," pp. 369–72.

58. In his 1917 article "20,000 Miles," p. 631, Rubinow acknowledged that most of the health insurance literature has "appeared in specialized magazines. American monthly magazines, which contributed so much to the spread of propaganda for workmen's compensation, have had comparatively little to say concerning health insurance." Rubinow felt that this might be "evidence that our fifteen-cent magazines have during the last five years changed from public forums to sources of public entertainment." But this reasoning failed to take account of the

fact that the workmen's compensation campaign, which was joined at high tide rather than spearheaded by the AALL, featured moralistic and emotional appeals about the dire effects of industrial accidents on workmen and their families. In Chapter 8 below, we will see similarities in the nationwide campaign for mothers' pensions, waged in part through women's magazines. The AALL-led health insurance campaign simply never did much to give emotional and moral drama to the favorable side of that cause, so it is not surprising that the mass-circulation magazines were little interested.

59. Lyon, "AALL Fight," p. 51.
60. Ibid., pp. 52–53.
61. The structure of the National Consumers' League is discussed in Chapter 7 below.
62. Pierce, "Activities of the AALL," p. 14.
63. I suggest in Chapter 5 that the one health insurance campaign that achieved partial legislative success, the 1919 New York effort that got a bill through the state Senate, involved the active support of an unusually dense network of women's associations that was also unusually closely interlocked with male-led reform groups in that state.
64. For arguments along these lines, see G. William Domhoff, *The Higher Circles* (New York: Random House, 1970), pp. 207–18; Domhoff, "Corporate-Liberal Theory and the Social Security Act: A Chapter in the Sociology of Knowledge," *Politics and Society* 15(3) (1986–87): 297–330; Jill Quadagno, *The Transformation of Old Age Security: Class and Politics in the American Welfare State* (Chicago: University of Chicago Press, 1988), pp. 110–11; J. Craig Jenkins and Barbara G. Brents, "Social Protest, Hegemonic Competition, and Social Reform: A Political Struggle Interpretation of the Origins of the American Welfare State," *American Sociological Review* 54(6) (Dec. 1989), pp. 897–900; and Jenkins and Breuts, "Reply: Capitalists and Social Security: What Did They Really Want?" *American Sociological Review* 56(1) (Feb. 1991), p. 131.
65. Pierce, "Activities of the AALL," pp. 21, 37.
66. Ibid., pp. 19, 36.
67. Irwin Yellowitz, *Labor and the Progressive Movement in New York State, 1897–1916* (Ithaca, NY: Cornell University Press, 1965), pp. 72–73. Pierce, "Activities of the AALL," p. 37, lists other wealthy donors: Thomas W. Lamont, Julius Rosenwald, R. J. Caldwell, Mrs. Dorothy Douglas, Mrs. Leonard Elmhirst, and John Randolph Haynes.
68. For example, analysts of business often say that Rockefeller interests clashed with Morgan interests in this period.
69. Pierce, "Activities of the AALL," ch. 4; Lyon, "AALL Fight," p. 47;

Irwin Yellowitz, "The Origins of Unemployment Reform in the United States," *Labor History* 9 (Fall 1968), pp. 353–56; Robert F. Wesser, "Conflict and Compromise: The Workmen's Compensation Movement in New York, 1890s-1913," *Labor History* 12 (1971): 345–72; and Joseph L. Castrovinci, "Prelude to Welfare Capitalism: The Role of Business in the Enactment of Workmen's Compensation Legislation in Illinois, 1905–12," pp. 265–87 in *Compassion and Responsibility: Readings in the History of Social Welfare Policy in the United States* (Chicago: University of Chicago Press, 1980).

70. Pierce, "Activities of the AALL," ch. 5; Anderson, "Health Insurance in U.S.," pp. 386–87; Visaltear, "Health Insurance in California," pp. 176–77; Numbers, *Almost Persuaded*, p. 85; and Forrest A. Walker, "Compulsory Health Insurance: 'The Next Great Step in Social Legislation,'" *Journal of American History* 16(2) (Sept. 1969), pp. 302–03.

71. Quoted from an IMA publication in Lyon, "AALL Fight," p. 46, n. 28. See also Donald F. Tingley, *the Structuring of a State: The History of Illinois, 1899–1928,* The Sesquicentennial History of Illinois, vol. 5 (Urbana: University of Illinois Press, 1980), p. 111; Robert H. Wiebe, *Businessmen and Reform: A Study of the Progressive Movement* (Chicago: Quandrangle Books, 1962), p. 213; and Steven J. Diner, *A City and Its Universities: Public Policy in Chicago, 1892–1919* (Chapel Hill: University of North Carolina Press, 1980), ch. 6.

72. Daniel Nelson, *Unemployment Insurance: The American Experience, 1915–1935* (Madison: University of Wisconsin Press, 1969); and Anderson, "Health Insurance in U.S.," p. 387. See also the NCF pamphlet cited in note 18.

73. J. Lee Kreader, "Isaac Max Rubinow: Pioneering Specialist in Social Insurance," *Social Service Review* 50 (Sept. 1976): 402–25.

74. On Hoffman, see Numbers, *Almost Persuaded*, pp. 18–22. See also a series of his anti–health insurance pamphlets in the Harvard College Library's "Industrial and Social Insurance, U.S.: Miscellaneous Pamphlets, 1917–1922." Most of these were slickly published by Prudential and pulled together arguments from dozens of speeches that Hoffman gave before professional associations, medical groups, and—especially—national and state associations of manufacturers and of insurance companies.

75. Furner, *Advocacy and Objectivity.*

76. Dr. A. F. Weber, "Labor Legislation, National and International," *Journal of the American Social Science Association* 45 (Sept. 1907), p. 36.

77. Ibid., p. 43.

78. Ibid.

79. On the role of socialists (including some who were members of the

AALL) in the early U.S. campaigns for social insurance, see Gordon J. Goldberg, "Meyer London and the National Social Insurance Movement, 1914–1922," *American Jewish Historical Quarterly* 65 (1975): 59–73. Many moderate socialists were fully part of "social progressivism."

80. Letter from John B. Andrews to William Cochran, Woodbrook, Maryland, January 5, 1915, as quoted in Lyon, "AALL Fight," pp. 171–72.

81. John R. Commons, "Is Class Conflict in America Growing and Is It Inevitable?" *American Journal of Sociology* 8(6) (May 1908), p. 757.

82. Haskell, *Emergence of Professional Social Science.*

83. This point is well made in Roy Lubove, "Economic Security and Social Conflict in America: The Early Twentieth Century, Part II," *Journal of Social History* 1(4) (Summer 1968), pp. 334–35.

84. These diagrams represent the AALL's vision of how labor-law administration worked (or should have worked) in these two states, not necessarily the reality.

85. John R. Commons, "Constructive Investigation and the Industrial Commission of Wisconsin," *Survey* 29 (Jan. 4, 1913): 440–48, quote on p. 440. See also John R. Commons and John B. Andrews, *Principles of Labor Legislation* (New York: Harper and Brothers, 1916), ch. 9; and "Labor Law Administration in New York," *ALLR* 7(2) (June 1917), entire issue.

86. Edward Berkowitz and Kim McQuaid, *Creating the Welfare State: The Political Economy of Twentieth-Century Reform,* 2nd ed., rev. and updated (New York and Westport, CT: Praeger, 1988), p. 47.

87. "Health Insurance: Tentative Draft of an Act," *ALLR* 6(2) (June 1916), pp. 264–65. The chart appeared at the front of *ALLR* 7(1) (March 1917).

88. I am indebted for this idea to Professor Bernard Silberman of the Department of Political Science, University of Chicago.

89. In 1915, AFL President Samuel Gompers quit his membership in the AALL during one such dispute about administrative reform in New York state. This incident is discussed in Chapter 4.

90. Seager, *Social Insurance.*

91. "Outline" appears in Seager's *Labor and Other Economic Essays,* pp. 131–48. On pp. 79–89, see also Seager's first statement along these lines, "Outline of a Program of Social Reform," which was originally published in *Charities and the Commons* 177 (Feb. 2, 1907): 828–32.

92. John B. Andrews, *Labor Problems and Labor Legislation* (New York: AALL, 1922).

93. See *ALLR* 3(1) (Feb. 1913), pp. 81–115; 3(2) (June 1913), pp. 191–201, 229–34.

94. Pierce, "Activities of the AALL," chs. 2–4.

95. Ibid., pp. 296–98.
96. "Practical Program," *ALLR* 5(2) (June 1915): 171–92. This was followed some months later by the AALL's attempt to supplement its own proposals with recommendations drawn from local and state experiences in coping with unemployment during the recession. See "Standard Recommendations," *ALLR* 5(3) (Nov. 1915), pp. 593–94.
97. Nelson, *Unemployment Insurance*, pp. 17–18. See also "Unemployment Insurance for Massachusetts: Draft of an Act with an Introduction and Notes" (Boston: Massachusetts Committee on Unemployment, 1916). Appropriately, this draft "submitted for discussion and criticism" started with a quote from Britain's William Beveridge.
98. An excellent discussion of debates over public measures to combat unemployment appears in Alex Keyssar, *Out of Work: The First Century of Unemployment in Massachusetts* (Cambridge and New York: Cambridge University Press, 1986), pp. 262–78.
99. *Report of the Special Commission on Social Insurance*, Feb. 1917, House doc. no. 1850 (Boston: Wright and Potter, State Printers, 1917).
100. Nelson, *Unemployment Insurance*, ch. 6.
101. *ALLR* 6(2) (June 1916), p. 121.
102. Numbers, *Almost Persuaded*, pp. 16–17.
103. *ALLR* 3(2) (June 1913), first three pages.
104. See Seager's "Outline of a Program of Social Legislation" (1907), pp. 141–44, and "Old Age Pensions" (1908), pp. 149–54, both in his *Labor and Other Economic Essays*.
105. See Seager's *Social Insurance*, chs. 5 and 6. In Chapter 5, I will analyze the reluctance of Seager and the AALL to make old-age pensions a priority.
106. John B. Andrews, "Outline of Work, 1914," *ALLR* 5(1) (March 1915), p. 153.
107. "Preliminary Standards for Sickness Insurance," *ALLR* 4(3) (Nov. 1914), pp. 595–96.
108. "Brief for Health Insurance," and "Health Insurance: Tentative Draft of an Act," *ALLR* 6(2) (June 1916), pp. 155–268.
109. Ibid., p. 236.
110. Irving Fisher, "The Need for Health Insurance," *ALLR* 7(1) (March 1917), p. 23.
111. Rubinow, "20,000 Miles Over the Land," p. 634.
112. See *ALLR* 6(2) (June 1916): facing the title page; and 8(4) (Dec. 1918), facing p. 316.
113. Walker, "Compulsory Health Insurance," p. 295, n. 22.
114. See the valuable discussion in Robert L. Church, "Economists as Experts: The Rise of an Academic Profession in the United States, 1870–

1920," pp. 571–609 in *The University in Society*, vol. 2, ed. Lawrence Stone (Princeton, NJ: Princeton University Press, 1975).

4. Help for the "Army of Labor"? Trade Unions and Social Legislation

1. Dr. A. F. Weber, "Labor Legislation, National and International," *Journal of the American Social Science Association* 45 (Sept. 1907), pp. 36–37.
2. Ibid., p. 37.
3. Hugh Heclo, *Modern Social Politics in Britain and Sweden* (New Haven: Yale University Press, 1974), pp. 165–78.
4. Ibid., pp. 78–90; and Bentley Gilbert, *The Evolution of National Insurance in Great Britain: The Origins of the Welfare State* (London: Michael Joseph, 1966), chs. 5–7.
5. Arthur Marwick, "The Labour Party and the Welfare State in Britain, 1900–1948," *American Historical Review* 73 (1967): 380–403.
6. *Hearings before the Committee on Labor, House of Representatives, 64th Congress, 1st Session, April 6 and 11, 1916, on H.J. Resolution 159, "A Resolution for the Appointment of a Commission to Prepare and Recommend a Plan for the Establishment of a National Insurance Fund for the Mitigation of the Evil of Unemployment"* (Washington: Government Printing Office, 1916), pp. 124, 135.
7. *American Federationist* 23(5) (May 1916): 333–57; 23(6) (June 1916):453–66; and 23(8) (Aug. 1916): 669–81.
8. *American Federationist* 23(5) (May 1916), p. 334. Among other articles in the *American Federationist*, see Samuel Gompers, "Labor versus Its Barnacles," 23(4) (April 1916): 268–74; Grant Hamilton, "Trade Unions and Social Insurance," 24(2) (Feb. 1917): 122–25; and Samuel Gompers, "Political Labor Party—Reconstruction—Social Insurance," 26(1) (Jan. 1919): 33–46.
9. Daniel Nelson, *Unemployment Insurance: The American Experience, 1915–1935* (Madison: University of Wisconsin Press, 1969), ch. 4.
10. *Report of Proceedings of the Thirty-Sixth Annual Convention of the American Federation of Labor*, Baltimore, MD, Nov. 13–25, 1916 (Washington, DC: Law Reporter Printing Co., 1916), p. 145.
11. For some examples, see United States Commissioner of Labor, *Workmen's Insurance and Benefit Funds in the United States*, Twenty-Third Annual Report, 1908 (Washington: Government Printing Office, 1909); Charles Richmond Henderson, "Industrial Insurance Benefit Features of the Trade-Unions," *American Journal of Sociology* 7(6) (May 1907): 756–78 (an account later incorporated into his 1909 book,

Industrial Insurance); and Boris Emmet, "Operation of Establishment and Trade-Union Disability Funds," *Monthly Labor Review* 5 (Aug. 1917): 217–36.

12. *Report of the Proceedings of the Thirty-Third Annual Convention of the American Federation of Labor*, Seattle, WA, Nov. 10–22, 1913 (Washington: Law Reporter Printing Co., 1913), p. 90.

13. Ibid., p. 89. An elaborate AFL proposal for public works to help the unemployed appears in *Report of the Proceedings of the Twenty-Eighth Annual Convention of the American Federation of Labor*, Denver, CO, Nov. 9–13, 1908 (Washington: National Tribune Co., 1908), p. 258. For a historical overview of AFL resolutions on public works to aid the unemployed, see *American Federation of Labor: History, Encyclopedia Reference Book* (Washington: AFL, 1919), pp. 391–92. See also the valuable discussion in Mollie Ray Carroll, *Labor and Politics: The Attitude of the American Federation of Labor toward Legislation and Politics* (New York: Arno Press and the New York Times, 1969; orig. 1923), pp. 110–12.

14. *Report of Proceedings of the Thirty-Fifth Annual Convention of the American Federation of Labor*, San Francisco, CA, Nov. 8–22, 1915 (Washington: Law Reporter Printing Co., 1915), pp. 313–15.

15. *Proceedings of Thirty-Sixth Annual AFL Convention* (1916), p. 144.

16. Grant Hamilton, "Proposed Legislation for Health Insurance," *Proceedings of the Conference on Social Insurance Called by the International Association of Industrial Accident Boards and Commissions*, Washington, DC, Dec. 5–9, 1916 in *Bulletin of the United States Bureau of Labor Statistics* 212 (1917) (Washington: Government Printing Office, 1917), p. 567. Gompers's "Address" appears on pp. 845–49.

17. *Report of the Proceedings of the Thirty-Eighth Annual Convention of the American Federation of Labor*, St. Paul, MN, June 10–20, 1918 (Washington: Law Reporter Printing Co., 1918), pp. 94, 282–83.

18. *Report of the Proceedings of the Thirty-Ninth Annual Convention of the American Federation of Labor*, Atlantic City, NJ, June 9–23, 1919 (Washington: Law Reporter Printing Co., 1919), pp. 144–45, 378–79; and *Report of the Proceedings of the Fortieth Annual Convention of the American Federation of Labor*, Montreal, Quebec, Canada, June 7–19, 1920 (Washington: Law Reporter Printing Co., 1920), pp. 176, 387. See also Carroll, *Labor and Politics*, pp. 105–109.

19. Samuel Gompers, "Not Even Compulsory Benevolence Will Do," *American Federationist* 24(1) (Jan. 1917): 47–48. See also Fred Greenbaum, "The Social Ideas of Samuel Gompers," *Labor History* 7 (1966): 35–61.

20. My account draws on Carroll, *Labor and Politics*, ch. 3; Sister Joseph M. Viau, *The Problem of Hours and Wages in American Organized Labor*

(New York: G. P. Putnam's Sons, 1939), pp. 46–60; and Philip Taft, *The A.F. of L. in the Time of Gompers* (New York: Harper and Brothers, 1957), ch. 9.

21. See *Proceedings of Thirty-Third Annual AFL Convention* (1913), pp. 59–64.

22. Ibid., p. 63.

23. Carroll, *Labor and Politics,* pp. 63–64.

24. *Proceedings of Thirty-Third Annual AFL Convention* (1913), p. 285.

25. *Report of the Proceedings of the Thirty-Fourth Annual Convention of the American Federation of Labor,* Philadelphia, PA, Nov. 9–21, 1914 (Washington: Law Reporter Printing Co., 1914), pp. 421–44.

26. Ibid., p. 421.

27. Ibid., pp. 443–44. See the final section of this chapter for a discussion of the minimal representation of state federations and their political interests at national AFL conventions.

28. *Proceedings of Thirty-Fifth Annual AFL Convention* (1915), pp. 484–504. This time, however, the AFL leadership prevailed by a minority, only because so many delegates abstained. The 1915 vote was 8,500 in favor of the Committee on Resolutions, 6,396 against, and 4,061 not voting.

29. Henry R. Seager, "American Labor Legislation" in his *Labor and Other Economic Essays,* ed. Charles A. Gulick, Jr. (New York: Harper and Brothers, 1931).

30. Ibid., pp. 285, 287.

31. Elizabeth Brandeis, *Labor Legislation,* in vol. 3 of *History of Labor in the United States, 1896–1932,* by John R. Commons and associates (New York: Macmillan, 1935), p. 557. Ironically, the AFL's highly visible opposition to general protective laws for men undercut these reformist movements at just about the time when the U.S. Supreme Court, through its 1917 decision in *Bunting v. Oregon,* seemed to back off from the hostile position it had taken toward such legislation in the 1905 *Lochner* decision. Court decisions on protective laws for men will be discussed in the next chapter.

32. Taft, *AFL in the Time of Gompers,* is an example of a classic work that omits to mention the Federation's endorsement of old-age pensions. An otherwise excellent recent work that fails to correctly identify the national Federation's stands on noncontributory old-age pensions as opposed to social insurance is Christopher Anglim and Brian Gratton, "Organized Labor and Old Age Pensions," *International Journal of Aging and Human Development* 25(2) (1987): 91–107. Jill Quadagno, *The Transformation of Old Age Security: Class and Politics in the American Welfare State* (Chicago: University of Chicago Press, 1988), ch. 3, cor-

rectly distinguishes among national AFL stances on social policies, yet mistakenly implies (p. 61) that the AFL acceptance of old-age pensions was due to socialist influence. As we shall soon see, the decisive leader inside the AFL was United Mine Workers official and eventually U.S. Representative William B. Wilson, a Democrat who became Secretary of Labor in the administration of President Woodrow Wilson.

33. *Report of the Proceedings of the Twenty-Second Annual Convention of the American Federation of Labor,* New Orleans, LA, Nov. 13–22, 1902 (Washington: Law Reporter Co., 1902), p. 86. The resolution added "provided . . . that such a wage-worker is a citizen of the United States and has lived in this country for at least 21 years continually at the time when the application for the pension is made."

34. The modal monthly rate under the 1890 Civil War pension law was $12.00 for elderly or disabled veterans. See *Annual Report of the Commissioner of Pensions to the Secretary of the Interior for the Year Ended June 30, 1902* (Washington: Government Printing Office, 1902), p. 62, exhibit no. 14c.

35. *Proceedings of Twenty-Second Annual AFL Convention* (1902), p. 112.

36. Ibid., pp. 135, 226. Kelly's resolution was simply treated as a repeat of Berger's.

37. Ibid., p. 135.

38. *Report of the Proceedings of the Twenty-Fourth Annual Convention of the American Federation of Labor,* San Francisco, CA, Nov. 14–26, 1904 (Washington: Law Reporter Printing Co., 1904), pp. 133, 205; *Report of the Proceedings of the Twenty-Fifth Annual Convention of the American Federation of Labor,* Pittsburgh, PA, Nov. 13–25, 1905 (Washington: Law Reporter Printing Co., 1905), pp. 156, 179; *Report of the Proceedings of the Twenty-Sixth Annual Convention of the American Federation of Labor,* Minneapolis, MN, Nov. 12–24, 1906 (Washington: Graphic Arts Printing Co., 1906), pp. 148, 235; and *Report of the Proceedings of the Twenty-Seventh Annual Convention of the American Federation of Labor,* Norfolk, VA, Nov. 11–23, 1907 (Washington: National Tribune Co., 1907), pp. 158, 218–19.

39. *Proceedings of Twenty-Seventh Annual AFL Convention* (1907), p. 218.

40. *Proceedings of Twenty-Eighth Annual AFL Convention* (1908), pp. 99–102 (quotes at 102).

41. Ibid., p. 260.

42. *Report of the Proceedings of the Twenty-Ninth Annual Convention of the American Federation of Labor,* Toronto, Canada, Nov. 8–20, 1909 (Washington: Law Reporter Printing Co., 1909), pp. 97–101, 119, 330–31. The AFL also called upon the Canadian Parliament to pass old-age pension legislation similar to Britain's 1908 law.

43. Ibid., p. 101. Wilson's "Brief," which was sent to the AFL Executive Council on June 11, 1909, appears at pp. 99–101.

44. Ibid., p. 98.

45. Wilson's stipulation that there could be no punishments, along with the absence of "good character" requirements in his bill, was also a way to get around a worry expressed by Gompers in 1908 that the government might use behavioral requirements for old-age pensions to control workers.

46. According to David Hackett Fischer, *Growing Old in America*, expanded ed. (New York: Oxford University Press, 1978), p. 171, Wilson's bill "was referred to the House Committee on Military Affairs, and never reported out." Wisconsin Congressman Victor Berger also introduced an old-age pension bill on July 31, 1911.

47. *Report of the Proceedings of the Thirtieth Annual Convention of the American Federation of Labor*, St. Louis, MO, Nov. 14–26, 1910 (Washington: Law Reporter Printing Co., 1910), p. 251 (this Convention reiterated support for Wilson's bill and pushed aside a more generous old-age pension proposal submitted by a delegate from the International Printing Pressmen's Union); *Report of the Proceedings of the Thirty-First Annual Convention of the American Federation of Labor*, Atlanta, GA, Nov. 13–25, 1911 (Washington: Law Reporter Printing Co., 1911), pp. 268–69; *Report of the Proceedings of the Thirty-Second Annual Convention of the American Federation of Labor*, held at Rochester, NY, Nov. 11–23, 1912 (Washington: Law Reporter Printing Co., 1912), pp. 52, 347; *Proceedings of Thirty-Third Annual AFL Convention* (1913), pp. 58, 376; and *Proceedings of Thirty-Fourth Annual AFL Convention* (1914), pp. 87–88, 327.

48. *Proceedings of Thirty-Sixth Annual AFL Convention* (1916), pp. 233, 357. On later developments, see the summary in Louis Leotta, Jr., "Abraham Epstein and the Movement for Social Security: 1920–1939" (Ph.D. diss., Columbia University, 1965), pp. 49–51.

49. Anglim and Gratton, "Organized Labor and Old Age Pensions"; and Quadagno, *Transformation of Old Age Security*, ch. 3.

50. *Proceedings of Twenty-Ninth Annual AFL Convention* (1909), p. 330.

51. Taft, *AFL in the Time of Gompers*, p. 23 and ch. 2 generally.

52. Christopher L. Tomlins, *The State and the Unions: Labor Relations, Law, and the Organized Labor Movement in America, 1880–1960* (Cambridge and New York: Cambridge University Press, 1985), pp. 69–74.

53. Andrew William John Thomson, "The Reaction of the American Federation of Labor and the Trades Union Congress to Labor Law, 1900–1935" (Ph.D. diss., Cornell University, 1968), p. 75. See also James

Holt, "Trade Unionism in the British and U.S. Steel Industries, 1880–1914: A Comparative Study," *Labor History* 18(1) (Winter 1977): 5–35.

54. Leo Wolman, "The Extent of Labor Organization in the United States in 1910," *Quarterly Journal of Economics* 30(3) (May 1916), p. 506.

55. This argument is featured in Quadagno, *Transformation of Old Age Security,* pp. 10–12 and ch. 3. For a classic formulation, see Michael Rogin, "Voluntarism: The Political Functions of an Antipolitical Doctrine," *Industrial and Labor Relations Review* 15(4) (July 1962): 521–35.

56. Quadagno, *Transformation of Old Age Security,* pp. 64–72.

57. William Green, "Trade Union Sick Funds and Compulsory Health Insurance," *American Labor Legislation Review* 7(1) (March 1917): 91–95; and *Report of the Proceedings of the Forty-First Annual Convention of the American Federation of Labor,* held at Denver, CO, June 13–25, 1921 (Washington: Law Reporter Printing Co., 1921), p. 332. See also the discussion in Nelson, *Unemployment Insurance,* p. 71.

58. See text and notes above; also Quadagno, *Transformation of Old Age Security,* p. 71.

59. Between 1910 and 1919, 31 percent of the U.S. labor force and 12 percent of the British labor force was employed in agriculture. For a series of tables comparing the socioeconomic characteristics of Britain, the United States, and the state of Massachusetts, see Ann Shola Orloff and Theda Skocpol, "Why Not Equal Protection? Explaining the Politics of Public Social Spending in Britain, 1900–1911, and the United States, 1880s-1920," *American Sociological Review* 49(6) (Dec. 1984), pp. 733, 736. See also Thomson, "Reaction to Labor Law," p. 673.

60. Thomson, "Reaction to Labor Law," pp. 672–73.

61. Mark Lawrence Kornbluh, "From Participatory to Administrative Politics: A Social History of American Political Behavior, 1880–1918" (Ph.D. diss., Johns Hopkins University, 1987), pp. 254–57 and ch. 5 generally.

62. Similarities between the late-nineteenth-century British and U.S. labor movements are discussed in Victoria C. Hattam, "Institutions and Politics: Working-Class Formation in England and the United States, 1830–1896" (paper presented at a conference on "The New Institutionalism," at the University of Colorado, Boulder, Jan. 12–13, 1990); and William Forbath, "Law and the Shaping of Labor Politics in the United States and England" (manuscript, UCLA Law School, 1990).

63. Reinhard Bendix, *Nation-building and Citizenship: Studies of Our Changing Social Order* (New York: John Wiley and Sons, 1964); and Ira Katznelson, "Working-Class Formation and the State: Nineteenth-Century England in American Perspective," pp. 257–84 in *Bringing the State Back In,* ed. Peter B. Evans, Dietrich Rueschemeyer, and

Theda Skocpol (Cambridge and New York: Cambridge University Press, 1985).

64. G. D. H. Cole, *A Short History of the British Working-Class Movement, 1789–1947,* rev. ed. (London: George Allen and Unwin, 1948), pp. 200–05.

65. Thomson, "Reaction to Labor Law," pp. 502–05.

66. My account of British organized labor's deepening involvement in national politics is based upon Ibid., pp. 505–33; Cole, *Short History;* and Forbath, "Law and Labor Politics in the United States and England."

67. Richard Oestreicher, "Urban Working-Class Political Behavior and Theories of American Electoral Politics, 1870–1940," *Journal of American History* 74(4) (March 1988), p. 1270. Mining areas, with their huge geographical concentrations of workers, were the principal places in the United States where workers could elect representatives to legislatures; indeed, three American miners including William B. Wilson were elected as Democrats to Congress in 1906. Yet British union miners, of whom there twice as many as U.S. union miners, could elect proportionately more representatives from smaller, parliamentary districts.

68. Thomson, "Reaction to Labor Law," pp. 675–77.

69. Susan Pedersen, "The Failure of Feminism in the Making of the British Welfare State," *Radical History Review* 43 (1989): 86–110.

70. William E. Forbath, "The Shaping of the American Labor Movement," *Harvard Law Review* 102(6) (April 1989), p. 1132.

71. Gerald Friedman, "Worker Militancy and Its Consequences: Political Responses to Labor Unrest in the United States, 1877–1914" (paper presented at the Annual Meeting of the Social Science History Association, Washington, DC, Nov. 1989), pp. 13–15.

72. Forbath, "Law and Labor Politics in the United States and England," pp. 30–34. During the 1890s, England had about 140 full-time mine and factory inspectors covering 190,000 workplaces, while in the United States in 1911 there were about 114 inspectors, over half less than full-time, covering some 513,000 workplaces.

73. Friedman, "Worker Militancy," p. 16. My account draws on pp. 16–26.

74. Oestreicher, "American Electoral Politics," p. 1263.

75. Kornbluh, "From Participatory to Administrative Politics," chs. 5 and 6.

76. Thomson, "Reaction to Labor Law," pp. 689–708; Oestreicher, "American Electoral Politics," pp. 1272–73; and Rogin, "Voluntarism," pp. 534–35.

77. This paragraph draws upon Thomson, "Reaction to Labor Law," ch. 7. See also Stephen J. Scheinberg, "Theodore Roosevelt and the A.F.of L.'s Entry into Politics, 1906–1908," *Labor History* 3 (1963): 131–48.

78. The impact of the courts on U.S. organized labor has been brilliantly analyzed by Victoria Hattam, "Unions and Politics: The Courts and American Labor, 1806–1896" (Ph.D. diss., Massachusetts Institute of Technology, 1987); Leon Fink, "Labor, Liberty, and the Law: Trade Unionism and the Problem of American Constitutional Order," *Journal of American History* 74(3) (Dec. 1987): 904–25; and Forbath, "The Shaping of the American Labor Movement." Forbath's article has now been turned into a book, *Law and the Shaping of the American Labor Movement* (Cambridge, MA: Harvard University Press, 1991); and Hattam's revised dissertation is forthcoming as *Labor Visions and State Power: The Origins of Business Unionism in the United States* (Princeton, NJ: Princeton University Press, 1992).

79. Forbath, "Shaping of American Labor Movement," p. 1133, including n. 78.

80. Ibid.

81. Samuel Gompers, *Seventy Years of Life and Labor: An Autobiography* (New York: E. P. Dutton, 1925), vol. 1, bk. 1, ch. 9, pp. 194, 197.

82. Tomlins, *The State and the Unions*, ch. 3.

83. Forbath, "Shaping of American Labor Movement," pt. 5; and Fink, "Labor, Liberty, and the Law."

84. From "A Verbatum [sic] Report of the Discussion of the Political Programme at the Denver Convention of the American Federation of Labor, December 15, 1894," as quoted in Forbath, "Law and Labor Politics in the United States and England," pp. 36–37. See also the useful discussion of the AFL's rejection of a Socialist alliance in Robin L. Einhorn, "Industrial Relations in the Progressive Era: The United States and Great Britain," *Social Service Review* 58(1) (March 1984): 98–116.

85. Forbath, "Law and Labor Politics in the United States and England," pp. 36–37.

86. From the President's Annual Report to the 1899 Convention, as quoted in Samuel Gompers, *Labor and the Common Welfare*, comp. and ed. Hayes Robbins (New York: E. P. Dutton, 1919), p. 45.

87. From the Feb. 1915 issue, as quoted in ibid., p. 54.

88. Irwin Yellowitz, *Labor and the Progressive Movement in New York State, 1897–1916* (Ithaca, NY: Cornell University Press, 1965), pp. 119–21, 138–42.

89. From U.S. Congress, Senate, Committee on Education and Labor, *Hearings on Relations between Capital and Labor*, vol. 1, 49th Congress,

1st Session (Washington: Government Printing Office, 1885), p. 289, as quoted in Gwendolyn Mink, *Old Labor and New Immigrants in American Political Development* (Ithaca, NY: Cornell University Press, 1986), p. 251.

90. Philip Taft, *Labor Politics American Style: The California State Federation of Labor* (Cambridge, MA: Harvard University Press, 1968), p. 5.
91. Thomson, "Reaction to Labor Law," pp. 678–79.
92. Gary M. Fink, *Labor's Search for Political Order: The Political Behavior of the Missouri Labor Movement, 1890–1940* (Columbia: University of Missouri Press, 1973), p. 167.
93. Christopher Anglim and Brian Gratton, "Organized Labor and Old Age Pensions," *International Journal of Aging and Human Development* 25(2) (1987), p. 92. Although they overlook the national Federation's 1909–1914 campaign for federal old-age pensions, Anglim and Gratton are right about its reluctance to push for state-level laws before the Depression.
94. Ibid., p. 95.
95. Quadagno, *Transformation of Old Age Security*, ch. 3. Her account of the Eagles as a cross-class association is more accurate than Anglim and Gratton's argument (p. 94) that the Eagles were a "working class fraternity." In the words of contemporary observer Charles Richmond Henderson, *Industrial Insurance in the United States* (Chicago: University of Chicago Press, 1909), p. 315, the "Order of Eagles is composed chiefly of artisans and professional men; few are low-paid laborers." The legislative effectiveness of the Eagles, as well as the content of the old-age pension bills they proposed, was rooted in the fraternity's cross-class social composition and in its organizational structure as a federation of local clubs. As with other widespread federated associations in American policy history, the Eagles were in an excellent position to shape local public opinion and lobby legislative representatives.
96. Quadagno, *Transformation of Old Age Security*, p. 62.
97. Ibid., p. 67.
98. Ibid., p. 65.
99. Fink, *Missouri Labor Movement*, pp. 53, 172, including n. 29.
100. Taft, *California State Federation of Labor*, p. 56.
101. *Report of the Commission on Old Age Pensions, Annuities, and Insurance*, Massachusetts House Document no. 1400 (Boston: Wright and Potter, State Printers, 1910), pp. 331–39.
102. Anglim and Gratton, "Organized Labor and Old Age Pensions," p. 100.
103. Ibid., pp. 99–100.

104. Fink, *Missouri Labor Movement,* pp. 174–75. Unfortunately, Fink does not make clear gender distinctions in his discussions of maximum hour and minimum wage legislation. Chapter 7 below discusses organized labor's stance toward such laws for women in particular. Even the Socialist-led Wisconsin State Federation of Labor briefly opposed minimum wage regulations for women workers in 1913; see Robert W. Ozanne, *The Labor Movement in Wisconsin: A History* (Madison; State Historical Society of Wisconsin, 1984), pp. 127–28.
105. Fink, *Missouri Labor Movement,* p. 174, including n. 35.
106. Ozanne, *Labor Movement in Wisconsin,* p. 123.
107. See note 25 above.
108. Eugene Staley, *A History of the Illinois State Federation of Labor* (Chicago: University of Chicago Press, 1930), p. 474. See also note 28 above.
109. This was the situation, for example, in New York; see Yellowitz, *Labor and the Progressive Movement in New York State,* p. 136.
110. *American Labor Legislation Review* 8(4) (Dec. 1918), p. 319.
111. John B. Andrews, "Report of Work—1919," *ALLR* 10(1) (March 1920), p. 74. I have not found the names of the additional three state labor federations that endorsed health insurance in 1919, but this was clearly past the peak of the national movement.
112. Ronald L. Numbers, *Almost Persuaded: American Physicians and Compulsory Health Insurance* (Baltimore: Johns Hopkins University Press, 1978), pp. 79, 81–82, 85. Before 1918, the New York State Federation was reluctant to support health insurance based on workers' contributions (rather than general taxation and employers' contributions). See Yellowitz, *Labor and Progressives in New York,* pp. 137–38.
113. "Health Insurance: Official Endorsement of the New York State Federation of Labor, with Report of Its Committee on Health" (New York: New York State Federation of Labor, 1918), pamphlet included in the Harvard College Library's "Industrial and Social Insurance, U.S.. 1917–1922: Miscellaneous Pamphlets."
114. Nelson, *Unemployment Insurance,* p. 18.
115. Ibid., pp. 70–71.
116. Ibid., p. 72.
117. Ibid., p. 72 and ch. 6; and Ozanne, *Labor Movement in Wisconsin,* pp. 129–33.
118. I devised this list by taking the top seventeen states in terms of value of manufactures per capita in 1910 (there was a significant gap between this group and the rest of the U.S. states on this measure in 1910). Then I dropped from the list seven small states with populations under 1.5 million apiece. The ten remaining states each had a total population of 2.3 million or more. Taken together, these large

and wealthy industrial states included 47 percent of the nation's population in 1910, and 67 percent of its total number of industrial wage earners.

119. Taft, *California State Federation of Labor,* p. 5.
120. Fink, *Missouri Labor Movement,* p. 219.
121. Ibid., p. 180.
122. Lorin Stuckey, *The Iowa State Federation of Labor, Bulletin of the State University of Iowa, Studies in the Social Sciences* 4(3) (Aug. 1916), p. 17.
123. Ibid.
124. Taft, *California State Federation,* p. 1. The role of organized labor in New York politics actually antedated the Federation, and was "crucial in breaking down the old laissez-faire concept of state government," in the words of Robert F. Wesser, "Charles Evans Hughes and the Urban Sources of Political Progressivism," *New York Historical Society Quarterly* 50 (1966), p. 370.
125. Taft, *California State Federation,* p. 1; Fink, *Missouri Labor Movement,* intro.; Stuckey, *Iowa State Federation,* ch. 1; and Keith L. Bryant, Jr., "Labor in Politics: The Oklahoma State Federation of Labor during the Age of Reform," *Labor History* 11(3) (1970), p. 261 and throughout (259–76).
126. AFL, *History, Encyclopedia, Reference Book,* p. 359.
127. Fink, *Missouri Labor Movement,* p. 165.
128. A Table of Voting Strength in 1912–1920 AFL Conventions appears in *Proceedings of Fortieth Annual AFL Convention* (1920), pp. 37–38.
129. The best overview appears in Taft, *California State Federation,* introduction.
130. Examples appear in the Harvard College Library's *Report[s] on Labor Legislation and Labor Record of Senators and Assemblymen,* issued by California State Federation of Labor, 1915–1935.
131. See Chapter 7 below.
132. Elizabeth Sanders, "Farmers and the State in the Progressive Era," pp. 183–205 in *Changes in the State: Causes and Consequences,* ed. Edward S. Greenberg and Thomas F. Mayer (Newbury Park, CA: Sage Publications, 1990); and Robert L. Morlan, *Political Prairie Fire: The Nonpartisan League, 1915–1922* (Minneapolis: University of Minnesota Press, 1955), pp. 65–66.
133. Quadagno, *Transformation of Old Age Security,* pp. 66–72.
134. Taft, *California State Federation,* p. 56.
135. Arthur J. Visaltear, "Compulsory Health Insurance in California, 1915–18," *Journal of the History of Medical and the Allied Sciences* 24 (1969), pp. 174–75.
136. Stuckey, *Iowa State Federation,* p. 24.

137. Thomas Ray Pegram, "Progressivism and Partisanship: Reformers, Politicians, and Public Policy in Illinois, 1870–1922" (Ph.D. diss., Brandeis University, 1988), p. 123.
138. Yellowitz, *Labor and Progressives in New York,* p. 24 and ch. 2 generally.

5. Progressive Era Politics and the Defeat of Social Policies for Workingmen and the Elderly

1. See Kenneth O. Morgan, "The Future at Work: Anglo-American Progressivism, 1870–1917," pp. 245–71 in *Contrast and Connection: Bicentennial Essays in Anglo-American History,* ed. H. C. Allen and Roger Thompson (Columbus: Ohio University Press, 1976); Charles L. Mowat, "Social Legislation in Britain and the United States in the Early Twentieth Century: A Problem in the History of Ideas," pp. 81–96 in *Historical Studies: Papers Read before the Irish Conference of Historians,* vol. 7, ed. J. C. Beckett (New York: Barnes and Noble, 1969); and Morton Keller, "Anglo-American Politics, 1900–1930, in Anglo-American Perspective: A Case Study in Comparative History," *Comparative Studies in Society and History* 22(3) (July 1980): 458–77.
2. Michael Freeden, *The New Liberalism: An Ideology of Social Reform* (London: Macmillan, 1973); and Francis H. Herrick, "British Liberalism and the Idea of Social Justice," *American Journal of Economics and Sociology* 4(1) (Oct. 1944): 67–79.
3. Pat Thane, *The Foundations of the Welfare State* (London: Longman, 1982), chs. 3, 5, and 6.
4. R. K. Webb, *Modern England: From the Eighteenth Century to the Present* (New York: Dodd, Mead, 1970), pp. 53–57.
5. K. B. Smellie, *A Hundred Years of English Government* (London: Duckworth, 1950), p. 69.
6. Ibid., pp. 69–70.
7. Emmeline Cohen, *The Growth of the British Civil Service, 1790–1939* (London: Allen and Unwin, 1941), ch. 7; and Herman Finer, *The British Civil Service* (London: Allen and Unwin, 1937), pp. 45–49.
8. Cohen, *Growth of Civil Service,* pp. 81–83; H. R. Greaves, *The Civil Service in the Changing State* (London: George C. Harrap, 1947), pp. 21–32; and Martin Shefter, "Party and Patronage: Germany, England and Italy," *Politics and Society* 7 (1977), pp. 434–37.
9. Roger Davidson and R. Lowe, "Bureaucracy and Innovation in British Welfare Policy, 1870–1945," in *The Emergence of the Welfare State in Britain and Germany, 1850–1950,* ed. W. J. Mommsen (London: Croom Helm, 1981), pp. 268–69.

10. Roger Davidson, "Llewellyn Smith and the Labour Department," pp. 227–62 in *Studies in the Growth of Nineteenth Century Government*, ed. Gillian Sutherland (London: Routledge and Kegan Paul, 1972).

11. Roy Douglas, *The History of the Liberal Party, 1895–1970* (London: Sidgwick and Jackson, 1971), pp. 1–17; H. J. Hanham, *Elections and Party Management: Politics in the Time of Disraeli and Gladstone* (London: Longmans Green, 1959); Barry McGill, "Francis Schnadhorst and the Liberal Party Organization," *Journal of Modern History* 34 (1962): 19–39; and Shefter, "Party and Patronage," pp. 438–41.

12. D. Collins, "The Introduction of Old Age Pensions in Great Britain," *Historical Journal* 8 (1965): 246–49; and José Harris, *Unemployment and Politics: A Study in English Social Policy, 1886–1914* (Oxford: Oxford University Press, 1972).

13. Bentley B. Gilbert, *The Evolution of National Insurance in Great Britain: The Origins of the Welfare State* (London: Michael Joseph, 1966), pp. 161–202.

14. The following account is based on ibid., pp. 202–32 and chs. 5–6; Hugh Heclo, *Modern Social Politics in Britain and Sweden* (New Haven: Yale University Press, 1974), pp. 78–90, 173–78; and J. R. Hay, *The Origins of Liberal Welfare Reforms, 1906–1914* (London: Macmillan, 1983).

15. H. V. Emy, "The Impact of Financial Policy on English Party Politics before 1914," *Historical Journal* 15 (1972): 103–31.

16. See esp. James Leiby, *Carroll Wright and Labor Reform: The Origins of Labor Statistics* (Cambridge, MA: Harvard University Press, 1960); and William R. Brock, *Investigation and Responsibility: Public Responsibility in the United States, 1865–1900* (New York and Cambridge: Cambridge University Press, 1984). Gerald D. Nash, "Bureaucracy and Reform in the West: Notes on the Influence of a Neglected Interest Group" *Western Historical Quarterly* 2(3) (July 1971): 295–305, argues that labor bureau officials in the western states were often in a stronger position than those in the East to investigate social conditions and recommend legislative changes.

17. Henry W. Farnam, "Practical Methods in Labor Legislation," *American Labor Legislation Review* 1(1) (January 1911), p. 8.

18. Andrew William John Thomson, "The Reaction of the American Federation of Labor and the Trades Union Congress to Labor Law, 1900–1935" (Ph.D. diss., Cornell University, 1968), p. 50.

19. Henry R. Seager, *Labor and Other Economic Essays*, ed. Charles A. Gulick, Jr. (New York: Harper and Brothers, 1931), p. 52. This article originally appeared in the *Political Science Quarterly* 19 (Dec. 1904): 589–611.

20. Ibid., p. 62.
21. From *Holden v. Hardy,* 169 U.S. 366 (1898), as quoted in Elizabeth Brandeis, *Labor Legislation,* in vol. 3 of John R. Commons, *History of Labor in the United States, 1896–1932* (New York: Macmillan, 1935), pp. 668–69.
22. From *People v. Lochner,* 177 N.Y. Reporter, p. 45, as quoted in Seager, "Attitude of American Courts," in *Essays,* p. 74.
23. Seager, "Attitude of American Courts," pp. 76–77.
24. Ibid., pp. 52–53.
25. Farnam, "Practical Methods," p. 7.
26. From *Lochner v. New York,* 198 U.S. 45 (1905), as quoted in Brandeis, *Labor Legislation,* pp. 670–71.
27. Brandeis, *Labor Legislation,* p. 671.
28. As explained in W. F. Dodd, "Social Legislation and the Courts," *Political Science Quarterly* 28(1) (March 1913), pp. 6–7, when state courts declared laws unconstitutional, citing the "due process" clauses of both state and federal constitutions, their decisions could not be appealed to the U.S. Supreme Court under the terms of the 1789 Judiciary Act, although decisions favorable to state statutes could be appealed to the U.S. Supreme Court. This provision of the Judiciary Act was finally amended by Congress in 1914, and thereafter state high court decisions could be appealed whether they were favorable or unfavorable to a statute.
29. Henry R. Seager, "The Constitution and Social Progress in the State of New York" (1915), in *Essays,* p. 260.
30. Dodd, "Social Legislation and the Courts," p. 5.
31. From *Ives v. South Buffalo Ry. Co.,* 201 N.Y., as quoted in Melvin I. Urofsky, "State Courts and Protective Legislation during the Progressive Era: A Reevaluation," *Journal of American History* 72(1) (June 1985), p. 86.
32. Henry R. Seager, "Adaptation of Written Constitutions to Changing Economic and Social Conditions," in *Essays,* pp. 197–99. This talk was delivered during a discussion of Frank J. Goodnow's "Judicial Interpretation of Constitutional Provisions" at the October 1912 Meeting of the American Academy of Political Science.
33. Seager, "Constitution and Social Progress in New York," pp. 259, 264–65.
34. Ibid., pp. 267–68.
35. Ibid., p. 258, n. 1; and Arthur J. Visaltear, "Compulsory Health Insurance in California, 1915–18," *Journal of the History of Medical and the Allied Sciences* 24 (1969), p. 181.
36. Urofsky, "State Courts and Protective Legislation," p. 64.
37. Visaltear, "Compulsory Health Insurance in California."

38. Urofsky's argument in "State Courts and Protective Legislation" is methodologically flawed, because he concentrates only on policy areas in which much legislation did pass. He does not consider areas where it might have been proposed but was not; nor does he pay much attention to modifications in proposals that were unsuccessfully put forward.

39. Seager, "Constitution and Social Progress in New York," p. 260.

40. See Frank J. Goodnow, "The Constitutionality of Old Age Pensions," *American Political Science Review* 5(194) (1911): 194–212. According to Susan Sterett in "Constitutionalism and Social Spending: Pennsylvania's Old Age Pensions in the 1920s," *Studies in American Political Development* 4 (1990): 231–47, anticipated constitutional obstacles were very important in limiting and shaping reform initiatives. She implies that such anticipated obstacles could prevent legislative initiatives altogether, but I doubt it. The 1907–1910 Massachusetts Commission looking into old-age pensions did give doubts about constitutionality as one of its many reasons for recommending against them; see *Report of the [Massachusetts] Commission on Old Age Pensions, Annuities and Insurance, January 1910,* House doc. no. 1400 (Boston: Wright and Potter, State Printers, 1910), pp. 238–39. But constitutional worries were *not* the reason for reformers' reluctance to campaign during the 1910s for the sort of federal, need-based old-age pensions advocated by the national AFL between 1909 and 1914. Goodnow did not see any constitutional bar to a federal old-age pension law in his 1911 article (and he also thought that state-level pensions for the indigent *might* pass constitutional muster). Certainly, despite any constitutional worries they may have had, reformers went ahead with the health insurance campaign of 1916–1920, and the AALL endorsed state-level old-age pensions during the 1920s. Reformers usually tried to pass social legislation, and then modified later bills to meet anticipated judicial objections after laws of a given sort were actually struck down. This suggests that worries about the courts influenced legislative campaigns, and could stop them, but did not prevent them from emerging in the first place.

41. See Chapter 3, note 93; and Chapter 7, notes 90, 91, and 92.

42. Seager, "Constitution and Social Progress in New York," p. 260. In his 1915 presidential address to the AALL, Seager also admitted that he had been wrong in supposing at the time that the 1905 *Lochner* decision would have "no lasting importance." See "American Labor Legislation," p. 279.

43. Lawrence Goodwyn, *Democratic Promise: The Populist Movement in America* (New York: Oxford University Press, 1976).

44. Leon Fink, *Workingmen's Democracy: The Knights of Labor and American*

Democracy (Urbana: University of Illinois Press, 1983); and William E. Forbath, "The Shaping of the American Labor Movement," *Harvard Law Review* 102(6) (April 1989), pts. 1 and 2.

45. I mean to include under the "Mugwump" rubric not just antipatronage Republicans but also reform-minded elites who became pro-Cleveland Democrats. My remarks draw from John M. Dobson, *Politics in the Gilded Age* (New York: Praeger, 1972), ch. 6; Ari Hoogenboom, *A History of the Civil Service Reform Movement, 1865–1883* (Urbana: University of Illinois Press, 1968); John G. Sproat, *"The Best Men": Liberal Reformers in the Gilded Age* (Chicago: University of Chicago Press, 1982); Martin J. Schiesl, *The Politics of Efficiency: Municipal Administration and Reform in America* (Berkeley and Los Angeles: University of California Press, 1977); and Stephen Skowronek, *Building a New American State: The Expansion of National Administrative Capacities, 1877–1920* (Cambridge and New York: Cambridge University Press, 1981), pp. 42–45.

46. Goodwyn, *Democratic Promise*, chs. 14–17; and Martin Shefter, "Trade Unions and Political Machines: The Organization and Disorganization of the American Working Class in the Late Nineteenth Century," pp. 197–276 in *Working-Class Formation: Nineteenth-Century Patterns in Western Europe and the United States,* ed. Ira Katznelson and Aristide R. Zolberg (Princeton, NJ: Princeton University Press, 1986).

47. Skowronek, *Building a New American State*, pt. 2.

48. Martin Shefter, "Party and Patronage: Germany, England and Italy," *Politics and Society* 7 (1977): 403–51.

49. This paragraph and the next draw especially upon Howard W. Allen and Jerome Clubb, "Progressive Reform and the Political System," *Pacific Northwest Quarterly* 65(3) (July 1974): 130–45; Walter Dean Burnham, "The System of 1896: An Analysis," ch. 5 in Paul Kleppner et al., *The Evolution of American Electoral Systems* (Westport, CT: Greenwood Press, 1981); Paul Kleppner, *Who Voted? The Dynamics of Electoral Turnout, 1870–1980* (New York: Praeger, 1982), ch. 4; and Mark Lawrence Kornblum, "From Participatory to Administrative Politics: A Social History of American Political Behavior" (Ph.D. diss., Johns Hopkins University, 1987).

50. Kleppner, *Who Voted?*, p. 57.

51. This process is nicely described in David P. Thelen, *Robert M. La Follette and the Insurgent Spirit* (Boston: Little, Brown, and Company, 1976).

52. Richard L. McCormick, "Political Change in the Progressive Era," pt. 3 of *The Party Period and Public Policy: American Politics from the Age of Jackson to the Progressive Era* (New York: Oxford University Press, 1986); and Martin Shefter, "Party, Bureaucracy, and Political Change in the United States," in *Political Parties: Development and Decay,* ed.

Louis Maisel and Joseph Cooper (Beverly Hills, CA: Sage Publications, 1978), pp. 229–37.

53. The concept of "social progressivism" is specified most effectively in Irwin Yellowitz, *Labor and the Progressive Movement in New York State, 1897–1916* (New York: Cornell University Press, 1965), chs. 3 and 4.

54. Allen F. Davis, *Spearheads for Reform: The Social Settlements and the Progressive Movement, 1890–1914* (New York: Oxford University Press, 1967); and Chapter 9 below.

55. Peter G. Filene, "An Obituary for 'The Progressive Movement,'" *American Quarterly* 22(1) (Spring 1970): 20–34; and Yellowitz, *Labor and Progressives in New York.*

56. Robert Buroker, "From Voluntary Association to Welfare State: The Illinois Immigrants' Protective League, 1908–1926," *Journal of American History* 58 (1971): 643–60.

57. Allen and Clubb, "Progressive Reform and the Political System."

58. William Graebner, "Federalism and the Progressive Era: A Structural Interpretation of Reform," *Journal of American History* 64 (1977): 331–57.

59. W. E. H. Lecky, "The Objections Summarized," in *Selected Articles on Old Age Pensions,* compiled by Lamar T. Beman, The Handbook Series, series II, vol. 1 (New York: H. W. Wilson Company, 1927), pp. 270–71; orig. in the *Independent* 51 (Oct. 5, 1899): 2662–65.

60. As quoted in Donald McMurry, "The Political Significance of the Pension Question, 1885–1897," *Mississippi Valley Historical Review* 9 (1922), pp. 34–35.

61. Edward H. Hall, "An Indignity to Our Citizen Soldiers: A Sermon Preached in the First Parish Church, Cambridge, June 1, 1890" (Cambridge, MA: John Wilson and Son, University Press, 1890), p. 12. Also of interest from this time period are an article arguing against Civil War benefits by a member of "The Sociological Group" of early social scientists and civil service reformers, which appeared as "Pensions and Socialism" in the *Century* 42(2) (June 1891): 179–88; and "Dependent Pension Bills; and the Race Problem at the South," a "Speech of Ex-Gov. D. H. Chamberlain before the Massachusetts Reform Club at Boston, February 8, 1890," accompanied by "Remarks on Pension Legislation by Mr. Frederick J. Stimson." Both the Hall Sermon and the speeches to the Reform Club are pamphlets in the collections of Harvard University's Widener Library.

62. On Booth, see Hugh Heclo, *Modern Social Politics in Britain and Sweden* (New Haven: Yale University Press, 1974), pp. 161–66. The parallel between Booth and Hale is drawn in the *Report of the Commission on Old Age Pensions,* p. 224.

63. Edward Everett Hale, "Universal Life Endowments," *Lend a Hand* 5(8) (Aug. 1890), p. 526.

64. Ibid., pp. 522–23, 525.

65. See, for example, the comment on Hale's advocacy in the 1906 *Springfield Republican* as rpt. in *Massachusetts Labor Bulletin* 11(1) (Jan. 1907), p. 42. This *Bulletin* was put out by the state's Bureau of Statistics of Labor, which clearly took a friendly interest in old-age pensions. Part III of the Bureau's 1905 Annual Report was devoted to "comparing the present expenditure for charity with the probable cost of a system of old-age pensions."

66. As reprinted in ibid., p. 43. The 1905–06 legislation is presented in *Labor Bulletin of the Commonwealth of Massachusetts,* no. 36 (June 1905), pp. 193–97.

67. *Report of the Commission on Old Age Pensions,* p. 7.

68. With around 200,000 constituents and substantial leverage in state-level politics during the 1910s, the Massachusetts Federation of Labor championed the cause of old-age pensions. In addition to the comments of Arthur Huddell below, see *Report of the [Massachusetts] Special Commission on Social Insurance, February 1917,* House doc. no. 1850 (Boston: Wright and Potter, State Printers, 1917), pp. 57–58; and Christopher Anglim and Brian Gratton, "Organized Labor and Old Age Pensions," *International Journal of Aging and Human Development* 25(2) (1987), pp. 99–101.

Although there was not much support for old-age pensions expressed in the public hearings convened by the 1907–1910 Commission on Old Age Pensions, this body worried about their potential popularity. And it later became unmistakable that noncontributory pensions were indeed very appealing to Massachusetts citizens. During 1915 and 1916, popular referenda were held with high voter participation in eight Massachusetts towns and city districts. Voters were asked to answer the question: "Shall the representative from this district be instructed to vote for non-contributory old-age pensions, so as to have the Commonwealth pension its deserving needy aged citizens, women and men, over sixty-five years of age and residents of the Commonwealth for at least fifteen years?" Old-age pensions were supported by more than a three-to-one margin in every referendum, as follows:

	YES	NO
Abington (1915)	671	185
Boston (1916)	6,147	1,076
(Wards 9, 10, 11)		

Brockton (1915)	7,215	1,341
Cambridge (1915)	8,697	2,718
Lawrence (1915)	5,082	1,303
Methuen (1915)	1,035	308
New Bedford (1916)	3,561	1,140
(Eighth Bristol District)		
Whitman (1915)	978	216

On these referenda, see *Report of the Special Commission on Social Insurance,* p. 57; and "Old-Age Pensions Poll a Strong Vote," *Survey* 35(9) (Nov. 27, 1915), p. 197.

69. *Report of the Commission on Old Age Pensions,* pp. 333–44.
70. Relying on standard biographical compendia, I have been unable to find anything about Mrs. M. R. Hodder or James T. Buckley (who may have been the employers' representative).
71. *Report of the Commission on Old Age Pensions,* p. 314; see also pp. 310–13.
72. Ibid., pp. 232–39 (where the phrases quoted in this paragraph are to be found) and 322–30.
73. Ibid., pp. 234–35; and Brian Gratton, "Social Workers and Old Age Pensions, " *Social Service Review* 57 (Sept. 1983): 403–15.
74. *Report of the Commission on Old Age Pensions,* pp. 237–38.
75. On Brooks's biography, see Table 5.
76. *Report of the Commission Old Age Pensions,* p. 238.
77. Louis D. Brandeis, "Massachusetts' Substitute for Old Age Pensions," *Independent* 65 (July 16, 1908): 125–28. See also Richard Abrams, *Conservatism in a Progressive Era: Massachusetts Politics, 1900–1912* (Cambridge, MA: Harvard University Press, 1964), pp. 140–42.
78. This 1907 statement by Brandeis is quoted in Alpheus Mason, *The Brandeis Way* (Princeton, NJ: Princeton University Press, 1938), p. 104.
79. *Report of the Commission on Old Age Pensions,* p. 323.
80. Abrams, *Conservatism,* p. 146; and Robert A. Silverman, "Nathan Matthews: Politics of Reform in Boston, 1890–1910," *New England Quarterly* 50 (1977), pp. 640–42.
81. Alexander Keyssar, *Out of Work: The First Century of Unemployment in Massachusetts* (Cambridge and New York: Cambridge University Press, 1986), p. 261.
82. For historical background, see Barbara Solomon, *Ancestors and Immigrants* (Cambridge, MA: Harvard University Press, 1956).
83. Silverman, "Politics of Reform in Boston." As added evidence that ethnic conflicts must be situated in relation to various national state-building experiences, Desley Deacon has pointed out to me that in Australia Irish immigrants were principal architects of the rationalized

civil service, which facilitated the enactment of modern welfare-state policies. In turn, many Australian Irish gained upward mobility through bureaucratic careers.

84. See the list of articles in Beman, *Selected Articles on Old Age Pensions*, pp. lxvii–lxix.

85. For background on this magazine, see Frank Luther Mott, *A History of American Magazines, 1885–1905* (Cambridge, MA: Harvard University Press, 1957), ch. 34, "The World's Work." One can also gain a sense of editorial policy from reading "The March of Events" at the beginning of each issue.

86. Ibid., pp. 773, 780. See the following articles from the period of Page's editorship of the *Forum:* Leonard Woolsey Bacon, "A Raid upon the Treasury," 6 (Jan. 1889): 540–48; Allen R. Foote, "Degradation by Pensions: The Protest of Loyal Volunteers," 12 (Dec. 1891): 423–32; H. W. Slocum, "Pensions: Time to Call a Halt," 12 (Jan. 1892): 646–51; John DeWitt Warner, "Half a Million Dollars a Day for Pensions," 15 (June 1893): 439–51; Charles M. Loeser, "The Grand Army as a Pension Agency," 15 (July 1893): 522–31; and S. N. Clark, "Some Weak Places in Our Pension System," 26 (1898): 306–20. Critical articles with somewhat more dispassionate titles and arguments continued into the 1900s.

87. Mott, *History of American Magazines*, p. 783.

88. Ibid., p. 777.

89. Robert Lincoln O'Brien, "Our Enormous Pension Roll," *World's Work* 8 (May 1904).

90. *World's Work* 20(6) (Oct. 1910): 13485–503; 21(1) (Nov. 1910): 13611–26; 21(2) (Dec. 1910): 13731–47; 21(3) (Jan. 1911): 13917–28; 21(4) (Feb. 1911): 13967–77; and 21(5) (March 1911): 14159–69. Brief editorial comments on pensions also appeared regularly in the magazine.

91. *World's Work* 23(2) (Dec. 1911): 188–96; 23(3) (Jan. 1912): 327–34; and 23(4) (Feb. 1912): 385–98. Adams's address in Boston appears in the Harvard University Widener Library's copy of the pamphlet reprinting the magazine articles. Adams was a member of the Massachusetts Reform Club referred to in note 61 above.

92. Charles Francis Adams, "Pensions—Worse and More of Them," *World's Work* 23(2) (Dec. 1911), p. 193.

93. "How Pensions Make Cowards," *World's Work* 23(4) (Feb. 1912), p. 379.

94. Ibid. This echoed the fearful projections about the future of U.S. pension politics in the 1912 introduction to Adams's "Civil-War Pension Lack-of-System" pamphlet. Adams believed that pensions would soon be extended to new categories of citizens. In what some might

suppose was an uncanny glimpse into what U.S. Social Security would become decades later, Adams declared (p. iii): "Under the system hitherto in vogue in this country of progressive pensions—that is, annual increases promised by candidates for office—it is not too much to say that at a not remote period the government will thus at each election be practically put up at auction. Each congressional candidate will travel through his district, hat in hand, promising to be more liberal in the way of pensions, etc., than his opponent."

95. Mott, *History of American Magazines,* p. 777. Indeed, during 1911–12, the Sherwood "Dollar-a-Day" Pension bill was debated but not ultimately passed in Congress. Upward adjustments of established benefits did continue, however.

96. Some flavor of press opinion, including articles which quoted Charles Francis Adams's pieces, can be found in the *Literary Digest* 42(3) (Jan. 21, 1911): 100–01; and 43(25) (Dec. 23, 1911): 1183–84.

97. As cited in Beman, *Selected Articles on Old Age Pensions,* p. 102.

98. As cited in ibid., p. 100.

99. Lippmann's article is reprinted in ibid., pp. 85–91 (quote on p. 89).

100. John G. Clark, "Reform Currents in Polite Monthly Magazines, 1880–1900," *Mid-America: An Historical Review* 47(1) (Jan. 1965): 3–23.

101. For those who cited Civil War pensions as a favorable precedent, see the Introduction to Part II of this book; and also M. Clyde Kelley, "The Need for Pensions," reprinted from the *Congressional Record,* June 10, 1913, in Beman, *Selected Articles on Old Age Pensions,* p. 215; and John Franklin Crowell, "Old-Age Pensions" pp. 775–77 in *Proceedings of the Conference on Social Insurance called by the International Association of Industrial Accident Boards and Commissions,* Washington, DC, Dec. 5–9, 1916, in *Bulletin of the United States Bureau of Labor Statistics,* no. 212 (June 1917) (Washington: Government Printing Office, 1917). The latter was a talk by the executive officer of the Chamber of Commerce of New York State. A straightforward argument for noncontributory old-age pensions that appeared (with reference to Civil War pensions) in 1911 was W. J. Ghent, "Pension Plans," reprinted from the *Independent* in Beman, *Selected Articles on Old Age Pensions,* pp. 141–44.

102. Charles Richmond Henderson, *Industrial Insurance* (Chicago: University of Chicago Press, 1909), p. 227.

103. Compare Seager's remarks in his "Outline of a Program of Social Reform" (1907), "Outline of a Program of Social Legislation with Special Reference to Wage-Earners" (1907), and "Old Age Pensions" (1908), all rpt. in his *Essays,* with the priorities set from 1912 onward

by the AALL's Committee on Social Insurance (a matter discussed in Chapter 3).

104. Henry Rogers Seager, *Social Insurance: A Program of Social Reform* (New York: Macmillan, 1910), p. 145.

105. Ibid., p. 144.

106. In addition to the *American Labor Legislation Review (ALLR)*, which chronicles the debates and policies of the AALL, see the noncommittal discussion in Industrial Commission of Wisconsin, "Report on Old Age Relief," March 1, 1915; and the New Jersey Commission report cited in note 108.

107. Such arguments appear very prominently in W. F. Willoughby's 1913 presidential address to the AALL, "Philosophy of Labor Legislation," *ALLR* 4(1) (March 1914): 37–46; Henry R. Seager's 1915 presidential address to the AALL, "American Labor Legislation," *ALLR* 6(1) (March 1916): 87–98; "Brief for Health Insurance," *ALLR* 6(2) (June 1916): 155–236; Irving Fisher's 1916 presidential address to the AALL, "The Need For Health Insurance," *ALLR* 7(1) (March 1917): 9–23; and Samuel McCune Lindsay's 1918 presidential address to the AALL, "Next Steps in Social Insurance in the United States," *ALLR* 9(1) (March 1919): 107–14. As Lindsay's speech exemplifies, AALL leaders in the 1910s occasionally indicated that they might like contributory old-age insurance along German lines, as well as contributory health and unemployment insurance. Notice also Lindsay's characterization (p. 114) of the AALL's support for the War Risk Insurance enacted for World War I veterans: "We have substituted the justice of insurance for the charity of pensions in the army."

108. *Report on Health Insurance by the New Jersey Commission on Old Age, Insurance and Pensions* (Rahway: New Jersey Reformatory Print, 1917), pp. 2–3.

109. For a classic argument along these lines, see Roy Lubove, *The Struggle for Social Security, 1900–1935* (Cambridge, MA: Harvard University Press, 1968), ch. 4.

110. In addition to the arguments of AFL President Samuel Gompers discussed in the previous chapter, see Ronald Numbers, *Almost Persuaded: American Physicians and Compulsory Health Insurance, 1912–1920* (Baltimore: Johns Hopkins University Press, 1978); Frederick L. Hoffman, *Failure of German Compulsory Health Insurance—A War Revelation* (Newark, NJ: Prudential Press, 1918); Hoffman, *Autocracy and Paternalism vs. Democracy and Liberty* (Newark, NJ: Prudential Press, 1918); and David Starr Jordan, "Governmental Obstacles to Insurance," *Scientific Monthly* 2 (Jan. 1916): 27–33.

111. Numbers, *Almost Persuaded,* p. 85; and Solon De Leon, "Year's Devel-

opments toward Health Insurance Legislation," *ALLR* 8(4) (Dec. 1918), pp. 316–17.

112. The social geography and political effectiveness of Progressive Era women's organizations are analyzed below in Part III.

113. Lecky, "The Objections Summarized," pp. 266–67.

114. Royal Meeker, "Social Insurance in the United States," from the *Proceedings of the National Conference of Social Work, 1917,* rpt. in Julia E. Johnson, comp., *Selected Articles on Social Insurance* (New York: H. W. Wilson Co., 1922), pp. 25–26.

115. Seager, *Social Insurance,* pp. 150–51.

116. Ibid., pp. 152–54.

117. Richard Martin Lyon, "The American Association for Labor Legislation and the Fight for Workmen's Compensation Laws, 1906–1942" (Ph.D. diss., Cornell University, 1952), p. 21. Actually, Montana passed a law in 1909 and New York in 1910, but both were soon declared unconstitutional.

118. Harry Weiss, "Employers' Liability and Workmen's Compensation," ch. 6 in Elizabeth Brandeis, *Labor Legislation,* in vol. 3 of *History of Labor in the United States,* by John R. Commons and associates (New York: Macmillan, 1935), p. 575.

119. Edward Berkowitz and Kim McQuaid, *Creating the Welfare State: The Political Economy of Twentieth-Century Reform* (New York: Praeger, 1980), p. 37.

120. Lawrence M. Friedman and Jack Ladinsky, "Social Change and the Law of Industrial Accidents," in *American Law and the Constitutional Order: Historical Perspectives,* ed. Lawrence M. Friedman and Harry N. Scheiber (Cambridge, MA: Harvard University Press, 1978), pp. 269–70.

121. Ibid., pp. 270–72.

122. Urofsky, "State Courts and Protective Legislation," p. 84.

123. See the discussion of the precedent-setting New York Court of Appeals decision of *Knisely v. Pratt* in Joseph Frederick Tripp, "Progressive Labor Laws in Washington State (1900–1925)" (Ph.D. diss., University of Washington, 1973), p. 62.

124. Ibid., p. 66.

125. Ibid., p. 63.

126. Friedman and Ladinsky, "Law of Industrial Accidents," p. 274.

127. Ibid., p. 272.

128. Urofsky, "State Courts and Protective Legislation," p. 84.

129. Ibid., p. 85.

130. Friedman and Ladinsky, "Law of Industrial Accidents," p. 273.

131. Ibid.

132. Berkowitz and McQuaid, *Creating the Welfare State,* p. 34, referring to Richard A. Posner, "A Theory of Negligence," *Journal of Legal Studies* 1(1) (Jan. 1972): 44–95.
133. Friedman and Ladinsky, "Law of Industrial Accidents," p. 274.
134. Ibid., p. 276.
135. Urofsky, "State Courts and Protective Legislation," p. 85.
136. Robert H. Bremner, *From the Depths: The Discovery of Poverty in the United States* (New York: New York University Press, 1956), p. 252, quoting from the article in *Leslie's Monthly Magazine* 58 (1904): 566–67.
137. Ibid., quoting from Arthur B. Reeve, "Our Industrial Juggernaut," *Everybody's Magazine* 16 (1907): 147–52.
138. Ibid., quoting from William Hard, *Injured in the Course of Duty* (New York: Ridgeway Co., 1910).
139. Crystal Eastman, *Work-Accidents and the Law* (New York: Russell Sage Foundation, 1910).
140. Ibid., p. 220.
141. Weiss, "Workmen's Compensation," p. 572.
142. Conflicts over workmen's compensation prior to 1909–10 illustrate organized labor's initial reluctance. According to Robert F. Wesser, "Conflict and Compromise: The Workmen's Compensation Movement in New York, 1890s-1913," *Labor History* 12 (1971): 348–49, the "first real attempt to implement the principle of compensation came in 1898, when the Social Reform Club in New York City sponsored a bill in the state legislature establishing a scheme of automatic payments to workmen injured in employment." But this bill was opposed by the Workingmen's Federation and died in committee. Labor opposition also helped to block British-style workmen's compensation bills proposed in 1904 by a Massachusetts investigatory committee chaired by Carroll Wright of the Bureau of Labor Statistics, and another proposed in 1907 by an Illinois investigatory commission. See Robert Asher, "Business and Workers' Welfare in the Progressive Era: Workmen's Compensation Reform in Massachusetts,1880–1911," *Business History Review* 43 (1969), pp. 455–47; and Joseph L. Castrovinci, "Prelude to Welfare Capitalism: The Role of Business in the Enactment of Workmen's Compensation Legislation in Illinois, 1905–12," in *Compassion and Responsibility: Readings in the History of Social Welfare Policy in the United States,* ed. Frank R. Breul and Steven J. Diner (Chicago: University of Chicago Press, 1980), pp. 268–69. Thinking in terms of fairness for worker litigants in the courts, American trade unions wanted to extend legislative limitations on employers' common-law defenses. If workmen's compensation were to be enacted, unions initially took the position that workers should retain the right to sue if

they thought they could do better in the courts. Employers, of course, would not accept such double jeopardy.

143. Wesser, "Workmen's Compensation in New York," pp. 354–58.

144. *Report of the Proceedings of the Thirtieth Annual Convention of the American Federation of Labor,* St. Louis, MO, Nov. 14–26, 1910 (Washington: Law Reporter Printing Co., 1910), pp. 262–63; and *Report of the Proceedings of the Thirty-Fourth Annual Convention of the American Federation of Labor,* Philadelphia, PA, Nov. 9–21, 1914 (Washington: Law Reporter Printing Co., 1914), pp. 80–82, 101, 322–26, 494. The story of Gompers's acceptance of workers' compensation—and his insistence that it was *not* a kind of social insurance—is told in Robert Asher, "The Ignored Precedent: Samuel Gompers and Workmen's Compensation," *New Labor Review,* no. 4 (Fall 1982): 51–77.

145. *Official Report of the Tenth Biennial Convention of the General Federation of Women's Clubs,* May 11 to May 18, 1910, Cincinnati, OH, comp. and ed. Mrs. Henry Hollister Dawson (Newark, NJ: GFWC, 1910), pp. 364–67 and 532.

146. Castrovinci, "Business and Workmen's Compensation in Illinois," p. 273.

147. Wesser, "Workmen's Compensation in New York," p. 346; and James Weinstein, *The Corporate Ideal in the Liberal State, 1900–1918* (Boston: Beacon Press, 1968), ch. 2.

148. Wesser, "Workmen's Compensation in New York," p. 346; and Castrovinci, "Business and Workmen's Compensation in Illinois," pp. 272–73, quoting Fred C. Schwedtman, *Cooperation or—What?* (New York: National Association of Manufacturers, 1912), p. 2, and citing Henry L. Rosenfield, *Cooperation and Compensation versus Compulsion and Compromise in Employers' Liability* (New York: Workmen's Compensation Publicity Bureau, 1911), p. 2.

149. Castrovinci, "Business and Workmen's Compensation in Illinois," quoting Schwedtman, *Cooperation,* p. 6.

150. Eliza K. Pavalko, "State Timing of Policy Adoption: Workmen's Compensation in the United States, 1909–1929," *American Journal of Sociology* 95(3) (Nov. 1989), p. 592. "Productivity" is measured as "the ratio of the total value of products in manufacturing to the number of wage earners" (p. 605). Pavalko offers a Marxist-sounding interpretation of this variable, but it could as well be interpreted in terms of modernization theories. Apparently, it gives strong weight to mining states as well as more generally industrial ones. In Pavalko's data base, the first two states to enact workmen's compensation were Montana (1909) and New York (1910), even though both of these laws were soon declared unconstitutional.

151. According to Castrovinci, "Business and Workmen's Compensation in

Illinois," organized business along with reformers primarily shaped the legislation in that state, while organized labor was divided about accepting the principle of workmen's compensation in place of employers' liability. According to Wesser, "Workmen's Compensation in New York," organized labor united to influence legislation in New York, while business groups were divided. Other patterns also occurred. For example, according to Tripp, "Progressive Labor Laws in Washington State," ch. 2, employers and labor in the lumber industry joined to shape that Washington's law, overcoming opposition from city-based industries.

152. On *Ives,* see Lyon, "AALL Fight for Workmen's Compensation," pp. 99–103; and Urofsky, "State Courts and Protective Legislation," pp. 86–87.

153. Weiss, "Workmen's Compensation," pp. 577–81; and Lubove, *Struggle for Social Security,* pp. 57–58.

154. Urofsky, "State Courts and Protective Legislation," p. 87; and Tripp, "Protective Labor Laws in Washington State," pp. 73–75.

155. Brandeis, *Labor Legislation,* pp. 682–83.

156. On the clogging of the courts, see Asher, "Workmen's Compensation Reform in Massachusetts," p. 456; Tripp, "Progressive Labor Laws in Washington State," p. 71; and Friedman and Ladinsky, "Law of Industrial Accidents," p. 273.

157. As quoted in Lloyd F. Pierce, "The Activities of the American Association for Labor Legislation in Behalf of Social Security and Protective Labor Legislation" (Ph.D. diss., University of Wisconsin, 1953), p. 161.

158. Ibid., p. 162; and pp. 162–63 and 171–73 for the contents of AALL standards and recommendations.

159. Berkowitz and McQuaid, *Creating the Welfare State,* p. 36. Pierce, "Activities of the AALL," pp. 171–74, gives specifics about the number of states that met AALL standards or amended their laws in the direction of the standards.

160. Berkowitz and McQuaid, *Creating the Welfare State,* p. 36.

161. Gerhard A. Ritter, *Social Welfare in Germany and Britain,* trans. Kim Traynor (Leamington Spa, Britain, and New York: Berg Publishers, 1986), pp. 62–64, 171–72; and Hay, *Origins of Liberal Welfare Reforms,* p. 55. See also Roy Hay, "Employers and Social Policy in Britain: The Evolution of Welfare Legislation, 1905–1914," *Social History* 4 (1977): 435–55.

162. Brandeis, *Labor Legislation,* ch. 8.

163. Berkowitz and McQuaid, *Creating the Welfare State,* p. 37; Weiss, "Employers' Liability and Workmen's Compensation," pp. 587–89; and Wallace D. Yaple, "Administration by Courts or by Commission?"

ALLR 5(1) (March 1915): 117–28. According to Weiss, prior to 1914 the states that left administration to the courts were Arizona, Maryland, Nebraska, New Jersey, New Hampshire, Kansas, Minnesota, and Rhode Island. Meanwhile, according to Yaple (p. 122) the "acts of Massachusetts, Connecticut, Ohio, California, Illinois, Michigan, Wisconsin, Iowa, Texas, Nevada, Oregon, West Virginia, New York and Washington provide for administration either by a single administerial officer, or by a board or commission, usually of three members."

164. "Three Years under the New Jersey Workmen's Compensation Law," *ALLR* 5(1) (March 1915): 31–104.

165. See, for example, the papers and discussion in Session II, "Administration by Commissions," AALL Conference, Chicago, Sept. 15–16, 1911, as reported in *ALLR* 1(4) (Dec. 1911), pp. 61–104.

166. Berkowitz and McQuaid, *Creating the Welfare State,* p. 39; and Weiss, "Employers' Liability and Workmen's Compensation," pp. 588–89.

167. Berkowitz and McQuaid, *Creating the Welfare State,* p. 40. See also Edward D. Berkowitz, *Disabled Policy: America's Programs for the Handicapped* (Cambridge and New York: Cambridge University Press, 1987), ch. 1.

168. John R. Commons, "Constructive Investigation and the Industrial Commission of Wisconsin," *Survey* 29 (Jan. 4, 1913), pp. 440–42.

169. Arthur J. Altmeyer, *The Wisconsin Industrial Commission,* University of Wisconsin, Studies in Social Science and History, no. 17 (Madison, 1932); Nelson, *Unemployment Insurance,* ch. 6; and Brandeis, *Labor Legislation,* pp. 649–59. Brandeis acknowledges that the Wisconsin system worked best in areas where non-zero-sum solutions were attainable, and did not handle direct conflicts of interest between labor and business as effectively. She also writes insightfully (p. 659) that "Wisconsin's complete centralization probably meant that the special problems of women and children were somewhat neglected while the major attention was directed to safety and workmen's compensation."

170. See the analysis in Edwin Amenta, Elisabeth S. Clemens, Jefren Olsen, Sunita Parikh, and Theda Skocpol, "The Political Origins of Unemployment Insurance in Five American States," *Studies in American Political Development* 2 (New Haven: Yale University Press, 1987): 137–82.

171. Brandeis, *Labor Legislation,* pp. 634–35; and Robert S. Maxwell, *La Follette and the Rise of the Progressives in Wisconsin* (Madison: State Historical Society of Wisconsin, 1956), p. 64.

172. Amenta et al., "Five American States," pp. 148–50.

173. Brandeis, *Labor Legislation,* p. 653.

174. Amenta et al., "Five American States," pp. 155–56.

175. Brandeis, *Labor Legislation,* pp. 632–45. See "Factory Inspection and Labor Law Enforcement," *ALLR* 3(1) (Feb. 1913), pp. 7–40; "Duties and Organization of State Labor Departments," *ALLR* 3(4) (Dec. 1913): 512–29 (and entire number). See also the section on "Administration of Labor Laws," *ALLR* 20(2) (June 1930): 143–80, esp. "Expenditures for Labor Law Administration," pp. 174–80, which summarizes a study by Elizabeth S. Johnson of the Department of Economics, University of Wisconsin.

176. Manfred Waserman, "The Quest for a National Health Department in the Progressive Era," *Bulletin of the History of Medicine* 49 (1975): 353–80. The following account draws repeatedly on this article.

177. For the General Federation endorsements, see resolutions unanimously adopted in *Official Report of the Tenth Biennial Convention* (1910), p. 535; and *Official Report of the Eleventh Biennial Convention of the General Federation of Women's Clubs,* June 25 to July 5, San Francisco, CA, comp. and ed. Mrs. George O. Welch (GFWC, 1912), p. 600.

178. For further background on the Committee, see William J. Schieffelin, "Work of the Committee of One Hundred on National Health," *Annals of the American Academy of Political and Social Science* 37 (March 1911): 77–86; and George Rosen, "The Committee of One Hundred on National Health and the Campaign for a National Health Department, 1906–1912," *American Journal of Public Health* 62 (Feb. 1972): 261–63.

179. The campaign to establish the Children's Bureau is analyzed in Chapter 9 below.

180. William Beveridge, *Unemployment: A Problem of Industry* (London: Longmans, 1909).

181. José Harris, *Unemployment and Politics: A Study in English Social Policy, 1886–1914* (London and New York: Oxford University Press, 1972), pts. 6 and 7.

182. John B. Andrews, "A Practical Program for the Prevention of Unemployment in America," *ALLR* 5(2) (June 1915): 172–92; see also the other papers and discussions at the AALL's Second National Conference on Unemployment, Philadelphia, Dec. 28–29, 1914, and reported in this number of the *Review.* An excellent discussion of the Massachusetts Committee appears in Keyssar, *Out of Work,* pp. 265–67.

183. Pierce, "Activities of the AALL," pp. 308–13.

184. John B. Andrews, "A National System of Labor Exchanges," 63rd Congress, 3rd Session, Senate doc. no. 956 (Washington: Government Printing Office, 1915).

185. William M. Leiserson, "A Federal Reserve Board for the Unemployed:

Outlines of a Plan for Administering the Remedies for Unemployment," *Annals of the American Academy of Political and Social Science* 69 (Jan. 1917): 103–17.

186. Ibid., p. 109.

187. See J. Michael Eisner, *William Morris Leiserson: A Biography* (Madison: University of Wisconsin Press, 1967), esp. ch. 3. For an early statement by Leiserson, see "The Problem of Unemployment Today," *Political Science Quarterly* 31(1) (March 1916): 1–24, where in very Beveridgean fashion he calls unemployment "A Political and Administrative, not a Theoretical Problem" (p. 1).

188. Henry R. Seager, "Coordination of Federal, State, and City Systems of Employment Offices," *ALLR* 8(1) (March 1918): 21–26. For arguments in favor of more centralized systems at the same forum, see M. B. Hammond, "Lessons from English War Experience in the Employment of Labor," pp. 21–37; and the comment during the "General Discussion" by George E. Barnett, Professor of Political Economy, Johns Hopkins University, pp. 55–57.

189. Frederic L. Paxson, "The American War Government, 1917–1918," *American Historical Review* 26 (1920): 54–76.

190. Ibid., pp. 74–76. Paxson notes that the USES was given its strongest powers on August 1, 1918, and that by "September, 1918, the organization of the American war government was complete." The Armistice ending World War I was signed in November 1918.

191. Margarett A. Hobbs, "A National Employment Service," *ALLR* 8(4) (Dec. 1918), p. 287.

192. Ibid.

193. Ibid., p. 288.

194. Lubove, *Struggle for Social Security,* p. 156.

195. Carroll H. Wooddy, *The Growth of the Federal Government, 1915–1932* (New York: McGraw-Hill, 1934), p. 373.

196. Hobbs, "National Employment Service," p. 289.

197. See I. W. Litchfield, "United States Employment Service and Demobilization," *Annals of the American Academy of Political and Social Science* 81 (1919): 19–27. See also Ordway Tread, "The United States Employment Service and the Prevention of Unemployment," along with other papers and discussions at the late December 1918 Annual Meeting of the AALL in Richmond, VA, Session III, "Problems of Demobilization," printed in *ALLR* 9(1) (March 1919): 73–103. The AALL continued for some time to fight for particular bills to charter a "federal-state" employment service. See *ALLR* 9(2) (June 1919): 195–98, and 10(2) (June 1920), pp. 121–22.

198. Frederic L. Paxson, "The Great Demobilization," *American Historical Review* 44(2) (Jan. 1939), p. 242. See also Ruth Kellogg, *The United States Employment Service* (Chicago: University of Chicago Press, 1933).
199. Shelby M. Harrison and collaborators, *Public Employment Offices: Their Purpose, Structure and Methods* (New York: Russell Sage Foundation, 1924), p. 89.
200. Wooddy, *Growth of Federal Government*, p. 372.
201. Raymond C. Atkinson, Louise C. Odencrantz, and Ben Deming, *Public Employment Service in the United States,* published by the Committee on Public Administration of the Social Science Research Council (Chicago: Public Administration Service, 1940), pp. 19–20.
202. Paul H. Douglas and Aaron Director, *The Problem of Unemployment* (New York: Macmillan, 1931), pp. 289–91.
203. I. M. Rubinow, *Social Insurance, with Special Reference to American Conditions* (New York: Arno Press, 1969; orig. 1913), p. 11.

Introduction to Part III

1. Jill Quadagno, *Aging in Early Industrial Society: Work, Family, and Social Policy in Nineteenth-Century England* (New York: Academic Press, 1982), p. 115.
2. The illustration in Figure 16 was borrowed by the AALL from the Women's Legislative Conference of New York. In that state, women's groups mobilized to an unusual degree in support of the AALL's legislative proposal for health insurance, probably because the National Consumers' League had its headquarters in New York and formed an interpersonal and organizational link between the AALL and the federated women's clubs and local Consumers' Leagues spread across the state. In the nation as a whole, many women's clubs may have been familiar with the idea of social insurance as one way to help women and children dependent on male breadwinners. But they did not initiate or strongly promote social insurance legislation during the early 1900s.
3. I do not repeat or document specific facts about the timing and incidence of maternalist social policies here, because these facts were given in the Introduction and appear again in Chapters 7, 8, and 9 in connection with the analysis of each individual type of legislation.

6. Expanding the Separate Sphere: Women's Civic Action and Political Reforms in the Early Twentieth Century

1. Richard Evans, *The Feminists: Women's Emancipation Movements in Europe, America and Australasia, 1840–1920* (London: Croom Helm, 1977), p. 44.

2. See James Henretta, *The Evolution of American Society, 1700–1815: An Interdisciplinary Analysis* (Lexington, MA: D. C. Heath, 1973); Philip J. Greven, Jr., *Four Generations: Population, Land, and Family in Colonial Andover, Massachusetts* (Ithaca, NY: Cornell University Press, 1970): and Michael Zuckerman, *Peaceable Kingdoms: New England Towns in the Eighteenth Century* (New York: Knopf, 1970).

3. Paula Baker, "The Domestication of Politics: Women and American Political Society, 1780–1920," *American Historical Review* 85(3) (June 1984), p. 623.

4. Carroll Smith-Rosenberg, *Disorderly Conduct: Visions of Gender in Victorian America* (New York: Knopf, 1985), pp. 85–86.

5. Barbara Welter, "The Cult of True Womanhood: 1820–1860," in *The American Family in Social-Historical Perspective*, ed. Michael Gordon (New York: St. Martin's Press, 1973), p. 225; Barbara Leslie Epstein, *The Politics of Domesticity: Women, Evangelism, and Temperance in Nineteenth-Century America* (Middletown, CT: Wesleyan University Press, 1981), p. 81; and Nancy F. Cott, *The Bonds of Womanhood: "Woman's Sphere" in New England, 1780–1835* (New Haven: Yale University Press, 1977), esp. ch. 2, "Domesticity."

6. Michael E. McGerr, *The Decline of Popular Politics* (New York: Oxford University Press, 1986), chs. 1 and 2; and Baker, "Domestication of Politics," pp. 627–29. The label "party period," referring to roughly 1830–1900, comes from Richard L. McCormick, "The Party Period and Public Policy: An Exploratory Hypothesis," *Journal of American History* 66 (Sept. 1979): 279–98.

7. Baker, "Domestication of Politics," p. 629.

8. Ibid., p. 628, n. 27.

9. Welter, "Cult of True Womanhood," p. 225.

10. Ruth M. Alexander, "'We Are Engaged as a Band of Sisters': Class and Domesticity in the Washingtonian Temperance Movement, 1840–1850," *Journal of American History* 75(3) (Dec. 1988): 763–85.

11. Sheila M. Rothman, *Woman's Proper Place: A History of Changing Ideals and Practices, 1870 to the Present* (New York: Basic Books, 1978), p. 22, emphasis added.

12. Welter, "Cult of True Womanhood," p. 242.

13. Susan Porter Benson, "Business Heads and Sympathizing Hearts: The Women of the Providence Employment Society, 1837–1858," *Journal of Social History* 12 (Winter 1978), pp. 302–03; emphasis originally in the organization's Annual Report, as quoted by Benson.

14. Ibid., p. 302. According to Benson, "The Providence Employment Society (PES) was typical of the meliorist urban reform organizations that flourished in antebellum American cities alongside the better-known perfectionist evangelical movements, such as abolitionism, temperance, and communitarianism."

15. Barbara Welter, "The Feminization of American Religion: 1800–1860," pp. 137–57 in *Clio's Consciousness Raised: New Perspectives on the History of Women,* ed. Mary S. Hartman and Lois Banner (New York: Harper and Row, 1976).

16. Smith-Rosenberg, *Disorderly Conduct,* p. 130. See also Mary P. Ryan, *Cradle of the Middle Class: The Family in Oneida County, New York, 1790–1865* (Cambridge and New York: Cambridge University Press, 1981), chs. 2 and 3; and Nancy A. Hewitt, *Women's Activism and Social Change: Rochester, New York, 1822–1872* (Ithaca, NY: Cornell University Press, 1984). Ryan's and Hewett's analyses differ from Smith-Rosenberg's, but they too emphasize women's activism in a variety of reform associations. Hewett offers intriguing insights into the possibly different class bases of different types of female-based associations.

17. William L. O'Neill, *The Woman Movement: Feminism in the United States and England* (London: Allen and Unwin, 1969), p. 20.

18. Smith-Rosenberg, *Disorderly Conduct,* p. 120.

19. Ibid., p. 115.

20. Ibid., p. 122.

21. Ibid., p. 110.

22. Ruth Bordin, *Woman and Temperance: The Quest for Power and Liberty, 1873–1900* (New Brunswick, NJ: Rutgers University Press, 1990; orig. 1981), p. 3, ch. 1 generally, and appendix, "Leadership Patterns in the WCTU"; and Katherine Harris, "Feminism and Temperance Reform in the Boulder WCTU," *Frontiers* 4(2) (Summer 1979): 19–24. For an overview of women's participation in male-led temperance activities before the Civil War, see Ian R. Tyrrell, "Women and Temperance in Antebellum America, 1830–1860," *Civil War History* 28(2) (June 1982): 128–52.

23. Ruth Bordin, "'A Baptism of Power and Liberty': The Women's Crusade of 1873–1874," in *Woman's Being, Woman's Place: Female Identity and Vocation in American History* ed. Mary Kelley (Boston: G. K. Hall, 1979), p. 283.

24. Bordin, *Woman and Temperance,* ch. 3; and Epstein, *Politics of Domesticity,* pp. 118–19.

25. Epstein, *Politics of Domesticity,* pp. 119–20.

26. June O. Underwood, "Civilizing Kansas: Women's Organizations, 1880–1920," *Kansas History* 7(4) (Winter 1984–85), p. 296.

27. Quotes are from Epstein, *Politics of Domesticity,* p. 121; and Rothman, *Woman's Proper Place,* p. 67.

28. Epstein, *Politics of Domesticity,* pp. 120–25; and Rothman, *Woman's Proper Place,* pp. 67–68.

29. Willard quoted in Epstein, *Politics of Domesticity,* pp. 129–30; and in Rothman, *Woman's Proper Place,* p. 69.

30. Epstein, *Politics of Domesticity,* p. 146.

31. Bordin, *Woman and Temperance,* ch. 8.

32. Lori D. Ginsberg, "Women and the Work of Benevolence: Morality and the Work of Politics in the Northeastern United States, 1820–1885" (Ph.D. diss., Yale University, 1985), ch. 5.

33. Ibid., ch. 6.

34. Ellen Carol DuBois, *Feminism and Suffrage: The Emergence of an Independent Women's Movement in America, 1848–1869* (Ithaca, NY: Cornell University Press, 1978); and Eleanor Flexner, *Century of Struggle: The Woman's Rights Movement in the United States* (Cambridge, MA: Harvard University Press, 1959), chs. 11 and 12. Not until the turn of the twentieth century did woman suffrage broaden into a truly mass movement, and this was coincident with the adoption of arguments for the vote emphasizing women's domestically related moral concerns.

35. Karen J. Blair, *The Clubwoman as Feminist: True Womanhood Redefined, 1868–1914* (New York: Holmes and Meier, 1980), ch. 5; and Brenda K. Shelton, "Organized Mother Love: The Buffalo Women's Educational and Industrial Union, 1885–1915," *New York History* 67 (April 1986): 155–76.

36. Margaret Gibbons Wilson, *The American Woman in Transition: The Urban Influence, 1870–1920* (Westport, CT: Greenwood Press, 1979), p. 101. As the president of the GFWC, Sarah Platt Decker, explained in "The Meaning of the Woman's Club Movement," *Annals of the American Academy of Political and Social Science* 28 (July-Dec. 1906), p. 202, the "great majority of the members of the Clubs and Federations are the homemakers, the thoughtful, earnest mothers and wives, who are giving their best efforts to the solution of the problems of their own and their children's lives. They are the 'Grand Army,' the majority, the ninety percent, who make the splendid, sturdy Americanism, which must be the hope of the future."

37. Blair, *Clubwoman as Feminist,* p. 118. This paragraph draws upon Blair's ch. 4. Wonderful glimpses into the activities of early local women's clubs can be found in Underwood, "Civilizing Kansas"; Mary D. Taylor, "A Farmers' Wives Society in Pioneer Days," *Annals of Iowa* 13(1)

(July 1921): 22–31; Ann M. Bowers, "White-Gloved Feminists: An Analysis of Northwest Ohio Women's Clubs," *Hayes Historical Journal* 4(4) (Fall 1984): 38–47; Stephanie Ambrose Tubbs, "Montana Women's Clubs at the Turn of the Century," *Montana: The Magazine of Western History* 36(1) (Winter 1986): 26–35; and Megan Seaholm, "Earnest Women: The White Woman's Club Movement in Progressive Era Texas, 1880–1920," (Ph.D. diss., Rice University, 1988), ch. 3.

38. Blair, *Clubwoman as Feminist*, pp. 15–31, 39–43.

39. As quoted in ibid., p. 95. See Blair's ch. 6 for details about the formation of the General Federation and the New York State Federation.

40. Patterns of organizational growth in "frontier" areas are well analyzed in Underwood, "Civilizing Kansas"; Seaholm, "Woman's Club Movement in Texas," chs. 3 and 4; and Tubbs, "Montana Women's Clubs."

41. Wilson, *American Woman in Transition*, p. 100; and Mary I. Wood, *The History of the General Federation of Women's Clubs for the First Twenty-Two Years of Its Organization* (New York: History Department, GFWC, 1912), p. 353.

42. This issue is in a partial collection held by the Widener Library at Harvard University. The Federation's official journals changed titles frequently over the years.

43. Blair, *Clubwoman as Feminist*, p. 97.

44. Marlene Stein Wortman, "Domesticating the Nineteenth-Century American City," *Prospects: An Annual of American Cultural Studies* 3 (1977), p. 548.

45. Seaholm, "Woman's Club Movement in Texas," pp. 264–65. This dissertation is the best source available on the dynamics of national-state-local interactions within the GFWC.

46. Rheta Childe Dorr, *What Eight Million Women Want* (New York: Kraus Reprint, 1971; orig. 1910), p. 327.

47. Mrs. T. J. Bowlker, "Woman's Home-Making Function Applied to the Municipality, " *American City* 6(6) (June 1912), p. 863. The entire issue of the journal contains valuable information on the civic activities of various women's clubs, as does Mary Ritter Beard's *Woman's Work in Municipalities* (New York: D. Appleton and Co., 1915).

48. Attributed to the GFWC Civic Section in Wood, *History of the GFWC*, p. 116. This statement was part of a proposal made by the Section at the Fourth Biennial Convention of the GFWC in Denver, CO, June 21–27, 1898.

49. Blair, *Clubwoman as Feminist*, p. 100.

50. As quoted in ibid., p. 106.

51. Dorr, *What Eight Million Women Want*, p. 328.

52. Rothman, *Woman's Proper Place*, pp. 97.

53. Ibid. See also Mary Madeleine Ladd-Taylor, "Mother-Work: Ideology, Public Policy, and the Mothers' Movement, 1890–1930" (Ph.D. diss., Yale University, 1986).

54. For indications of the early tensions between educators and the National Congress of Mothers, see Harry and Bonaro Overstreet, *Where Children Come First: A Study of the P.T.A. Idea* (Chicago: National Congress of Parents and Teachers, 1949), pp. 79–80, and *A History of the Maryland Congress of Parents and Teachers* (Baltimore: Maryland Congress of Parents and Teachers, 1965), p. 196.

55. This statement was for some years part of the "Aims and Purposes of the National Congress of Mothers," as listed in a box in each issue of the organization's official journal. See, for example, *Child-Welfare Magazine* 7(2) (Oct. 1912), p. 61.

56. See *Golden Jubilee History, 1897–1947* (Chicago: National Congress of Parents and Teachers, 1947), chs. 3 and 4. In 1908, the National Congress became "the National Congress of Mothers and Parent-Teacher Associations" (ibid., p. 52), but "Mothers" was not dropped until 1924 (ibid., p. 94). By that time, the association had recently experienced explosive growth, from 190,000 in 1920 to 532,000 in 1923, chiefly via the organization of school-based local groups, and it had begun to recruit its top officers from women who had spent many prior years as Congress officials (see ibid., chs. 5 and 6). A good discussion of the evolution of the National Congress into the P.T.A. appears in Steven L. Schlossman, "Before Home Start: Notes toward a History of Parent Education in America," *Harvard Educational Review* 46(3) (Aug. 1976): 436–67.

57. *Golden Jubilee History*, pp. 15–16.

58. Ibid., chs. 1–3; and Overstreet, *Children First*, pp. 42–43.

59. *Golden Jubilee History*, p. 17. That top-down methods of organization remained in operation after 1896–97 is made clear by a "Circular of Instructions and Suggestions for Workers and Others Interested in the National Congress of Mothers" that was used in the organization around 1900. This pamphlet, to be found in the Phoebe Apperson Hearst Papers (72/204 c) held by the Bancroft Library of the University of California at Berkeley, lays out a "Plan of Organization" (pp. 12–14). State Organizers are to be appointed by the Congress President for each unorganized state. These Organizers are to seek out "Mother Regents" for each county, who in turn should appoint a Sub-Regent for each city and town, to be in charge of organizing "such Mothers' and Homemakers' Clubs as she may deem wise."

60. The "Official Call" is reprinted in *The Work and Words of the National Congress of Mothers, Proceedings of the First Annual Session* [i.e. National

Congress] *of the National Congress of Mothers,* Washington, DC, Feb. 17–19, 1897 (New York: D. Appleton and Co., 1897), pp. vii–ix. Although the GFWC publicly welcomed the emergence of the Congress, a strictly personal letter of November 2, 1896, from GFWC President Ellen M. Henrotin to Mrs. Hearst (to be found in the Phoebe Apperson Hearst Papers 72/204c, Bancroft Library, University of California, Berkeley) makes it clear that the official GFWC endorsement was accompanied by ambivalence. Mrs. Henrotin reported to Mrs. Hearst that many thoughtful women "have said to me that they should not go to the National Congress of Mothers because they so strongly disapproved of a new organization being formed and pressed upon an over-burdened world . . . they feel that another National organization distinct in itself and not related to other associations is against the tendency of the age and to be deplored." Tactfully, Henrotin suggested that "whether the Executive Committee [of the National Congress decides to] form a separate organization or not," it might consider having the new Congress "formulate programs of study, traveling libraries on this subject and use the great organizations already in existence like the National Association of Teachers, [and] existing State Federations of Women's Clubs of which there are now twenty-three." This suggestion was not accepted, as the National Mothers' Congress went on to develop its own nationwide federal organization. Yet the two federations do often seem to have cooperated on substantive projects; and no doubt their memberships overlapped.

61. Mrs. Theodore W. Birney, "Address of Welcome," *Proceedings of the First Annual Session,* pp. 9, 7.

62. Mrs. Helen H. Gardner, "The Moral Responsibility of Women in Heredity," ibid., pp. 130–47, as quoted in Overstreet, *Children First,* pp. 67–69.

63. Birney, "Address of Welcome," p. 9.

64. Mrs. Frederic Schoff, "Message from the President of the Congress," *National Congress of Mothers Magazine* 1(1) (Nov. 1906), p. 2.

65. These statistics come from *Golden Jubilee History,* pp. 76, 197, 199; Overstreet, *Children First,* p. 196; and Rothman, *Woman's Proper Place,* p. 104.

66. "National Congress of Mothers, 1897–1907" (pamphlet in the Phoebe Apperson Hearst Papers, 72/204c, Bancroft Library, University of California, Berkeley), p. 11.

67. "President Roosevelt's Address," delivered March 10, 1908, rpt. in *Proceedings of the First International Congress in America for the Welfare of the Child, held under the auspices of the National Congress of Mothers,* Washington, DC, March 10–17, 1908 (National Congress of Mothers, 1908), p. 13.

68. Ibid., pp. 15, 14–15.

69. Ibid., p. 17.

70. Epstein, *Politics of Domesticity,* p. 121; and Blair, *Clubwoman as Feminist,* pp. 111–14.

71. Dorr, *What Eight Million Women Want,* pp. 315–16.

72. Blair, *Clubwoman as Feminist,* p. 119.

73. Florence Kelley was once married; but by the time she became a reform activist living in social settlements she was divorced, and another family shared in the care of her children.

74. Mabel Newcomer, *A Century of Higher Education for American Women* (New York: Harper, 1959), ch. 2; and Joyce Antler, "The Educated Woman and Professionalization: The Struggle for a New Feminine Identity, 1890–1920" (Ph.D. diss., State University of New York at Stony Brook, 1977), pp. 27–28.

75. See Helen Lefkowitz Horowitz, *Alma Mater: Design and Experience in the Women's Colleges from Their Nineteenth-Century Beginnings to the 1930s* (Boston: Beacon Press, 1984).

76. Newcomer, *Century,* p. 12.

77. Ibid., p. 14.

78. Ibid., p. 37, table 1. See also the discussion in Barbara Miller Solomon, *In the Company of Educated Women: A Century of Women and Higher Education in America* (New Haven: Yale University Press, 1985), ch. 4.

79. Newcomer, *Century,* p. 46, table 2.

80. Ibid.

81. William L. O'Neill, *The Woman Movement: Feminism in the United States and England* (London: George Allen and Unwin, 1969), p. 44.

82. Ibid., p. 57.

83. Martha Vicinus, *Independent Women: Work and Community for Single Women, 1850–1920* (Chicago: University of Chicago Press, 1985), p. 127.

84. See Roberta Wein, "Women's Colleges and Domesticity, 1875–1918," *History of Education Quarterly* 14(1) (Spring 1974): 31–47; and Joan G. Zimmerman, "Daughters of Main Street: Culture and the Female Community at Grinnell, 1884–1917," pp. 154–70 in *Woman's Being, Woman's Place,* ed. Mary Kelley (Boston: G. K. Hall, 1979).

85. Antler, "Educated Woman," pp. 27, 380–82.

86. Smith-Rosenberg, *Disorderly Conduct,* p. 253.

87. Antler, "Educated Woman," p. 419. See also Solomon, *Educated Women,* pp. 137–38.

88. John P. Rousmaniere, "Cultural Hybrid in the Slums: The College Woman and the Settlement House, 1889–1894," *American Quarterly* 22 (1970): 45–66. Rockford Seminary, attended by Jane Addams, seems to have had similarities to the institutions Rousmaniere discusses.

89. Ibid., p. 50.
90. Ibid., pp. 50, 55.
91. Ibid., p. 54.
92. Smith-Rosenberg, *Disorderly Conduct,* pp. 253–54.
93. Ibid., p. 254.
94. Allen F. Davis, *Spearheads for Reform: The Social Settlements and the Progressive Movement, 1890–1914* (New York: Oxford University Press, 1967).
95. From the constitution of the New York University Settlement, as quoted in Robert C. Reinders, "Toynbee Hall and the American Settlement Movement," *Social Service Review* 56(1) (March 1982), p. 43.
96. Davis, *Spearheads for Reform,* p. 8; Emily K. Abel, "Toynbee Hall, 1884–1914," *Social Service Review* 53(4) (Dec. 1979): 606–32; and Werner Picht, *Toynbee Hall and the English Settlement Movement,* rev. ed., trans. Lillian A. Cowell (London: G. Bells and Sons, 1914).
97. Vicinus, *Independent Women,* p. 215.
98. Abel, "Toynbee Hall," pp. 614–15.
99. Reinders, "Toynbee Hall and American Movement," p. 48.
100. George Lansbury, as quoted in Vicinus, *Independent Women,* p. 215.
101. As quoted in Abel, "Toynbee Hall," pp. 623.
102. Ibid., pp. 622–25.
103. See Standish Meacham, *Toynbee Hall and Social Reform, 1880–1914* (New Haven: Yale University Press, 1987), esp. ch. 6, "William Beveridge: 'Benevolent, Bourgeois Bureaucrat'"; and José Harris, *William Beveridge: A Biography* (Oxford and New York: Oxford University Press, 1977).
104. Davis, *Spearheads for Reform,* chs. 1 and 2; and Reinders, "Toynbee Hall and American Movement."
105. Davis, *Spearheads for Reform,* p. 12.
106. Reinders, "Toynbee Hall and American Movement," pp. 45–50.
107. See Daniel Levine, *Jane Addams and the Liberal Tradition* (Madison: State Historical Society of Wisconsin, 1971).
108. Allen Freeman Davis, "Spearheads for Reform: The Social Settlements and the Progressive Movement, 1890–1914" (Ph.D. diss., University of Wisconsin, 1959), p. 374. This dissertation contains material not subsequently included in Davis's book.
109. Picht, *English Settlement Movement,* p. 102, reports that in 1913 there were 246 women settlement residents as compared to 189 men; thus women were 56 percent of the English settlers.
110. Davis, "Spearheads for Reform," p. 5, including n. 17; and Smith-Rosenberg, *Disorderly Conduct,* p. 254, n. 20, citing a conversation with Allen Davis.

111. Picht, *English Settlement Movement,* p. 102.

112. Ibid., pp. 102–103.

113. As quoted in Reinders, "Toynbee Hall and American Movement," p. 45.

114. As quoted in Jill Conway, "Women Reformers and American Culture, 1870–1930," *Journal of Social History* 5 (1971–72), p. 174.

115. Stephen Kalberg, "The Commitment to Career Reform: The Settlement Movement Leaders," *Social Service Review* 49 (Dec. 1975), p. 626, n. 13.

116. Martha Vicinus makes a similar point in *Independent Women,* pp. 215–16.

117. There are excellent discussions of this issue in Antler, "Educated Woman"; and Ellen Fitzpatrick, *Endless Crusade: Women Social Scientists and Progressive Reform* (New York: Oxford University Press, 1990).

118. Vicinus, *Independent Women,* p. 244; and Meta Zimmeck, "Strategies and Stratagems for the Employment of Women in the British Civil Service, 1919–1939," *Historical Journal* 27(4) (1984): 901–24.

119. A similar argument appears in Kathryn Kish Sklar, "Hull House in the 1890s: A Community of Women Reformers" *Signs* 10(4) (Summer 1985): 658–77.

120. Sources for this paragraph are Ibid.; Smith-Rosenberg, *Disorderly Conduct,* p. 255; Rothman, *Woman's Proper Place,* pp. 125–26; Davis, *Spearheads for Reform,* pp. 128, 142; and Mark Leff, "Consensus for Reform: The Mothers'-Pension Movement in the Progressive Era," *Social Service Review* 47(3) (Sept. 1973), p. 250.

121. Biographical information on Hard and the quote from McDowell's letter appear in Janet Marie Wedel, "The Origins of State Patriarchy during the Progressive Era: A Sociological Study of the Mothers' Aid Movement" (Ph.D. diss., Washington University, 1975), pp. 311–12.

122. James J. Kenneally, "Women and Trade Unions, 1870–1920: The Quandary of the Reformer," *Labor History* 14 (1973): 42–55.

123. Allen F. Davis, "The Women's Trade Union League: Origins and Organization," *Labor History* 5 (1964): 3–17.

124. Ibid., p. 12.

125. Ibid., p. 6.

126. Diane Kirkby, "'The Wage Earning Woman and the State': The National Women's Trade Union League and Protective Labor Legislation, 1903–1923," *Labor History* 28(1) (1987): 54–74; and Nancy Schrom Dye, *As Equals and As Sisters: Feminism, the Labor Movement, and the Women's Trade Union League of New York* (Columbia: University of Missouri Press, 1980). These two scholars disagree about when and exactly why the WTUL became committed to campaigns for protective

legislation, but they agree that it was a major emphasis for the organization.

127. Robin Miller Jacoby, "The Women's Trade Union League and American Feminism," *Feminist Studies* 3 (1975): 126–40.

128. Robin Miller Jacoby, "Feminism and Class Consciousness in the British and American Women's Trade Union Leagues, 1890–1925," pp. 137–60 in *Liberating Women's History: Theoretical and Critical Essays,* ed. Berenice A. Carroll (Urbana: University of Illinois Press, 1976). See also Gladys Boone, *The Women's Trade Union Leagues in Great Britain and the United States of America* (New York: Columbia University Press, 1942).

129. According to William L. O'Neill, *Everyone Was Brave* (Chicago: Quadrangle Books, 1971), p. 95: "Except for the vastly larger NAWSA [National American Women's Suffrage Association], no other feminist group seems to have attracted upper-class women in such numbers." The NCL's Annual Reports show that President John Graham Brooks was often absent from Annual Meetings.

130. Louis Lee Athey, "The Consumers' Leagues and Social Reform, 1890–1923" (Ph.D. diss., University of Delaware, 1965), ch. 2; and Maud Nathan, *The Story of an Epoch-Making Movement* (Garden City, NY: Doubleday, Page and Co., 1926).

131. Information on numbers of state and local Consumers' Leagues appears in the NCL's Annual Reports.

132. A comprehensive biography of Florence Kelley, placing her in the context of the gender politics of turn-of-the-century America, is being prepared by Kathryn Kish Sklar. Meanwhile, see Josephine Goldmark, *Impatient Crusader* (Urbana: University Press of Illinois, 1953), ch. 5.

133. Allis Rosenberg Wolfe, "Women, Consumerism, and the National Consumers' League in the Progressive Era, 1900–1923," *Labor History* 16 (1975): 378–92; and Athey, "Consumers' Leagues and Social Reform."

134. The term "public mothers" comes from Smith-Rosenberg, who develops this argument in *Disorderly Conduct,* pp. 263–64.

135. Not all of the women reform leaders of the Progressive Era believed that women thought differently from men. See the discussion of the views of Julia Lathrop in Lela B. Costin, *Two Sisters for Social Justice: A Biography of Grace and Edith Abbott* (Urbana and Chicago: University of Illinois Press, 1983), p. viii. The fact remains, however, that even Lathrop was willing to speak to the GFWC as if she did believe that women had unique qualities, as we shall see in Chapter 9.

136. See Arthur Mann, ed., *The Progressive Era: Major Issues of Interpretation,* 2nd ed. (Hinsdale, IL: Dryden Press, 1975). For more recent assessments of the literature, see Peter G. Filene, "An Obituary for 'the

Progressive Movement,'" *American Quarterly* 22(1) (Spring 1970): 20–34; Richard L. McCormick, "Progressivism: A Modern Reassessment," ch. 7 in his *The Party Period and Public Policy* (New York: Oxford University Press, 1986); and Daniel T. Rodgers, "In Search of Progressivism," *Reviews in American History* 10 (Dec. 1982): 113–32.

137. Rodgers, "Search," pp. 123–27.

138. See esp. Nancy Schrom Dye, "'Sacred Motherhood': Women and Progressive Reform" (paper presented at the Annual Meeting of the Organization of American Historians, New York, April 1986); and Kathryn Kish Sklar, "Explaining the Power of Women's Political Culture in the Creation of the American Welfare State, 1890–1930," forthcoming in *Gender and the Origins of Welfare States in Western Europe and North America,* ed. Seth Koven and Sonya Michel (London and Boston: Routledge and Kegan Paul, expected 1992).

139. For an elegant study demonstrating this point, see Maureen A. Flanagan, "Gender and Urban Political Reform: The City Club and the Woman's City Club of Chicago in the Progressive Era," *American Historical Review* 95(4) (Oct. 1990): 1032–50.

140. Davis, *Spearheads for Reform,* chs. 8 and 9.

141. Jane Addams, "Political Reform," ch. 7 in her *Democracy and Social Ethics,* ed. Anne Firor Scott (Cambridge, MA: Harvard University Press, 1964).

142. Ibid., pp. 240, 266–67.

143. Julia C. Lathrop, "The Common Sense of Civil Service," *Official Report of the Thirteenth Biennial Convention of the General Federation of Women's Clubs,* May 24–June 2, 1916, New York City, comp. and ed. Mrs. Harry L. Keefe (GFWC, 1916), pp. 440–41.

144. Ibid., pp. 441–42.

145. Ibid., p. 445.

146. Mrs. G. H. Robertson, "The State's Duty to Fatherless Children," Address to the Congress of Mothers, Washington, DC, April 25, 1911, as published in *Child-Welfare Magazine* 6(5) (Jan. 1912), p. 157.

147. Ibid.

148. *Twenty Years' Work for Child Welfare by the National Congress of Mothers and Parent-Teacher Associations, 1897–1917* (Washington: National Congress of Mothers and Parent-Teacher Associations, 1917), p. 12.

149. See "Recommendations," *Proceedings of the First International Congress in America for the Welfare of the Child,* p. 348; "Resolutions Adopted by the Second International Congress on Child Welfare" (April 26–May 2, 1911, in Washington, DC), *Child-Welfare Magazine* 5(10) (June 1911), p. 193; "Report of National President, Mrs. Frederic Schoff, for 1912–1913–1914," in *Proceedings of the Third International Congress*

on the Welfare of the Child under the auspices of the National Congress of
Mothers and Parent-Teacher Associations, Washington, DC, April 22–27,
1914 (National Congress of Mothers and Parent-Teacher Associations,
1914), p. 32; and "Resolutions Adopted by the Third International
Congress on the Welfare of the Child," in ibid., p. 180.

150. *Twenty Years,* pp. 36–38; and "Report of the National President," in
Proceedings of the Third International Congress on the Welfare of the Child,
pp. 30–31.

151. "Report of the National President," in *Proceedings of the Third International Congress on the Welfare of the Child,* p. 31. Similar close relationships between federal agencies and private associations widely organized across the country developed in the areas of agriculture and
commerce. These arrangements allowed federal bureaus without bureaucratic capacities to reach into localities. Likewise, other progressive
reform groups sought to have voluntarily organized functions incorporated into public agencies; see Robert L. Buroker, "From Voluntary
Association to Welfare State: The Illinois Immigrants' Protective
League, 1908–1926," *Journal of American History* 58 (Dec. 1971): 643–
660.

152. *Twenty Years,* pp. 19, 21.

153. Anthony M. Platt, *The Child Savers: The Invention of Delinquency,* 2nd
ed. (Chicago: University of Chicago Press, 1977).

154. In addition to the resolutions passed at the yearly conventions of the
National Congress of Mothers, one can subtantiate this point by tracing articles that appeared in *Child-Welfare Magazine* and its precursors,
along with reports of the activities of state organizations that appeared
in each monthly issue of this official journal.

155. "Resolutions Adopted by the Second International Congress on Child
Welfare," p. 192.

156. Ibid., emphasis added.

157. Mrs. Frederic Schoff, as quoted in Mary S. Garrett, "Report of Department of Legislation" in *Proceedings of the Third International Congress
on the Welfare of the Child,* p. 62. "Kindergartners" were people, mostly
women, who advocated the spread of kindergartens and "kindergarten principles" of education throughout the United States at the turn
of the century. For background on this movement, which the National
Congress of Mothers strongly supported, see Karen Wolk Feinstein,
"Kindergartens, Feminism, and the Professionalization of Motherhood," *International Journal of Women's Studies* 3(1) (Jan.–Feb. 1980):
28–38.

158. See the historical account in Miss Georgie A. Bacon, "History of the
Civil Service Reform Committee," pp. 276–78 in the *Official Report of*

the Tenth Biennial Convention of the General Federation of Women's Clubs, May 11–18, 1910, Cincinnati, OH, comp. and ed. Mrs. Henry Hollister Dawson (Newark, NJ: GFWC, 1910).

159. See the reports of the state organizations in the Official Reports for each Biennial convention, especially from 1910 onward.

160. *Official Report of the Ninth Biennial Convention of the General Federation of Women's Clubs,* June 22–30, 1908, Boston, MA, comp. and ed. Mrs. John Dickinson Sherman (Chicago: GFWC, 1908), pp. 432–33.

161. As reported in the *Official Report of the Tenth Biennial* (1910), pp. 478–79.

162. *Official Report of the Eleventh Biennial Convention of the General Federation of Women's Clubs,* June 25–July 5, 1912, San Francisco, CA, comp. and ed. Mrs. George O. Welch (GFWC, 1912), p. 119.

163. Ibid., pp. 119–20.

164. Ibid., pp. 124–25.

165. *Official Report of the Twelfth Biennial Convention of the General Federation of Women's Clubs,* June 9–19, 1914, Chicago, IL, comp. and ed. Mrs. Harry L. Keefe (Bureau of Information, GFWC, 1914), p. 119.

166. In fact, General Federation leaders joined settlement leaders in legislative lobbying as early as the 1890s, although they were "out in front" of their membership at that time. See the account by Jane Addams, *Twenty Years at Hull-House,* with a foreword by Henry Steele Commager (New York: Signet, New American Library, 1961; orig. 1910), p. 150. Later examples of representative leadership lobbying will be cited below in discussions of the passage of mothers' pensions, protective labor laws, and the federal legislation for the Children's Bureau and the Sheppard-Towner Act.

167. See, for example, the tactical discussions in Mrs. Elizabeth Earl, "What Is Wasted Effort?" as reported in *Official Report of the Twelfth Biennial* (1914), pp. 544–46; in Mrs. George F. French, "Woman as Lobbyist," as reported in *Official Report of the Thirteenth Biennial* (1916), pp. 639–42; and in Seaholm, "Woman's Club Movement in Texas," pp. 474–78.

168. *Official Report of the Tenth Biennial* (1910), pp. 370–71.

169. Oakley, "Domestic Side of Civil Service Reform," in *Official Report of the Twelfth Biennial* (1914), p. 127. Oakley quoted the first two sentences from Abraham Lincoln, giving no citations.

170. *Official Report of the Tenth Biennial* (1910), p. 381.

171. As reported by Mrs. Albion Fellows Bacon, Secretary, in *Official Report of the Twelfth Biennial* (1914), p. 539.

172. An explicit outline of this process by a Michigan Federation leader appears in Mrs. Leota W. Keil, "The Outlook," in *Official Report of the*

Tenth Biennial (1910), pp. 283–86. Not all clubs responded at once, or ever. As of 1910, about one-sixth, or 531 out of 3,192 clubs in the General Federation, reported active involvement in legislative work, although still others had "appointed Legislative committees, showing a desire to work if called upon" (ibid., p. 376). And judging from the *Official Reports* of the Biennials, the Federation's calls to state and local affiliates did become more focused and better organized over the next several years, resulting in more frequent reports of activities on specific bills by state organizations.

173. Addams, "Women's Clubs and Public Policies," in *Official Report of the Twelfth Biennial* (1914), p. 26.

174. Miss Anna L. Clark, "What Civil Service Reform Means for Women," *Federation Bulletin: A Magazine for the Club Woman* 5(2) (Nov. 1907): 49–50.

175. Mrs. Leota W. Keil, "The Outlook," in *Official Report of the Tenth Biennial* (1910), p. 284.

176. Ibid., p. 286.

177. Ibid., p. 285.

178. Wood, *History of the GFWC*, p. 47.

179. Ibid., p. 103.

180. Ibid., p. 132.

181. *Official Report of the Ninth Biennial* (1908), p. 433.

182. *Official Report of the Twelfth Biennial* (1914), p. 325.

183. *Golden Jubilee History*, p. 17.

184. *Proceedings of the First Annual Session of the National Congress of Mothers*, p. 271.

185. Mrs. Edgar A. Hall, "The Press the Greatest Ally of the Congress," *National Congress of Mothers Magazine* 3(2) (Oct. 1908): 51.

186. Mrs. Edgar A. Hall, "Message from National Press and Publicity Committee," *Child-Welfare Magazine* 7(5) (Jan. 1913), p. 190. Mrs. Hall referred to the *Ladies Home Journal* article without giving its date. The *Journal's* relationship with the Congress was longstanding. Back in July 1905, for example, the *Journal's* lead article (in volume 12(8): 3–4) was a reprint of President Roosevelt's Address on "The American Woman as a Mother," delivered to the Congress of Mothers convention in March 1905.

187. Mary Ellen Waller, "Popular Women's Magazines, 1890–1917" (Ph.D. diss., Columbia University, 1987), p. 344.

188. Anna Steese Richardson, "Making Publicity Work," in *Proceedings of the Third International Congress on the Welfare of the Child*, pp. 44–48; and in *Child-Welfare Magazine* 8 (June 1914): 410–14.

189. Ibid., p. 44.

190. Ibid., p. 45.
191. Ibid., p. 46.
192. Ibid., p. 47. For evidence of the Congress's continuing practical interest in methods for reaching and using the press, see Mrs. Hence Orme (Chairman of Press and Publicity), "Do Not Hide Your Light under a Bushel," *Child-Welfare Magazine* 12(6) (Feb. 1918): 95–96.
193. On the importance of agenda-setting in setting the stage for legislative innovations, see John W. Kingdon, *Agendas, Alternatives, and Public Policies* (Boston: Little, Brown, 1984).
194. O'Neill, *Everyone Was Brave*, p. 88.
195. Elizabeth Brandeis, "Labor Legislation and the Constitution," ch. 9 of *Labor Legislation,* in vol. 3 of *History of Labor in the United States, 1896– 1932* by John R. Commons and associates (New York: Macmillan, 1935).
196. In *Ritchie v. People,* 155 Ill. 98 (1895), the Illinois Supreme Court invalidated an 1893 law mandating eight-hour days for women workers, arguing that the law violated equal protection and freedom of contract guarantees. New York's highest court subsequently cited the Ritchie precedent in striking down a law prohibiting night work for women in *People v. Williams,* 189 N.Y. (1907). For discussion of these decisions, see Brandeis, "Labor Legislation and the Constitution," pp. 662–63, and Melvin I. Urofsky, "State Courts and Protective Legislation during the Progressive Era: A Reevaluation," *Journal of American History* 72(1) (June 1985), p. 73.
197. Justice Gray's opinion in *Commonwealth v. Beatty,* 15 Pa. Super. 5, 8, 16 (1900), quoted in Urofsky, "State Courts and Protective Legislation," p. 74.
198. For discussion of *State v. Buchanan,* 29 Wash. 602 (1902), see Joseph F. Tripp, "Progressive Jurisprudence in the West: The Washington Supreme Court, Labor Law, and the Problem of Industrial Accidents," *Labor History* 24(3) (1983), p. 346. For discussion of *State v. Muller,* 48 Ore. 252, 254 (1906) and *Wenham v. State,* 65 Neb. 394 (1902), see Urofsky, "State Courts and Protective Legislation," p. 74.
199. From *Lochner v. New York,* 198 U.S. 45 (1905), as quoted in Brandeis, "Labor Legislation and the Constitution," p. 671.
200. From the Supreme Court's opinion in *Muller v. Oregon,* 208 U.S. 412 (1908), rpt. in Louis D. Brandeis and Josephine Goldmark, *Women in Industry,* intro. Leon Stein and Philip Taft (New York: Arno Press, 1969), pp. 6–7.
201. Ibid., p. 5.

7. Safeguarding the "Mothers of the Race": Protective Legislation for Women Workers

1. Marion Cotter Cahill, *Shorter Hours: A Study of the Movement Since the Civil War* (New York: Columbia University Press, 1932).

2. Elizabeth Brandeis, *Labor Legislation,* in vol. 3 of *History of Labor in the United States, 1896–1932* by John R. Commons and associates (New York: Macmillan, 1935), p. 540.

3. Ibid., ch. 3; and Florence P. Smith, *Chronological Development of Labor Legislation for Women in the United States,* rev. Dec. 1931, Bulletin no. 66-pt. 2, Women's Bureau, U.S. Department of Labor (Washington: Government Printing Office, 1932).

4. Brandeis, *Labor Legislation,* pp. 501–06.

5. J. Stanley Lemons, *The Woman Citizen: Social Feminism in the 1920s* (Urbana: University of Illinois Press, 1975), pp. 25–32.

6. Brandeis, *Labor Legislation,* pp. 461–64, 662–63; and Judith A. Baer, *The Chains of Protection: The Judicial Response to Women's Labor Legislation* (Westport, CT: Greenwood Press, 1978), pp. 31–32, 51–53.

7. My account of the Illinois events draws from Ralph Scharnau, "Elizabeth Morgan, Crusader for Labor Reform," *Labor History* 14 (1973): 340–51; Meredith Tax, *The Rising of Women: Feminist Solidarity and Class Conflict, 1880–1917* (New York and London: Monthly Review Press, 1980), pt. 2; Joseph Candela, "The Struggle to Limit the Hours and Raise the Wages of Working Women in Illinois, 1893–1917," *Social Service Review* 53(1) (March 1979): 15–34; and esp. Kathryn Kish Sklar, "Hull House in the 1890s: A Community of Women Reformers," *Signs* 10(4) (Summer 1985): 658–77.

8. Jane Addams, *Twenty Years at Hull-House,* with a foreword by Henry Steele Commager (New York: Signet, New American Library, 1961; orig. 1910), pp. 150–51.

9. Brandeis, *Labor Legislation,* pp. 466–71.

10. Ibid., pp. 662, 672.

11. Joseph F. Tripp, "Progressive Jurisprudence in the West: The Washington Supreme Court, Labor Law, and the Problem of Industrial Accidents," *Labor History* 24(3) (1983): 342–65.

12. Brandeis, *Labor Legislation,* p. 459; see also pp. 474–79.

13. Ibid., p. 459, nn. 14 and 15, and p. 474.

14. For discussion and examples, see Jacob Andrew Lieberman, "Their Sisters' Keepers: The Women's Hours and Wages Movement in the United States, 1890–1925" (Ph.D. diss., Columbia University, 1971), pp. 14–23; and Clara M. Beyer, *History of Labor Legislation for Women in Three States,* Bulletin no. 66-pt. 1, Women's Bureau, U.S. Department of Labor (Washington: Government Printing Office, 1929),

pp. 6, 19, 32–33, 121. Beyer's summary discussion (p. 6) strikes me as more pessimistic about the role of statistics bureaus in promoting new legislation than the facts in her case studies suggest.

15. Beyer, *History of Labor Legislation,* pp. 71–72.
16. Ibid., p. 4.
17. Ibid., pp. 3–4.
18. Ibid., p. 5.
19. Ibid., pp. 5–8 and ch. 3.
20. At the launching of the AALL, one of its founders, Professor Richard Ely, declared that "Our association draws no fixed line between legislation for adult males and for women and children." This statement from the first Annual Meeting of the AALL is quoted in Lieberman, "Their Sisters' Keepers," p. 92, n. 72.
21. Lloyd F. Pierce, "The Activities of the American Association for Labor Legislation in Behalf of Social Security and Protective Labor Legislation" (Ph.D. diss., University of Wisconsin, 1953), pp. 368–75.
22. The attitudes of early organized labor toward women workers are explored in James J. Kenneally, "Women and Trade Unions, 1870–1920," *Labor History* 14 (1973): 42–55.
23. Beyer, *Labor Legislation for Women,* p. 2, discusses such efforts by the New York metal polishers and the New York and Massachusetts molders. For the (limited) incidence across the states of laws of this sort, see Smith, *Chronological Development,* pp. 169–73. For a more general treatment of unions' motives for restricting women's work, see Alice Kessler-Harris, *Out to Work: A History of Wage-Earning Women in the United States* (New York: Oxford University Press, 1982), pp. 201–05.
24. A good overview of the AFL's changing positions appears in Brandeis, *Labor Legislation,* pp. 555–57.
25. Ibid., p. 557.
26. Ibid.
27. Beyer, *Labor Legislation for Women,* p. 17. For discussion of a similar situation in New York, see Irwin Yellowitz, *Labor and the Progressive Movement in New York State, 1897–1916* (Ithaca, NY: Cornell University Press, 1965), p. 103.
28. Ibid., p. 122; Scharnau, "Elizabeth Morgan, Crusader for Labor Reform"; and Dennis Irven Harrison, "The Consumers' League of Ohio: Women and Reform, 1909–1937" (Ph.D. diss., Case Western Reserve University, 1975), p. 35.
29. Beyer, *Labor Legislation for Women,* pp. 10–11, 120; and Diane Kirkby, "'The Wage-Earning Woman and the State': The National Women's Trade Union League and Protective Labor Legislation, 1903–1923," *Labor History* 28(1) (1987): 54–74.
30. Beyer, *Labor Legislation for Women,* p. 3.

31. Ibid., pp. 3, 122–24; and John L. Shover, "The Progressives and the Working Class Vote in California," *Labor History* 10(4) (Fall 1969): 584–601.

32. Joseph Frederick. Tripp, "Progressive Labor Laws in Washington State (1900–1925)" (Ph.D. diss., University of Washington, 1973), pp. 6, 81–83.

33. Harrison, "Consumers' League of Ohio," pp. 35–36.

34. Yellowitz, *Labor and Progressives in New York,* pp. 101–107; and Beyer, *Labor Legislation for Women,* p. 3 and ch. 3.

35. See the respective state Presidents' Reports in the "State News" section of *Child-Welfare Magazine* 13(10–11) (June-July 1919): 309, 320. For evidence of national leaders' support for the Women's Bureau, see ibid. 13(9) (May 1919), p. 249, and 16(10) (June 1922), p. 257.

36. Ibid. 8(7) (March 1914), p. 250.

37. *Summary Statement of the Work of the First Year of the National Consumers' League, May 1, 1899 to May 1, 1900* (New York: NCL, 1900), pp. 8, 10. Except for the years 1908–1909, 1910, and 1911, the NCL Annual Reports I cite were obtained on microfilm at the Schlesinger Library, Radcliffe College, Cambridge, Massachusetts.

38. *National Consumers' League Report for the Years 1914–1915–1916* (New York: NCL, 1917), p. 22.

39. Louis Lee Athey, "The Consumers' Leagues and Social Reform, 1890–1923" (Ph.D. diss., University of Delaware, 1965), p. 60 and ch. 3.

40. This pamphlet comes from the Schlesinger Library, Radcliffe College, Vertical Files, National Consumers' League #2. Although the pamphlet is undated, I have guessed at its approximate date based on when hour laws passed and when key court cases occurred.

41. *NCL Report for 1914–16,* p. 28.

42. For the directories I used, see *National Consumers' League Sixth Annual Report, Year Ending March 1, 1905* (New York: NCL, 1905), pp. 59–70; and *National Consumers' League Report for the Year Ending January 19, 1912* (New York: NCL, 1912), pp. 49–61. The twenty states that had leagues in 1905 were California, Colorado, Connecticut, Illinois, Iowa, Kentucky, Maine, Maryland, Massachusetts, Michigan, New Jersey, New York, Ohio, Oregon, Pennsylvania, Rhode Island, Tennessee, Utah, Vermont, and Wisconsin. The seventeen states that had leagues in 1912 were Connecticut, Delaware, Illinois, Indiana, Kentucky, Maine, Maryland, Massachusetts, Missouri, New Jersey, New York, Ohio, Oregon, Pennsylvania, Rhode Island, Tennessee, and Wisconsin.

43. Maud Nathan, *The Story of an Epoch-Making Movement* (Garden City, NY: Doubleday, Page and Co., 1926), pp. 144–45.

44. I base these assessments on the "Reports of the State Consumers' Leagues" helpfully summarized in ibid., appendix G, pp. 151, 160, 221. For Maine, one cannot conclude much, because Nathan (p. 167) simply says that the league of 1904–1913 did not send reports to the National League.
45. For information on these state leagues, see ibid., appendix G; and Athey, "Consumers' Leagues and Social Reform," esp. pp. 50–69. NCL Annual Reports also contain reports of the activities of state leagues, and this information is included at various points in ch. 3 of Lieberman, "Their Sisters' Keepers."
46. This is the argument of Harrison, "Consumers' League of Ohio."
47. Nathan, *Epoch-Making Movement,* appendix G, pp. 198–205.
48. "Report of the Committee on Legislation and the Legal Defense of Labor Laws," *NCL Report for 1912,* p. 27.
49. The discussion of Consumers' Leagues' geographical spread in this paragraph draws upon Athey, "Consumers' Leagues and Social Reform," pp. 47–49; Nathan, *Epoch-Making Movement,* appendix G; and the directories of the NCL Annual Reports.
50. Indications appear below of cooperation between the NCL and the GFWC. Cross-references frequently appear in the (respective) Annual and Biennial Reports of these associations.
51. Florence Kelley, "Twenty-five Years of the Consumers' League Movement," *Survey* 35 (Nov. 27, 1915), p. 212.
52. Clement E. Vose, "The National Consumers' League and the Brandeis Brief," *Midwest Journal of Political Science* 1 (Nov. 1957), p. 277, n. 18, citing a 1935 Consumers' League pamphlet.
53. Athey, "Consumers' Leagues and Social Reform," pp. 205–13. The following account is also based on Vose, "Brandeis Brief," pp. 276–79; and Josephine Goldmark, *Impatient Crusader: Florence Kelley's Life Story* (Urbana: University of Illinois Press, 1953), ch. 13.
54. The Brandeis brief is reprinted, along with the Court's decision, in Louis D. Brandeis and Josephine Goldmark, *Women in Industry,* intro. Leon Stein and Philip Taft (New York: Arno Press, 1969). A helpful discussion of the brief is to be found in Judith A. Baer, *The Chains of Protection: The Judicial Response to Women's Labor Legislation* (Westport, CT: Greenwood Press, 1978), pp. 57–61.
55. See Athey, "Consumers' Leagues and Social Reform," pp. 219–21. In 1917, the Supreme Court ruled in favor of an hour law for men in this case, but by that time the AFL had become opposed even to eight-hour statutes covering male workers, and this persuaded many state federations to oppose or deemphasize such laws, including the California Federation of Labor, which had previously worked for them.

See Gerald D. Nash, "The Influence of Labor on State Policy, 1860–1920: The Experience of California," *California Historical Quarterly* 42 (Sept. 1963), p. 244.

56. "Report of the Secretary," in *National Consumers' League, Tenth Report for Two Years Ending March 2, 1909,* published as *The Consumers' Control of Production: The Work of the National Consumers' League,* Supplement to the *Annals of the American Academy of Political and Social Science* (Philadelphia: American Academy of Political and Social Science, July 1909), p. 20. See also the minutes of "The Ninth Annual Session of the Council [1908]," ibid., p. 11, where Kelley reported about "carrying out the resolution of last year regarding investigation of working women and children." "In this investigation," Kelley reportedly said, "co-operation by State Leagues had not proved helpful. Successful comprehensive investigation carried out on a basis of voluntary co-operation seemed impossible. The investigation so far as it had gone had been carried on by one of the office staff of the National League."

57. As quoted in Josephine Goldmark, "Report of the Publication Committee," in ibid., p. 41.

58. Minutes of "The Ninth Annual Session of the Council," in ibid., p. 13.

59. Vose, "Brandeis Brief," p. 278. The phrases quoted come from the table of contents of Josephine Goldmark, *Fatigue and Efficiency: A Study in Industry,* a Russell Sage Foundation book, 3rd ed. (New York: Survey Associates, 1913), p. xi.

60. Athey, "Consumers' Leagues and Social Reform," p. 214.

61. Ibid., pp. 213–14.

62. *NCL Tenth Report,* p. 22.

63. "Report of the Secretary," in *National Consumers' League Report for the Year Ending March 1, 1910,* published as *The Work of the National Consumers' League During the Year Ending March 1, 1910,* Supplement to the *Annals of the American Academy of Political and Social Science* (Philadelphia: Academy of Political and Social Science, Sept. 1910), p. 18.

64. Addams, *Twenty Years at Hull-House,* p. 151.

65. As quoted in Mary I. Wood, *The History of the General Federation of Women's Clubs for the First Twenty-Two Years of Its Organization* (New York: History Department, GFWC, 1912), pp. 71–72.

66. Ibid., p. 109.

67. Ibid., p. 110. Later, the Federation apparently found it more practical to back off from eight-hour limits and call, instead, for a ten-hour limit for women workers. See *Official Report of the Ninth Biennial Convention of the General Federation of Women's Clubs,* Boston, MA, June 22–30, 1908, comp. Mrs. John Dickinson (Chicago: GFWC, 1908), p. 434.

68. Ibid., p. 111.
69. Ibid., pp. 125–26.
70. See ibid., pp. 134–35, 144–47, 173, 212, 242; *Report of the Ninth Biennial* (1908), p. 434; and *Official Report of the Thirteenth Biennial Convention of the General Federation of Women's Clubs,* May 24–June 2, 1916, comp. and ed. Mrs. Harry L. Keefe (GFWC, 1916), pp. 505–507.
71. *Official Report of the Tenth Biennial Convention of the General Federation of Women's Clubs,* Cincinnati, OH, May 11–18, 1910, comp. and ed. Mrs. Henry Hollister Dawson (Newark, NJ: GFWC, 1910), p. 360.
72. Wood, *History of the GFWC,* pp. 139, 145.
73. Ibid., pp. 145, 211–12, and 214; *Official Report of the Thirteenth Biennial* (1916), p. 634.
74. *Official Report of the Tenth Biennial* (1910), pp. 387–89.
75. *Official Report of the Ninth Biennial* (1909), p. 195.
76. Ibid., p. 233.
77. Ibid., p. 212.
78. *Official Report of the Tenth Biennial* (1910), p. 351. Since the eight-hour measure did not formally become law until 1911, the Washington Federation must have been talking about the initial steps in its enactment.
79. See the "State Reports" in the *Official Report of the Eleventh Biennial Convention of the General Federation of Women's Clubs,* San Francisco, CA, June 25–July 5, 1912, comp. and ed. Mrs. George O. Welch (GFWC, 1912), pp. 469, 475, 478, 485, 487, 489, 497, 505, 508, 520, 530, 532, 541.
80. See the "State Reports" in the *Official Report of the Twelfth Biennial Convention of the General Federation of Women's Clubs,* Chicago, IL, June 9–19, 1914, comp. and ed. Mrs. Harry L. Keefe (Bureau of Information, GFWC, 1914), pp. 287, 290, 292, 318, 333, 337.
81. See the "State Reports" in the *Report of the Thirteenth Biennial* (1916), pp. 224, 244.
82. James T. Patterson, "Mary Dewson and the American Minimum Wage Movement," *Labor History* 5(2) (Spring 1964), pp. 139–40; Lieberman, "Their Sisters' Keepers," ch. 7; and Athey, "Consumers' Leagues and Social Reform," ch. 7, "The Battle for the Minimum Wage."
83. *NCL Tenth Report,* p. 31.
84. Ibid.; *NCL Report for 1910,* p. 45; and *Report for Year Ending February 1, 1911, National Consumers' League,* published as *Work of National Consumers' League,* vol. 2 (Philadelphia: American Academy of Political and Social Science, 1911), p. 43. The publication of the magazine articles was reported in these Consumers' League Annual Reports.

85. The full citations are Elizabeth Beardsley Butler, *Women and the Trades: Pittsburgh, 1907–1908*, vol. 1 of the Pittsburgh Survey, in 6 vols. (New York: Charities Publication Committee, Russell Sage Foundation, 1909); and *Report on the Condition of Women and Child Wage-Earners in the United States*, 19 vols., U.S. Congress, Senate, 61st Congress, 2nd sess.; 62nd Congress, 1st and 2nd sess., doc. no. 645 (Washington: Government Printing Office, 1910–1915). Other studies published at this time included Edith Abbott, *Women in Industry: A Study in American Economic History* (New York: D. Appleton and Co., 1910); Annie M. MacLean, *Wage-Earning Women* (New York: Macmillan, 1910); and Louise M. Bosworth, *The Living Wage of Women Workers* (Philadelphia: American Academy of Political and Social Science, 1911).

86. Goldmark, *Impatient Crusader,* p. 133.

87. See Florence Kelley's discussion of the experiences of the Consumers' League of the City of New York in "Minimum-Wage Laws," *Journal of Political Economy* 20(10) (Dec. 1912), pp. 1005–06.

88. Athey, "Consumers' Leagues and Social Reform," pp. 171–73.

89. *NCL Tenth Report,* p. 18.

90. *NCL Report for 1910,* pp. 3, 21; and *NCL Report for 1911,* pp. 3, 51–52. For examples of John A. Ryan's writings, see *Living Wage* (New York: Macmillan, 1906); "Minimum Wage Legislation," *Catholic World* 96 (Feb. 1913): 577–86; and "Minimum Wage Laws to Date," *Catholic World* 100 (Jan. 1915): 433–42.

91. For writings by Arthur N. Holcombe see "Legal Minimum Wage in the United States," *American Economic Review* 2 (March 1912): 21–37; "Minimum Wage in Practice," *New Republic* 1 (Jan. 16, 1915): 16–18; and "What Is the Minimum Wage?" *Survey* 29 (Oct. 19, 1912): 74–76. For writings by Henry Rogers Seager, see "Minimum Wage as Part of a Program for Social Reform," *Annals of the American Academy of Political and Social Science* 48 (July 1913): 3–12; and "Theory of the Minimum Wage," *American Labor Legislation Review* 3 (Feb. 1913): 81–91.

92. See *Selected Articles on Minimum Wage,* comp. Mary Katherine Reely, Debaters' Handbook Series (White Plains and New York, NY: H. W. Wilson Co., 1917), which includes an excellent bibliography.

93. Margaret Dreier Robins, "The Minimum Wage," selection from her presidential address to the Fourth Biennial Convention, National Women's Trade Union League, St. Louis, June 2, 1913, rpt. in *Selected Articles on Minimum Wage,* p. 20; Beyer, *History of Labor Legislation for Women in Three States,* p. 56; and Gladys Boone, *The Women's Trade Union Leagues in Great Britain and the United States of America* (New York: Columbia University Press, 1942), pp. 112–16.

94. Goldmark, *Impatient Crusader,* pp. 132–41. Kelley's speech appears in *Survey* 33 (Feb. 6, 1915).

95. Donald Bruce Johnson, comp., *National Party Platforms,* vol. 1, *1840–1956,* rev. ed. (Urbana: University of Illinois Press, 1978), p. 177.

96. This account of the Massachusetts minimum wage campaign is based on Beyer, *Labor Legislation for Women in Three States,* pp. 55–61.

97. Brandeis, *Labor Legislation,* pp. 511–12.

98. Ibid., pp. 512–13; and Kelley, "Minimum-Wage Laws," p. 999.

99. In addition to the works by Athey, Beyer, Brandeis, Goldmark, and Kelley cited in the preceding notes for this section, my chief source on state-level activities is "Reports of the State Consumers' Leagues," appendix G in Nathan, *Epoch-Making Movement,* pp. 138–223. Nathan served for many years as the president of the New York Consumers' League and as the vice president of the National Consumers' League, and she summarizes the information that state leagues reported to the national level over the years, and gives the years that most leagues were in existence.

100. My assessment of the Indiana and Tennessee leagues is based on the information in ibid., pp. 160, 221; and my speculation about the Rhode Island league is based on ibid., pp. 214–21, where many efforts are discussed but *not* any campaign for a minimum wage law, and the statement is made that "Legislation for women has met with strong opposition because the state is industrial, and progress has therefore been slow."

101. See the useful comparison of the U.S. laws to those of Australia, New Zealand, and England in *The Development of Minimum-Wage Laws in the United States, 1912–1927,* Bulletin no. 61, Women's Bureau, U.S. Department of Labor (Washington: Government Printing Office, 1928), pp. 1–3.

102. See the arguments made in the works cited in notes 90–92 above.

103. Kelley, "Minimum-Wage Laws," p. 1009–10.

104. Ibid., p. 1003.

105. See the excellent discussion in Eli Zaretsky, "The Place of the Family in the Origins of the Welfare State," pp. 188–224 in *Rethinking the Family: Some Feminist Questions,* ed. Barrie Thorne with Marilyn Yalom (New York: Longmans, 1982), esp. pp. 211–18.

106. Kelley, "Minimum-Wage Laws," pp. 1002–03.

107. Diane Kirkby, "'The Wage Earning Woman and the State': The National Women's Trade Union League and Protective Labor Legislation, 1903–1923," *Labor History* 28 (1) (1987): 54–74.

108. "Minimum Wage Law Upheld in Oregon," *Survey* 31 (8) (Nov. 22,

1913), p. 191, characterizing the opinion of Judge Cleeton of the Circuit Court of Multnomah County, where the first challenge to the 1913 Oregon minimum wage law was adjudicated. See also Athey, "Consumers' Leagues and Social Reform," p. 224; and Goldmark, *Impatient Crusader,* p. 63.

109. Brandeis, *Labor Legislation,* p. 514. For the full story, see Norris C. Hundley, Jr., "Katherine Philips Edson and the Fight for the California Minimum Wage, 1912–1923," *Pacific Historical Review* 29 (1960): 271–85; and Jacqueline R. Braitman, "Katherine Philips Edson: A Progressive-Feminist in California's Era of Reform" (Ph.D. diss., University of California, Los Angeles, 1988), chs. 5 and 6.

110. Edith Hess, "State Regulation of Woman and Child Labor in Kansas," in *Collections of the Kansas State Historical Society, 1919–1922,* vol. 15, ed. William E. Connelley (Topeka: Kansas State Printing Plant, 1923), p. 306.

111. Ibid.

112. Ibid., p. 308. On the supporters of the minimum wage and other legislation for women in Kansas, see Robert Sherman La Forte, *Leaders of Reform: Progressive Republicans in Kansas, 1900–1916* (Lawrence: University Press of Kansas, 1974), pp. 220, 231, 241. Women could vote in Kansas after 1912, and an important leader of the Progressive Party movement, which pressured the Republicans toward many reforms, was Mrs. Eva Morley Murphey, an officer in both the Women's Christian Temperance Union and the Kansas Federation of Women's Clubs.

113. Kelley, "Minimum-Wage Laws," p. 1003.

114. Athey, "Consumers' Leagues and Social Reform," pp. 224–28.

115. Father O'Hara is quoted in "Minimum Wage Law Upheld in Oregon," p. 191.

116. Quoted and characterized from the 1913 and 1915 National Conventions of the National Association of Manufacturers by Joseph F. Tripp, "Toward an Efficient and Moral Society: Washington State Minimum-Wage Law, 1913–1925," *Pacific Northwest Quarterly* 67 (1976), p. 100, n. 10. See also the business and conservative arguments summarized in Lieberman, "Their Sisters' Keepers," pp. 296, 397–403; in Susan Lehrer, *Origins of Protective Labor Legislation for Women, 1905–1925* (Albany: State University of New York Press, 1987), pp. 66–71 and ch. 8; and in *Selected Articles on Minimum Wage.*

117. Lehrer, *Origins of Protective Legislation,* pp. 151–57.

118. Tripp, "Washington State Minimum-Wage Law."

119. W. M. W. Splawn, "A Review of the Minimum Wage Theory and Practice with Special Reference to Texas," *Southwestern Political Science*

Quarterly 1(4) (March 1921), p. 347, n. 1, summarizing information compiled by Miss Octavia Rogan of the State Library.

120. Robert L. Morlan, *Political Prairie Fire: The Non-Partisan League, 1915–1922* (Minneapolis: University of Minnesota Press, 1955), pp. 65–66 and ch. 10, esp. p. 237.

121. As quoted in Joseph L. Candela, "The Struggle to Limit the Hours and Raise the Wages of Working Women in Illinois, 1893–1917," *Social Service Review* 53(1) (March 1979), p. 24.

122. Brandeis, *Labor Legislation,* pp. 511–12; and Tripp, "Washington State Minimum-Wage Law," p. 101.

123. Candela, "Struggle to Limit Hours and Raise Wages in Illinois," p. 24.

124. Benjamin Parke De Witt, *The Progressive Movement: A Non-partisan, Comprehensive Discussion of Current Tendencies in American Politics* (New York: Macmillan, 1915), p. 257.

125. See the sources for Table 8.

126. *Official Report of the Eleventh Biennial* (1912), pp. 191–93; and *Official Report of the Twelfth Biennial* (1914), p. 360.

127. See the sources for Table 8.

128. See the respective State Reports in *Official Report of Twelfth Biennial* (1914), pp. 333, 293; and *Official Report of the Thirteenth Biennial* (1916), pp. 191, 212.

129. *Official Report of the Eleventh Biennial* (1912), pp. 191–92.

130. Hundley, "Edson and Fight for California Minimum Wage."

131. Beyer, *Labor Legislation for Women in Three States,* p. 129.

132. Ibid.

133. Ibid., pp. 129–30.

134. Ibid., p. 131.

135. See Candela, "Struggle to Limit Hours and Raise Wages in Illinois," p. 24; Brandeis, *Labor Legislation,* pp. 519–22 on Ohio; Beyer, *Labor Legislation for Women in Three States,* pp. 97–98 on New York; and Lieberman, "Their Sisters' Keepers," pp. 397–403 on New York, Ohio, Connecticut, and elsewhere. Lieberman stresses organized business opposition to proposed minimum wage bills.

136. J. Stanley Lemons, *The Woman Citizen: Social Feminism in the 1920s* (Urbana: University of Illinois Press, 1975), pp. 31–32.

137. Ibid., p. 26.

138. Ibid., p. 27.

139. Ibid. See also Lieberman, "Their Sisters' Keepers," pp. 356–60.

140. Athey, "Consumers' Leagues and Social Reform," p. 165.

141. Lemons, *Woman Citizen,* p. 27.

142. This was how the Secretary of Labor described the Bureau's purpose. He is quoted in *Second Annual Report of the Director of the Women's*

Bureau for the Fiscal Year Ended June 30, 1920, Women's Bureau, U.S. Department of Labor (Washington: Government Printing Office, 1920), p. 3.

143. Athey, "Consumers' Leagues and Social Reform," pp. 166–67; and Lemons, *Woman Citizen,* pp. 28–29.

144. *First Annual Report of the Director of the Woman in Industry Service for the Fiscal Year Ended June 30, 1919,* Woman in Industry Service, U.S. Department of Labor (Washington: Government Printing Office, 1919), pp. 6–8, 27–29.

145. Lemons, *Woman Citizen,* p. 30.

146. *First Annual Report of Woman in Industry Service* (1919), pp. 25–26.

147. Elizabeth Tilton, National Chairman of the Department of Legislation, "Welfare Legislation," *Child-Welfare Magazine* 16(10) (June 1922), p. 257.

148. Lemons, *Woman Citizen,* pp. 30–31.

149. Selected from 81 titles listed in "Publications of the Women's Bureau," *Women in Florida Industries,* Bulletin no. 80, Women's Bureau, U.S. Department of Labor (Washington: Government Printing Office, 1930), pp. 114–15.

150. A critical discussion of the 1928 Women's Bureau study appears in Sheila Rothman, *Woman's Proper Place* (New York: Basic Books, 1978), pp. 163–64.

151. Lemons, *Woman Citizen,* p. 138.

152. Smith, *Chronological Development of Labor Legislation for Women in the United States.*

153. As quoted in Athey, "Consumers' Leagues and Social Reform," pp. 226. I have relied heavily on Athey's ch. 8, "Legal Defense of Labor Legislation."

154. Florence Kelley, "The Minimum Wage Law in Oregon under Fire," *Survey* 31(24) (March 14, 1914): 740–41.

155. Brandeis, *Labor Legislation,* p. 690.

156. *Adkins v. Children's Hospital,* 261 U.S. 525, pp. 544–54, 557–59, as discussed and cited in Lieberman, "Their Sisters' Keepers," p. 414. See also the recent excellent discussion in Joan G. Zimmerman, "The Jurisprudence of Equality: The Women's Minimum Wage, the First Equal Rights Amendment, and *Adkins v. Childen's Hospital, 1905–1923," Journal of American History* 78(1) (June 1991): 188–225.

157. Lieberman, "Their Sisters' Keepers," pp. 423–34.

8. An Unusual Victory for Public Benefits: The "Wildfire Spread" of Mothers' Pensions

1. Children's Bureau, U.S. Department of Labor, *Mothers' Aid, 1931,* Publication no. 220 (Washington: Government Printing Office, 1933), p. 2.
2. Roosevelt's remarks are cited in Mark Leff, "Consensus for Reform: The Mothers'-Pension Movement in the Progessive Era," *Social Service Review* 47(3) (Sept. 1973), p. 399.
3. For this point, I am indebted to Matthew Crenson.
4. U.S. Congress, Senate, *Proceedings of the Conference on the Care of Dependent Children,* 60th Congress, 2nd sess., 1909, Senate doc. 721 (Washington: Government Printing Office, 1909), pp. 9–10; emphasis added. Many scholars have joined Mark Leff in misleadingly treating the 1909 Conference as the kickoff of the mothers' pension movement. The one account I have seen that cautions against this is Janet Marie Wedel, "The Origins of State Patriarchy during the Progressive Era: A Sociological Study of the Mothers' Aid Movement" (Ph.D. diss., Washington University, St. Louis, 1975), ch. 7, "The Origins of the Mothers' Aid Movement." This chapter and the next are very informative, especially on the role of William Hard of the *Delineator* magazine. However, even Wedel overlooks the evidence I present below about the early timing of the interventions by the National Congress of Mothers.
5. On the controversies, see Leff, "Consensus for Reform," pp. 402–04; Roy Lubove, *The Struggle for Social Security, 1900–1935* (Pittsburgh: University of Pittsburgh Press, 1986; orig. 1968), pp. 101–06; Horace Sorel Tishler, *Self-Reliance and Social Security, 1870–1917* (Port Washington, NY: Kennikat Press, 1971), ch. 7; and Susan Tiffin, *In Whose Best Interest? Child Welfare Reform in the Progressive Era* (Westport, CT: Greenwood Press, 1982), pp. 126–29.
6. For example, Mrs. Hannah Einstein, a member of the governing board of the United Hebrew Charities, was a strong proponent of mothers' pensions; and she served as a member of the New York State Commission on Relief of Widowed Mothers, which proposed such legislation in 1914.
7. Mary Ritter Beard, *Woman's Work in Municipalities* (New York: D. Appleton and Co., 1915), p. 251.
8. For the best quick overview of the arguments made for and against mothers' pensions see Edna D. Bullock, ed., *Selected Articles on Mothers' Pensions* (White Plains and New York, NY: H. W. Wilson Co., 1915). This volume was prepared as part of the Debaters' Handbook Series

for students, and it organizes and reprints magazine and journal articles from both sides of the public debate. It also offers an extensive bibliography. By the time it appeared, mothers' pension laws had already passed in 23 states (see p. 1).

9. Mary E. Richmond, "Motherhood and Pensions," *Survey* 29 (March 1, 1913), p. 775. Richmond was the director of the Charity Organization Department at the Russell Sage Foundation, and the *Survey* was the official organ of the National Council of Charities and Corrections. Her article was widely reprinted and also circulated as a pamphlet. It is only fair to point out that Richmond made additional arguments against mothers' pensions, some quite telling in light of what subsequently happened. Richmond objected to the barriers some mothers' pension bills would place in the way of women working outside the home; and she complained that the devotion of public resources to these pensions might delay other constructive policies, such as measures to improve public health or social services for children. In a private communication, Sonya Michel has pointed out to me that advocates of day care services for working mothers also tended to oppose mothers' pensions.

10. Ibid., pp. 776–78. The worries about political corruption evidenced in Richmond's article may account, in part, for the intensely negative reaction some leading social workers had against the short-lived efforts of one Henry Neil, an Illinois probation officer who tried to launch a national "Mothers' Pension League," based on membership dues, to promote this kind of legislation. This occurred after Mr. Neil played some role in passing the 1911 Illinois statute and in turning a 1907 Pennsylvania statute into a justification for making payments directly to widows rather than to charity organizations. The little information we have about the Mothers' Pension League comes from angry exchanges between Henry Neil and social workers. See "Henry Neil: Pension Agent," *Survey* 29(18) (Feb. 1, 1913): 559–61; and "The Henry Neil League for Mothers' Pensions" and "Communication," *Survey* 29(25) (March 22, 1913), pp. 849–51, 891.

11. Beard, *Woman's Work in Municipalities,* p. 251.

12. Quoted from a letter published in the *Survey* 30(22) (Aug. 30, 1913): p. 669, responding to Dr. Edward T. Devine, "Pensions for Mothers," *Survey* 30(14) (July 5, 1913): 457–60.

13. Lubove, *Struggle for Social Security,* p. 100; and L. A. Halbert, "The Widows' Allowance Act in Kansas City," *Survey* 31 (Feb. 28, 1914): 675–76.

14. Wedel, "Origins of State Patriarchy," pp. 264–65. See also Lubove, *Struggle for Social Security,* p. 100; and Libba Gage Moore, "Mothers'

Pensions: The Origins of the Relationship between Women and the Welfare State" (Ph.D. diss., University of Massachusetts, 1986), p. 126.

15. Moore, "Mothers' Pensions," p. 130. On the later involvement of Illinois women's groups in working for expansions of eligibility and funding for mothers' pensions, see the text and note 163 below.

16. Leff, "Consensus for Reform," pp. 400–01; and Charles Larsen, *The Good Fight: The Life and Times of Ben B. Lindsey* (Chicago: Quadrangle Books, 1972), pp. 73–74. According to Tiffin, *In Whose Best Interest,* pp. 122–23, other juvenile court judges active in campaigns for mothers' pensions included Judge Babst in Ohio and Judge Curtis Dwight Wilbur in California.

17. Leff, "Consensus for Reform," p. 405.

18. See Rubinow, *Social Insurance, With Special Reference to American Conditions* (New York: Arno Press and the New York Times, 1969; orig. 1913), pp. 436–38.

19. Edward T. Devine, "Pensions for Mothers," *American Labor Legislation Review* 3(2) (June 1913), p. 193. Devine stressed that he was speaking only as an individual, yet he explicitly invoked the collective thinking of the AALL's Committee on Social Insurance when arguing that mothers' pensions were not worthy of the social insurance label. He also predicted that mothers' pensions would overburden the courts designated to administer them and not necessarily protect children from abuse or neglect.

Discussion of Devine's talk at the AALL conference included a lengthy response from William Hard, an advocate of mothers' pensions (whose activities will be discussed below). Arguing that he, too, favored comprehensive social insurance, Hard pointed out that the United States was a long way from having it. He asserted that "Private charity is too puny for the task which confronts it" and that "the granting of money to mothers in the circumstances and for the purposes outlined in the so-called 'mothers' pension' laws is a public function *and, further, a public function of a kind to be utterly segregated from public poor law outdoor relief* . . . A 'mothers' pension,' or, to speak more strictly, a 'mothers' allowance,' is granted in return for services rendered . . . She gets the allowance for only such time as she renders services for it. She is not supported because [she is] a dependent. She is paid because [she is] an employee. And whose employee is she? To whom is she rendering services? I say to the community. It is the community that is profited by her having given home life to the children" (ibid., pp. 231–33).

20. Leff, "Consensus for Reform," p. 403.

21. Mention of Judge Porterfield's membership and the Eagles' support

for the 1911 Missouri law appeared in the *Eagle Magazine* (Spring 1989). The Eagles have long claimed a prominent role in the 1910s campaigns for mothers' pensions. See, for example, "The F.O.E. as Lawmaker," *Eagle Magazine* 9(10) (Oct. 1921), p. 4. Unfortunately, I have not been able to read through *Eagle Magazines* for the 1910s.

22. *Report of Proceedings of the Thirty-First Annual Convention of the American Federation of Labor,* Atlanta, GA, Nov. 13–25, 1911 (Washington: Law Reporter Printing Co., 1911), pp. 357–58.

23. On the cross-class characteristics of the Eagles and their cooperation with organized labor in campaigns during the 1920s for state-level old-age pensions, see Jill Quadagno, *The Transformation of Old Age Security: Class and Politics in the American Welfare State* (Chicago: University of Chicago Press, 1988), pp. 66–72. Issues of the *Eagle Magazine* contain friendly references to the AFL, and the records of AFL national conventions also contain periodic greetings from the Eagles. Many skilled workingmen were members of this and other fraternal organizations.

24. Leff, "Consensus for Reform," p. 405; and Hoyt Landon Warner, *Progressivism in Ohio, 1897–1917* (Columbus: Ohio State University Press, 1964), p. 404.

25. Leff, "Consensus for Reform," p. 406.

26. *National Party Platforms,* vol. 1, 1840–1956, rev. ed., comp. Donald Bruce Johnson (Urbana: University of Illinois Press, 1978), p. 177.

27. For the excellent analyses of women's magazines on which I am drawing, see Mary Ellen Waller, "Popular Women's Magazines, 1890–1917" (Ph.D. diss., Columbia University, 1987); and Mary Ellen Waller-Zuckerman, "'Old Homes in a City of Perpetual Change': Women's Magazines, 1890–1916," *Business History Review* 63 (Winter 1989): 715–56.

28. Waller-Zuckerman, "Women's Magazines," pp. 717, 745; and Harold A. Jambor, "Theodore Dreiser, the *Delineator* Magazine, and Dependent Children: A Background Note on the Calling of the 1909 White House Conference," *Social Service Review* 32 (March 1958), pp. 33–35, including n. 6. See also Frank Luther Mott, "The Delineator," in his *A History of American Magazines,* vol. 3 (Cambridge, MA: Harvard University Press, 1938), pp. 481–90.

29. Jambor, "*Delineator* Magazine," pp. 35–36.

30. For an example, see "The Delineator Child-Rescue Campaign," *Delineator* 71(1) (Jan. 1908): 97–103. This includes stories of "Baby Marion," "Baby Ernest," and a seven-year-old named Janet, along with letters from readers and celebrities and a list of prominent women and reformers who "supervised" the campaign.

31. Jambor, "*Delineator* Magazine," pp. 38–39 and pp. 35–36, n. 9. The note lists sixteen prominent women who were official sponsors of the Child-Rescue Campaign.
32. Ibid., passim.
33. For a good discussion of Hard, see Wedel, "Origins of State Patriarchy," pp. 302–11. Hard had previously written about women's work at *Everybody's* magazine.
34. As I indicated in Chapter 6, citing Mary McDowell's 1909 letter to Lillian Wald as quoted in ibid., pp. 311–12.
35. William Hard, "'With All My Worldly Goods I Thee Endow.' Yes, But Does He? The First of a Series of Notable Investigations," *Delineator* 78(4) (Oct. 1911); p. 217.
36. See William Hard, "'With All My Worldly Goods,'" ibid. 78(5) (Nov. 1911): 323; and "When the Law Calls the Children 'His' and Not 'Hers,'" ibid. 79(2) (Feb. 1912): 99–100.
37. See William Hard, "'With All My Worldly Goods': Letters, Letters, Letters, from South, North, West, East—and Every Letter a Link in the Chain of Evidence Which Binds Us to a Common Cause," ibid. 78(6) (Dec. 1911): 432; and "'With All My Worldly Goods': Our Overflowing Letter Box Reveals Many Intimate Problems—Help Us Solve Them," ibid. 79(1) (Jan. 1912): 19–20.
38. Ibid. 79(4) (April 1912): 287–88, 367–68. The following quotes appear respectively on pp. 288 and 287 (emphasis in original).
39. William Hard, "'With All My Worldly Goods I Thee Endow': Help From Clubwomen: One Million Organized American Women, through their National Convention, Endorse the Ideas to Which this Department of THE DELINEATOR is Dedicated," ibid. 80(4) (Oct. 1912), p. 295. The article begins on pp. 223–24 and celebrates Hard's appearance as a featured speaker at the 1912 Biennial of the GFWC in San Francisco. The Biennial passed a resolution embodying the legal improvements Hard recommended. Significantly, the 1912 GFWC Biennial also debated women's suffrage at length, but the Federation did not pass a resolution endorsing suffrage until 1914.
40. Mary O'Connor Newell, "Four Counties That Prefer Mothers to Orphan Asylums," *Delineator* 80 (Aug. 1912): 85–86.
41. The latter comment closely parallels the response that William Hard made to Edward Devine in the debate published by the AALL (see note 124).
42. *Delineator* 80(2) (Sept. 1912): 144. Indeed, Hard tended to give very detailed and specific advice on just when, at critical points in the legislative process, women should write to particular legislators. See

ibid. 79(4) (April 1912), p. 288, where two different letters are recommended; and 79(5) (May 1912), p. 390, where three letters are suggested.

43. *Delineator* 80(6) (Dec. 1912), contents page.
44. Ibid. 81(1) (Jan. 1913): 19–20.
45. Ibid. 81(2) (Feb. 1913): 85–86, 129.
46. Ibid. 81(3) (March 1913): 153.
47. Ibid. 81(4) (April 1913): 263, 314–17.
48. Wedel, "Origins of State Patriarchy," p. 323.
49. Alice Maxwell Appo, "House Bill No.626: A First Step toward the Endowment of Motherhood," *Collier's* 49 (Aug. 10, 1912): 20–21; and Frederic C. Howe and Marie Jenney Howe, "Pensioning the Widow and the Fatherless," *Good Housekeeping* 57 (Sept. 1913): 282–91. These references come from p. xviii of Edna D. Bullock, ed., *Selected Articles on Mothers' Pensions* (White Plains, NY: Wilson Co., 1915), which has a bibliography that shows many of the publications in which articles on mothers' pensions appeared. For circulation figures for 1914, see Waller, "Popular Women's Magazines," p. 344.
50. Leff, "Consensus for Reform," p. 406.
51. The Oregon Congress of Mothers mentioned many sources of support and inspiration for its 1912–13 campaign for mothers' pensions, including Hard's articles in the *Delineator*. See the quotation below in the text, and note 94.
52. "Our Christmas Wish for Women" (Dec. 1912).
53. Above I discussed the role of Federation leaders in the Child-Rescue Campaign. In April 1912, the *Delineator* 79(4): 336–37 started a regular feature aimed at the federated clubs called "The Modern Club Woman: Our Clearing-House for Women's Clubs," in which discussion programs were suggested, starting with a "program on civics" that included many legislative issues. And several of Hard's articles placed great emphasis on reform activities by women's clubs, including "Discovering the Laws About Women: A Nation-Wide Movement Which Will Make History," *Delineator* 79(5) (May 1912): 389–90, as well as "Help From Clubwomen" (Oct. 1912), "Motherless Children" (Jan. 1913) and "1913 Styles in Laws" (Feb. 1913).
54. *Official Report of the Eleventh Biennial Convention of the General Federation of Women's Clubs,* San Francisco, CA, June 25–July 5, 1912, comp. and ed. Mrs. George O. Welch (GFWC, 1912), p. 185.
55. Ibid., pp. 329–41.
56. Ibid., p. 600.
57. John Clayton Drew, "Child Labor and Child Welfare: The Origins and Uneven Development of the American Welfare State" (Ph.D. diss.,

Cornell University, 1987). This paragraph draws specifically on Drew's discussion of "The Private Widows' Scholarship Program," pp. 101–07.

58. This history appears in "Report of the Secretary," *Fourth Annual Report of the National Consumers' League, for the Year Ending March 4, 1903* (New York: NCL, 1903), pp. 19–20.

59. Mrs. A. O. Granger, "The Work of the General Federation of Women's Clubs Against Child Labor," *Annals of the American Academy of Political and Social Science* 25(3) (May 1905), pp. 516–17.

60. "Report of the Secretary," *NCL Fourth Annual Report,* p. 19.

61. These groups are mentioned in Drew, "Child Labor and Child Welfare," pp. 103–04.

62. *Official Report of the Tenth Biennial Convention of the General Federation of Women's Clubs,* Cincinnati, OH, May 11–18, 1910, comp. and ed. Mrs. Henry Hollister Dawson (Newark, NJ: GFWC, 1910), p. 319.

63. "State Reports," *Official Report of the Eleventh Biennial* (1912), pp. 491, 538.

64. "State Reports," *Official Report of the Twelfth Biennial Convention of the General Federation of Women's Clubs,* June 9–19, 1914, Chicago, IL, comp. and ed. Mrs. Harry L. Keefe (Bureau of Information, GFWC, 1914), pp. 282, 293, 320.

65. "State Reports," *Official Report of the Thirteenth Biennial Convention of the General Federation of Women's Clubs,* May 24–June 2, 1916, New York City, comp. and ed. Mrs. Harry L. Keefe (GFWC, 1916), pp. 198, 205, 210, 215, 224, 244.

66. Ibid., p. 186.

67. It is worth pointing out that some state organizations normally presented rather vague reports to the national Biennials, often indicating general support for legislation of interest to women and children, while other state organizations provided details about their support for particular bills or types of legislation. Thus, by relying primarily on explicit references in Official Reports of the Biennials, I have almost certainly underestimated the numbers of Federation state organizations that actually worked for mothers' pensions before or after 1915. I have learned about additional states where activities occurred by consulting various official histories of State Federations of Women's Clubs. But I have not been able to do this systematically; and in any event, such histories are unevenly detailed, and not available for all states.

68. The founding dates for state organizations appear in Mary I. Wood, *The History of the General Federation of Women's Clubs for the First Twenty-Two Years of Its Organization* (New York: History Department, GFWC,

1912), p. 353, and *Golden Jubilee History, 1897–1947* (Chicago: National Congress of Parents and Teachers, 1947), p. 199.

69. "The President's Desk," *Child-Welfare Magazine* 12(1) (Sept. 1917), p. 1.
70. Edwin D. Solenberger, "Placing Out Work for Children," *Proceedings of the First International Congress in America for the Welfare of the Child, held under the auspices of the National Congress of Mothers*, Washington, DC, March 10–17, 1908 (National Congress of Mothers, 1908), p. 291.
71. See the discussion of the National Congress and juvenile courts in Chapter 6. Note also that Judge Ben Lindsey spoke on the "Treatment of Erring and Dependent Children" at the 1908 International Congress (ibid.), so members were directly acquainted with him before he became an advocate of mothers' pensions.
72. Mrs. G. H. Robertson, "The State's Duty to Fatherless Children," *Child-Welfare Magazine* 6(5) (Jan. 1912): 156–60.
73. Mrs. Frederic Schoff, "The Evolution of the Mother's Pension," *Child-Welfare Magazine* 9(4) (Dec. 1914), p. 117. The fact that Mrs. Robertson was Tennessee state president comes from the report of Mrs. Seymour P. Mynders, chairman, Department of Labor, in the *Proceedings of the Third International Congress on the Welfare of the Child under the auspices of National Congress of Mothers and Parent-Teacher Associations*, Washington DC, April 22–27, 1914, pp. 64–65. Although I have not been able to find more information about her, it is clear that Mrs. Robertson was involved in charity work; and she refers in her address to the views of "Mrs. [Hannah B.] Einstein of New York," who was one of the few prominent charity leaders to favor mothers' pensions. Mrs. Einstein of the United Hebrew Charities was a member of the New York Commission that issued a hard-hitting and lengthy favorable report in March 1914. See State of New York, *Report of the New York State Commission on Relief of Widowed Mothers* (Albany: J. B. Lyon Co., 1914).
74. Robertson, "State's Duty," pp. 156–57.
75. Ibid., p. 158.
76. Ibid., pp. 158–59.
77. Ibid., p. 159.
78. Ibid., p. 160.
79. Schoff, "Evolution of the Mother's Pension," p. 117.
80. "Resolutions Adopted by Second International Congress on Child Welfare, National Congress of Mothers," *Child-Welfare Magazine* 5(10) (June 1911), p. 196.
81. *Proceedings of the Third International Congress on the Welfare of the Child* (1914), p. 179. Interestingly, this resolution advocated mothers' pensions "as the most effective method of checking truancy and child

labor." The resolution maintained that the "absence from home of wage-earning mothers contributes largely toward truancy" and held that truancy "is one of the first steps toward juvenile delinquency."

82. For evidence of this, see ibid., pp. 28 (where President Schoff reported that she had "urged the passage of the Mother's Pension laws in every state") and 64–65, as well as certain of the pieces in *Child-Welfare Magazine* cited above and below.

83. We know, for example, that the *Texas Motherhood Magazine* reprinted Mrs. Robertson's 1911 address, because an excerpt from the Texas article appears in Mary Richmond's 1913 *Survey* article "Motherhood and Pensions," rpt. in Bullock, ed., *Selected Articles,* p. 64.

84. *Child-Welfare Magazine* 7(9) (May 1913): 332; and 7(10) (June 1913): 418–20.

85. "Recognition of Motherhood," ibid. 7(9) (May 1913), p. 332.

86. Agnes H. Downing, "A Wider Pension Move," ibid. 7(2) (Oct. 1912): 59. Downing argued that "these unfortunate sisters of ours are usually very young girls, and because of the extreme difficulty of their finding work, their condition is pitiable in the extreme." State aid to "girl mothers," she suggested, would help keep them from further moral indiscretions. "There is no society better fitted to take an initial step in such a move than the Mothers' Congress. It is great enough to see a question like this in all its aspects, and its results not alone on the poor girls concerned and on their children but on the whole of society." The Congress did not officially adopt this position, however, and of the state-level laws passed during the Progressive Era, only Michigan's made explicit provision for unwed mothers.

87. The claim about "every state branch" appeared in "Recognition of Motherhood," ibid. 7(9) (May 1913): 332. We do know that the claim about every state branch was at least a little exaggerated, because the Maine Congress reported to the Third International Congress on the Welfare of the Child that "We have no Mothers' Pension Law, and have made no attempt to get one." This report was reprinted in *Child-Welfare Magazine* 8(11) (July 1914), p. 465. Some years later, the Maine Congress reversed itself and lobbied for the mothers' pension law that was passed in 1917; see ibid. 11(6) (Feb. 1917), p. 182, and 11(10) (June 1917), p. 302.

88. For documentation of the Congress's role in these states, see Appendix 2. All of these states enacted mothers' pensions during the 1910s, except for Mississippi, where the state branch reported activity in 1919 but the law did not pass until 1928.

89. Mabel Brown Ellis, "Mothers' Pensions," ch. 8 in *Child Welfare in Tennessee: An Inquiry by the National Child Labor Committee for the Ten-*

nessee Child Welfare Commission (Nashville: State of Tennessee, Department of Public Instruction, 1920), p. 511.

90. Lubove, *Struggle for Social Security,* p. 101.

91. Mary S. Gibson, comp., *A Record of Twenty-five Years of the California Federation of Women's Clubs, 1900–1925,* vol. 1 (California Federation of Women's Clubs, 1927), pp. 186–202. A list of the fifty-three women's organizations that were charter affiliates of the Women's Legislative Council of California appears on pp. 197–99. This pamphlet is held in the collections of the Bancroft Library of the University of California at Berkeley.

92. The letterhead of the California League for the Protection of Motherhood appears in the Phoebe Apperson Hearst Papers (72/204c), in the holdings of the Bancroft Library of the University of California at Berkeley. There is an October 10, 1912, letter from the secretary of the League to Mrs. Hearst, who was a leader of the National Congress of Mothers, soliciting support for a fundraiser for the mothers' pension campaign. There is also a subsequent handwritten letter acknowledging Mrs. Hearst's contribution and support for the cause.

93. See Wedel, "Origins of State Patriarchy," p. 364; Clara C. Park, "Widows' Pension in Massachusetts," *Child-Welfare Magazine* 6(10) (June 1912): 343; and Commonwealth of Massachusetts, *Report of the Commission on the Support of Dependent Minor Children of Widowed Mothers* (Boston: Wright and Potter, 1913).

94. Elizabeth Hayhurst, "How Pensions for Widows Were Won in Oregon," *Child-Welfare Magazine* 7(7) (March 1913): 248–49. Interestingly, the Oregon law did not include unmarried mothers, but it did cover women whose husbands were inmates in any Oregon state institution or were "physically or mentally unable to work." The law was reprinted in full at the end of Hayhurst's article.

95. Leff, "Consensus for Reform," pp. 400–01.

96. Quoted from the *Indianapolis Star,* Jan. 28, 1913, in Mary Richmond, "Motherhood and Pensions," *Survey* 29 (March 1, 1913). However, the state of Indiana did not enact a mothers' pension bill until 1919, so it obvious that sheer rhetoric of this sort did not always carry the day immediately in 1913.

97. Virginia Gray, "Innovation in the States: A Diffusion Study," *American Political Science Review* 67 (Dec. 1973), pp. 1182–83.

98. Ada J. Davis, "The Evolution of the Institution of Mothers' Pensions in the United States," *American Journal of Sociology* 35 (1930), p. 581. The affiliation of this author is listed as North Carolina College for Women.

99. The statistical study discussed here and below is documented in Susan

Lehmann, Marjorie Abend-Wein, Theda Skocpol, and Christopher Howard, "Class, Gender, and the Politics of Mothers' Pensions in the Early Twentieth-Century United States" (paper presented at the Annual Meeting of the American Sociological Association, Cincinnati, Aug. 25, 1991); and in Christopher Howard, Theda Skocpol, Susan Lehmann, and Marjorie Abend-Wein, "Government Institutions, Women's Associations, and the Enactment of Mothers' Pensions in the United States, 1910–1935" (paper presented at the Annual Meeting of the American Political Science Association, Washington, DC, Aug. 29, 1991).

100. See especially Jack L. Walker, "Innovation in State Politics," pp. 354–87 in *Politics in the American States: A Comparative Analysis,* 2nd ed., ed. Herbert Jacob and Kenneth N. Vines (Boston: Little, Brown, 1971).

101. Gray, "Innovation," p. 1183.

102. For the Progressive presidential votes, I used the numbers in *Historical Statistics of the United States, Colonial Times to 1970,* pt. 2, Bicentennial ed. (Washington: Government Printing Office, 1975), Series Y 135–186, p. 1078. States whose Progressive vote shares were more than two percentage points above the national average of 27.3 percent were Arizona (30%), California (41.89%), Iowa (32.93%), Kansas (32.88%), Maine (36.92%), Michigan (38.87%), Minnesota (37.72%), Nevada (30%), New Jersey (33.64%), North Dakota (30.23%), Pennsylvania (36.54%), South Dakota (50.43), Vermont (34.92%), Washington (35.40), and West Virginia (32.91%).

103. Leff, "Consensus for Reform," p. 405.

104. Davis, "Evolution of Mothers' Pensions," p. 584.

105. Ibid., p. 581.

106. Ibid., p. 583. Davis attributes this statement to "Michels," delivered in a 1927 class lecture at the University of Chicago.

107. Ibid., p. 581.

108. Ibid., pp. 583, 584.

109. Beard, *Woman's Work in Municipalities,* pp. 251, 255.

110. These findings correspond to central arguments in Drew, "Child Labor and Child Welfare."

111. Special circumstances, however, may explain why women's groups do not appear to have been central to the enactment of mothers' pensions in three of the thirteen states where I found no indication of endorsements (see Appendix 2). In Arizona, mothers' pensions passed along with old-age pensions in a 1914 popular referendum. In North Dakota, mothers' pensions were put through along with many other reforms by the agrarian-radical Non-Partisan League, which had just come to power in 1915. And in Nebraska it is possible that the Wom-

en's Christian Temperance Union was the most active major women's group. But I have not been able systematically to consult WCTU records to see if there is good information about state organizations' support for mothers' pensions.

112. From "Wildfire Spread of 'Widows' Pensions'—Its Start—Its Meaning—And Its Cost," *Everybody's Magazine* 32 (June 1915), as rpt. in Bullock, ed., *Selected Articles on Mothers' Pensions,* p. 87.

113. Illinois report in "State News," *Child-Welfare Magazine* 10(7) (March 1916); pp. 256–57.

114. Children's Bureau, U.S. Department of Labor, *Mothers' Aid, 1931,* Bureau Publication no. 220 (Washington, DC: Government Printing Office, 1933), p. 8. I am referring to "mothers" as the adult recipients of mothers' pensions, even though 1,012 "persons other than mothers" were receiving aid in 1931, mostly in the state of New York (ibid., p. 12).

115. Children's Bureau, U.S. Department of Labor, *The Administration of the Aid-to-Mothers Law in Illinois,* by Edith Abbott and Sophinisba Breckinridge, Publication no. 82 (Washington: Government Printing Office, 1921), pp. 65–67, 167.

116. Muriel W. Pumphrey and Ralph E. Pumphrey, "The Widows' Pension Movement, 1900–1930: Preventive Child-Saving or Social Control?" in *Social Welfare or Social Control?* ed. Walter I. Trattner (Knoxville: University of Tennessee Press, 1983), p. 61.

117. Ibid. For a similar argument, see Ann Vandepol, "Dependent Children, Child Custody, and the Mothers' Pensions: The Transformation of State-Family Relations in the Early 20th Century," *Social Problems* 29(3) (Feb. 1982): 221–35.

118. *Mother's Aid, 1931,* pp. 3–4.

119. Usually, but not always. According to ibid., pp. 11–12, a few deserted and divorced mothers received aid through administrative discretion in states where the statutes did not allow aid to mothers in those categories.

120. Ibid., pp. 11–13 and table A-I, p. 25.

121. Ibid., p. 3. Michigan allowed such aid from the start; and Nebraska and Tennessee also explicitly allowed aid to unmarried mothers by 1931. Of the 55 unmarried mothers reported as receiving aid in 1931, 17 were in Michigan, 14 were in Nebraska, and the rest were scattered across eleven other states where administrative discretion had presumably allowed from one to five such families headed by unmarried women to creep onto the rolls.

122. State of New York, *Report of the New York State Commission on Relief for Widowed Mothers,* transmitted to the Legislature, March 27, 1914 (Albany: J. B. Lyon Co., 1914), p. 21.

123. See Children's Bureau, U.S. Department of Labor, *A Tabular Summary of State Laws Relating to Public Aid to Children in Their Own Homes in Effect January 1, 1929 and the Text of the Laws of Certain States,* Chart no. 3, 3rd ed. (Washington: Government Printing Office, 1929).

124. As quoted in Pumphrey and Pumphrey, "Widows' Pension Movement," p. 58. These authors, who write from a point of view sympathetic to social workers, point out that the enforcement of social criteria in mothers' pension programs was part of the process of separating them from historically dishonorable poor-relief traditions.

125. An example is reproduced and eligibility criteria are discussed in Barbara J. Nelson, "The Gender, Race, and Class Origins of Early Welfare Policy and the Welfare State: A Comparison of Workmen's Compensation and Mothers' Aid," in *Women, Politics, and Change,* ed. Louise A. Tilly and Patricia Gurin (New York: Russell Sage Foundation, 1990), pp. 428–32.

126. See Children's Bureau, U.S. Department of Labor, *Administration of Mothers' Aid in Ten Localities with Special Reference to Health, Housing, Education, and Recreation,* by Mary F. Bogue, Publication no. 184 (Washington: Government Printing Office, 1928).

127. *Mothers' Aid, 1931,* p. 6.

128. Pumphrey and Pumphrey, "Widows' Pension Movement," p. 59.

129. On "friendly visiting" and its transformation into social work, see Roy Lubove, *The Professional Altruist: The Emergence of Social Work as a Career, 1880–1930* (Cambridge, MA: Harvard University Press, 1965).

130. Details about what social workers tried to do appear in Children's Bureau, *Mothers' Aid in Ten Localities.*

131. As quoted in Moore, "Mothers' Pensions," p. 170, from Children's Bureau, U.S. Department of Labor, *Standards of Aid to Children in Their Own Homes,* by Florence Nesbitt, Publication no. 118 (Washington: Government Printing Office, 1923), p. 32.

132. Moore, "Mothers' Pensions," pp. 156–57.

133. *Mothers' Aid, 1931,* p. 2; and Moore, "Mothers' Pensions," pp. 139–40.

134. Moore, "Mothers' Pensions," pp. 138–39, 159–61. Moore draws examples from reports about programs in Illinois, Minnesota, Massachusetts, New York, Rhode Island, Pennsylvania, and North Carolina.

135. State of Rhode Island and Providence Plantations, Bureau of Mothers' Aid, *Second Annual Report of the State Public Welfare Commission, 1925,* as quoted in Moore, "Mothers' Pensions," p. 182.

136. Emma O. Lundberg, "Aid to Mothers with Dependent Children," *Annals of the American Academy of Political and Social Science* 98 (Nov. 1921), p. 101; and Moore, "Mothers' Pensions," pp. 160, 185–86.

137. From records in the Archives of Washington University, St. Louis, as quoted in Wedel, "Origins of State Patriarchy," pp. 381–82.

138. David J. Rothman, "The State as Parent: Social Policy in the Progressive Era," in *Doing Good: The Limits of Benevolence,* by Willard Gaylin, Ira Glasser, Steven Marcus, and David Rothman (New York: Pantheon, 1978), p. 75.

139. See Chapter 2, note 100.

140. An excellent discussion of these points appears in Ann Shola Orloff, "Gender in Early U.S. Social Policy," *Journal of Policy History* 3(3) (1991): 249–81.

141. Contrasting U.S. workmen's compensation and mothers' pensions, Nelson in "Gender, Race, and Class Origins" argues that early U.S. benefits for women had moral criteria and administrative supervision, while benefits for (or including) men did not. As Orloff points out in "Gender in Early U.S. Social Policy," Nelson overlooks moral criteria for old-age pensions. I would also maintain that she romanticizes workmen's compensation, overlooking the many complaints by workers and unions about the niggardly benefits and the arbitrary and demeaning nature of compulsory examinations by physicians (who were sometimes beholden to employers, and motivated to minimize compensable injuries).

142. *Mothers' Aid, 1931,* pp. 5, 15–16.

143. Ibid., pp. 15–19.

144. Ibid., p. 13. See also table 2–4 and the accompanying discussion in Christopher Damon Howard, "The Early Fragmentation of the American Welfare State: A Comparative Study of Mothers' Pensions and Workmen's Compensation" (M.S. thesis, Massachusetts Institute of Technology, 1990), pp. 29–31.

145. Children's Bureau, U.S. Department of Labor, *Public Aid to Mothers with Dependent Children,* by Emma O. Lundberg, Publication no. 162 (Washington: Government Printing Office, 1926), p. 16.

146. *Mothers' Aid, 1931,* p. 23.

147. Ibid., pp. 23–24; and Emma O. Lundberg, "Progress of Mothers' Aid Administration," *Social Service Review* 2 (Sept. 1928), p. 455.

148. *Mothers' Aid, 1931,* pp. 16–18, 24. On the gap between statutory levels and actual costs of living, see *Public Aid to Mothers,* pp. 16–18.

149. *Mothers' Aid,* p. 17.

150. Ibid., p. 18. The eight cities with average grants of $60 or more were Washington, DC; Westchester County, NY; and Boston, Cambridge, Lynn, Somerville, Springfield, and Worcester, MA.

151. Ibid., pp. 17, 19, 24.

152. Ibid., p. 24.

153. Children's Bureau, U.S. Department of Labor, *Proceedings of the Conference on Mothers' Pensions,* Publication no. 109 (Washington: Government Printing Office, 1922), p. 11.

154. *Mothers' Aid in Ten Localities,* p. 8.

155. Elizabeth L. Hall, *Mothers' Assistance in Philadelphia, Actual and Potential Costs: A Study of 1010 Families* (Putnam, CT: Patriot Press, 1933), p. 5.

156. *Mothers' Aid in Ten Localities,* pp. 158–59; and Moore, "Mothers' Pensions," pp. 150–52.

157. These terms from original sources are quoted in Moore, "Mothers' Pensions," pp. 142, 149.

158. Ibid., pp. 179–81.

159. These results are reported in Lundberg, "Progress of Mothers' Aid Administration," pp. 449–50. As for the remaining percentages of the families' income: 2 percent came from relatives; 7 percent came from lodgers and boarders; and most of the remaining 4 percent came from "charitable relief." Lundberg observed (p. 50) that this and other studies spurred the Pennsylvania legislature in 1927 to raise the mothers' aid appropriation "to about 70 percent of the total deemed necessary for adequate aid. It is expected that this will enable the counties to wipe out their waiting lists, but it will not be possible to give the assistance found to be required for adequate aid in accordance with the budget needs of each family."

160. Ibid., p. 449.

161. These examples come from studies summarized in Moore, "Mothers' Pensions," pp. 181–84.

162. From arguments for mothers' pensions as summarized in "Both Sides: A Debate," *Independent* 80 (Nov. 9, 1914), p. 206, as quoted in Molly Ladd-Taylor, "Mother-Work: Ideology, Public Policy, and the Mothers' Movement, 1890–1930" (Ph.D. diss., Yale University, 1986), p. 248.

163. As quoted in Ladd-Taylor, "Mother-Work," pp. 248–49. As she points out, this statement from L. B. Hobhouse was much quoted in statements by proponents of mothers' pensions.

164. These points were made in a Jan. 2, 1990, letter to me from Joanne Goodwin. Her forthcoming dissertation is entitled "Gender, Politics, and Welfare Reform, Chicago 1900–1930" (Department of History, University of Michigan). For a resolution of the Illinois Congress of Mothers calling for the extension of programs under the Funds to Parents Act to all counties in the state, see *Child-Welfare Magazine* 9(11) (July 1915), p. 383.

165. For some examples, see the following reports in the "State News" sections of *Child-Welfare Magazine:* California in 9(8) (April 1915), pp. 272–73; Massachusetts in 10(7) (March 1916), pp. 256–57, and 11(8) (April 1917), p. 237; Tennessee in 11(9) (May 1917), p. 274; Pennsylvania in 9(4) (Dec. 1914), p. 138, 13(7) (March 1919), p. 208, and 13(10–11) (June-July 1919), p. 316; Idaho in 9(7) (March 1915), p. 242, and 13(10–11) (June-July 1919), p. 307; and Kansas in 14(1)

(Sept. 1919), p. 24. Also see the article "Mothers' Pension in Oregon" in 9(6) (Feb. 1915): 196–98, and the "President's Desk" discussion of the situation in Pennsylvania in 13(4) (Dec. 1918), p. 91. Pennsylvania mothers' pension programs were, by law, administered under the supervision of unpaid local boards of volunteer women, and this situation may well have helped to keep women's clubs in that state highly concerned about the proper administration and adequate funding of these programs.

166. Lundberg, "Progress of Mothers' Aid Administration," pp. 438, 455. For the 1920s, there are some indications of continuing interest by women's groups in the funding of mothers' pensions. According to Davis, "Evolution of Mothers' Pensions," p. 583, the League of Women Voters in Pennsylvania worked for increased appropriations for mothers' pensions. The New Hampshire Federation of Women's Clubs was working as late as 1929 for increases in the amount allocated to individual mothers; see *A History of the New Hampshire Federation of Women's Clubs, 1895–1940* (Bristol, NH: Musgrove Printing House, 1941), p. 128. See also the Goodwin dissertation cited in note 164.

9. Statebuilding for Mothers and Babies: The Children's Bureau and the Sheppard-Towner Act

1. *Twenty Years Work for Child Welfare by the National Congress of Mothers and Parent-Teacher Associations, 1897–1917* (Washington: National Congress of Mothers and Parent-Teacher Associations, 1917), pp. 36–38; and "Report of the National President, Mrs. Frederic Schoff, for 1912–1913–1914," in *Proceedings of the Third International Congress on the Welfare of the Child under the Auspices of the National Congress of Mothers and Parent-Teacher Associations*, April 22–27, 1914, Washington, DC (National Congress of Mothers and Parent-Teacher Associations, 1914), pp. 30–31.

2. J. Stanley Lemons, *The Woman Citizen: Social Feminism in the 1920s*, 2nd ed. (Chicago: University of Chicago Press, 1975), pp. 25–31. See also the discussion in the last section of Chapter 7.

3. *Report of the Chief of the Bureau of Home Economics*, in *Annual Reports of the Department of Agriculture for the Year Ended June 30, 1924* (Washington: Government Printing Office, 1924), pp. 1–2.

4. The text of the enabling act appears in *First Annual Report of the Chief, Children's Bureau to the Secretary of Labor for the Year Ended June 30, 1913* (Washington: Government Printing Office, 1914), p. 2.

5. *Third Annual Report of the Chief, Children's Bureau to the Secretary of Labor, Fiscal Year Ended June 30, 1915* (Washington: Government Printing Office, 1915), p. 5. Even though the Bureau's enabling legislation had

to be formally amended, the Bureau got exactly the increases it asked for at the end of the first year (see *First Annual Report,* p. 19).

6. Jacqueline K. Parker and Edward M. Carpenter, "Julia Lathrop and the Children's Bureau: The Emergence of an Institution," *Social Service Review* 55(1) (March 1981): 74; and *Tenth Annual Report of the Chief, Children's Bureau to the Secretary of Labor, Fiscal Year Ended June 30, 1922* (Washington: Government Printing Office, 1922).

7. Molly Ladd-Taylor, *Raising a Baby the Government Way: Mothers' Letters to the Children's Bureau, 1915–1932* (New Brunswick, NJ: Rutgers University Press, 1986), p. 28.

8. Ibid., p. 2.

9. Informed readers may notice that I am gently disagreeing with the centralized, monolithic, and hierarchical imagery of female welfare statebuilding offered in Robyn Muncy's interesting new book, *Creating a Female Dominion in American Reform, 1890–1935* (New York: Oxford University Press, 1991). Muncy works with an instrumental-professional and bureaucratic understanding of statebuilding that does not work well for the United States. At places such as pp. xii, 61, 62, 64, 93, and 161, she greatly overestimates the capacity of a handful of female reformist professionals to "construct" and "direct" what she calls "subordinate" networks of women's groups. In fact, the female reformers were responding to the orientations and organizational possibilities of the women's federations, even as the federations were responding to specific policy priorities suggested by the reformers. It was a two-way street, even in the centrally coordinated campaigns for the Children's Bureau and Sheppard-Towner. Moreover, in the campaigns for mothers' pension legislation waged across forty-some U.S. states during the 1910s, the initiative rested almost entirely with the federations of women's voluntary groups, while the social settlement women were only marginally involved (and were certainly not "directing" anything).

10. Nancy Pottishman Weiss, "Save the Children: A History of the Children's Bureau, 1903–1918" (Ph.D. diss. University of California, Los Angeles, 1974), pp. 51, 53.

11. Muncy, *Female Dominion,* p. 39.

12. Weiss, "Save the Children," pp. 48–49; James Johnson, "The Role of Women in the Founding of the United States Children's Bureau," in *"Remember the Ladies": New Perspectives on Women in American History,* ed. Carol V. R. George (Syracuse, NY: Syracuse University Press, 1975), pp. 183–84; and Louis J. Covotsos, "Child Welfare and Social Progress: A History of the United States Children's Bureau, 1912–1935" (Ph.D. diss., University of Chicago, 1976), ch. 1.

13. Johnson, "Role of Women," p. 184.

14. Parker and Carpenter, "Emergence of an Institution," p. 60.
15. Ibid.; these phrases are quoted from the 1909 White House Conference report (see note 4 to Chapter 8 above). On the effects of the Conference, see also Weiss, "Save the Children," pp. 59–65.
16. Johnson, "Role of Women," p. 186.
17. Covotsos, "Child Welfare and Social Progress," pp. 37–38.
18. Ibid., pp. 28–30, 38–39.
19. Johnson, "Role of Women," p. 185.
20. *Proceedings of the First International Congress in America for the Welfare of the Child, held under the auspices of the National Congress of Mothers,* Washington, DC, March 10–17, 1908 (National Congress of Mothers, 1908), p. 347; and "Resolutions Adopted by Second International Congress on Child Welfare, National Congress of Mothers," *Child-Welfare Magazine* 5(10) (June 1911); p. 196.
21. Samuel McCune Lindsay, "National Child Labor Committee," in *Official Report of the Eighth Biennial Convention of the General Federation of Women's Clubs,* St. Paul, MN, May 30–June 7, 1906, comp. and ed. Mrs. John Dickinson Sherman (Chicago: GFWC, 1906), p. 185. See also Owen R. Lovejoy, "Public Opinion and Child Labor," in ibid., pp. 249–56.
22. *Official Report of the Ninth Biennial Convention of the General Federation of Women's Clubs,* Boston, MA, June 22–30, 1908, comp. and ed. Mrs. John Dickinson Sherman (Chicago: GFWC, 1908), p. 434. See also "Report of the Legislative, Industrial and Child Labor Committee," p. 327.
23. *Official Report of the Tenth Biennial Convention of the General Federation of Women's Clubs,* May 11–18, 1910, Cincinnati, OH, comp. and ed. Mrs. Henry Hollister Dawson (Newark NJ: GFWC, 1910), "Report of the Legislative Committee," p. 372. See also "Conference of the Industrial and Child Labor Committee," p. 499.
24. *A Record of Twenty-Five Years of the California Federation of Women's Clubs, 1900–1925,* vol. 1, comp. Mary S. Gibson (California State Federation of Women's Clubs, 1927), p. 79. This is in the holdings of the Bancroft Library, University of California at Berkeley.
25. *Official Report of the Eleventh Biennial Convention of the General Federation of Women's Clubs,* June 25–July 5, 1912, San Francisco, CA, comp. and ed. Mrs. George O. Welch (GFWC, 1912), p. 484; see also pp. 471, 480, 487, 497.
26. Ibid., pp. 323–24, 596, 446–57 (for Lathrop's address, which will be discussed below).
27. Parker and Carpenter, "Emergence of an Institution," pp. 63–64.
28. The unusual leverage of the USDA within the early-twentieth-century

U.S. federal administration is analyzed in Theda Skocpol and Kenneth Finegold, "State Capacity and Economic Intervention in the Early New Deal," *Political Science Quarterly* 97(2) (Summer 1982): 255–78.

29. For the most telling evidence of this point, see Lathrop's rendition of the parallel scope of the USDA and the Children's Bureau in *First Annual Report of the Children's Bureau*, p. 5; and her explicit modeling of the infant and maternity health proposal (which eventually became the Sheppard-Towner Act) on the 1914 Smith-Lever Act establishing the Agricultural Extension Service, in *Fifth Annual Report of the Chief, Children's Bureau to the Secretary of Labor, Fiscal Year Ended June 30, 1917* (Washington: Government Printing Office, 1917), pp. 48–49.

30. *Official Report of the Eleventh Biennial, GFWC* (1912), pp. 447–48.

31. Lathrop's claims about following strict meritocratic procedures were a bit disingenuous. As Muncy argues in *Female Dominion*, pp. 49–52, she made use of all possible flexibilities in existing civil service rules in order to place ideologically congenial women in virtually all key positions within the Children's Bureau.

32. *Official Report of the Eleventh Biennial, GFWC* (1912), pp. 456, 447.

33. *Second Annual Report of the Chief, Children's Bureau, to the Secretary of Labor for the Fiscal Year Ended June 30, 1914* (Washington: Government Printing Office, 1914), p. 9.

34. *Third Annual Report of Children's Bureau*, p. 9.

35. *Second Annual Report of Children's Bureau*, p. 10.

36. Ibid.

37. *Official Report of the Eleventh Biennial, GFWC* (1912), p. 451.

38. *Third Annual Report of Children's Bureau*, p. 13; and Parker and Carpenter, "Emergence of an Institution," p. 68.

39. *Third Annual Report of Children's Bureau*, p. 13.

40. Ibid.; and *Second Annual Report of Children's Bureau*, p. 10.

41. *Third Annual Report of Children's Bureau*, pp. 13–14.

42. See, for example, Julia C. Lathrop, "Birth Registration—A Message to the Mothers' Congress," *Child-Welfare Magazine* 11(6) (Feb. 1917): 173–74. According to Parker and Carpenter, "Emergence of an Institution," p. 69. "By the end of 1919, the number of states in the birth registration area increased from ten to twenty-three."

43. *Third Annual Report of Children's Bureau*, p. 9.

44. *Fourth Annual Report of the Chief, Children's Bureau to the Secretary of Labor, for the Fiscal Year Ended June 30, 1916* (Washington: Government Printing Office, 1916), pp. 5–7; *Fifth Annual Report of Children's Bureau*, pp. 12–21; and *Sixth Annual Report of the Chief, Children's Bureau to the Secretary of Labor, for the Fiscal Year Ended June 30, 1918* (Washington: Government Printing Office, 1918), pp. 10–16.

45. Parker and Carpenter, "Emergence of an Institution," pp. 69–70.

46. Muncy, *Female Dominion*, pp. 63–64.

47. Dorothy Bradbury, "The Children's Advocate: The Story of the United States Children Bureau, 1903–1946," n.d., p. 79. Martha May Eliot Papers, Schlesinger Library, Radcliffe College, Boxes 28 and 29.

48. *Fourth Annual Report of Children's Bureau,* p. 12.

49. Ibid., pp. 12–13.

50. Ibid., pp. 13–14.

51. The Mothers' Congress published an appeal for cooperation: Julia C. Lathrop, "The Nation-Wide 1916 Baby Week," *Child-Welfare Magazine* 10(5) (Jan. 1916): 158. This first Baby Week came long after the GFWC's 1914 Biennial and a few months before its 1916 Biennial, so it could not be featured at either of these national conventions. But GFWC leaders reported close cooperation with Lathrop in promoting Baby Week; see *Official Report of the Thirteenth Biennial Convention of the General Federation of Women's Clubs,* New York City, May 24–June 2, 1916, comp. and ed. Mrs. Harry L. Keefe (GFWC, 1916) p. 161.

52. For a cross-section of many such reports, see "Reports of Presidents of State Federations," *Official Report of the Thirteenth Biennial, GFWC* (1916), pp. 173–245; and "The Reports Given by Presidents of State Branches, National Congress of Mothers and Parent-Teacher Associations at Nashville, Tennessee," *Child-Welfare Magazine* 11(1) (Sept. 1916): 22–38.

53. *Fifth Annual Report of Children's Bureau* (1917), p. 22.

54. Covotsos, "Child Welfare and Social Progress," p. 114.

55. *Fifth Annual Report of Children's Bureau* (1917), pp. 44–49.

56. *Official Report of the Thirteenth Biennial, GFWC* (1916), pp. 599–600.

57. The Bureau's studies of rural areas are summarized in Covotsos, "Child Welfare and Social Progress," pp. 103–05.

58. Ibid., p. 114.

59. Richard A. Meckel, *Save the Babies: American Public Health Reform and the Prevention of Infant Mortality, 1850–1929* (Baltimore: Johns Hopkins University Press, 1990), p. 195.

60. Covotsos, "Child Welfare and Social Progress," p. 121.

61. On the "Year of the Child" see *Sixth Annual Report of the Children's Bureau,* pp. 21–25; *Seventh Annual Report of the Chief, Children's Bureau to the Secretary of Labor, for the Fiscal Year Ended June 30, 1919* (Washington: Government Printing Office, 1919), pp. 6–12, 20; "National Child Welfare Program," presided over by Julia Lathrop, *Official Report of the Fourteenth Biennial Convention of the General Federation of Women's Clubs,* Hot Springs, AR, April 30–May 8, 1918, comp. Mrs. W. I. McFarland and ed. Mrs. Francis D. Everett (GFWC, 1918),

pp. 75–82; and the recurrent features that appeared in *Child-Welfare Magazine* in the March, April, Aug., and Sept. 1918 numbers, as well as in the June-July 1919 number. Moreover, according to *Child-Welfare Magazine* 14(7) (March 1920), p. 214, "In some states during the war period, the Congress took charge of the Children's Year Campaign under the Council of Defense." On the 1919 Conference, see *Seventh Annual Report of Children's Bureau* (1919), pp. 12–20.

62. See "State Quotas of Babies to Be Saved During Children's Year," *Child-Welfare Magazine* 12(8) (April 1918): 142–43; and "Conference on Child Welfare Standards Held in Washington, D.C., in May, 1919," ibid. 13(12) (Aug. 1919): 344–45.

63. Bradbury, "The Children's Advocate," p. 115.

64. As quoted in ibid., p. 132.

65. Full details of the legislative process appear in Joseph Benedict Chepaitis, "The First Federal Social Welfare Measure: The Sheppard-Towner Maternity and Infancy Act, 1918–1932" (Ph.D. diss., Georgetown University, 1968), ch. 2.

66. Covotsos, "Child Welfare and Social Progress," p. 123, including quotations from a letter by Julia Lathrop to Bleeker Marquette, Dec. 1, 1920, Children's Bureau Papers, Drawer 408, National Archives, Washington, DC.

67. Chepaitis, "First Federal Social Welfare Measure," pp. 58, 72–74, 76. The margin in the Senate vote on July 22, 1921, was 63 to 7, and the margin in the House vote on Nov. 19, 1921, was 321 in favor, 80 opposed, and 30 not accounted for. Oppositon came from some northeastern Republicans and southern Democrats.

68. Ibid., pp. 126–48; and Covotsos, "Child Welfare and Social Progress," pp. 134–41.

69. Quoted in Chepaitis, "First Federal Social Welfare Measure," p. 144, from the *Congressional Record,* 67th Congress, 1st sess., 1921, vol. 61, pt. 8, pp. 76945–46.

70. As quoted in Bradbury, "The Children's Advocate," p. 163.

71. Ibid., p. 130; Covotsos, "Child Welfare and Social Progress," pp. 135–37; and Sheila M. Rothman, *Woman's Proper Place* (New York: Basic Books, 1978), p. 303, n. 7.

72. Ibid., pp. 142–53. Rothman notes (p. 138) that in 1921 "the AMA found little interest within the profession" for all-out opposition to Sheppard-Towner. "Private physicians did not vigorously support the organization, because they did not believe that the programs offered by Sheppard-Towner would in any way compete with the services they offered to their private patients."

73. Meckel, *Save the Babies,* p. 210. For the importance and national cir-

culation of these women's magazines, see Mary Ellen Waller, "Popular Women's Magazines, 1890–1917" (Ph.D. diss., Columbia University, 1987), pp. 26, 344.

74. Chepaitis, "First Federal Social Welfare Measure," p. 48: Meckel, *Save the Babies,* p. 210.

75. *Official Report of the Fourteenth Biennial, GFWC* (1918), p. 471.

76. *Official Report of the Fifteenth Biennial Convention of the General Federation of Women's Clubs,* Des Moines, IA, June 16–23, 1920, comp. and ed. Mrs. Adam Weiss (GFWC, 1920), p. 463.

77. *Child-Welfare Magazine* 14(4) (Dec. 1919): 114.

78. See ibid. 14(6) (Feb. 1920), p. 165; 14(8) (April 1920), pp. 230–31; 14(9) (May 1920); pp. 261–62; 15(4) (Dec. 1920), p. 73. See also the President's Report to the Twenty-Fourth Annual Conference of the National Congress of Mothers and Parent-Teacher Associations, ibid. 14(11–12) (July-Aug. 1920), p. 342.

79. Bradbury, "The Children's Advocate," p. 146.

80. Ibid., pp. 122–23.

81. *Child-Welfare Magazine* 14(6) (Feb. 1920), p. 165.

82. "President's Desk," ibid. 14(9) (May 1920), pp. 261–62.

83. Ibid. 16(1) (Sept. 1921), p. 15.

84. Bradbury, "The Children's Advocate," p. 122.

85. Lemons, *The Woman Citizen,* p. 55.

86. Ibid., p. 155.

87. Ibid., p. 167.

88. As quoted in ibid., p. 166.

89. Ibid., pp. 157–58.

90. For background on Grace Abbott, see Lela B. Costin, *Two Sisters for Social Justice: A Biography of Grace and Edith Abbott* (Urbana: University of Illinois Press, 1983).

91. Ibid., pp. 134–36, 104–109. See also Abbott's discussion of criteria for approving state plans in *Tenth Annual Report of the Children's Bureau* (1922), pp. 8–9.

92. Covotsos, "Child Welfare and Social Progress," pp. 141–42.

93. Costin, *Two Sisters,* pp. 139–40.

94. Muncy, *Female Dominion,* p. 107.

95. *Official Report of the Sixteenth Biennial Convention of the General Federation of Women's Clubs,* Chautauqua, NY, June 20–30, 1922, comp. and ed. Mrs. Adam Weiss (Washington: GFWC, 1922), pp. 509, 511.

96. Ibid., p. 455.

97. Ibid., p. 496; see also Miss Mary E. Murphey's remarks on pp. 359–60.

98. Rothman, *Woman's Proper Place,* p. 140.

99. Ibid., pp. 140–41.
100. Covotsos, "Child Welfare and Social Progress," pp. 143–44.
101. *Fourteenth Annual Report of the Chief of the Children's Bureau to the Secreatary of Labor, Fiscal Year Ended June 30, 1926,* Children's Bureau, U.S. Deaprtment of Labor (Washington: Government Printing Office, 1926), p. 3.
102. See *Annual Reports* of the Children's Bureau, 1922–1929.
103. Ladd-Taylor, *Raising a Baby the Government Way,* esp. pp. 24–46.
104. See *Tenth Annual Report of Children's Bureau* (1922), pp. 8–9.
105. Rothman, *Woman's Proper Place,* pp. 140–41; and Children's Bureau, *Annual Reports, 1922–1929.*
106. Costin, *Two Sisters,* p. 136.
107. Ibid., pp. 137–38.
108. Ibid., pp. 136–37. See also Janet Geister, "The Child Welfare Special," American Child Hygiene Association, *Transactions* (1919): 214–22.
109. Meckel, *Save the Babies,* p. 212.
110. Covotsos, "Child Welfare and Social Progress," p. 144; Rothman, *Woman's Proper Place,* pp. 139–41 and 303, n. 12; and Muncy, *Female Dominion,* pp. 108–109.
111. Rothman, *Woman's Proper Place,* p. 141.
112. Ibid., p. 141 and 304, n. 18.
113. Ibid., p. 141.
114. Ibid., p. 139; and Ladd-Taylor, *Raising a Baby the Government Way,* p. 28.
115. Rothman, *Woman's Proper Place,* p. 139.
116. Ibid., pp. 139, 141.
117. Ibid., pp. 139–40.
118. Florence Brown Sherborn, "The Woman Physician and Her Obligation and Opportunity," *Woman's Medical Journal* 29 (April 1915), as quoted in Rothman, *Woman's Proper Place,* p. 140.
119. An undated memorandum in the archives of the U.S. Children's Bureau, as quoted in Rothman, *Woman's Proper Place,* p. 142 (and cited p. 304, n. 20).
120. Rothman, *Woman's Proper Place,* p. 142.
121. Except where otherwise noted, my discussion of the politics of Sheppard-Towner renewal relies on the richly detailed account in Chepaitis, "First Federal Social Welfare Measure," ch. 5.
122. Meckel, *Save the Babies,* p. 218.
123. Lemons, *The Woman Citizen,* p. 172.
124. These quotes from AMA resolutions appear in Meckel, *Save the Babies,* p. 216. The AMA's 1922 Resolution against "state medicine" defined it as "any form of medical treatment, provided, conducted, controlled

or subsidized by the federal or any state government, or municipality, excepting such service as is provided by the Army, Navy or Public Health Service, and that which is necessary for the control of communicable diseases, the treatment of mental disease, the treatment of the indigent sick, and such other services as may be approved by and administered under the direction of or by a local county medical society, and are not disapproved by the state medical society of which it is a component part."

125. James G. Burrow, *AMA: Voice of American Medicine* (Baltimore: Johns Hopkins Press, 1963), p. 161.

126. The most extreme attacks came from a formerly antisuffrage women's group, as Lemons explains in *Woman Citizen* (p. 173): "Senator Thomas A. Bayard of Delaware read into the *Congressional Record* a thirty-six-page petition and letter from the Woman Patriots. It purported to show the Bolshevist origins of the entire progressive program for children, which included the Sheppard-Towner Act, the Children's Bureau, child labor laws, and the child labor amendment. The petition traced an intricate web which joined the national women's organizations together in a conspiracy to Sovietize the United States. It was a feminist-socialist-communist plot under the leadership of women like Florence Kelley Wishnieweski. She was described as 'the ablest legislative general communism had produced.' The petition also denounced Jane Addams, Julia Lathrop, Grace Abbott, Carrie Chapman Catt, Mary Anderson, Maud Wood Park, Harriet Taylor Upton, Emily Newell Blair, Margaret Dreier Robbins, Hull House, the constituent organizations of the WJCC, the Federal Council of Churches, the Children's Bureau, the Women's Bureau, and the U.S. Department of Labor."

127. Letter from Florence Kelley to Grace Abbott, Jan. 15, 1927, as quoted in Clarke A. Chambers, *Seedtime of Reform: American Social Service and Social Action, 1918–1933* (Minneapolis: University of Minnesota Press, 1963), p. 51.

128. Chepaitis, "First Federal Welfare Measure," pp. 244–45. Other quotes from President Coolidge appear on pp. 216–17.

129. For a full account, see ibid., ch. 6. A list of these bills appears on pp. 279–80.

130. Lemons, *Woman Citizen*, p. 174.

131. The rest of this paragraph draws on the excellent discussion in Covotsos, "Child Welfare and Social Progress," pp. 150–60.

132. Lemons, *Woman Citizen*, p. 175.

133. Covotsos, "Child Welfare and Social Progress," p. 159.

134. Rothman, *Woman's Proper Place*, p. 125. See also Meckel, *Save the Babies*, pp. 217–18.

135. Rothman, *Woman's Proper Place,* p. 150.
136. Ibid., p. 143.
137. Chepaitis, "First Federal Welfare Program," p. 262; Lemons, *Woman Citizen,* pp. 164–65, 175; and Meckel, *Save the Babies,* pp. 216–17.
138. For indications that local doctors did not get as involved as the AMA leadership wanted, see Chepaitis, "First Federal Welfare Program," pp. 259–60.
139. Covotsos, "Child Welfare and Social Progress," p. 149.
140. Ibid., p. 153.
141. Chepaitis, "First Federal Welfare Program," pp. 246–49, 333–37.
142. Lemons, *Woman Citizen,* pp. 123–24, 172–73.
143. Covotsos, "Child Welfare and Social Progress," pp. 147–48, n. 2.
144. Chepaitis, "First Federal Welfare Program," p. 248.
145. *Golden Jubilee History, 1897–1947* (Chicago: National Congress of Parents and Teachers, 1947), pp. 197, 199.
146. The changes in the National Congress/PTA over time are cogently characterized in Steven L. Schlossman, "Before Home Start: Notes toward a History of Parent Education in America," *Harvard Educational Review* 46 (3) (Aug. 1976): 436–67. On the association's name changes, see p. 443, n. 21.
147. Lemons, *Woman Citizen,* p. 123.
148. Ibid.
149. Rothman, *Woman's Proper Sphere,* ch. 5.
150. See Nancy F. Cott, "Across the Great Divide: Women in Politics before and after 1920," in *Women, Politics, and Change,* ed. Louise A. Tilly and Patricia Gurin (New York: Russell Sage Foundation, 1990), esp. pp. 161–68.
151. Chepaitis, "First Federal Welfare Program," p. 142.
152. These aspirations can be traced most directly in the *Annual Reports* of the Children's Bureau, 1913–1929. Of course, the Bureau administered the federal child labor law, the Keating-Owen bill of 1916, until it was struck down by the Supreme Court nine months after its enforcement began. Grace Abbott was in charge; see Costin, *Two Sisters,* pp. 103–112.
153. Joanne L. Goodwin, "Mothers in Poverty: A Gender Analysis of Mothers' Pensions, 1911–1929" (paper presented at the Seventh Berkshire Conference on the History of Women, Wellesley College, June 19–21, 1987), p. 10; and discussions of mothers' pensions in the *Annual Reports* of the Children's Bureau. See also Bureau-sponsored studies of mothers' pensions by Emma O. Lundberg, a number of which are cited in the notes for Chapter 8 of this book.
154. On these speculations, see Children's Bureau, "Maternity Benefit," *Child-Welfare Magazine* 14(4) (Dec. 1919): 114–15, discussing a Bureau

study by Dr. Henry J. Harris on "Maternity Benefit Systems in Certain Foreign Countries" and stressing the study's conclusion that the "United States is the only one of the leading industrial countries of the world to have no system of state or national assistance to maternity." See also the discussion of "Unemployment and Child Welfare" in *Tenth Annual Report of Children's Bureau* (1922), pp. 16–17.

155. Costin, *Two Sisters,* p. 126.

156. From New York City Department of Health, *Annual Report, 1920,* p. 176, as excerpted by Rothman, *Woman's Proper Place,* pp. 124–25. I have further excerpted from her rendition.

157. Nancy F. Cott compares "the woman movement" of the nineteenth century to modern "feminism," which grew from tiny beginnings in the 1910s. See her introduction to *The Grounding of Modern Feminism* (New Haven: Yale University Press, 1987).

Conclusion: America's First Modern Social Policies and Their Legacies

1. This point is further discussed and documented in Edwin Amenta and Theda Skocpol, "Redefining the New Deal: World War II and the Development of Social Provision in the United States," pp. 81–122 in *The Politics of Social Policy in the United States,* ed. Margaret Weir, Ann Shola Orloff, and Theda Skocpol (Princeton, NJ: Princeton University Press, 1988).

2. See E. Cary Brown, "Fiscal Policies in the Thirties: A Reappraisal," *American Economic Review* 46(1956): 857–79; and Mark Leff, *The Limits of Symbolic Reform: The New Deal and Taxation, 1933–1939* (Cambridge and New York: Cambridge University Press, 1984).

3. An excellent discussion of the various factors contributing to the absence of social democracy in the United States appears in Gary Marks, *Unions in Politics: Britain, Germany, and the United States in the Nineteenth and Early Twentieth Centuries* (Princeton, NJ: Princeton University Press, 1989), especially ch. 6 on "American Exceptionalism in Comparative Perspective."

4. See John Ikenberry and Theda Skocpol, "The Political Formation of the American Welfare State in Historical and Comparative Perspective," *Comparative Social Research* 6 (1983): 87–148.

5. This theme is documented in Jerry Cates, *Insuring Inequality: Administrative Leadership in Social Security, 1935–54* (Ann Arbor: University of Michigan Press, 1983). Cates does not sufficiently appreciate the positive achievements of the Social Security administrators in building up universal U.S. social insurance programs that help less as well as more privileged Americans in a politically sustainable way.

6. A good overview of the transition from mothers' pensions to ADC appears in Winifred Bell, *Aid to Dependent Children* (New York: Columbia University Press, 1965).

7. See, for example, the eloquent statement by Sarah S. Brown, "Health Care Reform: What's In It for Mothers and Children?" (presented at the National Academy of Social Insurance, 4th Annual Conference and Membership Meeting, Jan. 30–31, 1992, Washington, DC).

8. Hugh Heclo, "Issue Networks and the Executive Establishment," pp. 87–124 in *The New American Political System,* ed. Anthony King (Washington: American Enterprise Institute, 1978).

9. See the insightful analysis in Jane J. Mansbridge, *Why We Lost the ERA* (Chicago: University of Chicago Press, 1986).

10. We learn much about these divisions in Kristin Luker, *Abortion and the Politics of Motherhood* (Berkeley and Los Angeles: University of California Press, 1984); and in Kathleen Gerson, *Hard Choices: How Women Decide about Work, Career, and Motherhood* (Berkeley and Los Angeles: University of California Press, 1986).

11. An explanation of how a new Family Security Program might improve contemporary U.S. social provision, while building on the best tendencies from the past, appears in my article "Sustainable Social Policy: Fighting Poverty without Poverty Programs," *The American Prospect* 1(2) (Summer 1990): 58–70.